A Survey of Basic Accounting

The Willard J. Graham Series in Accounting
Consulting Editor
Robert N. Anthony   Harvard University

A Survey of Basic Accounting

R. F. Salmonson, Ph.D., C.P.A.
Professor of Accounting
Michigan State University

Roger H. Hermanson, Ph.D., C.P.A.
Research Professor of Accounting
Georgia State University

James Don Edwards, Ph.D., C.P.A.
J. M. Tull Professor of Accounting
University of Georgia

1977

Revised Edition

RICHARD D. IRWIN, INC. Homewood, Illinois 60430
Irwin-Dorsey Limited   Georgetown, Ontario   L7G 4B3

Revised Edition

4 5 6 7 8 9 0 K 5 4 3 2 1 0 9

ISBN 0-256-01890-1
Library of Congress Catalog Card No. 76–24273
Printed in the United States of America

LEARNING SYSTEMS COMPANY—
a division of Richard D. Irwin, Inc.—has developed a
PROGRAMMED LEARNING AID
to accompany texts in this subject area.
Copies can be purchased through your bookstore
or by writing PLAIDS,
1818 Ridge Road, Homewood, Illinois 60430.

Preface

This revised edition of *A Survey of Basic Accounting* is designed for use by those who wish to obtain a basic understanding of the accountant's approach to measuring and reporting upon the economic activity, resources, and obligations of a business and how this information is used in decision making. Accounting topics are introduced and discussed under the assumption that the reader has no prior knowledge of accounting.

We have sought in this book to introduce financial and management accounting in a manner that emphasizes the output of the accounting process. While some attention is directed toward procedures and techniques used to accumulate accounting information, the major emphasis is on the contents of financial reports and the interpretation and possible uses of this information.

This revised edition incorporates new chapters on consolidated statements, standard costs, and responsibility accounting. It also uses journal entries to some extent in communicating concepts. The first 11 chapters of the book are devoted to a discussion of topics that relate largely to the determination and reporting of net earnings and financial position and the basic theory underlying financial statements of business corporations. Here again we have deliberately sought to emphasize certain subject matter because we believe knowledge of it is crucial in gaining an understanding of financial accounting and financial reporting. For example, attention is directed to the alternative approaches to accounting for inventories and plant assets since they may produce substantially different measurements of net earnings and of financial position. We also discuss matters such as the appraisal of financial position and the adequacy of earnings, stockholder's equity, debt financing and investments, changes in financial position, consolidated statements, and the theory underlying financial statements. We omit largely procedural matters such as bank reconciliation statements, petty cash and payroll accounting, and special-ized journals.

The remaining nine chapters deal with topics that are likely to be of concern to management in directing the internal affairs of a business. Topics discussed include the analysis and control of departmentalized retail operations; earnings determination, cost concepts, and cost systems in manufacturing operations; the development of relevant costs for use in decisions involving pricing, discontinuance of a product line or a department, and capital expenditures; responsibility accounting; profit planning and control through budgeting; taxes and tax considerations in decision making; and computer-based accounting systems. We believe knowledge of the topics included is essential to every reader who aspires to an executive position in business if he or she expects to understand accounting reports, plan and control the operations of a business, and communicate with other executives.

We have designed this text for use in a one-term survey-of-accounting course. It will provide the background necessary for students who have no prior knowledge of accounting to take further courses dealing with the accumulation, interpretation, and use of accounting information.

Various approaches may be taken in using this book in a one-quarter or one-semester course. For a course which is to be primarily "financial" in nature, attention could be focused on the first 11 chapters. If manage-ment accounting is to be emphasized, one could cover Chapters 1–3 and then concentrate on the last nine chapters. Alternatively, a balanced approach could be taken by covering all the chapters or by covering selected chapters from both groupings.

We also believe this book can be used with success in independent study. Much of the subject matter in this text has been enthusiastically received and widely used by business executives. It has been taught in seminars and conferences attended by mortgage bankers, management personnel from member companies of the Steel Service Center Institute, and by others whose primary concern has been with sales, production, and purchasing.

Questions, exercises, and problems are provided at the end of each chapter in sufficient quantity for use in classroom discussion and for assignment as homework. Their number has been increased in this revised edition. An instructor's manual is also available.

We are indebted to a number of members of the faculties of our respec-tive universities for helpful comments on the organization and content of this book. In addition, we would like to acknowledge specifically the assistance of V. Bruce Irvine, University of Saskatchewan; Gerald L. Johnson, California State University, Fresno; Larry N. Killough, Virginia Polytechnic Institute and State University; Lawrence Rittenberg, Univer-sity of Wisconsin; Deborah A. Wheless, Donald L. Wilson, Byron R. Wells, and John C. Richie, University of Georgia. Isabel L. Barnes and Rebecca Hooten provided capable and efficient service in typing the manuscript. But we, of course, bear full responsibility for any deficiencies in the text.

December 1976   R. F. SALMONSON
ROGER H. HERMANSON
JAMES DON EDWARDS

Contents

centages. Operating Cycle Concepts. Evaluating Financial Position Relationships: *The Current or Working Capital Ratio. Ideal Size of Ratio. The Quick or Acid Test Ratio. Satisfactory Acid Test Ratio. Cash Forecasts (budgets)—A Management Control. Cash Forecasts Illustrated. The Equity Ratio.* Evaluating the Efficiency of Asset Utilization: *Calculating Turnover Ratios. Accounts Receivable Turnover. Interpreting the Accounts Receivable Turnover Ratio. Number of Days' Sales Uncollected. Inventory Turnover. Significance of Inventory Turnover Ratios. Total Assets Turnover. Interpreting the Total Assets Turnover Ratio. Limitations in Evaluating Financial Position.*

chapter 1

Accounting—A Source of Financial Information

In our daily activities we make many decisions that consist of choosing between alternatives that have different expected outcomes. These decisions may be of a personal, political, social or economic nature, involving all aspects of life. Often, we are doubtful as to the course of action we should take to achieve a specific goal. This doubt, this uncertainty, can be reduced through the use of relevant information. In this text we are dealing with economic information.

Accounting is a primary source of information on economic activity. And, because economic activity includes the production, exchange, and consumption of scarce goods, it is found everywhere in our society. Thus, wherever economic resources are employed, an accounting is likely to be required to show what was accomplished at what cost or sacrifice. This is true whether the resources are used by individuals, business firms, or not-for-profit organizations such as churches, units of government, and hospitals.

ACCOUNTING DEFINED

Accounting is a systematic process of measuring and reporting to various users relevant financial information for decision making regarding the economic activity of an organization or unit. This information is primarily financial in nature, that is, it is stated in money terms.

The accounting process consists of a number of rather distinct functions. Accountants *observe* the economic scene and *select* (or identify) those events that are considered evidence of economic activity. (The purchase and sale of goods and services are examples.) Then, through the use of natural numbers, a monetary scale, and certain other general principles, they *measure* these selected events. As the next step, they *record* these measurements to provide a permanent history of the financial activities of the organization. In order to *report* upon what has happened, accountants *classify* their measurements of recorded events into meaningful groups. The preparation of financial statements and accounting reports frequently will require that accountants *summarize* these groups of measurements even further. Finally, accountants may be asked to *interpret* the contents of their statements and reports. Interpretation may involve explanation of the uses, meaning, and limitations of accounting information. It may also involve drawing attention to significant items through percentage and ratio analysis.

Accounting may also be defined as an *information system* designed to provide, through the medium of financial statements, relevant financial information. In designing the system, accountants keep in mind the types of users of the information (owners, managers, creditors, public officials, etc.) and the kinds of decisions they make that require financial information. Usually, the information provided relates to the economic resources owned by an organization, the claims against these resources, the changes in both resources and claims, and the results of using these resources for a given period of time.

THE PROFESSION OF ACCOUNTANCY

In our society, accountants are usually employed in (1) public accounting, (2) private industry, or (3) in the not-for-profit sector. Within each area, specialization is possible. An accountant may, for example, be an expert in auditing, systems development, budgeting, or cost or tax accounting.

Public Accounting

Accountants may offer their services to the general public for a fee in the same manner as do medical doctors and attorneys. They may be licensed by the state to practice as certified public accountants (CPAs) if they have met certain requirements, such as years of experience, and if they have passed a rigorous examination. This examination is prepared and graded by the American Institute of Certified Public Accountants (AICPA)—the accounting equivalent of the American Bar Association or the American Medical Association. CPAs typically offer their clients auditing, management advisory, and tax services.

Auditing.   A business is usually required to provide financial statements on its financial affairs when it seeks a loan or wishes to have its securities traded on a stock exchange. Users of such statements accept and rely upon them more readily when they are accompanied by an *auditor's report*.[1] This auditor's report contains the professional opinion of the CPA regarding the fairness of the statements. To be able to express an informed opinion, the CPA must conduct an audit of the accounting records, as well as seek supporting evidence from external sources.

Management Advisory Services. CPAs may be engaged to provide a wide range of what are called management advisory services. Typically, such services relate to the accounting process. Examples here include the design and installation of an accounting system, electronic processing of accounting data, inventory control, budgeting, or financial planning.

Tax Services. CPAs are often called upon for advice in the preparation of federal, state, and local tax returns. Here the objective is to use legal means to minimize the taxes paid. But of equal importance is the area known as tax planning. Proper tax planning requires that the tax effects, if any, of every business decision be known before the decision is made. There may be little chance to alter its tax effects after it is made.

Private or Industrial Accounting

Accountants employed by a single business are referred to as private or industrial accountants. They may be their employer's only accountant, or one of several hundred or more. They may or may not be CPAs. If they have passed an examination given by the Institute of Management Accounting (sponsored by the National Association of Accountants—an organization consisting largely of accountants in private industry), they will possess a Certificate in Management Accounting (CMA). As in public accounting, they may be specialists in providing certain services.

They may, for example, be engaged in the preparation of financial statements to be issued to external parties. Or they may be engaged in accumulating and controlling the costs of producing goods manufactured by their employer. They may be specialists in budgeting or in the design and installation of accounting systems. And they may serve as internal auditors being employed by a firm to see that its policies and procedures are being adhered to in its departments and divisions.

Accounting in the Not-for-Profit Sector

Many accountants, including CPAs, are employed by not-for-profit organizations, including governmental agencies at the federal, state, and local levels. Here again specialization is possible as, for example, in budgeting or systems design. But the governmental accountant is more likely to be concerned with the accounting for and control of tax revenues and their appropriation and expenditure. Accountants are also employed by

---

[1] For an example of an auditor's report, see the appendix to Chapter 11, page 278.

governmental agencies whose main function is the regulation of business activity—for example, the regulation by a state public service commission of public utilities.

It should also be noted that many accountants (including CPAs) are employed in the academic arm of the profession. Here attention is directed toward the teaching of accounting and to research into the uses, limitations, and improvement of accounting information and of the theories and procedures under which it is accumulated and communicated.

WHY ACCOUNTING INFORMATION IS USEFUL

The usefulness of accounting information in making decisions regarding economic resources has been noted. But little has been said about the decision-making process, to which attention is now directed.

The Decision-Making Process

Basically, as shown in the diagram in Illustration 1.1, any decision-making process involves (1) recognition of the existence of and the formulation of a problem, (2) determination of the alternative courses of action considered to be solutions to the problem, (3) prediction of the possible consequence or outcome of each of the alternatives considered, (4) selection of the preferred alternative as determined by reference to the decision maker's personal preferences or previously set goals, and (5) taking action to see that the alternative chosen is implemented.

The problem is caused, at least in part, by events occurring in the real world of human activity and scarce resources. Its existence must be recognized or there will be no decision. The nature of the problem must be understood so that alternatives, which are possible solutions to the problem, can be determined.

The list of alternatives should be complete, or the best solution may be overlooked. And the suggested actions should be competing. One need not choose between two approaches to solving a problem if one can have both.

Since they represent future expected happenings, the consequences associated with each alternative must be predicted. Because individuals

ILLUSTRATION 1.1

A Model of the Decision-Making Process

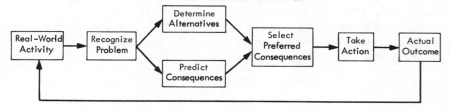

differ, they are likely to have different personal preferences. Thus, different decision makers may make different decisions even though they predict the same consequences from the same alternatives.

Note that implementing a decision causes events or happenings in the real world, which cause problems to arise. These problems, in turn, bring about a recycling of the whole process.

As a practical illustration, assume that a bank faces a problem: (1) it has received requests for loans from Company X and Company Y and cannot, because of a shortage of loanable funds, honor both requests; (2) it is in doubt as to which loan will meet its objectives relative to risk, interest earnings, use of the money, date of repayment, ability to repay, and similar matters; and (3) a loan to X differs from a loan to Y.

To solve the problem, the bank gathers information that will help it *predict the outcomes of granting each loan.* The predicted outcome of each loan will probably be based on such factors as the rate of interest that can be charged, how the money will be used, and when it will be repaid. Projected results of the alternatives will be compared with established objectives of the bank and a decision reached. This decision may be influenced by the personal preferences of the person making it. This person may conclude that, as far as the bank is concerned, a loan to X does not differ significantly from a loan to Y. But he or she may have a strong preference for loaning money to X because it intends to acquire pollution control equipment, while Y intends to acquire new smelting equipment.

In any event, a decision is made; and whether the loan is granted or not, or whether repaid or not if granted, the bank's relationship with its environment is now changed. This causes new problems requiring new information and further decisions.

In predicting the outcomes of the granting of each of the above loans, the bank undoubtedly relied heavily upon accounting information. Virtually every attempt to predict the future will involve a review of the past. And so, in making its predictions, the bank would have relied upon the accounting record of the past financial activities of each company.

In this example, the bank would be considered an external user of accounting information. But the same decision process would be employed, with accounting again supplying part of the information, in reaching a decision on an internal matter. For example, a business manager may have to decide whether to begin offering a new line of merchandise. Internal decisions requiring accounting information are now examined briefly.

Internal Decisions

In most companies, various levels of management make decisions that require accounting information. These decisions can be classified into four major types:

1. Financing decisions—deciding what amounts of capital are needed and whether it is to be secured from owners or creditors.
2. Resource allocation decisions—deciding how the total capital of a firm is to be invested, such as the amount invested in machinery.
3. Production decisions—deciding what products are to be produced, by what means, and when.
4. Marketing decisions—setting selling prices and advertising budgets; determining where a firm's markets are and how they are to be reached.

Managerial Accounting.   Managerial accounting is that part of the accounting discipline that provides information for the above types of management decisions. It ranges from the very broad (long-range planning) to the quite detailed (why costs varied from their planned levels). The information must usually meet two tests. It must be useful and not cost more to gather than it is worth. It generally relates to a part of a firm, such as a plant or a department, because this is where most of the decisions are made. It often is used to measure the success of managers in, for example, controlling costs and to motivate them to help a firm achieve its goals. And it is forward-looking, often involving planning for the future.

External Users and Their Decisions

The external users of accounting information and the types of questions for which answers are sought can be classified as follows:

1. Owners and prospective owners (stockholders and prospective stockholders in a corporation) and their advisers—financial analysts and investment counselors. Should an ownership interest be acquired in this firm? Or, if one is now held, should it be increased, decreased, or retained at its present level? Has the firm earned satisfactory profits?
2. Creditors and lenders. Should a loan be granted to the firm? Will the firm be able to pay its debts as they become due?
3. Employees and their unions. Does the firm have the ability to pay increased wages? Can it do so without raising prices? Is the firm financially able to provide permanent employment?
4. Customers. Will the firm survive long enough to honor its product warranties? Can a firm install costly pollution control equipment and still remain profitable? Are profit margins reasonable?
5. Governmental units. Is this firm, a public utility, earning a fair profit on its capital investment? How much taxes does it pay? In total, is business activity at a desired level for sound growth without inflation?
6. The general public. Are profit margins too high? Are they an increasing or decreasing part of national income? Are the firms in this industry contributing to inflation?

Except for some uses by governmental units, the information needs of the above users are usually met by providing a set of general-purpose financial statements. These statements are the end product of a process known as financial accounting.

Financial Accounting. It is the function of financial accounting to provide statements on a firm's financial position, changes in this position, and on the results of operations (profitability). These statements are usually published in a 20 to 60 page document known as the *annual report*. This report also contains the auditor's report or opinion as to the fairness of the financial statements, as well as considerable other information about the reporting company's activities, plans and expectations.

Financial accounting information generally relates to the firm as a whole, since outsiders can make decisions only on matters pertaining to the firm in its entirety, such as whether to extend credit to it. Such information is usually historical in nature, being a report upon what has happened. Because interfirm comparisons are often made, the information supplied must conform to certain standards or principles, called generally accepted accounting principles (GAAP).

Types of Business Firms

Although accounting information is equally essential in not-for-profit organizations, primary attention in this text will be paid to business firms. The three major types of firms and their distinctive features may be described as follows:

A *single (sole) proprietorship* is a business owned by one person who is also typically its manager. Since a business and its owner are not legally recognized as separate entities, the owner is personally responsible for the debts of the business. The accountant, however, treats the owner and the business as separate accounting entities.

A *partnership* is a business owned by two or more persons, called partners, who provide its capital and usually share in managing its affairs. Legally, each partner is personally responsible for the debts of the partnership (he is said to have unlimited liability) if they cannot be paid with partnership resources. But, for accounting purposes, each partner's personal activities must be clearly distinguished from partnership activities.

A *corporation* is a form of business organization created under the laws of a particular state. Ownership is evidenced by shares of capital stock that may be held by many stockholders and which may be readily bought and sold. The corporation operates under a charter issued by the state giving it a legal existence separate and distinct from its stockholders. The shareholders' responsibility for the corporation's debts is limited to the amount invested to acquire the shares owned. Here again, for accounting purposes, the corporation is considered a separate entity apart from its owners, creditors, managers, and employees. Because it is the major form of business in the United States, attention is directed to accounting for business corporations.

THE DEVELOPMENT OF FINANCIAL ACCOUNTING STANDARDS

As noted above, the financial statements a business firm issues to external parties must conform to certain standards or principles. These standards and principles have developed largely from accounting practice, as is discussed more fully in Chapter 11, and can, in some instances, be traced back for centuries. But accounting as we know it today has been shaped largely by four major accounting organizations, as is discussed below.

American Institute of Certified Public Accountants (AICPA)

The AICPA, an organization of CPAs in public and industrial practice, has been the dominant factor in the development of accounting standards over the past half century. In a 20-year period ending in 1959, its Committee on Accounting Procedure issued 51 *Accounting Research Bulletins* recommending certain principles or practices. From 1959 through 1973, the committee's successor, the Accounting Principles Board (APB), issued 31 numbered *Opinions* which CPAs generally were *required* to follow. These bulletins and opinions dealt with controversial issues. Through its monthly magazine, *The Journal of Accountancy,* its research division, and its other divisions and committees, the AICPA continues to influence the development of accounting standards and practices.

Financial Accounting Standards Board

The APB was replaced in 1973 with a new, independent, seven member, full-time Financial Accounting Standards Board (FASB). To date (1976), the FASB has issued 12 Statements of Financial Accounting Standards and 6 Interpretations of FASB statements of standards. The FASB is widely accepted as the major influence, in the private sector, in the development of new financial accounting standards.

U.S. Securities and Exchange Commission

Created under the Securities and Exchange Act of 1934, the Securities and Exchange Commission (SEC) administers a number of important acts dealing with the interstate sale of securities. The SEC has the power to prescribe in detail the accounting practices followed by companies required by law to file financial statements with it. This includes virtually every major U.S. business corporation. But rather than exercise this power, the SEC has adopted a policy of working closely with the accounting profession, especially the FASB, in the development of accounting standards.

American Accounting Association

Consisting largely of college instructors of accounting, the American Accounting Association (AAA) has sought to encourage research and study at a theoretical level into the concepts, standards and principles of accounting. It frequently publishes statements on such matters and supports the research efforts of individuals. In recent years, its quarterly magazine, *The Accounting Review,* has carried many articles reporting on research into the uses of accounting information.

FINANCIAL STATEMENTS OF BUSINESS ENTERPRISES

A modern business firm has many objectives or goals. They include providing well-paid jobs and comfortable working conditions for its employees, being a good citizen, generating satisfactory earnings, and maintaining a sound financial position. But the two primary objectives of every business firm are *profitability* and *solvency.* Unless a firm can produce satisfactory earnings and pay its debts as they become due, any other objectives a firm may have will never be realized simply because the firm will not survive.

The Statement of Financial Position

The statement of financial position (often called a balance sheet) presents measures of the assets, liabilities and owners' equity in a business firm as of a specific moment in time. Assets are things of value; they constitute the *resources* of the firm. They have value to the firm because of the uses to which they can be put or the things that can be acquired by exchanging them. In Illustration 1.2, the assets of the Hart Company amount to $35,670. They consist of current assets of cash and accounts receivable (amounts due from customers) and property, plant, and equipment consisting of delivery equipment and office equipment. Current assets consist of cash and other short-lived assets that are reasonably expected to be converted into cash or to be consumed or used up in the operations of the business within a short period, usually one year. Property, plant, and equipment refers to relatively long-lived assets that are to be used in the production or sale of other assets or services rather than being sold.

Liabilities are the debts owed by a firm. Typically, they must be paid

ILLUSTRATION 1.2

HART COMPANY
Statement of Financial Position
July 31, 1979

Assets			*Liabilities and Stockholders' Equity*		
Current Assets:			Current Liabilities:		
Cash	$12,470		Accounts payable	$ 600	
Accounts receivable	700		Notes payable	3,000	
		$13,170			$ 3,600
			Stockholders' Equity:		
Property, Plant, and Equipment:			Capital stock	$30,000	
			Retained earnings	2,070	
Delivery equipment	$20,000				32,070
Office equipment	2,500				
		22,500	Total Liabilities and Stockholders'		
Total Assets		$35,670	Equity		$35,670

at certain known moments in time. The liabilities of the Hart Company are both relatively short-lived current liabilities. They consist of accounts payable (amounts owed to suppliers) and notes payable (a written promise to pay) totaling $3,600.

The Hart Company is a corporation. It is customary to refer to the owners' interest in a corporation as stockholders' equity. Hart Company's stockholders' equity consists of $30,000 paid in for shares of capital stock and retained earnings (earnings not paid out to stockholders) of $2,070. All of these items will be discussed later in the text. At this point, simply note that the statement of financial position heading includes the name of the organization, the title of the statement, and the date of the statement. Also, note that the claims upon or interests in assets equal the assets—an equality explained later in this chapter.

The Earnings Statement

The purpose of the earnings statement (often called an income statement) is to report upon the profitability of a business organization for a stated period of time. In accounting, profitability is measured by comparing the revenues generated in a period with the expenses incurred to produce those revenues. *Revenue is defined as the product of the business organization*—the products it delivers or the services it renders. Revenues are usually measured by the assets customers are willing to surrender for the products or services. *Expense is defined as the sacrifice made or the cost incurred to produce revenue*. It is measured by the assets surrendered or consumed in serving customers. If revenues exceed expenses, net earnings result. If the reverse is true, the business is said to be operating at a loss. Illustration 1.3 contains the earnings statement of the Hart

ILLUSTRATION 1.3

HART COMPANY
Earnings Statement
For the Month of July 1979

Service revenues.................		$5,700
Expenses:		
Wages.......................	$2,600	
Gas and oil..................	400	
Rent........................	300	
Advertising..................	200	
Utilities.....................	100	
Interest......................	30	3,630
Net Earnings...................		$2,070

Company for the month of July 1979. It shows that revenues were generated by serving customers in the amount of $5,700. Expenses for the month amounted to $3,630 resulting in net earnings for the month of $2,070.

Note that the heading of an earnings statement always states the time period covered by the statement. Failure to do so would render it useless, or nearly so.

The Statement of Changes in Financial Position

Information on the *financing and investing activities* of a business may be helpful in appraising its continued profitability and solvency. Typically, a business needs cash to conduct its daily operations (pay for its expenses), pay debts that become due, and for expansion and investment. The needed cash is usually secured from owner investment, by borrowing, or from operating the business. The statement that reports on the financing and investing activities of a business is called the statement of changes in financial position. The APB issued, in 1971, its *Opinion No. 19* which requires that such a statement be presented whenever an earnings statement is published.

The statement of changes in financial position may focus upon cash inflows and outflows as it does for the Hart Company in Illustration 1.4 or it may highlight changes in working capital (defined as current assets less current liabilities). In either case, it provides information not readily obtainable from either the earnings statement or the statement of financial position. For example, it shows that the Hart Company received cash from its customers for services provided in the amount of $5,000 (total revenue of $5,700 less uncollected accounts receivable of $700). Deducting cash paid for expenses of $3,030 (total expenses of $3,630 less unpaid expenses of $600) leaves net cash provided by operations of $1,970. The statement then goes on to explain exactly how the cash increased by

ILLUSTRATION 1.4

HART COMPANY
Statement of Changes in Financial Position
For the Month of July, 1979

Cash provided (Inflows):

From operations:

Revenues	$ 5,000	
Less: Cash paid for expenses	3,030	
Cash from operations		$ 1,970
From other sources:		
Invested by owners	$30,000	
Borrowed under note payable	6,000	
Cash from other sources		36,000
Total cash provided (total inflows)		$37,970
Cash applied (Outflows):		
Purchase delivery equipment	$20,000	
Purchase office equipment	2,500	
Repayment of note payable	3,000	
Total cash applied (total outflows)		25,500
Increase in Cash for Month		$12,470

$12,470 for the month of July. Understanding the statement of changes in financial position requires some knowledge of accounting. For this reason, discussion is delayed until Chapter 9. The student who wishes to pursue the derivation of the amounts in Illustration 1.4 may turn to Illustration 1.5, page 18.

THE FINANCIAL ACCOUNTING PROCESS

Having briefly introduced the three principal financial statements, attention is now directed to the process underlying such statements.

The Accounting Equation

It has already been noted that in the statement of financial position presented in Illustration 1.2 the total assets of the Hart Company are equal to its liabilities and stockholders' equity. This equality follows from the basic assumption in accounting that the assets of a business are equal to the equities in those assets; that is, Assets = Equities. Assets have already been defined simply as things of value. In a more sophisticated sense, the accountant designates and records as assets all those economic resources owned by a business which can be measured. And all desired things, except those available in unlimited quantity without cost or effort, are economic resources.

Equities are interests in or claims upon assets. For example, assume that you purchased a new automobile for $5,000 by withdrawing $400 from your savings account and borrowing $4,600 from your credit union. Your equity in the automobile is $400 and that of your credit union is $4,600. The $4,600 can be further described as a liability. Your $400 equity is often described as the owner's equity or the residual equity or interest in the asset. Since, in the case of a corporation, the owners are the stockholders, the basic equation becomes:

$$\text{Assets} = \text{Liabilities} + \text{Stockholders' Equity}$$

This equation must always be in balance. The sum of the interests in assets must always be equal to the assets themselves. It is intuitively logical to hold that everything of value belongs to someone or to some organization.

The right side of the above equation is also looked upon in yet another manner—namely, it shows the sources of the existing stock of assets. Thus, liabilities are not only claims to assets but they also are sources of assets. And, in a corporation, all of the assets are provided by either creditors (liability holders) or owners (stockholders).

As a business engages in economic activity, the dollar amounts and the composition of its assets, liabilities, and stockholders' equity change. But the equality of the basic equation always holds.

Transaction Analysis

Our society is characterized by exchange. That is, the bulk of the goods and services produced are exchanged rather than consumed by their producers. From this it follows that much of the economic activity of our society can be observed from the exchanges that take place. In accounting, these exchanges (as well as other changes) are called *transactions*. They provide much of the raw data entered in the accounting system. There are several reasons why this is so. First, an exchange is a readily observable event providing good evidence that activity has occurred. Second, an exchange usually takes place at an agreed-upon price and this price provides a highly objective measure of the economic activity that has transpired. Thus, the analysis of transactions is a most important part of the financial accounting process.

To illustrate the analysis of transactions and their effects upon the basic accounting equation, the activities of the Hart Company that led to the statements in Illustrations 1.2, 1.3, and 1.4 are presented and discussed below. Assume that the Hart Company was organized as a corporation on July 1, 1979, and that in its first transaction it issued, for $30,000 cash, shares of capital stock to Jim Hart, his wife, and their son. Analyzed, the transaction increased the assets (cash) of the Hart Company by $30,000 and increased its equities (the capital stock element of stockholders' equity) by $30,000. Consequently, the transaction yields a basic accounting equation containing the following:

Assets   = Liabilities +   Stockholders' Equity
(Cash, $30,000)   (Capital Stock, $30,000)

As its next transaction, the company borrowed $6,000 from Mrs. Hart's father, giving its written promise to repay the amount in one year. As a result, the company cash is increased to $36,000 and, since the written promise to repay is a liability, liabilities are increased to $6,000, yielding a basic equation of:

Assets   =   Liabilities   + Stockholders' Equity
(Cash, $36,000) (Notes Payable, $6,000) (Capital Stock, $30,000)

As its third transaction, the Hart Company spent $20,000 for three delivery trucks and $1,500 for some office equipment. In this transaction the Hart Company received delivery equipment priced at $20,000 and office equipment priced at $1,500. It gave up cash of $21,500. This transaction thus does not change the totals in the basic equation, it merely changes the composition of the assets. The equation is as follows:

Assets	=	Liabilities	+	Stockholders' Equity
Cash.............. $14,500				
Delivery				
equipment.......... 20,000		Notes payable....... $6,000		Capital stock....... $30,000
Office equipment....... 1,500				
$36,000 =		$6,000 +		$30,000

Assume that as transaction four in the month of July, the Hart Company purchased an additional $1,000 of office equipment, agreeing to pay for it within 10 days after it receives a bill for it from the supplier. This transaction increases assets in the form of office equipment by $1,000. It also increases liabilities in the form of accounts payable (which are amounts owed to creditors for items purchased from them) by $1,000. The items making up the totals in the accounting equation now appear as follows:

Assets	=	Liabilities	+	Stockholders' Equity
Cash.............. $14,500				
Delivery				
equipment......... 20,000		Notes payable......... $6,000		Capital stock...... $30,000
Office equipment...... 2,500		Accounts payable...... 1,000		
$37,000 =		$7,000 +		$30,000

Revenue and Expense Transactions

Thus far the transactions presented have consisted of exchanges of or the acquisition of assets either by borrowing or by stockholder investment. But a business is not formed merely to acquire assets. Rather, it seeks to use the assets entrusted to it as a means of securing still greater amounts of assets. This is accomplished by providing customers with goods or services, with the expectation that the value of the assets received from customers will exceed the cost of the assets consumed or surrendered in serving them. This total flow of services rendered or goods delivered (as measured by assets received from customers) has already been defined as *revenue*. Thus, revenue is a source of assets. The cost of serving customers is called *expense*. It is measured by the cost of the assets surrendered or consumed. If revenues exceed expenses, net earnings exist. If not, a loss has been suffered.

Assume that as its fifth transaction in July the Hart Company renders delivery services for some of its customers for $4,800 cash. It is evident that cash has increased by $4,800. But what other change has occurred which, if properly recorded, would reflect the appropriate analysis of this transaction? The answer is that stockholders' equity would be increased by $4,800. The correctness of this response can be observed by noting that there is no corresponding increase in liabilities brought about by the rendering of the services, nor were any assets parted with. This leaves an increase in stockholders' equity as the only possible response. But more importantly, the basic objective of a business corporation in providing customers with goods and services is to bring about an increase in stockholders' equity. More will be said about this later.

Incorporating the effects of the revenue transaction upon the financial status of the Hart Company yields the following basic equation:

Assets		=	Liabilities		+	Stockholders' Equity	
Cash	$19,300		Notes			Capital	
Delivery equipment	20,000		payable	$6,000		stock	$30,000
Office equipment	2,500		Accounts payable	1,000		Retained earnings	4,800 (Service revenue)
	$41,800 =			$7,000 +			$34,800

Note that the increase in stockholders' equity brought about by the revenue transaction is recorded as a separate item, "Retained earnings." It cannot be recorded as capital stock. No additional shares of stock were issued. The expectation is that revenue transactions will yield net earnings. If net earnings are not distributed to stockholders, they are in fact retained, and the title "retained earnings" is quite descriptive. Subsequent chapters will show that, because of complexities in handling large numbers of transactions, revenues will be shown as affecting retained earnings only at the end of an accounting period. The procedure presented above is a shortcut used to explain why the accounting equation remains in balance.

Assume that as its sixth transaction in July the Hart Company performs services for customers who agree to pay $900 at a later date. The transaction consists of an exchange of services for a promise by the customer to pay later. It is similar to the preceding transaction in that stockholders' equity is increased because revenues have been earned. It differs because cash has not been received. But a thing of value, an asset, has been received. This is the claim upon the customer, the right to collect from him at the later date. Technically, such claims are called *accounts receivable*. But the important point is that accounting does recognize them as assets and does record them. The accounting equation, including this item, is as follows:

Assets		=	Liabilities		+	Stockholders' Equity	
Cash...............	$19,300		Notes			Capital	
Accounts			payable......	$6,000		stock.........	$30,000
receivable.........	900		Accounts			Retained	
Delivery equip-			payable......	1,000		earnings......	5,700 (Service
ment.............	20,000						revenue)
Office equip-							
ment.............	2,500						
	$42,700	=		$7,000	+		$35,700

To illustrate one more step in regards to accounts receivable, assume that $200 is collected from customers "on account," to use business terminology. The transaction consists of the giving up of claims upon customers in exchange for cash. The effects of the transaction are to increase cash to $19,500 and to decrease accounts receivable to $700. Note that this transaction consists solely of a change in the composition of the assets, not of an increase in assets resulting from the generation of revenue.

Attention may now be directed toward expenses. Suppose (transaction eight) that the Hart Company paid its employees $2,600 for services received in conducting business operations during the month of July. The transaction consists of an exchange of cash for employee services. A proper analysis of the transaction would appear to indicate an exchange of one form of asset for another. This seems especially true when one recognizes that business corporations generally will surrender assets only for other things of value, for other assets. But, because the value of the services typically has expired by the time payment is made, the accountant engages in a shortcut and treats the transaction as a decrease in an asset and in stockholders' equity. From a purely theoretical point of view, the transaction should be regarded as involving an increase in one asset (labor services) and a decrease in another (cash), and then a decrease in an asset (labor services) and a decrease in stockholders' equity because of the recognition of an expense—wages.

Let us further assume (as transactions 9 and 10) that the Hart Company paid cash of $300 as rent for truck storage space and office space and that it paid its utilities bill for July in the amount of $100. These transactions will be treated by the accountant as having the same effect upon the financial position of the company. They cause a decrease in the asset cash of $400 and a decrease in stockholders' equity of $400 because of the incurrence of rent expense of $300 and utilities expense of $100. Incorporating these two items and the wages of $2,600 cumulatively into our accounting equation, it now reads:

Assets	=	Liabilities	+	Stockholders' Equity	
Cash $16,500		Notes payable ... $6,000		Capital stock ... $30,000	
Accounts		Accounts payable 1,000		Retained	
receivable 700				earnings 2,700	Service revenue .. $5,700
Delivery					Less expenses:
equipment 20,000					Wages 2,600
Office equipment 2,500					Rent 300
$39,700 =		$7,000 +		$32,700	Utilities 100

Because of their similar effects, transactions 11 and 12 of the Hart Company may be treated simultaneously. Assume that the company received a bill for gasoline, oil, and other delivery equipment supplies consumed during the month in the amount of $400 and a bill for $200 for advertising in July. Both transactions would be treated by the accountant as involving an increase in a liability, accounts payable, and a decrease in stockholders' equity because of the incurrence of an expense. The accounting equation depicting the financial position of the Hart Company now reads:

Assets	=	Liabilities	+	Stockholders' Equity	
Cash $16,500		Notes payable ... $6,000		Capital stock ... $30,000	
Accounts		Accounts payable 1,600		Retained	
receivable 700				earnings 2,100	Service revenue .. $5,700
Delivery					Less expenses:
equipment 20,000					Wages 2,600
Office equipment 2,500					Rent 300
$39,700 =		$7,600 +		$32,100	Utilities 100
					Gas and oil ... 400
					Advertising 200

Next (transaction #13) the Hart Company paid the $1,000 balance due on the purchase of the office equipment (transaction #4). This reduced cash by $1,000 and reduced the debt owed to the equipment supplier, recorded as an account payable, by $1,000. Or, assets and liabilities are both reduced by $1,000.

Finally, (transaction #14) in reviewing his needs for cash at the end of the month, Mr. Hart decided that he would not need as much cash as he now holds. So, he paid $3,000 on the note owed to his father-in-law, plus interest of $30 for the month. This transaction decreased cash by the total amount paid out, $3,030. Of this amount, $3,000 was applied to reduce the principal amount owed on the notes payable and the remaining $30 consisted of the payment of interest expense—an element that reduces retained earnings. This transaction illustrates how a certain transaction may affect assets, liabilities, and stockholders' equity at the same time.

The basic equation as it stands after including the effects of transactions 13 and 14 is shown in the summary of transactions in Illustration 1.5.

ILLUSTRATION 1.5

HART COMPANY
Summary of Transactions
Month of July 1979

Trans-action	Explanation	Cash	Accts. Rec.	Del. Equip.	Office Equip.	Notes Payable	Accts. Payable	Capital Stock	Retained Earnings	
		Assets				= Liabilities		+ Stockholders' Equity		
	Beginning balances	$ 0	$ 0	$ 0	$ 0	$ 0	$ 0	$ 0	$ 0	
(1)	Issued stock for cash	+30,000						+30,000		
(2)	Borrowed money on note	+ 6,000				+ 6,000				
(3)	Purchased equipment for cash	−21,500		+20,000	+ 1,500					
(4)	Purchased equipment on account				+ 1,000		+ 1,000			
(5)	Service revenue for cash	+ 4,800							+ 4,800	(Service revenue)
(6)	Service revenue on account		+ 900						+ 900	(Service revenue)
(7)	Collection on account	+ 200	− 200							
(8)	Paid wages	− 2,600							− 2,600	(Wages expense)
(9)	Paid rent	− 300							− 300	(Rent expense)
(10)	Paid utilities bill	− 100							− 100	(Utilities expense)
(11)	Bill for gas and oil used						+ 400		− 400	(Gas and oil expense)
(12)	Bill for July advertising						+ 200		− 200	(Advertising expense)
(13)	Paid equipment bill	− 1,000					− 1,000			
(14)	Payment on note and interest	− 3,030				− 3,000			− 30	(Interest expense)
	Ending balances	$12,470	$ 700	$20,000	$ 2,500	$ 3,000	$ 600	$30,000	$ 2,070	
		+	+	+	=	+	+	+		
		$35,670				$3,600		$32,070		

SUMMARY OF TRANSACTIONS

The effects of all of the transactions entered into by the Hart Company in the first month of its existence upon its assets, liabilities, and stockholders' equity are summarized in Illustration 1.5. The ending balances in each of the columns are the dollar amounts reported in the statement of financial position in Illustration 1.2. The itemized data in the retained earnings column are the revenue and expense items reported in the earnings statement in Illustration 1.3. The reason for each change reported in the cash column is determined and reported in the statement of changes in financial position in Illustration 1.4. This summary further shows how the basic equation of Assets = Equities is subdivided into the five major elements of financial accounting: assets, liabilities, owners' equity, revenues, and expenses.

The Statement of Retained Earnings

The purpose of the statement of retained earnings is to explain the changes in retained earnings that occurred between two statement of financial position dates. Usually, these changes consist of the addition of net earnings (or deduction of net loss) and the deduction of dividends. Dividends are the means by which a corporation rewards its stockholders for providing it with capital.

The effects of a cash dividend transaction are to reduce cash and retained earnings by the amount paid out. In effect, the earnings are no longer retained but have been passed on to the stockholders; and this is one of the primary reasons why stockholders organize corporations.

The statement of retained earnings for the Hart Company for the month of July 1979, would be quite simple. Since the company was organized on July 1, there would be no beginning retained earnings balance. Net earnings of $2,070 would be added and, since no dividends were paid, this would also be the ending balance.

To provide a more effective illustration, assume that the Hart Company's net earnings for August were $1,500 (revenues of $5,600 less expenses of $4,100) and that it declared and paid dividends of $1,000. Its statement of retained earnings for August is shown in Illustration 1.6.

ILLUSTRATION 1.6

HART COMPANY
Statement of Retained Earnings
For the Month Ended August 31, 1979

Retained earnings, July 31.................	$2,070
Add: Net earnings for August............	1,500
	$3,570
Less: Dividends........................	1,000
Retained Earnings, August 31..............	$2,570

SOME BASIC CONCEPTS

The accountant, in seeking to provide useful information on economic activity, relies upon some basic concepts or assumptions. Those covered thus far, either explicitly or implicitly, are summarized briefly in the following paragraphs.

Entity

The information gathered in an accounting information system relates to a specific business unit or entity. This entity is deemed to have an existence separate and apart from its owners, creditors, employees, or other interested parties.

Transaction

Those events or happenings that affect the assets, liabilities, owners' equity, revenues, or expenses of an entity are called transactions and are recorded in the accounting system. For the most part, transactions consist of exchanges.

Duality

Every transaction has a two-sided or dual effect upon each of the parties engaging in it. Consequently, if information is to be complete, both sides or both effects of every transaction must be included in the accounting system.

Money Measurement

Economic activity is recorded and reported in terms of a common unit of measurement—the dollar. If not expressed in a common unit of measurement, accounting reports would be much less useful, if not unintelligible. Changes in the value of the dollar are usually ignored.

Cost

Most of the numbers entered in an accounting system are the bargained prices of exchange transactions. The result is that most assets (excluding cash and receivables) are recorded and reported at their cost of acquisition. Changes in the value of the asset are (with certain exceptions) usually ignored. This practice is usually defended on the grounds of objectivity and the absence of evidence that the acquiring firm would have been willing to pay more.

Periodicity

To be useful, information must be (among other things) timely and current. To provide such information, accountants assume that they can subdivide the life of an entity into periods and report upon its activities for those periods. The requirement of periodic reporting will require the use of estimates, thus making every accounting report somewhat tentative in nature.

Continuity

Unless strong evidence exists to the contrary, the accountant assumes that the entity will continue operations into the indefinite future. Consequently, assets that will be used up or consumed in future operations need not be reported at their current liquidation values.

All of these concepts or notions (as well as others) will be discussed in considerably greater detail in Chapter 11.

SUMMARY

Accounting is a systematic or organized means of gathering and reporting information on economic activity. The information provided is used by many external and internal parties, together with other information, for a wide range of decisions.

An accountant may be employed in public, private, or governmental accounting and may be a specialist in one of many fields of expertise such as auditing, budgeting, systems development, taxation, or financial reporting.

Internally, accounting information is used by various levels of management personnel. External users include actual and potential stockholders and creditors and their professional advisers; employees and their unions; customers; suppliers; governmental agencies; and the public at large. The basic end products of the financial accounting process are the statement of financial position, the earnings statement, the statement of changes in financial position, and the statement of retained earnings.

Most of the information reported in these statements is found originally in the transactions entered into by an entity. These transactions are analyzed and their effects recorded as increases or decreases in assets, liabilities, stockholders' equity, revenues, and expenses—the five basic elements of accounting. The framework for analysis is the basic equation of Assets = Equities expanded to Assets = Liabilities + Stockholders' Equity + Revenues − Expenses.

In providing useful information, accountants rely upon some basic concepts including those relating to the entity, transaction, duality, money measurement, cost, periodicity, and continuity.

QUESTIONS AND EXERCISES

1. Define accounting. What does the term "relevant" mean when speaking of accounting information? Give an example of relevant information.

2. Accounting has often been called the "language of business." In what respects would you agree with this designation? How might it be argued that it is deficient?

3. What is the relationship between accounting as an information system and economic resources?

4. Define asset, liability, and owners' equity.

5. How do liabilities and stockholders' equity differ? In what respects are they similar?

6. How do accounts payable and notes payable differ? How are they similar?

7. Define revenue. How is revenue measured?

8. Define expense. How is expense measured?

9. How does accounting information usually enter into the decision-making process?

10. Name four organizations that have or are playing an important role in the development of accounting standards. Describe each briefly.

11. What is a CPA? What are some of the services usually provided by a CPA?

12. What is the role of the accountant in private industry? What are some of the services provided by the industrial accountant?

13. What is a statement of financial position? This statement generally seeks to provide information relative to what aspect of a business?

14. What is an earnings statement? This statement generally provides information on what aspect of a business?

15. What information does a statement of changes in financial position provide? Why must a separate statement for such information be provided? Explain or illustrate.

16. What information does the statement of retained earnings provide?

17. What is a transaction? What use does the accountant make of transactions? Why?

18. What is the accounting equation? Why must it always balance?

19. Give an example from your personal life that you believe illustrates your use of accounting information in reaching a decision.

20. Give examples of transactions which would have the following effects upon the basic elements of accounting for a business:
    a. Increase cash; decrease some other asset.
    b. Decrease cash; increase some other asset.
    c. Increase an asset; increase a liability.
    d. Increase an expense; increase a liability.
    e. Increase an asset other than cash; increase revenue.
    f. Decrease an asset; decrease a liability.

21. What is the accounting entity assumption? Why is it needed?

22. What is the duality assumption of accounting? Why is it needed?

23. You are a young married person who three years ago purchased a home by borrowing $20,000 on a mortgage. You recently received an inheritance of $25,000 and are considering paying off the mortgage. What types of financial information would you seek in helping you arrive at a decision?

24. You have been elected to the board of deacons of your church. At the first meeting you attend, mention is made of building a new church. What accounting information would the board need in deciding whether or not to go ahead?

25. If, during 1979, retained earnings increased by $12,000, expenses amounted to $34,500, and dividends declared and paid amounted to $5,000, what were the revenues and net earnings for 1979?

PROBLEMS

1–1. Menomet, Inc., completes the following transactions.

Required: Show the effect of each transaction on the accounting equation of Assets = Liabilities + Stockholders' Equity. Prepare columns as shown below and enter the transactions in the proper columns.

Transactions:

July 1 The company is organized and receives its initial cash of $50,000 from issuing capital stock to the owners.

5 The company borrows $20,000 from its bank, giving a note.

7 The company buys $8,000 of delivery equipment from Madsen Motors on open account and agrees to pay for it within two weeks.

11 The company pays $8,000 cash to Madsen Motors on the debt of July 7.

17 The company receives $3,400 cash for services it performed to date.

24 The company pays $2,600 for employee services used in making deliveries to date.

Form for answer:

Date	Explanation	Assets	=	Liabilities	+	Stockholders' Equity
July 1	Cash—capital stock	$50,000 =				$50,000
5	Note payable	20,000 =		$20,000		

1–2. *Required:* Show the effect of each of the following transactions on the accounting equation of the Shenkir Company. Enter each transaction in the proper columns and show the balance of the equation after each transaction. Use the same form as in Problem 1 above but set up columns for each of the following:

Date	Equipment
Explanation	Notes payable
Cash	Capital stock
Accounts receivable	Retained earnings

Transactions:

May 1 The owners organize the corporation with initial cash of $70,000 received from the issuance of capital stock.

2 The company borrows $8,000 cash from the bank on a note.

7 The company buys $35,600 of equipment for cash.

11 Cash received for services performed to date is $4,800.

14 Services performed for customers who agree to pay within a month are $2,500.

15 Employee services received in operating the business to date are paid in cash, $4,300.

19 The company pays $3,500 on the note to the bank.

31 Interest paid to the bank for May is $35.

31 Customers of May 14 pay $800 of the amount they owe the company.

31 An order is received from a customer for services to be rendered next week which will be billed at $2,000.

1–3. The Dobson Company completes the following transactions. Show the effect of each transaction on the accounting equation. In a form similar to that used in Problem 1, set up columns with the following headings:

Date	Equipment
Explanation	Accounts payable
Cash	Capital stock
Accounts receivable	Retained earnings

Required: (1) Enter each transaction in the proper columns and show the balance of the equation after each transaction. (2) Prepare a statement of financial position as of April 30, 1979.

Transactions:

Apr. 1 The company is organized and receives $25,000 cash from the owners in exchange for capital stock issued.

4 The company buys equipment for cash, $15,600.

9 The company buys additional equipment which costs $950 and agrees to pay for it in 30 days.

15 Cash received for services performed to date is $800.

16 Amounts due from customers for services performed total $950.

30 Of the receivables (see April 16), $720 are collected in cash.

30 Various costs of operating the business during the month of $1,050 are paid in cash.

30 An order is placed for equipment advertised at $4,000.

1–4. The Gardner Drive-In operates an outdoor movie theatre.
Required: Prepare an earnings statement for the month of August 1979.

Transactions:

Aug. 2   Paid current month's rent for premises, $8,000.
     7   Cash received for admissions during the week, $4,800.
   14   Cash received for admissions during the week, $5,600.
   15   Paid semimonthly payroll, $6,400.
   21   Received cash of $3,200 for admissions during week.
   23   Sundry expenses paid in cash are $1,400.
   27   Advertising for month is $3,800.
   31   Paid semimonthly payroll, $6,800.
   31   Paid film rental, $10,000.
   31   Received $12,400 cash revenue from operators of popcorn and various other concessions for right to operate during August.
   31   Cash received for admissions from August 22–31 inclusive, $8,400.
   31   Paid a cash deposit of $850 to guarantee receipt of a special film to be shown in September.

1–5. Analysis of the transactions of the Maxwell Drive-In Theatre for the month of June 1979, discloses the following:

Ticket revenue	$25,600
Rent of premises and equipment	5,000
Film rental paid	8,900
Receipts from concessionaires (percentage basis)	5,000
Advertising expense	3,100
Wages and salaries	8,800
Utilities expense	1,350
Dividends paid	1,000

Statement of financial position figures at June 30 include the following:

Cash	$39,000
Franchise to show movies in area	8,000
Accounts payable	10,400
Capital stock	19,000
Retained earnings, June 1, 1979	15,150

Required:

a. Prepare an earnings statement for the month of June 1979.
b. Prepare a statement of retained earnings for the month of June 1979.
c. Prepare a statement of financial position at June 30, 1979.

1–6. The following data relate to the Parkett Corporation. At October 1, 1979, the statement of financial position of the company is as follows:

Cash.........................	$60,000	Accounts payable...........	$10,000
Accounts receivable..........	6,000	Capital stock..............	44,000
		Retained earnings...........	12,000
	$66,000		$66,000

Transactions:

Oct. 3 The company pays the accounts payable in the statement of financial position, $10,000.

7 The company receives cash of $2,400 for parking by daily customers during the week.

10 The company collects $4,800 of the accounts receivable in the statement of financial position at October 1.

14 Cash receipts for the week from daily customers are $1,200.

15 The company sets up a receivable of $1,000 as the amount due from Boyer Company for the right to park its fleet of cars during the remainder of October. The receivable is due November 10.

16 The company pays wages of $800 for the period October 1–15.

19 The company pays advertising expenses of $400 for October.

21 Cash receipts for the week from daily customers are $2,400.

24 The company incurred sundry expenses of $280 which will be due November 10.

31 Cash receipts for the last 10 days of the month from daily customers are $2,800.

31 The company pays wages of $1,000 for the period October 16–31.

31 Billings to monthly customers total $7,200 for October, exclusive of the Boyer Company.

31 The company pays rent for the premises for October, $6,400.

Required:

a. Show the effect of each transaction on the accounting equation, using the same format as in Problem 1 except that the items to be used are those in the statement of financial position above (for October 1).

b. Prepare an earnings statement for the month of October, 1979.

c. Prepare a statement of retained earnings for the month ended October 31, 1979.

d. Prepare a statement of financial position at October 31, 1979.

1–7.   Given below are the statements of financial position and the earnings statement of the Collins Company:

COLLINS COMPANY
Statement of Financial Position

Assets	May 31, 1979	June 30, 1979
Current Assets:		
Cash...	$5,000	$6,000
Accounts receivable.............................	—0—	2,000
Supplies.......................................	3,000	1,000
Total Assets...............................	$8,000	$9,000

Liabilities and Stockholders' Equity		
Liabilities.....................................	$2,000	$1,000
Capital stock...................................	5,000	5,000
Retained earnings...............................	1,000	3,000
Total Liabilities and Stockholders' Equity........	$8,000	$9,000

COLLINS COMPANY
Earnings Statement
For the Month Ended June 30, 1979

Revenue from services rendered..........		$8,000
Expenses:		
Salaries............................	$4,000	
Supplies used.......................	2,000	6,000
Net Earnings for June.................		$2,000

Required: From the information presented above, prepare a statement showing the cash inflows and cash outflows that resulted in the $1,000 increase in cash from May 31 to June 30, 1979.

chapter 2

The Process of Accumulating Financial Information

In Chapter 1 the effects of business transactions were shown as increases or decreases in the elements of the basic accounting equation. This approach was used as a way of securing easy understanding of some basic relationships. It is far too cumbersome to be used in actual practice, since even a small business enters into a large number of transactions every week.

The purpose of this chapter is to introduce the basic components of an accounting system and to provide illustrations of the information gathering process underlying financial statements. Here again, it is expected that knowledge of the process will aid in understanding the end products—the financial statements.

THE ACCOUNTING SYSTEM

The Account

Because even a small business may engage in hundreds of transactions, the effects of these transactions must be classified and summarized before they become useful information. The accountant's task is made somewhat easier because many business transactions are repetitive. Their effects can thus be classified into groups according to common characteristics. For example, hundreds of transactions may involve the receipt or spending of cash. As a result, a part of every transaction affecting cash will be recorded and summarized in a Cash account. An account will be set up whenever the data to be recorded in it are believed to constitute useful information. Thus, every business will have a Cash account simply because knowledge of the amount of cash owned is likely to be useful information.

An account may take a variety of forms, from various printed formats in which entries are written by hand to invisible encoding on magnetic tape. Although exact format is not important, several types will be illustrated. What is required is that an account readily accepts increases or decreases in the item for which it was set up. At the same time, it must allow the difference between the increases and decreases—the balance of the account—to be easily determined.

The number of accounts in an accounting system will depend largely upon the information needs of those interested in the business. As stated earlier, the primary requirement is that the account provide useful information. Thus, one account may be established for cash—the company's immediate spending power—rather than separate accounts for cash in the form of coins, cash in the form of currency, and cash in the form of deposits in banks, simply because the amount of cash is useful information while the form of cash is not.

The T-Account

The way an account functions is shown by use of a T-account. It is used in this text for illustrative purposes only (it is not a replica of a form of account generally used) and gets its name because it looks like a capital letter T. The name of the item to be accounted for (such as cash) is written across the top of the T. Increases are recorded on one side and decreases on the other side of the vertical line of the T.

Recording Changes in Assets and Equities. By convention, increases in assets are recorded on the left side of the account, decreases on the right side. For reasons to be explained later, the process is reversed for equities. Thus, a corporation would record the receipt of $10,000 for shares of its capital stock as follows (the number in parentheses is used to tie the two sides of the transaction together):

Cash		Capital Stock	
(1) 10,000			(1) 10,000

The transaction involves an increase in the asset (cash) which is recorded on the left side of the Cash account, and an increase in stockholders' equity in the form of capital stock which is recorded on the right side of the Capital Stock account.

Because liabilities are a subset of equities, changes in them are recorded in the same manner as for stockholders' equity—increases on the right side, decreases on the left. Note the consistency between the placement of amounts for assets and equities in the accounts and their presentation in the statement of financial position (see Illustration 1.2, page 10). Asset amounts are shown on the left side of the account and the left side of the statement of financial position; equity (liabilities and stockholders' equity) amounts are shown on the right side of the account and the right side of the statement of financial position. But for easy recollection of these rules, all that one need remember is that increases in assets are recorded on the left side of the account. Increases in equities are recorded in the opposite manner as for assets and, for any account, decreases are the opposite of increases.

Recording Changes in Expenses and Revenues.   To understand the logic behind the recording of changes in expense and revenue accounts it is necessary first to recall that all expenses and revenues could be recorded directly in Retained Earnings. Thus, the recording of (2) the receipt of $1,000 of cash from customers for services rendered and (3) the payment of $600 of cash to employees as wages could be recorded as follows:

Cash				Retained Earnings			
(2)	1,000	(3)	600	(3)	600	(2)	1,000

But since their dollar amounts are likely to be significant information, separate accounts are maintained for the various types of revenues and expenses. The recording rules for these are:

1. Since revenues increase stockholders' equity (and increases in stockholders' equity are recorded on the right side), it follows that increases in revenues should be recorded on the right side, decreases on the left.
2. Similarly, since expenses decrease stockholders' equity (and decreases in stockholders' equity are recorded on the left side), it follows that increases in expenses are recorded on the left, decreases on the right.

Following these rules, the service revenue and the wages mentioned above would be recorded in the following manner:

Cash				Service Revenue			
(2)	1,000	(3)	600			(2)	1,000

Wages Expense			
(3)	600		

Debits and Credits.   Before presenting a graphic summary of the recording rules discussed above, the technical accounting terms of debit and credit must be introduced. The accountant uses the term debit in lieu of saying "place an entry on the left side of an account" and credit for "place an entry on the right side of an account." While the terms debit (abbreviated Dr.) and credit (abbreviated Cr.) did have special meanings in their Latin origins, these have long been lost and no special significance should be attached to the terms. Debit means simply left side; credit, right side.

Note that since assets and expenses are increased by debits, these accounts normally have debit (or left side) balances. Conversely, liability, stockholders' equity, and revenue accounts are increased by credits and normally have credit (or right side) balances.

The balance of any account is obtained by summing the debits to the account, summing the credits to the account, and subtracting the smaller sum from the larger. If the sum of the debits exceeds the sum of the credits, the account has a debit balance. For example, the Cash account has a debit balance of $4,000, computed as total debits of $14,000 less total credits of $10,000, in the following T-account:

Cash

(1)	5,000	(2)	2,000
(3)	9,000	(4)	8,000

Similarly, the Accounts Payable account has a credit balance of $3,000:

Accounts Payable

(7)	10,000	(5)	7,000
		(6)	6,000

For the most part, the amounts entered into the various accounts are found in the transactions entered into by the business. Business transactions are first analyzed to determine the effects (increase or decrease) that they have upon the assets, liabilities, stockholders' equity, revenues, or expenses of the business. Then these increases or decreases are encoded into the special accounting terminology of debit and credit. For example, an increase in an asset is recorded as a debit in the proper asset account. When an asset account is debited, depending upon the transaction, there may be any of five credits:

1. Another asset account may be credited, that is, decreased.
2. A liability account may be credited, that is, increased.
3. A stockholders' equity account may be credited, that is, increased.
4. A revenue account may be credited, that is, increased.
5. An expense account may be credited, that is, decreased.

This double-entry procedure maintains the accounting equation in balance. The possibilities in every transaction can be analyzed similarly into debits and credits.

The rules of debit and credit may be presented in account form as follows:

Debits	Credits
1. Increase assets.	1. Decrease assets.
2. Decrease liabilities.	2. Increase liabilities.
3. Decrease stockholders' equity.	3. Increase stockholders' equity.
4. Decrease revenues.	4. Increase revenues.
5. Increase expenses.	5. Decrease expenses.

These rules may also be summarized graphically as shown below. Note especially the treatment of expense accounts as if they were merely subsets of the debit side of the Retained Earnings account. And remember that increases in expenses do tend to reduce what would otherwise be a larger growth in Retained Earnings; and if expenses are reduced, Retained Earnings will increase. The exact reverse holds true for revenues.

Assets	=		Liabilities	+		Stockholders' Equity	
An Asset Account			**A Liability Account**			**A Stockholders' Equity Account**	
Debit	Credit		Debit	Credit		Debit	Credit
+ In- creases	− De- creases		− De- creases	+ In- creases		− Decreases	+ Increases

					Expense Accounts		Revenue Accounts	
					Debit	Credit	Debit	Credit
					+ In- creases	− De- creases	− De- creases	+ In- creases

The Ledger

The accounts in an accounting system are customarily classified into two general groups: (1) the statement of financial position accounts (assets, liabilities, and stockholders' equity) and (2) the earnings statement accounts (revenues and expenses). Whether maintained in a bound volume, handwritten in loose-leaf form, or magnetically encoded on plastic tape and visible only as a computer printout, the accounts in an accounting system are collectively referred to as the ledger.

The list of the names of the accounts in an accounting system is known as the *chart of accounts.* Each account typically has an identification number as well as a name. For example, assets might be numbered from 100–199, liabilities from 200–299, stockholders' equity from 300–399, revenues from 400–499, and expenses from 500–599. The accounts would then, of course, be arranged in numerical sequence in the ledger.

The Journal

Every business transaction, under double-entry accounting, is analyzed as having a dual effect upon the entities engaging in it. And with the rare exception of transactions such as an exchange of land for land, almost every recorded business transaction will affect at least two ledger accounts. Since each ledger account shows only the increases and decreases in the item for which it was established, the entire effects of a single business transaction normally will not appear in any one account. For example, the Cash account contains only information with respect to changes in cash and does not show the exact accounts credited for sources of cash or the exact accounts debited for cash disbursements.

Therefore, if transactions are recorded directly in the accounts, it is quite difficult to ascertain the entire effects of any transaction upon an entity by looking at the accounts.[1] To remedy this deficiency, the accountant employs a book or a record known as a journal. A journal contains a chronological record of the transactions of a business. Because each transaction is initially recorded in a journal, a journal is often called a book of *original entry*. Here every business transaction is analyzed for its effects upon the entity and these effects are expressed in terms of debit and credit—the inputs of the accounting system.

The General Journal.   The general journal is the simplest form of journal. As shown in Illustration 2.1, it contains columns for:

1.   The date.
2.   The name of the account to be debited and the name of the account to be credited, shown on the following line and indented to the right. (Any necessary explanation of a transaction appears below the transaction, indented halfway between the debit and credit entry.)
3.   The ledger folio (L.F.) column; this will be explained in the section below headed "Cross-indexing."
4.   The debit column, in which the money amount of the debit is placed on the same line as the name of the account debited.
5.   The credit column, in which the money amount of the credit is placed on the same line as the name of the account credited.

---

[1] This would be true in an actual accounting system which is likely to contain scores of accounts, each on a separate page. But, if all of an entity's accounts can be represented by a group of T-accounts on a single page, the dual effects of a transaction can be easily observed. For this reason, we will make extensive use of the teaching technique of entering the effects of transactions directly into T-accounts.

A blank line should appear between entries for purposes of easy identification of a complete entry.

Journalizing

Journalizing is the act of entering a transaction in a journal. Information on the transactions to be journalized originates on a variety of source materials or documents such as invoices, cash register tapes, timecards, and checks issued. The activity recorded on these documents must be carefully analyzed to determine whether a recordable transaction has occurred. If so, the specific accounts affected, the dollar amounts of the changes, and their direction (whether increases or decreases) must also be determined. Then all of these changes must be translated into terms of debit and credit. As previously noted, the importance of proper analysis of business transactions cannot be overemphasized.

Posting

In a sense, a journal entry is a set of instructions. It tells the accountant to enter a certain dollar amount as a debit in a specific account. It also tells the accountant to enter a certain dollar amount as a credit in a specific account. The carrying out of these instructions is a process known as posting. In Illustration 2.1, the first entry directs that $10,000 be posted as a debit to the Cash account and as a credit to the Capital Stock account. The three-column balance type of accounts shown in that illustration for Cash and Capital Stock show that these instructions have been carried out. In other words, the entry has been posted.

After each entry is posted to an account, the balance of that account is determined and entered in the column headed "Balance." The "Dr." indicates a debit balance and the "Cr." a credit balance.

Cross-Indexing

The number of the ledger account to which the posting was made is placed in the ledger folio (L. F.) column of the journal. The number of the journal page *from* which the entry was posted is placed in the folio column of the ledger account. Posting is always from the journal to the ledger account. Cross-indexing is the placing of the account number in the journal and the placing of the journal page number in the account, as shown in Illustration 2.1.

Cross-indexing aids the tracing of any recorded transaction, either from the journal to the ledger or from the ledger to the journal. Cross-reference numbers usually are not placed in the L. F. column of the journal until the entry is posted; thereafter, the cross-reference numbers indicate that the entry has been posted.

ILLUSTRATION 2.1

GENERAL JOURNAL					Page 1
Date		Accounts and Explanation	L.F.	Debit	Credit
1979 May	1	Cash.................... Capital Stock.......... Cash invested in the business.	100 300	10,000	10,000
	2	Rent Expense............. Cash................. Rent for May 1979.	410 100	500	500
	3	Equipment............... Accounts Payable...... Tables and chairs, Diller Company.	110 201	2,200	2,200

GENERAL LEDGER
Cash   Account No. 100

Date		Explanation	Folio	Debit	Credit	Balance
1979 May	1 2		J 1 J 1	10,000	500	10,000 Dr. 9,500 Dr.

Equipment   Account No. 110

Date		Explanation	Folio	Debit	Credit	Balance
1979 May	3		J 1	2,200		2,200 Dr.

Accounts Payable   Account No. 201

Date		Explanation	Folio	Debit	Credit	Balance
1979 May	3	Diller Company	J 1		2,200	2,200 Cr.

Capital Stock   Account No. 300

Date		Explanation	Folio	Debit	Credit	Balance
1979 May	1		J 1		10,000	10,000 Cr.

Rent Expense   Account No. 410

Date		Explanation	Folio	Debit	Credit	Balance
1979 May	2		J 1	500		500 Dr.

Compound Journal Entries

The analysis of a business transaction often shows that more than two accounts are directly affected. In such cases the journal entry involves more than one debit or more than one credit or both. A journal entry with more than one debit or credit is a compound journal entry. An entry with one debit and one credit is a simple journal entry.

As an illustration of a compound journal entry:

J. T. Stine purchases $8,000 of machinery from the Myers Company, paying $2,000 cash with the balance due on open account. The journal entry for Stine is as follows:

```
Machinery................................................ 8,000
    Cash..................................................       2,000
    Accounts Payable, Myers Company.......................       6,000
    Machinery purchased from Myers Company, Invoice No. 42
```

Control of the Recording Process

As previously noted, increases in assets (and expenses) are recorded as debits and increases in equities (and revenues) as credits. The objective is to develop two sets of accounts, those with debit balances and those with credit balances, in a recording process such that the total of the accounts with debit balances agrees with the total of the accounts with credit balances. This provides an automatic check upon the arithmetic accuracy of the recording process.

The double-entry system of accounting requires, and the above examples illustrate, that the debits must equal the credits used to record each transaction properly. This equality of debits and credits for each transaction will always hold because both sides of the transaction are recorded. Note that this does not mean that the increases must equal the decreases. A perfectly valid transaction could involve an increase in both an asset and an equity account (the borrowing of money), a decrease in both an asset and an equity account (the repayment of a loan), as well as an increase in one account and a decrease in another. It is this equality of debits and credits, not of increases and decreases, that provides the important control device. If every transaction is recorded in terms of equal debits and credits, it follows that the total of the accounts with debit balances must equal the total of the accounts with credit balances.

The Trial Balance. This proof of the arithmetic accuracy of the recording process is accomplished by preparing a list of the accounts and their debit or credit balances. Such a list is called a trial balance. An example is found in Illustration 2.2. This is the trial balance for Jane's, Inc., which operates a dry cleaning business, at December 31, 1979, which is the end of its first year of operations. The balances reported are those found in the ledger after all of its transactions have been journalized and posted.

ILLUSTRATION 2.2

JANE'S, INC.
Trial Balance
December 31, 1979

	Debits	Credits
Cash...	$ 7,000	
Supplies on hand.................................	12,000	
Unexpired insurance..............................	4,000	
Equipment..	40,000	
Fixtures...	20,000	
Accounts payable.................................		$ 2,000
Notes payable....................................		10,000
Capital stock....................................		30,000
Sales..		145,000
Salaries expense.................................	72,000	
Advertising expense..............................	5,000	
Utilities expense................................	8,000	
Rent expense.....................................	12,000	
Payroll taxes, expense...........................	6,000	
Miscellaneous expense............................	1,000	
	$187,000	$187,000

While the inequality of the totals of the debits and credits columns would automatically indicate the presence of an error, the equality of the two totals does not indicate that the accounting undertaken has been error-free. Indeed, serious errors may have been made such as the complete omission of an important transaction or the recording of an entry in the wrong account as, for example, the recording of an expense as an asset.

Adjusting Entries

A trial balance is usually taken before the preparation of formal financial statements. Before the information in a trial balance can be used in the earnings statement and statement of financial position, the accountant must make sure that the accounts do indeed contain up-to-date information. An analysis of the accounts will usually reveal that some updating adjustments, called *adjusting entries,* are needed. Adjusting entries are needed because economic activity has taken place that is not evidenced by a transaction. Hence, it has not been recorded. Some examples of adjusting entries, based in part upon the data in the Jane's, Inc. trial balance in Illustration 2.2, are given below.

Supplies. Whenever supplies were purchased during the year, their cost was debited to an asset account called Supplies on Hand. These supplies were used during the year, but, because no exchange occurred, their use has not been recorded. An inventory, taken at year end, shows supplies on hand with a cost of $3,000. This means that the accounts should show an asset, Supplies on Hand, of $3,000 and an expense, Supplies Expense, of $9,000 since the supplies purchased but no longer on hand undoubtedly were used during the year. The adjusting entry, coded (*a*), brings the accounts to these balances:

Supplies on Hand		Supplies Expense	
Bal. 12,000	(*a*) 9,000	(*a*) 9,000	

In general journal form, the entry would read:

```
Supplies Expense............................................  9,000
    Supplies on Hand........................................           9,000
    To record supplies used during the year.
```

Unexpired Insurance.   The $4,000 balance in the Unexpired Insurance account represents the premium paid for insurance coverage for the years 1979 and 1980. Since one-half of the period covered by the premium paid has expired, one-half of the premium paid should be transferred from the asset account, Unexpired Insurance, to an Insurance Expense account. In journal form, the required entry would be:

```
Insurance Expense..........................................  2,000
    Unexpired Insurance.....................................           2,000
    To record insurance expense for the year.
```

Equipment and Fixtures.   The equipment and fixtures were acquired at the beginning of the year. Since they were used in generating revenue throughout the year, it is logical that some part of the cost of these assets be considered an expense for the year. This is true because these assets will eventually be scrapped due to "wear and tear" from usage. This wear and tear expense is called depreciation expense. Assuming that both the equipment and the fixtures have estimated useful lives of 10 years, the depreciation expense for the year for Jane's, Inc. is:

Depreciation Expense—Equipment: $40,000 ÷ 10 years = $4,000 per year
Depreciation Expense—Fixtures: $20,000 ÷ 10 years = $2,000 per year.

Using T-accounts, these depreciation amounts would be recorded as follows:

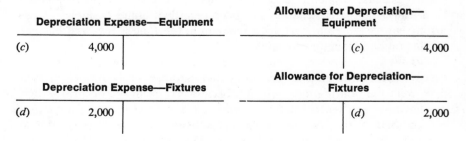

Depreciation Expense—Equipment		Allowance for Depreciation—Equipment	
(*c*) 4,000			(*c*) 4,000
Depreciation Expense—Fixtures		**Allowance for Depreciation—Fixtures**	
(*d*) 2,000			(*d*) 2,000

The depreciation expense recorded could be credited directly to the asset accounts, Equipment and Fixtures. But, for reasons given in Chapter 4, accountants prefer to use separate accounts, which are reported in the statement of financial position as deductions from the related asset accounts.

Accrued Salaries Payable. An analysis of the payroll records supporting the Salaries Expense account reveals that there are $3,000 of unpaid salaries at the end of the year. To have proper balances in the accounts, the following entry must be made:

Salaries Expense		Accrued Salaries Payable	
Bal.	72,000		
(e)	3,000	(e)	3,000

Because it is a debt that will be paid in the very near future, Accrued Salaries Payable is reported as a current liability. (Payroll taxes on this portion are ignored in this illustration.)

Accrued Interest Payable. No entry has been made to record the interest expense incurred and owed on the note payable. The note is dated January 2, 1979, and bears interest at a rate of 10 percent per year. The required entry would debit Interest Expense and credit Accrued Interest Payable for $1,000 (.10 × $10,000). The Interest Expense would be reported in the earnings statement and the Accrued Interest Payable would be reported as a current liability in the statement of financial position since it is also a short-term debt.

Accrued Federal Income Taxes Payable. Jane's, Inc. is subject to federal taxation of its taxable income. Assuming that its taxes payable are $4,000, the entry to record the income tax expense and the liability for such taxes is:

Federal Income Tax Expense		Accrued Federal Income Taxes Payable	
(g)	4,000	(g)	4,000

The above examples are but a few of the many adjusting entries that may be required. These entries have as their purpose the updating of the accounts to make them more accurate reflections of the assets, liabilities, owners' equity, revenues, and expenses of the business. After the posting of the adjusting entries, the accounts are ready for use in preparing the financial statements. The earnings statement for Jane's, Inc. is shown in Illustration 2.3. Its statement of financial position is in Illustration 2.4.

(The statement of changes in financial position is deliberately omitted at this time.) A statement of retained earnings could be prepared, but is also omitted here since it would show only the net earnings for the year of $16,000 and this would be the ending balance of retained earnings.

ILLUSTRATION 2.3

JANE'S, INC.
Earnings Statement
For the Year Ended December 31, 1979

Sales...		$145,000
Expenses:		
Salaries...	$75,000	
Advertising......................................	5,000	
Utilities..	8,000	
Rent..	12,000	
Payroll taxes expense.............................	6,000	
Insurance.......................................	2,000	
Supplies..	9,000	
Depreciation—Equipment...........................	4,000	
Depreciation—Fixtures............................	2,000	
Interest...	1,000	
Miscellaneous...................................	1,000	
Federal income taxes.............................	4,000	
Total Expenses...............................		129,000
Net Earnings......................................		$ 16,000

Closing Entries

One step remains in our illustration of the financial accounting process —a step known as "closing the books." As illustrated, after adjusting entries have been prepared and posted, the accounts contain basically two types of information: (1) information relating to the activities for the period just ended (reported in the earnings statement) and (2) information on financial condition (reported in the statement of financial position).

The first type of information is found in the expense and revenue accounts. As already indicated, these accounts are temporary subdivisions of the Retained Earnings account. They help the accountant fulfill a most important task—the determination of periodic net earnings. But after the financial statements for the period have been prepared, these temporary accounts have served their purpose. They must now be brought to a zero balance, or "closed" to use accounting jargon. In this way, information pertaining to the next period can be gathered in them.

The balance in each expense and revenue account is transferred to an account called Expense and Revenue Summary. This is a *clearing* account used only at the end of the accounting period. It summarizes the expenses

ILLUSTRATION 2.4

JANE'S, INC.
Statement of Financial Position
December 31, 1979

Assets			
Current Assets:			
Cash		$ 7,000	
Supplies on hand		3,000	
Unexpired insurance		2,000	$12,000
Property, Plant and Equipment:			
Equipment	$40,000		
Less: Allowance for depreciation	4,000	$36,000	
Fixtures	$20,000		
Less: Allowance for depreciation	2,000	18,000	54,000
Total Assets			$66,000

Liabilities and Stockholders' Equity		
Current Liabilities:		
Accounts payable	$ 2,000	
Notes payable	10,000	
Accrued salaries payable	3,000	
Federal income taxes payable	4,000	
Accrued interest payable	1,000	$20,000
Stockholders' Equity:		
Capital stock	$30,000	
Retained earnings	16,000	46,000
Total Liabilities and Stockholders' Equity		$66,000

and revenues for the period, with the difference between these two being either net earnings or a net loss. Since revenue accounts have credit balances, they are debited and Expense and Revenue Summary credited. Conversely, expense accounts have debit balances, so they are credited and Expense and Revenue Summary debited. The Expense and Revenue Summary now contains either a debit (net loss) or credit (net earnings) balance. It is then debited or credited to bring it to a zero balance. Retained Earnings is credited or debited to keep the entry in balance. With the making of this last entry, the books are closed. Note carefully that only expense and revenue accounts and the Expense and Revenue Summary account are closed. (If a separate Dividends account were used, it would be closed to Retained Earnings.)

The closing process, using T-accounts and assuming net earnings for the period, is as follows:

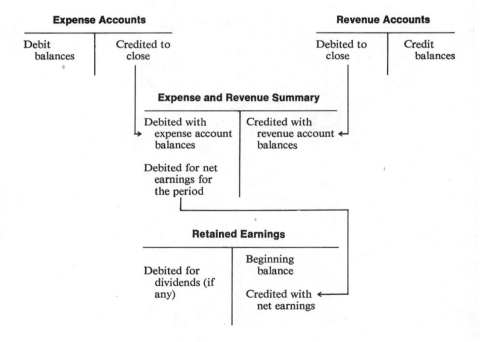

The balance in the Retained Earnings account after closing is correct as of the end of the period. It is reported in the statement of financial position.

For Jane's, Inc. the accounts to be closed are all of the expense and revenue accounts shown in the earnings statement in Illustration 2.3, on page 40. In journal form, its closing entries would read:

Sales..	145,000	
Expense and Revenue Summary.......................		145,000
To close the Sales revenue account.		

Expense and Revenue Summary...........................	129,000	
Salaries Expense......................................		75,000
Advertising Expense...................................		5,000
Utilities Expense.....................................		8,000
Rent Expense...		12,000
Payroll Taxes, Expense...............................		6,000
Insurance Expense....................................		2,000
Supplies Expense.....................................		9,000
Depreciation Expense—Equipment.....................		4,000
Depreciation Expense—Fixtures.......................		2,000
Interest Expense.....................................		1,000
Miscellaneous Expense................................		1,000
Federal Income Taxes Expense........................		4,000
To close the expense accounts for the year.		

Expense and Revenue Summary...........................	16,000	
Retained Earnings....................................		16,000
To close net earnings for the year to Retained Earnings.		

When the above entries are posted, all of the company's expense and revenue accounts will be reduced to a zero balance. Thus, they are ready to accumulate data on the operations for the year 1980. Note that Retained Earnings will have the same balance that it would have if all expenses and revenues had been entered directly in it. But the use of expense and revenue accounts permits classification of these elements and makes them readily available for reporting in the earnings statement.

The Financial Accounting Process Summarized

The steps involved in the operation of an accounting system are often referred to collectively as the accounting cycle. These steps include:

1. Journalizing transactions (and other events) in the journal.
2. Posting journal entries to ledger accounts.
3. Taking a trial balance of the accounts.
4. Journalizing the needed adjusting entries.
5. Posting the adjusting entries to the accounts.
6. Preparing the financial statements.
7. Journalizing the closing entries.
8. Posting the closing entries to the accounts.

SUMMARY

The basic components of an accounting system are the journal and the account. An account is the means or form used to summarize changes in the various types of assets, liabilities, owners' equities, revenues, and expenses of a business. By convention, asset and expense accounts are increased by entries on the left side of the account (called the debit side) and decreased by entries on the right side (called the credit side). Liability, stockholders' (owners') equity, and revenue accounts are increased by entries on the credit side, decreased by entries on the debit side. As a result, asset and expense accounts usually have debit balances, the others credit balances.

Recording increases and decreases in accounts in this manner yields two groups of accounts: (1) those with debit balances, and (2) those with credit balances. This provides an automatic check upon the arithmetic accuracy of the accounting process.

The ledger is the collection of accounts in an accounting system. The chart of accounts is a list of the names (and numbers) of the accounts in an accounting system.

Business activity is analyzed and certain transactions are recorded in a journal in a process known as journalizing. The journalized amounts are then posted to the ledger accounts. A trial balance is a list of all of the accounts in the ledger together with their debit or credit balances which, in total, must be equal. Adjusting entries are then prepared to bring the accounts up to date. Financial statements can then be prepared. Next, the expense and revenue accounts are closed, that is brought to a zero balance, to be ready to receive information on the next period's activities.

QUESTIONS AND EXERCISES

1. What is an account? What functions does it fulfill?
2. What are the two major components of an accounting system? What purpose does each fulfill?
3. Define debit and credit. Name the types of accounts that are increased by debits and decreased by credits and those that are increased by credits and decreased by debits.
4. Analyze the following transactions and indicate whether the accounts affected are debited or credited.
   a. Money is borrowed by the giving of a written promise to repay.
   b. Equipment is purchased on account.
   c. Services are rendered for customers who promise to pay later.
   d. Payments on account are received from customers.
   e. Cash is paid to employees for services rendered.
5. What are adjusting entries? In general, why must they be made?
6. What are closing entries? In general, why must they be made?
7. Which of the following could be and which cannot be a complete analysis of the effects of a transaction upon a business firm? Why?
   a. Increase a liability and increase an expense.
   b. Increase an asset and decrease a liability.
   c. Increase a revenue and decrease an expense.
   d. Decrease an asset and increase another asset.

e. Decrease an asset and increase a liability.

f. Decrease a revenue and decrease an asset.

g. Decrease a liability and increase a revenue.

8. What is a trial balance? What purposes are served by its preparation?

9. Give an example of an event that looks like a transaction, but which would not be recorded by the accountant.

10. What is a compound journal entry? Give an example.

11. List the steps taken to complete the accounting cycle.

12. The payment of $12,000 as the premium for one year of insurance coverage beginning on July 1 was debited to an Unexpired Insurance account. What adjusting entry is needed on December 31, the end of the accounting year?

13. You note that a trial balance shows an account entitled Supplies on Hand in the amount of $2,700. An inventory shows $300 of supplies actually on hand. What adjusting entry would be needed if financial statements were to be prepared?

14. The ledger of a business firm contains an account entitled Accrued Salaries Payable in the amount of $1,900. Where would this amount appear in the financial statements? Why? Would it be closed in the closing of the books? Why or why not?

15. The accountant of the A Company forgot to make an entry for $800 of accrued wages at the end of 1979. What is the effect of this omission upon net earnings for that year?

16. A firm borrows $10,000 on November 1 for 120 days with interest payable at the time of repayment of the loan at the rate of 9 percent per year. Prepare the adjusting entry needed on December 31.

PROBLEMS

2–1. *Required:*

a. Open T-accounts for the Hayden Company and enter transactions given below for the month of August 1979. Place the date of each transaction in the accounts.

b. Prepare a trial balance as of August 31, 1979.

Transactions:

Aug. 1 Issued capital stock for cash, $15,000.

3 Borrowed $12,000 from the bank on a note.

4 Purchased a truck for $3,300 cash.

6 Services are performed for customers who promise to pay later, $3,600.

7 Employee services received but not paid for, $700.

10 Collections are made for the services performed on August 6, $800.

11 The liability for employee services for the week ending August 7 is paid.

14 Supplies are purchased for use in future months, $300. They will be paid for next month.

17   A bill for $100 is received for gas and oil used to date.
25   Services are performed for customers who pay immediately, $4,500.
31   Employee services received but not paid for, $1,500.

2–2. *Required:*

a. Open proper T-accounts for the Bryan Service Company and enter the transactions given below for the month of July 1979. For identification, place the date of each transaction in the accounts.
b. Prepare a trial balance as of July 31, 1979.

Transactions:

July 2   Cash of $5,000 was received for capital stock issued to the owners.
      3   The company paid rent for July, $350.
      5   Office furniture was purchased for $3,000 cash.
      9   A bill for $500 for advertising for July was received and paid.
     14   Cash of $700 was received for fees for services to customers.
     15   Wages of $200 for the first half of July were paid in cash.
     20   The company sold services on open account to the Betz Company, $300. The account is to be paid August 10.
     22   Office furniture was acquired on account from the Martin Metal Company; the price was $400.
     30   Cash of $2,250 was received for fees for services to customers.
     31   Wages of $250 for the second half of July were paid in cash.

2–3. Completely adjusted (except for Federal income taxes, which are to be ignored) the accounts of the Farmer Company at June 30, 1979 are:

Equipment...............	$ 1,500	Service revenue.............	$8,000
Wages expense.............	4,000	Cash......................	9,270
Accounts receivable..........	1,030	Accounts payable............	800
Capital stock...............	10,000	Retained earnings............	?
Utilities expense............	1,000	Rent expense................	2,000
Depreciation expense.........	100	Allowance for depreciation....	100

Required:

a. Prepare an earnings statement for the month of June 1979.
b. Prepare a statement of financial position as of June 30, 1979.

2–4. Following are the transactions of the Akers Company for the month of May 1979:
(1) Issued capital stock for cash, $12,000.
(2) Purchased equipment on account, $7,200.
(3) Paid the rent for May, $500.
(4) Paid the equipment supplier (#2 above) $5,000 on account.
(5) Services rendered for customers for cash, $4,000; on account $6,000.
(6) Cash received from customers on account, $3,000.
(7) Paid employees for services rendered in May, $6,000.

(8) Accrued employee wages at the end of May, $1,000.
(9) The equipment is expected to last 120 months.

Required:

a. Set up T-accounts and record the above transactions and adjustments. (Ignore any possible Federal income taxes.)
b. Prepare an earnings statement for the month of May 1979.
c. Prepare a statement of financial position as of May 31, 1979.
d. Enter in the T-accounts the closing entries that would be required if May 31, 1979, is the end of the accounting period. (Key these entries *a, b,* and *c* in the T-accounts.)

2–5. Delano Cleaning Service, Inc., was organized July 1, 1979. The following account numbers and titles constitute the chart of accounts for the company:

Account No.	Account Name	Account No.	Account Name
101	Cash	332	Retained Earnings
102	Accounts Receivable	441	Cleaning Service Sales
111	Office Equipment	551	Salaries Expense
112	Cleaning Equipment	552	Insurance Expense
113	Service Truck	553	Service Truck Expense
221	Accounts Payable	554	Rent Expense
222	Notes Payable	555	Utilities Expense
331	Capital Stock	556	Cleaning Supplies Expense

Required:

a. Prepare ledger accounts for all of the above accounts except Retained Earnings.
b. Journalize the transactions given below for July 1979.
c. Post the journal entries to the ledger accounts.
d. Prepare a trial balance.

Transactions:

July 1 The company issued $30,000 of capital stock for cash.
      5 Office space was rented for July, and $600 cash was paid for the rental.
      8 Desks and chairs were purchased for the office, on account, $2,000.
     10 Cleaning equipment was purchased for $4,200; a note was given, to be paid in 30 days.
     15 Purchased a service truck for $18,000, paying $12,000 cash and giving a 60-day note to the dealer for $6,000.
     18 Paid for cleaning supplies received and already used, $300.
     23 Cleaning service sales, $1,800 cash.
     27 Insurance expense for July was paid, $450 cash.
     30 Paid for gasoline and oil used by the service truck in July, $60.
     31 Billed customers for cleaning services rendered, $4,200.
     31 Paid salaries for July, $5,400.
     31 Paid utilities bills for July, $450.

2–6. Given below is the trial balance of Windal Company, a computer programming and processing company:

WINDAL COMPANY
Trial Balance
June 30, 1979

	Debits	*Credits*
Cash.................................	$ 6,500	
Accounts receivable.....................	17,000	
Office equipment........................	50,000	
Allowance for depreciation..............		$10,000
Accounts payable.......................		5,400
Notes payable..........................		10,000
Capital stock...........................		10,000
Retained earnings (July 1, 1978)...........		12,700
Service revenue.........................		50,000
Office rent expense.....................	6,000	
Advertising expense.....................	2,200	
Salaries expense........................	15,740	
Supplies expense........................	540	
Miscellaneous expense...................	120	
	$98,100	$98,100

The unrecorded depreciation for the year ended June 30, 1979, on the office equipment is $10,000. The estimated Federal income taxes for the year amount to $3,400.

Required:

a. Prepare adjusting entries for the depreciation and the estimated Federal income taxes.
b. Prepare the earnings statement for the year ended June 30, 1979.
c. Prepare the statement of retained earnings for the year ended June 30, 1979.
d. Prepare a statement of financial position as of June 30, 1979.
e. Prepare closing entries.

2–7. The trial balance of the Mann Company at December 31 of the current year includes, among other items, the following account balances:

	Debits	*Credits*
Unexpired insurance.....................	$ 3,648	
Buildings..............................	79,000	
Allowance for depreciation of buildings....		$15,800
Salaries expense........................	55,000	
Prepaid rent...........................	24,000	

Additional information:

a. The debit balance in the Unexpired Insurance account is the advance premium for one year from September 1 of the current year.
b. The buildings are being depreciated over 25 years, with no salvage value expected.
c. Salaries accrued and payable at December 31 amount to $3,200.

d. The debit balance in Prepaid Rent is for a one-year period that started March 1 of the current year.

Required: Prepare the adjusting journal entries at December 31.

2–8. The balances of all of the Henge Company accounts as of June 1, 1979, were as follows:

Cash....................	3,200	Accounts payable..........	2,000
Accounts receivable........	4,300	Capital stock..............	5,000
		Retained earnings.........	500

The transactions (and certain other data) for the company for June were as follows:

(1) Services rendered to customers for cash, $4,000; on account, $8,000.

(2) Paid rent for the six months ending November 30, $3,000. (Record entire amount as prepaid rent.)

(3) Purchased equipment for cash, $4,800.

(4) Supplies purchased on account and used in June, $800.

(5) Receipts on account from customers, $11,000.

(6) Payments on account to suppliers, $1,400.

(7) Employee services received, $7,500; cash paid to employees, $6,500.

(8) Paid utility bill of $200.

(9) Paid dividend to stockholders, $300.

(10) Equipment has an expected life of four years.

(11) Adjust for prepaid rent that has expired.

Required:

a. Set up T-accounts and record the above data, including the beginning balances given above. (Ignore any possible Federal income taxes.)

b. Prepare an earnings statement for the month of June.

c. Prepare a statement of retained earnings for the month of June.

d. Prepare a statement of financial position as of June 30, 1979.

chapter 3

Sales, Cost of Goods Sold, and Inventories

As already noted, accountants seek to fulfill one of their most important tasks—the measurement of periodic net earnings—through a process of matching revenues and expenses by time periods. This chapter discusses the accounting for the major source of revenue for most business firms—sales of a product—and a major element of expense—the cost of the goods sold.

Attention is focused on the cost of goods sold not only because it is a relatively large expense but, as we shall see, because measures of its periodic amount may differ depending on which of several alternative accounting methods is employed.

SALES, COST OF GOODS SOLD, AND GROSS MARGIN

Accounting for Sales Revenue

The revenue of a company engaged in selling merchandise is typically recorded at the time of the completion of the sale (which is assumed to occur when the goods are delivered) and at the price agreed upon in the sales contract. Thus, a sale on account of a machine at a price of $3,000 would be recorded when the machine was delivered as follows:

Accounts Receivable		Sales	
(a)	3,000	(a)	3,000

Recording revenue at the time of sale is usually considered appropriate because (1) the revenue has been earned, that is, the seller has completed its part of the contract; (2) the revenue is readily measurable—the actual selling price is known; (3) legal title to the goods passes to the buyer; and (4) the revenue is realized—a valid asset has been received in an exchange with an outsider. Furthermore, the actual sale of the goods may be the critical event in a series of events that end in a sale. As a practical matter, revenue from the sale of goods is usually recorded when the goods are delivered in a valid sales transaction. But goods delivered on a consignment basis should not be recorded as sold. Here the goods remain the property of the shipper until sold by the party to whom consigned—the consignee.

Cost of Goods Sold—Perpetual Procedure

Firms securing revenue from the sale of goods usually keep a stock of such goods on hand which is called merchandise inventory. If prior to the above sale the seller had purchased three identical machines on account at a price of $1,800 each, this purchase transaction would, under what is known as *perpetual inventory procedure,* be recorded as follows:

Merchandise Inventory			Accounts Payable	
(b)	5,400		(b)	5,400

Merchandise inventory is a current asset account, and accounts payable is a current liability. Under perpetual procedure, a second entry is required at the time of sale to record the *expense* incurred as a result of transferring an asset, part of the inventory, to the customer:

Merchandise Inventory				Cost of Goods Sold	
(b)	5,400	(c)	1,800	(c)	1,800

The $1,800 in the above entry would be secured from supporting records called *stock cards* or *perpetual inventory cards.* These records show the dates, quantities, and prices of goods received and of those issued, and the quantities and prices of the goods on hand at any given moment in time.

Let us assume that $500 of other expenses were incurred in the week ending July 18, 1979, in which the above sale was the company's only sale. The earnings statement for the week would be as follows:

Sales..	$3,000
Cost of goods sold...	1,800
Gross margin..	$1,200
Other expenses..	500
Net Earnings...	$ 700

The difference between sales and cost of goods sold is called *gross margin* or *gross profit,* and the relationship between gross margin and sales is often expressed as a percentage called the gross profit or gross margin rate—40 percent in this instance ($1,200 ÷ $3,000).

Perpetual inventory procedure is widely used in companies that sell merchandise of high individual unit value, such as furs, jewelry, and autos. Because each unit has a high unit value, management finds it especially useful to know which merchandise is selling and which is not. Promotional activity and purchasing can be planned. Also, inventory shortages can be determined by comparing amounts shown on perpetual records with physical counts of the items on hand. Thus, the benefits derived from keeping detailed perpetual records are believed to exceed the cost of maintaining such records.

Cost of Goods Sold—Periodic Procedure

On the other hand, companies that sell goods with low unit values, such as greeting cards, nuts and bolts, and pencils, may find it too costly to maintain perpetual records for their merchandise. Such companies use periodic inventory procedure. Under this procedure, inventory is not updated in the accounts after every purchase and sale. Rather, the proper inventory balance is determined and recorded only after a physical count is taken of the goods on hand and the goods are properly priced. Such physical counts are usually taken once a year as a minimum. And cost of goods sold is determined only after the physical inventory has been taken.

The Purchases Account. Under periodic procedure, merchandise acquisitions are recorded in a separate Purchases account. A purchase of $40,000 of goods on account would then be recorded as a debit to Purchases and a credit to Accounts Payable. The cost of the goods sold in any period is then determined as follows:

> Merchandise Inventory (at beginning of period)
> + Purchases for the Period
> = Cost of Goods Available for Sale; this sum
> − Ending Inventory (goods on hand not sold)
> = Cost of Goods Sold (the expense for the period)

The computation of the cost of the goods sold can be included in the earnings statement, if desired, as shown in Illustration 3.1. Future examples will illustrate this periodic procedure only.

Returns and Allowances

Whenever goods are sold, some of them may be returned by the buyer to the seller for any of a variety of reasons. For example, assume that goods have been sold to a buyer on account in the amount of $5,000. This was recorded as a debit to Accounts Receivable and a credit to Sales of

ILLUSTRATION 3.1

X COMPANY
Partial Earnings Statement
For the Month Ended July 31, 1979

Sales...		$50,000
Cost of goods sold		
Inventory, July 1............................	$15,000	
Purchases..................................	40,000	
Cost of goods available for sale................	$55,000	
Less: Inventory, July 31.....................	22,000	
Cost of goods sold...........................		33,000
Gross Margin.................................		$17,000

$5,000 by the seller, and as a debit to Purchases and a credit to Accounts Payable of $5,000 by the buyer. Now goods with a sales price of $400 are returned. The entry on the seller's books—entry (a)—would be:

Sales Returns		**Accounts Receivable**		
(a) 400		Bal. 5,000	(a)	400

In journal form, the entry would read:

Sales Returns... 400
    Accounts Receivable....................................... 400
    To record return of goods by customer.

The entry on the buyer's books—entry (b)—would be:

Purchase Returns		**Accounts Payable**		
	(b) 400	(b) 400	Bal.	5,000

In journal form, the entry on the buyer's books would read:

Accounts Payable.. 400
    Purchase Returns.. 400
    To record return of goods to supplier.

The seller has credited the customer's account because the return has reduced the customer's obligation to pay. The customer (buyer) debited the vendor's account because the return reduced its obligation to the seller.

Occasionally, concessions will be granted from the originally agreed-upon price of a sale of merchandise because of blemishes, defects, or damage. Such price concessions are recorded in the same manner as returns, except that the accounts involved will be Sales Allowances and Purchase Allowances. Frequently, returns and allowances are recorded in combined Sales Returns and Allowances accounts and Purchase Returns and Allowances accounts.

Because sales returns and allowances represent actual cancellations of all or a part of a sale, they could be recorded directly as debits in the Sales account. For similar reasons, purchase returns and allowances could be recorded as credits in the Purchases account. But because, in a sense, returns and allowances represent or result from inefficiencies in operations, their amounts are likely to constitute significant information to management and others since the handling of returns can be costly to both buyers and sellers. (They amount to as much as 15 percent of sales in some businesses.) They are, therefore, recorded in separate accounts (called contra accounts) and often reported separately (as deductions from sales and purchases to arrive at net sales and net purchases) in the earnings statement.

Cash Discounts

Frequently when goods are sold on a credit basis, the buyer is permitted to pay an amount less than the full invoice price of the goods if payment is made within a stated period of time. Thus, an invoice might state credit terms of "2/10, n/30" (read as 2 10, net 30) which means that a 2 percent discount can be deducted from the total price of the invoice if the invoice is paid within 10 days from the invoice date. Thus, the payment within the discount period of a $1,000 invoice for merchandise sold under terms 2/10, n/30 and originally recorded at $1,000 would be recorded as follows:

Seller's Books

Accounts Receivable			Sales	
(a)	1,000	(b)	1,000	(a)	1,000

Cash		Sales Discounts	
(b)	980	(b)	20

Buyer's Books

Purchases		Accounts Payable		
(c)	1,000	(d)	1,000	(c)	1,000

Cash		Purchase Discounts	
Bal.	xxx	(d)	980	(d)	20

The Sales Discounts and Purchase Discounts accounts also are contra accounts to the Sales and Purchases accounts. This treatment reflects the preferred theoretical view that such discounts are adjustments of recorded revenue and cost.

An alternative consists of recording purchases at net invoice price and isolating in a separate account any discounts not taken. To illustrate, assume that a $1,000 invoice, terms 2/10, n/30, is recorded at net invoice price ($980) and paid after the discount privilege period has expired. The required entries are:

Purchases		**Accounts Payable**	
(*a*) 980		(*b*) 980	(*a*) 980

Cash		**Purchase Discounts Lost**	
Bal. xxx	(*b*) 1,000	(*b*) 20	

In journal form, the two entries required would be:

```
Purchases.........................................................  980
    Accounts Payable..............................................          980
    To record purchase of merchandise at net invoice price.

Accounts Payable..................................................  980
Purchase Discounts Lost...........................................   20
    Cash..........................................................        1,000
    To record payment of invoice after discount period had expired.
```

This procedure, in effect, applies the principle of management by exception by drawing attention to the exception rather than the routine, that is, to discounts *not* taken. Well-run businesses seldom fail to take all discounts offered simply because of the relative cost involved. For example, failure to take a 2 percent discount under credit terms of 2/10, n/30 is the equivalent of paying 2 percent for 20 days since the account is due 20 days after the discount period expires. Two percent for 20 days is roughly equivalent to an annual rate of interest of 36 percent.

Transportation-In

The cost a buyer incurs to have merchandise delivered is part of the total cost of the goods. But because the total freight costs incurred may be significant information, the receipt of a freight bill usually results in an entry debiting Transportation-In and crediting Accounts Payable.

The partial earnings statement shown in Illustration 3.2 illustrates the financial reporting of returns, allowances, discounts, and transportation-in.

ILLUSTRATION 3.2

FICTITIOUS COMPANY
Partial Earnings Statement
For the Year Ended December 31, 1979

Sales....................................			$100,000
Less: Sales returns and allowances.........		$ 4,000	
Sales discounts....................		1,000	5,000
Net sales.................................			$95,000
Cost of goods sold	*Raw materials &*		
Inventory, 1/1... *beginning Inventory - holding for sale*			$ 28,000
Purchases................................		$60,000	
Less: Purchase returns and allowances......	$5,000		
Purchase discounts..................	1,000	6,000	
Net purchases...........................		$54,000	
Transportation-in........................		3,000	57,000
Cost of goods available for sale.............			$ 85,000
Less: Inventory, 12/31....................			21,000	64,000
Gross Margin.............................			$31,000

Adjusting and Closing Entries

The data in Illustration 3.2 can be used to show the adjusting and closing entries required in the accounts of a merchandising firm. First an entry is needed to accumulate in one account all of the costs relating to the goods that were available for sale:

Cost of Goods Sold.......................................	85,000	
Purchase Returns and Allowances...........................	5,000	
Purchase Discounts.......................................	1,000	
Purchases...		60,000
Transportation-In..		3,000
Inventory..		28,000

The Cost of Goods Sold account now contains the cost of the goods available for sale. But not all of the goods have been sold. An inventory of $21,000 remains on hand. This must be set up as an *asset,* which leads to the following entry:

Inventory..	21,000	
Cost of Goods Sold....................................		21,000

Now the revenue and revenue contra accounts can be closed:

Sales..	100,000	
Sales Returns and Allowances.........................		4,000
Sales Discounts......................................		1,000
Expense and Revenue Summary........................		95,000

The Cost of Goods Sold account would be closed along with the other expense accounts in an entry involving a debit to Expense and Revenue Summary and a credit to each of the individual expense accounts, as already illustrated.

Bad Debts

A seller doing business on a credit basis faces the virtual certainty that some customers' accounts will ultimately prove uncollectible. For example, assume that a seller because of past experience expects to collect only $95,000 out of $100,000 of accounts receivable outstanding at year-end. Normally, this would require the following entry:

Bad Debts Expense		Allowance for Doubtful Accounts	
(a)	5,000	(a)	5,000

This entry serves two purposes: (1) Uncollectible accounts are charged as an expense in the year the sale giving rise to them was made; that is, a proper matching is secured when, say, uncollectible accounts arising from credit sales made in 1979 are charged as an expense in 1979. (2) The accounts receivable at year-end are properly valued at their *net realizable value*—the amount of cash expected to be collected.

The Bad Debts Expense account is shown as an operating expense in the earnings statement. The Allowance for Doubtful Accounts is a contra account (reduction account) to Accounts Receivable and is credited rather than crediting Accounts Receivable directly because it is not known at this time which customers' accounts will actually prove uncollectible. A typical reporting of the $100,000 of accounts receivable and the related allowance for doubtful accounts of $5,000 is to include the following in the current assets section of the statement of financial position:

Accounts receivable (less estimated uncollectibles of $5,000)........... $95,000

Subsequent Write-Offs. Later, when an account is determined to be uncollectible, an entry is made debiting the Allowance for Doubtful Accounts and crediting Accounts Receivable. Note that this entry has no effect upon net earnings or upon the valuation of the accounts receivable. The expense and the reduced valuation for the asset were recognized when the adjusting entry for estimated uncollectibles was made. The write-off entry merely gives recognition to an event that was anticipated when the allowance was established.

If, by chance, an error was made in writing off an individual customer's account (as shown by the collection of the account), an entry is made debiting Accounts Receivable and crediting the Allowance for Doubtful Accounts. Then the cash collection is recorded as a debit to Cash and a credit to Accounts Receivable.

INVENTORY MEASUREMENT

A crucial step in the determination of net earnings is the measurement of the ending inventory of the period. This is true not only because it affects net earnings but also because it affects measurements of current assets, total assets, gross margin, retained earnings, and total stockholders' equity. How this happens will be explained later when the questions of what to include as part of the cost of the inventory and which of several measurement methods should be used are discussed.

The Basic Rule

Chapter 4 of *Accounting Research Bulletin 43* states that "the primary basis of accounting for inventories is cost . . ." and further stipulates that "a departure from the cost basis . . . is required when the utility of the goods is no longer as great as . . ." their cost. Thus, inventories are usually reported in the statement of financial position at a dollar amount described as *cost or market, whichever is lower*.

In applying this general or basic rule, several problems exist. As discussed below, these include:

1. What costs should be included as part of the cost of the inventory?
2. What is the cost of the inventory when goods have been purchased at different unit costs?
3. What constitutes evidence of a decline in the utility of goods and how is it measured?

Inventory Cost—Possible Inclusions

In principle, the cost of inventory includes all costs incurred, directly or indirectly, to acquire the goods and place them in position and condition for sale. Thus, cost includes the net invoice price of the goods plus. insurance in transit, transportation charges, receiving, handling and storage costs, and duties. But, as a practical matter, these related costs are often omitted from inventory cost because (1) they are not material in amount relative to the total cost of the goods purchased, or (2) there is no easy way to allocate these costs to individual units of merchandise. Also, because they are immaterial, purchase discounts are on occasion not deducted from invoice price in determining inventory cost.

Inventory Costing Methods

As already indicated, the cost of the goods available for sale (beginning inventory plus purchases) must be apportioned between ending inventory and cost of goods sold. But how are these costs to be apportioned when goods have been acquired at different unit costs? For example, suppose at the beginning of a month a retailer has three units of a product on hand, one acquired at $10, another at $11, and the third at $12. Suppose that during the month two units were sold. What is their cost? Is it $21, the cost of the first and second units? Or $22, the cost of the first and third units? Or $23, the cost of the second and third units? Or should it be $22 determined as two units at an average cost of $11? Four inventory costing methods have been developed to solve this type of problem. They are: (1) specific identification, (2) first-in, first-out (Fifo), (3) last-in, first-out (Lifo), and (4) weighted average.

The data in Illustration 3.3 are assumed for the beginning inventory, purchases, and sales of a given product in order to illustrate the application of these four inventory costing methods.

The total goods available for sale consisted of 80 units with a total cost of $854. Of the units available, 60 were sold, producing sales revenue of $940, and 20 units were left on hand in inventory. Our task now is to apportion the $854 between cost of goods sold, an expense, and ending inventory, an asset.

Specific Identification. This method calls for the assignment of a known actual cost to a particular identifiable unit of product. The specific product involved is usually identifiable through the use of a serial number plate or identification tag. The method is quite appropriately applied when large, readily identifiable units of product are purchased and sold, for example, automobiles.

To illustrate, assume that the 20 units of product on hand at the end of the year in Illustration 3.3 are definitely known to consist of 10 from the August 12 purchase and 10 from the December 21 purchase. The ending inventory then is shown in Illustration 3.4.

The cost of the ending inventory of $222 would be deducted from the total cost of goods available for sale of $854 to get the cost of goods sold of $632.

The specific identification method results in the cost of goods sold, and inventory being stated in terms of the actual cost of the actual units sold and on hand. Thus, costs are matched against revenues with a high

ILLUSTRATION 3.3

Inventory, Purchases, and Sales Data

Product X, Model No. 12

Beginning Inventory and Purchases				Sales			
Date	No. of Units	Unit Cost	Total Cost	Date	No. of Units	Price	Total
1/1 inventory..	10	$10.00	$100.00	3/8...........	10	$15.00	$150.00
3/2...........	10	10.40	104.00	7/5...........	10	15.00	150.00
5/28..........	20	10.50	210.00	9/7...........	20	16.00	320.00
8/12..........	10	11.00	110.00	11/27.........	20	16.00	320.00
10/12.........	20	10.90	218.00				
12/21.........	10	11.20	112.00				
Total.........	80		$854.00		60		$940.00

ILLUSTRATION 3.4
Ending Inventory under Specific Identification

From Purchase of—	No. of Units	Cost Each	Total Cost
August 12	10	$11.00	$110.00
December 21	10	11.20	112.00
Total	20		$222.00

degree of precision. The method is used most logically to account for "big ticket" items, such as autos and trucks, because each unit tends to be unique. Also, the selling price of such items tends to be based on a markup over a specifically identified cost.

The method is criticized by some because it may result in two identical units of product being included in the inventory at different prices even if, because they are identical, they have the same utility. But supporters would contend that this is entirely logical and consistent with the cost basis of asset measurement. The method is also indicted by some as theoretically unacceptable because earnings may be manipulated when it is used. If higher earnings are desired, ship the units with the lower cost. If lower earnings are desired, ship the high cost units.

But the major deficiency in the specific identification method is that it is simply too costly and too time consuming to apply. This would be true where large quantities of many different types of products with low unit costs are purchased and sold.

First-In, First-Out (Fifo).   Good merchandising policy usually calls for moving oldest goods first, if at all possible. In reality, in most businesses, the actual physical flow of goods *is* first-in, first-out and has to be to avoid substantial losses from spoilage as in the case of dairy products and fresh produce. Since conforming the flow of costs through the accounting system to the actual physical flow of goods seems intuitively logical, the first-in, first-out method of inventory measurement results.

The application of the Fifo method results in the latest costs being included in inventory, while the older costs are charged to cost of goods sold. The method may be applied even in those circumstances in which goods do not flow in a first-in, first-out manner.

Fifo Applied under Periodic Procedure.   Since, in the data presented in Illustration 3.3, the inventory consists of 20 units, under the Fifo method these units would be priced as shown in Illustration 3.5.

The ending inventory thus includes the costs of the latest purchases, and the balance of the cost of the goods available for sale (consisting of older costs) is charged to cost of goods sold. The ending inventory is $221, and this sum will be deducted from the total cost of goods available for sale of $854 to get the cost of goods sold of $633.

ILLUSTRATION 3.5

Fifo Cost of Ending Inventory under Periodic Procedure

From Purchase of—	No. of Units	Unit Price	Total Cost
December 21	10	$11.20	$112.00
October 12	10	10.90	109.00
Total	20		$221.00

Last-In, First-Out (Lifo). Under Lifo, the cost of the last goods purchased are charged against revenues as the cost of the goods sold, while the inventory is composed of the costs of the oldest goods acquired. Tax regulations provide that if Lifo is used for tax purposes it must be used in general financial reports. Note that although the costs of the goods purchased are assumed to flow in a last-in, first-out manner, this does not mean that the goods physically flow in this manner.

In order to determine the cost of the ending inventory, list the goods in the beginning inventory and continue listing subsequent purchases until enough units have been listed to equal the number in the ending inventory. Illustration 3.6 shows the determination of the ending inventory for the data listed in Illustration 3.3.

The cost of the ending inventory of $204 would be deducted from the cost of the goods available for sale of $854 to show a cost of goods sold of $650. Note that in this example the costs charged against revenues as the cost of the goods sold are all fairly current or recent costs. The inventory, however, consists of a March 2 cost and the cost of the beginning inventory, which may actually have been incurred many years ago.

Fifo and Lifo Compared. Much has been written in recent years concerning the relative merits of Fifo and Lifo. Lifo's appeal can be tied directly to the long-run tendency toward rising prices experienced in this country since the early 1930s. An example will make this point clear.

Suppose that Company A has one unit of a given product on hand which cost $10. The unit is sold for $15, other expenses of sale amount to $3.50, the tax rate is 50 percent, and the unit is replaced for $11 prior

ILLUSTRATION 3.6

Lifo Cost of Ending Inventory

From Purchase of—	No. of Units	Unit Cost	Total Cost
Beginning inventory	10	10.00	$100.00
March 2	10	10.40	104.00
Total	20		$204.00

to the end of the accounting period. Under Fifo accounting net earnings are computed as follows:

Net sales	$15.00
Cost of goods sold	10.00
Gross margin	$ 5.00
Expenses	3.50
Net operating margin	$ 1.50
Federal income taxes (50 percent rate)	0.75
Net Earnings	$ 0.75

According to the above schedule the company is selling this product at a price sufficient to produce net earnings. But consider the following:

Cash secured from sale	$15.00
Expenses and taxes paid ($3.50 + $0.75)	4.25
Cash available for replacement and for dividends	$10.75
Cost to replace	11.00
Additional Cash Required to Replace Inventory	$ 0.25

Thus, Company A, which is reporting net earnings, finds itself unable to replace its inventory without securing additional cash. But note what happens when Lifo is used as the method of inventory pricing:

Net sales	$15.00
Cost of goods sold	11.00
Gross margin	$ 4.00
Expenses	3.50
Net operating margin	$ 0.50
Federal income taxes	0.25
Net Earnings	$ 0.25

The $0.25 of net earnings is matched by an increase in cash that is available for distribution as dividends or for other purposes:

Cash secured from sale	$15.00
Expenses and taxes ($3.50 + $0.25)	3.75
Cash available for replacement and dividends	$11.25
Cash spent to replace unit sold	11.00
Cash Available for Dividends (or Other Uses)	$ 0.25

Because the unit sold was replaced before the end of the year, the effect of using Lifo increased cost of goods sold $1.00 ($11.00 − $10.00). This, in turn, reduced taxable income by $1.00 and, with a 50 percent tax rate, reduced federal incomes taxes by 50 cents. Some of Lifo's popularity thus is due to its ability to minimize current tax payments in periods of rising prices which is what has occurred in our economy over recent years.

But Lifo is supported on theoretical grounds in that it tends to match costs and revenues on a more reasonable basis than Fifo. The earnings statement reports sales and the most recent costs of making those sales when Lifo is used. Thus, the earnings reported reflect operating results and do not include gains from holding inventory in periods of rising prices —"inventory profits" as they are called. The inventory profit in the above example was $1.00—the difference between the cost to replace the unit sold at the time of sale ($11) and its actual cost ($10). Lifo is also supported by accountants who believe that selling prices are most likely to be based upon replacement cost and that Lifo cost most closely approximates replacement cost.

On the other hand, Fifo advocates point out that Lifo matches the cost of *un*sold goods (because goods usually move in a first-in, first-out manner) against sales revenue. Lifo also tends to yield an inventory amount that, after a period of rising prices, is substantially below the inventory's current replacement cost. The net earnings reported under Lifo can also be manipulated to a certain extent by purchasing, or not purchasing, goods near the end of the accounting year when unit costs have changed. If smaller earnings are desired, increase the amount of purchases at current high costs, and, under Lifo, these high costs will be charged to cost of goods sold. If higher earnings are desired, delay making purchases and charge to cost of goods sold some of the older, lower costs in inventory.

Weighted Average Method. Under this method the total number of units purchased plus those on hand at the beginning of the year is divided into the total cost of the purchases plus the cost of the beginning inventory in order to derive a weighted unit cost. This unit cost is then multiplied by the number of units in the ending inventory to arrive at the cost of the inventory. Illustration 3.7 shows the application of this procedure.

ILLUSTRATION 3.7
Application of Weighted Average Method

Purchase Date	No. of Units Purchased	Unit Cost	Total Cost
1/1 inventory	10	$10.00	$100.00
3/2	10	10.40	104.00
5/28	20	10.50	210.00
8/12	10	11.00	110.00
10/12	20	10.90	218.00
12/21	10	11.20	112.00
	80		$854.00

Weighted average unit cost is $854 ÷ 80, or $10.675.
Ending inventory then is $10.675 × 20 .... 213.50
Cost of Goods Sold $640.50

Differences in Cost Methods Summarized. Illustration 3.8 summarizes the cost of goods sold, ending inventories, and gross margins which will result from the application to the same data of the four basic cost methods of pricing ending inventory.

Note that each of the above methods produces a different inventory measurement and gross margin. As might be expected, since the trend of prices was upward during the period, Lifo shows the highest cost of goods sold and the lowest gross margin.

Which Is the "Correct" Method? All of the above methods are considered acceptable, and no one of them can be considered the only "correct" one. Each method is attractive in particular circumstances. The application of Lifo results in matching current cost with current revenue, and makes it more likely that any net earnings reported can be distributed

ILLUSTRATION 3.8

**Summary of Effects of Employing Different Inventory Methods
with Same Basic Data**

	Specific Identification	Fifo	Lifo	Weighted Average
Sales	$940.00	$940.00	$940.00	$940.00
Cost of goods sold				
Beginning inventory	$100.00	$100.00	$100.00	$100.00
Purchases	754.00	754.00	754.00	754.00
Cost of goods available for sale	$854.00	$854.00	$854.00	$854.00
Ending inventory	222.00	221.00	204.00	213.50
Cost of goods sold	$632.00	$633.00	$650.00	$640.50
Gross Margin	$308.00	$307.00	$290.00	$299.50

as dividends without impairing the level of operations. Lifo is actually a partial answer to the problems encountered in accounting under inflationary conditions. Also Lifo reduces the amount of taxes payable currently under these conditions.

On the other hand, Lifo often charges against revenues the cost of goods *not* sold. And it permits manipulation of net earnings simply by changing the time at which additional purchases of merchandise are made. If precision in the matching of *actual historical cost* with revenue is desired, Fifo or specific identification are to be preferred. But earnings may also be manipulated under the specific identification method, as they may be under the simple weighted average method. Under the latter method the purchase of a large amount of goods at a relatively high price after the last sale of the period will change the average unit cost of the goods charged to the Cost of Goods Sold account. Only under Fifo is the manipulation of earnings *not* possible. But because net earnings under this method in periods of rising prices may have to be reinvested in inventory in order to maintain a given level of sales volume, these earnings are considered fictitious by many accountants and dubbed "paper profits."

There is also some evidence to suggest that companies have changed their method of inventory measurement simply to conform with other companies in their industry. And further, a company may employ different methods for different inventories.

Inventories at Less than Cost

As already noted, Chapter 4 of *Accounting Research Bulletin 43* requires a departure from the cost basis for inventories when the utility of the goods is less than their cost. Such loss of utility may be evidenced by damage or obsolescence or by a decline in the selling price of the goods.

Net Realizable Value. Damaged, obsolete, shopworn goods are not to be carried in inventory nor reported in the financial statements at an amount greater than their net realizable value. Net realizable value is defined as estimated selling price less costs to complete and dispose of the goods. For example, assume that an auto dealer has on hand one auto that has been used as a demonstrator. The auto was acquired at a cost of $3,600 and had an original sales price of $4,200. But, because it has been used and it is now late in the model year, the net realizable value of the auto is estimated at:

Estimated selling price	$3,500
Estimated maintenance and selling costs	300
Net realizable value	$3,200

The auto would be written down for inventory purposes from $3,600 to $3,200. In this way, the $400 would be treated as an expense in the period in which the decline in utility took place. If net realizable value exceeds cost, the item would of course be carried at cost. Accountants generally frown upon recognizing profits before goods are sold.

Inventories at Cost or Market, Whichever Is Lower

Pricing inventories at the lower of cost or current market price has a long history of acceptance in accounting. The method is based, in part, upon the assumption that if the purchase price in the market in which the firm buys has fallen, the selling price has fallen or will fall. This is not always a valid assumption.

The term "market" as used in this context means replacement cost in terms of the quantity usually purchased. In the application of the method, it is still necessary to determine cost (by either the specific identification, Fifo, Lifo, or average method).

The method uses market values only to the extent that these values are less than cost. If the inventory at December 31, 1979, has a cost of $20,000 and a market value of $21,000, this increase in market value is not recognized. To do so would be to recognize revenue prior to the time of sale.

On the other hand, if market value is $19,400, the inventory may be written down to market value from cost and a $600 loss recognized on the grounds that the inventory has lost some of its revenue-generating ability. Thus, the entry made anticipates a reduced selling price when the goods are actually sold.

Application of the Method. As shown in Illustration 3.9, the lower-of-

ILLUSTRATION 3.9
Application of Lower-of-Cost or-Market Method

Item and Class	Quantity	Unit Cost	Unit Market	Total Cost	Total Market	Lower of Cost or Market By Classes	Lower of Cost or Market By Units
Class A							
A1..........	100	$8.00	$6.90	$ 800	$ 690		$ 690
A2..........	200	5.00	4.25	1,000	850		850
				$1,800	$1,540	$1,540	
Class B							
B1..........	500	3.00	3.40	$1,500	$1,700		1,500
B2..........	300	4.00	3.90	1,200	1,170		1,170
				$2,700	$2,870	2,700	
				$4,500	$4,410	$4,240	$4,210

cost-or-market method may be applied to each item in the inventory, to each class in the inventory, or to the total inventory. Each method of application is considered acceptable, although tax regulations require application to individual items whenever feasible.

The inventory in Illustration 3.9 could be reported at $4,210, $4,240, or $4,410 and each of these measurements referred to as the lower of cost or market. When applied to each individual item, all possible losses are consistently anticipated. But this may be unduly conservative as the inventory may be written down even though there has been an actual increase in its total market value.

Gross Margin Method of Estimating Inventory

The gross margin method is an estimating procedure used to approximate the amount of an inventory for the following purposes:

1. To obtain an inventory at the end of each month of a fiscal period except the last. The inventory cost so computed is used in the monthly financial statements.
2. As a method of verifying a previously determined ending inventory amount.

The gross margin method is a substitute method used to arrive at an inventory amount and is based on the assumption that the *rate* of gross margin realized is highly stable from period to period; the method is satisfactory only if this assumption is correct.

To illustrate the gross margin method of computing the inventory, assume that the Sweet Company has for several years maintained a rate of gross margin on sales of 40 percent. From this fact and the data given below the approximate inventory of December 31, 1979, may be determined as shown in Illustration 3.10.

Inventory, January 1, 1979	$ 30,000
Purchases of merchandise in 1979	390,000
Sales of merchandise in 1979	600,000

Because the gross margin method is based on the assumption that the gross margin rate in the *current* period is the *same* as in prior periods, which, of course, may not be true, it generally is not an accurate enough method to be used for the year-end statements. One of the other methods described in this chapter or the retail method discussed in Chapter 13 should be used, preferably in conjunction with a physical inventory.

ILLUSTRATION 3.10
Computation of the Inventory, December 31, 1979

Inventory, January 1, 1979		$ 30,000
Purchases		390,000
Cost of merchandise available for sale		$420,000
Less estimated cost of sales:		
Sales	$600,000	
Gross margin (40% of $600,000)	240,000	
Estimated cost of sales		360,000
Inventory, December 31, 1979		$ 60,000

SUMMARY

Revenue generated by the selling activities of a business is usually recorded when the goods are delivered with the intent of making a sale. At that time, the revenue is measurable, earned, and realized.

The major expense incurred in making sales to customers—the cost of the merchandise delivered—may be recorded at the time of sale (perpetual procedure) or at the end of the period (periodic procedure). The difference between sales revenue and the cost of the goods sold is called gross margin. Merchandise delivered may be returned or price concessions may be granted for any of a number of reasons. These returns and allowances are adjustments of recorded revenues or purchases and are recorded in separate contra accounts. Cash discounts are viewed and recorded similarly.

To obtain a proper matching of expense and revenue and to report a proper valuation for accounts receivables, the estimated uncollectible accounts arising from a year's sales are charged to bad debts expense and credited to an allowance for doubtful accounts.

Inventory cost theoretically includes the net invoice price of the goods and the cost of transportation-in, insurance in transit, receiving, handling, storage, and duties. As a practical matter, invoice cost alone is often used.

The cost of the inventory may be determined by attaching known invoice costs to specifically identified goods or by assuming a pattern of cost flows—Fifo, Lifo, or average. Each method will yield different reported amounts for inventory and net earnings. Management faces the task of choosing the method it will use, and this choice may be influenced by many factors including the methods employed by other members of the industry. Generally, the method chosen will be used over a period of years because generally accepted accounting principles prohibit indiscriminate switching between methods. Such switching would open the door to manipulation of reported net earnings and would yield information lacking in consistency between years.

Generally accepted accounting principles usually require the write-down from cost to market value (replacement cost) of those goods whose selling prices have fallen or are expected to fall before the goods are sold. Damaged, obsolete, or shopworn goods should be inventoried at their net realizable value, if less than cost.

Inventories can, if necessary, be estimated by using the gross margin method.

QUESTIONS AND EXERCISES

1. Why does an understated ending inventory understate net earnings (before income taxes) by the same amount?

2. In what respects are a purchase return and a purchase allowance similar? How do they differ?

3. Conceptually, what should the cost of the inventory include?

4. Explain the meaning of the phrase "to take a physical inventory."

5. What is the effect of a failure to include in inventory the cost of transportation, insurance in transit, and other handling and receiving costs?

6. Show how reported net earnings can be manipulated by a company using Lifo in pricing its inventory. Why is the same manipulation not possible under Fifo?

7. In what three different ways can the lower-of-cost-or-market method of inventory measurement be applied?

8. State several of the advantages of recording revenue at the time of the making of a credit sale. State one disadvantage of this practice.

9. Under what operating conditions will the gross margin method of computing an inventory produce approximately correct amounts?

10. Explain how perpetual procedure affords control over inventory.

11. Give some examples of the types of decisions management might make using information obtained from perpetual inventory stock cards.

12. What kind of an account is sales returns? Why is such an account used?

13. The Grosse Company inventory records show:
    Inventory
        1/1 .... 500 units at $6.00 = $3,000
    Purchases
        2/14 .... 300 units at 5.40 = 1,620
        3/18 .... 800 units at 5.25 = 4,200
        7/21 .... 600 units at 5.70 = 3,420
        9/27 .... 600 units at 5.40 = 3,240
      11/27 .... 200 units at 5.85 = 1,170
      12/31 .... Inventory = 1,300 units
    a. Present a short schedule showing the measurement of the ending inventory using the Fifo method.
    b. Repeat using the Lifo method.

14. The White Company's inventory of a certain product consisted of 8,000 units with a cost of $11 each on January 1, 1979. During 1979 numerous units of this product were purchased and sold. Also, during 1979 the purchase price to the White Company of this product fell steadily until at year-end it was $9. The inventory at year-end consisted of 12,000 units.
    State which of the two methods of inventory calculation, Lifo or Fifo, would have resulted in the higher reported net earnings and explain briefly.

15. The Black Company had the following inventory transactions during 1979:
      1/1   Inventory, 100 units at $4 = $400.
      1/31   January sales were 20 units.
      2/28   February sales totaled 30 units.
      3/1   Purchased 50 units at $4.20.
      8/31   Sales for March through August were 40 units.
      9/1   Purchased 10 units at $4.80.
      12/31   September through December sales were 55 units.
    Determine the cost of the December 31, 1979, inventory and the cost of the goods sold for the year 1979 using the weighted average method.

16. Your assistant prepared the following schedule to assist you in pricing the inventory under the cost or market, whichever is lower, method applied on an item-by-item basis. What is the amount of the ending inventory?

Item	Count	Unit Cost	Unit Market	Total Cost	Total Market
A...............	200	$18.00	$17.00	$ 3,600	$ 3,400
B...............	200	8.00	9.00	1,600	1,800
C...............	600	6.00	6.00	3,600	3,600
D...............	1,000	10.20	10.40	10,200	10,400
Total........				$19,000	$19,200

17. Roll Company follows the practice of taking a physical inventory at the end of each calender year accounting period to establish the ending inventory amount for financial statement purposes. Its financial statements for the past few years indicate a normal gross margin of 20 percent.

On July 18, a fire destroyed the entire store building and contents. The records were in a fireproof vault and are intact. These records, through July 17, show:

Merchandise inventory, January 1.........................	$ 50,000
Merchandise purchases..................................	1,350,000
Purchase returns.......................................	15,000
Transportation-in......................................	85,000
Sales...	1,550,000
Sales returns..	50,000

The company was fully covered by insurance and asks you to determine the amount of its claim for loss of merchandise.

18. Jimmy's Store has a television set on hand at year end that cost $300 and which it expected to sell for $400. But, because the set has been used as a display model its estimated selling price is only $250. Estimated reconditioning costs and selling commission amount to $40. At what dollar amount should this set be included in the year-end inventory? Why?

PROBLEMS

3–1. Hart Company, which uses periodic inventory procedure, purchased merchandise as follows:
 (1) $5,000 from Luigi Company, terms 2/10, n/30.
 (2) $4,000 from Williams Company, terms 2/10, n/30.
 The Luigi invoice was paid within the discount privilege period; the Williams invoice was paid late.

Required:

 a.   Set up T-accounts and record the above transactions assuming the invoices were originally recorded at their gross amounts.
 b.   Repeat part (a), assuming the invoices are to be recorded originally at their net invoice amounts.

3–2. Following are selected, summarized transactions of the Bunker Corporation (which uses periodic inventory procedure) for the year 1979:
   (1) Sales on account, $500,000, terms 2/10, n/30.
   (2) Sales returns and allowances amounted to $10,000.
   (3) Customers remitted $392,800 in settlement of $400,000 of accounts.
   (4) Purchases on account, $400,000; terms 2/10, n/30.
   (5) Purchase returns and allowances amounted to $12,000.
   (6) Transportation-in costs incurred on account, $16,000.
   (7) Payments on account, $353,200, in settlement of $360,000 of accounts.
   (8) Bad debts are estimated at 1 percent of sales less sales returns and allowances.

   Required:
   a. Set up T-accounts and record the above transactions.
   b. Assume the inventory on January 1 was $44,000 and on December 31 was $72,000 and that operating expenses and taxes amount to $70,000. Prepare an earnings statement for the year. (Include in the statement the determination of gross margin.)

3–3. Following are data relating to the beginning inventory and purchases of the Sandy Barr Company for the year 1979:

January 1 inventory	1,400 @ $4.20
Purchases:	
February 2	1,000 @ 4.00
April 5	2,000 @ 3.48
June 15	1,200 @ 3.40
September 20	1,400 @ 3.20
November 28	1,800 @ 3.60

   A physical count showed 2,200 units of this product on hand at the end of the year.

   Required: Compute the cost of the ending inventory and the cost of the goods sold under each of the following methods:
   a. Fifo.   b. Lifo.   c. Weighted average.

3–4. The Drayer Corporation was organized on January 1, 1977, to deal in a product whose resale price reacts promptly to changes in cost. Unit prices rose during the three years ended December 31, 1979. Selected data for 1977–79 are:

Year Ended December 31	Inventory		Annual Data	
	Fifo	Lifo	Purchases	Sales
1977	$3,200	$2,400	$14,400	$16,200
1978	4,000	2,800	12,000	19,000
1979	6,600	4,000	14,800	16,400

Required:

a. Compute the gross margin for each of the three years under Fifo and under Lifo.

b. Comment on your answer to (*a*).

3–5. The Busby Co. began business on July 1, 1978, selling a single product. For the year ending June 30, 1979, 15,000 units were sold at $10 each. Purchases consisted of 10,000 units on July 1 at $4 and 10,000 units on December 18 at $5. Jim Graves, the accountant for Busby Co., prepared the following earnings statement for the year ended June 30, 1979, for presentation to the board of directors:

Sales...	$150,000
Cost of goods sold.............................	67,500
Gross margin...................................	$ 82,500
Expenses.......................................	40,000
Net earnings (before taxes)....................	$ 42,500

At the board meeting, members of the board questioned Jim's use of the average cost method in determining the cost of goods sold and the cost of the ending inventory. One member indicated a preference for Lifo, another preferred Fifo. And yet another asked about the effects of using Fifo or Lifo and the direction of price changes. The board directed Jim to prepare the information desired by various members and to report at the afternoon meeting of the board.

Required:

a. Using the above information, prepare two earnings statements similar to the one given above, one using Fifo, the other using Lifo, for presentation to the board. Assume Busby Co. uses periodic inventory procedures.

b. Repeat part (*a*) using all of the same information except assume that the July 1 purchases cost $5 each, while the December purchases cost $4 each.

c. What facts are revealed by the statements in (*a*) and (*b*) that should be brought to the board's attention?

3–6. The accountant for the Schafer Corp. prepared the following schedule of the company's December 31, 1979, inventory, and used the lower of total cost or total market in determining the cost of goods sold for the year:

Item	Quantity	Unit Cost	Unit Market	Total Cost	Total Market
A.........	4,000	$6.00	$6.00	$24,000	$24,000
B.........	3,000	4.00	3.60	12,000	10,800
C.........	6,000	2.00	1.60	12,000	9,600
D........	8,000	1.00	1.20	8,000	9,600
				$56,000	$54,000

Required:

a. State whether the method used is an accepted way of applying the cost or market, whichever is lower method.

b. Compute the dollar amount of the inventory under an alternative way of applying this method.

c. What would be the effect on net earnings (before taxes) of using the alternative method?

d. If the 3,000 units of product B are obsolete and shopworn so that they can be sold for an estimated $2 each, less total delivery charges of $75, at what amount should they be included in inventory?

3–7. Given below are data relating to the December 31, 1979, inventory of the McDonald Company:

Item	Quantity	Unit Cost	Unit Market
1....................	3,000	$4.00	$3.80
2....................	6,000	3.20	3.60
3....................	2,000	3.00	3.20
4....................	5,000	5.60	5.00
5....................	4,000	5.00	5.20
6....................	1,000	3.60	3.20

Required:

a. Compute the ending inventory applying the cost or market, whichever is lower, method to the total inventory.

b. Repeat (a) applying the method to individual items.

c. What would be the effect on net earnings before income taxes of using the method applied to individual items rather than to total inventory?

3–8. You are the chief accountant of the Marple Company and your assistant has been applying the cost or market, whichever is lower, method to your company's December 31, 1979 inventory. Your assistant brings the following data to your attention:

Item	Units	Unit Cost
Product R—This item has been selling extremely well. Its retail price was recently raised 20 percent because replacement cost increased from $100 to $120 per unit....	10	$100
Product S—The retail price on this item has been reduced because of a lack of demand. The cost to replace this item has also been reduced from $60 to $50 each............	40	60
Product T—The units on hand of this item are obsolete and damaged to such an extent that it will cost more to repair them than they can be sold for after repair.......	4	20
Product U—The cost of replacing this item has dropped 5 percent, but Marple has a contract to sell all of these items at their regular selling price, which includes normal markup......................................	100	10
Product V—This product is being discontinued. Sales price is to be reduced from $50 to $25, with disposal costs of $2 each expected.................................	50	50
Product W—This item was shipped to Marple by Baker on a consignment basis with Marple to pay only for units sold.....................................	20	75

Remainder—No problems encountered. At cost or market, whichever is lower, their dollar amount is $28,000.

Required:

a. Compute the cost or market, whichever is lower, dollar amount for the ending inventory. State the amount assigned to each of the above items separately.

b. For the six items above, state the reason for the unit dollar amount you assigned in part (*a*).

3–9. Ramos Company recently asked Guerre Corporation to sell merchandise to it on a credit basis. Guerre asked for current financial statements before granting the request. Ramos does not wish to incur the cost of taking a physical inventory, which it normally takes only at the end of its fiscal year, December 31. Financial statements for the previous three years ending on December 31, 1978, show that Ramos has consistently earned a gross margin on net sales of 40 percent. The accounts show, for the seven months ending on July 31, 1979, the following:

Expenses (for seven months)	$164,000
Sales	628,500
Purchases	363,000
Purchase returns	3,000
Sales returns	18,500
Inventory, January 1, 1979	46,000

Required:

a. Indicate, in general terms, how inventories can be estimated so that financial statements can be prepared for interim periods.

b. Estimate the July 31, 1979, inventory of the Ramos Company.

c. Prepare an earnings statement for Ramos for the seven months ended July 31, 1979.

d. Upon what factor used in preparing the earnings statement in (*b*) does the accuracy of the statement depend very heavily? Explain.

chapter 4

Plant and Intangible Assets; Depreciation, Depletion, and Amortization

Business assets are commonly classified as current and noncurrent assets depending upon the amount of time expected to expire before they are consumed or used up in the operations of the business. For many businesses the noncurrent category consists largely of property, plant, and equipment (often described simply as plant or fixed assets) and intangible assets.

PLANT AND INTANGIBLE ASSETS IN GENERAL

Types of Plant Assets

1. *Land.* Land used as a building site is usually considered to have an unlimited life and is generally not used up in production.
2. *Depreciable plant assets and equipment.* Such assets eventually become worthless due to physical wear and tear or obsolescence. In essence, they are consumed indirectly over long periods of time in the operation of a business.
3. *Natural resources.* These resources are consumed directly through mining, lumbering, or other extraction.

Intangible Assets

Intangible assets do not have any physical features. They have value because they confer business advantages upon their owners. Some examples are patents, copyrights, leases, and goodwill. Most intangibles are considered to have a finite life, but it has been argued that some, for example, goodwill, may have indefinite lives.

Periodic Costs Relating to Plant and Intangible Assets

Plant assets may be viewed as consisting of bundles of service potentials. For most assets, these service potentials are used up over a period of time through physical use, obsolescence, deterioration, or expiration of a certain right. The general approach in accounting is to allocate the cost of such service potentials in a systematic and rational manner to the periods which benefit by their use. If an asset's ability to provide services does not decline with use, as in the case of land, none of its cost is allocated to the period.

Depreciation is an estimate of the service potential which was used up or consumed during the period. Under depreciation accounting, the cost of a plant asset (less its salvage value) is allocated over its estimated useful life. Depreciation is usually debited to a Depreciation account and credited to an Allowance for Depreciation or Accumulated Depreciation account. The Allowance for Depreciation account (or Accumulated Depreciation account) is considered a contra account to the asset. It reduces the carrying value of the asset on the statement of financial position.

The subsequent treatment of the recorded depreciation will depend upon the nature of the services received from the asset. When related to the manufacturing operation, it will usually be considered in the computation of the cost of goods produced for the period. When related to general and administrative items such as an office building, it is charged to expense. If used in the construction of an asset, the cost is capitalized (debited to an asset account).

Depletion is the exhaustion of a natural resource, such as a coal mine. It is caused by the physical removal of part of the resource. The amount of depletion recognized in a period is an estimate of the cost (or other basic value) of the resource extracted or mined in that period. It is recorded first in a depletion account with the reduction in the asset credited directly to the asset account or to a separate allowance for depletion. This depletion cost is combined with other mining or extractive costs to arrive at the total cost of the ore mined. This total cost is, in turn, divided between cost of goods sold (which is an expense account) and inventory of ore on hand (which is an asset account) according to to the amount of ore sold.

Intangible assets are *amortized*. That is, their cost is allocated to the periods that benefit from their use. For example, the cost of a patent is amortized over the periods in which its exclusive rights confer benefits upon a company and the products it produces.

Sometimes evidence exists which suggests that plant and intangible assets could be sold at prices which differ substantially from their recorded costs. The accounting requirement of realization (meaning, loosely, that an exchange must take place) typically bars the recording of market prices greater than cost until the asset is sold. Also, it is generally considered inappropriate to record a loss by writing down an asset from cost to a lower market value if the cost of the asset is expected to be recovered fully from the future revenues produced by the asset. Consequently, plant and intangible assets are seldom reported at amounts other than cost or an unamortized or undepreciated portion thereof.

PLANT ASSETS

Cost Basis of Measurement

In most cases, plant assets are recorded initially at cost. This cost includes all reasonable and necessary expenditures to prepare the asset for use.

Land.   The cost of land includes the contract purchase price; option cost; attorney fees; cost of title search; fees for recording the transfer of title; taxes in arrears assumed by the purchaser; local assessments for sidewalks, streets, sewers, and water mains; and cost of grading.

Building.   If a building is purchased, its cost includes the contract purchase price, the costs of remodeling and repairing the building for the purposes of the new owner, unpaid taxes assumed by the purchaser, legal costs, and real estate broker commissions. When land and the buildings on it are purchased for one lump sum, the total cost should be apportioned so that separate ledger accounts may be established for land and for buildings; this may be accomplished by a competent appraisal. Separation is necessary so that proper depreciation charges on the buildings will be included in the computation of net earnings.

If a building is constructed rather than purchased outright, the cost may be more difficult to determine. But it will generally include payments to contractors, architects' fees, building permits, taxes during construction, salaries of officers supervising construction, and insurance during construction.

To illustrate, assume that as part of its expansion program, Tyler Corporation purchased an old farm on the outskirts of Bridgeport, Connecticut, as a factory site. The company paid $100,000 for this property. In addition, the company agreed to pay back taxes of $6,000 on this property. The attorneys' fees and other legal costs related to the purchase of the farm amounted to $630. The farm buildings were demolished at a net cost of $4,000 (cost of removal less salvage value of lumber, etc.), and a factory was constructed at a cost of $125,000. Building permits and architects' fees amounted to another $12,500. Finally, the company paid an assessment of $5,000 to the city for water mains, sewers, and street paving.

The cost of the land and building is computed as follows:

	Land	Building
Cost of factory site......................	$100,000	
Back taxes.............................	6,000	
Attorneys' fees.........................	630	
Demolition.............................	4,000	
Factory construction....................		$125,000
Building permits.......................		12,500
City assessment........................	5,000	
	$115,630	$137,500

All of the costs relating to the purchase of the farm and the razing of the old buildings can be assigned to the land account because none of the old buildings purchased with the land is to be used. The real goal was to purchase the land, but the land was not available without taking the buildings also. Instead of the condition described, one or more of the old buildings could have been remodeled for use by Tyler Corporation. It would then have been necessary to decide what part of the cash purchase price of the farm, the back taxes, and the legal fees was allocable to such buildings and what portion of the acquisition cost plus remodeling costs would have been included in the cost of the new factory. These costs would have been apportioned using the appraised values. For instance, assume that the land was appraised at two thirds of the total value and the buildings at one third. Then two thirds of the acquisition cost would be assigned to the land and one third to the buildings.

Machinery and Equipment.   If machinery or equipment is acquired by purchase, its cost includes the invoice price, transportation charges, insurance in transit costs, the costs of any attachments or accessories, testing costs, if any, and the cost of installation.

Noncash Acquisitions and Gifts of Plant Assets

Although generally acquired by purchase for cash or on account, plant assets are sometimes acquired in a noncash exchange for assets other than cash, by the issuance of stocks or bonds, or are received as gifts. In such exchanges, the assets received are recorded at their fair market values. Fair market value is determined from either the value of the asset received or the item given up, whichever is the more clearly determinable. Thus, plant assets received in an exchange for securities having a ready market value are recorded at the market value of the securities given up. If the securities given up do not have a ready market value, the cash purchase price at which the asset could have been acquired should be used. In the absence of fair market values or cash purchase prices, values determined by a professional appraiser may be used. As a last resort, assets received in noncash exchanges may be recorded at the cost or book value of the assets surrendered. But it should be understood fully that the cost of an old asset may be a poor and even misleading indication of the economic importance of the new asset.

In any exchange of noncash assets, the accountant's task is to find the most suitable value to assign to the assets received. Generally, one uses the fair market value of the assets received or of the assets given up or equities issued, whichever is the more clearly evident.

To illustrate, assume that on July 14, 1979, the Ogden Company acquired, in exchange for 100 shares of its common stock, land next to its factory for use as a parking lot. At the start of negotiations, the owner of the property quoted a price of $7,500 for the land. The common stock of the Ogden Company has a par value of $60 per share and a market value on July 14, 1979, of $71.50 per share. Similar plots of land in the city are selling for $6,900. The best evidence of the fair market of the items exchanged is the $7,150 market value of the 100 shares of stock. The fact that similar property in the city is selling for less is not relevant here. Ogden Company obviously wanted the nearby land enough to be willing to give up stock that could be sold in the market for $7,150. In the absence of a market price for the shares exchanged, the price at which similar property is selling probably would be used. But every tract of land is unique—there is no other exactly like it.

DEPRECIATION OF PLANT ASSETS

Significance of Depreciation

As indicated earlier, the accountant seeks to allocate in a systematic and rational manner the cost of a plant asset to the various periods in its useful life. An attempt must be made to measure periodic depreciation because, for most businesses, depreciation is a very large and important cost factor. And it is through recognition of periodic depreciation charges that plant asset costs are converted to operating costs.

Factors Affecting Depreciation Estimates

In order to estimate periodic depreciation, the following three factors must be considered:

1. Cost.
2. Estimated salvage value. Salvage or scrap value is the amount expected to be received on the date the asset will be retired or otherwise disposed of.

3. Estimated useful life. This may be expressed in years, months, working hours, or units of production.

Because it is not possible to measure the exact amount of depreciation to be assigned to each period of an asset's life, a number of different methods of computing periodic depreciation exist.

When appraising the various methods of computing depreciation, it is important to remember the main causes of depreciation. To oversimplify, depreciation is caused chiefly by physical deterioration, inadequacy, obsolescence, or a combination of these factors. The appropriate method should take these factors into account. For instance, a machine may be capable of producing units for ten years. But if it will be obsolete (in the sense of too costly to operate in relation to a new machine) in five years, then five years should be its estimated life.

Depreciation Methods

Straight-Line Depreciation. This method assigns the same amount of asset cost to each year of the asset's life. Periodic depreciation is computed as follows:

$$\text{Depreciation per Period} = \left(\frac{\text{Cost} - \text{Estimated Salvage Value}}{\text{Expected Useful Life in Years}} \right)$$

Thus, if a company has a machine that cost $6,500 and has an estimated useful life of four years and a salvage value of $500, the annual depreciation charge would be $1,500 computed as follows:

$$\text{Depreciation} = \frac{\text{Cost} - \text{Salvage Value}}{\text{Expected Useful Life}} = \frac{\$6,500 - \$500}{4 \text{ years}} = \underline{\$1,500} \text{ per year}$$

Straight-line depreciation may also be expressed as a percentage rate, computed as 100 percent divided by expected useful life. In the above example the rate is 25 percent (100% ÷ 4) per year. The depreciation computation for the year would be $6,000 × 25 percent = $1,500. Similarly an asset with a five-year life would have a 20 percent rate; one with 10 years would have a 10 percent rate; and so on.

The straight-line method is based on two assumptions. They are (1) that the asset will be used at a fairly constant rate, and (2) that wear and deterioration will all occur in direct proportion to elapsed time.

The main advantage of the straight-line method is its simplicity. Its use is suggested whenever the conditions cited above are present and when repairs and maintenance are incurred evenly during the life of the asset or are relatively immaterial. The straight-line method is not considered appropriate when one of the following circumstances exists: (1) the machine is not expected to operate with equal efficiency throughout its life, or

(2) repair and maintenance costs are expected to be higher in later years (see example on page 84) resulting in an increased total cost of operating the asset.

Units-of-Production Method.   If usage is the main factor causing expiration of an asset, it may be desirable to base depreciation charges on physical output. A depreciation charge per unit may be obtained by dividing the original cost of the asset less salvage value by the estimated number of units to be produced by the asset during its useful life. The periodic depreciation charge is obtained by multiplying the rate per unit by the output for the period.

For example, assume that on March 1, 1979, Jay Corporation purchased a machine at a total cost of $100,000. The machine is expected to have an eight-year useful life, during which time it is expected to produce about five million units of product. Its scrap value at the end of that time is estimated to be $10,000. During 1979, 900,000 units of product are processed by this machine. Depreciation for the year under the units of production method would be $16,200, computed as follows:

$$\frac{\$100,000 - \$10,000}{5,000,000 \text{ units}} = \$0.018 \text{ per unit; } \$0.018 \times 900,000 \text{ units} = \$16,200$$

The units-of-production method of depreciation is not widely used because it is difficult to determine the output from a single machine. The units method does not take into account the loss in value that might occur when a machine is idle.

Accelerated (or Declining-Amount) Depreciation.   The 1954 Revenue Act first allowed taxpayers to use a fixed percentage on declining balance and a sum-of-the-years'-digits method of computing depreciation—so-called accelerated (or declining-amount) methods or simply accelerated depreciation. Later laws and amendments have continued this permission. Under these methods larger amounts of depreciation are recorded in the earlier years of the life of an asset than in the later years. These methods are often preferred because the increased depreciation charges in the early years reduce taxable earnings and thereby reduce the amount of federal income taxes which must be paid in those years.

Theoretical support for these methods also exists. Their use seems especially appropriate when the service-rendering or revenue-producing ability of the asset declines through time, when the value of the asset declines more in early years and less in later years of its life, or when repairs and other maintenance costs increase through time.

Double-Declining Balance Depreciation.   Under this method, the straight-line rate of depreciation is doubled, and the doubled rate is applied to the declining balance of the asset—its net book (or carrying) value. The asset is depreciated down to its salvage value. Thus, salvage value is not deducted from cost before applying the percentage in calculat-

ILLUSTRATION 4.1
Double-Declining Balance Method Depreciation Schedule

End of Year		Periodic Depreciation	Accumulated Depreciation	Net Book Value
				$16,000.00
1.	(20% of $16,000.00)	$3,200.00	$ 3,200.00	12,800.00
2.	(20% of $12,800.00)	2,560.00	5,760.00	10,240.00
3.	(20% of $10,240.00)	2,048.00	7,808.00	8,192.00
4.	(20% of $ 8,192.00)	1,638.40	9,446.40	6,553.60
5.	(20% of $ 6,553.60)	1,310.72	10,757.12	5,242.88
6.	(20% of $ 5,242.88)	1,048.58	11,805.70	4,194.30
7.	(20% of $ 4,194.30)	838.86	12,644.56	3,355.44
8.	(20% of $ 3,355.44)	671.09	13,315.65	2,684.35
9.	(20% of $ 2,684.35)	536.87	13,852.52	2,147.48
10.		147.48*	14,000.00	2,000.00

* To depreciate asset down to salvage value of $2,000.

ing depreciation. Illustration 4.1 contains an example of the application of this method in depreciating a $16,000 asset over its estimated 10-year useful life. In this example the 10 percent straight-line rate of depreciation is doubled, giving a depreciation rate of 20 percent.

In practice, business firms often switch to the straight-line method in the last few years to bring the book value down to the salvage value.

Sum-of-the-Years'-Digits Depreciation. This method also produces larger depreciation charges in the early years of an asset's useful life. The estimated life years of an asset are added together and used as the denominator in a ratio formed in which the number of years of life remaining from the beginning of the year is the numerator.[1] This ratio is then multiplied by *cost less estimated salvage value* to compute the periodic depreciation as is illustrated below for a plant asset costing $19,000, with an estimated life of five years and salvage value of $1,000:

```
Sum of the years' digits: 1 + 2 + 3 + 4 + 5 = 15
Depreciation
    Year 1: 5/15 of $18,000................................  $ 6,000
    Year 2: 4/15 of $18,000................................     4,800
    Year 3: 3/15 of $18,000................................     3,600
    Year 4: 2/15 of $18,000................................     2,400
    Year 5: 1/15 of $18,000................................     1,200
        Total Depreciation................................   $18,000
```

At the beginning of year 1 there are five years of life remaining. Thus, the ratio used to compute the depreciation charge for year 1 is 5/15.

---

[1] The denominator used in the sum-of-the-years'-digits method can be determined from the following formula where S = sum of the digits and N = number of years of estimated life:

$$S = \frac{N(N + 1)}{2}$$

ANALYSIS OF THE VARIOUS METHODS

The different effects of the straight-line method and the double-declining balance method of depreciation are shown in the following illustration. Assume a company has purchased a group of machines costing $50,000 with an expected useful life of eight years. Salvage value is assumed to be $5,000. In addition, because of the nature of the machines, maintenance costs will be $1,000 the first year and will increase $500 each year. Computation of the yearly costs are computed for the straight-line method and the double-declining balance method and are as follows:

$$\text{Straight-Line Depreciation} = \frac{\$50,000 - \$5,000}{8} = \frac{\$45,000}{8}$$

$$= \$5,625 \text{ per Year}$$

Double-Declining Balance Depreciation Rate $= 12\frac{1}{2}$ Percent (Straight-Line Rate) $\times 2 = 25$ Percent per Year.

Year	Straight-Line Depreciation	Double-Declining Balance Depreciation	Maintenance Costs
1..............	$5,625	$12,500	$1,000
2..............	5,625	9,375	1,500
3..............	5,625	7,031	2,000
4..............	5,625	5,274	2,500
5..............	5,625	3,955	3,000
6..............	5,625	2,966	3,500
7..............	5,625	2,225	4,000
8..............	5,625	1,674*	4,500

* Extra depreciation of $5 in last year to adjust to salvage value.

Illustration 4.2 on page 84 shows markedly different total cost patterns. Total annual costs (depreciation + maintenance) using the straight-line method increase each year and are highest in the later years. Using double-declining balance depreciation, total annual costs tend to decrease rather sharply at first and then to level out in the last years. Different results will, of course, be obtained with different patterns for repairs and maintenance costs.

Depreciation on Assets Acquired or Retired during the Accounting Period

Various methods are used to depreciate plant assets that are acquired or retired during an accounting period. One commonly used method is to consider all plant assets purchased on or before the fifteenth day of the month as having been purchased on the first day of the month and to consider all plant assets purchased after the fifteenth day of the month

ILLUSTRATION 4.2

Straight-Line Depreciation Compared with Double-Declining Balance Depreciation

Straight-Line Depreciation

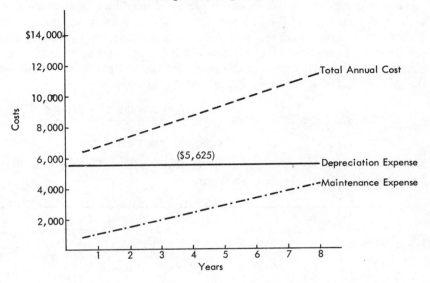

Double-Declining Balance Depreciation

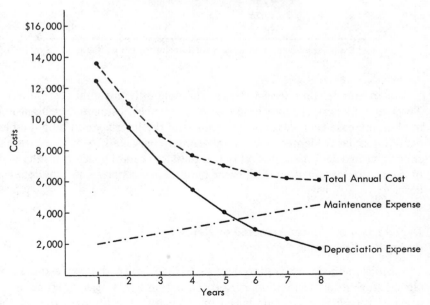

as having been purchased on the first day of the following month. For example, assume that a company, whose fiscal year ends on June 30, purchases a machine on February 14, 1979. The machine would be treated as though it had been purchased on February 1. Assuming that the machine has a $12,500 cost, a $500 salvage value, and ten year estimated useful life, the straight-line depreciation expense for the fiscal year ending June 30, 1979, would be $500(5/12 × .10 × $12,000). On the other hand, if the machine had been purchased on February 18, it would be treated as though it were purchased on March. 1. In this case, the straight-line depreciation expense would be $400(4/12 × .10 × $12,000).

When the double-declining balance or the sum-of-the-years'-digits depreciation method is used, more computations are required when an asset is acquired or retired during the accounting period. To illustrate, assume that on July 1, 1979, A Company purchased equipment for $30,000. The equipment, which has a $3,000 salvage value and a five year estimated useful life, is depreciated by the sum-of-the-years'-digits method. During 1979, the equipment was used for half a year; the 1979 depreciation expense would be $4,500 (1/2 × 5/15 × $27,000). The 1980 depreciation expense would be $8,100 computed as follows:

$$
\begin{array}{ll}
& 1/2 \times (5/15 \times \$27,000) = \$4,500 \\
+ & 1/2 \times (4/15 \times \$27,000) = \underline{3,600} \\
& 1 \text{ year} \qquad\qquad\qquad\quad \underline{\underline{\$8,100}}
\end{array}
$$

Revisions of Estimated Useful Life

When events show that the original estimated useful life of an asset is not correct, the annual depreciation charge should be revised to reflect the remaining useful life of the asset. The net book value (less salvage) of the asset at the start of the current period is divided by the number of life periods expected to remain. The result is the revised annual depreciation charge applicable to the current and succeeding years. For example, assume that a company using straight-line depreciation has a machine that originally cost $16,000 and has an estimated salvage value of $2,000 at the end of its useful life. The balance in the allowance for depreciation account (based on a life estimate of 10 years) stands at $5,600 at the end of the fourth year of the asset's life. In the fifth year it is estimated that the asset will last another 10 years, including the current year. The revised annual depreciation charge would be $840 [$16,000 − ($5,600 + $2,000) ÷ 10].

CAPITAL AND REVENUE EXPENDITURES

Expenditures which are directly related to plant assets are often made during the period of ownership and use of such assets at times other than the date of purchase. These expenditures are classified as capital expenditures or expenses.

Expenditures Capitalized in Asset Accounts

Expenditures for new or used assets, additions to existing assets, or betterments or improvements to existing assets are capital expenditures. They should be debited to asset accounts because they add to the total service-rendering ability of the assets. For example, if a company made a major planned repair to an asset right after purchasing it, the major repair would be considered part of the cost of obtaining the service potentials of the asset.

Expenditures Capitalizable as Charges to Allowance for Depreciation

Sometimes during the life of a plant asset, expenditures are made as a result of a decision that it is more economical to overhaul and repair an existing machine rather than to replace it at that specific time. Such expenditures usually extend the life of the asset; that is, they change the quantity but not the quality of the services provided by the asset. Because they will benefit future periods, these expenditures are properly capitalizable. But because there is no visible, tangible addition to or improvement of the asset, they are often debited to the allowance for depreciation account. Such expenditures are viewed as canceling a part of the past accumulated depreciation.

Similarly, expenditures for major repairs which do not extend the life of an asset are often debited to the allowance for depreciation (with an increase in subsequent depreciation charges) in order to avoid distorting periodic net earnings by expensing them. In this manner the cost of major repairs is spread over a number of years.

To illustrate, assume a company has a machine which has been depreciated on the straight-line basis with an estimated life of 10 years. Salvage value is considered insignificant. At the end of six years its net book value is as follows:

Original cost	$40,000
Allowance for depreciation	24,000
Book value	$16,000

At the end of the sixth year, the company overhauled the machine and this extended its life three years beyond the original estimate, or to 13 years altogether. The major repair cost of $5,000 would be debited to the allowance for depreciation account giving a net book value as follows:

```
Original cost.........................................    $40,000
Allowance for depreciation ($24,000 − $5,000).............    19,000
Net book value.......................................    $21,000
```

The revised depreciation charge per year would be $3,000 ($21,000 ÷ 7 year remaining life.)

Expenditures Charged to Periodic Expense

Expenditures for expected amounts of normal repair and part replacements are treated as periodic expenses because of their recurring nature and because they do not add to the service-rendering ability of the asset above that acquired at the time of purchase or extend its life. Such ordinary recurring expenses are referred to as revenue expenditures. Estimates of the yearly depreciation charge on an asset are usually based upon the assumption that the asset will be properly maintained and that the normal repair costs will be expensed as they are incurred. Thus, regular maintenance (oiling a machine) and normal repairs (replacing a minor part) are usually charged to expense as incurred as revenue expenditures.

Company Policy and Expenditures on Plant Assets

Conceptually, capital expenditures can be distinguished from ordinary repair and maintenance expenses. But the distinction is difficult to make in practice. As a result, the accounting for expenditures on plant assets is often guided by the unit of property concept or the establishment of arbitrary minimums for capitalization.

Unit of Property Concept. Under this concept an expenditure on a plant asset for anything less than a complete replacement of the unit of property is charged to expense. For example, under this concept, the cost of replacing the motor of a truck would be charged to expense if the truck were considered the unit of property. Theoretically, the cost of the new motor should be added to the asset account and the cost of the old motor would be removed from the asset account.

Arbitrary Minimums. As a matter of managerial policy, expenditures for plant assets, such as the $4.95 cost of a wastebasket, may be expensed immediately because the benefits which result from the application of depreciation accounting procedures to such items would not be worth the cost involved. Similarly, a firm may decide to capitalize all repair costs incurred on a specific asset in a single act of repair in excess of an arbitrary amount, say $500, while expensing those of a lesser amount. The arbitrary nature of these practical rules should be recognized. They have little, if any, support in theory mainly because they tend to misstate assets.

Disposal of Plant Assets

The disposal of a plant asset by sale, scrapping, theft or destruction may require recognition of a gain or loss. Assume, for example, that a company sells a machine for $7,000 cash which cost $31,000 and on which $22,000 of depreciation has been accumulated. The entry for the sale would be:

Cash	Machinery	Allowance for Depreciation
(1) 7,000	Bal. 100,000 | (1) 31,000	(1) 22,000 | Bal. 40,000

Loss on Sale of Machinery
(1)   2,000

In journal form, the entry would read:

```
Cash................................................... 7,000
Allowance for Depreciation............................ 22,000
Loss on Sale of Machinery.............................. 2,000
    Machinery.........................................          31,000
    To record loss on sale of machinery.
```

If more than $9,000 is received, a gain account would be credited for the difference between $9,000 and the amount received. Gains or losses on the disposal of plant assets are reported in the earnings statement, frequently as elements of "other revenue" or "other expense."

Analysis of Gains or Losses

The gain or loss on the disposal of an asset may result from the various estimates used to determine a depreciation charge. Errors may occur in estimating salvage value, useful life, pattern of use, or company maintenance policies. Computed gains and losses may vary considerably depending on the depreciation method used. For instance, an asset being depreciated by an accelerated method would be less likely to show a loss earlier in its life than would an identical asset being depreciated by the straight-line method. Gains and losses, of course, can also occur because of changed economic conditions. These changes include changes in the value of the dollar and in the supply and demand conditions for the asset.

PLANT ASSET EXCHANGES

Certain plant assets are often acquired in circumstances which involve the trade-in of an old asset along with the payment of cash. In such cases, the cash outlay is referred to as "boot". Accounting for the asset exchange depends upon whether the assets are similar or dissimilar and whether a gain or loss is indicated. For example, trading in an old automobile for a new automobile would involve similar assets. On the other hand, trading in machinery for an automobile would involve dissimilar assets.

If similar assets are exchanged and a loss is indicated, the new asset is recorded at its cash price (the amount which would have to be paid without the trade-in). In this case, the loss *is* recognized. If the exchange involves similar assets and a gain is indicated, the new asset is recorded at the sum of the cash ("boot") paid and the net book value of the old asset. The gain is *not* recognized. If dissimilar assets are exchanged, the new asset is recorded at its cash price regardless of whether a gain or loss is indicated. Thus, when dissimilar assets are involved, both gains and losses are recognized, but when similar assets are exchanged only losses are recognized. Each of the four cases is illustrated below.

Exchange of Similar Plant Assets; Recognition of Loss

Assume that $38,000 cash and delivery truck No. 1, which cost $40,000 and on which $25,000 of depreciation has been accumulated, are exchanged for delivery truck No. 2, which has a cash price of $50,000. There is a $3,000 loss on the exchange, computed as follows:

Cost of delivery truck No. 1	$40,000
Accumulated depreciation	25,000
Net book value	$15,000
Trade-in allowance ($50,000–$38,000)	12,000
Loss on exchange	$ 3,000

The entry for the exchange would be:

Cash			Delivery Trucks			Allowance for Depreciation		
Bal. 90,000	(1)	38,000	Bal. 150,000 (1) 50,000	(1)	40,000	(1) 25,000	Bal. 50,000	

Loss on Exchange of Delivery Trucks	
(1) 3,000	

In journal form, the entry would read:

Delivery Trucks	50,000	
Allowance for Depreciation	25,000	
Loss on Exchange of Delivery Trucks	3,000	
Cash		38,000
Delivery Trucks		40,000
To record loss on exchange of delivery trucks.		

Delivery truck No. 1 and its accumulated depreciation balance are removed from the accounts by a $40,000 credit to Delivery Trucks and a

$25,000 debit to the Allowance for Depreciation. Delivery truck No. 2 is recorded at its cash price by a $50,000 debit to Delivery Trucks. The $3,000 loss is recorded as a debit to Loss on Exchange of Delivery Trucks.

Exchange of Similar Plant Assets; Nonrecognition of Gain

To illustrate the nonrecognition of a gain when similar assets are exchanged, assume that in the preceding example the trade-in allowance amounted to $17,000 instead of $12,000 and that $33,000 was paid in cash. In this case there would be a $2,000 gain on the transaction, computed as follows:

Trade-in allowance	$17,000
Net book value of old asset	15,000
Gain on exchange	$ 2,000

According to *APB Opinion No. 29,* the gain should not be recognized. Instead, the new delivery truck (No. 2) should be recorded at $48,000 (the sum of the cash paid, $33,000, and the net book value of delivery truck No. 1, $15,000). The entry for the exchange would be:

Cash			Delivery Trucks			Allowance for Depreciation		
Bal. 90,000	(1)	33,000	Bal. 150,000	(1)	40,000	(1) 25,000	Bal.	50,000
			(1) 48,000					

In journal form, the entry would read:

Delivery Trucks	48,000	
Allowance for Depreciation	25,000	
Cash		33,000
Delivery Trucks		40,000
To record exchange of delivery trucks.		

Exchange of Dissimilar Plant Assets; Recognition of Loss

When dissimilar assets are exchanged, a loss is recognized when the trade-in allowance is less than the book value of the old asset. The new asset is recorded at its cash price. For example, assume that a computer is exchanged for a delivery truck. The computer cost $28,000 and has a related accumulated depreciation balance of $25,000. The delivery truck has a cash price of $40,000. The truck is obtained by trading the computer and paying $38,000 cash. Therefore, there is a $1,000 loss on the exchange, computed as follows:

Cost of computer	$28,000
Accumulated depreciation	25,000
Net book value of old asset	$ 3,000
Trade-in allowance ($40,000–$38,000)	2,000
Loss on exchange	$ 1,000

The following entry would be made to record the transaction:

Cash		Computers		Allowance for Depreciation—Computers	
Bal. 90,000	(1) 38,000	Bal. 28,000	(1) 28,000	(1) 25,000	Bal. 25,000

Delivery Truck		Loss on Exchange	
(1) 40,000		(1) 1,000	

In journal form, the entry would read:

```
Delivery Truck.........................................   40,000
Allowance for Depreciation—Computers...................   25,000
Loss on Exchange.......................................    1,000
    Cash..............................................              38,000
    Computers.........................................              28,000
        To record loss on exchange of dissimilar plant assets.
```

Exchange of Dissimilar Plant Assets; Recognition of Gain

When a gain occurs on the exchange of dissimilar plant assets, the gain is recognized in the accounts, and the new asset is recorded at its cash price. For example, in the preceding illustration involving the computer and delivery truck, assume that the trade-in allowance was $5,000 instead of $2,000 and that $35,000 was paid in cash. The gain would be $2,000–$5,000 trade-in allowance less $3,000 book value. The delivery truck would be recorded at $40,000, its cash price. The following entry would be made:

Cash		Computers	
Bal. 90,000	(1) 35,000	Bal. 28,000	(1) 28,000

Allowance for Depreciation—Computers		Delivery Truck	
(1) 25,000	Bal. 25,000	(1) 40,000	

Gain on Exchange	
	(1) 2,000

In journal form, the entry would read:

Delivery Truck...	40,000	
Allowance for Depreciation—Computers...................	25,000	
Cash..		35,000
Computers.......................................		28,000
Gain on Exchange.................................		2,000

To record gain on exchange of dissimilar plant assets.

Plant Asset Exchanges and Tax Rules

The Internal Revenue Code bars the recognition of gains and losses when similar assets are exchanged. According to the tax rules, a new asset would be recorded at the sum of the cash paid plus the net book value of the old asset. Thus, in the first illustration the new delivery truck would be recorded at $53,000 ($38,000 cash paid plus $15,000 book value) and a loss would not be recognized for tax purposes.

LEASES

A *lease* is an agreement or contract which grants a right to operate or use property for a specific period of time. The person or organization which grants the right is referred to as the *lessor*. The person or organization which receives the right to use or operate property is called the *lessee*.

The accounting treatment for leases on the books of the lessee differs depending upon whether the lease is classified as a capital lease or an operating lease. If the lease meets any one of five specified criteria, it is classified as a capital lease. All other leases are classified as operating leases. In this text, we will assume that all leases mentioned are operating leases. Rental payments under operating leases are charged to expense in the periods for which they are incurred.

Leasehold Improvements and Leaseholds

Often, a lessee will improve leased property by, for example, erecting a building on leased land or by making major changes remodeling a leased building. Normally, the cost of these improvements will be recorded in a Leasehold Improvements account and amortized over the shorter term of the life of the lease or the useful life of the improvements. Straight-line amortization is common, although accelerated methods may be used to obtain a better matching of expense and revenue.

To illustrate, assume that a company leases a tract of land at an annual rental of $10,000 plus a $60,000 nonrefundable advance payment on the lease. The advance payment is called a Leasehold and is to be amortized over the life of the lease. The company immediately erects a building at a cost of $150,000 on the leased property. The lease runs for 20 years, while the physical life of the building is estimated at 25 years. Assuming the company uses the straight-line amortization method, the total annual expense to be recognized on the lease and the leasehold improvement is $20,500, computed as follows:

Annual rental.	$10,000
Amortization of advance payment ($60,000 ÷ 20 years).	3,000
Depreciation on the building ($150,000 ÷ 20 years).	7,500
	$20,500

In this case the building was amortized over the life of the lease since it was less than the useful life of the building. The company will be able to use the services of the building only for the period of the lease.

Although a leasehold is an intangible asset, leaseholds and leasehold improvements are typically reported in the plant asset section of the statement of financial position.

NATURAL RESOURCES

Natural resources, such as mines, quarries, and timber stands, should be originally recorded in the accounts at cost of acquisition plus cost of development. Natural resources are later carried in the accounts at total cost minus *depletion*. Depletion is a cost allocation brought about by removal of a physical quantity of the resource.

Depletion charges may be computed by dividing the total cost of acquisition and development by the estimated number of units—tons, barrels, or board feet—in the property. This is known as the unit method of computing depletion. To illustrate, assume that $1,000,000 was paid for a mine estimated to contain 800,000 tons of ore. The unit (per ton) depletion charge would be $1,000,000 ÷ 800,000 tons, or $1.25 per ton. If, in 1979, 80,000 tons of ore were extracted, the depletion charge would be 80,000 × $1.25 or $100,000. This $100,000 would be recorded in a separate Depletion account and either as a direct credit to the Mineral Deposits account or in a separate Allowance for Depletion account. For example, the T-accounts would appear as follows:

Depletion		Mineral Deposits	
100,000		Balance 1,000,000	100,000

The Depletion account contains the material cost of the ore mined. It is combined with labor and other mining costs to arrive at the total cost of the ore mined. This total cost is then divided between cost of goods sold and inventory.

To illustrate, assume that in addition to the depletion cost of $100,000, mining labor costs for 1979 amounted to $210,000 while all other mining costs (depreciation, property taxes, supplies used, power, similar costs) amounted to $90,000. The total cost of mining 80,000 tons then would be $400,000, and the cost per ton would be $5. If 70,000 tons were sold, the earnings statement would show cost of ore sold at $350,000, and the statement of financial position would show inventory of ore on hand at $50,000.

It is often necessary to revise the depletion charge per unit when evidence indicates that the original estimate of the number of units in the property was wrong. When a change in estimate occurs, the unallocated cost is spread over the estimated remaining units. Referring to the above example, assume that in 1980 it is estimated that there are 750,000 tons (instead of 720,000 tons) of ore remaining in the mine. The depletion charge per ton for 1980 would be $1.20 [($1,000,000 − $100,000) ÷ 750,000 tons].

INTANGIBLE ASSETS

Sources of Intangible Assets

Intangible assets arise from:

1. Superior entrepreneurial capacity or management "know-how": *goodwill.*
2. Exclusive rights granted by governmental authority: *trademarks, patents, copyrights,* and *franchises.*

The intangible assets of a business are closely related to the manufacturing or merchandising activities of the business. The problem of their valuation is often just a part of the problem of the valuation of the entire business.

The costs of intangible assets are recorded upon acquisition. The major criteria in recording an intangible become (1) identification of the outlay and (2) reasonable grounds for thinking that future benefits will be obtained from the outlay.

In general, intangible assets are amortized over the shorter of their expected economic life or their legal life. Patents and copyrights (legal life may be changed) have legal lives of 17 and 28 years respectively. The legal life is the maximum period of life; quite often, though, such assets will become useless before the end of that period. Thus if the expected useful life of a patented production process is five years, amortization should be based on the five-year period.

Patents. Patents are grants made by the federal government which give an inventor the sole right to make, use, or sell an invention for a period of 17 years. Patents are recorded at cost and are amortized over the shorter of their expected economic (useful) life or legal life. For example, assume that Curry Company purchased patent rights to a machine invented by Denton Company. The patent rights cost $30,000 and have a 10 year estimated economic life. The following entry would be made each year for ten years to amortize the cost of the patent rights:

Amortization of Patents		Patents		
3,000		Bal.	xxx	3,000

The Patents account may also be debited for the costs of successful lawsuits brought in defense of a patent.

Copyrights. A copyright is a grant by the federal government which gives a specific person or organization the sole right to reproduce, publish, and sell a literary, musical, or artistic work. Although it has a legal life of 28 years, (this may be changed as of January 1, 1978), a copyright is usually amortized over its economic life (since economic life is shorter than legal life in most cases.) But, since the cost of a copyright is usually small, the amount is often charged directly to an expense account instead of an asset account.

Goodwill. Goodwill is best viewed as an intangible value attached to an entity which results primarily from the skill of its management. A firm may be continuously generating goodwill. Such goodwill may be represented by a superior marketing organization, product reputation, marketing channels, technical know-how, and astute management. Such factors, though, are hard to identify and value. Thus the value of goodwill is often described as the value of the entity over the sum of the fair values of its net discernible assets. It arises because management has the ability to use the resources of the entity to produce an above-average rate of earnings per dollar of investment. This means that the proof of the existence of goodwill is found in the ability to generate superior or above-average earnings.

A Goodwill account will appear in the records only if the goodwill has been purchased. Goodwill cannot be purchased separately; an entire business or a portion of it must be purchased. The amount debited to a Goodwill account will equal the total price paid for a going business less the excess of the fair market values assigned to the assets over the total amount of the liabilities.

To illustrate the recording and amortization of Goodwill, assume that Little Company purchases Small Company for $900,000. The fair market value of Small's assets totals $1,460,000 and the amount of its liabilities totals $580,000. Purchased goodwill amounts to $20,000. This is equal to $900,000 − ($1,460,000 − $580,000). The $20,000 is debited to a Goodwill account. Assume the estimated life of the Goodwill is 10 years. Amortization for each of the 10 years would be $2,000 and would be recorded by the following entry in the first year:

Goodwill			Amortization of Goodwill	
Bal.	20,000	(1)	2,000	(1)	2,000

Although goodwill cannot be amortized for tax purposes, *Opinion No. 17* of the Accounting Principles Board of the American Institute of Certified Public Accountants requires that goodwill be amortized by periodic charges to expense over a period not to exceed 40 years. If its estimated life is less than 40 years, it would be amortized over the shorter period. The reasoning behind the opinion is that the value of the purchased goodwill eventually disappear. Other goodwill may be generated in its place, but the organization is not equipped to value the regenerated goodwill. An analogy can also be made to the purchase of a machine. Both goodwill and the machine are purchased because they will generate a stream of revenue in the future. In both cases, it is proper to spread the cost over the period of expected benefit.

Research and Development Costs

Prior to 1975, research and development costs were often capitalized as intangible assets when future benefits were expected from their incurrence. Since it was often difficult to determine the costs applicable to future benefits, many firms expensed all such costs as they were incurred. Other firms capitalized those costs which related to proven products and expensed the rest as incurred. As a result of these varied accounting practices, the Financial Accounting Standards Board (in FASB Statement No. 2) ruled that all research and development costs, other than those directly reimbursable by government agencies and others, must be expensed at the time they are incurred. Such immediate expensing is justified on the grounds that the amount of costs applicable to the future cannot be measured with any high degree of precision, that doubt exists as to whether any future benefits will be received, and that even if future benefits are expected they cannot be measured. As a result of the new ruling, research and development costs will no longer appear as an intangible asset on the statement of financial position.

SUMMARY

Noncurrent assets are the assets used in a business over a long period of time and are generally referred to as plant assets. The assets represent bundles of service potentials which are expected to yield positive benefits in the future. A further breakdown of the noncurrent assets is made to separate tangible assets (those with physical substance) and intangible assets (those based on legal rights, superior earning power, or licenses, etc.).

The noncurrent assets can be further divided into those items whose service potentials do not expire, for example, land used as a building site, and those assets which lose their service potentials over a period of time, for example, machinery. Proper accounting calls for the allocation of the costs of the assets whose service potentials expire to the periods benefiting from their use. Such an allocation is referred to as *depreciation* of plant assets, *depletion* of natural resources, or *amortization* of intangible assets.

The proper method for allocating the cost of the assets to the periods benefited will depend on many factors including the nature of the revenue patterns, the expected useful life of the asset, and the maintenance policy of the firm. Three main approaches exist in allocating the cost: (1) straight-line method, where the cost of the asset less salvage value is allocated in equal amounts to each year of the expected life of the asset; (2) accelerated method, where decreasing portions of the cost are allocated to each year; and (3) the units-of-production method, where the cost allocated to each year is based upon the number of units produced. The units method is used most often in computing depletion charges.

Intangible assets are recorded when purchased or when a specific expenditure benefiting future periods can be identified. The costs of intangible assets are usually amortized over the shorter of (1) their economic life or (2) their legal life. Goodwill is a special intangible associated with a business as a whole and is recognized only upon the purchase of a total entity or a large portion thereof. Goodwill may have an indefinite, though finite life, and should be amortized over its expected economic life. The period of amortization should not exceed 40 years. Plant and intangible assets are generally reported at cost less allowances for depreciation, depletion, or amortization.

QUESTIONS AND EXERCISES

1. Bruce Company is offered $50,000 for a tract of land carried in its accounts at $20,000. Should it accept the offer? Why or why not?

2. What is the logic underlying the accounting requirement that depreciation, depletion, or amortization be recorded periodically on virtually every plant asset?

3. What accounting treatment would you recommend for each of the following (that is, record as an asset, an expense, or charge to the allowance for depreciation)?
    a. Cost of new air conditioning equipment installed in leased building.
    b. The cost of painting an owned factory building. Such painting must be done every three years.
    c. Cost of installing a new battery in an owned automobile. Battery will last two to three years.

    d. Cost of rebuilding the transmission in an owned truck. Transmission should last the remaining life of the truck.

4. Distinguish between depreciation, depletion, and amortization. Name two assets subject to depreciation. To depletion. To amortization.

5. Distinguish between tangible and intangible assets. Classify the assets named in Question 4 accordingly.

6. What is the measure of the gain or loss when a depreciable asset is sold for cash?

7. In an exchange of plant assets, at what amount would the new asset be recorded under each of the following conditions? Would a gain or loss be recognized in each case? Would the tax treatment differ in each case?
    a. Similar assets exchanged at a loss.
    b. Similar assets exchanged at a gain.
    c. Dissimilar assets exchanged at a gain.
    d. Dissimilar assets exchanged at a loss.

8. Distinguish between patents and copyrights.

9. Distinguish between leaseholds and leasehold improvements.

10. M Company leased land for a 25-year period beginning on July 1, 1979, at an annual rental of $10,000. The company then erected one building on the land and placed the building in operation on January 1, 1980. The building has an estimated physical life of 30 years. Over what period of time should the building be depreciated? Why?

11. Why does a businessman generally favor quick write-off of depreciable assets? Can you cite any practical reason for a business to change from an accelerated to the straight-line depreciation method?

12. A certain store enjoys a reputation for fair dealing with its customers, employees, and suppliers; is favorably located; seems to enjoy repeated visits from loyal customers; and retails high-quality merchandise. Does it follow that such a store possesses goodwill? Would it be recorded?

13. A Company purchased all of the assets of B Company for $700,000. A Company duly recorded the acquired current assets at their estimated fair market values of $300,000 and the acquired plant assets at their appraised values of $350,000. The president of the company wanted to dispose of the remaining $50,000 by charging it to the Retained Earnings account. Would you support this treatment of the $50,000? Why or why not? What does the $50,000 represent?

14. What accounting treatment should be accorded research and development costs?

15. For $320,000 cash, the Box Company purchased a tract of land and two buildings. The company intended to demolish the old factory building and to remodel and use the office building. An appraiser employed by the company placed appraised values of $120,000 on the land, $120,000 on the old factory building, and $160,000 on the office building. The factory building was demolished at a cost of $16,000, while the office building was remodeled at a cost of $32,000. Compute the cost at which each of the above assets should be carried in the company's accounts.

16. Barker Company purchased a new machine on January 2, 1979, at a cost of $80,000. The machine is expected to last five years and to have no salvage value at the end of that time. Assuming a 50 percent federal income tax rate, how much would the income taxes payable for 1979 and 1980 be reduced if the company used the double-declining balance rather than the straight-line method of computing periodic depreciation?

17. B Company purchased a machine for $48,000 on January 2, 1976, and proceeded to depreciate it over five years on a straight-line basis. No salvage value is expected. On December 31, 1980, before recording depreciation for 1980, B Company decided that the machine would last a total of eight years. Compute the depreciation to be recorded on the machine in 1980.

18. Queen Company paid $1,200,000 for the mineral rights, estimated at 6,000,000 tons, in a certain tract of land. In the first year of operating the property, Queen Company extracted 600,000 tons of ore and sold 400,000 tons. What part of the $1,200,000 is to be considered an expense of this first year of operations?

19. Barker Stores leased a tract of land and a building for a 20-year period beginning January 1, 1979, paying $80,000 in cash and agreeing to make annual payments equal to 1 percent of the first $1,000,000 of sales and ½ percent of all sales in excess of $1,000,000 but with the provision that the minimum annual payment would be at least $12,500. Compute the rent expense for 1979 assuming sales of $1,400,000.

20. Quite often a company will use an accelerated method of depreciation for tax purposes and the straight-line method for financial reporting purposes. As a financial manager, would you recommend such a policy? Why?

21. Discuss the correct accounting for expenditures on research and development.

PROBLEMS

4–1. Bryson Company planned to erect a new factory building and a new office building in Warren, Michigan. Preliminary studies showed two possible sites were available and desirable. Bryson Company then paid $5,000 to the owner of each site for a 90-day option to buy. Further studies showed the second site to be preferable. An appraisal report on this property showed:

Item	Appraised Value
Land.	$260,000
Building.	140,000
Orchard.	100,000

After considerable negotiation the company and the owner had reached the following agreement. Bryson Company was to pay $184,000 in cash in addition to the option, issue to the owner 3,000 shares of its common stock, assume a $130,000 mortgage note on the property, assume accrued interest of $4,800 on the mortgage note, and assume unpaid property taxes of $9,000. Bryson Company's common stock had previously been issued at $50 per share. The stock had a market value of $56 per share on the date the agreement was signed. Bryson Company paid $42,000 cash for broker and legal services in acquiring the property. Shortly after acquisition of the property, Bryson Company sold the fruit on the trees for $4,400, remodeled the building into an office building at a cost of $68,000, and removed the trees from the land at a cost of $10,000. Construction of the factory building is to begin in a week.

Required: Prepare schedules showing the proper valuation of the assets acquired by the Bryson Company.

4–2.   Hard Company acquired a machine on July 1, 1979, at a cash cost of $48,000 and immediately spent $2,000 to install it. The machine was estimated to have a useful life of eight years and a scrap value of $4,000 at the end of this time. It was further estimated that the machine would produce 1,000,000 units of product during its life. In the first year the machine produced 200,000 units.

Required: Compute the depreciation for the fiscal year ended June 30, 1980, if the company chooses to use—
a.   The straight-line method.
b.   The sum-of-the-years'-digits method.
c.   The double-declining balance method.
d.   The units-of-production method.

4–3.   Jarrell Company purchased a machine on January 2, 1977, at an invoice price of $142,600. Transportation charges amounted to $2,000, and $3,400 was spent to install the machine. Costs of removing an old machine to make room for the new amounted to $1,200, and $200 was received for the scrapped material in the old machine.

Required:

a.   State the amount of depreciation that would be recorded on the machine for the first year on a straight-line basis and on a double-declining balance basis, assuming an estimated life of eight years and no salvage value expected at the end of that time.
b.   Compute the depreciation for the year ended December 31, 1979, assuming a revised total life expectancy for the machine of 12 years; assume that depreciation has been recorded through December 31, 1978, on a straight-line basis.

4–4.   Barton Company purchased a new 1979 model automobile on September 1, 1979. The list price of the new car was $6,800, and the company received a trade-in allowance for a 1977 model of $2,500. The 1977 model had been acquired on September 1, 1977, at a cost of $3,400. Depreciation has been recorded through September 1, 1979 on a double-declining balance basis with four years of useful life expected.

4. Plant and Intangible Assets   101

Required:

Compute the gain or loss on the exchange and the dollar amount at which the new auto will be recorded using the tax method.

4–5. *a.* Newberry Company purchased a tract of land and a building having appraised values of $315,000 and $525,000, respectively. The terms of the sale were $423,000 cash, with Newberry Company to assume the responsibility to repay a $270,000 mortgage note, as well as $9,000 of accrued interest on the mortgage note and $34,000 of unpaid property taxes. Newberry intends to use the building as an office building.

Required: Compute the cost of each of the assets acquired.

b. Martin Company secured a lease on a building and tract of land for a 40-year period beginning July 1, 1971, by paying $88,000 immediately in cash and agreeing to make annual payments each June 30 of $22,000. Effective July 1, 1981, Martin Company subleased this property to the Brice Company at an annual rental of $50,000 payable each July 1 for the year in advance for the remaining 30 years of life in its lease. On July 2, 1981, Martin Company paid a broker a commission of $36,000 for services in arranging the sublease.

Required: Determine the amounts of revenue and expense to be recorded relative to these leases by the Martin Company for the fiscal year ended June 30, 1982.

4–6. The King Mining Company acquired on January 2, 1979, ore deposits at a cash cost of $2,646,000. The ore deposit contains an estimated 4,200,000 tons, but present technology will allow the economical extraction of only 90 percent of the total deposit. Machinery, equipment, and temporary sheds are installed at a cost of $352,000. These assets will have no further value to the company when the ore body is exhausted; they have a physical life of 12 years. In 1979, 500,000 tons of ore are extracted; future annual production is expected to increase to 600,000 tons and then fall to around 335,000 tons per year. In any event, the company expects the mine to be exhausted in 10 years.

Required:

a. Compute the depletion charge for 1979.
b. Compute the depreciation charge on the machinery and equipment for 1979 under each of the following methods: (1) straight-line, (2) double-declining balance, and (3) units-of-production.
c. Which depreciation method do you believe to be most appropriate in the circumstances cited?

4–7. The Harrisburg Company acquired a machine for $45,000 on September 5, 1979, and spent $2,000 on accessories that were required to get the machine ready for use. It has been estimated that the machine will have a 9-year useful life and a $2,000 salvage value and that it will produce 750,000 units of product during its life. The machine produced 5,000 units during 1979 and 85,000 units during 1980.

Required: Compute the depreciation for the years ended December 31, 1979, and 1980, if the company uses—
a.   The straight-line method.
b.   The sum-of-the-years'-digits method.
c.   The double-declining balance method.
d.   The units-of-production method.

4–8.   Baker Company is to purchase all of the assets and assume all of the liabilities of the Hayes Company. The purchase price is $600,000. The fair market values of Hayes Company's assets total $750,000 and the fair market values of its liabilities total $200,000.

Required:

a.   Compute the amount of goodwill purchased by the Baker Company.
b.   Assume the goodwill has an estimated life of 20 years, and compute the periodic amortization charge.

4–9.   The following information is presented for the Webber Corporation:

Sales	$1,000,000
Expenses (excluding depreciation)	700,000
Earnings before depreciation and taxes	$ 300,000

The company, which is in its first year of operation, has plant assets consisting of machinery having a cost of $760,000, an estimated life of eight years, and no salvage value expected at the end of that time. It is subject to a corporate federal income tax rate of 50 percent.

Required:

a.   Compute the annual depreciation on the machinery under the straight-line method and under the double-declining balance method for each of the first three years.
b.   Compute the tax savings for each of the first three years if the company used the double-declining balance method rather than the straight-line method for tax purposes.

chapter 5

Stockholders' Equity

The corporation is the major form of business enterprise in terms of economic power in this country. One of the reasons for this is that huge amounts of capital can be raised by a corporation by the sale of shares of its stock to the public. Hence, the owners' interest in a corporation is usually called stockholders' or shareholders' equity. Other advantages of the corporation include the stockholders' limited liability and the ease of transferring ownership by selling the shares of stock owned. Here, limited liability means that a stockholder is not responsible (liable) for the debts of the corporation. The stockholder can lose only the amount invested.

The goals of accounting for stockholders' equity are to show the *sources* of *equity* capital and the *rights* of the various capital investors in the corporation. In addition to capital invested by owners, equity capital may be obtained by retention of earnings in the corporation. The corporation may also obtain capital by issuing bonds or short-term debt. Accounting for this type of capital is discussed in another chapter, but it should be noted that the rights of equity capital holders rank below those of debt holders. This means that in times of economic hardship, all legal liabilities must be met before equity holders can share in the assets of the business. Thus, the major risks and rewards of a business lie with those who provide equity capital.

Capital Stock Authorized, Issued, and Outstanding

The corporate charter will state the maximum number of shares and the par value, if any, per share of each class of stock that the corporation is authorized to issue, thus the term *authorized shares*. The total ownership interest in a corporation rests with the holders of its *outstanding shares* of stock—that is, the shares authorized and *issued* and currently held by stockholders. If, for example, a corporation is authorized to issue 30,000 shares of common stock but has issued only 14,000 shares, the holders of the 14,000 shares are the sole owners of the corporation.

Each outstanding share of stock of a given class has identical rights and privileges with every other outstanding share of that class. Shares authorized but not yet issued are referred to as *unissued shares*. These shares possess no rights.

CLASSES OF CAPITAL STOCK

Common Stock

Every corporation will have common stock outstanding. The primary rights of the *common* stockholder include the right to (1) share in earnings when they are declared as dividends; (2) subscribe to additional offerings of the same stock in proportion to the amount currently held; (3) share in assets upon liquidation; and (4) share in management through the election of a board of directors which guides the broad policy decisions of the business. The equity of the common stockholders is often referred to as the residual equity in a corporation, meaning that all other claims rank ahead of the claims of the common stockholders. It is to the common stockholder that the primary risks and rewards of ownership accrue.

Preferred Stock

Often, a corporation may, for various reasons, need more equity capital than that provided by the common stockholders. Usually, the corporation will need to attract a different type of investor—one that is more interested in stable earnings on an investment. To do this, a class of stock granting certain preferences and called *preferred stock* may be issued. Usually preferred stock is *preferred as to dividends,* although it can also be *preferred as to assets* in case of liquidation.

If stock is *preferred as to dividends,* its holders are entitled to a specified dividend per share before the payment of any dividend on the common stock. A stock preferred as to dividends is *cumulative* if all *dividends in arrears* (required dividends not paid in prior years) on this stock and the current dividend must be paid before dividends can be paid on the common stock. If a preferred stock is *noncumulative,* a dividend which is not paid in any one year does not need to be paid in any future year. Because omitted dividends are lost forever, noncumulative preferred stocks hold little attraction for investors and are seldom issued.

Dividends in arrears are never shown as a liability of the corporation since they are not a legal liability until declared by the board of directors.

Since the amount of dividends in arrears may influence the decisions of users of a corporation's financial statements, such dividends should be and usually are disclosed in a footnote.

If stock is preferred as to assets in case of liquidation, its holders are entitled to receive par value or a larger specified amount per share (called liquidation value) before the common stockholders receive any distribution of assets.

The issuance of preferred stock may have other advantages for the corporation: (1) since preferred stocks often have no voting rights, their issuance will not weaken the control of the common stockholders, and (2) the return (dividend) usually is fixed and thus provides for *financial leverage* to the common stockholders.

Financial Leverage.   Financial leverage is the use of debt or preferred stock to increase (or perhaps decrease) earnings per share to common stockholders. Favorable financial leverage results when earnings per share (EPS) increase because of the issuance of preferred stock or debt. As an example of financial leverage, assume that the organizers of a corporation have two possible ways of getting capital: (1) issue 40,000 shares of $10 par value common stock for $400,000, or (2) issue 20,000 shares of $10 par value common stock for $200,000 and 2,000 shares of $100 par, 8 percent preferred stock for $200,000. Assume that net earnings of $80,000 per year are expected. The earnings to the common stockholders on a per share basis (net earnings, less preferred dividends, divided by number of common shares outstanding) and as a percentage of original investment are shown in Illustration 5.1. Favorable leverage results when debt or preferred stock is used to increase the earnings per share of the common shareholders. In Illustration 5.1 the earnings per share of common stock is greater with preferred stock outstanding, and therefore, at that level of earnings there is favorable financial leverage. The result is $3.20 per share with the preferred stock and $2.00 without the preferred stock.

Financial leverage works in both ways. If earnings in the above example should drop to $20,000, the corresponding earnings per common share would be $0.20 for the corporation with preferred stockholders and $0.50 for the all-common-stock corporation. Thus, in certain cases, the risks of financial leverage may offset the advantages. This is also true for long-term debt, which is another means of obtaining leverage.

ILLUSTRATION 5.1

	With Preferred	*Without Preferred*
Net earnings	$80,000	$80,000
Preferred dividends	16,000	0
Net earnings to common stock	$64,000	$80,000
Number of common shares outstanding	20,000	40,000
Earnings per share of common stock	$ 3.20	$ 2.00

Convertible Preferred Stock.   In recent years large amounts of new preferred stock have been issued in corporate mergers or acquisitions. The preferred stock issued was often convertible; that is, the holder of the stock could exchange it when desired for shares of common stock of the same corporation at a conversion ratio stated in the preferred stock contract.

Convertible preferred stock is attractive to the investor because of (1) the stability of dividends, and (2) the opportunity to participate in the growth of the corporation through the conversion privilege. Issuing preferred stock is also attractive to a corporation because it avoids the use of debt that will have to be repaid and that bears interest which must be paid regardless of the level of earnings.

To illustrate this latter attraction, assume that the Olsen Company issued 2,000 shares of 8 percent, $100 par value convertible preferred stock at $100 per share. The stock can be converted at any time into four shares of Olsen common stock which has a current market value of $25 per share. Assume further that in the next several years the company's earnings increase sharply and that it increases the dividend on the common stock from $1.50 to $3.00 per share. The common stock now sells at $50 per share. The holder of one share of preferred stock could convert the stock into four shares of common stock and increase the annual dividend from $8 (from the preferred) to $12 (from the common). Or if one so desired, one could sell the preferred share at a substantial gain since the preferred stock would sell in the market for about $200—the market value of the four shares of common into which it is convertible. Or one may continue to hold it in the expectation of realizing an even larger gain at a later date.

Statement of Financial Position Presentation

As previously noted, the statement of financial position should show the sources of capital and the rights of the various holders. It should also indicate the status of issued and unissued shares. To illustrate, assume that a corporation is authorized to issue (1) 20,000 shares of $100 par value, 8 percent, cumulative, convertible preferred stock, all of which have been issued and are outstanding; and (2) 400,000 shares of $10 par value common stock of which 160,000 shares have been issued at par and are outstanding. The stockholders' equity section of the statement of financial position (assuming $600,000 of retained earnings) would be:

Stockholders' Equity
Preferred stock—$100 par value, 8% cumulative, convertible;
   authorized, issued, and outstanding 20,000 shares......... $2,000,000
Common stock—$10 par value; authorized 400,000 shares;
   issued and outstanding 160,000 shares.................   1,600,000 $3,600,000
Retained earnings.......................................   600,000
   Total Stockholders' Equity........................... $4,200,000

A footnote to the statement of financial position would state the rate at which the preferred stock is convertible into common stock.

Shares with Par Value. Each share of capital stock—common or preferred—will, according to the terms of the charter of the issuing corporation, be of *par value* or of *no-par value*. The par value, if any, will be stated in the corporate charter and will be printed on the stock certificates. Par value may be of any amount.

Par value serves two purposes. It is the amount per share that is recorded in the capital stock account for each share outstanding. Secondly, the par value of the outstanding shares is often the legal or stated capital of the corporation. A corporation is forbidden by law to declare dividends or to acquire its own stock if such action will reduce stockholders' equity below the legal capital of the corporation. If stock is issued at a discount from par, the stockholder may be liable to the creditors up to the total discount from par value.

Par value is not an indication of the amount of stockholders' equity per share (book value per share, as it is called) that is recorded in the accounting records of the corporation. The stockholders' equity consists of paid-in or contributed capital and retained earnings, and the latter may be either positive or negative. Nor does par value give any clue to the market value of the stock because market value is based largely upon investors' expectations concerning future earnings and dividends and general market prospects.

Shares without Par Value. It is possible to have common stock without par value. Quite often, though, such stock will have a stated value. This stated value, like par value, may be set at any amount by the board of directors. The accounting treatment for par value stock and stated value stock is the same. The shares are carried in the capital account at either the par or stated value. Any proceeds in excess of par or stated value should be recorded in a separate paid-in capital account.

As an illustration, assume that the DeWitt Corporation, which is authorized to issue 20,000 shares of capital stock without par value, assigned a stated value of $15 per share to its stock. The 20,000 authorized shares were issued for cash at $20 per share. The entry would appear as follows:

Cash	400,000	
Common Stock		300,000
Paid in Capital in Excess of Stated Value		100,000

The stockholders' equity section of the statement of financial position would be as follows:

Stockholders' Equity
Common stock—no par value, stated value, $15; 20,000 shares authorized, issued, and outstanding	$300,000
Paid-in capital in excess of stated value	100,000
Total Stockholders' Equity	$400,000

The $100,000 received over and above the stated value of $300,000 should be carried permamently as paid-in capital because it is a part of the capital originally contributed by the stockholders. The stated capital of the DeWitt Corporation, however, is $300,000—the stated value of the shares issued.

Shares without Par or Stated Value. If a corporation issues shares without par value to which no stated value is assigned or required by law, the entire amount received is credited to the capital stock account. The entire amount received for such shares, to which no stated value is assigned or required by state law, is the amount of stated capital.

In the above illustration of the DeWitt Corporation, if no stated value was assigned to the shares the entry would have been:

```
Cash...................................................  400,000
      Common Stock......................................          400,000
```

The stockholders' equity section of the company's statement of financial position would be:

```
Stockholders' Equity
Common stock—no par or stated value; 20,000 shares
   authorized, issued, and outstanding....................  $400,000
      Total Stockholders' Equity.........................   $400,000
```

Recording Capital Stock Issues

The issuance of common stock or preferred stock may be preceded by the subscription of the stock by the future stockholders. If handled in one transaction, the entry is usually not recorded until cash is received.

Quite often stock will be issued through underwriters who guarantee the corporation a fixed price per share and make a commission by selling at a slightly higher price to the public. To illustrate, assume that an underwriter guaranteed the sale of 300,000 shares at $20 per share net to the company. Selling price to the public was $21. Authorized shares are 500,000, and par value is $10 per share. The entry to record the receipt of the net proceeds would be:

```
Cash.................................................  6,000,000
      Common Stock....................................          3,000,000
      Paid in Capital in Excess of Par Value..........          3,000,000
```

After completion of the transaction, the stockholders' equity section of the statement of financial position would be:

```
Stockholders' Equity
Common stock—$10 par value; authorized 500,000
   shares, issued and outstanding 300,000 shares..........  $3,000,000
Paid-in capital in excess of par value...................   3,000,000
      Total Stockholders' Equity.........................   $6,000,000
```

The computation is as follows:

Gross proceeds, 300,000 × $21	$6,300,000
Underwriter's charge	300,000
Proceeds to company	$6,000,000
Par value, 300,000 × $10	3,000,000
Capital in excess of par	$3,000,000

Typically only $6,000,000 is recorded as the capital received, since it represents the net proceeds to the company.

Values Associated with Capital Stock

Book Value. The book value of a corporation is the total of the recorded net asset values of a corporation, or simply the total stockholders' equity. When only common stock is outstanding, *book value per share* is computed by dividing stockholders' equity by the number of shares outstanding. For example, if a corporation has stockholders' equity consisting of Capital Stock of $100,000 and Retained Earnings of $50,000 and has 10,000 shares outstanding, the book value per share is $15 ($150,000 ÷ 10,000 shares).

When two or more classes of capital stock are outstanding, the computation of book value per share is more complex. The usual approach is to assume that the assets and liabilities are liquidated at book value. Preferred shareholders typically are entitled to at least par value plus cumulative dividends in arrears. The provision in the preferred stock contract will govern and may, for example, state specifically the amount the holder of the preferred stock is entitled to receive in *liquidation* (the liquidation value) in addition to cumulative dividends, if any.

As an illustration assume that the Celoron Company's stockholders' equity is as follows:

Stockholders' Equity	
Preferred stock—$50 par value, 8%, cumulative, 8,000 shares	$ 400,000
Common stock—$10 par value, 400,000 shares	4,000,000
Paid-in capital in excess of par value—preferred	40,000
Retained earnings	600,000
Total Stockholders' Equity	$5,040,000

Assume that the preferred stock has a liquidation value of $52 and that dividends on the preferred stock have not been paid this year. The book values for each class of stock are shown in Illustration 5.2.

Relationship of Book Value, Par Value, and Market Value. Par value and book value are related only to the extent that the par value of the

ILLUSTRATION 5.2

		Total	Per Share
Total stockholders' equity......................		$5,040,000	
Book value of preferred stock (8,000 shares):			
Liquidation value ($52 × 8,000)...............	$416,000		
Dividends (1 year at $32,000).................	32,000	448,000	$56.00
Book value of common (400,000 shares)...........		$4,592,000	11.48

stock is one element of stockholders' equity—on which book value is computed. Book value and market value are related only to the extent that the market forces consider book value important. But market value is more dependent on (1) the company's future earning power and possible dividend payments, (2) the present financial position of the company, and (3) the current state of the economy and other general stock market influences. Thus, a share of common or preferred stock may sell in a market for much more or much less than its book value or more or less than its par value.

OTHER SOURCES OF PAID-IN (OR CONTRIBUTED) CAPITAL

The goal of paid-in capital accounts is to show the sources of capital. An account is usually established for each source of capital, for example, preferred stock, common stock, capital in excess of par from common stock issuance, and so forth. The major source of capital is investment by stockholders. But, sometimes a company may receive donated capital. This often happens when a city donates land and a building to a corporation to encourage it to locate in that city. Proper recording would show the source as paid-in capital—donations. For example, assume the Chamber of Commerce gave a building worth $30,000 and land worth $12,000 to a corporation. The entry required is:

Land..	12,000	
Building...	30,000	
Paid in Capital—Donations.............................		42,000

Other changes in the capital accounts might include: (1) capitalization of retained earnings through issuance of a stock dividend (discussed later in this chapter); (2) "gains" on treasury stock transactions (discussed later in this chapter); and (3) revaluation of assets.

To illustrate the reporting of capital, the following stockholders' equity section of a statement of financial position is presented:

Stockholders' Equity

Paid-In Capital		
Preferred stock—$100 par value; authorized, issued and outstanding 4,000 shares.......... $ 400,000		
Common stock—no par value; stated value $5 per share; authorized, issued, and outstanding 200,000 shares.................... 1,000,000	$1,400,000	
Paid-in capital in excess of par or stated value		
From preferred stock issuances............. $ 40,000		
From stock dividend...................... 1,000,000		
From donations. . .~.................... 10,000	1,050,000	
Total Paid-In Capital...................		$2,450,000
Capital from appreciation of land................		100,000
Retained earnings...............................		400,000
Total Stockholders' Equity..............		$2,950,000

RETAINED EARNINGS

In general the stockholders' equity in a corporation is made up of two elements: (1) paid-in (or contributed) capital and (2) retained earnings. Retained earnings is the term used to describe the increase in stockholders' equity resulting from profitable operation of the corporation. As such, it shows the source of assets received but not distributed to stockholders as dividends. Thus, both categories indicate the source of assets received by the corporation—actual investment by the stockholder and investment by the stockholder in the sense of dividends forgone. For now, the balance in the Retained Earnings account will be viewed as the difference between (1) the net earnings of the corporation during its existence to date and (2) the sum of dividends declared during the same period. Dividends are usually declared only when retained earnings exist.

When the Retained Earnings account has a negative (or debit) balance, a deficit exists. It is shown under that title as a negative amount in the stockholders' equity section of the statement of financial position.

DIVIDENDS

Dividends are distributions by a corporation to its stockholders. The normal dividend is a cash dividend; but other types of assets, such as marketable securities, may be distributed. A corporation may also distribute additional shares of its own capital stock as dividends.

Since they are the means by which the owners of a corporation share in the earnings of the corporation, dividends are usually charged against retained earnings. They must be declared by the board of directors. The significant dates concerning dividends are the date of declaration, the date of record, and the date of payment. For example, the board of directors may declare, on June 5, 1979, a cash dividend of $1.25 per share payable on July 10 to stockholders of record on July 1, 1979. The date of declaration is the date the action of the board becomes effective, creating the liability for dividends payable. The date of record is used to determine to whom the dividends will be paid. The date of payment is the date of actual payment.

Cash Dividends

Assume that the statement of financial position of a company shows among others the following balances:

Assets	Stockholders' Equity
Cash.................. $10,000	Retained earnings........ $15,000

On January 21, 1979, a cash dividend of $2,000 is declared, to be paid on March 1 to stockholders of record on February 5, 1979. The entry needed is:

Retained Earnings...	2,000	
Dividends Payable......................................		2,000

After recording the effects of the dividend declaration, a partial statement of financial position would show:

Assets	Current Liabilities	
Cash..................... $10,000	Dividends payable...	$ 2,000
	Stockholders' Equity	
	Retained earnings....	13,000

Until paid, a legally declared cash dividend is a current liability of the declaring corporation. When the dividend is paid on March 31, the entry needed would be:

Dividends Payable...	2,000	
Cash..		2,000

Stock Dividends

Quite often, a company will declare a dividend to be paid in the company's stock instead of in cash. There are a number of reasons a company might do this: (1) it is a means of declaring a dividend without draining cash which is needed for other purposes; (2) the additional shares available to be traded may create a more active market for the stock; and (3) the corporation may desire more permanent capital which it can obtain by transferring retained earnings to capital stock and capital in excess of par.

Stock dividend declarations usually call for the distribution of more shares of the same class of stock as that held by the stockholders—in other words, more common stock to common stockholders. Stock dividends have no effect on the total amount of stockholders' equity. They either decrease retained earnings and increase paid-in capital by an equal amount or transfer amounts between paid-in capital accounts. Stock dividends decrease book value per share. This is because more shares are outstanding with no increase in total stockholders' equity.

Stock dividends do not affect the individual stockholder's percentage ownership in the corporation. For example, if Judy Smith owns 1,000 shares in a corporation having 100,000 shares of stock outstanding, she owns 1 percent of the outstanding shares. After a 10 percent stock dividend she will still own 1 percent of the outstanding shares—1,100 owned with 110,000 outstanding. For this reason, the receipt of a stock dividend does not represent income to its holder.

Amount Transferred to Capital for Stock Dividends. When stock dividends are declared, what amount should be transferred from retained earnings to more permanent capital? Legal requirements usually specify that the amount transferred must at least equal the par value of the additional stock issued.

Accounting Research Bulletin No. 43 distinguishes between stock dividends and *stock split-ups* or stock splits. It takes the position that a stock dividend seeks to give stockholders some separate evidence of their interest in the retained earnings of the corporation without distributing assets. A stock split-up, on the other hand, has the goal of reducing the market price of each share by increasing the number of shares outstanding.

Many investors view stock dividends as distributions of earnings to the extent of the fair value of the shares received. Also, in many instances, the stock distributions are so small as to have no apparent effect on the market price of the previously held shares. Under these circumstances, *Accounting Research Bulletin No. 43* recommended capitalizing retained earnings to the extent of the fair value of the shares issued. But whenever the dividend is greater than 20 or 25 percent, only the amount legally required is capitalized.

Recording Stock Dividends. Assume that a corporation is authorized to issue 50,000 shares of $20 par value common stock, of which 30,000 shares are outstanding. Its stockholders' equity section appears as follows:

```
Stockholders' Equity
    Paid-In Capital
        Common stock—$20 par value; authorized 50,000
            shares, issued and outstanding 30,000 shares........ $  600,000
        Retained earnings....................................      500,000
                Total Stockholders' Equity...................   $1,100,000
```

Its board of directors now declares a 10 percent stock dividend (3,000 shares). The market price of the stock on the date of the dividend declaration is $54 per share. Assuming that the shares to be issued are to be accounted for at market value, the entry for the declaration of the **dividend** would be as follows:

```
Retained Earnings (3,000 shares × $54)..................... 162,000
    Common Stock........................................          60,000
    Paid-in Capital—From Stock Dividend.................          102,000
```

After recording the stock dividend, stockholders' equity would be:

```
Stockholders' Equity
    Paid-in Capital
        Common stock—$20 par value; authorized 50,000
            shares, issued and outstanding 33,000 shares........ $  660,000
        From stock dividend.............................          102,000
        Retained earnings...............................          338,000
            Total Stockholders' Equity....................      $1,100,000
```

Now assume that the same corporation had declared a 50 percent rather than a 10 percent stock dividend. In this case, the shares issued would be accounted for at par value. The entry for the declaration and issuance would have been:

```
Retained Earnings (15,000 shares × $20)................... 300,000
    Common Stock....................................          300,000
```

After issuance of the 50 percent stock dividend, stockholders' equity would appear as follows:

```
Stockholders' Equity
    Paid-In Capital
        Common stock—$20 par value; authorized 50,000
            shares, issued and outstanding 45,000 shares........ $  900,000
        Retained earnings...............................          200,000
                                                                $1,100,000
```

Stock Splits

A stock split is not a dividend; it does not affect the balances in the stockholders' equity accounts. The effect of a stock split is to increase the number of shares outstanding and to decrease the par or stated value. Proportional ownership of the stock remains the same. For example, assume Company A has $400,000 (20,000 shares of $20 par value) of common stock outstanding. The board of directors declares a 2 for 1 stock split. After the split, there would be $400,000 (40,000 shares of $10 par value) of common stock outstanding. A person who had previously owned 200 shares or 1 percent of the outstanding shares would now own 400 shares which would still be 1 percent of the outstanding shares. No formal entries are required for a stock split.

TREASURY STOCK

Nature of Treasury Stock

Treasury stock is capital stock, either preferred or common, which has been issued and reacquired by the issuing corporation. It has not been canceled, and it is legally available for reissuance. Treasury stock and unissued capital stock differ in that treasury stock has been issued at some time in the past, while unissued capital stock has never been issued.

Treasury stock may be acquired by purchase, or in settlement of a debt. The corporation laws of most states consider treasury stock as issued but not outstanding. Treasury shares cannot be voted, and dividends are not paid on them.

Generally, as a matter of law, when a corporation acquires treasury stock at a cost (not as a gift), an equal amount of retained earnings is not available for dividends until the treasury stock is reissued or formally retired. As a result, the cost of treasury stock typically will not exceed the amount of retained earnings at the date of its acquisition. Thus, dividends plus treasury stock purchases must not impair the legal (or stated) capital of the corporation. If a corporation is subject to such a law, the retained earnings available for dividends are limited to the amount of retained earnings in excess of the cost of the treasury shares.

Treasury Stock in the Statement of Financial Position

The acquisition of treasury stock is normally recorded by a debit to a Treasury Stock account and a credit to Cash for its cost as follows:

```
Treasury Stock...................................  75,000
    Cash .......................................          75,000
```

It should not be reported as an asset on the statement of financial position. Rather, it is reported as a deduction from the sum of the paid-in capital and retained earnings as follows:

```
Stockholders' Equity
    Common stock—authorized and issued, 40,000 shares; par
        value $10 per share, of which 5,000 shares are in the treasury.......  $400,000
    Retained earnings (including $75,000 restricted by acquisition
        of treasury stock)..........................................   500,000
            Total..................................................  $900,000
    Less: Treasury stock at cost, 5,000 shares......................    75,000
            Total Stockholders' Equity.............................  $825,000
```

Treasury Stock Transactions

To illustrate the accounting for treasury stock, assume that the Hillside Corporation, whose stockholders' equity consists solely of capital stock and retained earnings, acquired 2,000 shares of its capital stock for $70,000. Two months later, when the market price of the stock was $40 per share, it issued 800 shares to officers and employees as bonuses. A year later, when it needed cash, it sold the rest of the shares at $30 each. The entries required are:

(1) Treasury Stock (2,000 shares × $35)..................... 70,000
         Cash... 70,000

(2) Salaries and Bonuses Expense (800 shares × $40).......... 32,000
         Treasury Stock (800 shares × $35).................. 28,000
         Paid-in Capital—Treasury Stock Transactions........ 4,000

(3) Cash (1,200 shares × $30)............................ 36,000
         Paid-in Capital—Treasury Stock Transactions............ 4,000
         Retained Earnings.................................. 2,000
         Treasury Stock (1,200 shares × $35)................ 42,000

In T-account format they would appear as follows:

	Cash		Treasury Stock		Paid-In Capital—Treasury Stock Transactions	
Bal. xxx						
(3) 36,000	(1) 70,000	(1) 70,000	(2) 28,000	(3) 4,000	(2) 4,000	
			(3) 42,000			

Salaries and Bonuses Expense		Retained Earnings	
Bal. xxx		(3) 2,000	Bal. xxx
(2) 32,000			

The acquisition of the shares is recorded at cost ($70,000). The issuance of the 800 shares as bonuses requires a debit to the Salaries and Bonuses Expense account for the market value of the shares, a credit to Treasury Stock for the cost of the shares, and a credit to a paid-in capital account for the excess of the fair value of the shares over their cost. When the remaining shares are issued, the deficiency of issue price from cost is charged against Paid-In Capital—Treasury Stock Transactions until the credit balance in the account is exhausted. The remaining deficiency is then charged to Retained Earnings.

If at the end of the fiscal year the Paid-In Capital—Treasury Stock Transactions account contained a positive (credit) balance, it would be reported in the statement of financial position below capital stock as Paid-In Capital in Excess of Par (or Stated) Value. The "gain" on the transaction represents an increase in invested capital.

EXTRAORDINARY ITEMS AND PRIOR PERIOD ADJUSTMENTS

In the determination of net earnings, more useful information is provided if revenues generated and expenses incurred in the normal operations of a business are reported separately from unusual, nonrecurring gains and losses. In addition, a more useful presentation results if certain unusual, nonrecurring items are reported in the retained earnings statement rather than the earnings statement. In recognition of the above facts, the Accounting Principles Board, in *Opinion No. 9* (December 1966), recommended that unusual, nonrecurring items that have an effect on earnings or losses be classified as either extraordinary items (reported in the earnings statement) or prior period adjustments (reported in the retained earnings statement).

Extraordinary Items

According to APB *Opinion No. 30* extraordinary items are those which are unusual in nature and which occur infrequently. It should be emphasized that items must meet both conditions—unusual nature *and* infrequent occurrence—in order to be classified as extraordinary. Examples include gains or losses which are the direct result of a major casualty (a flood), an expropriation, or a prohibition under a newly enacted law or regulation. Such items are to be included in the computation of periodic net earnings, and disclosed separately in the earnings statement. Also, according to *Statement of Financial Accounting Standards No. 4*, gains and losses from the early extinguishment of debt are extraordinary items. Gains or losses directly related to ordinary business activities are not extraordinary items regardless of their size. For example, material writedowns of uncollectible receivables, obsolete inventories, and intangible assets are not extraordinary items.

Prior Period Adjustments

Prior period adjustments are reported in the statement of retained earnings. They consist of those material adjustments which (1) are directly and specifically related to business activities of a prior period, (2) are not the result of economic events occurring after the prior period, (3) result primarily from determinations made by persons outside the business, and (4) could not be estimated with reasonable accuracy prior to this determination. Prior period adjustments are expected to be rare. They exist mainly because the uncertainty surrounding events and transactions in prior periods was so great that their accounting effects could not be determined at that time.

Examples of prior period adjustments include material assessments or settlements of income taxes, settlements of contracts through renegotiation, and amounts paid to settle litigation or other similar claims. (A *proposed* FASB would change all of this. If adopted prior period adjustments would consist almost solely of corrections of mistakes.)

In the statement of retained earnings, prior period adjustments are treated as adjustments of the opening balance of retained earnings. But normal recurring corrections or adjustments, which follow inevitably from the use of estimates in accounting practice, are not to be treated as prior period adjustments.

Accounting for Tax Effects

Most extraordinary items and prior period adjustments will affect the amount of income taxes payable with the result that questions arise as to proper reporting procedure. To prevent distortions, *Opinion No. 9* recommends that extraordinary items and prior period adjustments be reported net of their tax effects, as shown in Illustration 5.3.

ILLUSTRATION 5.3
ANSON COMPANY
Earnings Statement
For the Year Ended December 31, 1979

Net sales...		$41,000,000
Other revenue......................................		2,250,000
Total revenue..................................		$43,250,000
Cost of goods sold...............................	$22,000,000	
Administrative, selling, and general expenses.......	12,000,000	34,000,000
Net earnings before income taxes.................		$ 9,250,000
Federal income taxes.............................		4,625,000
Net earnings before extraordinary item and the cumulative effect of an accounting change........		$ 4,625,000
Extraordinary Item:		
Gain on retirement of debt.....................	$40,000	
Less tax effect.............................	20,000	20,000
		$ 4,645,000
Cumulative effect on prior years' earnings of changing to a different depreciation method......		20,000
Net Earnings......................................		$ 4,665,000
Earnings per share of common stock:		
Net earnings before extraordinary item and the cumulative effect of an accounting change......		$ 4.625
Extraordinary item.............................		.020
Cumulative effect on prior years' earnings of changing to a different depreciation method....		.020
Net Earnings...................................		$ 4.665

Accounting Changes

A company's net earnings and financial position can be materially altered by changes in accounting methods. A change in inventory valuation method (for example, from Fifo to Lifo) or a change in depreciation method (for example, from straight-line to accelerated) would be examples of accounting changes. According to APB *Opinion No. 20* a company should consistently apply the same accounting methods from one period to another. But, a change may be made if the newly adopted method is preferable and if the change is adequately disclosed in the financial statements. In the period in which an accounting change is made, the nature of the change, its justification, and its effect on net earnings must be disclosed in the financial statements. Also, the cumulative effect of the change on prior years' earnings must be shown on the earnings statement for the year of change.

Illustrative Statements

Financial statements illustrating the treatment of extraordinary items, prior period adjustments, and the cumulative effect of an accounting change are presented in Illustrations 5.3 and 5.4. They are based on the assumption that the Anson Company in 1979 had a gain of $40,000 on the retirement of debt which is taxable income. Also, the company paid $1,200,000 in the current year as a result of the renegotiation of the price of a contract completed three years ago. The company changed depreciation methods in 1979, and the cumulative effect of the change amounted to $20,000. The company has 1,000,000 shares of common stock outstanding. The current tax rate is assumed to be 50 percent.

A number of important considerations in financial reporting are presented in Illustrations 5.3 and 5.4: (1) earnings of $4,625,000 before the extraordinary item and cumulative effect of an accounting change are more

ILLUSTRATION 5.4

ANSON COMPANY
Statement of Retained Earnings 1979
For the Year Ended December 31, 1979

Retained earnings, January 1, 1979......................	$5,000,000
Prior Period Adjustment	
Contract negotiation settlement	
(net of tax effect of $600,000).......................	600,000
	$4,400,000
Add: Net Earnings......................................	4,665,000
Total...	9,065,000
Deduct: Dividends.....................................	500,000
Retained Earnings, December 31, 1979..................	$8,565,000

representative of the continuing earning power of the company because normal amounts of income taxes have been deducted in arriving at this amount; (2) the gain on the retirement of debt and the negotiated contract settlement are reported at their actual impact on the company—that is, less their effect on the amount of taxes currently payable; and (3) earnings per share are reported both before and after the extraordinary item and cumulative effect of an accounting change.

SUMMARY

The goal in accounting for stockholders' equity is to show the sources of capital contributed to the corporation and to show the relevant claims held by the capital contributors. The corporation obtains equity capital (as opposed to debt capital) from three main sources: (1) the common stockholders, (2) the preferred stockholders, and (3) earnings retained in the business. Most of the risks and rewards of ownership lie with the holders of common stock. Preferred stock is often issued to attract potential investors who are more interested in stability of return. Recent preferred stock issues have been convertible into common stock in an attempt to make them more attractive.

Most stock issued will have either a par value or a stated value. If so, this amount is credited to a capital stock account. All proceeds in excess of par or stated value are recorded in separate capital in excess of par (or stated) value accounts.

Book value can be computed for common and preferred stock. Book value per share amounts usually differ from either the par value or market value of the shares.

Dividends are distributions of retained earnings and are usually paid in cash. But it is quite common for companies to declare stock dividends in which additional shares are issued to the current holders. The issuance of small stock dividends (less than 20 to 25 percent) results in capitalizing a portion of retained earnings equal to the current market value of the shares issued. The issuance of a large stock dividend (more than 20 to 25 percent) often results in capitalizing retained earnings equal to the par value of the shares issued.

A stock split increases the number of shares outstanding and decreases the par or stated value of each share. It has no effect upon the stockholders' equity account balances.

Treasury stock is stock acquired by the issuing company. It is generally held for possible issuance to employees or for other reasons. The cost of the stock, if any, is considered a reduction of total equity and is shown as a deduction from total stockholders' equity—not as an asset.

The Accounting Principles Board in its *Opinion No. 9* and *Opinion No. 30* has distinguished between extraordinary items (to be shown in the earnings statement) and prior period adjustments (which are in a sense corrections of the beginning retained earnings balance). Prior period adjustments should be quite rare. In either case, the prior period adjustment or extraordinary item should be shown net of its tax effect, if any.

APB Opinion No. 20 states that when an accounting change is made, the cumulative effect of the change on prior years' earnings must be shown on the earnings statement for the year of change.

QUESTIONS AND EXERCISES

1. What are the basic rights associated with a share of capital stock assuming there is only one class of stock outstanding?

2. A corporation has outstanding 5,000 shares of 8 percent, $50 par value, cumulative preferred stock. Dividends on this stock have not been declared for two years. Is the corporation liable to its preferred stockholders for these dividends? How should they be shown in the statement of financial position, if at all?

3. Explain why a corporation might issue a preferred stock that is both convertible into common stock and callable.

4. Assuming there is no preferred stock outstanding how can the "book value" per share of common stock be determined? Of what significance is it? What is its relationship to market value per share?

5. One hundred shares of $50 par value common stock are issued to the promoters of a corporation in exchange for land needed by the corporation for use as a plant site. Experienced appraisers have recently estimated the value of the land to be $8,500. At what amount would it be appropriate to record the acquisition of the land? Why?

6. What are the two component parts of the stockholders' equity in a corporation? Explain the difference between them.

7. What is the effect of each of the following on the total stockholders' equity of a corporation; (a) declaration of a cash dividend, (b) payment of a cash dividend, and (c) issuance of a stock dividend?

8. The following dates are associated with a cash dividend of $100,000: July 15, July 31, and August 15. Identify each of the three dates. What is the accounting impact of each date?

9. One of the problems faced by the accountant in accounting for stock dividends is determining the amount that should be transferred out of retained earnings into capital accounts for the shares issued. How has this issue been resolved?

10. Distinguish carefully between extraordinary items and prior period adjustments. Explain why it is important that the two be carefully distinguished.

11. Arden Company's statement of financial position shows total assets of $800,000, liabilities of $300,000, and stockholders' equity of $500,000. B owns 400 of Arden's 20,000 shares of outstanding common stock. Arden now declares and issues a 10 percent stock dividend. Compute the book value per share and in total of B's investment in Arden (a) before the stock dividend and (b) after the stock dividend.

12. Distinguish between a stock dividend and a stock split. How does accounting treat each?

13. How does the declaration of a cash dividend on preferred stock affect the reported earnings of a corporation? How does it affect the earnings available to the common stockholder?

14. What does the balance in retained earnings mean to an investor? Why might a corporation with a $4 million balance in retained earnings need to raise additional capital to finance a $1 million plant expansion?

15. What are some of the significant similarities and differences between a 20-year bond and a cumulative preferred stock? Why might an investor desire a preferred stock, and why might a corporation be interested in issuing preferred stock?

16. What is treasury stock? Where does it appear on the statement of financial position?

PROBLEMS

5–1. Rex Company has 2,000 shares of cumulative preferred stock with a $4 annual dividend per share and 10,000 shares of no-par value common stock outstanding. No dividends were paid in 1979 or 1980. At the beginning of 1981, the company had a deficit of $10,000. During 1981 it had net earnings of $70,000.

Required: Assume a dividend of $2 per share was declared on the common stock and compute the December 31, 1981, balance in retained earnings.

5–2. The Stanley Company issued all of its 5,000 shares of authorized preferred stock on July 1, 1978, at $105 per share. The preferred stock has a par value and liquidation value of $100 per share and is entitled to a cumulative basic preference dividend of $8 per share. Stanley also issued its 20,000 authorized shares of $15 stated value common stock on this date at $40 per share.

On June 30, 1980, the end of its second fiscal year of operations, the company's retained earnings amounted to $95,000. No dividends have been declared or paid on either class of stock since the date of issue.

Required:

a. Prepare the stockholders' equity section of the Stanley Company's June 30, 1980, statement of financial position.
b. Compute the book value of each class of stock.

5–3. Andrews Brothers, Inc., is a corporation in which all of the outstanding preferred and common stock is held by the four Andrews brothers. The brothers have an agreement stating that upon the death of one brother, the remaining brothers will purchase from his estate his holdings of stock in the company at book value. The agreement also stipulates that the land owned by the company be valued at fair market value, that inventory be valued at its current replacement cost, and that whatever other adjustments are needed to place the accounts on a sound accounting basis be made prior to computing book value.

The stockholders' equity accounts of the company on June 30, 1979, the date of the death of James Andrews, show:

Liquidation value, $100 per share

Preferred stock—6 percent, $100 par value; $100 liquidation value; 4,000 shares authorized, issued, and outstanding......................	$ 400,000
Paid-in capital in excess of par—preferred.........	20,000
Common stock—no-par value, stated value, $5; 60,000 shares authorized, issued, and outstanding..	300,000
Paid-in capital from recapitalization.:::..........	300,000
Retained earnings.............................	40,000
	$1,060,000

The fair market value of the land held by the company and carried in its accounts at $40,000 is $100,000, and the current replacement cost of the inventory is $32,000 more than the amount at which it is carried in the accounts, although no improper accounting is involved. It is also agreed by the three remaining brothers and the accountant representing Mrs. James Andrews that the accounts fail to include a proper accrual of $20,000 for pensions payable to employees. No dividends have been paid on the preferred stock, which is cumulative in the last one-half year.

James Andrews, at the time of his death, held 2,000 shares of preferred stock and 10,000 shares of common stock of the company.

Required: Compute the amount which the remaining brothers must pay to the estate of James Andrews for the preferred and common stock which he held at the time of his death.

5–4. The stockholders' equity section of the Sanchez Company's June 30, 1979, statement of financial position is:

Capital stock—common, $50 par value, authorized 5,000 shares; issued and outstanding 4,000 shares....	$200,000
Retained earnings.............................	120,000
	$320,000

The board of directors, on June 30, 1979, declared a $5 cash dividend payable on July 31 to stockholders of record as of July 15.

Required:

a. Assuming no change in the amount of retained earnings except that caused by the dividend and no change in the number of shares

outstanding between June 30 and July 31, compute the book value per share of common stock—
- (1) Just prior to the declaration of the dividend.
- (2) Just after the declaration of the dividend.
- (3) Just after the payment of the cash dividend.
- b. Assume that instead of a cash dividend a 5 percent stock dividend is issued on August 15 and is to be recorded at $70 per share (the market price on the declaration date). Show how this would affect the book value per share assuming no change in retained earnings except that caused by the dividends.

5–5. On January 1, 1979, the Morino Corporation's stockholders' equity section appeared as follows:

Stockholders' Equity

Paid-In Capital:		
Preferred stock—$100 par value; authorized, issued and outstanding 5,000 shares	$500,000	
Common stock—$10 par value; authorized 50,000 shares; issued and outstanding 20,000 shares	200,000	$ 700,000
Retained Earnings		300,000
Total Stockholders' Equity		$1,000,000

Required:

- a. Prepare a stockholders' equity section on July 1, 1979, after the issuance of a 10 percent stock dividend to common stockholders. Market value per share at date of declaration was $65.
- b. Ignore part *a* and prepare a stockholders' equity section on July 1, 1979, after a 2 for 1 common stock split. Market value per share before the split was $65.

5–6. The following information relates to the Goldberg Corporation for the year 1979 or on the dates indicated:

Net earnings for the year	$160,000
Dividends declared on common stock	20,000
Dividends paid on common stock during 1979	25,000
Dividends declared on preferred stock	8,000
Dividends received on investments	2,000
Retained earnings, January 1	405,000
Amount over par value received from preferred stock issued during the year	4,000

Required: Prepare a statement of retained earnings for the year ended December 31, 1979.

5–7. Selected account balances of the Barnes Corporation at December 31, 1979, are:

Capital from appreciation of land................... 150,000
Bonds payable, 7 percent, due May 1, 1981......... 600,000
Common stock—no par value; 100,000 shares
  authorized, issued, and outstanding; stated value
  of $10 per share.............................. 1,000,000
Retained earnings................................ 285,000
Dividends payable (in cash declared December 15
  on preferred stock)............................ 8,000
Accrued lawsuit damages.......................... 160,000
Preferred stock—8 percent, par value $100; 1,000
  shares authorized, issued, and outstanding........ 100,000
Paid-in capital from donation of plant site......... 50,000
Paid-in capital in excess of par value—preferred..... 4,000

Required: Present in good form the stockholders' equity section of the statement of financial position.

5–8. The stockholders' equity of the Cornplanter Company as of December 31, 1979, consisted of 20,000 shares of authorized and outstanding $10 par value common stock, paid-in capital in excess of par of $100,000, and retained earnings of $200,000.

Following are selected transactions for 1980:

May 1   Acquired 4,000 shares of its own common stock at $25.
June 1   Reissued 1,000 shares at $28.
Oct. 1   Declared a cash dividend of $1 per share to holders as of
           October 14.
      15   Reissued 1,400 shares at $23.
Dec. 31   Paid the cash dividend declared on October 1.

The net earnings for the year were $30,400. No other transactions affecting retained earnings occurred during the year.

Required:

a. Prepare journal entries to record the treasury stock and dividend transactions.
b. Prepare the stockholders' equity section of the December 31, 1980, statement of financial position.
c. Compute the book value per share as of December 31, 1980.

5–9. Selected accounts of the Hammond Company for the year ended December 31, 1980, are:

Sales, net....................................... $960,000
Interest expense................................. 80,000
Cash dividends on common stock.................. 160,000
Selling and administrative expense............... 240,000
Cash dividends on preferred stock............... 80,000
Rent revenue.................................... 440,000
Cost of goods sold.............................. 640,000
Flood loss (has never occurred before)............. 240,000
Interest revenue................................. 80,000
Other revenue................................... 120,000
Depreciation and maintenance on rental
  equipment.................................... 160,000
Stock dividend on common stock.................. 400,000
Litigation loss.................................. 480,000
Cumulative effect on prior years' earnings of
  changing to a different depreciation method....... 40,000

The applicable federal income tax rate is 50 percent. All above items of expense, revenue, and loss are includable in the computation of taxable income. The litigation loss resulted from a court award of damages for patent infringement on a product the company produced and sold in 1976 and 1977 and which was discontinued in 1977. The cumulative effect of the accounting change amounts to an increase of $40,000. Retained earnings as of January 1, 1980, were $5,600,000.

Required: Prepare an earnings statement and a statement of retained earnings for 1980.

chapter 6

Debt Financing
and Investments

In Chapter 5, stockholders' equity was discussed as a source of capital. Now the other source of capital is discussed—short- and long-term debt. Also discussed is the topic of investments in the financial obligations of others, since the discussion involving investments in the bonds of others is quite similar to the discussion of bonds payable.

SHORT-TERM FINANCING

Let us identify some of the reasons a business may need short-term financing; that is, why it may need to use the bank's or some other creditor's money for short periods of time. A business usually expects the cash inflow from the sale of goods or services to exceed the cash outflow for the purchase of goods for resale or the purchase of supplies, labor services, utilities, and so on. This is especially so when we realize that some expenses, such as depreciation expense, do not involve an outflow of cash in the current period. But at certain times in the life of a business the inflow of cash may not be greater than the outflow of cash from operations. This can be caused by: (1) the delay in the receipt of cash due to giving customers credit terms on amounts due (although this is at least partly offset by the use of credit on its own purchases in order to delay the payment of cash); (2) the seasonal buildup of inventory, such as that which occurs in department stores just before the Christmas holiday; or (3) an expansion in operations caused by an expected future increase in sales. Some of the ways in which a business can obtain short-term financing are discussed below.

Short-Term Commercial Bank Loans

When the above happens, a business may go to a commercial bank to borrow on a short-term basis. When the loan is granted the bank normally asks the borrower to sign a promissory note. A promissory note is an unconditional promise in writing made and signed by the borrower (the maker) obligating the borrower to pay the lender (the payee) or someone else who legally acquired the note a certain sum of money on demand or at a definite time. Normally, only the maker and the payee are parties to the instrument, but sometimes others who legally acquire the note or guarantee payment also become parties.

Nature of Interest. Most notes bear an explicit (or stated) charge for interest. Interest is the fee charged for use of money through time. It is an expense to the maker of the note and a revenue to the payee of the note. In commercial transactions interest is commonly figured on the basis of 360 days per year. The elapsed time in a fraction of a year between two stated days is computed by counting the exact number of days—omitting the day the money is borrowed but counting the day it is paid back. A note falling due on a Sunday or a holiday is due on the following business day.

Assume that we desire to calculate the interest on a $1,000 note: the interest rate is 6 percent, and the life of the note is 60 days. It can be done thus:

$$\text{Principal} \times \text{Rate of Interest} \times \text{Time} = \text{Interest}$$

$$\$1,000 \ \times \ \frac{6}{100} \ \times \ \frac{60}{360} = \$10$$

Giving Your Own Note to the Bank. In instances in which a borrower presents his own noninterest-bearing note to a bank with a request for a loan, the bank computes the amount of interest on the face value of the note, deducts the amount computed from the face value, and gives the balance, the proceeds, to the borrower. The amount deducted is often called bank discount, and the process of computing the amount is referred to as discounting. To illustrate this process, assume that a bank discounts a customer's $20,000, 90-day, noninterest-bearing note at 6 percent. The discount would be $300, and this sum would be deducted from the $20,000 and the remainder of $19,700 given to the customer.

To show how this would be recorded in the accounts assume that the above transaction occurred on December 1, 1979. It could be recorded by the borrower as follows:

Cash	Notes Payable—Discount	Notes Payable
12/1 19,700	12/1 300	12/1 20,000

Note that the borrower does not receive $20,000, but $19,700. Since the borrower will pay $300 for the use of this sum for a period of 90 days, the rate of interest is actually higher than 6 percent. (If $300 is the interest on $20,000 at 6 percent for 90 days, then $300 is more than 6 percent on $19,700 for 90 days.) Note also that the bank must discount this note in order to introduce interest into the transaction. If the bank advanced $20,000 on this noninterest bearing note, it would not earn any interest from this loan because at maturity it will receive only $20,000.

The Notes Payable—Discount account used above is a contra account to Notes Payable. Assuming that December 31, 1979, is the end of the borrower's accounting period, it would be necessary to record interest expense for the month of December as follows (the debit and credit are dated 12/31, and the debit balance of $300 shown in Notes Payable—Discount is the balance in the account *before* making the latest entry):

Interest Expense		Notes Payable—Discount	
12/31 100		Bal. 300	12/31 100

In the current liability section of the December 31, 1979, statement of financial position, the note and the discount would appear as follows:

Notes payable...	$20,000	
Less: Discount..	200	$19,800

When the note is paid at maturity the accounts would be affected as follows (maturity date is March 1, 1980):

Cash		Notes Payable—Discount		Notes Payable	
Bal. xxx	3/1 20,000	Bal. 200	3/1 200	3/1 20,000	Bal. 20,000

Interest Expense	
3/1 200	

In journal entry form this transaction would appear as follows:

Notes Payable...	20,000	
Interest Expense...	200	
Cash...		20,000
Notes Payable—Discount...............................		200

The above changes reduce the Notes Payable—Discount and Notes Payable accounts to zero balances. Notice that the difference in the cash paid out ($20,000) and that originally received ($19,700) is equal to the total interest expense ($300). The interest relates to a 90-day period, 30 days of which fall in the year ending December 31, 1979, and 60 days fall in the following year. Thus, the amount charged to interest expense should be $100 in 1979 and $200 in 1980.

An alternative approach is to compute interest on the amount requested, add this to the amount requested, and draw a note for the total of the two. Thus the borrower would sign a 90-day, noninterest-bearing note for $20,300 and would receive $20,000. At the date of borrowing the entry would be:

Cash		Notes Payable—Discount		Notes Payable	
a) 20,000		*a)* 300			*a)* 20,300

The borrowing could alternatively be done by giving a $20,000, 90-day, 6 percent interest-bearing note. At the date of borrowing the required entry is:

Cash		Notes Payable	
a) 20,000			*a)* 20,000

At maturity the borrower pays both the face amount of the note and interest at the rate stated in the note on that face amount (a total of $20,300). The $300 paid over and above the $20,000 face of the note represents interest expense to the borrower.

Notes Arising from Business Transactions

A company may have notes receivable and/or notes payable arising from transactions with customers or suppliers. When a company is the maker of a note with a supplier as the payee, the company has *received* short-term financing from that supplier. When a company is the payee of a note and a customer is the maker, the company has *supplied* short-term financing to that customer. A note may result from the conversion of an overdue open account or directly from merchandise transactions. To illustrate, assume that on October 6, 1979, Fox Company, the payee, receives from Kent Company, the maker, a 60-day, $18,000 note. The interest rate is 8 percent and the note results from the previous sale (on October 4) of merchandise by Fox Company to Kent Company. The interest will be earned over the life of the note and will not be paid until maturity, December 5, 1979. The entries for both the payee and the maker are:

Fox Company, Payee

To record sale:

Accounts Receivable				Sales			
10/4	18,000					10/4	18,000

To record receipt of note:

Notes Receivable				Accounts Receivable			
10/6	18,000			Bal.	18,000	10/6	18,000

To record receipt of principal and interest:

Cash				Notes Receivable			
12/5	18,240			Bal.	18,000	12/5	18,000

Interest Revenue			
		12/5	240

Kent Company, Maker

To record purchase:

Purchases				Accounts Payable			
10/4	18,000					10/4	18,000

To record giving of note:

Accounts Payable				Notes Payable			
10/6	18,000	Bal.	18,000			10/6	18,000

To record payment of principal and interest:

Cash				Notes Payable			
Bal.	xxx	12/5	18,240	12/5	18,000	Bal.	18,000

Interest Expense			
12/5	240		

A note is *dishonored* if the maker fails to pay it at maturity. The payee of the note may debit either Accounts Receivable or Dishonored Notes Receivable and credit Notes Receivable for the face of the note. If interest is due, it should be debited to the same account to which the dishonored note is debited and credited to Interest Revenue. The maker should merely debit the amount of interest incurred to Interest Expense and credit Interest Payable. Sometimes when a note cannot be paid at maturity the maker either pays the interest on the original note or includes it in the face of a new note given to take the place of the old note.

Discounting Notes Receivable

When a company issues its own note payable to a bank, it is directly liable to the bank at the maturity date of the loan. Such notes payable are shown in the statement of financial position as liabilities.

Instead of borrowing directly, a company may use another method of obtaining short-term financing from a bank. A note receivable held by the company may be endorsed and then discounted at a bank. The bank gives the company cash in exchange for the note. Thus, a note receivable discounted arises. The company which discounts the note receivable is contingently, instead of directly, liable to the lending bank; that is, the company must pay the bank the amount due at maturity only if the maker of the note fails to pay the obligation.

The cash proceeds from notes receivable discounted are computed as follows:

1. Determine the maturity value of the note (face value plus interest). This is the amount the bank will collect at maturity. For a noninterest-bearing note, the face of the note equals the maturity value. For an interest-bearing note, the face of the note plus interest for the life of the note equals the maturity value.
2. Determine the discount period; that is, count the exact number of days from the date of discounting to the date of maturity. Exclude the date of discounting but include the date of maturity in the count. The discount period, of course, can never be longer than the life of the note.
3. Using the rate of discount charged by the bank, compute the discount on the maturity value (principal plus interest) for the discount period.
4. Deduct the bank discount from full value at maturity. The result is the cash proceeds.

The contingent liability for the notes receivable discounted is usually shown in the accounts by recording the face value of the note in a Notes Receivable Discounted account. This is done even though the contingent liability includes the interest. If the original maker does not pay the bank at the maturity date, the company which discounts the note will be held liable.

Example. Assume that on May 4, 1979, Carlson Company received a $10,000 note from Thomas. The note bears interest at 6 percent and matures in 60 days from May 4. On May 14, 1979, Carlson Company discounted the note at the Michigan National Bank at 8 percent. The discount and the cash proceeds are determined as follows:

Face value of note...................................	$10,000.00
Add: Interest at 6% for 60 days.......................	100.00
Maturity value..	$10,100.00
Less: Bank discount on $10,100 at 8% for 50 days........	112.22
Cash proceeds..	$ 9,987.78

The entry would be as follows:

Cash		Interest Expense		Notes Receivable Discounted	
5/14 9,987.78		5/14 12.22			5/14 10,000.00

If the proceeds had exceeded the book value of the note, the difference would have been credited to an Interest Revenue account.

Statement of Financial Position Presentation of Notes Receivable Discounted. In the above illustration a statement of financial position prepared for Carlson Company as of December 31, 1979, should show a contingent liability in the amount of $10,000 for notes receivable discounted. Assume that the total of all notes receivable is $70,000. One acceptable method of presenting this information in the statement of financial position is:

Assets

Current Assets	
Cash...	$xx,xxx
Accounts receivable....................................	xx,xxx
Notes receivable (Note 1).............................	60,000

    Note 1: At December 31, 1979, the company is contingently liable for $10,000 of customers' notes receivable (in addition to the $60,000 shown) which it has endorsed and discounted at the local bank.

Although the contingent liability is actually for the note plus the accrued interest to maturity ($10,100), for convenience it is customarily shown only for the face of the note ($10,000).

Discounted Notes Receivable Paid by Maker. When a note receivable has been discounted, it is usually the duty of the endorsee (the holder) to present the note to the maker for payment at maturity. Sometimes the note designates the place of payment. If the maker pays the endorsee (the bank in the above illustrations) at maturity, the endorser is thereby relieved of contingent liability. If the note is not paid at maturity, the endorsee can collect from the endorser who, in turn, can try to collect from the maker.

Assume that Thomas (above) pays his $10,000 note plus interest of $100 to the Michigan National Bank on July 3, 1979—the note's maturity date. Carlson Company, which discounted the note at the bank, has been relieved of the possibility of being held liable on the note and, therefore, will show the following changes in its accounts.

Notes Receivable				Notes Receivable Discounted			
5/4	10,000	7/3	10,000	7/3	10,000	5/14	10,000

These changes reduce Thomas' Notes Receivable account and the related Notes Receivable Discounted account on Carlson's books to zero balances.

If Thomas dishonors the note at maturity instead of paying it, the Michigan National Bank will collect the principal ($10,000), interest ($100), and any protest fee (assume it is $5) from Carlson Company. Besides removing the note from the Notes Receivable and Notes Receivable Discounted accounts as shown above, Carlson Company will also show the following changes in its accounts:

Cash		Accounts Receivable	
xxx	10,105	10,105	

Carlson Company will then try to collect $10,105 from Thomas. If this cannot be done; the $10,105 should be removed from the Accounts Receivable account and treated as a loss from bad debts.

LONGER TERM FINANCING

Although it is conceivable that once a company begins operations it can finance the acquisition of additional long-term or plant assets out of operating cash flows, this is often not possible, nor is it desirable (leverage). It is quite common for companies to use long-term sources of financing to acquire these assets. Chapter 5 discussed the use of capital stock to acquire long-term funds. This chapter discusses some of the more common forms of long-term debt financing.

Notes Payable

Notes payable may be either short term or long term but they are usually short term. Since these have been discussed earlier we will not deal with them again in this section except to say that when payables (or receivables) have maturities *exceeding* approximately one year they are to be recorded at their present cash value.[1] The procedure is similar to that used in calculating the proceeds of a discounted bank loan. To illustrate, assume we are the maker of a $1,000 face value note, bearing no explicit rate of interest, which is due one year from its date. (Even though this does not exceed "approximately one year" and technically would not have to be recorded at its present value, we will assume the company chooses to do so.) Assume also that the rate of interest to be used in reducing this note to its present value is 8 percent. To solve for the present value we have to ask the question, "What amount if invested at 8 percent would grow to $1,000 one year from now?" If we let *"x"* equal that amount, our formula would be:

$$x + 0.08x = \$1,000$$
$$1.08x = \$1,000$$
$$x = \frac{\$1,000}{1.08}$$
$$x = \$925.93$$

Assuming the note payable resulted from the purchase of a machine, it would be recorded as follows:

Machinery	Notes Payable—Discount	Notes Payable
a) 925.93	a) 74.07	a) 1,000

At the due date, $1,000 would be paid to the payee and $74.07 would be (or would have been) recorded as interest expense. The accounting for the interest in this type of transaction is quite similar to that used when a company discounts its own note at the bank.

Mortgage Notes Payable

Another form of long-term financing is a mortgage note payable. This is a note payable that is secured by a mortgage; that is, an obligation to give up certain property that has been pledged to the payee in case the maker defaults on the payments. Most of us become familiar with this form of financing when we purchase a home. Business firms also sometimes use this method of financing when they acquire assets such as buildings.

This form of financing will be illustrated by assuming that a company acquires a small building. The company makes a constant lump-sum payment each month (exclusive of real estate taxes) which at first pays mostly

---

[1] Accounting Principles Board, "Interest on Receivables and Payables," *Opinion No. 21* (AICPA, August 1971).

interest and very little principal. Assume that the mortgage on the building is $35,000, the interest rate is 8 percent, and the life of the note is 25 years. There are mortgage payment schedule books which indicate that the monthly payment for principal and interest is $271. Here is how the first two months' and the last month's payments are applied:

	Monthly Payment	Interest at 8% on Principal Balance	Payment on Principal ($271 less interest)	Principal Balance
Date of purchase......				$35,000.00
1st month..........	$271	$233.33	$ 37.67	34,962.33
2nd month..........	271	233.08	37.92	34,924.41
⋮	⋮	⋮	⋮	⋮
300th month..........	271	2.00	269.00	0

Notice that interest is calculated on the latest principal balance. For instance, when the first $271 payment is made interest is calculated as follows:

$$\frac{\$35,000 \times 0.08}{12} = \$233.33$$

It is necessary to divide by 12 because the interest rate is 8 percent per *year* and we are calculating the amount for one *month*. The excess of the payment over the interest is applied against the principal ($37.67 in the first payment above). Thus, the principal balance decreases slowly (but more rapidly each month) so that the last $271 payment at the end of 25 years pays interest (approximately $2) on the remaining principal balance (approximately $269) and then reduces the principal balance to zero.

Since the building is pledged (or mortgaged) as security for the loan, if the company does not keep up the payments the party to whom payment is due can foreclose on the mortgage and take over the building. As a practical matter, many lending institutions are quite lenient in allowing a few back payments to be made up rather than taking this drastic step.

Bonds Payable

Bonds are one of the longest term debt issues commonly used by companies. A bond is a written promise made by the borrower to pay back the face amount of the bond at a determinable future date together with interest at a stated rate and at stated dates (usually semiannually). Bonds may or may not be secured by a mortgage against specific property.

Accounting for the Issuance of Bonds. The bond indenture (the overall contract between the issuer and the bondholders) sets forth the total amount of bonds that may be issued. The bonds may all be issued at one time or a portion at one date and the remainder later.

Assume that the Valley Company issued on June 1, 1979, $1,000,000 of its $1,500,000 authorized first-mortgage, 9 percent, 10-year bonds (dated June 1, 1979) at face value of $1,000,000. This transaction would be recorded in the accounts as follows:

Cash	Bonds Payable
6/1 1,000,000	6/1 1,000,000

Recording Bond Interest.   Interest on most bonds is paid semiannually, as required by the provisions of the bond indenture. We will assume that the interest is paid directly by the borrower to the bondholders. It would be recorded as follows:

Cash	Bond Interest Expense
Bal. xxx	12/1 45,000	12/1 45,000

The Price Received for a Bond Issue.   The price a bond issue will bring when offered to investors, or the price at which a bond sells in the market, often may differ from its face or maturity value. Basically, a bond issue will sell at a price higher (lower) than its face or maturity value if the rate of interest offered in the bonds is higher (lower) than that which can be secured from similar bonds of other issuers. The effect of a premium or discount on a bond is to change the rate of interest offered by the bond to the effective rate desired by the investor.

In purchasing a bond, an investor actually acquires two promises from the issuer of the bond: (1) the promise to pay the stated principal amount on a given date—the maturity date—and (2) a promise to pay periodic interest at stated intervals throughout the life of the bond. Thus, a $1,000, 20-year, 8 percent bond, dated October 1, 1979, which calls for semiannual interest payments on each April 1 and October 1, contains two promises. The issuer promises to pay $1,000 to the holder on October 1, 1999, and to pay $40 each April 1 and October 1 through October 1, 1999, beginning on April 1, 1980.

If an investing company desired an 8 percent rate of interest from such a bond, it would offer to purchase it at face value. It would invest $1,000 and receive $80 of interest per year—exactly an 8 percent rate. But suppose the company would invest in such a bond only if it could earn a 10 percent rate. Since the rate in the face of the bond (the nominal or coupon rate) cannot be changed, the investing company can change the rate at which interest is actually earned only by changing the price paid for the bond. The method for determining the price which a company would be willing to pay for a bond is discussed in the Appendix to this chapter (page 150).

Bonds Issued at a Discount. To illustrate the accounting for bonds issued at a discount, assume that on July 1, 1979, the Western Company issues $1,000,000 of first-mortgage, 9 percent, 10-year bonds for $980,000, or at 98 percent of face value. The bonds call for semiannual interest payments and mature on July 1, 1989. At issuance the accounts would be affected as follows:

Cash	Discount on Bonds Payable	Bonds Payable
7/1 980,000	7/1 20,000	7/1 1,000,000

Note that in recording bonds payable on the issuer's books, the bonds are carried at their face value in one account and the discount (or premium) in another. It is customary in accounting to record liabilities at the amount expected to be paid at maturity, excluding interest unless it has actually accrued.

Accounting for Bond Discount. To the issuing corporation, bond discount represents a cost of using funds just as it is a form of additional interest earnings to the investor. Thus the total cost of borrowing includes the total interest currently paid in cash plus the total discount which is paid as a lump sum at maturity. Both items must be spread equitably over the life of the bonds, although no disbursement is made for the amount of discount until the debt is paid at or before maturity.

Thus, the original amount in the Discount on Bonds Payable account should be charged to expense over the period of time between the date on which the bonds were issued and their maturity date. The amount charged to expense is usually computed on a straight-line basis, that is, equal amounts are charged to expense for equal periods of time elapsed. How often this adjusting entry will be made will depend upon how often the company prepares financial statements. This may be monthly, quarterly, semiannually, or annually, with monthly statements rather common.

To illustrate, assume that the Western Company, which issued $1,000,000 of 10-year, 9 percent bonds at 98, uses a calendar year accounting period and prepares semiannual financial statements. The total discount of $20,000 must be written off over the 10 years of life in the bonds. The annual charge is $2,000, and the charge per interest period (six months) is $1,000. The entry required on December 31, 1979, would be (recall that the bonds were issued on July 1, 1979):

Bond Interest Expense	Discount on Bonds Payable	Accrued Bond Interest Payable
12/31 46,000	7/1 20,000 | 12/31 1,000	12/31 45,000

Under the straight-line method illustrated, the total interest cost for each six months is the $45,000 which must be paid currently plus $1,000 of the $20,000 of discount which will be paid at maturity, or a total of $46,000.

The straight-line discount accumulation method shown is widely used because of its simplicity and ease of application. An alternative, and the theoretically correct method which yields slightly different results, embraces the use of the effective rate of interest. This method is covered in the Appendix to this chapter.

Each time a statement of financial position is prepared, the remaining balance in the Discount on Bonds Payable account will be shown as a deduction from bonds payable. The bonds payable, except for amounts maturing currently, are usually shown in the long-term liability section of the statement of financial position. At the end of the 10th year of the bonds' life—after 20 interest payments have been made—the balance in the Discount on Bonds Payable account will be zero; the entire amount will have been charged to expense.

Bonds Issued at a Premium. Bonds are issued at a premium, (at more than face value) when the interest rate specified on the face of the bonds is higher than the market rate of interest for similar bonds. Investors are willing to pay a premium because the periodic interest payments are larger than they require to purchase the bonds at face value. Thus, investors literally purchase some of the interest to be paid periodically by the issuing company. The total interest cost to the company, then, will not be the total of all of the cash interest payments made but will be this sum less the amount of premium received.

To illustrate, assume that $1,000,000 of 9 percent, 10-year, first-mortgage bonds are issued for $1,100,000. The total of the periodic interest payments to be made on the bonds is $90,000 per year for 10 years, or a total of $900,000. But this will not be the total expense to the company. The company literally returns to the investors a part of the premium they paid for the bonds each time that it pays the periodic interest. Remember, the premium exists because the periodic interest payment promised by the bonds is larger than that necessary to induce investors to buy the bonds at their face value. This, in turn, makes the bonds attractive to investors causing them to bid up the price offered for the bonds. The investors have then actually purchased in advance a part of each periodic interest payment; and in this way, they have invested more capital in the business issuing the bonds than simply the face value of the bonds. And so a part of each periodic payment to the investors must be viewed as a partial return of the investors' capital.

At the date of issuance the required entry is:

Cash	Premium on Bonds Payable	Bonds Payable
1,100,000	100,000	1,000,000

Accounting for Bond Premium. The typical accounting treatment for bond premium is to amortize the original amount by crediting interest expense with an equal amount each accounting period between the issue date of the bonds and their maturity date. This is called straight-line amortization. To continue the above illustration, the amount of premium amortized each year would be $10,000 ($100,000 ÷ 10 years). If the company issuing these bonds prepares monthly statements, the following entry would be recorded at the end of each month in the life of the bonds:

Bond Interest Expense		Premium on Bonds Payable		Accrued Bond Interest Payable	
a) 6,666.67		a) 833.33	Bal. 100,000		a) 7,500

The debit to Premium on Bonds Payable is $10,000 ÷ 12 = $833.33. The net monthly interest cost recorded is $6,666.67 ($7,500 − $833.33), which, adjusted for rounding, would equal an annual cost of $80,000. This $80,000 can be verified in another manner. The total interest payments over the life of the bonds amount to $900,000; the premium is $100,000; and the net total interest cost is $800,000. Dividing this by 10 years, an annual cost of $80,000 is obtained.

When a statement of financial position is prepared, the remaining balance in the Premium on Bonds Payable account will be added to the amount of Bonds Payable which, except for currently maturing amounts in some instances, is shown in the long-term liabilities section.

Bonds Issued between Interest Dates. Frequently, bonds are issued between interest dates. In this case, the bond investor usually pays for both the bond and the interest accrued from the last interest payment date to the date of purchase. On the interest date following the interim date of purchase, the accrued interest will be collected by the bondholder when a check is received for the interest for the entire period. The company is obligated, by contract, to pay the bondholders interest for the full six months on the interest payment date *regardless* of how long these holders have owned the bonds. Since the bond purchaser has paid for the interest which had accrued to the purchase date, it would be improper not to give recognition to this fact in determining the bond interest expense for the first interest period after issuance.

To illustrate, assume that the Carson Company issues $100,000 of 9 percent bonds four months after the last interest date at face value plus accrued interest. The accrued interest is equal to $100,000 × 0.09 × 1/3 = $3,000. The entry to record the issuance is:

Cash		Accrued Bond Interest Payable		Bonds Payable	
Bal. xxx			a) 3,000		a) 100,000
a) 103,000					

Assuming no action has been taken to record the interest accrued for the two months prior to the payment of the semiannual interest, the Carson Company will make the following entry in its accounts at the time of semiannual payment:

Cash			Bond Interest Expense			Accrued Bond Interest Payable		
Bal. xxx	b)	4,500	b)	1,500		b) 3,000	Bal.	3,000

The net interest expense to the Carson Company is $1,500 ($100,000 × 0.09 × 1/6) which represents interest for the two months from the date of issuance to the succeeding interest date. Bonds issued at a discount or premium could be issued between interest dates. Such examples only involve a little more complicated arithmetic, but the same general concepts apply. This situation will not be dealt with in this text.

Redeeming Outstanding Bonds. At the maturity date the bonds are to be redeemed at their face value. Assuming interest for the last period has already been paid, the redemption would be recorded as follows:

Cash			Bonds Payable		
Bal. xxx	c)	100,000	c) 100,000	Bal.	100,000

If bonds are redeemed before their maturity date, any difference between the amount paid and the book value is treated as a gain or loss on retirement. Book value is equal to the face value plus the pro rata share of any remaining premium or minus the pro rata share of any remaining discount. The gains and losses from such transactions are totaled and, if material in amount, are classified as an extraordinary item in the earnings statement, net of the related income tax effect. (This is required under FASB *Statement No. 4*.)

INVESTMENTS

Just as there may be a temporary need for cash, as discussed earlier, so might there be a temporary surplus of cash. When this occurs the company sometimes invests the surplus in the securities (bonds or stocks) of others to earn a small amount of revenue. When there is again a need for the funds, the securities are sold (hopefully at not less than was paid for them).

But there may be other, longer term, reasons for investing in the securities of others. These include the desire to (1) establish an affiliation with another business, (2) acquire control over another business, or (3) secure a continuing stream of revenue from the investment over a period of years.

Reporting Securities in the Statement of Financial Position

The generally stated guides as to how securities should be classified in the statement of financial position tend to emphasize intent and may be summarized as follows:

1. If the securities held are readily marketable, they should be shown as current assets if they will be converted into cash in the normal operating cycle of the business. If they will not be converted, they should be considered noncurrent assets and reported in the investments section of the statement.
2. If the securities are not readily marketable, they may not be classified as current assets, unless they mature in the coming operating cycle and there is no doubt as to their redemption.

The primary classification criterion is *intent* of management.

Valuation of Debt and Equity Securities Held

Investments in Bonds. For investments in bonds, the most common basis of valuation is cost whether classified as current assets or long-term investments. Cost usually consists of price paid plus broker's commission. An exception to this practice is made when a *substantial* and *apparently permanent* decline in the value of the bonds occurs. Then these bond investments are written down to market by debiting Loss on Market Decline of Bond Investments and crediting Bond Investments.

Once bond investments are written down, it is not permissible to write them back up to even their original cost if market prices advance in the future. Gain or loss is simply recorded for the difference between the sales proceeds and the amount at which the bonds are carried in the accounts when they are sold.

Marketable Equity Securities. For investments in common stock which represent less than 20 percent of the outstanding shares of the issuing company, the most common basis of valuation until recently has been cost, whether classified as current assets or long-term investments. Cost usually consists of price paid plus broker's commission. An exception to this practice was made when a *substantial* and *apparently permanent* decline in the value of the securities occurred. Then these investments were written down to market by debiting Loss on Market Decline of Securities and crediting either Marketable Securities or Investments, whichever is applicable.

Once securities were written down, it was considered the same as recognizing unrealized revenue to write them back up to even their original cost if market prices advanced in the future. Gain or loss was simply recorded for the difference between the sales proceeds and the amounts at which the securities were carried in the accounts when they were sold.

The FASB in its *Statement No. 12* "Accounting for Certain Marketable Securities" changed the method of accounting for marketable securities.[2] It requires the use of the lower of cost or market method for those companies now carrying marketable *equity* securities at cost (with certain limited exceptions).

Marketable equity securities are to be carried at the lower of total cost or total market for all securities classified as current *taken as a group* and for securities classified as noncurrent *taken as a group*. For the securities classified as current, any excess of total cost over total market is to be debited to an account such as Net Unrealized Loss on Current Marketable Equity Securities, which is to be shown in the earnings statement. The credit is to a valuation allowance account such as Allowance for Market Decline of Current Marketable Equity Securities. The entry would appear as follows (assuming cost is $500 above market):

```
Net Unrealizable Loss on Current Marketable Equity Securities....... 500
    Allowance for Market Decline of Current Marketable Equity
    Securities...............................................       500
```

Any later recovery in total market price (up to the amount of the original cost) is to be debited to the valuation allowance and credited to an account such as Net Unrealized Gain on Current Marketable Equity Securities, which would be shown in the earnings statement. The entry would appear as follows (assuming market value increased by $400):

```
Allowance for Market Decline of Current Marketable Equity
Securities...................................................... 400
    Net Unrealized Gain on Current Marketable Equity Securities....   400
```

Any "temporary" losses on noncurrent equity securities (long-term investments) are to be charged to a stockholders' equity account (but not be charged against net earnings) and credited to a valuation allowance account. The account debited might be entitled, Net Unrealized Loss on Noncurrent Marketable Equity Securities. Thus, the entry might be as follows (assuming cost exceeds market by $1,000):

```
Net Unrealized Loss on Noncurrent Marketable Equity Securities.. 1,000
    Allowance for Market Decline of Noncurrent Marketable Equity
    Securities..............................................        1,000
```

Later recoveries up to cost would be debited to the allowance account and credited to the unrealized loss account as follows (assuming market value increases by $1,700):

```
Allowance for Market Decline of Noncurrent Marketable Equity
Securities..................................................... 1,000
    Net Unrealized Loss on Noncurrent Marketable Equity
    Securities.............................................         1,000
```

---

[2] Financial Accounting Standards Board, "Accounting for Certain Marketable Securities," *Statement No. 12* (December 1975), pp. 31.

Thus, the entry would increase stockholders' equity by $1,000 (not $1,700), but would not increase reported earnings. If a loss on an individual noncurrent security is determined to be "permanent," it is to be written down to market as a *realized* loss charged against earnings. The entry would be (assuming a permanent loss of $1,400):

Realized Loss on Noncurrent Marketable Equity Securities......... 1,400
    Investment in Noncurrent Marketable Equity Securities........   1,400

Any subsequent recovery in market value would be ignored until the security is sold.

When a company holds 20 percent or more of the voting stock (common stock) of another company it normally has the ability to exercise significant influence over the operations of that company. In these situations the company is required[3] to use the equity method of accounting for its investment. Under the equity method, the investor initially records the investment at cost and then adjusts the carrying amount to recognize its share of the other company's earnings or losses after the date of acquisition. Dividends received are deducted from the investment. We shall not deal with this method further. We shall assume that investments in the common stock of others represent less than 20 percent of the outstanding shares.

Accounting for Bond Investments

Bonds are often purchased at a premium or discount—that is, at an amount greater or less than their face (maturity) value. The reason why bonds sell at a premium or discount was covered previously.

Some of the effects of recording the acquisition of bonds and the earning of interest revenue are discussed below. In the illustrations which follow, rounded dollar amounts are used merely for the sake of keeping the illustrations simple.

Bonds Purchased at a Discount or Premium. Earlier in the chapter when bonds were *issued* at a discount or premium the discount or premium was recorded in a separate account. But when bonds are *purchased* at a discount or premium no separate account is used for the discount or premium.

To illustrate, assume that Andrews Company on July 1, 1979, purchased $1,000,000 of 9 percent, 10-year first-mortgage bonds of the Western Company for $980,000 (this example is the opposite side of the transaction where bonds were issued by Western Company at this amount on page 138). The interest dates are July 1 and January 1. The bond investment would be recorded as follows:

---

[3] Accounting Principles Board, "The Equity Method of Accounting for Investments in Common Stock," *Opinion No. 18* (AICPA, March 1971).

Bond Investments			Cash		
7/1	980,000			7/1	980,000

The total amount carried to the Bond Investments account is the total cost of acquiring the bonds. This usually consists of the price paid for the bonds, broker's commission, and perhaps postage and other miscellaneous delivery charges. (These latter charges are ignored in the example.) No useful purpose is served by recording the face value of the bonds in one account and the difference between face value and total cost in another.

If the bonds are to be held to maturity, that is, if they are considered long-term investments, the premium is amortized or the discount is accumulated over the remaining life of the bonds. Usually this is done on a straight-line basis. In this example the $20,000 discount is to be accumulated over the 10 years that the company will hold the bonds. The annual amount is $2,000, and the amount per interest period (six months) is $1,000. The entry required on December 31, 1979, would be (recall that the bonds were purchased on July 1, 1979):

Bond Investments			Accrued Interest Receivable		
Bal.	980,000		12/31	45,000	
12/31	1,000				

			Interest Revenue		
				12/31	46,000

In journal entry form this would appear as follows:

```
Bond Investments...........................................    1,000
Accrued Interest Receivable................................   45,000
    Interest Revenue.......................................            46,000
```

Interest receivable is calculated as follows:

$$\$1,000,000 \times .09 \times \tfrac{1}{2} = \$45,000 \text{ per 6 months}$$

The Andrews Company's statement of financial position as of December 31, 1979, would show accrued interest receivable of $45,000 as a current asset. The bonds will be shown in the investments section of that statement at $981,000.

If the bonds had been purchased at a premium of $20,000 instead of at a discount the entry to record the purchase would have been:

Bond Investments		Cash	
7/1 1,020,000		7/1 1,020,000	

The entry required at December 31 would have been:

Bond Investments		Accrued Interest Receivable	
Bal. 1,020,000	12/31 1,000	12/31 45,000	

Interest Revenue	
	12/31 44,000

In journal entry form this latter entry would appear as follows:

```
Accrued Interest Receivable................................ 45,000
     Bond Investments........................................          1,000
     Interest Revenue........................................         44,000
```

The Andrews Company's statement of financial position as of December 31, 1979, would have shown accrued interest receivable of $45,000 and bond investments of $1,019,000.

Bonds Purchased between Interest Dates. Assume that the $100,000 of 9 percent bonds of the Carson Company (described on page 140) are purchased by Braxton Company at face value plus four months of accrued interest. (They were purchased four months after the most recent interest date.) The accrued interest is equal to $100,000 \times .09 \times \frac{1}{3} = $3,000. The entry to record the purchase is:

Bond Investments		Interest Receivable Accrued		Cash	
a) 100,000		a) 3,000		Bal. xxx	a) 103,000

If no action has been taken to record the interest accrued for the two months prior to the receipt of the semiannual interest, the Braxton Company will make the following entry in its accounts at the time it receives the first interest check:

Cash		Accrued Interest Receivable		Interest Revenue	
b) 4,500		Bal. 3,000	b) 3,000		b) 1,500

The net interest revenue is $1,500 ($100,000 × .09 × ⅙) which is interest for the two months from the date of purchase to the first interest date.

Bonds purchased at a discount or premium could, of course, be purchased between interest dates. This situation will not be dealt with in this text.

Accounting for Stock Investments

When the common or preferred stocks of other corporations are acquired, they should be recorded at cost, which is the cash outlay or the fair value of the asset given in exchange. Since the stock acquired will usually be purchased from another investor through a broker, cost will normally consist of the price paid for the stock, plus a commission to the broker. For example, assume that Brewer Corporation purchased 1,000 shares of Cowen Corporation common stock at $15 per share through a broker who charged $100 for services rendered in acquiring the stock. Brewer Corporation would record the transaction as follows:

Cash				Stock Investments	
Bal.	xxx	a)	15,100	a)	15,100

Cash Dividends on Investments. The usual accounting procedure followed in recording the receipt of dividends on stock investments is to debit Cash and credit Dividend Revenue when the cash dividend check is actually received. This is the method of accounting for dividends which is acceptable for tax purposes and is widely followed by investors.

An alternative will be required when a dividend is declared in one accounting period which will not be received until the following period. Assume that the Cowen Corporation declared a cash dividend of 20 cents per share on December 1, 1979, payable on January 15, 1980, to stockholders of record as of December 20, 1979. Under these circumstances an entry should be made either on December 20 or as an adjusting entry on December 31 as follows:

Dividends Receivable				Dividend Revenue	
b)	200			b)	200

When the dividend is collected on January 15, the entry would be a debit to Cash and a credit to the Dividends Receivable account. In this manner the dividend is recorded as revenue in the period in which it is *earned*.

Stock Dividends and Stock Splits. A stock dividend consists of the distribution by a corporation of additional shares of its stock to its stockholders. Usually the distribution consists of additional common stock to common stockholders. Such a distribution is not considered to be a revenue-producing transaction to the holders of the stock. A stock dividend is viewed simply as having the effect of dividing the stockholders' equity into a larger number of smaller pieces. It simply increases the number of shares held by an investor, but it does not change an investing company's percentage ownership of the outstanding shares.

Thus, the accounting for stock dividends consists only of a notation in the accounts of the number of shares received and a change in the average per share cost of the shares held. For example, if 100 shares of XYZ Company common stock were held, which cost $22 per share, and the XYZ Company distributes a 10 percent stock dividend, the number of shares held is increased to 110 and the cost per share is now $20 ($2,200 ÷ 110 shares = $20 per share).

Similarly, when a corporation splits its stock, the only accounting entry required is a notation indicating the receipt of the additional shares. If Smith Company owned 1,000 shares of Jones Company common stock and Jones Company split its stock on a two-for-one basis, Smith Company would own 2,000 shares after the split and the cost per share would be halved.

Sale of Stock Investments.   When stock holdings are sold, the realized gain or loss on the sale is the difference between the net proceeds received and the cost of the shares sold.[4] Assume, for example, that 100 shares of Thacker Company common stock are sold for $75 per share. The broker deducted the commission and other taxes and charges of $62 prior to making remittance to the seller. If the seller's cost was $5,000, the required entry is:

Cash		Stock Investments		Realized Gain on Sale of Investments	
a) 7,438		Bal. 5,000	a) 5,000		a) 2,438

The realized gain on sale of investments is shown in the earnings statement regardless of whether the securities were classified as current or noncurrent marketable equity securities.

SUMMARY

This chapter has been concerned with financing activities and investments in the financial obligations of others. It includes both short-term and long-term items.

---

[4] Financial Accounting Standards Board, *Statement No. 12,* p. 5.

When a business finds itself in a position in which cash outflows temporarily exceed cash inflows, it may have to seek short-term financing. It may decide to borrow from a commercial bank by giving its own note payable. It may seek to borrow from suppliers by delaying the time of payment for goods purchased. (This often results in notes payable to those suppliers.) Or, it may decide to sell (or discount) to a bank notes receivable which it obtained from customers. In this latter instance, the business is contingently liable for the note; that is, if the maker of the note does not pay the bank at maturity, the company will have to pay the note.

Longer term financing is sometimes necessary to acquire additional long-term assets such as property, plant, and equipment. Notes payable are sometimes used for this purpose. Long-term notes must be recorded at their present value (while short-term notes are usually recorded at their face value). Quite often these notes are secured by a mortgage on certain property. A mortgage is a conditional transfer of property which is actually transferred to the payee if the maker does not meet his obligations under the terms of the note. A common form of mortgage notes payable is that arising from the purchase of a home. Businesses sometimes use this same form of long-term financing. Bonds are one of the longest term debt issues commonly used. Bonds may or may not be secured by a mortgage against specific property.

A bond is a written unconditional promise to pay the principal at a determinable future date together with interest at a stated rate and at stated dates (usually semiannually). Bonds may be issued at face value or at a premium or discount. Bond premiums and discounts are typically allocated to the remaining life of the bonds in equal amounts to equal periods of time. When bonds are issued between interest dates, the investor will pay for both the bond and the interest accrued from the last interest payment date to the date of acquisition.

One company may acquire and hold the securities of another issuer as a temporary investment of otherwise idle cash, for purposes of control or affiliation, or for long-term revenue purposes. The intent of management is the criterion used to classify readily marketable securities as either current assets or long-term investments. Securities have traditionally been valued at cost regardless of whether classified as current assets or long-term investments. But if there were a significant and apparently permanent decline in value below cost, they were written down to market. FASB *Statement No. 12* "Accounting for Certain Marketable Securities" requires that marketable equity securities be carried at the lower of total cost or market for each of two categories, current and noncurrent.

When bonds are purchased at a premium or a discount with the expectation that they will be held to maturity, the premium or discount is usually amortized or accumulated on a straight-line basis over the remaining life of the bonds.

Investments in stock of other companies are recorded at cost with dividends thereon usually taken into revenue at time of receipt. An exception is where the equity method must be used. Stock dividends and stock splits merely change the number of shares owned and the cost per share. When stock investments are sold, the difference between the selling price (less commissions and other charges) and cost is recorded as a realized gain or loss.

APPENDIX

This appendix discusses the concepts of compound interest, present value, and present value of an annuity, their use in determining the price of a bond issue, and the effective rate of interest method for accumulating the discount on bonds payable.

Compound Interest.   Interest is compounded when periodically its amount is computed and added to the base to form a new amount upon which the interest for a later period is to be computed. For example, an investment of $1,000 at 3 percent compound interest would grow to $1,060.90 in two periods at compound interest, but only to $1,060 at simple interest. At simple interest, the interest for each period would be $30 for a total of $60. At compound interest, the interest for the first period would be $30 and the amount of the investment at the end of the first period would be $1,030 ($1,000 × 1.03). Interest for the second period would be $30.90 ($1,030 × 0.03) and the amount of the investment would be $1,060.90 ($1,030 × 1.03) at the end of the second period.

Note that the $1,060.90 amount was derived by multiplying $1,000 × 1.03 × 1.03. Since 1.03 × 1.03 is equal to $(1.03)^2$, a shortcut can be employed in the calculation. The amount of the investment at the end of the second period is simply $1,000 $(1.03)^2$, which equals $1,000 × 1.0609, or $1,060.90. From this the formula for the compound amount of 1 can be derived as being $(1 + i)^n$ where i is the interest rate per period and n is the number of periods involved.

The task of computing the sum to which any invested amount will grow at a given rate for a stated number of periods is facilitated through the use of interest tables. From Appendix Table I (at the end of the text), the amount to which an investment of $1 at 3 percent for three periods will grow can be determined as being $1.092727. The amount to which an investment of $1,000 would grow would simply be 1,000 times this amount.

Present Value.   In the illustrations above, the future amount of a given investment was found by multiplying the investment by $(1 + i)^n$, where i was the interest rate involved and n the number of periods of life. Since present value is exactly the reverse of a future sum, it is found by dividing the future sum by $(1 + i)^n$. Thus, the present value of $1,000 due in one period at 3 percent is equal to $1,000 ÷ (1.03). Or the computation can be expressed as $1,000 × 1/(1.03) which is equal to $1,000 × 0.970874, or $970.87. Thus, $970.87 invested at 3 percent per period will grow to exactly $1,000 in one period.

The present value of $1,000 due in two periods then is simply $1,000 ÷ (1.03)². Here again the computation can be expressed as $1,000 × 1/(1.03)², which simplifies to $1,000 × 0.942596, or $942.60. Appendix Table II contains the present values of $1 at different interest rates for different periods of time. The use of the table can be illustrated by determining the present value of $10,000 due in 40 periods at 3 percent. The present value of 1 due in 40 periods at 3 percent per period is given as 0.306557. The present value of $10,000 due in 40 periods at 3 percent then is $3,065.57 ($10,000 × 0.306557).

Present Value of an Annuity. An annuity may be defined as a series of equal payments equally spaced in time. The present value or worth of such a series may be desired information for certain types of decisions. The approach to the problem of valuing annuities can be illustrated by finding the present value, at 3 percent per period, of an annuity calling for the payment of $100 at the end of each of the next three periods. It would be possible, through the use of Table II in the Appendix, to find the present value of each of the $100 payments as follows:

```
Present value of $100 due in—
    1 period  is 0.970874 × $100 = $ 97.09
    2 periods is 0.942596 × $100 =   94.26
    3 periods is 0.915142 × $100 =   91.51
Total present value of three
    $100 payments.............. $282.86
```

Such a procedure could become quite tedious if the annuity consisted of 50 to 100 or more payments. Fortunately, tables are also available showing the present values of an annuity of $1 per period for varying interest rates and periods. See Table III in the Appendix. Thus, a single figure can be obtained from the table which represents the present value of an annuity of $1 per period for three periods at an interest rate of 3 percent per period. This figure is 2.828611, and when multiplied by $100, the number of dollars in each payment, yields the present value of the annuity as $282.86.

Determining the Price of a Bond. The concepts discussed above will now be employed to illustrate the computation of the price of a bond issue.

In determining the price of a bond, the life of the bond is always stated in terms of interest payment periods, and the effective rate used in seeking amounts from the interest tables is the annual effective rate divided by the number of interest periods in one year.

Assume that bonds with a $100,000 face value and 10 percent face rate of interest are issued at a price which will yield the investor a return of 12 percent. The issue date is July 1, 1979 and the maturity date is July 1, 1982 (this unrealistically short life is used for sake of keeping the illustration simple). The price the investor would pay is calculated as shown:

Present value of the promise to pay principal is $100,000
times the present value of $1 due in 6 periods at 6%,
or $100,000 × .704961 (from Appendix Table II). $70,496.10

Present value of the promise to pay periodic interest is
$5,000 times the present value of an annuity of $1 for 6
periods at 6%, or $5,000 × 4.917324 (from Appendix
Table III). 24,586.62

Total Price. $95,082.72

Thus, the amount of the discount is $100,000 − $95,082.72 = $4,917.28.

The Effective Rate of Interest Method for Accumulating the Discount. The following table shows how this discount would be accumulated over the life of the bonds. The yield rate must be known to make the calculations required under this method. Notice that the amount accumulated increases each period rather than remaining constant as it would under the straight-line method ($819.55 per 6-month period under the straight-line method).

Discount Accumulated by the Effective Rate of Interest Method

Date	Cash Credit	Interest Expense Debit	Discount on Bonds Payable Credit	Carrying Value of Bonds Payable
7/1/79				$ 95,082.72
1/1/80	$ 5,000[1]	$ 5,704.96[2]	$ 704.96[3]	95,787.68[4]
7/1/80	5,000	5,747.26	747.26	96,534.94
1/1/81	5,000	5,792.10	792.10	97,327.04
7/1/81	5,000	5,839.62	839.62	98,166.66
1/1/82	5,000	5,890.00	890.00	99,056.66
7/1/82	5,000	5,943.34[5]	943.34	100,000
	$30,000	$34,917.28	$4,917.28	

[1] $100,000 × 10% × ½ = $5,000
[2] $95,082.72 × 12% × ½ = $5,704.96
[3] $5,704.96 − $5,000 = $704.96
[4] $95,082.72 + $704.96 = $95,787.68
[5] Actually this came to $5,943.40, but was reduced to make the carrying value come to $100.000

QUESTIONS AND EXERCISES

1. A fellow student makes the following comment: "There is no such thing as a noninterest-bearing note. Accountants only account for them that way when the interest is included in the face amount of the note." Comment.

2. Brown gives his 90-day, $15,000, 8 percent note to Blue in exchange for merchandise. Using T-accounts give the entries each will make on the maturity date assuming payment is made.

3. In Question 2 above give the entries for each at the maturity date assuming Brown defaults.

4. Day Kreuzburg goes to the bank and asks to borrow $1,000 at 9 percent for a 60-day period. Using T-accounts show how to record the proceeds received for each of the following alternatives:

    a. He signs a note for $1,000. Interest is deducted from the face amount in determining the proceeds.

    b. He receives $1,000 and signs a note for the interest plus the amount borrowed.

    c. He receives $1,000 and signs an interest-bearing note for that amount. The interest is to be paid at the maturity date.

5. Using T-accounts give the entries at the maturity date for each of the alternatives given in Question 4 assuming the loan is repaid. Also assume that repayment is made before the end of the accounting period.

6. Carefully explain the main problem encountered in classifying marketable securities in the statement of financial position.

7. Describe the accounting for bonds purchased at a discount when conditions exist requiring that they be held to maturity. Would the accounting differ if the bonds were readily marketable and represented a temporary investment of seasonally idle cash?

8. The December 31, 1979, statement of financial position of the BMI Corporation shows, under a section heading entitled "Investments and Advances," U.S. government securities (at cost less amortized premium), $100,780. What might be the reason for classifying these securities as "investments" rather than as "current assets"?

9. Explain briefly the accounting for stock dividends and stock splits from the investor's point of view.

10. The Hall Corporation purchased $100,000 of the bonds of Reston Corporation, 40 percent of whose stock it already owns. The bonds were purchased at 104 on July 1, 1979, pay interest semiannually on July 1 and January 1 at 9 percent per annum (year), and mature on July 1, 1984. The market value of these bonds on December 31, 1979, is 102 ¾. State exactly what items, their amounts, and where each would appear in the financial statements for the calender year 1979 as a result of the above transactions.

11. Book Company purchased on July 1, 1979, 100 shares of Case Company common stock at 47 plus a commission of $50. Book received a cash dividend of 50 cents per share on August 12, 1979. On November 1, Book sold all of the above shares for $59 per share, less commissions and taxes of $55. Record all of the above in Book Company's T-accounts.

12. When bonds are issued between interest dates, why is it appropriate that the issuing corporation should receive cash equal to the amount of accrued interest in addition to the issue price of the bonds?

13. Thayer Company issued $200,000 of 10-year, 10 percent bonds at 102 on January 1, 1979, the date of the bonds.
    a. Was the market rate of interest for these bonds higher or lower than 10 percent?
    b. What is the amount of bond interest expense for 1979 assuming straight-line amortization of the bond premium?

14. If in the preceding question the bonds had been issued at 95, what would have been the interest expense for 1979?

15. (This question is based on the Appendix to the chapter.)
    Assume that the Adams Company offered on July 1, 1979, $100,000 of 10 percent bonds calling for semiannual interest payments on January 1 and July 1, which mature on July 1, 1999, to investors at a price to yield 8 percent. What sum of money would the Adams Company receive if all the bonds were purchased immediately to yield 8 percent?

PROBLEMS

6–1. On November 1, 1979, the Scruggs Company discounted its own $16,000, 90-day noninterest-bearing note at 9 percent at the First National Bank.

Required: Using T-accounts give the entries required on Scruggs' books as of November 1, December 31 (the company's closing date), and at maturity date.

6–2. Following are selected transactions of the Beyers Company:
    Oct. 31 Discounted its own 30-day, $20,000, noninterest-bearing note at the First State Bank at 9 percent.
    Nov. 8   Received a $10,000, 30-day, 9 percent note from the Schultz Company in settlement of an account receivable. The note is dated November 8.
          15 Purchased merchandise by issuing its own 90-day note for $9,600. The note is dated November 15 and bears interest at 8 percent.
          20 Discounted the Schultz Company note at 10 percent at the First State Bank.
          30 The First State Bank notified the Beyers Company that it had charged the note of October 31 against the company's checking account.

Required: Assume that all notes falling due after November 30 were paid in full on their due dates by their respective makers. Give the journal entries required on Beyers' books for each of the above transactions and each of the necessary adjustments assuming a fiscal year accounting period ending on November 30. Also give the journal entries required on Beyers' books for payment of the notes due after November 30.

6–3. Susan, Inc., issued $200,000 of 8 percent, 10-year bonds at 98. Interest is payable semiannually. Dana Corporation also issued $200,000 of 8 percent, 10-year bonds, but received a price of 102 for its bonds. These bonds also call for semiannual interest payments. Assume both bond issues are dated and issued on July 1, 1979.

Required: Using T-accounts, show the entries to record the issuance of both bond issues and to record the interest expense and the payment of interest for the first semiannual period. Assume both companies have a calendar year accounting period. Which company is actually paying the lower interest rate? Why?

6–4. On January 1, 1979, Krogman, Inc., issued $100,000 of 10 percent, 20-year bonds at 106. Interest is payable on January 1 and July 1. The bond indenture provides that the company may retire any or all of the bonds on any interest payment date subsequent to July 1, 1983, at a price equal to 105 percent of face value. On January 1, 1984, Krogman, Inc., redeemed $40,000 of its outstanding bonds. The company's accounting period ends on December 31.

Required: Prepare entries in T-account format to record the issuance of the bonds, the first semiannual interest payment, and the entries necessary on January 1, 1984.

6–5. The Stabler Company acquired on July 15, 1979, 300 shares of Hix Company $100 par value common stock at 97 plus a broker's commission of $180. On August 1, 1979, Stabler Company received a cash dividend of 60 cents per share. On November 3, 1979, it sold 150 of these shares at 105 less a broker's commission of $120. On December 1, 1979, the Hix Company issued the shares comprising a 100 percent stock dividend declared on its common stock November 18.

Required:

a. Present entries in T-account format to record all of the above data.
b. If the remaining shares are to be held for affiliation purposes—Hix Company has become a major customer—indicate how they should be shown in the statement of financial position. Assume the market value is $13,800.

6–6. (This problem is based on the Appendix to the chapter.)

Assume that Buckner Company offered on July 1, 1979, $100,000 of 10 percent bonds calling for semiannual interest payments on January 1 and July 1, which mature on July 1, 1982, to investors at a price to yield 8 percent.

Required:

a. Calculate the amount which the Buckner Company would receive if all the bonds were purchased immediately to yield 8 percent.
b. Prepare a table similar to the one in the Appendix to the chapter showing how the premium would be amortized under the effective rate of interest method.

chapter 7

Evaluation of
Financial Position

PURPOSE OF FINANCIAL STATEMENTS

Financial statements are issued to communicate useful financial information to interested parties. If this objective is not met, the statements serve no purpose. But careful analyses and interpretations made by the users of financial statements will often clarify and add to their usefulness and thus aid communication.

Managers, employees, current and prospective stockholders, current and prospective creditors, business counselors, and executives of trade associations are among those who at one time or another will be interested in the financial statements of a specific firm. For example, a commercial bank loan officer will decide whether or not to grant a loan after the firm's financial statements have been analyzed. The loan officer will pay particular attention to the firm's ability to meet its obligations. Similarly, a stockholder may decide to sell stock in the company after analyzing the company's financial statements and comparing its earnings history with that of another firm.

Statement analysis is used to establish and present the relationships and trends which are inherent in the data contained in financial statements. Therefore, it is essential that the user of the statements become skilled in the use of available techniques for analyzing financial statements. Several of these analytical techniques are presented in this chapter.

COMPARATIVE FINANCIAL STATEMENTS

Nature and Purpose

Comparative financial statements present the statements of the same firm for a number of accounting periods in such a manner that changes and trends can be analyzed. The usefulness of financial statements is greatly enhanced when they are presented in this manner. The nature of and trends in changes which affect an enterprise can be seen far more clearly by the reader in comparative statements than in the statements for a single period.

To illustrate, a statement of financial position dated December 31, 1980, shows an accounts receivable balance of $500,000. That information by itself tells the reader only that there is a receivables balance and that it equals $500,000. If the reader were also told that on December 31, 1979, the receivables balance was $250,000 and that the balance was increased by $250,000 during 1980—an increase of 100 percent—the balance of $500,000 on December 31, 1980, becomes more meaningful. Data from the December 31, 1979, statement of financial position have provided a standard for comparison which makes interpretation of the December 31, 1980, statement of financial position easier.

Methods of Comparison—Illustrated

Comparisons of financial statement data can be expressed as:

1. Absolute increases and decreases for an item from one period to the next or from a base period which is more than one period removed.
2. Percentage increases and decreases for an item from one period to the next or from a base period which is more than one period removed.
3. Percentages of an aggregate total.
4. Trend percentages; or
5. Ratios.

The first three of these methods have been used in preparing the following comparative financial statements which will serve as a basis for the analyses presented in this chapter. Ratios are employed in the analyses which follow. The statements presented are:

Exhibit A: Comparative statements of financial position, Illustration 7.1.
Exhibit B: Comparative statements of earnings and retained earnings, Illustration 7.2.
Schedule B–1:   Comparative schedules of selling and administrative expenses, Illustration 7.3.
Schedule B–2:   Comparative schedules of other expenses and revenues, Illustration 7.4.

These statements are presented here where they will be easy to find for reference while studying this chapter and the next. The "Other Expenses" and "Other Revenues" categories include earnings statement items which are not directly related to the regular operations of the business.

The comparative statements of financial position of the Knight Cor-

ILLUSTRATION 7.1

THE KNIGHT CORPORATION   *Exhibit A*
Comparative Statements of Financial Position
December 31, 1979 and 1980

	December 31		Increase or Decrease* 1980 over 1979		Percentage of December 31	
	1980	1979	Dollars	Percentage	1980	1979
Assets						
Current Assets:						
Cash	$ 80,215	$ 54,980	$25,235	45.9	12.6	10.0
Accounts receivable, net	124,171	132,550	8,379*	6.3*	19.5	24.0
Notes receivable	55,000	50,000	5,000	10.0	8.7	9.1
Inventories	110,825	94,500	16,325	17.3	17.4	17.1
Prepaid expenses	3,640	4,700	1,060*	22.6*	.6	0.9
Total Current Assets	$373,851	$336,730	$37,121	11.0	58.9R	61.1
Property, Plant, and Equipment:						
Land	$ 21,000	$ 21,000	-0-	-0-	3.3	3.8
Building	205,000	160,000	$45,000	28.1	32.3	29.0
Less: Allowance for depreciation .	(27,040)	(22,355)	(4,685)	21.0	(4.3)	(4.1)
Furniture and fixtures	83,200	69,810	13,390	19.2	13.1	12.7
Less: Allowance for depreciation .	(20,800)	(14,100)	(6,700)	47.5	(3.3)	(2.5)
Total Plant Assets	$261,360	$214,355	$47,005	21.9	41.1	38.9
Total Assets	$635,211	$551,085	$84,126	15.3	100.0	100.0
Liabilities and Stockholders' Equity						
Current Liabilities:						
Accounts payable	$ 70,310	$ 64,560	$ 5,750	8.9	11.1	11.7
Notes payable	20,000	15,100	4,900	32.4	3.1	2.7
Taxes accrued	36,830	30,200	6,630	22.4	5.8	5.5
Total Current Liabilities	$127,140	$109,860	$17,280	15.7	20.0	19.9
Long-Term Liabilities:						
Mortgage notes payable, land and building 7%, 1982	43,600	60,750	17,150*	28.2*	6.9	11.0
Total Liabilities	$170,740	$170,610	$ 130	†	26.9	30.9
Stockholders' Equity:						
Common stock, par value $10 per share	$240,000	$200,000	$40,000	20.0	37.8	36.3
Retained earnings	224,471	180,475	43,996	24.4	35.3	32.7R
Total Stockholders' Equity ..	$464,471	$380,475	$83,996	22.1	73.1	69.0R
Total Liabilities and Stockholders' Equity ..	$635,211	$551,085	$84,126	15.3	100.0	100.0R

† Less than one half of 1 percent.
R Rounding error.

ILLUSTRATION 7.2

THE KNIGHT CORPORATION   *Exhibit B*
Comparative Statements of Earnings and Retained Earnings
For the Years Ended December 31, 1979 and 1980

	Year Ended December 31		Increase or Decrease* 1980 over 1979		Percentage of Net Sales	
	1980	*1979*	*Dollars*	*Percentage*	*1980*	*1979*
Gross sales	$995,038	$775,836	$219,202	28.3	100.9	101.3
Less: Sales returns and allowances	8,650	10,321	1,671*	16.2*	0.9	1.3
Net sales	$986,388	$765,515	$220,873	28.9	100.0	100.0
Cost of goods sold						
Inventories, January 1	$ 94,500	$ 85,150	$ 9,350	11.0	9.6	11.1
Net purchases	639,562	510,290	129,272	25.3	64.8	66.7
	$734,062	$595,440	$138,622	23.3	74.4	77.8
Inventories, December 31.......	110,825	94,500	16,325	17.3	11.2	12.4
Cost of goods sold	$623,237	$500,940	$122,297	24.4	63.2	65.4
Gross Margin	363,151	264,575	98,576	37.3	36.8	34.6
Less: Selling Expenses,						
Schedule B–1	$132,510	$ 84,898	$ 47,612	56.1	13.4	11.1
Administrative Expenses,						
Schedule B–1	120,345	98,642	21,703	22.0	12.2	12.9
	$252,855	$183,540	$ 69,315	37.8	25.6	24.0
Net operating earnings	$110,296	$ 81,035	$ 29,261	36.1	11.2	10.6
Less: Net other expenses,						
Schedule B–2	3,000	2,800	200	7.1	.3	.4
Net earnings before federal						
income taxes	$107,296	$ 78,235	29,061	37.1	10.9	10.2
Deduct: Federal income taxes ..	48,300	31,700	16,600	52.4	4.9	4.1
Net earnings, to retained earnings .	$ 58,996	$ 46,535	$ 12,461	26.8	6.0	6.1
Retained earnings, January 1	180,475	146,440	34,035	23.2		
	$239,471	$192,975	$ 46,496	24.1		
Deduct: Dividends declared						
and paid	15,000	12,500	2,500	20.0		
Retained Earnings, December 31	$224,471	$180,475	$ 43,996	24.4		

poration, Illustration 7.1, set forth certain relationships. Management can establish these relationships by means of analysis, and use them as guidelines when it makes business decisions. For example, the comparative statements of financial position in Illustration 7.1 show (among other items):

1. The dollar amount of each asset, liability, and stockholders' equity item and the total of each class of assets, liabilities, and stockholders' equity on December 31, 1979, and on December 31, 1980.
2. The increase or decrease in dollar amounts of each of the items listed in (1) above, by comparison of December 31, 1980, balances with

ILLUSTRATION 7.3

THE KNIGHT CORPORATION   *Schedule B–1*
Comparative Schedules of Selling and Administrative Expenses
For the Years Ended December 31, 1979 and 1980

	Year Ended December 31		Increase or Decrease* 1980		Percentage of Net Sales	
	1980	*1979*	*Dollars*	*Percentage*	*1980*	*1979*
Selling Expenses						
Advertising	$ 28,632	$18,105	$10,527	58.1	2.9	2.4
Salesmen's salaries	69,225	45,900	23,325	50.8	7.0	6.0
Rent of sales office	10,150	7,200	2,950	41.0	1.0	0.9
Payroll taxes	9,366	4,050	5,316	131.3	1.0	0.5
General sales office expense and depreciation	15,137	9,643	5,494	57.0	1.5	1.3
Total Selling Expenses (Exhibit B)	$132,510	$84,898	$47,612	56.1	13.4	11.1
Administrative Expenses						
Officers' and office salaries	$ 90,132	$74,957	$15,175	20.2	9.1	9.8
Bad debts expense	1,100	2,500	1,400*	56.0*	0.1	0.3
Telephone and light	10,300	7,200	3,100	43.1	1.0	0.9
Taxes, payroll, and other	9,853	7,450	2,403	32.3	1.0	1.0
General administrative office expenses and depreciation	8,960	6,535	2,425	37.1	1.0	0.9
Total Administrative Expenses (Exhibit B)	$120,345	$98,642	$21,703	22.0	12.2	12.9

ILLUSTRATION 7.4

THE KNIGHT CORPORATION   *Schedule B–2*
Comparative Schedules of Other Expenses and Revenues
For the Years Ended December 31, 1979 and 1980

	Year Ended December 31		Increase or Decrease* 1980 over 1979		Percentage of Net Sales	
	1980	*1979*	*Dollars*	*Percentage*	*1980*	*1979*
Other Expenses						
Interest expense	$9,325	$10,850	$1,525*	14.1*	0.9	1.4
Total Other Expenses	$9,325	$10,850	$1,525*	14.1*	0.9	1.4
Other Revenues						
Gain on sale of plant assets	6,325	8,050	1,725*	21.4*	0.6	1.0
Net Other Expenses (Exhibit B)	$3,000	$ 2,800	$ 200	7.1	0.3	0.4

those of December 31, 1979. For example, it is shown that on December 31, 1980, as compared with December 31, 1979:

a. Total current assets have increased $37,121, while total current liabilities have increased $17,280. This increase in the Knight Corporation's working capital (current assets less current liabilities) could have resulted from (1) retention of earnings, (2) conversion of plant assets to current assets through sale, (3) long-term borrowing, and/or (4) the issuance of more capital stock. Further examination of the comparative statements of financial position and the earnings statement will reveal that the first and last of these possibilities have actually brought about the improvement in the current position.

b. Total assets have increased $84,126, while total liabilities have increased only $130, and total stockholders' equity has increased $83,996 of which $40,000 represents an increase in outstanding capital stock. Thus, it is established that by retention of earnings and by more investment in the corporation on the part of the stockholders, the stockholders' equity in the corporation has been greatly increased while the equity of the creditors has been only slightly increased.

3. The percentage increase or decrease in each of the items listed in (1) above—December 31, 1980, balances are compared with December 31, 1979 balances. For example, inspection of the comparative statements of financial position shows that:

Current assets have increased by 11 percent, while current liabilities have increased by 15.7 percent; total assets have increased by 15.3 percent, while total liabilities have increased by less than one half of 1 percent, and total stockholders' equity has increased by 22.1 percent. These percentages express the increases and decreases in terms which, in many cases, convey more meaning than do the increases and decreases expressed in dollar amounts.

Trend Percentages

Trend percentages (also referred to as index numbers) are a useful means for comparing financial statements for several years. They emphasize changes or trends that have occurred over a period of time. They are calculated by:

1. Selecting a base year.
2. Assigning a weight of 100 percent to the amounts appearing on the base year financial statements.
3. Expressing the amounts shown on the other years' financial statements as a percentage of their corresponding base year financial statement amounts. (In other words, divide the other years' amounts by the base year amounts.)

As an example, assume the following information is given.

	1978	1979	1980	1981
Sales...............................	$350,000	$367,500	$441,000	$485,000
Cost of Goods Sold.................	200,000	196,000	230,000	285,000
Gross Margin......................	$150,000	$171,500	$211,000	$200,000
Operating Expenses.................	145,000	169,000	200,000	192,000
Net Earnings before Taxes...........	$ 5,000	$ 2,500	$ 11,000	$ 8,000

Letting 1978 be the base year, the trend percentages would be calculated as follows:

1. Divide the amounts shown for "Sales" by $350,000.
2. Divide the amounts shown for "Cost of Goods Sold" by $200,000.
3. Divide the amounts shown for "Gross Margin" by $150,000.
4. Divide the amounts shown for "Operating Expenses" by $145,000.
5. Divide the amounts shown for "Net Earnings before Taxes" by $5,000.

After all the divisions have been made, the resulting trends would appear as follows:

	1978	1979	1980	1981
Sales....................................	100	105	126	139
Cost of Goods Sold......................	100	98	115	143
Gross Margin...........................	100	114	141	133
Operating Expenses......................	100	117	138	132
Net Earnings before Taxes...............	100	50	220	160

In reviewing the trends, one should pay close attention to the trends for interrelated items. Also, trend percentages simply indicate changes and the direction of changes; they do not explain the basic reasons for the changes. But, by looking at the trend percentages, management can determine which areas of the business need to be investigated and analyzed more closely.

OPERATING CYCLE CONCEPTS

Familiarity with the term "operating cycle" will help one to understand the various ratios and financial relationships to be discussed in this chapter and in the following chapter. The operations of a typical business represent numerous operating cycles in various stages of completion. The operating cycle may be started with the introduction of cash and/or other assets into the business. These assets are then converted to goods or services that can be sold. When the asset is sold, either cash is received or a receivable is created. When cash is collected either from a cash sale or from accounts receivable, the cycle is complete. The above operating cycle may be referred to as a cash-to-cash cycle. Other cycles may be used to represent receivables, inventory, plant assets, debt, and owner's equity cycles.

The debt cycle begins when a company incurs a current liability by, for example, purchasing goods or services on account or borrowing money from a bank. The debt cycle ends when the company disburses cash to satisfy the obligation. The company has the use of the short-term debt capital for a certain average length of time before cash is disbursed to satisfy the obligation. By comparing the length of the cash-to-cash cycle with the length of the debt cycle, one can assess whether or not the company takes too much time converting current assets into cash. For example, assume the lengths are 150 days for the cash-to-cash cycle and 100 days for the debt cycle. Thus, the company collects cash every 150 days and pays out cash every 100 days. In order for the company to be able to pay its current liabilities as they become due, the current assets must be at least 1.5 (150/100) times the current liabilities. If the ratio of current assets to current liabilities is less than 1.5, the company may have a difficult time satisfying its obligations. This ratio, known as the current ratio, is discussed further in the next section.

The cash-to-cash, debt, and plant asset operating cycles are presented in the illustrations below. Thinking in terms of cycles will aid in understanding ratios and turnover figures.

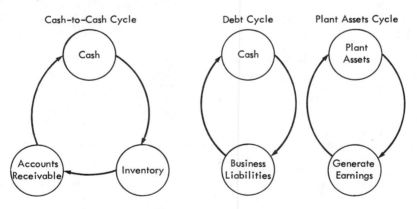

EVALUATING FINANCIAL POSITION RELATIONSHIPS

It is generally recognized that logical relationships exist between certain pairs of items that appear in the statement of financial position, certain pairs that appear in the earnings statement, and other pairs of which one appears in one statement and one in the other. For convenience, the ratios of items that appear only in the statement of financial position are treated first.

The Current or Working Capital Ratio

Working capital is the excess of current assets over current liabilities. The ratio which relates these two categories to each other is known as the current ratio or working capital ratio. It is used to help measure the ability of a company to meet its maturing current liabilities and to indicate the strength of its working capital position. The amount of working capital expressed in dollars does not provide an adequate index of the ability to pay current debts. The current ratio provides a better index.

The current ratio is computed by dividing total current assets by total current liabilities:

$$\text{Current Ratio} = \frac{\text{Current Assets}}{\text{Current Liabilities}}$$

The ratio is usually stated in terms of the number of dollars of current assets to one dollar of current liabilities (although the dollar signs usually are omitted). Thus, if current assets total $75,000 and current liabilities total $50,000, the ratio is usually expressed as 1.5:1 or 1.5 to 1.

To illustrate the superiority of the current ratio over net working capital as a measure of debt-paying ability, consider the following example. Assume that Company A and Company B have current assets and current liabilities as of December 31, 1979, as follows:

	Company A	Company B
Current assets..........................	$11,000,000	$200,000
Current liabilities......................	10,000,000	100,000
Working capital........................	$ 1,000,000	$100,000
Current ratio..........................	1.1 to 1	2 to 1

Company A has 10 times as much working capital as Company B. But Company B has a superior debt-paying ability since it has two dollars of current assets for each dollar of current liabilities, while Company A has only $1.10 of current assets for each $1 of current liabilities.

Short-term creditors are especially interested in the working capital ratio. They expect to receive payment from the conversion of inventories and accounts receivable into cash. They are not as concerned with long-range earnings as investors are. Therefore, they concentrate on the current, short-term financial position. They are more interested in the short and

ILLUSTRATION 7.5

	December 31		Amount of Increase
	1980	1979	
Current Assets (*a*).................	$373,851	$336,730	$37,121
Current Liabilities (*b*)..............	127,140	109,860	17,280
Working Capital (*a* − *b*)............	$246,711	$226,870	$19,841
Current Ratio (*a* ÷ *b*)..............	2.94:1	3.07:1	

intermediate term operating prospects of a firm and whether it will be able to meet current operating commitments.

The current ratios for the Knight Corporation are in Illustration 7.5.

Ideal Size of Ratio

Actually, the "ideal" size of the current ratio depends upon the industry, the methods of buying and selling, the methods of financing in general, the season of the year, and many other factors. An acceptable current ratio for a well-established and well-managed company might be too low for a new company, for an expanding company, or for a poorly managed company. For most lines of business, certain limits can be established between which a current ratio is regarded as generally acceptable. A current ratio below the lower limit, for example, may spell potential financial trouble; a current ratio above the upper limit may indicate unproductive use of assets. To illustrate, a current ratio of less than, say, 2.3 to 1 may be considered dangerous because a company may not be able to pay its bills when due. A current ratio of more than, say, 5 to 1 may be too conservative; that is, it may indicate that too many assets are idle and are not being profitably employed. In the latter case, idle cash or cash obtained by reducing inventories might be invested in long-term assets or returned to stockholders. Thus, it should be remembered that every ratio is satisfactory within a given range and becomes unsatisfactory as it leaves that range in either direction.

The working capital position of the Knight Corporation appears to have been satisfactory on both of the dates shown above. But, in spite of the apparently favorable position, comparison with appropriate standards, such as typical current ratios within the industry in which the Knight Corporation operates, is necessary.

Managements of firms are continually faced with the dilemma of meeting the liquidity goal or meeting the profitability goal. On the one hand, they would like to have enough cash and near cash on hand so that any bills coming due can be paid with a minimum of advance planning. On the other hand, they would like to keep the balances of idle cash and near cash assets on hand as small as possible and put the remainder to work increasing earnings. A wise management will make a compromise between safety and profitability. When the management of a company does not do this, the current ratio is likely to fall outside the acceptable range.

The Quick or Acid Test Ratio

The acid test ratio (or quick ratio) is the ratio of cash, net receivables, and marketable securities (known as quick assets) to current liabilities:

$$\text{Acid Test Ratio} = \frac{\text{Quick Assets}}{\text{Current Liabilities}}$$

Inventories and prepaid expenses are excluded from this computation because they may not be readily convertible into cash. Short-term creditors are especially interested in this ratio since it relates the "pool" of cash and immediate cash inflows to immediate cash outflows.

For the Knight Corporation, acid test ratios are presented in Illustration 7.6.

ILLUSTRATION 7.6

	December 31		Amount of Increase
	1980	1979	
Cash, accounts, and notes receivable (a)....................	$259,386	$237,530	$21,856
Current liabilities (b)...............	127,140	109,860	17,280
Net quick assets (a − b).............	$132,246	$127,670	$ 4,576
Acid test ratio (a ÷ b)...............	2.04:1	2.16:1	

Satisfactory Acid Test Ratio

In deciding whether or not the acid test ratio is satisfactory, a good starting point is to consider the quality of the receivables and the marketable securities. An accumulation of poor quality receivables or temporary investments on which losses are likely at the time of their disposition could cause an acid test ratio to appear deceptively favorable. As for the Knight Corporation, there appears to be little immediate danger of insolvency since it has over $2.00 of quick assets for every dollar of short-term debt.

Cash Forecasts (budgets)—A Management Control

While the current and quick ratios are indicators of short-term debt-paying ability, they usually must be supplemented by other information for credit purposes. One very important schedule often requested by loan officers in banks, for instance, is the *cash budget* or *cash forecast*. The cash forecast shows gross cash inflows (receipts) and outflows (disbursements) anticipated as well as the resulting net cash inflow or outflow expected (usually on a monthly basis for short-term credit purposes).

To be effective and efficient, management must anticipate the future cash requirements of the business and make sure that adequate amounts of cash will be available when payments become due. In addition, management should not keep excessive amounts of idle, unproductive cash on hand; such cash should be temporarily invested in other assets until it is needed. It is usually necessary for management to forecast cash receipts and disbursements several months in advance. To do so, management must analyze the cash receipts and disbursements of prior periods and consider any necessary adjustments for expected changes. The illustration which follows should provide some insight into the process by which management prepares a cash forecast.

Cash Forecasts Illustrated

The information outlined below was collected and analyzed prior to the preparation of the formal cash forecast for the Lewis Toy Company.

a. Estimated sales (40 percent for cash; 60 percent on credit)

August.........................	$32,000
September.......................	29,000
October.........................	34,000
November.......................	42,000
December.......................	50,000

b. Collections on credit sales are estimated as follows:

Month of sale....................	20%
First month following sale..........	60%
Second month following sale........	20%

c. Estimated net purchases (all on credit)

September.......................	$25,000
October.........................	30,000
November.......................	40,000
December.......................	35,000

d   Payments for purchases are estimated as follows:

Month of sale....................	80%
Month following sale..............	20%

e. Other estimated monthly cash expenses:

Salaries and wages................	$ 9,000
Advertising......................	500
Insurance and taxes...............	1,600
Miscellaneous expenses............	2,600

f. A cash dividend payment of $1,000 is scheduled for November.

g. Cash balance, October 1, 1979, $31,000.

The cash forecast for the Lewis Toy Company for the last quarter of 1979 appears below.

LEWIS TOY COMPANY
Cash Forecast
October, November, December, 1979

	October	November	December
Cash balance, beginning of month..............	$31,000	$20,260	$ 5,120
Cash receipts:			
Cash sales...................................	13,600	16,800	20,000
Collections on credit sales....................	18,360	20,760	25,200
Total cash available...................	$62,960	$57,820	$50,320
Cash disbursements:			
Purchases...................................	$29,000	$38,000	$36,000
Salaries and wages...........................	9,000	9,000	9,000
Advertising.................................	500	500	500
Insurance and taxes..........................	1,600	1,600	1,600
Dividend payments...........................	0	1,000	0
Miscellaneous...............................	2,600	2,600	2,600
Total cash disbursements...............	$42,700	$52,700	$49,700
Cash balance, end of month..................	$20,260	$ 5,120	$ 620

The figures shown for October's cash receipts and for cash disbursements for purchases are derived by the following computations:

Cash sales = (40% of $34,000) = $13,600

Collections on credit sales:
  From August sales   = (.60 × $32,000 × .20) = $ 3,840
  From September sales = (.60 × $29,000 × .60) = $10,440
  From October sales   = (.60 × $34,000 × .20) = $ 4,080
                                                  $18,360

Cash disbursements for purchases:
  For September purchases = (20% of $25,000)   = $ 5,000
  For October purchases   = (80% of $30,000)   = $24,000
                                                  $29,000

By preparing the cash forecast, management can decide whether or not adequate amounts of cash will be provided to meet the maturing commitments of the company. If estimated cash receipts are less than estimated cash disbursements, management can plan in advance for loans to meet the shortages. On the other hand, if large amounts of cash are expected to be idle for some period of time, management can investigate investment opportunities at an early date to decide how the excess cash can be most profitably used.

The Equity Ratio

The following data shown in Illustration 7.7, taken from the comparative statements of financial position in Illustration 7.1, disclose the sources of the assets of the Knight Corporation on December 31 of 1980 and 1979.

ILLUSTRATION 7.7

	December 31, 1980		December 31, 1979	
	Amount	*Percent*	*Amount*	*Percent*
Current liabilities..................	$127,140	20.0	$109,860	20.0
Long-term liabilities................	43,600	6.9	60,750	11.0
Total Liabilities..................	$170,740	26.9	$170,610	31.0
Common stock....................	$240,000	37.8	$200,000	36.3
Retained earnings.................	224,471	35.3	180,475	32.7
Total Stockholders' Equity........	$464,471	73.1	$380,475	69.0
Total Equity (equal to Total Assets)...............	$635,211	100.0	$551,085	100.0

It is apparent that the stockholders of the Knight Corporation have increased their proportionate equity in the assets of that company, both through additional investment in the company's common stock and through retention within the business of the company's earnings.

The equity ratio is equal to the proportion of owners' equity to total equity (or to total assets):

$$\text{Equity Ratio} = \frac{\text{Owner's Equity}}{\text{Total Equity}}$$

The equity ratio, must be carefully interpreted. From a creditor's point of view, a high proportion of owners' equity is desirable because a high percentage indicates the existence of a large protective buffer for creditors in the event the company suffers a loss. But, from an owner's point of view, a high proportion of owners' equity may or may not be desirable. If borrowed funds can be used by the business to generate earnings in excess of the net after tax cost of the interest on such borrowed funds, a lower percentage of owners' equity may be desirable. For example, assume that Dorton Company has $10,000,000 of 8 percent bonds payable in its capital structure, which after taxes have a net cost of $400,000, assuming a 50 percent tax rate. If the Dorton Company can employ the $10,000,000 in such a way as to produce earnings in excess of the $400,000 net after-tax cost of the borrowed funds and to increase earnings per share, it may decide that borrowing is advantageous. Use of borrowed funds to such an advantage is termed successful "trading on the equity" or "favorable *financial leverage.*"

The following is a brief illustration of the effect on the Knight Corporation if it were more leveraged (i.e., had a larger proportion of debt.) Assume that Knight Corporation could have financed its present operations with $50,000 of 8 percent bonds instead of 5,000 shares of common stock. The effect on earnings for 1980 would be as follows, assuming a marginal federal income tax rate of 50 percent:

Earnings as presently stated (Illustration 7.2)................ $58,996
Net additional interest on bonds .50 (8% × 50,000).......... 2,000
Adjusted earnings..................................... $56,996

As shown, net earnings would be less. But there would be 5,000 fewer shares outstanding. Therefore, earnings per share would be increased to $3.00 ($56,996 ÷ 19,000) from $2.46 ($58,996 ÷ 24,000). Many companies have introduced larger portions of debt into their capital structures to increase earnings per share. But these companies will also show a larger drop in earnings per share when earnings go down than will those which are financed largely by common stock.

It should also be pointed out that too low a percentage of owners' equity (too much debt) may be hazardous from the owners' standpoint. A period of business recession may result in operating losses and shrinkages in the values of assets (such as receivables and inventories) leading to an inability to meet fixed payment for interest and principal on the debt. This in turn may cause stockholders to lose control of the company. The company may be forced into liquidation.

The relative equities of owners and creditors may be expressed in several ways. To say, for example, that creditors hold a 26.9 percent equity in the assets of the Knight Corporation on December 31, 1980, is equivalent to saying that the stockholders hold a 73.1 percent interest. In many cases, the relationship is expressed as a ratio of owners' equity to debt. Such a ratio for the Knight Corporation would be 2.23 to 1 ($380,475 ÷ $170,610) on December 31, 1979, and 2.72 to 1 ($464,471 ÷ $170,740) on December 31, 1980.

At times analysts may be interested in the ratio of long-term debt to owners' equity:

$$\text{Long-Term Debt to Owners' Equity Ratio} = \frac{\text{Long-Term Debt}}{\text{Owners' Equity}}$$

In computing this ratio it is assumed that current liabilities are for financing current operations, and attention is focused on the risk inherent in the longer term capital structure. For the Knight Corporation, the long-term debt to owners' equity ratio was 0.09 to 1 in 1980 ($43,600 ÷ $464,471) and 0.16 to 1 in 1979 ($60,750 ÷ $380,475).

EVALUATING THE EFFICIENCY OF ASSET UTILIZATION

The previous discussions were concerned largely with the possible significant relationships between items appearing on the statement of financial position. These ratios are of limited significance because they do not take into consideration the results that have been obtained from the use of assets. The primary purpose of business is to use assets to generate earnings. The following discussion covers some of the significant relationships that exist between operating data and items in the statement of financial position. It deals with some of the techniques used to determine whether assets are being used efficiently and whether sufficient earnings are being generated.

Calculating Turnover Ratios

Significant relationships between items appearing on different financial statements are sometimes best expressed as turnovers, often called turnover ratios. A turnover expresses the number of times during a period—usually a year—that an asset or group of assets was disposed of or converted into another asset or group of assets. For example, the turnover of accounts receivable indicates the number of times the accounts receivable were collected or converted into cash during a given period. In general, *turnovers measure the efficiency with which the assets are used* and may disclose under- or overinvestment in assets.

Accounts Receivable Turnover

The turnover of accounts receivable is computed by dividing net sales by net accounts receivable, that is, accounts receivable after deducting the balance of the allowance for doubtful accounts:

$$\text{Accounts Receivable Turnover} = \frac{\text{Net Sales}}{\text{Net Average Accounts Receivable}}$$

Ideally, the divisor should be computed by averaging the end-of-month balances or end-of-week balances of net accounts receivable outstanding during the period, although often only the beginning-of-year and end-of-year balances are averaged. The net sales figure should include only sales on account (credit sales). But, if cash sales are relatively small or if their proportion to total sales remains fairly constant from year to year, reliable results can be obtained by the use of the total net sales figure appearing on the earnings statement.

Illustration 7.8 shows the computations of the accounts receivable turnovers for the Knight Corporation for 1980 and 1979:

ILLUSTRATION 7.8

	1980	1979	Amount of Increase or Decrease*
Net sales (a)................................	$986,388	$765,515	$220,873
Accounts receivable, net, December 31 (b).......	124,171	132,550	8,379*
Turnover of accounts receivable (a ÷ b).........	7.94	5.77	

As a general rule when computing ratios in which one element is from the statement of financial position and the other is from the earnings statement, an average of the statement of financial position item should be used. An average is used so that the statement of financial position item will be for the period (usually a year) rather than for a moment in time. It can then be related to an earnings statement item which is also for the period. But if the balance in a given account fluctuates widely during the year, then more refined averages should be used, such as those obtained from quarterly, monthly, weekly, or even daily observations.

The divisor used in each of the above computations is the net accounts receivable at year-end. Beginning balances for the first of the two years' financial statements presented are not available in the report. Thus, to be consistent, year-end balances are used in computing the turnover ratios for both 1980 and 1979. This procedure will be employed in most of the illustrations which follow and will produce meaningful ratios if it can be assumed that the year-end balance fairly represents the actual average balance for the year.

Interpreting the Accounts Receivable Turnover Ratio

A rather high turnover ratio for accounts receivable always means that the accounts have a relatively short average life. Since the probability that an account will be collected often decreases as it ages, a high turnover ratio is usually favorable. Thus, the increase in the turnover, such as the Knight Corporation experienced in 1980, is encouraging. The turnover ratio is dependent upon many factors, such as the terms of credit extended to customers (whether 2/10, n/30, or n/60, for example), collection policies, and general business conditions. Comparisons of turnover figures with those of prior years and with those of other companies in the same line of business are essential to proper interpretation.

The average investment in accounts receivable represents funds which if freed could be invested elsewhere. If a company with an accounts receivable turnover of three times a year and an average accounts receivable balance of $100,000 could increase the turnover to six times a year, the average accounts receivable balance could be reduced by $50,000. Assuming the $50,000 could be reinvested by the company in additional plant and equipment at 12 percent, the increase in earnings would be $6,000. This, of course, assumes that customers are not driven away by the policies used to increase the accounts receivable turnover rate.

It is possible, of course, to go too far in attempting to increase the turnover of accounts receivable. The company may, through strict collection or screening policies, be driving away trustworthy (but slow-paying) customers. The careful manager will determine what accounts receivable turnover rate is desirable by weighing all of these factors.

Number of Days' Sales Uncollected

Some accountants and analysts prefer to evaluate the quality of accounts receivable by estimating the number of days' sales which remain uncollected at year-end. To do this, the net accounts receivable at year end are expressed as a percentage of the net sales for the year. The net sales figure should include only sales on account. This percentage is then multiplied by the number of days in the year (often assumed to be 360, but 365 could also be used); the result is the approximate number of days' sales remaining uncollected at year-end. The formula is:

Number of Days' Sales Uncollected

$$= \frac{\text{Net Accounts Receivable at Year End}}{\text{Net Sales}} \times 360$$

For the Knight Corporation, the number of days' sales uncollected at year-end for 1980 and 1979 is shown in Illustration 7.9.

ILLUSTRATION 7.9

	1980	1979
End of year net accounts receivable (a).................	$124,171	$132,550
Net sales for year (b)...............................	986,388	765,515
Ratio of (a) to (b).................................	12.59%	17.32%
Number of days' sales outstanding (assuming 360 days in a year)................................	45	62

The essential difference between the number of days' sales outstanding (uncollected) and the accounts receivable turnover rate is that the latter will include the average accounts receivable for the year if adequate information is available, while the former ratio uses only the year-end receivables balance. The number of days' sales outstanding is preferred by some because it provides more current information, although this may not represent the typical situation.

The ratios for the Knight Corporation indicate significant improvement in the collection of accounts receivable. The ratio may be viewed even more favorably when the rather large increase in sales is noted. But a proper and complete interpretation of this ratio requires consideration of credit and collection policies, general business conditions, and comparable data applicable to other dates and other companies.

Inventory Turnover

The turnover of inventory is obtained by dividing the cost of goods sold for a given period by the average inventory for the same period:

$$\text{Inventory Turnover} = \frac{\text{Cost of Goods Sold}}{\text{Average Inventory}}$$

An average of the January 1 and December 31 inventories may not be representative of the inventories held throughout the year. When possible, it is advisable to obtain an average of all the month-end inventories of the year plus the beginning of year inventory, as explained earlier.

Significance of Inventory Turnover Ratios

The turnover of inventory indicates the speed with which inventories are sold and replenished. The greater the number of times per year that the inventory can be sold and replaced, the smaller is the amount of capital necessary to produce a given volume of sales and the larger is the return on the money invested in the inventories. For the Knight Corporation the inventory turnover ratios for 1980 and 1979 are shown in Illustration 7.10.

ILLUSTRATION 7.10

	1980	1979	Amount of Increase
Cost of goods sold (a)	$623,237	$500,940	$122,297
Inventories			
January 1	$ 94,500	$ 85,150	$ 9,350
December 31	110,825	94,500	16,325
Total	$205,325	$179,650	$ 25,675
Average inventory (b)	102,663	89,825	
Turnover of inventory (a ÷ b)	6.07	5.58	

In 1980 the inventories were turned over more often (once every two months $\frac{360}{6.07} = 59$ days) than in 1979. If an inventory could be purchased and sold daily, only one day's inventory-capital requirement would be necessary to produce the annual sales volume, and the investment in inventories would be reduced to a minimum. Other things being equal, the more times per year an investment in inventory can be sold and reinvested, the more favorable are the earnings results. Also, a rapid turnover tends to prevent the accumulation of obsolete items. Of course, an attempt at too rapid a turnover may result in inventory shortages that delay the filling of sales orders, thereby causing customer dissatisfaction. Also, because of high ordering and processing costs and discounts on larger size orders, the optimum economic order quantity may indicate that reorders should be made less often and in larger quantities. As in the case of most ratios, there is a *range* that is favorable.

Total Assets Turnover

The turnover of total assets shows the relationship between dollar volume of sales and total assets used in the business:

$$\text{Total Assets Turnover} = \frac{\text{Net Sales}}{\text{Total Assets}}$$

This ratio is a measure of the efficiency of the use of the capital invested in the assets, assuming a constant margin of earnings on each dollar of sales. The larger the dollar volume of sales made per dollar of invested capital, the larger will be the earnings on each dollar invested in the assets of the business. For the Knight Corporation the total assets turnover ratios for 1980 and 1979 are shown in Illustration 7.11.

In 1979, each dollar of total assets produced $1.39 of sales; and in 1980, each dollar of total assets produced $1.55 of sales, or an increase of $0.16 of sales per dollar of investment in the assets.

ILLUSTRATION 7.11

	1980	1979	Amount of Increase
Net sales (a)........................	$986,388	$765,515	$220,873
Total assets at end of year (b)..........	635,211	551,085	84,126
Turnover of total assets (a ÷ b)........	1.55	1.39	

Interpreting the Total Assets Turnover Ratio

This ratio includes in the denominator not only plant assets but all assets. By analyzing this ratio over time, management can determine if the sales volume is sufficient relative to the commitment of total capital invested in the business. If management finds that the turnover of total assets has been declining over time, it may decide to investigate more thoroughly. It can do this by carefully analyzing the turnovers of the individual groupings of assets such as receivables, inventories, plant assets, and other assets. By improving any one of these ratios, all other things being equal, the turnover ratio of total assets will be improved.

Management may find that the turnover ratio of total assets has been increasing over time. As the volume of sales continues to grow, it may decide (by analyzing individual asset turnover rates as well) that more funds must be invested in inventory, in accounts receivable, or in plant assets.

The turnover ratio of total assets is a rather broad measure of the efficient use of capital. It may indicate that problems exist, but without further anlysis it does not identify the specific problem. It may be a composite of satisfactory and unsatisfactory turnovers. It is of greatest value when used with measures of profitability. The use of turnover ratios in evaluating relative profitability is discussed in the next chapter.

Limitations in Evaluating Financial Position

Financial statements presented in comparative form for several accounting periods facilitate analysis of changes and possible trends. Generally, three to five years is a minimum time period necessary for evaluation. There is no substitute for informed judgment in financial analysis. Percentages and ratios are useful *guides* to aid comparisons. The sophisticated financial analyst uses these tools to uncover potential corporate strengths and weaknesses. The analyst should try to discover the *basic causes* behind apparent changes and trends. For example, declining earnings may be a result of poor management, declining product demand, poor cost control, an inefficient sales force, and so forth. By examining key items on financial statements, the analyst can make *informed* judgments on the probability of continued profitability or reversal of losses.

Companies do not operate in an economic vacuum. It is important to place financial statement analysis within an industry context. Acceptable current ratios, gross margin percentages, debt to equity ratios, and so forth, vary widely depending upon the industry in which the company operates. Even within an industry legitimate variations may exist. For example, a retail discount store may operate at a relatively low gross profit percentage. This does not necessarily mean that its operating philosophy is inferior to that of its higher margin competitors. Also, within the same company over time, small percentage declines may indicate potential trouble. For example, a small percentage decline in gross margin percentage may be a danger signal because large dollar amounts may be involved. Conversely, if selling expenses are rising with respect to sales revenue, greater effort may be required to stimulate product demand which may be dwindling. Although the dollar amounts involved may be quite small, ignoring this ratio could prove costly. A change in the selling expense/sales ratio may be the first indicator of a long-term downward trend in profits.

SUMMARY

The usefulness of the financial statements of a given entity may be greatly increased when they are presented in comparative form for two or more accounting periods. Trends which cannot otherwise be seen may be quickly noted; and in this way, truly significant information may be obtained.

The analysis made possible by comparative statements usually includes the computation of increases or decreases in financial statement items and in classes of items in both absolute dollar terms and percentages. The use of percentages aids the comparison of widely varying dollar amounts which if not expressed in percentages may appear to signal major changes when in fact, major changes did not occur. On the other hand, attaching undue significance to a rather large percentage change may be avoided if absolute dollar changes are also shown. Analysis is easier when both dollar and percentage changes are shown. Trend percentages are useful for comparing financial statements for several years. They are calculated by dividing the base year amounts into the amounts for other years. They indicate favorable and unfavorable changes that may need investigation.

The analysis of comparative statements of financial position usually includes the computation of the ratio of current assets to current liabilities, that is, the current ratio. This ratio is viewed as an index of immediate debt-paying ability. A ratio satisfactory for one company may not be satisfactory for another because conditions vary from industry to industry and from company to company. Every ratio is satisfactory within a given range and becomes unsatisfactory as it leaves that range in either direction. A more severe test of immediate debt-paying ability is found in the quick or acid-test ratio. This ratio is computed by dividing the total of cash and near cash assets (net receivables and marketable securities) by total current liabilities. Cash forecasts which show anticipated cash receipts and cash disbursements are often prepared to insure that adequate cash will be available to meet maturing commitments.

The ratio of stockholders' equity to total equities (the equity ratio) is often computed and used as an index of long-run solvency and safety. This ratio implies that there is less risk for a business which has a high percentage of its assets supplied by stockholders. But a ratio that is too high may indicate that management is not increasing earnings per share by taking advantage of financial leverage.

Since, in business, assets are acquired and funds are invested to secure earnings, it follows that the ratios having the greatest significance are those which relate the asset or the investment to its earnings. Ratios of this type are heavily relied upon as indicators of progress and effectiveness.

The evaluation of the effectiveness of the use of assets is often undertaken through calculation and interpretation of turnover ratios. In general, turnover ratios relate the amount of assets employed to the volume of business secured. Such ratios are usually calculated by dividing the average asset balance into the earnings statement measure of activity, usually net sales. Since the earnings statement item covers a period of time, it follows that the asset balance should also be for the same period of time rather than for one point in time.

The accounts receivable turnover ratio is used to evaluate the quality of the accounts receivable through a determination of their average period of collection. The inventory turnover ratio is computed in an attempt to determine whether a sufficient volume of business is being generated in relation to the amount of inventory kept on hand.

The total assets turnover ratio is computed to determine whether the volume of business generated is adequate relative to the amount of capital invested in the business. As is true for all turnover ratios, the general implication is that the higher the ratio the better. The operating goal of management is to expand the volume of business relative to the amount of assets employed with the expectation of increasing the profitability of the business.

But caution must be exercised in placing too much emphasis on the various ratios. They are tools which aid in looking at the underlying forces of a business. As such, they indicate areas for further inquiry. There is no "correct" set of ratios for a given firm.

QUESTIONS AND EXERCISES

1. Indicate how each of the following ratios or measures is calculated:
    a. Current ratio (or working capital ratio).
    b. Quick ratio (or acid test ratio).
    c. Equity ratio.
    d. Accounts receivable turnover.
    e. Number of days' sales uncollected.
    f. Inventory turnover.
    g. Total assets turnover.
2. Under what conditions might the stockholders prefer an equity ratio of less than 100 percent? What is this situation called?
3. a. In general, what are turnover ratios and what are they designed to measure?
    b. If Company A has an inventory turnover of 4 and Company D has an inventory turnover of 2, is Company A performing better than Company D?
4. Define working capital and list four possible sources of an increase in the working capital of a business.
5. Define the following two frequently used terms:
    a. Current assets.
    b. Normal operating cycle.
6. State the primary purpose that comparative financial statements serve and at least three of the five ways in which comparisons of financial statement data can be expressed.
7. How are trend percentages calculated, and how are they used?
8. How do the following transactions affect the working capital of a company?

a. A sale of merchandise amounting to $9,000 on account (at a profit).
b. A sale of merchandise amounting to $9,000 for cash (at a profit).
c. A purchase of $300 of office supplies on account.
d. A payment of $200 on the company's 30-day note held by Little Town State Bank.
e. A net increase in accounts receivable during the normal operating period.
f. A net increase in accounts payable during the normal operating period.
g. A net decrease in prepaid expenses during the normal operating period.
h. A net decrease in the federal tax liability during the normal operating period.

9. Can you think of a situation in which the current ratio is very misleading as an indicator of short-term debt-paying ability? Does the quick ratio offer a remedy to the situation you have described? Describe a situation in which the quick ratio will not suffice either.

10. Company Y operates in an industry in which all of the other firms have current ratios which fall between 2.5 to 1 and 4 to 1. Company Y has a ratio of 2 to 1. The company decides to sell a plant asset and to lease it back in order to improve its current position. The proceeds of the sale increase current assets by 40 percent. What is the new current ratio? Is the company in a stronger financial position than it was before?

11. The higher the accounts receivable turnover rate the better off is the company. Do you agree? Why?

PROBLEMS

7–1. The statement of financial position of H. L. Eidson Printing Company, as of June 30, 1979, is shown below.

The management team has decided to spend an additional $1,000,000 on plant expansion and to divide another $500,000 equally between financing expansion of inventories and receivables. This $1,500,000 expansion will approximately double the business volume. Market research and forecasts assure disposal of all the new volume at the same price level, and profit forecasts indicate that net earnings from operations will rise to $660,000. It appears the tax rate will be about 40 percent.

The necessary funds can be secured under the following alternative arrangements;

(1) Finance entirely by issuance of additional common stock. Assume the issue price would be $75 per share.

(2) Finance two thirds with bonds, one third with additional common stock. The bonds would be 20-year, 7 percent, and the issue price of the stock is assumed to be $80. Assume the bonds are issued at face value.

H. L. EIDSON PRINTING COMPANY
Statement of Financial Position
June 30, 1979

Assets

Current Assets:

Cash.................................	$ 80,000	
Receivables (net)........................	520,000	
Inventories.............................	600,000	
Other current assets.....................	50,000	$1,250,000

Property, Plant, and Equipment:

Land....................................	$ 55,000	
Building (net of depreciation)...............	345,000	
Equipment (net of depreciation).............	800,000	1,200,000
Total Assets.......................		$2,450,000

Liabilities and Stockholders' Equity

Current Liabilities:

Accounts payable........................	$ 268,000	
Notes payable...........................	292,000	$ 560,000
Long-term debt, due in 1985, 6% bonds.......		400,000

Stockholders' Equity:

Common stock ($10).....................	$1,000,000	
Retained earnings........................	490,000	1,490,000
Total Liabilities and Stockholders' Equity		$2,450,000

Pertinent information from the earnings statement for the year ended June 30, 1979, is:

(1)	Net earnings after income taxes................	$219,000
(2)	Income taxes.............................	146,000
(3)	Interest expense...........................	35,000
(4)	Net earnings from operations................	400,000

Required:

a. Compute the following ratios for the current situation and indicate what the ratios are expected to be under each of the two financing arrangements (assume the investments in the plant and current assets are made immediately):
    (1) Current ratio.
    (2) Quick ratio.
    (3) Equity ratio.

b. Should the investment be made? If so, what financing method would you recommend?

7–2. This information was obtained from the annual reports of Corbert Truck Manufacturers:

	1978	1979	1980	1981
Net accounts receivable.......	$ 90,000	$ 180,000	$ 240,000	$ 330,000
Net sales..................	800,000	1,100,000	1,250,000	1,600,000

Required:

a. Assume a 360-day year. If cash sales account for 40 percent of all sales and credit terms are always 1/10, n/60, determine all turnover ratios possible and the number of days' sales in accounts receivable at all possible dates.

b. Comment on the effectiveness of the credit policy.

7–3. The statement of financial position for Martinez, Inc., has been given to you by your supervisor who would like you to compute certain ratios, showing your computations in detail.

MARTINEZ, INC.
Statement of Financial Position
June 30, 1979

Assets

Current Assets:

Cash.	$ 300,000	
Marketable securities.	200,000	
Accounts receivable.	570,000	
Inventory.	610,000	$1,680,000

Property, Plant, and Equipment:

Plant assets, cost.	$3,400,000	
Less: Allowance for depreciation.	800,000	2,600,000
Total Assets.		$4,280,000

Liabilities and Stockholders' Equity

Current Liabilities:

Accounts payable.	$ 230,000	
Bank loans.	150,000	$ 380,000

Long-term Liabilities:

Mortgage notes payable, due in 1982.	$ 400,000	
Bonds payable, 6%, due December 31, 1984...	600,000	1,000,000
Total Liabilities.		$1,380,000

Stockholders' Equity:

Common stock (par value, $100).	$2,000,000	
Retained earnings.	900,000	2,900,000
Total Liabilities and Stockholders' Equity		$4,280,000

The company's earnings statement for the year shows: net sales, $3,500,000; cost of goods sold, $2,500,000; interest expense, $65,000; net earnings after taxes, $190,000; earnings before interest and taxes, $395,000. The June 30, 1978, inventory was $580,000.

Required: Determine the following ratios: (*a*) current ratio, (*b*) acid test ratio, (*c*) inventory turnover, (*d*) number of days' sales in accounts receivable, (*e*) equity ratio, and (*f*) turnover of total assets.

7–4. The following information relates to the Reef Company for 1979:

    a. Estimated sales (35% for cash; 65% on credit)

February	$45,000
March	55,000
April	70,000
May	60,000
June	50,000

    b. Collections on credit sales are estimated as follows:

Month of sale	30%
First month following sale	60%
Second month following sale	10%

    c. Estimated net purchases (all on credit)

March	$30,000
April	28,000
May	25,000
June	22,000

    d. Payments for purchases are estimated as follows:

Month of sale	60%
Month following sale	40%

    e. Other estimated monthly cash expenses:

Salaries and wages	$5,000
Insurance	2,000
Administrative	3,000

    f. A large advertising campaign is planned for the second quarter of 1979. The advertising bill for $6,000 must be paid during April.

    g. A dividend payment of $10,000 is scheduled for June 18.

    h. An outstanding loan of $15,000 must be paid during the second quarter of 1979. Payments of $5,000 are to be made each month.

    i. Cash balance, April 1, 1979, $22,000.

Required: Prepare a cash forecast for April, May, and June of 1979. Include a schedule which shows computations for cash receipts and for cash disbursements for purchases.

7–5. Bradford Products, Inc., has a current ratio on December 31, 1979, of 2 to 1. If the following transactions were completed on that date, indicate (a) whether the amount of working capital would have been increased, decreased, or unaffected by each of the transactions; and (b) whether the current ratio would have been increased, decreased, or unaffected by each of the transactions. (Consider each independently of the others.)

    (1) Sold building for cash.

    (2) Exchanged old equipment for new equipment. (No cash was involved.)

    (3) Declared a cash dividend on preferred stock.

    (4) Sold merchandise on account (at a profit).

(5)   Retired mortgage notes which would have matured in 1985.
(6)   Issued stock dividend to common stockholders.
(7)   Paid cash for a patent.
(8)   Temporarily invested cash in government bonds.
(9)   Purchased inventory for cash.
(10) Wrote off an account receivable as uncollectible.
(11) Paid the cash dividend on preferred stock.
(12) Purchased a computer and gave a two-year promissory note, due December 31, 1981.
(13) Collected accounts receivable.
(14) Borrowed from bank on a 120-day promissory note.

7–6. The following information was taken from the statement of financial position of the Kaplan Corporation as of June 30, 1980, and June 30, 1979.

	June 30, 1980	June 30, 1979
Cash	$140,000	$ 52,000
Accounts receivable (net)	180,000	172,000
Inventory	280,000	310,000
Prepaid expenses	20,000	22,000
Land	310,000	310,000
Buildings (net of depreciation)	105,000	110,000
Accounts payable	194,000	138,000
Other accrued liabilities	56,000	62,000
Mortgage bonds payable (due 8/15/88)	140,000	140,000
Common stock (par $50)	500,000	500,000
Paid-in capital in excess of par value	25,000	25,000
Retained earnings	120,000	111,000

Required:

a. Compute the following for each year:
    (1) Working capital.
    (2) Working capital ratio.
    (3) Acid test ratio.
b. Comment on the above analysis as a basis for evaluating Kaplan Corporation's short-run debt-paying ability.

7–7. The following are statements of financial position of the Whitehurst Steel Distributors, Inc., as of August 31, 1980, and August 31, 1979.

WHITEHURST STEEL DISTRIBUTORS, INC.
Statements of Financial Position
August 31, 1980, and August 31, 1979

	August 31, 1980	August 31, 1979
Assets		
Cash....................................	$ 45,000	$ 15,000
Accounts receivable.......................	6,000	9,000
Inventory...............................	33,000	51,000
Plant assets.............................	28,500	30,000
Total Assets.......................	$112,500	$105,000
Liabilities and Stockholders' Equity		
Accounts payable.........................	$ 6,000	$ 6,000
Common stock...........................	60,000	60,000
Retained earnings........................	46,500	39,000
Total Liabilities and Stockholders' Equity	$112,500	$105,000

Required:

a. What were the net earnings for 1980, assuming no dividend payments?

b. What was the primary source of the large increase in the cash balance from 1979 to 1980?

c. What are the two primary sources of assets for Whitehurst Steel Distributors, Inc.?

d. What other comparisons and procedures would you suggest be used in completing the analysis of the statement of financial position begun above?

7–8. The following data are taken from the records of Burton Company:

	December 31, 1980	December 31, 1979
Current liabilities.......................	$ 95,000	$130,000
Long-term liabilities....................	100,000	200,000
Common stock.........................	150,000	100,000
Retained earnings.....................	88,000	65,800

Required:

a. Show the sources of the company's assets in percentages as of both year-end dates.

b. Compute the percentage of stockholders' equity to total assets as of both year-end dates.

c. Comment briefly on the results of your computations.

chapter 8

Appraisal of Earning Power; and Price-Level Accounting

APPRAISING EARNING POWER FROM A TOTAL ENTITY VIEWPOINT

Businesses are formed to generate earnings. But a level of earnings can hardly be viewed in an absolute sense only. The appraisal of earning power involves the relationship between earnings and some investment base. For example, net earnings may be related to net sales or to total assets. A meaningful ratio may be that relating operating earnings to operating assets. One popular ratio expresses net earnings as a percentage of average stockholders' equity.

Net Earnings as a Percentage of Net Sales

Net earnings as a percentage of net sales is obtained by dividing the net earnings for the period by the net sales for the same period:

$$\text{Net Earnings to Net Sales} = \frac{\text{Net Earnings}}{\text{Net Sales}}$$

This ratio measures the proportion of the sales dollar which remains after the deduction of all expenses. For the Knight Corporation the computations are shown in Illustration 8.1 (the financial statements are those presented in Chapter 7).

ILLUSTRATION 8.1

	1980	1979	Amount of Increase
Net earnings (a).....................	$ 58,996	$ 46,535	$ 12,461
Net sales (b).......................	986,388	765,515	220,873
Ratio of net earnings to net sales (a ÷ b)	5.98%	6.08%	

Distorting Factors

Although the ratio of net earnings to net sales indicates the net margin of earnings on each dollar of sales, a great deal of care must be exercised in its use and interpretation. The amount of net earnings is equal to net operating earnings plus nonoperating revenues and less nonoperating expenses and taxes. Thus, it is affected by the methods used to finance the assets of the firm. To illustrate the possible misinterpretation of this ratio, consider Illustration 8.2 which shows the partial earnings statements for the calendar year 1979 for Companies X, Y, and Z, each of which had net sales of $2,000,000.

ILLUSTRATION 8.2

	Company X	Company Y	Company Z
Net operating earnings..................	$436,000	$460,000	$220,000
Interest expense.........................		(60,000)	
Federal income taxes...................	(202,780)	(185,500)	(101,860)
Net earnings before extraordinary item.....	$233,220	$214,500	$118,140
Gain on early retirement of debt.			
(net of tax effect).....................			150,000
Net earnings.........................	$233,220	$214,500	$268,140
Ratio of net earnings to net sales..........	0.117	0.107	.134

Assume that all of the companies used nearly the same amount of assets in 1979. Which company's operations are the most efficient?

Although Company Z has the highest ratio of net earnings to net sales, Company Y is the most efficient company as far as operations are concerned. It is able to earn $460,000 on sales of $2,000,000, which is more than either of the other two companies earned. Illustration 8.2 shows the possible misinterpretation of the net earnings to net sales ratio when assets are financed by interest-bearing debt and when large nonoperating items are involved.

The Determination of Earning Power on Operating Assets

The best measure of earnings performance without regard to the sources of assets is the relationship of net operating earnings to operating assets. Net operating earnings exclude nonoperating revenues (such as extraordinary gains on the early retirement of debt and interest earned on investments), nonoperating expenses (such as interest paid on obligations), and federal income taxes. Operating assets are all assets actively used in producing operating revenue. Examples of excluded (that is, nonoperating) assets are land held for future use, a factory building being rented to someone else, and long-term bond investments.

Elements in Earning Power

There are two elements in the determination of earning power (also referred to as return on operating assets). They are the operating margin and the turnover of operating assets. The operating margin can be expressed in formula form as follows:

$$\text{Net Operating Margin} = \frac{\text{Net Operating Earnings}}{\text{Net Sales}}$$

In Chapter 7 the total assets turnover was discussed and was said to be inadequate as an independent measure of earnings performance. But when slightly changed and used in combination with the net operating margin, it becomes an excellent measure of earnings performance as shown below. If nonoperating assets are excluded (as they should be), this ratio becomes the "turnover of operating assets" represented by the formula:

$$\text{Turnover of Operating Assets} = \frac{\text{Net Sales}}{\text{Operating Assets}}$$

The turnover of operating assets is described as the sales made for each dollar invested in operating assets.

The earning power of a firm is equal to the net operating margin multiplied by the turnover of operating assets. The more a company earns per dollar of sales and the more sales it makes per dollar invested in operating assets, the higher will be the return per dollar invested. Earning power may be expressed by the following formula:

Earning Power = Net Operating Margin × Turnover of Operating Assets

or,

$$\text{Earning Power} = \frac{\text{Net Operating Earnings}}{\text{Net Sales}} \times \frac{\text{Net Sales}}{\text{Operating Assets}}$$

Since the net sales amount appears as both a numerator and a denominator, it can be cancelled out, and the formula for earning power becomes:

$$\text{Earning Power} = \frac{\text{Net Operating Earnings}}{\text{Operating Assets}}$$

But it is more useful for analytical purposes to leave the formula in the form which shows margin and turnover separately.

Securing Desired Earning Power

Companies that are to survive in the economy must attain some minimum degree of earning power. But this minimum can be obtained in many different ways. To illustrate, consider a grocery store and a jewelry store, each with an earning power of 8 percent on operating assets. The grocery store normally would tend to have a low margin and a high turnover while the jewelry store would have a higher margin and a lower turnover:

	Margin	× Turnover	= Earning Power
Grocery store.	2%	× 4.0 times =	8%
Jewelry store.	20%	× 0.4 times =	8%

The earning power figures for the Knight Corporation for 1980 and 1979 are calculated as shown in Illustration 8.3.

ILLUSTRATION 8.3

	1980	1979	Amount of Increase
Net operating earnings (a).	$110,296	$ 81,035	$ 29,261
Net sales (b).	986,388	765,515	220,873
Net operating margin $(a \div b = c)$.	11.18%	10.59%	
Net sales (d).	$986,388	$765,515	$220,873
Total assets (all operating assets) (e).	635,211	551,085	84,126
Turnover of operating assets $(d \div e = f)$	1.55	1.39	
Earning power $(c \times f)$.	17.33%	14.72%	

As was stated earlier, earning power is the best measure of the profitability of the firm without regard to the sources of the assets. It is concerned with the earning power of the company as a bundle of assets not with the determination of which sources of the assets are favored in the division of earnings.

APPRAISING EARNING POWER FROM THE VIEWPOINT OF LONG-TERM SUPPLIERS OF CAPITAL

Net Earnings as a Percentage of Stockholders' Equity

From the stockholders' point of view, an important measure of the earnings-producing ability of a company is the relationship of net earnings to stockholders' equity or the rate of return on stockholders' equity. Stockholders are interested in the ratio of operating earnings to operating assets as a measure of the efficient use of assets. But they are even more interested in knowing what part of the earnings stream generated remains for them after other capital suppliers have been paid for providing capital.

Net earnings as a percentage of stockholders' equity (also called return on owners' investment) is obtained by dividing the net earnings for the period by the total stockholders' equity. For the Knight Corporation, the ratios for 1980 and 1979 are shown in Illustration 8.4.

The use of average total stockholders' equity for the period would have been preferable. It should be noted by reference to the statements of financial position, Illustration 7.1, Chapter 7, that the amount of capital stock increased by $40,000 during the year 1980. If this additional capital stock were issued at any time during 1980 except at the beginning of the year, average stockholders' equity would be smaller and the rate of return on stockholders' investment (net earnings ÷ average stockholders' equity) for 1980 would be higher. In any event the increase in this ratio shown in Illustration 8.4 will be looked upon favorably.

ILLUSTRATION 8.4

	1980	1979	Amount of Increase
Net earnings (a).....................	$ 58,996	$ 46,535	$12,461
Total stockholders' equity (b).........	464,471	380,475	83,996
Ratio of net earnings to stockholders' equity (a ÷ b).....................	12.70%	12.23%	

Influence of Financing Methods and Taxation

The method of financing a business has an impact on the ratio of net earnings to stockholders' equity. Because of differences in the methods of financing a business, two companies with equal rates of earning power on operating assets (and therefore fairly similiar earnings before interest and taxes, assuming insignificant amounts of nonoperating revenues and expenses other than interest on long-term debt) may show different returns on stockholders' equity. To illustrate this, assume companies A and B each have $4,000,000 of total capital. Company A has received all its assets from stockholders, while Company B has received $2,500,000 from stockholders and $1,500,000 (at 8 percent) from long-term creditors. Because of the different long-term methods of financing, the ratios of net earnings to stockholders' equity differ as shown in Illustration 8.5.

The higher ratio of net earnings to stockholders' equity earned by Company B was due to factors other than the efficiency with which assets were employed. It results from the fact that funds were borrowed at an 8 percent rate of interest but after taxes have a net cost to the company of approximately 4 percent, and these funds were put to work earning over 8 percent ($400,000/$4,000,000 = 10 percent). Thus it would be a mistake to say that the management of Company B is a more efficient employer of assets than is the management of Company A.

ILLUSTRATION 8.5

	Company A		Company B	
Assumed earnings before interest				
and taxes.......................		$400,000		$400,000
Less interest (8% on $1,500,000)........		0		120,000
Balance...........................		$400,000		$280,000
Less taxes				
At 20% on first $25,000..............	$ 5,000		$ 5,000	
At 22% on next $25,000.............	5,500		5,500	
At 48% on remainder...............	168,000	178,500	110,400	120,900
Earnings after taxes.................		$221,500		$159,100
Ratio of net earnings to stockholders'				
equity...........................		5.54%		6.36%

Earnings per Share

When preferred stock is outstanding, a portion of the net earnings must be assigned to the preferred stock with the remainder left for the common stock. To determine the rate of earnings (or dollars earned per share) on the common stock, it is necessary to identify the portion of net earnings belonging to the various classes of stock outstanding.

Most preferred stock issues provide for preference over common stock for a specific limited dividend per share with no participation rights beyond this amount. In this case it is necessary to deduct from the net earnings for the period only the annual dividends to which preferred stockholders are entitled. The remainder is then divided by the number of shares of common stock outstanding in order to compute the earnings per share of common stock:

$$\text{Earnings Per Share of Common Stock} = \frac{\text{Earnings Available to Common Shareholders}}{\text{Number of Shares Outstanding}}$$

When extraordinary gains or losses (see Chapter 5) are included in net earnings, Accounting Principles Board *Opinion No. 9* requires that separate per share amounts be shown for net earnings before extraordinary items; for the net amount of the extraordinary items, if any (net of their tax effects); and for net earnings. Thus a company which has suffered a loss on the early retirement of debt might include the following in its earnings statement for the year:

Per share of common stock—	
Net earnings before extraordinary loss...................	$ 2.00
Loss on early retirement of debt, net of tax...............	(0.23)
Net Earnings...	$ 1.77

Annual preferred dividend requirements, if any, must be deducted in computing the $2 as well as the $1.77.

Effect of Stock Splits and Stock Dividends

In comparing earnings per share for successive periods, it is important to note the changes in the number of shares outstanding; otherwise, there is the risk of misinterpreting apparent trends. If additional shares are issued, for example, by means of a stock dividend or a stock split, earnings per share before and after the issue are not comparable without adjustment. A stock dividend consists of the issuance of additional shares of common stock to common stockholders as a dividend. A stock split occurs when a company replaces, say, each of its existing and outstanding shares of $10 par value common stock with two shares of new $5 par value common stock.

A 100 percent stock dividend and a two for one stock split will both double the number of shares of stock outstanding. Earnings of $10 per share before any change in the number of shares are equivalent to $5 per share after either the two for one stock split or the 100 percent stock dividend. In both of these situations, the old shares are simply converted into a larger number of shares. Even if the split or the dividend occurred very late in a given year, the earnings per share for that year would be stated as $5 per share for the year. No attempt is made to average the number of shares outstanding at different times during the year as is often done when additional shares are issued for cash or other property. The reason is that the stock split or the stock dividend is not viewed as being a change in substance. It is simply a division of the stockholders' interest into more pieces.

When comparing earnings per share before and after a stock split, the earnings per share should be adjusted to the same basis. Assume a company reports earnings per share as follows: 1978, $1.00; 1979, $1.25; 1980, $.75. But, a 2 for 1 stock split occurred in 1980. The first two years' figures should be adjusted for the stock split in order to be comparable to the 1980 figure. Thus, earnings per share would be $.50 for 1978 and $.625 for 1979. Then the proper trend can be seen:

Year	Earnings per Share
1978	$.50
1979	.625
1980	.75

Investors often attach great importance to the amount of earnings per share of common stock since it tends to have an effect on the market price of the shares held. It is, therefore, important that consistent methods of accounting be followed from period to period in arriving at and reporting net earnings. Where inconsistencies exist, the effect upon reported earnings should be disclosed.

For the Knight Corporation, which had no preferred stock outstanding in either 1980 or 1979 and no extraordinary items, earnings per share of common stock are computed as shown in Illustration 8.6.

ILLUSTRATION 8.6

	1980	1979	Amount of Increase
Net earnings (a).....................	$58,996	$46,535	$12,461
Average number of shares of common stock outstanding (b)................	22,000	20,000	2,000
Earnings per share of common stock (a ÷ b)...........................	$2.68	$2.33	

Effect of Shares Issued for Assets

In interpreting the above illustration it is important to note that although the Knight Corporation increased its outstanding common stock by 4,000 shares in 1980, the increase in the average number of shares outstanding was only 2,000. The above computation assumes that the 4,000 shares were issued on June 30. Having 4,000 shares outstanding for one-half year is equivalent to having 2,000 shares outstanding during all of the year. Hence, the average number of shares outstanding increased by 2,000.

The treatment here is different from that for stock dividends or stock splits. When new shares are issued for assets, or outstanding shares are reacquired by the company, it is best to compute the average number of shares outstanding during the period. Earnings per share of common stock are then reported on an average basis for the entire year rather than being based on amounts which were true for only a part of the year.

To illustrate, assume that as of January 1, 1979, Barnes Corporation had 100,000 shares of common stock outstanding. On June 30, 1979, it distributed a stock dividend of 10 percent; and on October 1, 1979, it issued 40,000 shares for cash. Earnings available to common stockholders for 1979 amount to $480,000. The average number of shares outstanding is computed as follows:

$$(110,000 \times 9/12) + (150,000 \times 3/12) = 120,000$$

The 10,000 shares issued because of a stock dividend are treated as though they were outstanding for the full year. Thus the computation shows 110,000 shares outstanding for nine months and 150,000 shares outstanding for the last three months.

The earnings per share are:

$$\$480,000 \div 120,000 = \$4$$

Price-Earnings Ratio and Yield on Common Stock

The earnings per share are often compared to the market value of the shares as follows:

$$\frac{\text{Earnings per Share}}{\text{Market Price per Share}} = \text{Earnings Yield (or Earnings Rate) on Market Price}$$

Suppose, for example, that a company had earnings per share of common stock of $2 and that the quoted market price of the stock on the New York Stock Exchange was $30. The earnings yield (or earnings rate) on market price would be:

$$\frac{\$2}{\$30} = 6\tfrac{2}{3} \text{ Percent}$$

This ratio when inverted is called the price-earnings ratio. In the case just cited the price-earnings ratio is:

$$\text{Price-Earnings Ratio} = \frac{\text{Market Price per Share}}{\text{Earnings per Share}} = \frac{\$30}{\$2} = 15 \text{ to } 1$$

Investors would say that this stock is selling at 15 times earnings or at a multiple of 15. They might have a multiple in mind as being the proper one that should be used to judge whether the stock was underpriced or overpriced. Different investors will have different estimates of the proper price-earnings ratio for a given stock and also different estimates of the future earnings prospects of the firm. These are two of the factors which cause one investor to sell stock at a particular price and another investor to buy at that price.

The dividend paid per share of common stock is also of much interest to common stockholders. When the dividend is divided by the market price per share, the result is the "dividend yield."

If the company referred to immediately above paid a $1.50 per share dividend, the dividend yield would be:

$$\text{Dividend Yield} = \frac{\text{Dividend per Share}}{\text{Market Price per Share}} = \frac{\$1.50}{\$30.00} = 5 \text{ Percent}$$

One additional step is to divide the dividend per share by the earnings available per share to determine the "payout ratio" as follows:

$$\text{Payout Ratio} = \frac{\text{Dividend per Share}}{\text{Earnings per Share}} = \frac{\$1.50}{\$2.00} = 75 \text{ Percent}$$

A payout ratio of 75 percent means that the company paid out 75 percent of the earnings per share in the form of dividends. Certain investors are attracted by the stock of companies that usually pay out a large percentage of their earnings while other investors are attracted by the stock of companies which retain and reinvest a large percentage of their earnings. The tax status of the investor, as discussed in Chapter 19, has a great deal to do with this. Investors in very high tax brackets often prefer to have the company reinvest the earnings with the expectation that this will result in share price appreciation which would be taxed at capital gains rates when the shares are sold. Dividends are taxed at ordinary income rates which can be much higher than capital gains rates.

Number of Times Interest Is Earned

Another relationship which focuses attention upon the position of a particular class of investor—in this case, the bondholder—is the ratio of earnings available for bond interest charges to the amount of such charges:

$$\text{Number of Times Interest is Earned} = \frac{\text{Earnings Before Interest and Taxes}}{\text{Interest Expense}}$$

For example, if the amount of earnings before interest and income taxes is $100,000 and the bond interest for the period is $10,000, the ratio is 10 to 1. In such a case the bond interest is said to have been earned 10 times.

Bondholders are interested in knowing whether the company is earning enough so that even if a drop in earnings should occur, it could continue to earn enough to meet its interest payments. It is true that interest must usually be paid regardless of whether earnings are sufficient to cover it. It is also true that a company probably could not continue to pay interest in excess of net earnings before interest and taxes for a long period of time. Thus, the bondholders are interested in knowing the likelihood that they will continue to receive their interest.

The number of times that the present interest is earned is one measure of a company's ability to meet interest payments. And, of course, since bond interest is deductible for income tax purposes, net earnings before bond interest and income taxes is used since there would be no tax if bond interest were equal to or greater than before-interest-and-tax net earnings. If other interest-bearing obligations are outstanding, the ratio is computed using total interest expense.

Number of Times Preferred Dividends Are Earned

Preferred stockholders, like bondholders, must usually be satisfied with a fixed rate of return on their investments. They are interested in the likelihood of the company being able to make preferred dividend payments each year. This can be measured by computing the number of times preferred dividends are earned. It can be computed as follows:

$$\text{Times Preferred Dividends Earned} = \frac{\text{Net Earnings after Income Taxes}}{\text{Preferred Dividends}}$$

Suppose a company has earnings after income taxes of $48,000 and has $100,000 (par value) of 8 percent preferred stock outstanding. The number of times the preferred dividends are earned would be:

$$\frac{\$48,000}{\$8,000} = 6 \text{ times}$$

The higher this rate, the higher is the probability that the preferred stockholders will receive their dividends each year. While the analogy is far from perfect, a finance company would be much more likely to expect to continue to receive payments on a loan from an individual who is earning eight times the required periodic payment than one who is earning only twice the payment.

Yield on Preferred Stock

Preferred stockholders compute yield in a manner similar to the computation of dividend yield for common stockholders. This is possible because preferred stock has no maturity date.

Suppose a company has 2,000 shares of $100 par value, 8 percent preferred stock outstanding which has a current market price of $110 per share. The yield would be computed as follows:

$$\text{Yield} = \frac{\text{Dividend per Share}}{\text{Market Price per Share}} = \frac{\$8}{\$110} = 7.27 \text{ Percent}$$

Through the use of yield rates, different preferred stocks having different annual dividends and different market prices can be compared.

LIMITATIONS OF RATIO ANALYSIS

Ratios Not Infallible Indicators

The techniques for disclosing relationships between financial statement items presented in this chapter and in the preceding chapter by no means constitute a complete collection of such analytical tools. It seems important, before closing the discussion of statement analysis through the use of ratios, to offer certain words of caution. There is some danger that enthusiasm for the techniques of statement analysis in judging a business enterprise has gone too far, at least in some instances. Ratios are not to be regarded as a substitute for judgment; they are merely clues which focus attention on certain relationships, some of which may be worthy of further study.

Ratios which have little or no meaning should be avoided; they are likely to promote confusion rather than understanding. For example, the ratio of plant assets to current liabilities would seem to have little significance.

Need for Comparable Data

Analysts must be sure that their comparisons are valid—whether the comparisons be of items for different periods or dates or for items of different companies. It is essential that consistent accounting practices be followed from period to period if interperiod comparisons are to be made. It is the accountant's duty, of course, to disclose any changes in method or departures from consistent practice, if they are material. Footnotes to financial statements, for example, may be used to reveal the effect of those practices which are not consistent.

Influence of External Factors

Facts and conditions not disclosed by the financial statements may affect the interpretation of the statements. A single event of very great importance to the company may have been largely responsible for a given relationship. For example, a new product may have been suddenly put on the market by a competitor, making it necessary for the company under study to sacrifice its stock of a product abruptly rendered obsolete at very reduced prices. Such an event would affect the percentage of gross margin to net sales severely, yet there may be little or no chance that such an event would happen again, or it may indicate that the company has not been doing enough of its own product development.

The backdrop of general business conditions and conditions within the business or industry of the company under study must be considered. A downward trend in earnings, for example, may be less alarming to a stockholder if it can be established that the trend in the industry or in business in general is also downward rather than limited to the corporation in which an investor holds stock.

Consideration should be given to the possible seasonal nature of the business firm under study. If the statement of financial position date coincides with the seasonal peak in the volume of business, for example, the ratio of current assets to current liabilities may acceptably be much lower than if the statement of financial position date falls in a season of low activity.

Need for Comparative Standards

Relationships between financial statement items become much more meaningful when suitable standards are available for comparison. Comparison with standards provides a starting point for the analysts' thinking and leads them to further study and, ultimately, to conclusions and business decisions. Such standards consist of (1) those which the analysts have in their own minds, as a result of their experience and observation; (2) those provided by the records of past performance and position of the business under study; and (3) those provided by accounting data of other enterprises—for example, data available through trade associations, universities, research organizations, and governmental units.

The Effect of Changes in the General Purchasing Power of the Dollar

One of the most powerful factors influencing the comparability of financial statements in recent years has been the change in the general level of prices or the change in the general purchasing power of the dollar. General purchasing power refers to the ability to buy all goods and services with a specific quantity of money, say, one dollar. Actually, there is an inverse relationship between the general level of prices and the general purchasing power of the dollar. As the price level rises, the general purchasing power of the dollar declines—a situation commonly referred to as inflation. For example, if prices double within a certain period of time the purchasing power of the dollar declines by 50 percent or one-half. Less frequently, the general level of prices declines and the general purchasing power of the dollar increases. That is, if prices decline by 50 percent or one-half, the general purchasing power of the dollar doubles. This situation is usually called deflation. But inflation has generally prevailed in the United States.

When analyzing financial statements for several years, one must keep in mind the impact that inflation has on comparability; otherwise, incorrect conclusions may be drawn. For example, the dollar amount of sales appearing on the earnings statement may have doubled within ten years. But if the firm's selling prices have changed with the general level of prices, which has doubled or tripled within the same ten years, then the physical volume of goods sold has either remained constant or decreased.

General price-level changes affect both the earnings statement (as evidenced by the discussion of sales) and the statement of financial position. Assets purchased in different years and with dollars representing different amounts of general purchasing power are all added together on the statement of financial position. Most of the items appearing on this statement are stated at historical cost. Suppose a company purchased a machine in 1975 for $20,000. Then in 1980, it purchased an identical machine for $30,000. Both of these assets appear on the statement of financial position at historical cost less accumulated depreciation—thus, 1975 dollars are added to 1980 dollars.

It is possible that general purchasing power financial statements will someday be required in the United States.[1] The objectivity of historical cost is maintained in these statements, but general price indexes are used to convert the historical costs to dollars of current purchasing power. It is important for the reader to understand that general purchasing power financial statements do not intend to present replacement costs, appraisal values, or any other current value measurements. The historical costs are

---

[1] There is also a possibility that financial statements containing at least some current value information will be required instead of having purchasing power statements. (The Securities and Exchange Commission requires this in certain reports filed with it.)

simply restated (by means of a price index) in terms of current dollars in order to disclose the effects of changes in the general price level.

Conversion Process

The conversion process is accomplished by (1) multiplying the historical-dollar amount by the price index existing on the date of the latest statement of financial position and (2) dividing the result obtained in step (1) by the price index existing on the date of purchase, incurrence, or issuance. For example, suppose land was purchased for $100,000 when the price index was 105. At December 31, 1980, the price index is 147. The land would appear on the December 31, 1980, price level adjusted statement of financial position at $140,000, computed as follows:

(1) $100,000 × 147 = $14,700,000
(2) $14,700,000 ÷ 105 = $140,000

Monetary and Nonmonetary Items

When preparing general purchasing power financial statements, a distinction must be made between monetary items and nonmonetary items. Monetary items are those assets and liabilities whose dollar amounts are fixed by contract and do not vary with changes in the general price level. They include cash, notes and accounts receivable, notes and accounts payable, accrued receivables and payables, bonds payable, certain prepaid expenses and investments in debt instruments. The common characteristic of monetary items is their claim to a fixed amount of dollars. (Notice that the examples listed include both current and noncurrent assets and liabilities.) All other items are nonmonetary—their values change with changes in the general price level. Inventories, supplies, plant assets, investments in capital stock, capital stock, premium on capital stock (paid-in capital in excess of par value), retained earnings, and intangibles are all nonmonetary items.

Purchasing Power Gains and Losses

Purchasing power gains and losses result from holding monetary items while changes occur in the general price level. During inflation, purchasing power losses result from holding monetary assets and purchasing power gains result from maintaining monetary liabilities. During inflation, each dollar held will buy fewer and fewer goods and services. But, if one pays off a debt after a period of inflation, the dollars paid back are worth less than the dollars borrowed. There has been a purchasing power gain. On the other hand, during deflation, purchasing power gains result from holding monetary assets and purchasing power losses result from having monetary liabilities. Each dollar held will buy more real goods and services.

The Value of General Purchasing Power Financial Statements

In periods of rapid inflation, incorrect conclusions can be drawn from financial statements if general price-level changes are ignored. General purchasing power financial statements emphasize the effects of inflation on financial position and the results of operations. Therefore, when investors analyze financial statements, their attention is directed towards the impact of inflation. They can then evaluate the firm in dollars which represents the same purchasing power. In the case of comparative statements presented for 1979 and 1980, the 1979 statements would be expressed in 1980 dollars. Thus, all figures would represent dollars of equal purchasing power.

SUMMARY

Analysis of comparative earnings statements usually consists of the computation of absolute and percentage changes between years, as well as the presentation of the various items in the earnings statements as percentages of net sales. Attention is usually centered upon changes in net sales, gross margin, operating expenses, net operating earnings, and net earnings.

Appraising earning power generally involves relating earnings to some base—sales, assets, or stockholders' equity. The ratio of net earnings to net sales shows in a final sense what part of each sales dollar a given company was able to earn for its stockholders. But the value of this ratio as an analytical tool is lessened considerably through the inclusion of nonoperating revenues and expenses, extraordinary gains and losses, and federal income taxes. The earning power ratio which relates net operating earnings to net operating assets excludes these distorting factors and is, therefore, the best measure of managerial effectiveness.

The ratio of net earnings to stockholders' equity expresses what a given company was able to earn for its stockholders from all sources as a percentage of the stockholders' investment. This ratio may be affected substantially by the means employed to finance a given company. It should be used with care in comparing two companies that use different financing methods.

The most widely used single statistic regarding a business is probably its earnings per share of common stock. Earnings per share of common stock is often related to the market price of the stock through the price-earnings ratio. This ratio is widely used to indicate whether a stock is relatively expensive or cheap. It also shows, through its reciprocal, the amount a company was able to earn per share as a percentage of the market price of the stock. Thus, a stock with a price-earnings ratio of 20 to 1 earned 5 percent on the market price of its stock.

The dividend yield on a share of common stock is simply its current dividend expressed as a percentage of its current market price, while the payout ratio shows the percentage of current earnings paid out in dividends.

The likelihood that bondholders will continue to receive their periodic interest payments is suggested by the number of times interest is earned. The number of times preferred dividends are earned is computed to indicate the probability that the preferred stockholders will continue to receive their annual dividends.

Ratios should be used with caution and as clues indicating areas requiring further investigation. Ratios should be computed from comparable data if intercompany or interperiod comparisons are to be made. Ratios should be interpreted in the light of known external factors, such as the introduction by a competitor of a superior product. One of the most serious limitations of ratio analysis is the failure to account for changes in the level of prices over a period of years. Since they emphasize the effect of price-level changes on financial position and results of operations, general purchasing power financial statements may be more valuable to an investor than historical-dollar statements in periods of inflation. Historical-dollar statements are converted to general purchasing power financial statements by the use of a general price-level index.

QUESTIONS AND EXERCISES

1. Indicate how each of the following ratios or measures is calculated:
   a. Payout ratio.
   b. Earnings per share of common stock.
   c. Price-earnings ratio.
   d. Earnings yield on common stock.
   e. Yield on preferred stock.
   f. Times interest earned.
   g. Times preferred dividends earned.
   h. Return on stockholders' equity.

2. a. What is the best measure of the profitability of a firm without regard to the sources of the assets?
   b. What is the size of this measure for a company with these statistics:
      (1) Net Sales = $75,000.
      (2) Net Operating Earnings = $12,000.
      (3) Operating Assets = $80,000.
      (4) Other Assets = $15,000.

3. How is earning power on operating assets determined? Is it possible for two companies with "operating margins" of 5 percent and 1 percent, respectively, to both have an earning power of 20 percent on operating assets? How?

4. The Coggins Company had 3,000 shares of $50 par value, 7 percent, preferred stock outstanding. Net earnings after taxes were $42,000. The market price per share was $70.

    a. How many times were the preferred dividends earned?

    b. What was the yield on the preferred stock assuming the regular preferred dividends were declared and paid?

5. The Beaumont Company reports that earnings per share were: 1978, $2.50; 1979, $3.00; and 1980, $2.00. Assume that the company split its stock two for one (in effect gave every stockholder two shares for each share held) in July of 1980. The company made no mention of this in reporting the earnings per share in 1980. Is this misleading? If so, how would you correct the situation?

6. The Sabre Company had 60,000 shares of common stock outstanding on January 1, 1980. On April 1, 1980, the company issued an additional 20,000 shares for cash. The earnings available for common stockholders in 1980 were $141,000. What is the amount the company should report as earnings per share of common stock?

7. Through the use of turnover ratios explain why a firm might seek to increase the volume of its sales even though such an increase can be secured only at reduced prices.

8. Cite some of the possible deficiencies in accounting information especially as regards its use in analyzing a particular company over a 10-year period.

9. a. Using the net earnings to net sales ratio and the data below for Companies X, Y, and Z, determine which company appears to be the most efficient generator of net earnings.

    b. Explain how the computations in part (a) might be misleading.

	Company X	Company Y	Company Z
Net operating earnings............	$ 350,000	$ 300,000	$ 400,000
Interest expense.................	(60,000)		
Federal income taxes.............	(132,700)	(138,000)	(192,000)
Net earnings before extraordinary item........................	$ 157,300	$ 162,000	$ 208,000
Gain on early retirement of debt...		200,000	
Net earnings....................	$ 157,300	$ 362,000	$ 208,000
Net sales......................	$1,500,000	$1,500,000	$1,500,000

10. Distinguish between monetary items and nonmonetary items. Classify the following items as either monetary or nonmonetary:

    (1) Cash   (6) Patents
    (2) Retained Earnings   (7) Common Stock
    (3) Bonds Payable   (8) Land
    (4) Merchandise Inventory   (9) Accounts Payable
    (5) Accounts Receivable   (10) Buildings

11. What are purchasing power gains and losses on monetary items? When do these gains and losses occur?

PROBLEMS

8–1. *Part I:* Refer to the information in Problem 1, Chapter 7, the H. L. Eidson Printing Company, and compute the following ratios for the current situation and indicate what the ratios are expected to be under each of the two financing arrangements.

    a. Earnings per common share.

    b. Rate of return on stockholders' equity.

    Part II: Which method of financing do you think would be better? Give your reasons for the choice, assuming you were the financial vice president of H. L. Eidson Printing Company. Consider the long-term debt to equity ratio.

8–2. Refer to the information in Problem 3, Chapter 7, and compute the following ratios. Show your computations in detail.

    a. Ratio of net earnings to stockholders' equity.

    b. Earnings per share of common stock.

    c. Number of times bond interest is earned.

    d. Ratio of net earnings to total assets.

8–3. The market prices of the preferred and common stock of Alfred's, Inc. have remained relatively stable over the past year at $80 for the preferred and $12 for the common. Other data extracted from the company's financial statements over the past two years, 1979 and 1980, are as follows:

	1979	1980
8% bonds payable...............................	$2,000,000	$2,000,000
6% preferred stock, $100 par value, noncumulative, nonparticipating (assume no change in 1979, change in 1980 occurred on 1/1).........................	500,000	750,000
Common stock, $10 par value (assume no change in 1979 or 1980).................................	2,500,000	2,500,000
Retained earnings (assume zero balance at 1/1/79)......	60,000	140,000
Net earnings after taxes (assume 50% tax rate).........	90,000	190,000
Dividends declared and paid.......................	30,000	110,000

Required:

    a. Using year-end rather than average amounts to simplify computations, compute the following ratios for each year: (1) earnings per share of common stock; (2) number of times bond interest is earned; (3) rate of return on common stockholders' equity; (4) rate of return on total stockholders' equity; (5) price earnings ratio for common stock; (6) yield on preferred stock, (7) earnings yield on common stock; and (8) payout ratio on common stock.

    b. Comment briefly on the results of this ratio analysis.

8–4. In 1980 the Compu-anal-iser Corporation reported $320,000 net operating earnings on $1,100,000 of net sales. An examination of its statement of financial position indicates that total assets of $800,000 are composed of $700,000 of operating assets and $100,000 of other assets.

Required:

a. Compute the net operating margin.
b. Compute the operating asset turnover.
c. What is the earning power of the operating assets?
d. Indicate how each of the following discoveries would affect the earning power calculation made in (c) (consider each independently):
  (1) Accrued administrative expenses of $20,000 were not reflected in the financial statements prepared.
  (2) Ending inventory was understated by $40,000 in the financial statements.
  (3) Accounts receivable were overvalued by $50,000 in the financial statements.
e. Compute the earning power of the operating assets considering the combined effect of all three items under (d).

8–5. The Union Tire Company is considering an expansion program to be financed by the issuance of $500,000 of 8 percent bonds. The company expects that such an expansion would increase earnings before interest and taxes by $90,000. The company has in the recent past been earning a return, before taxes, of 11 percent on stockholders' equity of $1,200,000.

Required:

a. Compute the rate of return on stockholders' equity assuming the expansion program is undertaken as described, that no other capital changes occur, that all company expectations are fulfilled, and that the tax rate is 50 percent.
b. Would you recommend the expansion program under the assumptions of part (a)? Why?

8–6. Martha Johnson is a potential investor involved in making a decision in which of three companies to invest (by buying the company's stock on one of the stock exchanges). The companies' shares are selling at about the same price. The long-term capital structures of each are as follows:

	Company A	Company B	Company C
Bonds with an 8% interest rate.......			$ 500,000
Preferred stock with a 5% dividend rate..............................		$ 500,000	
Common stock, $10 par	$1,000,000	500,000	500,000
Retained earnings..................	80,000	80,000	80,000
Total Long-Term Equity.......	$1,080,000	$1,080,000	$1,080,000
Number of common shares outstanding.......................	100,000	50,000	50,000

One of the advisors at a brokerage house believes that each of the companies will earn $50,000 per year before interest and taxes. Another advisor claims that each of them will earn about $200,000 per year before interest and taxes.

Required: Compute each of the following, assuming first the estimate made by the first advisor is used and then the one made by the second advisor is used:

a. Earnings to common stockholders assuming the first $25,000 of earnings are taxed at 22 percent, the remainder at 48 percent.
b. Earnings per share of common stock outstanding.
c. Rate of return on total stockholders' equity.

Which stock should she select if she believed the first advisor? Which one should she select if she believed the second advisor? Why?

Are the stockholders as a group (common and preferred) better off with or without the use of long-term debt in the above companies?

8–7. The following information was taken from the December 31, 1979 and 1980 statements of financial position for the Hyberger Company.

	1979	1980
8% Mortgage bonds payable	$500,000	$ 500,000
6% Preferred stock, $50 par	400,000	600,000
Common stock, $20 par	800,000	1,000,000
Retained earnings	95,000	140,000

Net earnings after taxes were: 1979, $99,000; 1980, $136,000. Assume a 50 percent tax rate.

Required: Using the information presented above, compute the following for each year:

a. Number of Times Bond Interest Earned
b. Earnings per Share of Common Stock
c. Rate of Return on Common Stockholders' Equity
d. Rate of Return on Total Stockholders' Equity

Reporting Changes in
Financial Position

Users of the conventional financial statements of a company—the earnings statement, the statement of retained earnings, and the statement of financial position—often find that these statements do not readily provide answers to questions they are raising. These questions include: How much working capital was generated by operations? Why is such a profitable firm able to pay only such meager dividends? How much was spent for new plant and equipment and where did the company get the means to purchase it?

The statement which will provide this desired information is called the statement of changes in financial position and is discussed in this chapter. APB *Opinion No. 19,* issued by the Accounting Principles Board, requires that this statement be provided as a basic financial statement for each period for which an earnings statement is presented.[1]

THE STATEMENT OF CHANGES IN FINANCIAL POSITION

Basic Objectives and Content

The broad objectives of the statement of changes in financial position are (1) to summarize the financing and investing activities of the company, including an indication of the amount of working capital provided by operations; and (2) to help explain and disclose the changes in financial position that occurred during the period, such as the conversion of a substantial amount of long-term debt into common stock. The statement is

---

[1] AICPA, *Opinions of the Accounting Principles Board, No. 19,* "Reporting Changes in Financial Position," (New York, March 1971), par. 7.

designed to provide information relating to the management of the financing and investing activities of the company. These activities are a vital part of the successful administration of any company.[2]

Currently, the concepts, terminology, and form of the statement of changes in financial position are in a transitional stage. Accounting Principles Board *Opinion No. 19* permits considerable flexibility in form. The statement of changes in financial position presented in this text will be similar in format and terminology to those widely used in recent practice.

Typically, these statements contain two major sections. One is headed "Financial Resources Provided" and shows the sources of the flows of financial resources (funds) into the company. The other is headed "Financial Resources Applied" and shows how the financial resources flowing into the company were used. (Refer to Illustration 9.5 on page 219 to examine the format of the statement.) In the past such statements often were broadly referred to as funds flow statements and carried the formal titles of "statement of sources and applications of funds" or "statement of sources and uses of funds." Because such statements usually showed the flows of working capital into and out of the firm, an alternative title was "statement of sources and uses of working capital." Following the definite preference expressed by the Board in APB *Opinion No. 19,* this text will use the title "statement of changes in financial position."

Uses of the Statement of Changes in Financial Position

The information contained in the statement of changes in financial position is useful to many parties for a variety of reasons.

Management Uses.   The information may cause management to change its dividend policy in order to conserve working capital. Or, management may decide that in light of the working capital generated by operations, a certain amount can be safely invested in plant and equipment. Or, the information may clearly reveal the need for additional financing to take advantage of capital expenditure opportunities that seem highly profitable. And the statement highlights the all-important relationship between working capital generated by operations and all other sources and uses of working capital, and financial resources provided and applied which did not affect working capital.

Creditor and Investor Uses.   Information contained in the statement of changes in financial position may be used by both creditors and investors. These groups make decisions on whether to invest (or disinvest) in the debt or equity securities issued by a given company. *Projections* of such

---

[2] The statement of changes in financial position may highlight the amount of cash provided by operations and still be in accord with APB *Opinion No. 19.* Current practice, however, tends heavily to emphasize working capital from operations and our illustrations and discussion will follow this practice.

information can provide valuable insights into such matters as (1) whether dividends are likely to be increased; (2) how future capital expenditures are likely to be financed; and (3) whether a firm appears capable of meeting its debts as they come due. Typically, projections of the future are based upon study of the immediate past.

Preparing the Statement of Changes in Financial Position

Illustration 9.1 shows the financial resources provided (inflows) and the financial resources applied (outflows) which are reported in the statement of changes in financial position. A careful study of this illustration should be helpful in understanding the concepts presented in the remainder of the chapter.

ILLUSTRATION 9.1

Graphic Illustration of Flows Represented in the Statement
of Changes in Financial Position

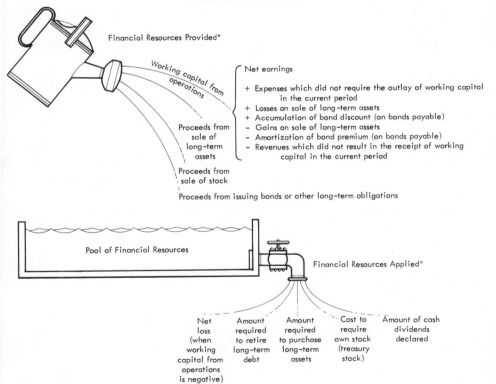

* If Financial Resources Provided exceeds Financial Resources Applied there is an increase in working capital, and vice versa. While financial resources provided and applied which did not affect working capital are included, the amounts offset each other.

Working Capital from Operations. The amount of working capital generated by operations has long been recognized as one of the most important single figures that can be determined for most businesses. Over the long run, a successful business will acquire plant and other assets, retire long-term debt, and pay dividends largely from working capital from operations. Revenue-producing activities associated with service to customers generate this working capital.

Typically, the measurement of working capital from operations begins with net earnings. This follows because sales of goods and services bring new current assets into the business, usually cash or receivables. Expenses for the most part decrease working capital, either through decreases in current assets or increases in current liabilities. But because of the inclusion of expenses which do not require the use of working capital, (e.g., depreciation) net earnings are not likely to measure the exact amount of working capital generated by operations. Adjustments must be made for revenues not producing working capital and expenses not consuming working capital.

The following illustration is presented to explain the adjustment needed when net earnings contain an expense not requiring working capital:

Sales (represented by receipts of cash and receivables)......		$230,000
Operating expenses consuming working capital (represented by credits to current asset or current liability accounts)...	$180,000	
Depreciation (recorded by credits to allowance for depreciation accounts, which are related to plant assets and are *not* current assets or current liabilities).............	12,000	192,000
Net Earnings..		$ 38,000

The parenthetical expressions above indicate that one item in the earnings statement data presented—depreciation—does not result in either an increase or decrease in working capital. Unlike most expenses, depreciation does not decrease current assets or increase current liabilities. Since this is true, it follows that the amount of working capital generated by operations is not $38,000 (the net earnings amount) but $50,000. This amount is computed as follows:

Working capital from sales...............................	$230,000
Working capital consumed by expenses....................	180,000
Working capital from operations.........................	$ 50,000

A more common way of showing the working capital generated by operations in the statement of changes in financial position is as follows:

Working capital provided by operations	
Net earnings..	$38,000
Add: Expenses not requiring the outlay of working capital in the current period—depreciation....................	12,000
Working capital from operations.........................	$50,000

Because the purpose of the statement of changes in financial position is to show gross flows rather than simply net changes, the first method of reporting has considerable merit. But the second method is almost universally employed because it is easily tied into net earnings reported in the earnings statement.

Depreciation is only one example of an expense that does not require working capital. Others are the amortization of patents, leases, and leaseholds, and the recording of depletion expense. In fact, adjustment is required for any expense that is recorded by a debit to an expense account and a credit to a long-term asset account. The asset account may be credited directly or by means of a credit to a contra account (e.g., Allowance for Depreciation).

The periodic amortization of recorded amounts of bond premium or bond discount also affects net earnings through its effect on interest expense. The following situation illustrates the premium case. Assume that a company received $102,000 for $100,000 face value, of 20-year, 9 percent, semiannual interest-bearing bonds ($4,500 of interest is paid each six months). The amount received in excess of the face value of the bonds is called a premium and is credited to Premium on Bonds Payable. The credit balance in this account is reported in the statement of financial position as an addition to Bonds Payable (a long-term liability). Since the premium is not paid back to investors at maturity date, it serves to reduce the interest cost on the bonds to less than 9 percent per year. The annual interest expense is determined as follows:

Total interest to be paid in cash ($100,000 × 0.09 × 20 years)..	$180,000
Less premium received on issuance......................	2,000
Total net interest cost....................................	$178,000
Cost per year (divide by 20).............................	$ 8,900

An entry would be made annually debiting Premium on Bonds Payable and crediting Interest Expense for $100. The interest actually paid would be recorded by a debit to Interest Expense and a credit to either Cash or Accrued Interest Payable, both elements of working capital, for a total of $9,000 per year.

The amount of interest expense deducted in arriving at net earnings is $8,900, whereas the decrease in working capital is $9,000. Net earnings will overstate the working capital from operations by this $100 difference. The $100 of bond premium amortized must therefore be deducted in order to convert net earnings to working capital provided by operations.

When bonds are issued at a discount (at an amount less than face value) the discount is also allocated over the life of the bonds. This amount is an addition to, rather than a deduction from, the amount of interest paid currently. The amount of expense recorded is therefore larger than the drain on working capital. The discount must be added to net earnings to convert it to a measure of working capital from operations.

Whether or not operations produce or consume working capital in a firm operating at a net loss depends upon the size of the items included in determining the net loss that did not require or produce working capital. For example, if a company reports a net loss of $50,000 occurring after deducting $80,000 of depreciation, then $30,000 of working capital was provided by operations. But if a loss of $50,000 is shown with only $15,000 of depreciation deducted, then operations have consumed rather than provided $35,000 of working capital. Typically, the $35,000 is reported as an application of working capital.

Other Significant Financing and Investing Activities

In addition to reporting the working capital provided by operations, the statement of changes in financial position should clearly disclose:

1. The use of working capital to acquire long-term assets—investments; property, plant, and equipment; and intangibles.
2. The other sources of working capital such as the sale of noncurrent assets and the issuance of long-term debt or shares of stock.
3. The use of working capital to pay dividends to stockholders.
4. All changes of a significant financial or investment nature which do not involve the use of working capital. Examples of these are the conversion of long-term debt or preferred stock into common stock and the issuance of long-term debt or preferred or common stock for noncurrent assets.

Changes in items reported in the statement of financial position which do not constitute significant investment or financial activity do not have to be reported in the statement of changes in financial position. Examples here are stock dividends and stock splits.

THE SCHEDULE OF CHANGES IN WORKING CAPITAL

In APB *Opinion No. 19,* the Board stated that a statement or schedule showing the details making up the net change in working capital should be presented when a statement of changes in financial position is presented. Such a schedule is shown in Illustration 9.4.

THE STATEMENT OF CHANGES IN FINANCIAL POSITION ILLUSTRATED

The following extended illustration is based upon the assumption that the accountant has prepared the basic financial statements for The Standard Corporation (see Illustrations 9.2 and 9.3) and is now turning to the statement of changes in financial position. Additional information

ILLUSTRATION 9.2

THE STANDARD CORPORATION
Statement of Earnings and Retained Earnings
For the Year Ended December 31, 1979

Gross sales..		$1,475,000
Less: Sales returns and allowances..................		10,800
Net sales..		$1,464,200
Cost of goods sold		
Inventories, January 1............................	$115,300	
Net purchases....................................	883,450	
Cost of goods available for sale................	$998,750	
Inventories, December 31.........................	127,600	
Cost of goods sold.............................		871,150
Gross margin.......................................		$ 593,050
Less: Operating expenses		
Bad debts expense..............................	$ 7,320	
Depreciation expense...........................	34,300	
Salaries..	215,000	
Sundry selling expenses........................	90,000	
Taxes, payroll, and other.......................	26,000	
General administrative expenses..................	123,780	
Total Operating Expenses......................		496,400
Net earnings from operations.......................		$ 96,650
Other revenue		
Interest earned.................................	$ 1,950	
Gain on sale of long-term investments.............	1,700	3,650
		$ 100,300
Other expense		
Interest expense................................	$ 3,800	
Loss on sale of equipment........................	900	4,700
Net earnings before federal income taxes..............		$ 95,600
Deduct: Federal income taxes......................		45,250
Net earnings to retained earnings.....................		$ 50,350
Retained earnings, January 1.......................		84,100
		$ 134,450
Deduct: Dividends declared........................		18,000
Retained Earnings, December 31.....................		$ 116,450

of the type needed will be provided as required in order to illustrate the type of analyses undertaken in the preparation of the statement of changes in financial position.

The comparative statements of financial position in Illustration 9.3 have already been expanded to include a column showing the net increase or decrease in each item between December 31, 1978, and December 31, 1979. From the increase-decrease column it is a simple matter to prepare the comparative schedule of working capital shown in Illustration 9.4. Each of the current assets and current liabilities is listed along with its balance, the change in its balance, and its effect on working capital.

Each increase in a current asset results in an increase in working capital, as, for example, the $5,400 increase in cash. Similarly, a net decrease in

ILLUSTRATION 9.3

THE STANDARD CORPORATION
Comparative Statement of Financial Position
December 31, 1978 and 1979

	1979	1978	Increase Decrease*
Assets			
Current Assets:			
Cash	$ 46,300	$ 40,900	$ 5,400
Accounts receivable	119,980	107,000	12,980
Allowance for doubtful accounts	(7,820)	(6,000)	(1,820)
Marketable securities	3,000	–0–	3,000
Inventories	127,600	115,300	12,300
Prepaid expenses	3,100	4,700	1,600*
Total Current Assets	$292,160	$261,900	$30,260
Investments	$ 17,000	$ 25,000	$ 8,000*
Property, Plant, and Equipment:			
Land	$100,000	$ 80,000	$20,000
Buildings	175,000	130,000	45,000
Allowance for depreciation—buildings	(29,750)	(26,500)	(3,250)
Equipment	198,000	175,000	23,000
Allowance for depreciation—equipment	(57,650)	(43,100)	(14,550)
Total Property, Plant, and Equipment	$385,600	$315,400	$70,200
Total Assets	$694,760	$602,300	$92,460
Liabilities and Stockholders' Equity			
Current Liabilities:			
Accounts payable	$ 74,620	$ 64,900	$ 9,720
Notes payable	15,000	20,000	5,000*
Advances from customers	1,000	900	100
Accrued interest payable	800	1,070	270*
Other accrued liabilities	9,890	12,230	2,340*
Estimated federal income tax liability	12,000	14,100	2,100*
Total Current Liabilities	$113,310	$113,200	$ 110
Long-Term Liabilities:			
Mortgage note payable, 9 percent (on land and buildings)	$ 35,000	$ –0–	$35,000
Bonds payable, 9% due 1983	40,000	40,000	–0–
Total Long-Term Liabilities	$ 75,000	$ 40,000	$35,000
Total Liabilities	$188,310	$153,200	$35,110
Stockholders' Equity:			
Common stock, stated value $50	$390,000	$365,000	$25,000
Retained earnings	116,450	84,100	32,350
Total Stockholders' Equity	$506,450	$449,100	$57,350
Total Liabilities and Stockholders' Equity	$694,760	$602,300	$92,460

ILLUSTRATION 9.4

THE STANDARD CORPORATION
Comparative Schedule of Working Capital
December 31, 1978 and 1979

	December 31		Working Capital	
	1979	1978	Increase	Decrease
Current Assets:				
Cash................................	$ 46,300	$ 40,900	$ 5,400	
Accounts receivable....................	119,980	107,000	12,980	
Allowance for doubtful accounts.........	(7,820)	(6,000)	(1,820)	
Marketable securities...................	3,000	–0–	3,000	
Inventories...........................	127,600	115,300	12,300	
Prepaid expenses.......................	3,100	4,700		$ 1,600
Total Current Assets.............	$292,160	$261,900		
Current Liabilities:				
Accounts payable.....................	$ 74,620	$ 64,900		9,720
Notes payable........................	15,000	20,000	5,000	
Advances from customers..............	1,000	900		100
Accrued interest payable...............	800	1,070	270	
Other accrued liabilities................	9,890	12,230	2,340	
Estimated federal income tax liability.....	12,000	14,100	2,100	
Total Current Liabilities..........	$113,310	$113,200		
Working Capital......................	$178,850	$148,700		
Net increase in working capital..........				30,150
			$41,570	$41,570

any current asset results in a decrease in working capital. Conversely, increases in current liability accounts represent decreases in working capital (accounts payable, for example). Likewise, decreases in current liability accounts represent increases in working capital.

The schedule of changes in working capital as shown in Illustration 9.4 shows the changes in the elements of the working capital of The Standard Corporation. But it does not explain what caused the $30,150 net increase in working capital. One of the purposes of the statement of changes in financial position is to indicate these causes. As the analysis below explains, these causes lie primarily in the changes in the noncurrent accounts shown in the comparative statements of financial position. Bear in mind that the effect of net earnings and dividends is reported in retained earnings.

Adjustment of Net Earnings to Working Capital
Provided by Operations

Operations are a major source of working capital for most corporations, and modern financial analysis tends to highlight this source. Thus, a logical starting point in preparing the statement of changes in financial position is to convert reported net earnings to working capital provided by operations. As already noted, most of the items reported in the earnings statement either decrease or increase working capital. Depreciation is the most common item included in net earnings which does not either increase or decrease working capital. In the earnings statement in Illustration 9.2, $34,300 of depreciation was deducted in arriving at net earnings of $50,350. Thus, to arrive at the effect of operations on working capital, the $34,300 must be added back to net earnings. Because the loss on sale of equipment of $900 does not consume working capital but is similar to depreciation in that both are write-offs of part of the cost of a plant asset, it is added back to net earnings. (The details of this transaction will be provided later. It is sufficient for now to note the similarity of the loss to depreciation.) In fact, working capital is increased by the amount of proceeds realized from the sale of the equipment. Since the loss is not a part of operations and did not consume working capital, it is added back to net earnings.

A third adjustment is required to convert net earnings to working capital provided by operations; this time for a different reason. The comparative statement of financial position shows a decrease in investments of $8,000, while the earnings statement shows a gain from the sale of investments of $1,700. From this it follows that the investments were sold for $9,700. This is the amount that will be shown in the statement of changes in financial position as the working capital provided by the sale of the investments. But note that if the $1,700 gain is included in working capital provided by operations *and* in working capital provided by the sale of investments, it is counted twice. Since, technically, the sale of investments is not a part of operations, the preferred procedure is to deduct any gain from such sales from net earnings to arrive at working capital from operations. (Losses, of course, would be added back.) With these adjustments, the working capital provided by operations amounts to $83,850 and would be shown in the statement of changes in financial position as follows:

Working Capital Provided:
From operations:

Net earnings...............................		$50,350
Add: Expenses not requiring outlay of working capital in the current period:		
Depreciation..........................	$34,300	
Loss on sale of equipment..............	900	35,200
		$85,550
Less: Gain on sale of investments.............		1,700
Working capital provided by operations...		$83,850

Note carefully that the treatment accorded losses in the statement of changes in financial position depends upon the nature of the item causing the loss. If, for example, the loss in the above illustration had resulted from the sale of a current asset, such as temporary investments, and the loss was included in the determination of net earnings, no adjustment to net earnings would be required in deriving working capital provided by operations. The loss on the sale of a current asset is a loss that reduces working capital. The sale of part of a temporary investment in marketable securities having a cost of $2,000 for $1,800 cash reduces working capital by $200. Thus, if the loss is included in the determination of net earnings, as it should be, no adjustment is needed.

Analysis of Changes in Noncurrent Accounts

One of the items to be reported in the statement of changes in financial position is the net change in working capital. Consequently, once the change in working capital has been determined (see Illustration 9.4), no further attention need be paid to the individual components of working capital—cash, accounts receivable, accounts payable, and so forth. The changes in all of these accounts are summarized and reported as one amount. Thus, in our analysis of changes in financial position, we need not concern ourselves with whether cash increased or decreased when we analyze the changes in the noncurrent accounts. All that we need to know is whether the change affected working capital or was part of a significant financing or investing transaction. If so, it must be reported in the statement of changes in financial position.

The changes which we must analyze to see whether they should be so reported are summarized below. They consist of all of the changes shown in the noncurrent accounts in the comparative statements of financial position for December 31, 1978, and December 31, 1979.

	Increase	Decrease
Investments...............................		$8,000
Land....................................	$20,000	
Buildings...............................	45,000	
Allowance for depreciation of buildings.......	3,250	
Equipment...............................	23,000	
Allowance for depreciation of equipment......	14,550	
Mortgage note payable.....................	35,000	
Common stock, stated value, $50 per share....	25,000	
Retained earnings.........................	32,350	

Let us assume that the following information also is available:

1. There were no purchases of investments during the year. Investments with a cost of $8,000 were sold for $9,700.
2. One transaction took place in which land and buildings valued at $65,000 were acquired, subject to a 9 percent mortgage note of $35,000 on the buildings.

3. During the year the corporation disposed of equipment which had an original cost of $20,000 and which had been depreciated to the extent of $16,500 at date of sale.
4. All of the common stock was issued for cash.

We are now prepared to analyze each of the above changes in the noncurrent accounts to see if it affected working capital or was part of a significant investing or financing transaction. Changes of either type must be reported in the statement of changes in financial position.

Investments. We have already indicated that the gain on the sale of investments must be deducted from net earnings to show the entire amount received from the sale as a source of working capital. We know that the $8,000 change in investments actually produced $9,700 of working capital. The statement of changes in financial position would show:

> Other sources of working capital:
> Sale of investments................................... $9,700

Land and Buildings. The increases in the land and buildings accounts were the result of a single transaction. The acquisition of these long-term assets was financed in part by an increase in a long-term debt, the mortgage note of $35,000, and in part by the use of working capital. The acquisition of these assets would be reported in the statement of changes in financial position as follows:

> Working capital applied:
> Land... $20,000
> Building...   10,000
>
> Financial resources applied which did not affect working capital:
> Building acquired by assuming the liability on a
> mortgage note...................................... $35,000

The assumption of liability on the mortgage note would be reported:

> Financial resources provided which did not affect working capital:
> Assumption of liability on mortgage note to acquire
> building... $35,000

Before the issuance of Accounting Principles Board *Opinion No. 19,* it was not uncommon to report only the $30,000 effect on working capital of transactions such as the above as an element of funds applied. Such a procedure is now considered deficient. The merger wave of the 1960s showed very clearly that a company could engage in highly significant transactions which do not affect working capital. It could, for example, double the amount of assets owned by issuing common stock for plant and equipment. Consequently, under APB *Opinion No. 19,* a transaction involving a change in a noncurrent asset and a noncurrent equity must be reported as both a provision of financial resources and an application of financial resources. Similarly, exchanges of one type of noncurrent asset for another and one type of noncurrent equity for another must also be reported in both financial resources provided and financial resources applied. Stock dividends and stock splits are exceptions.

Equipment. The Equipment account shows a net increase of $23,000 in spite of the fact that some equipment was sold during the year. The net change in this account must be analyzed further to allow the reporting of the working capital provided and applied. The amount shown under "Other sources of working capital" from the sale of the equipment is the amount received at time of sale, computed as follows:

Cost of equipment sold....................................	$20,000
Less: Allowance for depreciation..........................	16,500
Book value of equipment sold.............................	$ 3,500
Less: Loss on sale of equipment (from earnings statement)......	900
Working capital received (sales price of the equipment).........	$ 2,600

The cost of the additional equipment acquired during the year must have exceeded $23,000 (the net increase in that account) by an amount equal to the cost of the equipment sold, which was credited to the account. Thus, the statement of changes in financial position would show working capital applied to purchase of equipment of $43,000, computed as follows:

Cost of equipment sold (credited to equipment account)........	$20,000
Net increase in equipment account (debit increase)............	23,000
Working capital applied to purchase equipment..............	$43,000

The equipment account must have been debited for purchases of equipment amounting to $43,000 if the account increased $23,000 in spite of a $20,000 credit to the account.

Allowance for Depreciation. The $17,800 net increase in the two allowance for depreciation accounts ($3,250 for buildings plus $14,550 for equipment) is the result of the credits from recording the depreciation charges for the year ($34,300) and the debit entered to remove the $16,500 applicable to the equipment sold. The effect of the change in these two accounts on working capital has already been explained in the adjustment of net earnings and in the treatment of the equipment sold.

Mortgage Note Payable. The manner in which the change in the Mortgage Note Payable account will appear in the statement of changes in financial position has already been presented.

Common Stock. Since $25,000 of stated value common stock was issued for $25,000 cash, the statement of changes in financial position would show working capital provided by the issuance of common stock of $25,000. Had the stock been issued at an amount greater than stated value, the excess would appear as an increase in a separate stockholders' equity account. But the statement of changes in financial position would simply show the total amount received under "Other sources of working capital."

Retained Earnings.   The statement of retained earnings and the earnings statement reveal that net earnings for 1979 amounted to $50,350 and that dividends declared during the year amounted to $18,000. The difference between these two figures fully explains the $32,350 net increase in retained earnings. The net earnings amount has already been included as a source of working capital from operations. The dividends of $18,000 represent an application of working capital, since they reduced working capital by $18,000 at the time of declaration (the creation of the current liability account, Dividends Payable, reduced working capital).

Had the Retained Earnings account changed for any other reason, the cause of the change must be determined in order to decide whether it should be reported in the statement of changes in financial position. The transfer of an amount from one stockholders' equity account to another does not affect working capital and usually is not a transaction possessing investment or financial significance. Such transactions would not be reflected in the statement of changes in financial position.[3]

The Statement of Changes in Financial Position Illustrated

All available information relating to working capital, the changes in working capital, and other significant financing and investing activities during 1979 has now been examined and analyzed, making possible the presentation of the statement of changes in financial position shown in Illustration 9.5. This statement shows that of the total financial resources provided over one half consisted of working capital provided by operations. The working capital provided by operations was adequate not only to cover the dividends for the year but also to finance approximately one half of the expansion in assets, including the increase in working capital. This latter increase may very well be a permanent increase necessary to support the corporation's expanded level of business activity.

If the statement in Illustration 9.5 and a request for a $250,000, five-year loan were presented to The Standard Corporation's banker, the banker would be quick to note that the company apparently has the ability to pay off the loan in approximately three years by using the working capital provided by operations. The banker would also note that the company keeps dividends well under the amount of working capital generated by operations.

Note that in the statement of Illustration 9.5, the increase in working capital agrees with the change in working capital shown in Illustration 9.4.

See the Appendix on page 222 for a precise methodology for identifying

---

[3] Such a transfer that does represent a significant financial transaction should be reported. An example would be the conversion of preferred stock into common stock (see paragraph 8 of APB *Opinion No. 19* of the Accounting Principles Board).

ILLUSTRATION 9.5

THE STANDARD CORPORATION
Statement of Changes in Financial Position
For the Year Ended December 31, 1979

Financial resources provided:

Working capital provided:

By operations:

Net earnings...............................		$50,350	
Add: Expenses not requiring outlay of working capital in current period:			
Depreciation............................	$34,300		
Loss on sale of equipment.................	900	35,200	
		$85,550	
Deduct: Gain on sale of investments..............		1,700	
Working capital provided by operations...............			$ 83,850
Other sources of working capital:			
Sale of investments............................			9,700
Sale of equipment..............................			2,600
Issuance of common stock.......................			25,000
Total working capital provided................			$121,150
Financial resources provided which did not affect working capital:			
Assumption of liability on mortgage note to acquire building..............................			35,000
Total financial resources provided.....................			$156,150

Financial resources applied:

Working capital applied:

Acquisition of land..............................			$ 20,000
Acquisition of building...........................			10,000
Acquisition of equipment.........................			43,000
Payment of dividends............................			18,000
Total working capital applied..................			$ 91,000
Financial resources applied which did not affect working capital:			
Building acquired by assuming the liability on a mortgage note.........................			35,000
Total financial resources applied.....................			$126,000
Increase in working capital..........................			30,150
Total...			$156,150

the amounts to be reported in the statement of changes in financial position. It is called the T-account method.

Statement of Changes in Financial Position Which Emphasizes Cash Flow

The statement of changes in financial position may emphasize cash provided from or used in operations rather than working capital.[4] If so, the

---

[4] It may alternatively emphasize cash and temporary investments combined or all quick assets (see paragraph 11 of APB *Opinion 19*). But statements with this format are so rare that we will ignore them in our discussion.

changes in other elements of working capital (all other current assets and the current liabilities) should be shown as sources or uses of cash in the statement.

As when the working capital concept was emphasized, the effects of other financing and investing activities should also be shown separately in such a statement of changes in financial position.

This form of the statement of changes in financial position is ideally suited to an entity which does not distinguish between current and non-current liabilities (such firms are relatively rare) but may be used by any entity which believes this format will be the most informative in its circumstances. Since it is seldom used in practice, illustration of this form will be left to textbooks designed for more advanced courses. Thus, when we are discussing the statement of changes in financial position we will be using the working capital format.

CASH FLOW AND FINANCIAL ANALYSIS

Currently, business periodicals and other literature often refer to an amount described as "cash flow." The amount presented usually is computed by adding to net earnings the depreciation (and possibly other expenses not requiring working capital) of the period. This cash flow amount often is divided by the number of shares outstanding and its per share amount compared with earnings per share. Some analysts and investment services draw specific attention to this comparison in their discussions of the relative merits of various issues of common stock as investment media.

Cash Flow—A Misnomer

But cash flow computed in this manner is really a misnomer since it does not measure the actual flow of cash into a company either from its operations or in total, except by accident. Many adjustments must be made to convert net earnings to cash flow from operations. For example, cash received from customers may be larger or smaller than net sales depending upon whether accounts receivable increased or decreased from the beginning to the end of the year. Cost of goods sold may differ sharply from purchases if inventories are reduced. And purchases may differ from cash paid to suppliers if accounts payable increased or decreased during the year. Many other expenses may be recognized in amounts different from the amount of cash paid out relative to the expense simply because of changes in prepaid expense or accrued liabilities.

Actually, cash flow computed in this simplified manner may, in some instances, yield a significant amount because it is a fair approximation of the working capital provided by operations. Unfortunately, the use of the term "cash flow" is quite misleading. Working capital, not cash, is involved; and a company's working capital may consist largely of accounts receivable and inventories but very little cash. Even if net earnings plus depreciation does measure cash flow into an enterprise, emphasis only upon cash flow *in* can be misleading. It fails to give recognition to the many possible uses of cash, especially for replacement of depreciable assets consumed in generating the cash flow from operations.

Cash Flow and Net Earnings. A more serious matter is the conceptual flaw in designating a sum consisting of net earnings and depreciation as cash earnings or implying that cash flow is a better measure of profitability than is net earnings. The increasing employment of depreciable assets makes it inappropriate to designate any amount as earnings that does not include a charge for the use of such assets. The accrual system of accounting was developed to provide a more meaningful and representative measure of periodic profitability than can be obtained from the difference between cash receipts and cash disbursements. Analysis of such receipts and disbursements may yield important information for specific purposes, such as cash forecasting. Reliance on a "cash earnings" amount for evaluation of an enterprise's well-being, however, represents a regression to cash basis accounting. Earnings per share still provides a better measure of profitability than does a "cash flow" amount.

SUMMARY

The statement of changes in financial position has increased in importance in recent years and is now required for each period for which an earnings statement is presented. The statement is designed to provide information relating to the financing and investing activities of a firm. As such, the statement shows the sources and uses of working capital during the period, and all other significant financial or investment changes that took place during the period. The main items presented are (1) the amount of working capital generated through operations; (2) the other sources of working capital; (3) financial resources provided which did not affect working capital; (4) working capital applied; and (5) financial resources applied which did not affect working capital.

Current practice emphasizes the *changes in working capital* as the basic element of the statement. Preparation begins by identifying the total change in working capital. Net operating earnings are a source of working capital. But the earnings must be adjusted for certain expenses, such as depreciation, that do not have an effect on working capital. Likewise they must be adjusted for gains and losses on asset disposals, the net proceeds of which are reported elsewhere in the statement. In addition to changes in working capital, APB *Opinion No. 19* requires disclosure of all other changes which are of a significant financial or investment nature. The Appendix to this chapter provides an illustration of a method that is helpful in preparing this statement.

The statement of changes in financial position may emphasize cash provided from or used in operations rather than working capital. Under this format all changes in other current assets and in current liabilities are shown as sources or uses of cash. Significant financing and investing activities not involving cash are also included.

Often, financial analysts will draw attention to the cash flow of the firm computed by adding depreciation to the net earnings of the period. Such a concept is a misnomer as it does not fully recognize all the cash changes during a period. Conceptually, it may wrongly imply that cash flow is a better measure of profitability than is net earnings. This can be particularly misleading where large amounts of depreciable assets are employed. Net earnings under the accrual method of accounting provide the better measure of a firm's profitability.

APPENDIX

The purpose of this Appendix is to provide a precise methodology for discovering the amount of working capital provided by operations and the amounts of other financing and investing activities. As already illustrated, the preparation of a statement of changes in financial position consists of a careful analysis of all of the changes in the noncurrent accounts. Consequently, we will first establish T-accounts for all noncurrent accounts and record in these accounts the change in each over the period. The Standard Corporation's Land account is shown as an example:

Land

20,000	

We also will set up a T-account for Working Capital from Operations to help us analyze earnings statement data to derive this amount. And we will use one account, really a master account, titled Financial Resources Provided and Applied which will, when completed, contain virtually all of the data needed for the statement of changes in financial position. In this account we will record the change in working capital for the period in the same manner as we have for land as shown above. The complete procedure is illustrated below using The Standard Corporation data presented and analyzed earlier in this chapter.

The Methodology Illustrated

The complete set of T-accounts needed to analyze the activities of The Standard Corporation for the year ended December 31, 1979, is presented on page 224–25. Each entry is keyed with a number and is discussed below.

We will start with data taken from the earnings statement. Entry 1 involves a debit to Working Capital from Operations and a credit to Retained Earnings. The reason for recording in this manner is that from a statement of financial position point of view, net earnings serve to increase retained earnings and working capital.

Entry 2 consists of a debit to Working Capital from Operations and a credit to a combined Allowances for Depreciation—Buildings and Equipment. Since the amount of depreciation expense recorded was not classified as between buildings and equipment, we simply combined the two allowance accounts. Recall that depreciation is an expense deducted in arriving at net earnings that does not reduce working capital. The amount of working capital from operations is larger than the amount of net earnings reported because depreciation was recorded.

Entry 3 consists of a debit to Financial Resources Provided and Applied of $2,600, a debit to Working Capital from Operations of $900, a debit to Allowances for Depreciation—Buildings and Equipment of $16,500, and a credit to Equipment of $20,000. Equipment costing $20,000 and on which $16,500 of depreciation had been recorded was sold for $2,600, that is, at a loss of $900. The $2,600 must be recorded as working capital provided. The $900 is added to Working Capital from Operations because it did not reduce working capital from that source but did reduce net earnings—our initial measure of working capital from operations. Like depreciation, it is not a working capital item.

Continuing our analysis of earnings statement and retained earnings statement data, we come to dividends. As shown in Entry 4, these are recorded as a debit to Retained Earnings of $18,000 and as a credit to Financial Resources Provided and Applied of a similar amount. As we have already noted, the declaration of cash dividends reduces working capital and retained earnings.

Turning next to the noncurrent accounts, we note that a net decrease of $8,000 occurred in the Investments account resulting, according to the additional data, from the sale of investments for $9,700. Entry 5 properly records this transaction in our T-accounts as a debit to Financial Resources Provided and Applied of $9,700, a credit to Investments of $8,000, and a credit to Working Capital from Operations of $1,700. As previously discussed, this latter credit is needed to remove working capital provided by the sale of investments from Working Capital from Operations.

The next change is the $20,000 increase in the Land account. From the additional data we know that land and buildings were acquired for cash and the assumption of liability on a mortgage note. Because we wish to report all investing and financing activities, we record the assumption of liability on the mortgage note in a somewhat different manner. We debit Financial Resources Provided and Applied and credit Mortgage Note

Payable for $35,000 (Entry 6). Then, in Entry 7, we debit Land for $20,000 and Buildings for $45,000 and credit Financial Resources Provided and Applied for $20,000 and $45,000. In this way, we include the effects of a significant financing and investing transaction that only partially affected working capital. As shown in Illustration 9.5 on the statement of changes in financial position, the $45,000 amount for the acquisition of buildings is split into the $10,000 which consumed working capital and the $35,000 which did not consume working capital. Note that we have now fully accounted for the changes in the Land and Buildings accounts.

The next account is the Equipment account which shows a net change of $23,000 and in which we have already recorded a credit of $20,000. Since we have no additional information, we can only make the logical assumption that equipment was purchased at a total cost of $43,000. Entry 8 thus reflects a debit to Equipment and a credit to Financial Resources Provided and Applied of $43,000.

We have apparently fully accounted for the changes in the next account, Allowances for Depreciation—Buildings and Equipment, because the credit to the account of $34,300 when offset by the debit of $16,500 yields a net credit change of $17,800. The same is true for the Mortgage Note Payable and Retained Earnings accounts—the items entered account fully for the net change in the account.

Entry 9 records the issuance of common stock for cash by debiting Financial Resources Provided and Applied and crediting Common Stock for $25,000.

We have now completed our analysis of all of the noncurrent accounts. The entries in these accounts reflect the net change in each account. We need only transfer the balance in Working Capital from Operations to Financial Resources Provided and Applied. This transfer is shown in Entry 10.

Financial Resources Provided and Applied

		30,150		
(3)	Sale of equipment	2,600	(4) Dividends	˙18,000
(5)	Sale of investments	9,700	(7) Acquisition of land	20,000
(6)	Mortgage note assumed	35,000	(7) Acquisition of buildings	45,000
(9)	Issuance of common stock	25,000	(8) Acquisition of equipment	43,000
(10)	From operations	83,850		

Working Capital from Operations

(1)	Net earnings	50,350	(5) Gain on sale of investments	1,700
(2)	Depreciation	34,300	(10) Working capital from opera-	
(3)	Loss on sale of equipment	900	tions	83,850

Investments			Land		Buildings	
	8,000		20,000		45,000	
(5)	8,000	(7)	20,000	(7)	45,000	

Equipment			Allow. for Depreciation—Buildings and Equipment		Mortgage Note Payable	
23,000				17,800		35,000
(8) 43,000	(3) 20,000	(3) 16,500	(2) 34,300			(6) 35,000

Retained Earnings		Common Stock	
	32,350		25,000
(4) 18,000	(1) 50,350		(9) 25,000

The Financial Resources Provided and Applied account now contains nearly all of the information needed to prepare the statement of changes in financial position. Missing are the details showing the conversion of net earnings to working capital from operations, and these are readily available in the Working Capital from Operations account. The account will also have to be analyzed for non-working capital financial resources provided and applied. Entry 6 shows the $35,000 of financial resources provided by assumption of liability on the mortgage note. The details of the transaction will have to be analyzed to learn that the $35,000 was applied to acquisition of the building. Separate accounts could be used for such transactions, but this is seldom worthwhile. Such transactions occur infrequently, are few in number, and are so significant that their details are known to the accountant. In the Financial Resources Provided and Applied account, the sum of the debits is $156,150 while the credits total to $126,000. The difference between these two amounts equals the change in working capital ($30,150) during the period.

QUESTIONS AND EXERCISES

1. If the net earnings of a company for a given period amount to $40,000, does this mean that there has been a similar increase in working capital? Why or why not?

2. Show, by means of an example, how information contained in the statement of changes in financial position can assist management in making a decision.

3. Indicate the major types of activity that are to be reported in the statement of changes in financial position. What use of working capital might be called involuntary? Why?

4. The financial press frequently carries comments similar to the following: "New equipment purchases of $325,000 were financed by net earnings and depreciation." Comment.

5. The annual report of the Brice Company reports net earnings of $2.34 per share, down slightly from last year. But, at the annual stockholders' meeting, the president noted with pride that cash flow per share was up substantially from last year to the current level of $7.10 per share. What is cash flow? Why might cash flow per share be up while earnings per share are down? How valid is the concept of cash flow?

6. Which transaction—the declaration or the payment of a dividend—is reported in the statement of changes in financial position? Why?

7. Explain why a company reporting a net loss for a given period might actually have a positive flow of working capital from operations.

8. A company purchased land valued at $20,000 and a building valued at $40,000 by issuing a check for $10,000, signing an interest-bearing note for $15,000, and assuming the liability on a mortgage of $35,000. How should this information be reported in the statement of changes in financial position?

9. A company received $6,000 cash for a machine which cost $10,000 and on which depreciation of $6,000 has been recorded. The gain was included in net earnings. Indicate how the above data should appear in the statement of changes in financial position.

10. A company sold its stock investment in another company for $18.3 million. Its statement of changes in financial position for the year of sale included one item under the heading "Other sources of working capital" as follows:

Proceeds from sale of stock in Alexander Company (net of gain of $8.5. million included in net earnings)................................. $9,800,000

Indicate your agreement or disagreement with the above reporting and your supporting reasoning.

PROBLEMS

9–1. The comparative statement of financial position and the earnings statement for Guy, Inc., are as follows:

GUY, INC.
Comparative Statement of Financial Position

	September 30	
Assets	*1979*	*1978*
Cash...	$ 42,000	$ 15,000
Accounts receivable...........................	108,000	129,000
Inventory.....................................	95,000	81,000
Prepaid expenses.............................	9,000	5,000
Equipment and fixtures.......................	75,000	57,000
Allowance for depreciation...................	(21,000)	(15,000)
Total Assets..........................	$308,000	$272,000
Liabilities and Stockholders' Equity		
Accounts payable............................	$ 52,000	$ 46,000
Accrued expenses payable....................	9,000	11,000
Federal income taxes payable.................	38,000	35,000
Dividends payable...........................	6,000	5,000
Capital stock...............................	100,000	100,000
Retained earnings...........................	103,000	75,000
Total Liabilities and Stockholders' Equity.	$308,000	$272,000

GUY, INC.
Earnings Statement
For Year Ended September 30, 1979

Net sales.....................................		$800,000
Cost of goods sold...........................	$400,000	
Selling and administrative expenses.............	320,000	720,000
Net earnings before taxes.....................		$ 80,000
Federal income taxes.........................		38,000
Net Earnings................................		$ 42,000

Additional Data:

(1)   Depreciation of $6,000 is included in selling and administrative expenses.

(2)   Dividends declared and paid during the year amounted to $14,000.

Required:

a.   Compute the change in working capital. 16,000

b.   Prepare a statement of changes in financial position.

9–2.   Following are comparative financial position data and a statement of retained earnings for the year ended May 31, 1979, for Miles, Inc. (in thousands of dollars):

	May 31	
	1979	*1978*
Cash......................................	$ 60	$ 56
Marketable securities........................	20	24
Accounts receivable, net......................	116	144
Inventories.................................	140	100
Investments in subsidiary.....................	85	80
Land......................................	65	50
Buildings and equipment.....................	450	380
Patents....................................	14	16
Total..............................	$950	$850

	May 31 1979	May 31 1978
Accounts payable..........................	$ 90	$ 64
Taxes payable.............................	16	12
Allowance for depreciation..................	80	60
Bonds payable.............................	200	200
Common stock, $100 par...................	400	400
Retained earnings.........................	164	114
Total..............................	$950	$850

Statement of Retained Earnings

Balance, May 31, 1978......................	$114
Net earnings...............................	100
	$214
Dividends declared.........................	50
Balance, May 31, 1979......................	$164

Additional Data:

(1) Additional shares of stock of the subsidiary company were acquired for cash.
(2) A tract of land adjacent to land owned was purchased during the year.
(3) Depreciation of $32,000 and patent amortization of $2,000 were charged to expense during the year.
(4) New equipment with a cost of $82,000 was purchased during the year, while fully depreciated equipment with a cost of $12,000 was scrapped and discarded.

Required:

a. Prepare a comparative schedule of working capital.
b. Prepare a statement of changes in financial position.

9–3. The comparative statement of financial position and the earnings statement for the Cook Company are as follows:

COOK COMPANY
Comparative Statement of Financial Position

Assets	April 30 1979	April 30 1978
Cash..	$ 51,000	$ 61,000
Marketable securities.............................	12,000	20,000
Accounts receivable, net..........................	98,000	60,000
Inventories.......................................	250,000	100,000
Prepaid expenses.................................	10,000	15,000
Total Current Assets.........................	$421,000	$256,000
Land...	60,000	65,000
Buildings and equipment..........................	330,000	250,000
Allowance for depreciation........................	(80,000)	(65,000)
Total Assets.............................	$731,000	$506,000

Liabilities and Stockholders' Equity

Accounts payable.................................	$100,000	$ 60,000
Bank loans..	60,000	–0–
Accrued expenses payable..........................	32,000	15,000
Federal income taxes payable......................	70,000	75,000
Total Current Liabilities......................	$262,000	$150,000
Bond payable (8%).................................	200,000	200,000
Premium on bonds payable..........................	1,800	2,000
Capital stock—common, $100 par...................	200,000	140,000
Capital in excess of par...........................	10,000	–0–
Retained earnings.................................	57,200	14,000
Total Liabilities and Stockholders' Equity....	$731,000	$506,000

COOK COMPANY
Earnings Statement
For Year Ended April 30, 1979

Net sales...		$800,000
Less: Cost of goods sold..........................	$500,000	
Selling and administrative expenses..............	140,000	640,000
Net earnings from operations.......................		$160,000
Gain on sale of land..............................		8,000
		$168,000
Loss on sale of marketable securities..................	$ 1,000	
Interest expense....................................	18,800	
Loss on sale of equipment..........................	4,200	24,000
Net earnings before income taxes.....................		$144,000
Federal income taxes...............................		70,000
Net Earnings......................................		$ 74,000

Additional Data:

(1) Dividends of $30,800 were declared during the year.
(2) Equipment sold during the year had an original cost of $20,000, and depreciation of $12,000 had been recorded to time of sale.
(3) The capital stock was issued for a building valued at $70,000 erected on company property.
(4) Premium on bonds payable of $200 was amortized during the year.

Required:

a. Compute the change in working capital.
b. Prepare a statement of changes in financial position.

9–4. The comparative statement of financial position for the Winkle Corporation is as shown on the next page.

WINKLE CORPORATION
Comparative Statement of Financial Position

	June 30	
	1979	1978
Assets		
Current assets....................................	$ 360,000	$235,000
Investment in stock of affiliated company............	175,000	150,000
Buildings...	380,000	280,000
Allowance for depreciation—buildings...............	(60,000)	(50,000)
Equipment..	470,000	400,000
Allowance for depreciation—equipment..............	(160,000)	(120,000)
Total Assets...............................	$1,165,000	$895,000
Liabilities and Stockholders' Equity		
Current liabilities................................	$ 180,000	$120,000
Five-year note payable............................	100,000	–0–
Capital stock, par $100............................	800,000	700,000
Retained earnings.................................	85,000	75,000
Total Liabilities and Stockholders' Equity......	$1,165,000	$895,000

Additional Data:

(1) Net earnings for year ended June 30, 1979, were $50,000.
(2) Dividends declared, $40,000.
(3) Stock was issued at par for cash.
(4) No equipment or building retirements occurred during the year.
(5) The five-year note was issued to pay for a building erected on land leased by the company.
(6) Additional shares of stock of the affiliated company were acquired for cash.
(7) Equipment was also purchased for cash.

Required:

a. Show the change in working capital.
b. Prepare a statement of changes in financial position.

9–5. The comparative statement of financial position and the earnings statement and statement of retained earnings for the Roberts Corporation are as follows:

ROBERTS CORPORATION
Comparative Statement of Financial Position

	December 31	
	1979	1978
Assets		
Cash...	$ 15,000	$ 20,000
Accounts receivable................................	122,000	98,000
Inventories..	122,000	112,000
Unexpired insurance...............................	3,000	4,000
Total Current Assets........................	$262,000	$234,000
Land..	50,000	30,000
Buildings...	200,000	100,000
Allowance for depreciation—buildings................	(25,000)	(20,000)
Equipment..	225,000	215,000
Allowance for depreciation—equipment..............	(115,000)	(100,000)
Total Assets...............................	$597,000	$459,000

Liabilities and Stockholders' Equity

Accounts payable..................................	$ 82,000	$ 80,000
Dividends payable................................	12,000	10,000
Federal income taxes payable......................	35,000	30,000
Accrued salaries and wages payable..................	4,000	3,000
Accrued expenses payable..........................	6,000	4,000
Total Current Liabilities......................	$139,000	$127,000
Bonds payable—9 percent..........................	100,000	100,000
Total Liabilities..............................	$239,000	$227,000
Capital stock—common............................	300,000	200,000
Capital in excess of par...........................	15,000	–0–
Retained earnings.................................	43,000	32,000
Total Liabilities and Stockholders' Equity........	$597,000	$459,000

ROBERTS COPORATION
Earnings Statement and Statement of Retained Earnings
For Year Ended December 31, 1979

Sales (net)..		$900,000
Cost of goods sold.................................		600,000
Gross margin......................................		$300,000
Salaries and wages.................................	$150,000	
Depreciation.......................................	27,000	
Insurance...	2,000	
Other expenses (including interest)....................	50,000	
Loss on sale of equipment...........................	1,000	230,000
Net earnings before federal income taxes...............		$ 70,000
Federal income taxes...............................		35,000
Net earnings.......................................		$ 35,000
Retained earnings, December 31, 1978................		32,000
		$ 67,000
Less: Dividends....................................		24,000
Retained Earnings, December 31, 1979................		$ 43,000

Additional Data:

(1) Equipment having an original cost of $10,000 and on which $7,000 of depreciation was recorded was sold at a loss of $1,000. Equipment additions were for cash.

(2) All of the additional capital stock issued during the year, plus $5,000 of cash, was exchanged for land and a building.

Required:

a. Compute the change in working capital.

b. Prepare a statement of changes in financial position.

chapter 10

Consolidated Financial Statements

Parent and Subsidiary Corporations

In many cases, one corporation owns a majority (more than 50 percent) of the outstanding voting common stock of a second corporation. In such cases, both corporations exist as separate legal entities; neither of the corporations is dissolved. The corporation which owns a majority (more than 50 percent) of the outstanding voting common stock of another corporation is referred to as the *parent* company. The corporation controlled by the parent company is known as the *subsidiary* company.

When a large enterprise is operated as a parent company controlling its subsidiaries, each corporation maintains its own accounting records. But, since the parent and its subsidiaries are *controlled* by a central management and are related to each other, the parent company is required to prepare one set of financial statements as if the parent and its subsidiaries taken together constitute a single enterprise. The term *consolidated statements* refers to the financial statements that result from combining the parent's financial statement amounts with those of its subsidiaries. Preparation of consolidated statements is discussed in the following sections. Consolidated statements must be prepared when one company owns more than 50 percent of the outstanding voting common stock of another company (and, thus, exerts control over the other company) and the two companies are engaged in similar or related businesses. A bank and a manufacturing company is a case in which the businesses are so dissimilar that consolidated statements would not be prepared.

Elimination Entries

In preparing consolidated financial statements, it is necessary to eliminate intercompany transactions to show the assets, liabilities, stockholders' equity, revenues, and expenses as if the parent and its subsidiaries were a single economic enterprise. The items remaining on the financial statements of the subsidiaries (after eliminations have been made for intercompany transactions) are combined with the corresponding items on the parent's financial statements.

One elimination will offset the parent company's investment in the subsidiary against the stockholders' accounts of the subsidiary. This elimination is required because the parent company's investment in the stock of the subsidiary actually represents an equity in the net assets of the subsidiary. Thus, unless the investment is eliminated, the same resources will appear twice on the consolidated statement of financial position (as the investment and as the assets of the subsidiary). The elimination is necessary to avoid double counting the owners' equity.

Intercompany receivables and payables (due from and owed to companies in the consolidated group) also must be eliminated during the preparation of consolidated statements. For example, assume the parent company owes the subsidiary $5,000 as evidenced by a $5,000 note receivable on the subsidiary's books and a $5,000 note payable on the parent's books. These balances would be eliminated by offsetting the note receivable against the note payable. No debt is owed to or due from any one outside the consolidated enterprise. Similarly, other intercompany balances would be eliminated when consolidated statements are prepared.

CONSOLIDATED STATEMENT OF FINANCIAL POSITION AT TIME OF ACQUISITION

Acquisition at Book Value

To combine the assets and liabilities of a parent company and its subsidiaries, a work sheet similar to the one shown below is prepared. The first two columns show the assets, liabilities, and stockholders' equity of the parent and subsidiary as they would appear on each corporation's individual statement of financial position. The pair of columns labeled Eliminations allows intercompany items to be offset and consequently eliminated from the consolidated statement. The final column shows the amounts that will appear on the consolidated statement.

This particular work sheet (Illustration 10.1) was prepared to consolidate the accounts of P Company and its subsidiary, S Company, on January 1, 1979. P Company acquired S Company on January 1, 1979, by purchasing all of its outstanding voting common stock for $106,000, the book value of the stock (common stock of $100,000 and retained earnings of $6,000).

Two elimination entries are required in this example. When P Company acquired the stock of S Company, P Company made the following entry:

Investment in S Company		Cash	
106,000			106,000

The investment appears as an asset on P Company's statement of financial position. By buying the subsidiary's stock, the parent in effect acquires an equity or ownership interest in the subsidiary's assets. Thus, if both the investment and the subsidiary's assets appear on the consolidated statement of financial position, the same resources will be counted twice. The common stock and retained earnings accounts of the subsidiary also represent an equity in the subsidiary's assets. Therefore, it is necessary to offset P's investment in S Company against S Company's stockholders' equity accounts so that the subsidiary's assets appear only once on the consolidated statement. This elimination is accomplished by entry (a) on the work sheet.

Entry (b) is required to eliminate the effect of an intercompany transaction (intercompany debt in this case). On the date it acquired S Company, P Company loaned S Company $5,000—which is recorded as a $5,000 note receivable on P's books and a $5,000 note payable on S's books. If the elimination entry is not made on the work sheet, the consolidated statement of financial position will show $5,000 owed to the con-

ILLUSTRATION 10.1

P COMPANY and S COMPANY
Work Sheet for Consolidated Statement of Financial Position
January 1, 1979 (date of acquisition)

	P Company	S Company	Eliminations Debit	Eliminations Credit	Consolidated Amounts
Assets					
Cash	26,000	12,000			38,000
Notes Receivable	5,000			(b) 5,000	
Accounts Receivable, net	24,000	15,000			39,000
Inventory	35,000	30,000			65,000
Investment in S Company	106,000			(a) 106,000	
Equipment, net	41,000	15,000			56,000
Buildings, net	65,000	35,000			100,000
Land	20,000	10,000			30,000
	322,000	117,000			328,000
Liabilities and Stockholders' Equity					
Accounts Payable	18,000	6,000			24,000
Notes Payable		5,000	(b) 5,000		
Common Stock	250,000	100,000	(a) 100,000		250,000
Retained Earnings	54,000	6,000	(a) 6,000		54,000
	322,000	117,000	111,000	111,000	328,000

solidated enterprise by itself. Actually, from the viewpoint of the consolidated entity, neither an asset nor a liability exists. Therefore, entry (*b*) is made on the work sheet to eliminate both the asset and the liability.

In making elimination entries, it is important to understand that *the entries are made only on the consolidated statement work sheets; no entries are made in the accounts of either P Company or S Company.*

Acquisition of Subsidiary at a Cost above or below Book Value

In the previous illustration, P Company acquired 100 percent of S Company at a cost equal to book value. But, in some cases subsidiaries may be acquired at a cost greater than or less than book value. For example, assume P Company purchases 100 percent of S Company's outstanding voting common stock for $125,000. The book value of the stock is $106,000. Cost exceeds book value by $19,000. P Company may have paid more than book value for either or both of two reasons: (1) P Company may believe that the fair value of the subsidiary's assets exceeds the assets' book values, or (2) P Company may think that the subsidiary's earnings prospects justify paying a price greater than book value.

According to the Accounting Principles Board, in cases where cost exceeds book value because of above average earnings prospects, the excess should be labeled as goodwill on the consolidated statement of financial position.[1] On the other hand, if the excess is attributable to the belief that certain assets of the subsidiary are undervalued then the value of the assets should be increased to the extent of the excess. In Illustration 10.2, it is assumed that the $19,000 excess of cost over book value is attributable to above average earnings prospects. As a result, the excess is identified as goodwill on the consolidated statement of financial position (Illustration 10.3). Elimination entry (*b*) in Illustration 10.2 is the same as for the first illustration. Entry (*a*) involves debits to the subsidiary's common stock and retained earnings accounts and to an account labeled excess of cost over book value and a credit to the parent's investment account. After these elimination entries are made, the remaining amounts are combined and extended to the column labeled consolidated amounts. The amounts in this column are then used for preparing the consolidated statement of financial position shown in Illustration 10.3.

Under some circumstances, a parent company may pay less than the book value of the subsidiary's net assets. In such cases, it is highly unlikely that a "bargain" purchase has been made. The most logical explanation for the price paid is that some of the subsidiary's assets are overvalued. The Accounting Principles Board requires that the excess of book value

---

[1] Accounting Principles Board, "Business Combinations," *Opinion No. 16* (AICPA, August 1970).

ILLUSTRATION 10.2

P COMPANY and S COMPANY
Work Sheet for Consolidated statement of Financial Position
January 1, 1979 (date of acquisition)

	P Company	S Company	Eliminations Debit	Eliminations Credit	Consolidated Amounts
Assets					
Cash	7,000	12,000			19,000
Notes Receivable	5,000			(b) 5,000	
Accounts Receivable, net	24,000	15,000			39,000
Inventory	35,000	30,000			65,000
Investment in S Company	125,000			(a) 125,000	
Equipment, net	41,000	15,000			56,000
Buildings, net	65,000	35,000			100,000
Land	20,000	10,000			30,000
Excess of cost over book value			(a) 19,000		19,000
	322,000	117,000			328,000
Liabilities and Stockholders' Equity					
Accounts Payable	18,000	6,000			24,000
Notes Payable		5,000	(b) 5,000		
Common Stock	250,000	100,000	(a) 100,000		250,000
Retained Earnings	54,000	6,000	(a) 6,000		54,000
	322,000	117,000	130,000	130,000	328,000

over cost be used to reduce proportionately the value of the noncurrent assets.[2] If the noncurrent assets are reduced to zero before the excess of book value over cost is fully eliminated, the remaining amount of excess should be reported as a deferred credit (Excess of Book Value over Cost) on the consolidated statement of financial position. Deferred credits, which will be allocated to future operations, are often located between liabilities and stockholders' equity on the statement of financial position.

Acquisition of Less Than 100 Percent of Subsidiary

Sometimes a parent company acquires less than 100 percent of the outstanding voting common stock of a subsidiary. For example, assume P Company acquires 80 percent of S Company's outstanding voting common stock. P Company is the majority stockholder, but there exist minority stockholders who own 20 percent of the stock. These minority stockholders have a *minority interest,* as it is called, in the subsidiary's net assets and share in the subsidiary's earnings with the parent company.

[2] Ibid.

ILLUSTRATION 10.3

P COMPANY and S COMPANY
Consolidated Statement of Financial Position
January 1, 1979

Assets

Currents Assets:

Cash...	$ 19,000	
Accounts Receivable, net............................	39,000	
Inventory..	65,000	
Total Current Assets...........................		$123,000

Property, Plant, and Equipment:

Equipment, net.....................................	$ 56,000	
Buildings, net......................................	100,000	
Land...	30,000	
Total Property, Plant, and Equipment............		186,000
Goodwill...		19,000
Total Assets...............................		$328,000

Liabilities and Stockholders' Equity

Liabilities:

Accounts Payable..................................		$ 24,000

Stockholders' Equity:

Common Stock.....................................	$250,000	
Retained Earnings..................................	54,000	
Total Stockholders' Equity......................		304,000
Total Liabilities and Stockholders' Equity.....		$328,000

When preparing a consolidated statement of financial position for a partially owned subsidiary, only part of the subsidiary's stockholders' equity is eliminated. That part of the common stock and retained earnings which relates to the minority stockholders is established on the consolidated statement work sheet as the minority interest.

Illustration 10.4 shows what elimination entries are required when P Company purchases 80 percent of S Company's stock for $100,000. The book value of the stock owned by P Company is $84,800 (80 percent of $106,000). The excess of cost over book value amounts to $15,200 and can be attributed to S Company's above average earnings prospects. On the consolidated statement of financial position, the $15,200 excess will be identified as goodwill (Illustration 10.5).

The minority stockholders have an equity of $21,200 in the net assets of the consolidated enterprise (Illustration 10.5). The amount of the minority interest appears between the liabilities and stockholders' equity sections of the consolidated statement of financial position. (Actually, there is some disagreement as to whether the minority interest is a liability or a part of stockholders' equity.)

ILLUSTRATION 10.4

P COMPANY and S COMPANY
Work Sheet for Consolidated Statement of Financial Position
January 1, 1979 (date of acquisition)

	P Company	S Company	Eliminations Debit	Eliminations Credit	Consolidated Amounts
Assets					
Cash	32,000	12,000			44,000
Notes Receivable	5,000			(b) 5,000	
Accounts Receivable, net	24,000	15,000			39,000
Inventory	35,000	30,000			65,000
Investment in S Company	100,000			(a) 100,000	
Equipment, net	41,000	15,000			56,000
Buildings, net	65,000	35,000			100,000
Land	20,000	10,000			30,000
Excess of cost over book value			(a) 15,200		15,200
	322,000	117,000			349,200
Liabilities and Stockholders' Equity					
Accounts Payable	18,000	6,000			24,000
Notes Payable		5,000	(b) 5,000		
Common Stock	250,000	100,000	(a) 100,000		250,000
Retained Earnings	54,000	6,000	(a) 6,000		54,000
Minority Interest				(a) 21,200	21,200
	322,000	117,000	126,200	126,200	349,200

EARNINGS, LOSSES, AND DIVIDENDS OF A SUBSIDIARY

If a subsidiary is operated profitably, there will be an increase in its net assets and retained earnings. When the subsidiary pays dividends, both the parent company and the minority stockholders will share in the distribution. Earnings and dividends will be recorded in the accounting records of the subsidiary just as they are recorded for other corporations.

The Accounting Principles Board requires the parent company to record its share of the subsidiary's earnings or losses as they are reported by the subsidiary. The parent company's share of the subsidiary's earnings is debited to the Investment in S Company account and credited to an account labeled Revenue from Investment in S Company. For example, assume the subsidiary S Company mentioned in the preceding illustrations earned $20,000 during 1979, P Company owns 80 percent of S Company. P Company would record its share of the earnings in the following manner:

Investment in S Company		**Revenue from Investment in S Company**	
Bal.	100,000		
a)	16,000	a) 16,000	

ILLUSTRATION 10.5

P COMPANY and S COMPANY
Consolidated Statement of Financial Position
January 1, 1979

Assets

Current Assets:

Cash...	$ 44,000	
Accounts receivable, net............................	39,000	
Inventory...	65,000	
Total Current Assets...........................		$148,000

Property, Plant, and Equipment

Equipment, net....................................	$ 56,000	
Buildings, net.....................................	100,000	
Land...	30,000	
Total Property, Plant, and Equipment............		186,000
Goodwill..		15,200
Total Assets..............................		$349,200

Liabilities and Stockholders' Equity

Liabilities:

Accounts payable..................................		$ 24,000
Minority interest..................................		21,200

Stockholders' Equity:

Common stock....................................	$250,000	
Retained earnings.................................	54,000	
Total Stockholders' Equity......................		304,000
Total Liabilities and Stockholders' Equity.....		$349,200

The $16,000 debit to the investment account increases the parent's equity in the subsidiary. The $16,000 credit to the earnings account will be closed to the Expense and Revenue Summary account and then to P Company's Retained Earnings account.

If the subsidiary incurs a loss the parent company debits a loss account and credits the investment account for its share of the loss. For example, assume S Company incurs a loss of $10,000 in 1980. Since P Company still owns 80 percent of S Company, P Company would record its share of the loss as follows:

Loss from Investment in S Company			**Investment in S Company**		
			Bal.	116,000	
b)	8,000				*b)* 8,000

The $8,000 debit is closed first to the Expense and Revenue Summary and then to Retained Earnings; the $8,000 *credit* reduces P Company's equity in the subsidiary.[3]

---

[3] Amortization of the goodwill over a period not to exceed 40 years is required

When a subsidiary declares and pays a dividend, the assets and retained earnings of the subsidiary are both reduced by the amount of the dividend payment. When the parent company receives its share of the dividends, it debits the asset received (cash, in this case) and credits the investment account. For instance, assume S Company declares a cash dividend of $8,000 in 1979. P Company's share of the dividend amounts to $6,400 and is recorded as follows:

Cash			Investment in S Company		
Bal.	xxx		Bal.	116,000	
c)	6,400		c)		6,400

The receipt of the dividend reduces the parent's equity in the subsidiary as shown by the credit to the investment account.

Consolidated Financial Statements at a Date after Acquisition

The investment account on the parent company's books increases and decreases as the parent company records its share of the earnings, losses, and dividends reported by the subsidiary. Consequently, the balance in the investment account is not usually the same after acquisition as it is on the date of acquisition. Therefore, the amounts eliminated on the consolidated statement work sheet will be different from year to year.

As an illustration, assume the following facts:

1. P Company acquired 100 percent of the outstanding voting common stock of S Company on January 1, 1979. P Company paid $121,000 for an equity of $106,000. The excess of cost over book value (sometimes referred to as a *differential*) is attributable to S Company's high earnings prospects.
2. During 1979, S Company earned $20,000 from profitable operations.
3. On December 31, 1979, S Company paid a cash dividend of $8,000.
4. S Company has not paid the $5,000 it borrowed from P Company at the beginning of 1979.

---

by the APB. Thus, the following entries are required on P company's books in 1979 and 1980 to amortize goodwill ($15,200) over 40 years.

```
1979   Revenue from Investment in S Company ............. 380
          Investment in S Company ................................ 380
1980   Loss from Investment in S Company ................. 380
          Investment in S Company ............................... 380
```

P Company actually records its share of the net earnings (loss) of S Company less (plus) the amortization of goodwill.

Changes in the values of limited life assets are likely to require other adjusting entries on the parents books, which are beyond the scope of this text.

5. Including its share of S Company's earnings, P Company earned $31,000 during 1979.
6. P Company paid a cash dividend of $10,000 during December 1979.

A work sheet for consolidated financial statements for December 31, 1979, appears in Illustration 10.6.

The elimination entries are explained below:

Entry (a): During the year, S Company earned $20,000. P Company increased its investment account balance by $20,000 for its share of S's net earnings. The first entry (a) on the work sheet eliminates the subsidiary's earnings from the investment account and P Company's revenue. It reverses the entry made on the books of P Company to recognize the parent's share of the subsidiary's earnings.

Entry (b): When S Company paid its cash dividend, P Company debited cash and credited the investment account for $8,000. The second entry (b) offsets parts of the entries originally made by P Company and S Company. That is, P's investment account is debited and S's dividends account is credited.

Entry (c): This entry is familiar. It eliminates the original investment account balance and the subsidiary's stockholders' equity accounts as of the date of acquisition. It also establishes an amount which represents the excess of cost over book value.

After the first three entries are made, the investment account contains a zero balance from the viewpoint of the consolidated entity.

Entry (d): According to APB *Opinion No. 17*, goodwill must be amortized over a period of time which cannot exceed forty years.[4] In this case, goodwill is being amortized over twenty years which results in $750 being written off as expense each year.

Entry (e): This entry is also familiar. It eliminates the intercompany debt of $5,000.

After the eliminations have been made, the corresponding amounts are added together and placed in the consolidated amounts column. The entire net earnings row in the earnings statement section is carried forward to the net earnings row in the statement of retained earnings section. Likewise, the complete ending retained earnings row in the statement of retained earnings section is carried forward to the retained earnings row in the statement of financial position section. The final column of the work sheet is then used in the preparation of the consolidated earnings statement (Illustration 10.7), the consolidated statement of retained earnings (Illustra-

---

[4] Accounting Principles Board.

ILLUSTRATION 10.6

P COMPANY and Subsidiary S COMPANY
Work Sheet for Consolidated Financial Statements
December 31, 1979

	P Company	S Company	Eliminations Debit	Eliminations Credit	Consolidated Amounts
Earnings Statement:					
Revenue from Sales	397,000	303,000			700,000
Revenue from Investment in S Company	20,000		(a) 20,000		
Cost of Goods Sold	(250,000)	(180,000)			(430,000)
Expenses (excluding dep. and amort. and taxes)	(100,000)	(80,000)			(180,000)
Depreciation Expense	(7,400)	(5,000)			(12,400)
Amortization of Goodwill			(d) 750		(750)
Income Tax Expense	(28,600)	(18,000)			(46,600)
Net Earnings-carried forward.	31,000	20,000			30,250
Statement of Retained earnings:					
Retained Earnings–January, 1					
P Company	54,000				54,000
S Company		6,000	(c) 6,000		
Net Earnings—brought forward.	31,000	20,000			30,250
	85,000	26,000			84,250
Dividends:					
P Company	(10,000)				(10,000)
S Company		(8,000)		(b) 8,000	
Retained Earnings—December 31 carried forward	75,000	18,000			74,250
Statement of Financial Position:					
Assets					
Cash	38,000	16,000			54,000
Notes Receivable	5,000			(e) 5,000	
Accounts Receivable, net	25,000	18,000			43,000
Inventory	40,000	36,000			76,000
Investment in S Company	133,000		(b) 8,000	(c) 121,000 (a) 20,000	
Equipment, net	36,900	12,000			48,900
Buildings, net	61,700	33,000			94,700
Land	20,000	10,000			30,000
Excess of cost over book value			(c) 15,000	(d) 750	14,250
	359,600	125,000			360,850

ILLUSTRATION 10.6 (continued)

	P Company	S Company	Eliminations Debit	Eliminations Credit	Consolidated Amounts
Liabilities and Stockholders' Equity					
Accounts Payable	19,600	2,000			21,600
Notes Payable	15,000	5,000	(e) 5,000		15,000
Common Stock	250,000	100,000	(c) 100,000		250,000
Retained Earnings— brought forward	75,000	18,000			74,250
	359,600	125,000	154,750	154,750	360,850

ILLUSTRATION 10.7

P COMPANY and Subsidiary S COMPANY
Consolidated Earnings Statement
For the Year Ended December 31, 1979

Revenue from Sales		$700,000
Cost of Goods Sold		430,000
Gross Margin		$270,000
Expenses (excluding depreciation, amortization, and taxes)	$180,000	
Depreciation Expense	12,400	
Amortization of Goodwill	750	
Income Tax Expense	46,600	239,750
Net Earnings		$ 30,250

P COMPANY and Subsidiary S COMPANY
Consolidated Statement of Retained Earnings
For the Year Ended December 31, 1979

Retained Earnings, January 1, 1979	$ 54,000
Net Earnings	30,250
	$ 84,250
Dividends	10,000
Retained Earnings, December 31, 1979	$ 74,250

ILLUSTRATION 10.8

P COMPANY and Subsidiary S COMPANY
Consolidated Statement of Financial Position
December 31, 1979

Assets

Current Assets:

Cash	$ 54,000	
Accounts receivable, net	43,000	
Inventory	76,000	
Total Current Assets		$173,000

Property, Plant, and Equipment:

Equipment, net	$ 48,900	
Buildings, net	94,700	
Land	30,000	
Total Property, Plant, and Equipment		173,600
Goodwill		14,250
Total Assets		$360,850

Liabilities and Stockholders' Equity

Current Liabilities:

Accounts payable	$ 21,600	
Notes payable	15,000	
Total Liabilities		$ 36,600

Stockholders' Equity:

Common stock	$250,000	
Retained earnings	74,250	
Total Stockholders' Equity		324,250
Total Liabilities and Stockholders' Equity		$360,850

tion 10.7), and the consolidated statement of financial position (Illustration 10.8).

PURCHASE VERSUS POOLING OF INTERESTS

Throughout the illustrations in this chapter, it has been assumed that the parent company acquired the subsidiary's common stock in exchange for cash. Such a business combination is classified as a *purchase*. A purchase would also result if the acquiring company issued debt securities or assets other than cash. But, in some cases, one company issues common stock in exchange for common stock of another company. In such a situation, it appears that the stockholders of both companies maintain an ownership interest in the combined company. Such a business combination is classified as a *pooling of interests* (if it meets all the pooling criteria cited in APB *Opinion #16*).

Given the circumstances surrounding a particular business combination, only one of the two methods—purchase or pooling of interests—is appropriate. It should be emphasized that the purchase and pooling of interests methods are not alternatives which can be applied to the same situation. APB *Opinion No. 16* specified certain conditions that must be met before a business combination can be classified as a pooling of interests.[5] If all of the conditions are met, then the resulting business combination *must* be accounted for as a pooling of interests. Otherwise, the purchase method must be used to account for the combination.

When the pooling of interests method is used, the parent company's investment is recorded at the parent's share of the book value of the subsidiary's net assets and not at the market value of the parent's common stock given in exchange. This differs from the purchase method in which an investment is recorded at the amount of cash given up or at the fair market value of the assets or stock given up, or the fair market value of the stock received, whichever can be the most clearly and objectively determined.

Since the investment is recorded at the book value of the subsidiary's net assets, under the pooling of interest method, there can be no goodwill or deferred credit from consolidation. The subsidiary's retained earnings which exist on the date of acquisition become a part of the consolidated retained earnings, whereas under the purchase method the subsidiary's retained earnings at date of acquisition do not become part of consolidated retained earnings. Also, under the pooling of interests method all the earnings of a subsidiary for the year in which it is acquired are included in the consolidated earnings for the year of acquisition. On the other hand, only that portion of the subsidiary's earnings which arise after the date of acquisition are included in consolidated earnings under the purchase method.

From the above discussion, it should be apparent that significant differences exist between earnings statement amounts and statement of financial position amounts when the different methods are used. (Remember only one method is appropriate for a given set of circumstances.) For instance, under the purchase method, any excess of cost over book value must be used to increase the value of assets that are undervalued or be recognized as goodwill from consolidation. Thus, more depreciation and amortization will be recorded under the purchase method when cost exceeds book value. The result is that consolidated net earnings are less under the purchase method than under the pooling of interests method. (Remember that under the pooling of interests method asset values are not increased and goodwill is not recognized upon consolidation.) Similarly, since the subsidiary's earnings for the entire year in which it was acquired are included in consolidated net earnings under the pooling of interests method, consolidated net earnings for the year of acquisition also would be larger under the pooling of interests method than under the purchase

---

[5] Accounting Principles Board.

method. Because of the differences just illustrated, it is important that the appropriate method of accounting be used for a particular business combination.

Abuses of Pooling

Prior to APB *Opinion No. 16,* the pooling of interests method was used in cases where it really was not applicable. In other words, its use was subject to abuse. Four common abuses of pooling are illustrated below:

1. Acquisition of smaller companies at year-end so that the earnings of the smaller companies can be combined with the parent's earnings (or used to offset the parent's loss) to increase net earnings and earnings per share.
2. Acquisition of a company having several plants whose fair market values are much greater than their book values. In this case the plants would be recorded as assets at their rather low book value, say, $200,000. The next year one of the plants would be sold for its fair market value of, say, $800,000. The result of the sale would be a $600,000 gain which would instantly increase net earnings and earnings per share.
3. Issuance of odd securities which could be traded in one year later for either common stock or cash. Odd securities were issued so that (1) the combination could be accounted for as a pooling of interests and (2) stockholders of the subsidiary could receive cash shortly if they did not want common stock.
4. Accounting for an acquisition as "part-purchase, part-pooling". In some cases, a certain number of stockholders would refuse to accept common stock or odd securities. They wanted cash immediately. Thus, some companies accounted for part of the acquisition as a purchase and the other part as a pooling of interests. APB *Opinion No. 16* has helped to reduce these abuses of pooling.

USES AND LIMITATIONS OF CONSOLIDATED STATEMENTS

Consolidated statements are of primary importance to the stockholders, managers, and directors of the parent company. The parent company benefits from the earnings, asset increases, and other financial strengths of the subsidiary. Likewise, the parent company suffers from a subsidiary's losses or other financial weaknesses.

On the other hand, consolidated statements are of very limited use to the creditors and minority stockholders of the subsidiary. The subsidiary's creditors have a claim against the subsidiary alone; they cannot look to the parent company for payment. Likewise, the minority stockholders do not benefit or suffer from the parent company's operations. They benefit only from the subsidiary's earnings, asset increases, and financial strengths; they suffer only from the subsidiary's losses and financial weaknesses. Therefore, the subsidiary's creditors and minority stockholders are more interested in the subsidiary's individual financial statements than in the consolidated statements.

SUMMARY

A corporation that owns a majority of the outstanding voting common stock of another corporation is called a *parent company*. The corporation controlled by the parent company is known as a *subsidiary company*. Consolidated statements are the financial statements that result from combining the parent's financial statement amounts with those of its subsidiaries. When preparing consolidated statements, a work sheet is a valuable tool on which the necessary elimination entries can be made. Such entries are required to eliminate certain intercompany items to show the assets, liabilities, stockholders' equity, revenues, expenses, and dividends as if the parent and its subsidiaries were a single economic enterprise. Included in the items to be eliminated are the parents' investment account, the subsidiary's stockholders' equity accounts, and intercompany receivables and payables as well as intercompany revenues, expenses, and dividends. No elimination entries are made on the books of either the parent or the subsidiary.

In certain instances, a parent company may acquire a subsidiary at a cost above or below book value. Any excess of cost over book value must be used to increase the value of the subsidiary's undervalued assets or be recognized as goodwill from consolidation. Any excess of book value over cost must first be used to reduce the values of the noncurrent assets; the remaining excess should be reported as a deferred credit.

When a parent company acquires less than 100 percent of the outstanding voting common stock of a subsidiary a minority interests emerges. The minority stockholders have an interest in the subsidiary's net assets and share the subsidiary's earnings with the parent company.

The Accounting Principles Board requires the parent company to account for its share of the subsidiary's earnings, losses, and dividends as they are reported by the subsidiary. Earnings increase the investment while losses and dividends reduce the investment.

A business combination will be classified as a purchase or a pooling of interests. A purchase results when the acquiring company exchanges cash, other assets, debt securities (and sometimes, preferred and common stock) for the net assets or common stock of another company. A pooling of interests results if the acquiring company issues common stock in exchange for common stock *and* if the business combination satisfies certain conditions stated in APB *Opinion No. 16*. Only one of the methods—purchase or pooling of interests—is appropriate (correct) given the circumstances surrounding a particular business combination. The two methods result in different earnings statement and statement of financial position amounts.

Consolidated statements are of primary importance to the stockholders, managers, and directors of the parent company. On the other hand, the minority stockholders and creditors of the subsidiary company are more interested in the subsidiary's individual financial statements.

QUESTIONS AND EXERCISES

1. What is (are) the purpose(s) of preparing consolidated financial statements?

2. Why is it necessary to make elimination entries on the consolidated statement work sheet? Are these elimination entries also posted to the accounts of the parent and subsidiary? Why or why not?

3. Why might a corporation pay an amount in excess of book value for a subsidiary's stock? Why might it pay an amount less than the book value of the subsidiary's stock?

4. The item "Minority Interest" often appears as one amount in the stockholders' equity section of the statement of financial position. What does this item represent?

5. How do a subsidiary's earnings, losses, and dividends affect the investment account of the parent?

6. On January 1, 1979, Company A acquired 85 percent of the outstanding voting common stock of Company B. On that date, Company B's stockholders' equity section appeared as follows:

> Common stock, $20 par; 10,000 shares authorized,
> issued, and outstanding......................... $200,000
> Retained earnings................................ 50,000
> Total Stockholders' Equity................... $250,000

Compute the difference between cost and book value in each of the following cases

a. Company A pays $212,500 cash for its equity.

b. Company A pays $250,000 cash for its equity.

c. Company A pays $195,000 cash for its equity.

d. Company A issues some of its own common stock; the resulting business combination must be accounted for as a pooling of interests.

7. Company Y purchased 90 percent of Company Z's outstanding voting common stock on January 2, 1979. Company Y paid $150,000 for an equity of $135,000—$90,000 of common stock and $45,000 of retained earnings. Company Z earned $18,000 during 1979 and paid cash dividends of $6,000.

a. Compute the balance in the investment account on December 31, 1979.

b. Compute the amount of the minority interest on (1) January 2, 1979 and (2) December 31, 1979.

8. When must each of the following methods be used to account for a business combination?

a. Purchase.

b. Pooling of interests.

9. List four differences that exist between the purchase and pooling of interests methods of accounting for business combinations.

10. Why are consolidated financial statements of limited usefulness to the creditors and minority stockholders of a subsidiary?

PROBLEMS

10–1. The Robins Company acquired 100 percent of the outstanding voting common stock of the Warner Company on January 1, 1979, for $76,000. On the date of acquisition, the statements of financial position for the two companies were as follows:

	Robins Company	Warner Company
Assets		
Cash	$ 6,000	$14,000
Accounts Receivable	14,000	18,000
Notes Receivable	10,000	6,000
Inventory	25,000	15,000
Investment in Warner Company	76,000	
Equipment, net	22,000	28,000
Total Assets	$153,000	$81,000
Liabilities and Stockholders' Equity		
Accounts Payable	$ 16,000	$ 5,000
Notes Payable	12,000	
Common Stock—$20 par	100,000	60,000
Retained Earnings	25,000	16,000
Total Liabilities and Stockholders' Equity	$153,000	$81,000

Also on January 1, 1979, Robins Company borrowed $6,000 from Warner Company; the debt is evidenced by a note.

Required: Prepare a work sheet for a consolidated statement of financial position on the date of acquisition.

10–2. On January 1, 1979, Medlin Company acquired 80% of the outstanding voting common stock of the Hamby Corporation for $90,000. The January 1, 1979, statements of financial position for the two companies are shown below:

	Medlin Company	Hamby Corporation
Assets		
Cash..	$ 12,000	$ 9,000
Accounts receivable...........................	10,000	12,000
Inventory.....................................	30,000	26,000
Investment in Hamby Corporation..............	90,000	
Equipment, net...............................	15,000	9,000
Buildings, net................................	45,000	32,000
Land...	8,000	10,000
Total Assets.............................	$210,000	$98,000
Liabilities and Stockholders' Equity		
Accounts payable.............................	$ 10,000	$ 5,000
Common stock—$10 par........................	160,000	80,000
Retained earnings............................	40,000	13,000
Total Liabilities and Stockholders' Equity.......	$210,000	$98,000

Medlin Company was willing to pay an amount greater than the book value of Hamby Corporation's stockholders' equity for two reasons:

(1)   It believed that the equipment owned by Hamby Corporation was undervalued. It was felt that the equipment should be valued at $12,000 as opposed to $9,000.

(2)   The company believed that the remaining excess of cost over book value could be justified on the basis of the subsidiary's excellent earnings expectations.

Required:

a.   Prepare a work sheet for a consolidated statement of financial position on the date of acquisition.

b.   Prepare a consolidated statement of financial position for January 1, 1979.

10–3.   The Adams Company acquired 100 percent of the outstanding voting common stock of the Belcher Company on January 2, 1979, for $300,000. On the date of acquisition, the statements of financial position for the two companies were as follows:

	Adams Company	Belcher Company
Assets		
Cash..	$ 35,000	$ 20,000
Accounts receivable...........................	26,000	16,000
Notes receivable..............................	40,000	10,000
Inventory.....................................	55,000	26,000
Investment in Belcher Company.................	300,000	
Equipment, net...............................	72,000	50,000
Buildings, net................................	210,000	110,000
Land...	85,000	45,000
Total Assets.............................	$823,000	$277,000

Liabilities and Stockholders' Equity

Accounts payable......................................	$ 13,000	$ 15,000
Notes payable...	10,000	12,000
Common stock—$10 par..............................	600,000	200,000
Retained earnings.....................................	200,000	50,000
Total Liabilities and Stockholders' Equity..........	$823,000	$277,000

The excess of cost over book value is attributable to the above average earnings prospects of Belcher Company and to the belief that Belcher Company's equipment and buildings are undervalued. The fair values are believed to be $70,000 for the equipment and $120,000 for the buildings. On the date of acquisition, Belcher Company borrowed $8,000 from Adams Company; the debt is evidenced by a note.

Required:

a. Prepare a work sheet for a consolidated statement of financial position on the date of acquisition.
b. Prepare a consolidated statement of financial position for January 2, 1979.

10–4. Refer to problem 3. Assume the following are the adjusted balances for the Adams Company and the Belcher Company on December 31, 1979.

	Adams Company	Belcher Company
Cash...	$ 39,000	$ 35,000
Accounts Receivable.............................	42,000	20,000
Notes Receivable................................	35,000	5,000
Inventory, Dec. 31..............................	55,000	31,900
Investment in Belcher Company....................	310,000	
Equipment, net.................................	68,400	47,500
Buildings, net..................................	201,600	105,600
Land..	85,000	45,000
Cost of Goods Sold..............................	200,000	70,000
Expenses (excl. depr. taxes, and amort.)...............	80,000	30,100
Depreciation Expense............................	12,000	6,900
Income Tax Expense.............................	65,000	21,000
Dividends Declared..............................	60,000	12,000
Total Debits................................	$1,253,000	$430,000
Accounts Payable...............................	$ 15,000	$ 20,000
Notes Payable..................................	16,000	10,000
Common Stock—$10 par..........................	600,000	200,000
Retained Earnings...............................	200,000	50,000
Revenue from Sales..............................	400,000	150,000
Revenue from Investment in Belcher Company..........	22,000	
Total Credits................................	$1,253,000	$430,000

There is no intercompany debt at the end of the year.

Required: Prepare a work sheet for consolidated financial statements on December 31, 1979.
(On January 2, 1979, the equipment and buildings had remaining lives of 20 and 25 years, respectively; goodwill is to be amortized over 20 years.)

10–5. Using the work sheet prepared for Problem 4, prepare the following items:
  a. Consolidated earnings statement for the year ended December 31, 1979.
  b. Consolidated statement of retained earnings for the year ended December 31, 1979.
  c. Consolidated statement of financial position for December 31, 1979.

chapter 11

The Basic Theory Underlying Financial Accounting

Some of the theoretical concepts presented in this chapter have been dealt with directly in previous chapters. Others have been presented only indirectly. No attempt has been made to present a complete model of accounting theory. This chapter provides such a model.

Accounting theory has been defined as a set of basic concepts or assumptions and related principles and standards that explain and guide the accountant's actions in identifying, measuring, and communicating economic information.[1] What constitutes accounting theory and what its purposes are have been the subject of debate for years. And the issues are yet unresolved. Accounting practices are guided by a group of important ideas that collectively are called "generally accepted accounting principles." This chapter deals with the nature of some of these principles and the objectives sought by their application.

THE GENERAL OBJECTIVES OF FINANCIAL ACCOUNTING

As business' financial historians, accountants provide a "history quantified in money terms of economic resources and obligations of a business enterprise and of economic activities that change these resources and ob-

---

[1] American Accounting Association, *A Statement of Basic Accounting Theory*, (Sarasota, Fla.: AAA, 1966), pp. 1–2.

ligations."[2] The information gathered is reported to both internal and external users. Neither group would know much about the financial activities of a modern business corporation without such information.

For external users, the information is in the form of general purpose financial statements (see the Appendix to this chapter for examples). It is believed that such statements will serve the common needs of several classes of users if they provide the following:

1. Reliable financial information about economic resources and obligations.
2. Reliable information about changes in net resources (resources less obligations) of an enterprise that result from its profit-directed activities.
3. Financial information that assists in estimating the future capacity of an enterprise to generate earnings.
4. Information about changes in resources and obligations resulting from sources other than profit-directed activities, such as transactions between an entity and its owners, and information about working capital and other fund flows.
5. Adequate disclosure of other information, such as accounting policies and depreciation and inventory methods, that is relevant to statement users' needs.[3]

The Sources of Accounting Principles

Accounting principles are man-made and have been derived largely from accounting practice. Practice in turn has been subject to many influences, some of the more important of which are discussed below.

Federal Income Taxation.   The acceptance for income tax purposes of the accelerated depreciation methods and of the Lifo inventory method did much to further discussion and spread of these methods to financial accounting. But the most notable impact is found in U.S. Supreme Court decisions, in tax cases, which firmly established realization as a major principle of accounting, as is discussed further below.

Federal Securities Legislation.   The stock market crash in 1929 led directly to government intervention in the securities markets and to the establishment, in 1934, of the Securities and Exchange Commission (SEC). The SEC has the power to prescribe the accounting practices of most U.S. business corporations. Although it has issued nearly 200 *Accounting Series Releases,* the SEC has followed a basic policy of co-

---

[2] American Institute of Certified Public Accountants, *Statements of the Accounting Principles Board, No. 4* "Basic Concepts and Accounting Principles Underlying Financial Statements of Business Enterprises," (New York: AICPA, 1970), par. 41.

[3] Ibid. par. 77–81.

operating with the accounting profession (the AICPA and now the FASB) in the development of accounting principles.

The American Accounting Association. Since 1936, the AAA has published a number of statements on accounting principles, including the 1966 *A Statement of Basic Accounting Theory*. Most of the AAA statements sought to provide a general framework of principles, rather than solutions to specific problems. The 1966 statement, for example, set four standards—relevance, quantifiability, freedom from bias, and verifiability—to which information must conform before it is admitted to the accounting system.

The Accounting Research Bulletins. Starting in 1939, the Committee on Accounting Procedure of the AICPA issued over the next 20 years a total of 51 *Accounting Research Bulletins* which were largely suggested solutions to practical problems. The rules (discussed in Chapter 3) of the cost-or-market method of inventory measurement are illustrative of the content of these bulletins.

The Accounting Principles Board and the Accounting Research Division. In 1959, the council of the AICPA approved the organization of the Accounting Principles Board and the Accounting Research Division with the stated objective:

> . . . to advance the written expression of what constitutes generally accepted accounting principles, for the guidance of its members and of others. This . . . means a continuing effort to determine appropriate practice and to narrow the areas of difference and inconsistency in practice.[4]

The ARD published three *Accounting Research Studies* (Nos. 1, 3, and 7) dealing with accounting principles. None was formally adopted by the APB as an authoritative statement of principles. Instead, the AICPA, in 1970, published *Statement of the Accounting Principles Board, No. 4.* Although never formally adopted by the board, *Statement No. 4* is the most complete statement of accounting principles published to date. Portions of this statement have already been cited.

In *Statement No. 4* the board erected a general structure of accounting theory by dividing the basic concepts of accounting into (1) objectives—general and qualitative, the first of which was presented above; (2) basic features, which will be presented below; (3) basic elements—assets, liabilities, owners' equity, revenues, expenses, and net earnings; (4) pervasive principles, which are discussed below; (5) modifying conventions, such as conservatism; (6) broad operating principles, such as the recording of exchange prices; and (7) detailed accounting principles, such as the requirement that goodwill be amortized over a period not to exceed 40 years.

---

[4] American Institute of Certified Public Accountants, *Organization and Operation of the Accounting Research Program and Related Activities* (New York: AICPA, 1959), p. 9.

APB Opinions. The APB, an official "spokesman" for the AICPA, issued a total of 31 *Opinions* on a variety of topics. References to some of these *Opinions* have been made in previous chapters. The APB *Opinions* are, for the practicing CPA, generally accepted accounting principles in the subject matter areas covered. Whenever financial statements are presented following principles that differ from board *Opinions,* the CPA must insist upon full disclosure of the circumstances that lead to this decision.

The Financial Accounting Standards Board. The APB was replaced in 1973 by a new, seven member, full-time, paid, independent board called the Financial Accounting Standards Board. This board is currently the major voice of the private sector on financial accounting principles (standards). The FASB has adopted the APB Opinions as they then existed and has issued a number of statements of accounting standards as well as a number of interpretations of its own statements and of APB *Opinions.*

The rest of this chapter discusses the generally accepted accounting principles that currently guide the accountant in identifying, measuring, and reporting upon economic activity. They are the principles that give accounting a degree of uniformity from period to period and between firms.

QUALITATIVE OBJECTIVES

Every discipline is based upon certain fundamental premises or assumptions. Our law, for example, assumes a person is innocent until proven guilty; the physicist assumes that energy can neither be created nor destroyed; the mathematician, that every integer has a successor. And parts of economic theory rely heavily upon the assumption of diminishing marginal utility.

Accountants recognize that implicit in their discipline are certain basic notions that distinguish it from other disciplines. These are discussed below, beginning with the seven qualitative objectives of financial accounting as stated by the APB.[5]

Relevance

For information to be relevant it must be pertinent or bear upon a decision. Relevance is the *primary* qualitative objective. If information is not relevant, it is useless even though it meets the other objectives fully. And it is for its lack of relevance that accounting information is under serious attack today. For example, it is argued that the fact that a tract of land cost its owner $1 million over 40 years ago is irrelevant (except for possible tax implications) to any user for any decision that must be made today. These attacks have encouraged research into the types of information that are relevant to users.

---

[5] American Institute of Certified Public Accountants, *Statement No. 4,* par. 88–94.

Understandability

This objective is important on the simple grounds that information must be understood if it is to be useful. Information should be presented in a form and expressed in terminology that a user understands. But the complexity of economic activity makes it impossible to always reduce it to simple terms. It follows that users must aid their own cause by acquiring some understanding of business and accounting terminology, as well as financial reporting practices.

Verifiability

Accounting information is considered verifiable when it would be substantially duplicated by other independent measurers using the same measurement methods. The requirement that accounting information be based upon objective evidence is based upon the demonstrated needs of users for reliable, unbiased financial information. This is especially needed when parties with opposing interests (credit seekers and credit grantors) rely upon the same information. The reliability of information is enhanced if it is verifiable.

But accounting information will never be free of subjective opinion and judgment. It will always possess varying degrees of verifiability. Some measurements can be supported by canceled checks and invoices. Others, such as periodic depreciation charges, can never be verified because of their very nature. Thus, financial information in many instances is verifiable only in that it represents a consensus as to what would be reported if the same procedures had been followed by other accountants.

Neutrality

Financial accounting information should be neutral—it should not favor one group over another. It should meet the common needs of many users rather than the particular needs of specific users. It is not sufficient that the information be verifiable, since biased information can be verified. For example, inventories under the lower-of-cost-or-market method can be verified. But, since only declines in, and not increases to, market value have been recognized, one may question whether they meet the objective of neutrality.

Timeliness

The utility of information decreases with age. It is likely to be much more useful to know what the net earnings for 1978 were in early 1979 than to receive this information a year later. And if information is to be of any value in decision making, it must be available before the decision is made. If not, it is useless. In determining what constitutes timely information, consideration must be given to the other qualitative objectives and to the cost of gathering information. For example, a timely estimated amount for uncollectible accounts may be more valuable than a later, verified actual amount.

Comparability

When comparable financial information is presented, the differences and similarities noted will arise from the matters being reported upon and not from their accounting treatment. Comparable information will reveal relative strengths and weaknesses in a single firm through time and between two or more firms at the same point in time.

The accounting requirement of consistency leads to comparability of financial information for a single firm through time. Consistency generally requires adherence to the same accounting principles and reporting practices through time. It bars indiscriminate switching of principles or methods (such as changing depreciation methods every year). It does not bar changes in principles if the information needs of users are better served by the change. But disclosure of the change and, if material, its effects are required.[6]

Comparability between firms is more difficult to achieve because the same activities may be accounted for in different ways. For example, B may use the Lifo and accelerated depreciation methods, while C accounts for identical activities using Fifo and straight-line depreciation methods. A high degree of interfirm comparability will not exist until it is required that the same activities be accounted for in the same manner.

Completeness

Completeness requires that all financial accounting information meeting the other six qualitative objectives be reported. All significant information is to be disclosed in a manner that aids understanding and avoids misleading implications. This disclosure may be made in (1) the body of the financial statements, (2) in the notes to such statements, (3) in special communications, and (4) in the president's letter in the annual report.

In addition to changes in accounting principles, disclosure usually must be made of unusual activities (loans to officers); changes in expectations (losses on inventory); long-term obligations entered into that are not recorded by the accountant (lease of a factory building for 20 years); new arrangements with certain groups (pension and profit-sharing plans for employees); significant events that occur after the date of the statements (such as the loss of a major customer); and the accounting policies (major

---

[6] American Institute of Certified Public Accountants, Accounting Principles Board *Opinion No. 20,* "Accounting Changes" (New York: AICPA, 1971).

principles and their manner of application) followed in preparing the financial statements.[7]

THE BASIC FEATURES OF FINANCIAL ACCOUNTING

Many of what the APB calls basic features are characteristics of the environment in which the financial accounting process is applied.[8] They form the foundation that supports present generally accepted accounting principles. Some of these features were presented and discussed briefly in Chapter 1.

Accounting Entity

All accounting information pertains to a specific unit or area of interest called the entity. This entity is viewed as having an existence apart from its owners, creditors, employees, and other interested parties. For the corporation, this separate existence is confirmed by law. But the boundaries of the accounting entity may differ from those of the legal entity, since financial information may relate to a corporation and its subsidiary corporations as a single business. An accounting entity may exist where it is not supported by a legal entity, as in a single proprietorship. Here the business, not the individual, is the accounting entity. Financial statements must identify the entity for which they are prepared; and their content must be limited to reporting the activities, resources, and obligations of that entity.

Going Concern

In financial accounting, the entity is viewed as continuing indefinitely in operation unless evidence to the contrary exists. This assumption is justified because experience shows that continuity is highly probable for most entities. Yet if liquidation appears likely, financial information should not be reported based on the assumption of continuity.

The expectation of continuity is often used to justify the use of cost rather than market value as a basis for measuring assets. While significant for an entity in liquidation, market values are alleged to be of no significance to an entity that intends to use rather than sell its assets. On the other hand, the expectation of continuity permits the accountant to treat certain costs as assets. For example, printed advertising matter may be on hand to be used to promote a special sale next month. It may have little, if any, value to anyone but its owner. But it is treated as an asset because its owner is expected to continue operating long enough to benefit from it.

---

[7] American Institute of Certified Public Accountants, Accounting Principles Board *Opinion No. 22*, "Disclosure of Accounting Policies" (New York: AICPA, 1972).

[8] American Institute of Certified Public Accountants, *Statement No. 4*, par. 132.

Measurement of Economic Resources and Obligations

Financial accounting is primarily concerned with the measurement of economic resources and obligations and of changes in both. Basically, only those activities, resources, and obligations that can be quantified (measured in numbers) are of concern to financial accounting. Quantified data are generally more useful than verbal data. Accounting is not concerned with the economic concepts of satisfaction and welfare, nor is it directly concerned with the sociological and psychological aspects of economic activity.

Time Periods

To provide useful information to external parties for decision making at various points in the life of an entity, the accountant must subdivide the life of the entity into periods and prepare reports on the activities of those periods. In order to aid comparisons, the time periods usually are of equal length. The length of the period must be stated in the financial statements. Only in this way can useful information on what is a never-ending stream of activity be reported.

Measurement in Money Terms

Accounting measurements normally will be expressed in money terms. The unit of measure (the dollar in the United States) is identified in the financial statements.

This does not mean that all measurements of economic activity must be stated in monetary terms to be useful. It may, for example, be pertinent to know that a plant is operating at 50 percent of its capacity. But the full economic significance of this bit of information cannot be known until it is translated into money terms.

The monetary unit, the dollar, also provides accountants with a common unit of measure in reporting upon economic activity. Think, for a moment, about preparing a statement of financial position without using the dollar as a unit of measure. Such a statement would probably be of little value.

Stable Unit. In making money measurements, accountants have typically ignored fluctuations in the value of the unit of measure—the dollar. Thus, a portion of the cost of a building acquired in 1940 is deducted, without adjustment for change in the value of the dollar, from revenues earned in, and expressed in, 1979 dollars in arriving at the net earnings for 1979. The 1940 and 1979 dollars are treated as equal units of measure, even though substantial price inflation has occurred between the two years. The inflation experienced in the 1970s once again caused renewed interest to be expressed in the problem of adjusting financial statements for changes in the general level of prices.

Accrual Basis

Financial statements provide a better description of the financial status and operations of a firm when prepared under the accrual rather than the cash basis of accounting. Under the cash basis, which is used primarily in small service-rendering firms, revenues and most expenses are recorded at the time of cash receipt or cash payment. Under the accrual basis, changes in resources (assets) and obligations (equities), including revenues and expenses, are recorded much more nearly at the time that they actually occur. For example, revenues are recorded when services are rendered or products are sold and delivered, even if not paid for immediately in cash. Similarly, expenses are recorded as incurred in the period benefited—for example, employee services are recorded in the period received, which may not be the same period in which payment is made. The accrual basis reflects the fact that considerable economic activity can occur that is not matched by a concurrent cash flow.

Exchange Prices

Financial accounting measurements consist largely of the prices found in exchanges of economic resources. Typically, past exchange prices are used and called historical costs when applied to many assets. But, at times, a current exchange price or a future exchange price may be used. For example, both replacement cost and expected selling price are used in determining "market" under the lower-of-cost-or-market inventory method. But, on the whole, financial accounting is concerned largely with past exchange prices rather than current values.[9]

Approximation and Judgment

Accounting measurements are often based upon estimates. To provide periodic financial information, estimates must often be made of such things as expected uncollectible accounts and the useful lives of depreciable assets. Periodic depreciation charges can never be anything but estimates. Because they depend on future events, estimates of the net realizable value of accounts receivable must be uncertain and tentative. This uncertainty precludes precise measurement and makes estimates necessary.

---

[9] But this appears to be changing. Due largely to the "double-digit" rate of inflation in the mid-70s, accountants are becoming increasingly interested in "current value accounting." The SEC has also been responsible for much of this interest. As stated in *Accounting Series Release No. 190*, the SEC requires that certain companies required to file financial statements with the Commission disclose in their annual reports (in footnotes or in a separate section) the current replacement cost of inventories, cost of goods sold, productive capacity (plant assets, except land), and depreciation, depletion, and amortization. As of this writing, some departure from the historical cost basis of asset valuation seems imminent.

Yet, because they represent the exercise of judgment by an informed accountant, these estimates are often quite accurate. And it is this need to exercise judgment that prevents one from stating the financial accounting process as a set of inflexible rules, an example of which might be: Depreciate all trucks over three years.

General Purpose Financial Information

The results of the financial accounting process are presented in general-purpose financial statements. They are presented to external parties and to top-level internal managers in the belief that they will serve the common needs of these and other users. This does not mean that special-purpose financial information cannot be developed from accounting records. For example, the information demanded by an insurance company which has been asked for a loan may differ from the information it would receive if it sought to purchase some of the potential borrower's shares of stock in the market.

Fundamentally Related Financial Statements

The statements that are the end product of the financial accounting process are fundamentally related because they are based on the same data. For example, the net earnings shown on the earnings statement must be carried to the statement of retained earnings before that statement can be completed. The ending balance on the statement of retained earnings must be carried to the statement of financial position to bring the assets and equities on this statement into agreement.

Substance over Form

In some instances the economic substance of a transaction may conflict with its legal form. For example, a contract which is legally a lease may, in fact, be a purchase. This is true for a three-year contract to rent an auto at a stated monthly rental with the lessee to receive title to the auto at the end of the lease period upon the payment of a nominal sum (say, $1). When the two conflict, the accountant records economic substance rather than legal form.

Materiality

A statement, fact, or item is material if it is significant enough to influence the decisions of an informed investor, creditor, or other interested party. One way of determining whether an item is material is to look at its relative size. A $10,000 item of expense in a firm with net earnings of

$30,000 would seem to be material. But the same amount in a larger, more profitable, corporation may not be material. If an item is considered immaterial, it may be handled without regard to accounting principles. Thus, the cost of a minor asset, such as a wastebasket, may be charged to expense in the period it is acquired rather than set up as an asset and depreciated over its useful life.

But there is more to materiality than dollar amounts. The very nature of an item may make it material. For example, it may be quite significant to know that a certain corporation is securing its overseas business by bribing the employees of a foreign government. Or that certain U.S. corporations are making illegal political contributions. How to assess the significance of such actions is proving to be a serious problem for accountants.

Conservatism

Basically, the modifying convention of conservatism embraces the idea of being cautious or prudent. Many accounting measurements are estimates and involve the exercise of judgment. In such cases, conservatism tells the accountant "to play it safe." Playing it safe usually involves making sure that, if in error, all estimates are in error in such a way as to yield lower reported net assets and net earnings than might otherwise be reported.

Conservatism may be applied with varying degrees of severity in different firms, causing decreased comparability in their financial information. This may cause investors to act in a manner not in their best interest. They may, for example, sell shares of stock in a firm because its earnings did not meet their expectations. But this failure may have been due solely to a conservative measurement of inventories. Thus, a fine line exists, in many instances, between conservative and incorrect accounting.

Other Modifying Conventions

In addition to conservatism, the board identified two other conventions that modify the strict application of generally accepted accounting principles: (1) emphasis upon earnings or income determination, and (2) application of judgment of the accounting profession as a whole.[10] Both of these are incorporated in the remaining discussion.

THE MAJOR PRINCIPLES

Although there exists no authoritative statement of generally accepted accounting principles, accountants agree that certain principles dominate accounting practice. These principles are presented and discussed below.

---

[10] Ibid., par. 172–74.

The Initial Recording Principle

Stated briefly, this principle is: Transfers of resources are recorded in the accounting system at the time of exchange and at the prices agreed upon in the exchange.[11] Thus, for any firm, this principle determines to a large extent (1) what goes into the accounting system, (2) when it is recorded, and (3) the amounts at which assets, liabilities, owners' equity, revenues, expenses, and net earnings are recorded. As applied to certain assets, the principle is often called the "cost principle," meaning that these assets are recorded at cost. But use of the term "exchange price principle" is to be preferred because it seems inappropriate to refer to liabilities, revenues, owners' equity, and certain assets such as cash and accounts receivable as being measured in terms of their cost.

The Matching Principle

A most fundamental principle of accounting is that net earnings can be determined by matching the expenses incurred with the periodic revenues they generate.[12] The logic of the principle stems from the fact that wherever economic resources are employed someone will want to know what was accomplished and at what cost. Every appraisal of economic activity will involve matching sacrifice with benefit. And knowledge of sacrifice and benefit is usually considered far more valuable than knowledge of the stock of resources. So it is in accounting. The earnings statement is generally considered more important than the statement of financial position.

In applying the matching principle, revenue is the independent variable. It is recognized through application of the realization principle, as discussed and illustrated below.

Revenue Recognition

Revenue is defined as the product or service provided by a firm. It is best measured by the amount of cash expected from the customer. The generation of revenue usually consists of a never-ending stream of activity. A question thus arises as to when this revenue, this added utility, should be recorded, that is, credited to a revenue account. The general answer is that the revenue should be earned and realized before it is recognized.

The Earning of Revenue. In a broad sense, all of the activities of a firm to create additional utility constitute the earning process. The actual

---

[11] Ibid., par. 145.

[12] The APB refused to use the term "matching" in *Statement No. 4,* stating that the term has too many meanings. But the process of matching is implicit in its discussion. For example: "Income determination in accounting is the process of identifying, measuring, and relating revenue and expenses of an enterprise for an accounting period" is one of the board's "pervasive" principles. (Ibid., par. 147.)

receipt of cash from a customer may have been preceded by many events including (1) placing advertisements, (2) calling on the customer several times, (3) submission of samples, (4) acquisition of raw materials, (5) manufacture of the goods, and (6) delivery of the goods. Costs were undoubtedly incurred for these activities. And revenue was actually being generated by these activities, even though accountants refuse to recognize it until time of sale. This refusal is based upon their requirement that revenue be realized before it is recognized.[13]

The Realization of Revenue.   As a general principle, revenue is considered realized at the time of sale for merchandise transactions and when services have been performed in service transactions. Legally, a sale occurs when title to the goods passes to the buyer. As a practical matter, accountants generally record revenue when goods are delivered.

The advantages of recognizing revenue at time of sale include: (1) the delivery of the goods is a discernible event; (2) the revenue is measurable; (3) the risk of loss due to price decline or destruction of the goods has passed to the buyer; (4) the revenue has been earned, or substantially so; and (5) because the revenue has been earned, expenses can be determined thus allowing net earnings to be determined. As discussed below, the disadvantage of recognizing revenue at time of sale is that the revenue may not be recorded in the period in which the activity creating it occurred.

Cash Collection as Point of Revenue Recognition.   Some small firms record revenues and expenses at the time of cash collection and payment. This procedure is known as the cash basis of accounting. It is acceptable primarily in service enterprises which do not have substantial credit transactions or inventories, and in accounting for installment sales.

Installment Basis of Revenue Recognition.   When the selling price of goods is to be collected in installments and considerable doubt exists as to collectibility, the installment basis of accounting may be employed. Under this basis, the gross margin on a sale is treated as being realized proportionately with the cash collected from customers. If this gross margin rate is 40 percent, then 40 cents of every dollar collected on the installment accounts receivable represents realized gross margin. For example, assume a stereo system costing $300 is sold for $500, with payment to be made in 10 equal installments of $50 each. If four installments are collected in the year of sale, the realized gross margin taken into net earnings is $80 ($4 \times \$50 \times .40$). In the next year it will be $120 ($6 \times \$50 \times .40$), if the final six installments are collected.

This method is accepted for tax purposes. But, because it delays the recognition of revenue beyond the time of sale, it is accepted for accounting purposes only when extreme doubt exists as to the collectibility of the installments due.

---

[13] In *Statement No. 4* the board combines the earning of revenue and the realization of revenue into a single pervasive principle called *realization* (Ibid., par. 150).

Revenue Recognition on Long-Term Construction Projects. The revenue created by completing a long-term construction project can be recognized under two methods: (1) the completed-contract method or (2) the percentage-of-completion method. Under the completed-contract method, no revenue is recognized until the period in which the contract is completed, and then all of the revenue is recognized even though the contract may have required three years to complete. The costs incurred on the project are carried forward in inventory accounts and are charged to expense in the period in which the revenue is recognized. This approach is similar to recognizing revenue at the time of sale. It suffers from the disadvantage of recognizing no revenue or net earnings from a project in periods in which a major part of the revenue-producing activity may have occurred.

Under the percentage-of-completion method, revenue and net earnings are recognized periodically on the basis of the estimated stage of completion of the project. To illustrate, assume that a firm has a contract to erect a dam at a price of $44 million. By the end of the first fiscal year, it had incurred costs of $30 million and expected to incur $10 million more. The contract would be considered 75 percent complete, since $30 million of an expected $40 million of costs have been incurred. Consequently, $33 million of revenue and $3 million of earnings would be recognized on the contract in the fiscal year. Accountants believe the use of this method results in a clearer reflection of the actual underlying activities. It is an example of the use of the modifying convention calling for the exercise of the judgment of the accounting profession as a whole.

Collections of Revenue before It Is Earned. Sometimes cash is collected before goods are delivered or services rendered; in effect, future revenues are collected. Such receipts should not be credited to a revenue account, since no revenue has been earned. Such receipts give rise to a liability and they should be credited to an account that reveals their nature, such as Unearned Subscription Revenue or Advances by Customers. In the period in which the goods are delivered or the services performed, this account can be debited and the regular revenue account (Sales or Service Revenue) credited.

Expense Recognition

Expense is defined as the resources or service potentials consumed in generating revenue. Since resources and service potentials are assets, expense may also be defined as asset expirations voluntarily incurred to produce revenue. The television set delivered by a dealer to a customer for cash can readily be thought of as an asset expiration to produce revenue. Similarly, the services of a television station employed to advertise a product can be thought of as expiring to produce revenue. Losses, on the other hand, may be distinguished as involuntary asset expirations not related to the production of revenue. Fire losses are an example.

The Measurement of Expense.   Since many assets used in operating a business are measured in terms of historical cost, it follows that many expenses, being expired assets, are measured in terms of the historical cost of the assets expired. Other expenses are paid for currently and are measured in terms of their current cost. Note that in a transaction recorded as a debit to Advertising Expense and a credit to Cash, it is not the asset, cash, that expires. The actual transaction consists of an exchange of cash for advertising services—an asset. The accountant, anticipating that the services will have expired by the end of the accounting period, records the expenditure as an expense. By this shortcut, an adjusting entry will be avoided. But this is merely an expedient accounting technique. No one knowingly buys expenses, that is, expired assets.

The Timing of Expense Recognition.   The matching principle implies that a cause-and-effect relationship exists between expense and revenue, that is, expense is the cause of revenue.[14] For certain expenses, the relationship is readily seen, as in the case of goods delivered to customers. When a direct cause-and-effect relationship cannot be seen, the costs of assets with limited lives may be charged to expense in the periods benefited on a systematic and rational allocation basis.[15] Depreciation of plant assets is an example. In other instances, the relationship between expense and revenue can only be assumed to exist, as in the case of a contribution to the local community fund. Consequently, the recognition of expense, as a practical matter, is often guided by the concepts of product costs and period costs.

Product costs are those costs incurred directly and indirectly in the acquisition and manufacture of goods. Included are the invoice costs of goods, as well as freight and insurance-in-transit costs. For manufacturing firms, product costs include all costs of raw materials as well as the direct labor and indirect costs of operating a factory to produce goods (see Chapters 13 and 14). Such costs are deemed to attach to the goods produced; are carried in inventory accounts as long as the goods are on hand; and are charged to expense when the goods are sold. Thus, a precise matching of the expense cost of goods sold and its related revenue is obtained.

Period costs are the remaining costs incurred and consist primarily of selling and administrative expenses. Under this concept, expenses are matched with revenues by periods because matching by transactions is

---

[14] In *Statement No. 4* this is called the "pervasive principle of associating cause and effect" (ibid., par. 157).

[15] In *Statement No. 4* this is called the "pervasive principle of systematic and rational allocation" (ibid., par. 159).

simply not possible.[16] Thus, period costs are expensed in the period incurred because (1) they relate to the current period's revenue—the local supermarket's weekly newspaper advertisement is an example; (2) the cost must be incurred every period and there is no measurable build-up of benefits—officers' salaries are an example here; (3) there is no measurable relationship with any segment of revenue, yet the cost must be incurred to remain in business—the cost of the annual audit is an example; and (4) the amount of cost to be carried forward cannot be measured in a nonarbitrary manner—as might be true for the costs of an employee training and apprenticeship program.

Before leaving these principles, let us illustrate how completely they dominate what is reported in the financial statements:

The initial recording principle directs that assets be initially recorded at cost. The realization principle requires that increases in the value of assets not be recorded until realized through an exchange. Thus, assets are reported at cost, or at undepreciated cost if they are being systematically and rationally amortized in adherence to the matching principle.

In seeking to adhere to the matching principle, a firm may defer the cost of a major promotional campaign to introduce a new product. These costs are reported as an asset and amortized over future periods even though they represent nothing of value to anyone but the firm incurring them.

Many firms include among their liabilities an item titled "Deferred Federal Income Taxes (Payable)." This item does not represent an obligation to transfer assets or to provide services. But, as discussed in Chapter 19, it arises solely from a matching of federal income tax expense with net earnings before taxes.

BROAD OPERATING AND DETAILED ACCOUNTING PRINCIPLES

Underlying the major principles presented above is a set of broad operating principles. This set consists of a group of principles that guides the actual operation of an accounting system.[17] They indicate which events are to be recorded and which are not, and how the selected events are to be measured. They show how the principle of initial recording of exchange prices is to be applied to exchanges that affect assets, liabilities, owners' equity, revenues, and expenses. These principles also indicate broadly the accounting to be applied to (1) transfers such as gifts, donations, lawsuit losses, fines, and thefts, (2) events favorable and unfavorable to the firm, such as changes in the market values of assets owned, and (3) internal

---

[16] In *Statement No. 4* this is called the "pervasive principle of immediate recognition" (ibid., par. 160).

[17] Ibid., par. 181–201.

events such as the manufacture of goods. Some of these broad operating principles relate to financial reporting, specifying the financial statements that must be presented, the classifications of items within these statements, and providing for the reporting of earnings per share.

These broad operating principles are not dealt with here because most of them are presented and discussed in depth in other chapters. For the same reason, the detailed accounting principles used to implement the major and broad operating principles will not be discussed here.[18] Examples of these are the Fifo method of inventory pricing and the straight-line depreciation method. One of the purposes of this chapter has been to put these more detailed accounting principles in place in a model of theory underlying financial accounting. For examples of the type of financial reporting that emerges from application of all of the above principles, see the appendix to this chapter.

SUMMARY

In recent years, financial accounting practice has been guided by a group of important ideas that are collectively called generally accepted accounting principles. These principles have been relied upon in fulfilling the general objective of providing reliable information about economic resources and obligations.

Accounting principles are man-made and have evolved through the years in response to many influences including federal income tax laws and regulations, securities legislation, organizations such as the AICPA, AAA, SEC, and FASB, individual writers, and industry practices. The AICPA has been especially influential through publications such as the *Accounting Research Bulletins,* the APB *Opinions,* the *Accounting Research Studies,* and the *Statements of the Accounting Principles Board.* The FASB, which replaced the APB in 1973, has also issued a number of statements of accounting standards.

The discussion in this chapter followed roughly the model of theory provided by the APB in its *Statement No. 4.* This model consisted of:

1. General and qualitative objectives.
2. Basic features.
3. Basic elements.
4. Pervasive principles.
5. Modifying conventions.

---

[18] No list of detailed principles is included in *Statement No. 4.* Rather, the board draws attention to the absence of such an authoritative list and then notes the possible sources of such detailed accounting principles—the *Opinions* of the APB, the *Accounting Research Bulletins,* textbooks, and so on (ibid., par. 202–206). Statements of the FASB, the APB's successor, would, of course, be considered authoritative now.

6. Broad operating principles.
7. Detailed accounting principles.

Among the major, pervasive principles of accounting are (1) the initial recording of exchange prices, (2) the matching of expenses and revenues, and (3) the realization principle. Revenue is the independent variable in the matching process and may be recognized (1) at time of sale or performance of services, (2) at time of cash collection, (3) under the installment method, or (4) as production progresses, depending upon the underlying circumstances. Expense recognition is guided largely by the (1) matching, (2) systematic and rational allocation, and (3) immediate recognition principles. To a large extent, the principles of initial recording of exchange prices, matching, and realization determine not only the content of the earnings statement but also the content of the statement of financial position.   .

APPENDIX

Presented in this appendix are significant portions of the Annual Report for 1975 of Interlake, Inc. and its consolidated subsidiaries. Included are: (1) a page of 1975 financial highlights, (2) the statement of consolidated income and retained earnings, (3) the consolidated balance sheet, (4) the statement of changes in consolidated financial position, (5) notes to consolidated financial statements, (6) report of independent accountants, (7) management's operating and financial review, (8) a five-year financial summary of operations, and (9) management's discussion of the summary of operations. These items are presented as being illustrative of the financial reporting practices followed by a modern business corporation in reporting to its stockholders and to other external parties. Several explanatory comments of the above items are needed.

1. Your authors prefer the terminology of earnings statement and net earnings in the statement reporting on operations and the term statement of financial position to balance sheet, although the terminology employed by the company is fully acceptable and, indeed, more widely used.

2. The item "Future Income Taxes" in Illustration 11.3 and discussed in Notes 1 and 11 in Illustration 11.5 is explained and discussed in Chapter 19.

3. The financial statements are for Interlake, Inc. and a number of wholly owned and partially owned corporations called subsidiaries (see Note 1 in Illustration 11.5). The item "Minority Interests in Subsidiaries" in the Consolidated Balance Sheet represents the stockholders' equity of the owners of the shares of stock of subsidiary companies not owned by Interlake (as was discussed in Chapter 10).

ILLUSTRATION 11.1

Interlake, Inc.
1975 Highlights

Interlake, Inc. is engaged in two main businesses: metals and material handling. In metals, we manufacture and sell iron, steel and related products as an integrated steel producer. . . plus silicon metal, ferroalloys and ferrous metal powders. In material handling, we're involved in packaging and storage products and systems, fabricated products and material handling equipment.

For The Year (In thousands)	% Change '75-'74	1975	1974	1973
Net sales of continuing operations	7.9	$640,831	$593,764	$425,999
Income of continuing operations	(1.4)	39,706	40,263	17,950
Net income	(11.9)	34,375	38,999	16,784
Cash flow	(2.4)	52,388	53,678	30,713
Capital expenditures	40.8	35,884	25,486	12,773
Cash dividends paid	(26.7)	8,075	11,013	7,373
At Year End (In thousands)				
Working capital	15.0	$109,421	$ 95,143	$ 98,021
Current ratio	25.0	2.0 to 1	1.6 to 1	2.5 to 1
Property, plant and equipment—net	7.4	202,621	188,746	155,265
Long-term debt, less current maturities	15.3	85,599	74,216	60,367
Shareholders' equity	9.0	264,046	242,134	214,056
Shares outstanding	(3.5)	5,405	5,603	5,597
Per Share Statistics (Restated for 3-for-2 stock split)				
Income of continuing operations	2.1	$ 7.34	$ 7.19	$ 3.15
Net income	(8.9)	6.35	6.97	2.95
Cash dividends paid	(23.9)	1.50	1.97	1.30
Shareholders' equity at year-end	13.0	48.85	43.22	38.24

Quarterly Results—1975 and 1974 (In millions—except per share statistics)

	Sales*				Income*				Net Income				Stock Price Range				Dividends	
			Amount		Per Share				Amount		Per Share		1975		1974		Per Share	
	1975	1974	1975	1974	1975	1974	1975	1974	1975	1974	1975	1974	High Low		High Low		1975	1974
1st	$186.5	$125.0	$14.0	$ 4.8	$2.55	$ .86	$ 7.7	$ 4.7	$1.39	$ .83	21⅝ 18		17⅜ 13⅞		$ .33	$ .30
2nd	153.9	149.6	4.4	11.7	.84	2.08	5.4	11.4	1.02	2.04	23⅜ 19½		18⅝ 16		.33	.33
3rd	143.2	158.9	10.9	14.5	2.01	2.59	10.9	14.3	2.01	2.56	25⅞ 20⅝		18⅛ 14⅞		.34	.34
4th	157.2	160.3	10.4	9.3	1.94	1.66	10.4	8.6	1.93	1.54	26½ 23¾		19⅝ 14⅜		.50	1.00
Year	$640.8	$593.8	$39.7	$40.3	$7.34	$7.19	$34.4	$39.0	$6.35	$6.97	26½ 18		19⅝ 13⅞		$1.50	$1.97

*Of continuing operations

Sales and Earnings by Business (In millions)

		Sales				Earnings*			
		1975	%	1974	%	1975	%	1974	%
Metals	Iron	$110.1	17	$103.0	17	$50.7	66	$45.5	58
	Steel	171.4	27	202.6	34				
	Silicon Metal/Ferroalloys	48.6	7	55.1	9	8.1	11	13.3	17
	Metal Powders	30.4	5	34.0	6	4.0	5	3.5	4
Material Handling	Packaging/Fabricated Products	109.1	17	119.2	20	5.7	7	9.8	13
	Material Handling/Storage	171.2	27	79.9	14	8.8	11	6.6	8
		$640.8	100%	$593.8	100%	$77.3	100%	$78.7	100%

*Of continuing operations before unallocated corporate items and income taxes.

ILLUSTRATION 11.2

Interlake, Inc.

Statement of Consolidated Income and Retained Earnings
For the Years Ended December 28, 1975 and December 29, 1974

	1975	1974
Sales and Revenues:		
Net sales of continuing operations	$640,831,084	$593,763,666
Other revenues	9,492,783	9,277,879
	650,323,867	603,041,545
Costs and Expenses:		
Cost of products sold (Note 6)	457,733,049	447,726,271
Depreciation, depletion and amortization (Note 1)	19,287,194	15,337,132
Selling and administrative expenses	74,984,861	45,996,124
State, local and miscellaneous taxes	19,283,832	14,427,498
Interest expense	9,861,363	5,934,395
	581,150,299	529,421,420
Income of Continuing Operations before Taxes on Income	69,173,568	73,620,125
Provision for Income Taxes (Note 11)	29,467,000	33,357,000
Income of Continuing Operations	39,706,568	40,263,125
Loss from Discontinued Operations, net of applicable income taxes (Note 9)	5,331,238	1,264,432
Net Income for the Year	34,375,330	38,998,693
Retained Earnings at Beginning of Year	157,577,049	129,591,281
	191,952,379	168,589,974
Deduct Cash Dividends Paid ($1.50 per share in 1975 and $1.97 per share in 1974) (Note 4)	(8,075,091)	(11,012,925)
Retained Earnings at End of Year	$183,877,288	$157,577,049
Per Share of Common Stock (Note 4):		
Income of Continuing Operations	$7.34	$7.19
Loss from Discontinued Operations	(.99)	(.22)
Net Income	$6.35	$6.97

(See notes to consolidated financial statements)

ILLUSTRATION 11.3

Interlake, Inc.

Consolidated Balance Sheet
December 28, 1975 and December 29, 1974

Assets	1975	1974
Current Assets:		
Cash	$ 2,860,359	$ 5,071,634
Certificates of deposit	5,728,920	1,647,987
Marketable securities, at cost which approximates market	149,441	3,557,451
Receivables, less allowance for doubtful accounts of $2,470,000 in 1975 and $2,450,000 in 1974	81,636,139	106,136,415
Inventories (Note 1):		
Raw materials and supplies	57,339,376	60,121,078
Semi-finished and finished products	60,790,986	66,332,308
Other current assets	7,986,684	7,578,937
Total current assets	216,491,905	250,445,810
Investments and Other Assets:		
Affiliated companies (Note 1)	12,057,200	5,618,392
Iron ore interests (Notes 1 and 12)	21,704,676	22,367,676
Other investments and deferred charges	9,906,916	8,322,342
Construction funds held by trustees	5,712,428	9,568,928
Goodwill (Note 1)	11,619,402	11,294,208
	61,000,622	57,171,546
Property, Plant and Equipment, at cost (Note 1):		
Land and mineral properties, less depletion	14,128,400	14,718,260
Plant and equipment	467,675,404	438,286,832
	481,803,804	453,005,092
Less—Depreciation and amortization	279,183,259	264,258,709
	202,620,545	188,746,383
	$480,113,072	$496,363,739

Liabilities and Shareholders' Equity	1975	1974
Current Liabilities:		
Accounts payable	$ 58,567,310	$ 85,713,329
Salaries and wages	15,890,461	14,801,873
Taxes other than income taxes	8,154,881	7,356,939
U.S. and foreign income taxes (Notes 8 and 11)	13,484,385	28,002,250
Notes payable	10,090,457	16,700,482
Current maturities of long-term debt (Note 2)	883,702	2,728,285
Total current liabilities	107,071,196	155,303,158
Long-Term Debt (Note 2)	85,599,287	74,216,174
Other Long-Term Liabilities	10,202,481	8,399,620
Future Income Taxes (Note 1)	12,041,761	13,316,205
Minority Interests in Subsidiaries	1,152,494	2,994,775
Shareholders' Equity:		
Common stock, par value $1 a share; authorized 10,000,000 shares; issued 6,381,948 shares in 1975 and 6,385,692 shares in 1974 (Note 4)	98,221,862	98,418,612
Retained earnings (Note 3)	183,877,288	157,577,049
	282,099,150	255,995,661
Less—Cost of common stock held in treasury (976,919 shares in 1975 and 782,932 shares in 1974) (Note 4)	18,053,297	13,861,854
	264,045,853	242,133,807
	$480,113,072	$496,363,739

(See notes to consolidated financial statements)

ILLUSTRATION 11.4

Interlake, Inc.

Statement of Changes in Consolidated Financial Position
For the Years Ended December 28, 1975 and December 29, 1974

	1975	1974
Financial Resources Were Provided By:		
Income of continuing operations	$ 39,706,568	$ 40,263,125
Depreciation, depletion and amortization	19,287,194	15,337,132
Equity in undistributed earnings of affiliates and joint ventures	(3,224,345)	(2,763,421)
Future income taxes	(1,274,444)	(657,558)
Loss from discontinued operations, net of applicable income taxes	(5,331,238)	(1,264,432)
Increase in other long-term liabilities	1,802,861	2,143,995
Working capital provided from operations	50,966,596	53,058,841
Long-term borrowings	14,140,149	11,100,000
	65,106,745	64,158,841
Financial Resources Were Used For:		
Capital expenditures, less net book value of retirements and sales of $1,161,892 in 1975 and $1,454,876 in 1974	34,722,000	24,031,361
Reduction of long-term debt	2,757,036	4,008,218
Cash dividends	8,075,091	11,012,925
Purchase of Company common stock	5,080,950	—
Acquisitions, net of working capital acquired	—	18,882,968
Purchase of minority interests	1,925,925	—
Investment in affiliated companies and joint ventures	2,551,463	—
Increase (decrease) in construction funds held by trustees	(3,856,500)	8,998,327
Other	(427,277)	103,855
	50,828,688	67,037,654
Increase (decrease) in working capital	$ 14,278,057	$ (2,878,813)
Increase (Decrease) In Working Capital Comprises:		
Cash, certificates of deposit and marketable securities	$ (1,538,352)	$ (8,971,257)
Receivables	(24,500,276)	44,118,481
Inventories	(8,323,024)	49,055,819
Other current assets	407,747	2,244,323
Accounts payable and salaries and wages	26,057,431	(48,597,260)
Taxes payable	13,719,923	(23,140,699)
Notes payable	6,610,025	(16,700,482)
Current maturities of long-term debt	1,844,583	(887,738)
	14,278,057	(2,878,813)
Working capital at beginning of year	95,142,652	98,021,465
Working capital at end of year	$109,420,709	$ 95,142,652

(See notes to consolidated financial statements)

ILLUSTRATION 11.5

Interlake, Inc.

Notes to Consolidated Financial Statements
For the Years Ended December 28, 1975 and December 29, 1974

NOTE 1—Summary of Significant Accounting Policies

Principles of Consolidation—The consolidated financial statements include the accounts of all majority-owned domestic and foreign subsidiaries. Investments in corporate joint ventures and companies owned 20% to 50% are accounted for by the equity method. Such investments are carried at cost plus equity in undistributed earnings.

Translation of Foreign Currencies—Starting with 1975, the financial statements of foreign operations have been translated in accordance with provisions of the Financial Accounting Standards Board Statement Number 8. This change, had it been applied retroactively, would not have resulted in a material restatement of prior year financial results and had no material effect on 1975 operating results. Exchange adjustments of immaterial amounts have been reflected in earnings.

Inventories—Inventories are stated at the lower of cost or market value. Cost of domestic inventories is determined principally by the last-in first-out method, which is less than current costs by $69,460,000 and $53,962,000 at December 28, 1975 and December 29, 1974, respectively. Cost of inventories of foreign subsidiaries is determined principally by the first-in first-out method.

Property, Plant and Equipment and Depreciation—For financial reporting purposes, plant and equipment are depreciated principally on a straight-line method over the estimated useful lives of the assets. Costs of significant renewals and betterments, including furnace relines, are capitalized. Depreciation claimed for income tax purposes is computed by use of accelerated methods. Income taxes applicable to differences in depreciation claimed for tax purposes and that reported in the financial statements is charged or credited to future income taxes, as appropriate. Provision for depletion of mineral properties is based on tonnage rates which are expected to amortize the cost of such properties over the estimated amount of mineral deposits to be removed.

Goodwill—Goodwill represents the excess of the purchase price over the fair value of the net assets of acquired companies and is amortized on a straight-line basis over a period of approximately thirty years. In 1975 the Company extended its amortization policy to include goodwill arising from acquisitions occurring prior to November 1, 1970. This change had no significant effect on 1975 operating results.

Investment Tax Credits—The full amount of investment tax credits claimed for tax purposes is reflected in income in the year the related property is placed in service.

Pension Plans—The Company has several pension plans which cover substantially all employees. These plans generally follow the basic pension pattern of the steel industry. The provision for pension cost includes current costs plus interest on and amortization of unfunded prior service cost over a period of approximately 25 years. The Company's policy is to fund pension cost accrued.

NOTE 2—Long-Term Debt and Credit Arrangements

Long-term debt of the Company consists of the following:

	December 28, 1975	December 29, 1974
8.80% debentures, due annually $2,500,000 1978 to 1995, and $5,000,000 in 1996	$ 50,000,000	$ 50,000,000
4⅞ % debentures, due $1,500,000 in 1976 and $2,477,000 in 1977	2,683,000	3,374,000
Obligations under long-term lease agreements	16,300,000	16,300,000
11¼ % notes payable, due annually in varying installments from 1980 to 1998	4,362,000	—
Bank term loans, due 1977, repayable in pound sterling, interest at 1½ % over the interbank rate	9,103,500	—
Other	4,034,489	7,270,459
	86,482,989	76,944,459
Less—Current maturities	883,702	2,728,285
	$ 85,599,287	$ 74,216,174

At December 28, 1975, 4⅞ % debentures with a face value of $1,294,000 were held in the treasury by the Company. These may be used in meeting the 1976 sinking fund requirement and have been applied as a reduction of current maturities of long-term debt.

The long-term lease obligations relate principally to pollution control facilities which are being accounted for as plant and equipment as funds are expended. The interest rates on these obligations vary from 6.00% to 7.88%. Principal payments begin in 1981 ($500,000) and continue in varying annual amounts through 1999.

During 1975 the Company entered into a loan agreement to sell $10,000,000 of 11¼ % notes to finance the Company's share of construction costs for a coal mining venture. A commitment fee of ½ % per annum is payable on funds not borrowed.

On April 28, 1975 the Company entered into a revolving credit agreement with a group of banks which permits short-term borrowings up to a maximum of $15,000,000 until April 27, 1977 at the prime rate of interest on notes dated March 7, 1976 or prior and at ¼ % over the prime rate thereafter. A commitment fee of ½ % per annum is payable quarterly on the average unused amount of credit. There were no borrowings outstanding at December 28, 1975.

In connection with the revolving credit agreement and other domestic lines of credit, the Company has entered into informal arrangements to maintain average compensating balances of 12% for the unused lines and an additional 7% for any borrowings. The Company's estimated average float exceeded the bank deposits required under these arrangements.

ILLUSTRATION 11.5 (continued)

NOTE 3—Retained Earnings

Under the most restrictive terms of agreements relating to outstanding loans, the Company may not as of December 28, 1975 pay cash dividends or repurchase the Company's capital stock in amounts aggregating more than $73,500,000.

NOTE 4—Capital Stock

In August, 1975 the Board of Directors declared a three-for-two stock split effected in the form of a 50% stock dividend on all common shares outstanding and held in the treasury. Common stock, stock option and per share data for 1975 and 1974 have been restated to reflect the stock split.

Earnings per share of common stock were computed based on the weighted average number of shares outstanding which was 5,412,904 shares in 1975 and 5,598,207 shares in 1974. In February, 1975 the Company purchased 241,950 shares of its common stock for $5,080,950. Shares purchased are being held in the treasury.

At December 28, 1975, 153,925 treasury shares of common stock were reserved for outstanding stock options under the 1965 Stock Option Plan, 435 for distribution under a deferred compensation plan, and 822,559 were unreserved. During both 1975 and 1974, 864 treasury shares were distributed under the deferred compensation plan.

The Company's authorized capital stock includes 1,000,000 shares of serial preferred stock, $1 par value per share, none of which has been issued.

NOTE 5—Stock Options

In 1965 the shareholders approved a Qualified Stock Option Plan for the Company's officers and key employees. Under the plan, options were available for grant until December 31, 1974 to purchase common stock for periods not longer than five years from the date of grant and at prices not less than the market value at date of grant. Options are exercisable 33⅓% annually, on a cumulative basis, beginning one year from date of grant. Options outstanding at December 28, 1975 expire at varying dates until 1979.

In April, 1975 the shareholders approved a non-qualified Stock Option Plan for the Company's officers and key employees. Under the plan, options may be granted until December 31, 1984 to purchase common stock for periods not longer than ten years from the date of grant and at prices not less than the market value at date of grant. Options are exercisable 33⅓% annually, on a cumulative basis, beginning one year from date of grant. The total number of shares which may be issued pursuant to this plan may not exceed 375,000 shares. At December 28, 1975, 320,325 options were available for grant.

Changes in the number of shares of common stock under option during the years ended December 28, 1975 and December 29, 1974 were as follows:

	1975	1974
Options outstanding at beginning of year	217,500	184,350
Options granted— Per share—$22.00 in 1975 and $17.21 in 1974	54,975	72,300
Options exercised— Per share—$15.42 to $18.75 in 1975 and $15.42 in 1974	(47,099)	(4,800)
Options cancelled	(16,776)	(34,350)
Options outstanding at end of year: Number of shares	208,600	217,500
Exercise price per share	($15.79-$22.00)	($15.42-$18.75)
Options exercisable at end of year	98,075	109,971

NOTE 6—Significant Transaction

In 1975 cost of products sold includes a $10,000,000 favorable settlement from a supplier in connection with a long-term coal supply contract. The settlement, recorded in the third quarter of 1975, increased net income $5,000,000.

NOTE 7—Acquisition

In October, 1974 the Company acquired substantially all of the outstanding ordinary and preference shares of Dexion-Comino International Limited, a producer of storage and material handling products with manufacturing operations principally in Europe, for an aggregate cash cost of $22,080,000. The acquisition was accounted for using the purchase method. The consolidated financial statements for 1975 and 1974 include Dexion's operating results for the thirteen months ended December 28, 1975 and month of November, 1974.

Had the acquisition occurred at the beginning of 1974, pro forma consolidated net sales, net income and net income per share of continuing operations for 1974, after giving effect to appropriate purchase accounting adjustments, would have been $697,802,000, $42,401,000 and $7.57, respectively.

NOTE 8—Foreign Operations

The Company's foreign subsidiaries, affiliates and joint ventures are located principally in Canada and Western Europe. Net assets of foreign companies at December 28, 1975 and December 29, 1974 and results of operations for the years then ended were as follows:

	1975	1974
Net assets	$ 56,435,000	$62,935,000
Net sales	150,655,000	66,648,000
Earnings before taxes and unallocated corporate items	12,109,000	7,239,000

Had Dexion been acquired at the beginning of 1974 (see Note 7), pro forma net sales and earnings before taxes and unallocated corporate items for the year ended December 29, 1974 would have been $157,284,000 and $14,662,000, respectively.

No provision for U.S. income taxes on unremitted earnings of foreign companies has been made as it is anticipated that any U.S. taxes on dividend distributions will be substantially offset by foreign tax credits.

NOTE 9—Discontinued Operations

In April, 1975 the Company adopted a plan to dispose of its Howell Division (furnishings and gas products) and, as of May 25, 1975, the Company sold substantially all assets of the business. Results of operations for the year ended December 29, 1974 have been restated to reflect the discontinued operations as a separate caption.

Results of operations of the Howell Division for the five months ended May 25, 1975 and year ended December 29, 1974 and loss on disposition were as follows:

	1975	1974
Net sales	$9,678,238	$30,029,855
Loss from discontinued operations to measurement date, less related income tax benefits of $574,000 in 1975 and $1,341,000 in 1974	$ 565,238	$ 1,264,432
Loss on disposal of assets from discontinued operations (including operating losses of $643,000 during phase-out period), less related tax benefits of $3,820,000	4,766,000	—
	$5,331,238	$ 1,264,432

ILLUSTRATION 11.5 (concluded)

NOTE 10—Pension Plans

Pension costs were $15,737,000 in 1975 and $13,314,000 in 1974. The actuarially computed value of vested benefits per the latest actuarial reports exceeded the market value of the pension fund assets by approximately $64,000,000 and $55,000,000 as of December 28, 1975 and December 29, 1974, respectively. The Company anticipates that the vesting requirements of the Employee Retirement Income Security Act, to become effective in 1976, will increase vested benefits approximately $16,000,000.

NOTE 11—Income Taxes

The provisions for taxes on income of continuing operations for the years ended December 28, 1975 and December 29, 1974 consist of:

	1975	1974
Currently payable:		
U.S. Federal (less investment credits of $3,320,000 in 1975 and $621,000 in 1974)	$21,938,000	$27,977,000
State and foreign	8,206,000	5,330,000
Deferred	(677,000)	50,000
	$29,467,000	$33,357,000

The effective tax rates are lower than the statutory rate due principally to investment tax credits, equity in earnings of affiliated companies and percentage depletion allowances.

As of December 28, 1975 Federal income tax returns for the years 1965 through 1971 have been examined and returns for the years 1972 and 1973 were in process of examination. A number of adjustments have been proposed, one of which involves the determination of the cost of ore from one of the Company's iron ore interests and could result in certain of these costs being disallowed as a tax deduction. The Company believes that its position on this issue has merit and should not result in any significant adjustment.

NOTE 12—Commitments

With respect to the Company's interests in two mining joint ventures, the Company is required to take its ownership proportion of production for which it is committed to pay its proportionate share of the operating costs of these projects, either directly or as a part of the product price. Such costs include, as a minimum and regardless of the quantity of ore received, annual interest and sinking fund requirements of the funded debt of these projects of approximately $3,500,000 through 1983, and lesser amounts thereafter through 1991.

Noncancelable leases for pollution control facilities have been capitalized. All other lease commitments, considered in the aggregate, are not material in relation to the operations of the Company.

NOTE 13—Proposed Acquisition

In November, 1975 the Company signed a letter of intent to acquire all of the outstanding common and preferred stock of Arwood Corporation, a manufacturer of investment castings and die castings, for approximately 423,000 shares of Interlake common stock. The proposed merger is subject to approval by Arwood Corporation shareholders, a favorable tax ruling and resolution of other matters.

ILLUSTRATION 11.6

Report of Independent Accountants

To the Board of Directors and Shareholders of Interlake, Inc.

In our opinion, the accompanying consolidated balance sheets and the related statements of consolidated income and retained earnings and the statements of changes in consolidated financial position present fairly the financial position of Interlake, Inc. and its subsidiaries at December 28, 1975 and December 29, 1974, and the results of their operations and the changes in their financial position for the years then ended, in conformity with generally accepted accounting principles consistently applied. Our examinations of these statements were made in accordance with generally accepted auditing standards and accordingly included such tests of the accounting records and such other auditing procedures as we considered necessary in the circumstances.

Price Waterhouse & Co

Chicago, Illinois
January 30, 1976

ILLUSTRATION 11.7

Operating/Financial Review

Worldwide sales for 1975 reached a new record due to the inclusion of a full year of the storage products operations of Dexion-Comino International Limited, acquired in late 1974. Interlake experienced a strong first quarter benefiting from large backlogs at the end of 1974. The next six months saw demand slacken, but the year ended with a strengthening fourth quarter. The near record earnings performance of continuing operations is attributable to the company's ability to hold down operating expenses and to maintain or, when possible, to increase selling prices to recover cost increases.

The key financial achievements in 1975 were:
• Net sales of continuing operations in 1975 reached $640.8 million for an increase of $47 million, or 7.9%, from 1974 sales of $593.8 million. Material handling and storage products sales accounted for the increase with declines experienced in Interlake's other businesses.

• Income of continuing operations was at a near record level in 1975 totaling $39.7 million, within 2% of the record 1974 performance of $40.3 million of continuing operations. The lower average number of common shares outstanding in 1975 allowed net income of continuing operations per common share of $7.34 to exceed by 2% the comparable $7.19 per share in 1974 (restated for the three-for-two stock split in October, 1975). The company purchased 241,950 shares during the year.

• Capital expenditures of $35.9 million exceeded the record of $25.5 million achieved in 1974 by $10.4 million, or 41%. Expansion projects accounted for 32% of the corporate total—the highest amount in over a decade.

• Financial condition continued to improve with a cash flow of $52.4 million, record working capital of $109.4 million at year-end, and an improved current ratio of 2.0 to 1 compared to 1.6 to 1 at the end of 1974.

Operating Results
The restructuring of Interlake's material handling businesses created the Packaging and Fabricated Products Division and the Material Handling/ Storage Division; this action recognized the broadening worldwide scope of the company's operations. The sale of the furnishings and gas products business further altered the line-up of Interlake's major components. Interlake's 1975 sales reached an eighth consecutive record year because a general decrease in volume in the metals businesses was overcome by record sales in the material handling businesses. Sales by Interlake's continuing businesses in 1975 and 1974 were:

(In millions)	1975 Amount	1975 %	1974 Amount	1974 %
Iron/Steel	$281.5	44%	$305.6	51%
Silicon Metal/Ferroalloys	48.6	7	55.1	9
Metal Powders	30.4	5	34.0	6
Packaging/Fabricated Products	109.1	17	119.2	20
Material Handling/ Storage	171.2	27	79.9	14
	$640.8	100%	$593.8	100%

This detail illustrates the greater diversification achieved through the 1974 acquisitions in material handling and storage products.

Iron/Steel
Decreased volume highlighted the results of 1975 as sales of $281.5 million reached 92% of record 1974 sales of $305.6 million. After the first quarter, demand evaporated quickly and recovery was slow but noticeable in the fourth quarter. Each of Interlake's major product groups of pig iron, molten iron, flat rolled steel, rolled steel products and tubular steel products realized reduced volume in 1975.

Iron tonnage shipped fell 27% below 1974 volume. In 1975, pig iron sales moved away from customer allocation and allowed replenishment of depleted coke and pig iron inventory levels caused by coal shortages due to the coal miners' strike and a furnace outage for reline in 1974. The overall drop in volume in 1975 was attributed to increased pig iron imports of 60% over the 1974 period and lower scrap prices coupled with dramatically reduced foundry activity. Imports from Canada, Japan, Hungary and Sweden were indicative of surpluses due to the general low level of world demand. In addition, molten iron for ingot molds dropped from the record 1974 level as steel industry activity diminished.

Shipments of flat rolled steel products outperformed the other products in the iron and steel business. Volume of 486,000 net tons represented a 12% decrease from 1974.

Tubular products sales in the form of spiral weld and line pipe realized a 52% fall-off from 1974. The decrease in expansion and drilling activity by oil transmission and producing companies was related to government controls and an uncertain energy policy.

Silicon Metal/Ferroalloys
Demand for silicon metal persisted at modestly reduced levels in 1975; however, shipments of ferrochrome alloys declined 52% and led an overall volume drop of 37% from 1974. Sales of $48.6 million in 1975 fell 12% from the $55.1 million recorded in 1974. Selling price increases in late 1974 and early 1975 aided the sales performance.

Imports of low priced high carbon ferrochromes, coupled with a general decline in the steel industry generated a decline in demand for ferrochrome products.

Silicon metal volume to the two principal markets of the chemical and secondary aluminum industries remained fairly strong in 1975.

The second silicon metal furnace at Selma, Alabama, completed in December, 1975, will increase production capacity by about one-third.

Net Sales
(in millions)

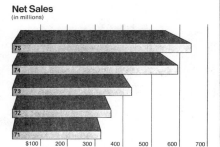

ILLUSTRATION 11.7 (continued)

Metal Powders

Accelerated quarterly demand throughout 1975 typified the sales pattern for metal powders. Sales of $30.4 million in 1975 were 11% below the 1974 total of $34.0 million. However, volume declined 24% below the record 1974 level. Major declines in pre-mixed and high alloy powders led the volume drop which extended to all grades of powders. Price increases in 1975 averaged less than 5%. Resurgence of the major automobile manufacturers and related parts producers led the recovery during the year. The fourth quarter demand saw a return to customer allocations as a major repair program preempted use of the second tunnel kiln until early 1976. These high demand levels provide an optimistic outlook for next year.

Packaging/Fabricated Products

Increased placements of strapping equipment throughout the world brightened an otherwise depressed year. Total sales in 1975 of $109.1 million fell 8%, primarily in domestic markets as illustrated below:

(In millions)	1975 Amount	%	1974 Amount	%
Domestic	$ 72.2	66%	$ 79.4	67%
International	36.9	34	39.8	33
	$109.1	100%	$119.2	100%

Domestic sales were aided by a full year's sales of pressed steel and bronze products which were part of the A. J. Bayer acquisition in December, 1974.

Steel strapping prices were increased in October, 1975, in response to increased employment and material costs. These increases, coupled with the full year's impact of 1974 price increases, added $10.0 million to 1975 sales over those in 1974.

Volume declines in steel and non-metallic strapping mirrored the sluggish industrial economies of the U.S., Europe, and Mexico and the strike hampered paper and lumber industries in Canada. Slippage in domestic stitching wire volume was aggravated further by severe weather conditions in Central America and a slow recovery from the damage to our banana plantation customers. In total, volume in steel packaging products fell 28% from 1974; the decline in international markets was held to 20%.

Our Belgian and English subsidiaries were particularly successful in steel strapping machine placements in 1975. European equipment activity increased 42% over 1974. Major installations included a rod compactor system for the British Steel Corporation, and the completion of a hot coil strapping system in Luxembourg.

Material Handling/Storage

Significant backlogs at the end of 1974 were eroded during the year and sales levels deteriorated except in Canada and England. Sales of $171.2 million in 1975 were more than double the 1974 total of $79.9 million. However, the inclusion of a full year's results of Dexion-Comino International Limited, acquired in October, 1974, and the conveyor business of A. J. Bayer, acquired in December, 1974, more than accounted for the increase.

Engineered storage systems buoyed sales within the United States by holding at 1974 levels for the year; slotted angle and pallet rack sales fell 18% in the face of retrenchment of capital investment and a recessionary economy. The acquisition of the Dexion plant in Newburgh, New York provided the desired geographic flexibility of production facilities necessary to economically service all U.S. markets. However, reduced production activity followed the sales trends at Newburgh and at the Lodi, California and Pontiac, Illinois plants.

The expanded Canadian production facilities, completed in 1974, allowed the solicitation of major orders for 1975 delivery. This volume sustained the high level of sales activity

in the first half and allowed the full year's results to approximate the 1974 level.

United Kingdom sales and exports showed surprising strength and accounted for $50.5 million of the 1975 total. This performance matched the comparable pre-acquisition sales level and overshadowed modest volume declines. Intensified export activity in oil producing countries overcame sluggishness in more established markets. Economic declines in other European markets and in Australia took a severe toll on the sales of the other international subsidiaries.

Operating Profit

Income before taxes and unallocated corporate items of continuing operations was $77.3 million, compared with $78.7 million in 1974. This performance was better than volume declines would indicate and was attributable to tight costs controls, the full year's benefit of much needed 1974 price increases, and the contributions of acquired businesses.

The comparative income by major businesses in 1975 and 1974 were:

(In millions)	1975 Amount	%	1974 Amount	%
Iron/Steel	$50.7	66%	$45.5	58%
Silicon Metal/Ferroalloys	8.1	11	13.3	17
Metal Powders	4.0	5	3.5	4
Packaging/Fabricated Products	5.7	7	9.8	13
Material Handling/ Storage	8.8	11	6.6	8
	$77.3	100%	$78.7	100%

Iron/Steel

Earnings growth of 11% for iron and steel brought income to a record $50.7 million in 1975 from the $45.5 million reported in 1974. Income gains over 1974 were limited to the iron operations and were aided by:
- a $10.0 million settlement of a dispute with a raw material supplier.
- increased income from the operations of Olga Coal in which Interlake has a 37% interest.

An extended strike at our 10.2% owned Wabush ore mine in Canada had an adverse impact on these results; however, with reduced demand, blast furnace operations were not affected.

The earnings performance of steel operations was down from the 1974 level primarily because of the decline in tubular steel products and increased costs of raw materials, fuels, and labor.

Silicon Metal/Ferroalloys

The impact of reduced shipments and higher costs lowered 1975 income of the silicon metal and ferroalloy business to $8.1 million from the record $13.3 million in 1974. Reduced electrical power delays and improved operating efficiencies limited the income drop. Significant increases in labor, electrical energy, and raw material costs added to the depressing effect of lower volume on income. Income on all major products fell from the record 1974 levels.

ILLUSTRATION 11.7 (continued)

Income

Metal Powders
The demand surge experienced in the fourth quarter aided the income performance of metal powders. Income for 1975 of $4.0 million increased 14% over the $3.5 million recorded in 1974. Lower scrap prices tended to limit the impact of increases in the costs of other goods and services, primarily fuels. Because of low demand early in the year, strict cost controls were prescribed and retained throughout the recovery in the last nine months of the year; this permitted income performance to exceed sales performance.

Packaging/Fabricated Products
The impact of the volume declines in steel strapping and stitching wire reduced the 1975 income of packaging and fabricated products to $5.7 million from $9.8 million in 1974. Production, personnel, and service cost reductions in the year and improved earnings of international subsidiaries prevented a further deterioration in realized income. The favorable effects of selling price increases were significantly eroded by increased costs of raw materials and labor.

Material Handling/Storage
The earnings growth trend of material handling and storage products continued into 1975. Income of $8.8 million increased 33% over the record $6.6 million in 1974. This performance was achieved by the maintenance of 1974 earnings level at domestic operations, a 27% gain in Canadian results, and additions to income from acquisitions.

In the United Kingdom, the acquired Dexion operations generated income at over 90% of the pre-acquisition amounts and bucked the generally gloomy trend of industrial results. The Continental European operations were less satisfactory because of depressed economic conditions.

The start-up costs of the new rack manufacturing facility at Kilnhurst, England cut income in 1975 and realized sales fell below expectations.

Kawatetsu-Interlake Ltd., Interlake's entry into the Japanese storage rack market, is proceeding on schedule. 1975 income was adversely affected by the pre-operating expenses of the joint venture marketing company. Initial production and sales are anticipated in the first quarter of 1976. New production and marketing facilities and staff were essentially in place at the end of 1975 to launch the drive for a major share of this important world market.

Income of continuing operations in 1975 reached $39.7 million, but fell 1.4% from the record $40.3 million in 1974. Income per common share rose 2% to $7.34 from $7.19 in 1974. This per share improvement reflects a purchase of shares, in 1975, which reduced the average common shares outstanding 3.3% from the 1974 average. Income included $3.3 million, or $.61 per share of U.S. investment tax credits related to the increased capital spending level and the higher rate allowed in 1975; this compares to $.6 million, or $.11 per share in 1974.

The beneficial impact of the investment tax credits, equity in earnings of affiliated companies and percentage depletion allowances available on the company's ore and coal mining interests reduced the effective income tax rate to 42.6% in 1975 compared with 45.3% in 1974.

Cash requirements for acquisitions in 1974 and capital spending in 1975 reduced cash available for short-term investment; as a result, interest income in 1975 declined to one-third of the 1974 amount. Interest expense of $9.9 million in 1975 was 68% above the $5.9 million recorded in 1974; a full year's cost of financing pollution control facility expenditures and of the debt of acquired companies accounted for the significant increase. Other corporate expenses, unallocated to operations, rose modestly from 1974.

Discontinued Operations
As of May 25, 1975, certain assets and the business of the Howell Division (home furnishings and gas products) were sold, resulting in 1975 in a loss on disposal of $4,766,000 net of income taxes. In addition, a loss from operations of the discontinued Howell Division of $565,000, net of income taxes, was realized in 1975.

Dividends
Cash dividends on common stock totaled $8.1 million in 1975 and represented a payout of 23.5% on net income. The reinvestment of earnings for the extensive capital program in 1975 minimized the need for additional debt. On November 25, 1975, the regular cash dividend on restated shares was

Net Income and Common Dividends
(In millions)

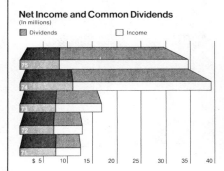

Capitalization
(in millions)

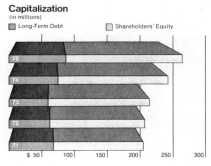

ILLUSTRATION 11.7 (concluded)

raised by 50% over the previous rate to bring the total 1975 payout to $1.50. The indicated dividend for 1976 would be $2.00. For 1974, a year-end extra raised total dividends paid to $11.0 million, or $1.97 on the restated common shares.

Financial Condition

The company's financial condition improved during 1975 and is in a strong position to capitalize on business opportunities in 1976. Cash flow of $52.4 million was close to last year's record of $53.7 million. Major requirements for available funds were:
- capital expenditure programs totaling $35.9 million
- increased working capital requirements of $14.3 million
- purchase of company common stock for $5.1 million
- investments in the Japanese joint venture and Scotts Branch Mine which totaled $2.5 million.

During the year, temporary cash requirements in excess of funds generated were provided by issuance of commercial paper and draw-downs on established worldwide revolving credit agreements. In addition, $3.9 million of funds available under long-term leases to finance facilities at Beverly, Ohio, and Selma, Alabama were used.

Shareholders' equity increased 9.0% from the end of 1974 to $264.0 million at December 28, 1975. This increase and the lower net income resulting from the Howell Division disposal and loss from operations reduced the return on shareholders' average equity to 13.7% in 1975 compared with 17.2% in 1974.

A summary of the key financial ratios indicates:

	At Dec. 28, 1975	At Dec. 29, 1974
Working Capital Ratio	2.0 to 1	1.6 to 1
Quick Asset Ratio	.8 to 1	.7 to 1
Debt/Total Capitalization	24%	23%

Capital Expenditures

1975 capital spending was at the highest level ever and exceeded depreciation for the second consecutive year. Capital expenditures of $35.9 million in 1975 were $10.4 million above the 1974 amount. A comparison of the nature of capital spending in 1975 compared to 1974 indicates the increasing demand for earnings adequate to support expansion and environmental control projects:

	1975	1974
• for replacement and improvements using new and better equipment which will also contribute to lower costs	48%	60%
• for expansion which provides for future growth and profits	32%	29%
• for pollution control devices to assure a better environment in our host communities and the nation	20%	11%

Capital spending was dominated by the silicon metal/ferroalloys business which represented 44% of the corporate total. Spending included the completion of a second furnace for the production of silicon metal at Selma, Alabama, and installation of fume control facilities at both the Beverly, Ohio and Selma, Alabama plants.

The iron and steel business accounted for 36% of the total spending and included major expenditures for the initial phase of blast furnace rehabilitation programs at Chicago and Toledo.

Other capital projects in 1975 included:
- expanded production facilities at the Lodi, California storage products plant
- product improvement and expansion equipment at the Pontiac, Illinois storage products plant
- upgrading of equipment to produce strapping tools at Riverdale

At the end of 1975, the unexpended balance of approved capital projects were about 40% of the $27.9 million at the end of 1974 and approximated the spending proportions by type of project realized in 1975.

Capital Expenditures and Depreciation
(in millions)

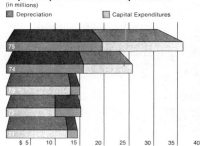

Capital Expenditures–By Type
(in millions)

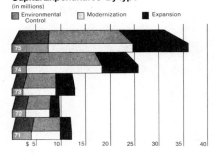

ILLUSTRATION 11.8

Interlake, Inc.

Five Year Financial Summary of Operations

(Amounts in thousands—except per share statistics)

For the Year (1)		1975	1974	1973	1972	1971
Net Sales of Continuing Operations		$640,831	$593,764	$425,999	$353,552	$319,921
Other Revenues		9,493	9,278	7,034	1,532	1,295
		650,324	603,042	433,033	355,084	321,216
Cost of Products Sold and Operating Expenses		571,290	523,488	398,948	327,992	296,893
Interest Expense		9,861	5,934	5,322	5,497	4,721
		581,151	529,422	404,270	333,489	301,614
Income Before Taxes on Income		69,173	73,620	28,763	21,595	19,602
Provision for U.S. and Foreign Income Taxes		29,467	33,357	10,813	9,016	7,701
Income of Continuing Operations		39,706	40,263	17,950	12,579	11,901
Income (loss) from Discontinued Operations		(5,331)	(1,264)	(1,166)	393	623
Net Income	Amount	34,375	38,999	16,784	12,972	12,524
	% of Net Sales	5.4%	6.6%	3.9%	3.7%	3.9%
	% of Average Shareholders' Equity	13.7%	17.2%	8.0%	6.3%	6.0%
Earnings per Common Share (2)— Income of Continuing Operations		7.34	7.19	3.15	2.11	1.92
Net Income		6.35	6.97	2.95	2.17	2.02
Cash Flow (net income, depreciation and future income taxes)		52,388	53,678	30,713	26,982	25,354
Cash Dividends	Amount	8,075	11,013	7,373	7,158	7,400
	Per Share (2)	1.50	1.97	1.30	1.20	1.20
	% of Net Income	23.5%	28.2%	43.9%	55.2%	59.1%
Capital Expenditures (excluding assets of acquired businesses)		35,884	25,486	12,773	9,818	12,146
Depreciation		19,287	15,337	15,042	15,077	13,923
At Year End						
Working Capital	Amount	$109,421	$ 95,143	$ 98,021	$ 90,040	$ 86,839
	Current Ratio	2.0 to 1	1.6 to 1	2.5 to 1	2.5 to 1	2.6 to 1
Property, Plant and Equipment (net)		202,621	188,746	155,265	153,697	159,304
Long-Term Debt (less current maturities)		85,599	74,216	60,367	62,923	68,115
Future Income Taxes		12,042	13,316	13,974	15,816	16,883
Common Shareholders' Equity	Amount	264,046	242,134	214,056	208,295	206,171
	Shares Outstanding (2)	5,405	5,603	5,597	5,820	6,017
	Per Share (2)	48.85	43.22	38.24	35.79	34.26
Common Stock Price Range (2)		26½—18	19⅝—13⅞	19⅜—13⅛	21⅜—17⅜	20¼—16⅛
Price Earnings Ratio (based upon year-end stock price)		4.09	2.56	4.75	8.82	9.24
Number of Shareholders		24,504	24,624	24,898	25,036	25,919
Number of Employees		10,502	13,391	10,272	9,440	9,224

(1) 1974 and prior years have been restated to exclude operating results of the Howell Division (home furnishings and gas products), which was sold in 1975 as described in the Operating/Financial Review.

(2) Restated to reflect the 3-for-2 share split in October, 1975.

ILLUSTRATION 11.9

Management's Discussion of Summary of Operations

Sales

Net sales of continuing operations reached a record level in 1975 for the eighth consecutive year. Sales of companies acquired in 1974 aided the 1975 performance as a general decline was experienced in other segments of Interlake.

(In millions)	1975	1974	1973	1972	1971
Iron	$110.1	$103.0	$ 78.6	$ 62.7	$ 57.9
Steel	171.4	202.6	142.4	131.3	112.5
Silicon Metal/ Ferroalloys	48.6	55.1	32.9	22.4	24.3
Metal Powders	30.4	34.0	26.5	17.2	13.8
Packaging/Fabricated Products	109.1	119.2	95.6	77.9	75.1
Material Handling/ Storage	171.2	79.9	50.0	42.1	36.3
	$640.8	$593.8	$426.0	$353.6	$319.9

The significant sales increases in 1973 and 1974 were related to strong demand and higher selling prices. In 1973, shipments in excess of annual production capacity were realized and depleted inventory levels; selling price increases accounted for one-fourth of the sales gain.

In 1974, the lifting of price controls allowed selling price increases to help recover costs of the previous two years; higher selling prices accounted for 36% of the year-to-year improvement. Strong demand and sales of acquired companies accounted for the balance of the sales growth in 1974.

Other Revenues

Other revenues include interest income, gains on the sale of corporate properties, and rent and royalty income.

In 1973, Interlake sold a parcel of vacant land in Canada and an office building in London. The pre-tax gain on the sale of these two properties of approximately $3.5 million is included in other revenues. Also, in 1973, interest income increased more than $1 million from the previous year. Other revenues in 1974 include sales of vacant land in Burnham, Illinois and idle equipment.

Interest income in 1974 increased $1.9 million from 1973 as a result of higher yields and higher average cash balances on hand during most of the year. Also included in other revenues in 1974 and in 1975 is rental income from the lease of the Erie coke facility.

In 1975, increased royalty income and sales of idle equipment more than offset a decrease in interest income.

Cost of Products Sold and Operating Expenses

Cost of products sold and operating expenses in 1974-75 averaged 88.7% of sales compared with an average of 93.1% in the 1971-73 period. Most of the improvement in this ratio was due to selling price increases, following the suspension of government price controls, which allowed recovery of cost increases experienced in 1974 and earlier years.

Throughout this period, raw materials, power, labor, and most other costs incurred by Interlake have steadily increased. In addition, depreciation expense, which reflects the company's investment in improved facilities, and state and local taxes, which are largely outside of the company's control, have risen in recent years—especially in 1975. Also, the inclusion of a full year of operations for Dexion-Comino International Limited caused increases in all cost categories. However, 1975 costs did benefit from a $10 million settlement with a raw material supplier and reduced operating activity permitted reductions in maintenance and repair expenses, which had increased significantly during the 1973-74 period of very high operating levels.

Interest Expense

Interest expense rose sharply in 1975 due to a combination of higher interest rates and a higher average indebtedness resulting from a full year of Dexion's financing requirements and increased financing of pollution control facilities and the Scotts Branch coal mining venture. The period 1972-1974 had interest expense at a relatively stable level following the issuance of $50,000,000 of 8.8% debentures in 1971.

U.S. and Foreign Income Taxes

The tax provisions are at an effective rate lower than the statutory tax rate principally due to percentage depletion allowances, equity in earnings of affiliated companies, and investment tax credits as follows:

Year	1975	1974	1973	1972	1971
Effective tax rate	42.6%	45.3%	37.6%	41.8%	39.3%

The lower rate in 1973 was due to the real estate transactions mentioned previously, which were subject to minimal income taxes under the applicable foreign tax regulations. The higher rates in 1974 and 1975 reflect increased operating income subject to income taxes at normal rates.

Summary of Earnings by Line of Business

Earnings in 1975 were the second best in Interlake's history. Overall volume declines from 1974 adversely affected the earnings of each principal line of business. However, a $10 million settlement from a raw material supplier, the full year's benefit of price increases in 1974, and cost reduction measures limited the earnings decline.

(In millions)	1975	1974	1973	1972	1971
Iron/Steel	$50.7	$45.5	$16.7	$18.5	$13.0
Silicon Metal/ Ferroalloys	8.1	13.3	2.1	1.3	4.5
Metal Powders	4.0	3.5	1.5	(.4)	.1
Packaging/ Fabricated Products	5.7	9.8	8.6	4.3	4.7
Material Handling/ Storage	8.8	6.6	4.8	2.9	1.9
	77.3	78.7	33.7	26.6	24.2
Corporate items	(8.1)	(5.1)	(4.9)	(5.0)	(4.6)
Income of continuing operations before taxes	$69.2	$73.6	$28.8	$21.6	$19.6

( ) denotes loss or expense

Results of Foreign Operations
(in millions)

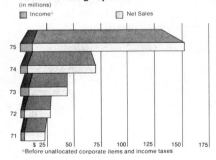

°Before unallocated corporate items and income taxes

4. Particular attention should be paid to the rather substantial amounts of additional information and explanation presented in Illustration 11.5, Notes to Consolidated Financial Statements. Note 1 is especially informative since it discloses the accounting policies followed in developing the amounts for the various statements, such as use of the straight-line method of computing periodic depreciation charges.

5. A strong trend has emerged in recent years toward making more informative disclosures in corporate annual reports. Many of these additional disclosures are included in response to SEC requirements. Examples include (1) management's review of operations and financial results (Illustrations 11.7 and 11.9), (2) the reporting of quarterly results, and of (3) sales and earnings by major lines or categories of business (both in Illustration 11.1). The premise underlying these added disclosures is that management knows better than anyone else why operating and financial results differ from those of preceding years and, therefore, should be called upon to explain and to further enlighten readers.

QUESTIONS AND EXERCISES

1. Why would it be desirable to have an authoritative set of generally accepted accounting principles?

2. Indicate some of the things the AICPA has done to try to develop a set of generally accepted accounting principles.

3. What are generally accepted accounting principles? What is the source of such principles? Where might one find a list of such principles?

4. What is the primary qualitative objective of accounting? Why is it considered primary?

5. What is meant by the term "accrual basis of accounting?" What is its alternative?

6. How might it be argued that the statement of financial position is misnamed?

7. What two requirements generally must be met before revenue will be recognized in a period? What would you consider the ideal time to recognize revenue? Why?

8. Under what circumstances, if any, is the receipt of cash an acceptable time to recognize revenue?

9. The statement of financial position of a firm shows marketable securities at cost of $100,000. You look up the current market value of these securities and determine them to be worth $250,000. Why are the securities reported at $100,000 and the $150,000 increase ignored? Isn't the firm better off by $150,000?

10. Define expense. What principles guide the recognition of expense?

11. Assets are sometimes referred to as deferred costs. Comment on the validity of this designation.

12. What is meant by the accounting term "conservatism"? How does it affect the amounts reported in the financial statements?

13. What is the principle of initial recording of exchange prices? What is the significance of adhering to this principle?

14. The financial statements in the annual report of a company include an account entitled "Unearned Subscription Revenue." What kind of an account is this, and in what statement would it be reported? What is the most probable disposition of the account?

15. If accountants did not record exchanges at the prices agreed upon in those exchanges, what might they use as an alternative? What are some of the implications of using the alternative?

16. How are consistency and full disclosure related?

17. What does it mean when accountants say they emphasize substance over form?

18. A building was purchased on January 1, 1974, for $40,000. By December 31, 1978, it had a net book value of $32,000 and a market value of $50,000. The building was completely destroyed by fire on January 1, 1979. Cash received from the insurance company amounted to $36,000. What is the amount of the gain or loss that the accountant would record? Is the accounting record in accord with the economic facts given? If not, why not?

PROBLEMS

11–1. Given below are the contract prices and costs relating to all of the Jones Construction Company's long-term construction contracts (all dollar amounts are in millions):

	Contract Price	Costs Incurred Prior to 1979	Costs Incurred In 1979	Costs Yet to Be Incurred
On contracts completed in 1979................	$ 8.0		$7.0	–0–
On incomplete contracts........	24.0	$4.0	8.0	$8.0

General and administrative expenses for 1979 amounted to $500,000.

Required:

a. Compute the earnings before taxes for 1979 using the completed contract method of accounting for earnings and revenues from construction contracts.

b. Repeat part (a) assuming employment of the percentage-of-completion method.

11–2. Swampe Company sells real estate lots under terms calling for a small down payment and monthly installment payments spread over a number of years. Following are data relating to the company's operations for its first three years of existence:

	1978	1979	1980
Gross margin rate........................	45%	48%	50%
Cash collected in 1980 from installment sales made in.........................	$80,000	$100,000	$120,000

Sales in 1980 amounted to $400,000, while general and administrative expenses amounted to $100,000.

Required:

a. Compute the net earnings before taxes for 1980 assuming revenues and earnings are to be computed under the completed sales method. (Sales revenue is recognized in the year of sale.)
b. Repeat part (a) using the installment method of accounting for sales and gross margin.

11–3. Jackson, Inc. reported net earnings for 1979 of $520,000. An audit of the company's accounting records shows that the following items were not considered when the net earnings were computed:
(1) New contracts for services to be rendered in 1980 in the amount of $20,000 were received in 1979.
(2) Employee services received in 1979 with a cost of $3,000 were not recorded because they had not been paid.
(3) It was estimated that $6,000 of accounts receivable at the end of the year would not be collected. (The balance in the Allowance for Doubtful Accounts is zero.)
(4) The sum of $25,000 was paid to an advertising agency to begin work on a large-scale promotional campaign for a new product to be introduced next year.

Required:

a. Compute the corrected net earnings for 1979, ignoring federal income taxes.
b. Compute the net effect of the proper accounting for the above items on the amount of assets owned by the company.
c. Explain briefly, by reference to specific principles or concepts, the reasons for the corrections you made.

11–4. The Crooch Company reported the following financial position as of December 31, 1979:

Assets......................................	$750,000
Liabilities..................................	150,000
Stockholders' equity........................	600,000

Net earnings before taxes were $100,000 for 1979. You discover in your audit of the company's records that:
(1) The company wrote off $25,000 of its merchandise inventory to expense on the grounds that selling prices might decline.

(2) Sales orders of $20,000 were recorded as sales revenue and debited to accounts receivable.

(3) No entry was made to accrue employee wages in the amount of $8,000 at the end of the year because these wages were not paid until 1980.

(4) The net book value of a machine of $8,000 was charged to expense because the machine was used to make a special product which is now obsolete. The machine could be used for another 10 years in the manufacture of this product. There is no other use for the machine at this time and no future use can be seen at this time.

(5) The company had its buildings appraised on December 31, 1979, and as a result recorded a $50,000 increase in its buildings account and in a stockholders' equity account called Capital from Appreciation.

Required:

a. Prepare a schedule starting with reported net earnings which shows the corrections to be made to arrive at the correct net earnings (ignore income taxes).

b. Prepare another schedule with three columns in which are entered first the amounts for assets, liabilities, and stockholders' equity for December 31, 1979. Show by means of plus and minus the needed corrections for these items to arrive at corrected amounts.

c. Justify the position you took on each of the above items by reference to generally accepted accounting principles.

11–5. For each of the numbered items listed below, state the letter or letters of the principles used to justify the accounting procedure followed:

A—Accounting entity	F—Matching principle
B—Conservatism	G—Period cost (or principle of immediate recognition of expense)
C—Earning principle of revenue recognition	H—Realization principle
D—Going concern	I—Systematic and rational allocation principle of expense recognition
E—Initial recording at exchange prices principle	J—Stable dollar assumption

(1) The ending inventory was recorded at $60,000 using the cost of market, whichever is lower method. The cost of the inventory was $64,000.

(2) A truck purchased in January was reported at 80 percent of its cost even though its market value at year end was only 70 percent of its cost.

(3) One-half of the premium paid on January 2 for a two-year term of insurance coverage was charged to expense.

(4) The collection of $10,000 of cash for services to be performed next year was reported as a current liability.

(5) The president's salary was treated as an expense of the year even though he spent most of his time planning the next two years' activities.

(6) No entry was made to record that the company received an offer of $100,000 for land carried in its accounts at $60,000.

(7) A stock of printed stationery, checks and invoices with a cost of $2,000 was treated as a current asset at year end even though it had no value to others.

(8) A tract of land acquired for $35,000 was recorded at that price even though it was appraised at $40,000 and the company would have been willing to pay that amount if pushed.

(9) Paid and charged to expense the $1,500 paid to Bill Bunker for rent of a truck owned by him. Bill Bunker is president of the company and also owns all of its outstanding stock.

(10) Recorded the $5,000 of interest collected on $100,000 of 5 percent bonds as interest revenue even though the general level of prices increased 8 percent during the year.

11–6. By following the most conservative accounting practices permitted, its accountant determined that the Blake Company can report a loss of $60,000 for income tax purposes in 1979, its first year of operation. But the top management of the company is concerned about reporting such a loss for financial reporting purposes because it is planning on seeking outside financing for some additional equipment. It calls upon you as an expert accountant to review the accounting practices followed. You discover the following information relating to the loss that can be reported for tax purposes:

(1) Construction revenue has been recorded on a completed contract basis. Six contracts with a total price of $800,000 were partially completed during the year, with costs of $120,000 incurred out of a total expected costs of $480,000.

(2) Only $20,000 of gross margin realized through installment collections was included in arriving at the net loss of $60,000. Installment sales for the year were $400,000; cost of goods sold was $300,000. There is little doubt about the collection of the installment receivables.

(3) The ending inventory was $62,000, using Lifo. Under Fifo it would have amounted to $70,000.

(4) Accelerated depreciation for the year amounted to $24,000. Under the straight-line method it would have been $16,000.

Required: Prepare a schedule showing how the above items would change the reported net loss to net earnings (before income taxes) if they were accounted for in an acceptable, yet less conservative way

chapter 12

Earnings Measurement in Retail Departments

DEPARTMENTALIZED NATURE OF RETAIL BUSINESS OPERATIONS

Many retailing business organizations actually conduct a number of different types of activities or deal with a number of different products within the framework of the single organization. A large department store, for example, typically will have a men's clothing department whose manager is assigned resources and personnel to assist in performing the function of marketing men's clothing. The manager also will have the right to call on others in the business for legal advice, financing, accounting, and similar services which are available to all departments.

Uses for Departmentalized Data

When a retail business operates more than one department or sells more than one class of merchandise, the need for information pertaining to each department or line of merchandise arises. This information is needed by management in order to determine the overall profitability of the department and to evaluate the performance of individuals in carrying out their assigned duties. If such information is available, management is in a position to make informed decisions regarding questions such as whether additional resources should be devoted to the department, whether the manager of the department should be relieved of his or her duties, whether costs incurred in a department are in line with expectations, and whether prices should be changed in an attempt to increase the profitability of the department. This illustrates the point that internal users have different informational needs than outsiders. Insiders are concerned with resource allocation decisions within an organization, while outsiders are usually not primarily concerned with these matters.

APPROACHES TO APPRAISING A DEPARTMENT'S PERFORMANCE

Indices of Profitability

The specific accounting records maintained for each department in a multidepartment retail business will vary according to the information desired by management. But since the general goal of all business is the generation of net earnings, some measure of profitability undoubtedly will be desired. A number of alternative measures or indices of profitability may be computed. The older and more well-known measures are *gross margin* and *net earnings.* A more modern measure, and one currently receiving considerable support, is the *contribution to indirect expenses*. This latter measure is sometimes referred to as the contribution to overhead or simply as the *contribution concept*. Using assumed data, the relationship of each of these measures to the others is portrayed in the following example:

Sales..	$5,000
Cost of goods sold......................................	3,000
Gross margin...	$2,000
Direct expenses...	1,600
Contribution to indirect expenses.........................	$ 400
Indirect expenses.......................................	250
Net Earnings (before Federal Income Taxes)...............	$ 150

As used above, the term *direct expenses* refers to those expenses which are clearly incurred for the benefit of a given department and which would be eliminated if the department was eliminated. The salary paid to a salesman who works only in a given department is an example of a direct expense.

Indirect expenses consist of those expenses which are incurred for the benefit of many departments and can only be identified with a given department through allocation on some fair and reasonable basis. The salary of the general sales manager for the corporation is an example of an indirect expense.

Objectivity versus Relevance

The measures of departmental performance—gross margin, contribution to indirect expenses, and net earnings—are presented in order of decreasing objectivity. The computation of departmental gross margin requires only knowledge of net sales and cost of goods sold. Since both of these amounts can be measured relatively accurately, the measurement of gross margin is relatively accurate. While somewhat more difficult, the determination of a department's direct expenses is possible without accepting purely arbitrary allocations of expense. Thus, there is a degree of objectivity in any measurement of a department's contribution to indirect expenses. But the computation of net earnings by departments inevitably involves the allocation of some expenses to the departments on some arbitrary basis simply because there is no possible way of measuring directly the amount applicable to a department. For example, how much of the annual contribution to local charities should be allocated to each department? No exact measurement is possible.

Yet, it would seem that as an ideal, management would prefer accurate measurements of net earnings by departments. The earnings of the department could be related to the resources employed by the department in generating the earnings. This information is used to calculate a valuable index of profitability—return on investment. But, while highly relevant, the necessity of allocating certain expenses in order to calculate departmental net earnings causes these earnings amounts to be of questionable objectivity.

The Contribution Concept

In choosing between deriving gross margin or net earnings for a given department, the accountant is confronted by a dilemma: Which is preferable—highly objective but somewhat less relevant data, or highly relevant but considerably less objective data? Instead of choosing between the two, many accountants choose an alternative. They deduct from each department's net sales only the direct expenses of the department and use this as a measure of the department's contribution to indirect expenses and, hopefully, to net earnings. It is this concept, and variations of it, which is stressed in modern profitability or responsibility accounting systems.

Direct and Indirect Expenses and Cost Objectives

In discussing direct and indirect costs it is necessary to have a cost objective in mind. A cost objective might be a product, a department, a sales territory, and so on. A direct expense is one which is incurred *to benefit* or which is *caused by* the existence of the cost objective. Thus, if the cost objective were eliminated, the direct expense would be eliminated. Direct expenses may be fixed or variable in nature—that is, they may vary with volume or remain relatively constant as volume changes.

For certain decisions the most relevant measurement of departmental activity may be the amount by which the revenues exceed the variable expenses of the department. This contribution to fixed costs concept, or "contribution margin" concept as it is called, is discussed in Chapter 16.

DETERMINING DEPARTMENTAL GROSS MARGINS

While gross margin as a measure of performance leaves much to be desired, it is an important variable in overall profitability. The factors which produce gross margin—sales and costs of goods sold—can be varied, and a satisfactory gross margin can be secured in several ways. For example, a high rate of gross margin per dollar of sales and a relatively low volume of sales may produce as much gross margin as a low margin rate and a high volume of sales. Gross margins thus reveal the relationship between sales revenue and the major element of expense—cost of goods sold.

Sales and Sales Contra Accounts

If gross margins are to be computed by .departments, the net sales revenue for each department must first be determined. This net revenue is determined by deducting from sales the various sales adjustments or contra items such as sales discounts and sales returns and allowances.

Purchases and Related Accounts

Since the other factor in determining gross margins by departments is the cost of goods sold, adequate accounts or records must be maintained for those factors affecting cost of goods sold. Usually required will be departmental totals for purchases, purchase returns, purchase allowances, purchase discounts, inventories, and transportation-in. Adequate records also must be maintained for original markup, additional markup and additional markup cancellations, and markdown and markdown cancellations. This information is needed so that the retail method of inventory determination (discussed below) can be applied.

Departmental Inventories

Unless perpetual inventory records are maintained, the determination of cost of goods sold will require information on the cost of the beginning and ending inventories. Such information can be secured through the taking of physical inventories or by some estimation process. The monthly departmental inventories in a merchandising company usually are determined through use of the *retail inventory method or procedure*. This procedure is used because monthly financial statements usually are desired and because the taking of a physical inventory is a costly and time-consuming activity. Inventories are determined on a departmental rather than store-wide basis because gross margin rates may differ substantially between departments.

The Retail Method of Determining Inventory

The retail method is used by a wide variety of companies which sell goods directly to the ultimate consumer. In such companies, each item of merchandise usually is marked or tagged with its retail or selling price. The result is that the goods are referred to and inventoried at their retail prices.

In skeletal form, the retail method consists first of determining the ending inventory at retail prices:

Beginning Inventory at Retail Prices
+ Purchases at Retail Prices
= Goods Available for Sale at Retail Prices; this sum
− Sales (which are, of course, at retail prices)
= Ending Inventory at Retail Prices

In order to convert the ending inventory at retail prices to cost, the relationship between cost and retail prices must be known. This requires that information on the beginning inventory and purchases be accumulated so that goods available for sale can be expressed in terms of *cost* and *retail prices*. This cost/retail price ratio is then applied to sales to determine cost of goods sold and to the ending inventory at retail to reduce it to cost. This procedure is shown in Illustration 12.1.

The $186,000 on the line entitled "Cost of goods sold and sales" is the amount of sales in the department for the month of January and is taken from the accounting records. The $111,600 is the cost of goods sold during the month found by applying the cost/retail price ratio of 60 percent to the sales of $186,000. Deducting these two amounts, $111,600 and $186,000, from the $132,000 and $220,000 amounts on the preceding

ILLUSTRATION 12.1

Inventory Calculation Using the Retail Method

	Cost	Retail Price
Inventory, January 1, 1979............................	$ 12,000	$ 20,000
Purchases, net......................................	120,000	200,000
Cost/retail price ratio:		
$132,000/$220,000, or 60%......................	$132,000	$220,000
Cost of goods sold and sales (cost is 60% of retail). . .	111,600	186,000
Inventory, January 31, 1979 (cost is 60% of retail)......	$ 20,400	$ 34,000

line—goods available for sale at cost and at retail—gives the January 31, 1979, inventory for the department at cost and at retail.

Retail Method Terminology. A number of items enter into the determination of the cost/retail price ratio of a given department's merchandise in addition to the *initial markup*—the difference between cost and the selling prices first established. Selling prices may be increased later giving rise to *additional markups* which increase the gross margin rate and amount. Some of these additional markups may be cancelled leaving *net additional markups*. Similarly, selling prices may be reduced below the originally established levels giving rise to *markdowns,* some of which may be cancelled leaving *net markdowns*. The cost/retail price ratio is also affected by purchase returns and allowances, purchase discounts, and transportation-in.

To illustrate these factors, assume the data in Illustration 12.2 are for the Baxter Company for the month of June, 1979.

The data in Illustration 12.2 are used in Illustration 12.3 to show the computation of the cost of the June 30 inventory of the clothing department. The cost of goods sold of $29,400 shown in Illustration 12.3 can be obtained in two ways. One way is to multiply the $49,000 figure in the retail column by 60%. Another way is to deduct the $51,000 inventory (at cost) figure from the $80,400 cost of goods available for sale figure (shown in the cost column).

A similar computation for the furnishings department would show an ending inventory of $21,700 as of June 30, 1979. You may want to see if you can arrive at this figure.

To a certain extent the retail inventory method is a perpetual inventory method since it does provide a total dollar valuation at retail price of a departmental inventory through the use of accounting records. But it is not a complete perpetual method since it does not include the maintenance of records of the number of units of each item of merchandise in inventory. On the other hand, it is not uncommon to find perpetual records

ILLUSTRATION 12.2

	Clothing Department		Furnishings Department	
	Cost	Retail	Cost	Retail
Inventory, May 31......................	$50,000	$83,000	$19,000	$29,000
Sales.....................................		48,900		14,800
Sales returns...........................		900		500
Purchases...............................	30,000	50,000	12,000	20,000
Purchase returns.......................	1,200	2,000	600	1,000
Purchase discounts.....................	500		200	
Transportation-in......................	2,100		800	
Net additional markups................		3,000		2,000
Net markdowns.........................		1,000		700

ILLUSTRATION 12.3

Retail Method of Inventory Pricing

BAXTER COMPANY
Clothing Department—Inventory Computation
June 30, 1979

	Cost	Retail
Inventory, May 31	$50,000	$ 83,000
Purchases	30,000	50,000
Purchase returns	(1,200)	(2,000)
Purchase discounts	(500)	
Transportation-in	2,100	
Net additional markups		3,000
Total (ratio of cost to retail is 60%)	$80,400	$134,000
Sales		$ 48,900
Less sales returns		900
Net sales		$ 48,000
Plus net markdowns		1,000
Total deductions	29,400	$ 49,000
Inventory, June 30, 1979 ($85,000 × 60% cost ratio)	$51,000	$ 85,000

maintained in terms of quantities for merchandise such as ladies' high-fashion clothing and so-called "big-ticket" items—stereo and television sets, washers, dryers, and refrigerators.

The reliability of the ending inventory at retail is usually tested by comparing it with a physical inventory. This is taken at least once a year and frequently more often if management has any reason to doubt the accuracy of the results obtained under the retail method. Because it provides an independently determined inventory figure, the retail method serves as an excellent control device over inventory. For example, an inventory shortage can be uncovered by comparing the ending inventory computed by the retail method with the amount obtained by taking a physical inventory.

Earnings Statement with Departmental Gross Margins

Using the data presented above, an earnings statement for the month of June, 1979, can now be prepared. Such a statement may be quite condensed, as discussed later, or may show the calculation of departmental gross margins in considerable detail, as in Illustration 12.4. Operating expenses are not detailed in this illustration. The classification and reporting of operating expenses is discussed and illustrated in following sections.

The earnings statement showing gross margins by departments for the Baxter Company shows that the clothing department contributes by far the larger absolute amount of gross margin, $18,600 as against $5,000. Expressing gross margin as a percentage of net sales reveals that the

ILLUSTRATION 12.4

Earnings Statement with Departmental Gross Margins

BAXTER COMPANY
Earnings Statement
For Month Ended June 30, 1979

	Clothing Department		Furnishings Department		Total	
Sales...........................		$48,900		$14,800		$63,700
Less: Sales returns..............		900		500		1,400
Net sales......................		$48,000		$14,300		$62,300
Cost of goods sold						
Inventory, 5/31/79.............	$50,000		$19,000		$ 69,000	
Purchases.....................	$30,000		$12,000		$ 42,000	
Less: Purchase returns........	(1,200)		(600)		(1,800)	
Purchase discounts......	(500)		(200)		(700)	
Net purchases.................	$28,300		$11,200		$ 39,500	
Add: Transportation-in.......	2,100		800		2,900	
Cost of purchases..............	$30,400		$12,000		$ 42,400	
Cost of goods available for sale..	$80,400		$31,000		$111,400	
Less: Inventory 6/30/79......	51,000		21,700		72,700	
Cost of goods sold........		29,400		9,300		38,700
Gross margin (percentages)........	(38.75)	$18,600	(34.97)	$ 5,000	(37.88)	$23,600
Operating expenses (details omitted here).........................						14,600
Net operating earnings...........						$ 9,000
Other revenue						
Interest revenue..............						100
Net earnings before income taxes...						$ 9,100
Estimated federal income taxes....						3,200
Net earnings....................						$ 5,900

clothing department also has the higher gross margin rate, 38.75 percent as against 34.97 percent. The overall gross margin rate is 37.88 percent. These data may be analyzed further by management in an effort to see whether the furnishings department's sales, prices, and gross margin rates might not be improved and brought into better relationship to those of the clothing department.

Combined Monthly and Year-to-Date Earnings Statements

Illustration 12.5 contains an earnings statement showing monthly as well as year-to-date departmental and total gross margins as well as total monthly and year-to-date net earnings. Such a statement is an excellent means of reviewing quickly the progress of the company for the month and for the year to date. Such statements are usually rather highly condensed, although as much detail as is desired may be presented either in the body of the statement or in supporting schedules.

The statement presented in Illustration 12.5 highlights, as it is designed

ILLUSTRATION 12.5

Monthly and Year-to-Date Earnings Statement

BAXTER COMPANY
Earnings Statement
For the Month and Twelve Months Ended June 30, 1979

	Clothing Department		Furnishings Department		Total	
	June	Twelve Months	June	Twelve Months	June	Twelve Months
Net sales.....................	$48,000	$480,000	$14,300	$120,000	$62,300	$600,000
Cost of goods sold............	29,400	279,200	9,300	74,800	38,700	354,000
Gross margin.................	$18,600	$200,800	$ 5,000	$ 45,200	$23,600	$246,000
Gross margin percentages......	(38.75)	(41.83)	(34.97)	(37.67)	(37.88)	(41.00)
Operating expenses (details omitted here)..............					14,600	187,000
Net operating earnings.........					$ 9,000	$ 59,000
Other revenue................					100	1,000
Net earnings before income taxes					$ 9,100	$ 60,000
Estimated federal income taxes..					3,200	21,000
Net Earnings.................					$ 5,900	$ 39,000

to do, gross margin amounts and percentages. Note that the gross margin percentage for the month of June was lower for each of the departments and in total than it was for the year to date. This information might cause management to undertake an investigation seeking to find the underlying reasons. Or a comparison of the current year's statements with those of prior years might indicate that the relationships shown this year are to be expected.

From the information contained in the earnings statement, it would be quite incorrect to conclude that June was a relatively unsatisfactory month in terms of the absolute amount of earnings. It contributed $5,900 of net earnings to an annual total of only $39,000, a far greater than pro rata amount. This statement illustrates clearly that care must be exercised so as not to place too much emphasis on gross margins. Additional information may be needed for truly intelligent decision making.

Determining Departmental Net Earnings

The determination of departmental net earnings involves the allocation of a number of expenses to the various departments. And this allocation process can be performed with varying degrees of accuracy. The resulting net earnings, then, are only as reliable as the least reliable of the expense allocation methods. If this method is used, the basis of all allocations should be made known to users and the limitations of the allocations should be clearly understood.

Classifying Expenses

Expenses may be classified according to a *natural* classification, a *functional* classification, or a combination of the two.

Natural Classification.   In some published annual reports to stockholders, expenses are classified according to a *natural* or *object of expenditure* classification. That is, expenses are shown as employees' salaries and wages, depreciation, taxes, cost of purchased materials used, and so on. Under this classification the salary of the president and the wages of the janitor or stock boy are presented as employees' salaries and wages.

Functional Classification.   The natural classification does not serve well for purposes of control or appraisal of departmental or individual performance. For such purposes, a *functional* classification is better. A functional classification of an employee's wage or salary would describe it as selling, administrative, or delivery expense, and so forth. That is, expenses are classified according to the task accomplished through their incurrence. For example, advertising expenses are incurred to sell merchandise. The function is selling, or it might be called promotion. The way in which expenses are functionally classified varies considerably from company to company.

Natural and Functional Classification.   As might be expected, the advantages of both systems of classification can be secured through a system of classification using both concepts. Thus, payroll taxes can be further subclassified into payroll taxes—salesmen's salaries; payroll taxes—sales office salaries; payroll taxes—delivery wages; payroll taxes—office salaries, and so forth.

Relating Expenses to a Department

When operating expenses are to be charged to the various departments, the allocation bases should have some foundation in logic. The accountant approaches this problem in a number of ways.

Direct Expenses.   First of all, direct expenses should be assigned to the department which if eliminated would cause the expense to be eliminated. Salesmen's salaries are the prime example of this type of expense, if, of course, salesmen are employed in only one department.

Indirect Expenses.   All expenses which would *not* be eliminated if the department was to be closed are indirect expenses and must be allocated to the departments. Indirect expenses ideally are allocated on the basis of *benefits* received. This idea is based on the matching concept in accounting, that is, that expenses incurred should be matched against the revenues they generate. In practice, this ideal can seldom be implemented with a high degree of precision. Because benefits are often impossible to measure, indirect expenses frequently are allocated on the basis of *causality*. That is, the expense is allocated to the department having the authority to order its incurrence. The assumption here is that the department would not incur the expense if it did not expect to benefit. Also, the allocation process is much more objective if causality rather than benefits is the criterion of allocation employed.

The allocation of indirect expenses is further complicated by the fact that the incurrence of an expense may not result in the receipt of essentially the same service or product in the several departments. This problem is referred to as a problem of joint costs. A cost is a *joint cost* if its incurrence results in the receipt of two or more essentially different services or products.

The classic example used to illustrate joint costs is the cost incurred in occupying two different floors of a building. It is a well-known fact that a square foot of space on the fifth floor of a building used for retailing activities will not bring as much rent as a square foot of space on the first floor. The units are not homogeneous, and thus the building occupancy cost is a joint cost. Therefore, the relative value of each square foot of space must be considered in order to obtain reasonable allocations of the building occupancy cost.

Expense Allocations Illustrated

To illustrate the allocation of expenses between departments, it is assumed that the Baxter Company classifies its expenses by five major functions: building occupancy, promotion, salesmen, buying, and administrative. The allocation of its expenses to the clothing and furnishings departments for the year ended June 30, 1979, is shown in Illustration 12.6. The bases for the various allocations are discussed below.

Building Occupancy Expenses. Building occupancy expenses consist of depreciation and insurance on a building, heat and light, repairs and maintenance, cleaning, and similar expenses. It is assumed that none of

ILLUSTRATION 12.6

Expense Distribution Sheet

BAXTER COMPANY
Expense Distribution
For Year Ended June 30, 1979

Type of Expense	Total	Clothing Department			Furnishings Department		
		Total	Direct	Indirect	Total	Direct	Indirect
Building occupancy.....	$ 24,000	$ 8,000		$ 8,000	$16,000		$16,000
Promotion.......	28,000	22,000	$13,000	9,000	6,000	$ 3,000	3,000
Salesmen.............	50,000	39,000	39,000		11,000	11,000	
Buying...............	43,000	34,400		34,400	8,600		8,600
Administrative.........	42,000	35,000	7,000	28,000	7,000		7,000
	$187,000	$138,400	$59,000	$79,400	$48,600	$14,000	$34,600

these expenses can be specifically assigned to either department, although in an actual case some of these expenses may be direct. The available space is occupied 50 percent by the furnishings department, and the remaining 50 percent by the clothing department. The furnishings department occupies the more valuable space as it is located at the front of the store in the hope that its merchandise will attract impulse or spur-of-the-moment buying from passersby. For this reason it is charged with more than 50 percent of the total building occupancy expense, with the balance allocated to the clothing department.

Promotion Expenses.   The bulk of the promotional expenses is incurred to advertise clothing department items. The company advertises primarily in local newspapers, with some direct mail circulars and some special sale announcements sent out on postal cards to credit customers. Occasionally, time is purchased on local radio and television stations to promote special sales. The cost of the advertising specifically related to the clothing and furnishings departments for the year is $13,000 and $3,000. The remaining $12,000 is allocated to the clothing and furnishings department in the amounts of $9,000 and $3,000. This ratio is determined from company policy of attempting to devote three fourths of the time or space of any advertisement to the clothing department's merchandise.

Salesmen's Expenses.   This category of expense includes all of the costs of employing salesmen—their salaries and commissions, all payroll taxes and other forms of "fringe" benefits. Delivery costs incurred on an individual package basis from a delivery service are also included in this category and charged directly to the department involved. Thus, all of these expenses can be specifically assigned to a given department.

Buying Expenses.   Two full-time buyers are employed by the Baxter Company. Neither buyer specializes in any particular type of merchandise. Efforts in the past to trace buying expenses specifically to a given department have not been very successful and have included a number of rather arbitrary assumptions about time spent. Consequently, these costs are allocated between the two departments on the basis of net purchases.

When buying costs are so allocated, the manner of computing the amounts allocated is:

$$\frac{\$275,200}{\$344,000} \times \$43,000 = \$34,400 \text{ Clothing Department}$$

$$\frac{\$68,800}{\$344,000} \times \$43,000 = \$8,600 \text{ Furnishings Department}$$

Administrative Expenses.   Included in this category are the salaries of the officers of the company, the salary of a secretary, liability and officer life insurance expense, legal fees, contributions, bad debts, stationery, supplies, and postage. A careful analysis of these expenses shows that a total of $7,000 can be specifically charged to the clothing department. These expenses include, among others, bad debts, legal fees, and collection agency charges with respect to uncollectible and slow-paying accounts. Since it is assumed that there are virtually no sales on account in the furnishings department, these expenses can all be charged to clothing.

For sake of simplicity, and because there is no better alternative, the remaining administrative expenses are allocated between the departments on the basis of relative net sales. Since clothing net sales are $480,000 and furnishings net sales are $120,000, the remaining $35,000 is allocated in the ratio of 80/20, or $28,000 and $7,000.

Departmentalized Earnings Statement

With all of the operating expenses allocated to the two departments, as shown in Illustration 12.6, an earnings statement showing net earnings by departments can be drawn as is shown in Illustration 12.7. Some of

ILLUSTRATION 12.7
Earnings Statement Showing Departmental Net Earnings

BAXTER COMPANY
Departmentalized Earnings Statement
For Year Ended June 30, 1979

	Clothing Department		Furnishings Department		Total	
Sales.....................		$489,000		$123,000		$612,000
Less: Sales returns.........		9,000		3,000		12,000
Net sales...................		$480,000		$120,000		$600,000
Cost of goods sold						
Inventory, July 1, 1978.....	$ 50,000		$20,000		$ 70,000	
Purchases.................	$290,000		$74,000		$364,000	
Less: Purchase returns.....	(10,000)		(4,000)		(14,000)	
Purchase discounts...	(4,800)		(1,200)		(6,000)	
Net purchases............	$275,200		$68,800		$344,000	
Add: Transportation-in..	24,000		6,000		30,000	
Cost of purchases........	$299,200		$74,800		$374,000	
Cost of goods available						
for sale...............	$349,200		$94,800		$444,000	
Less: Inventory, June						
30, 1979..............	70,000		20,000		90,000	
Cost of goods sold....		279,200		74,800		354,000
Gross margin..............		$200,800		$ 45,200		$246,000
Operating expenses						
Building occupancy........	$ 8,000		$16,000		$ 24,000	
Promotion................	22,000		6,000		28,000	
Salesmen.................	39,000		11,000		50,000	
Buying...................	34,400		8,600		43,000	
Administrative...........	35,000	138,400	7,000	48,600	42,000	187,000
Net earnings from operations		$ 62,400		$ (3,400)		$ 59,000
Interest revenue.............		1,000				1,000
Net earnings before taxes.....		$ 63,400		$ (3,400)		$ 60,000
Federal income taxes.........		22,190		(1,190)		21,000
Net Earnings...............		$ 41,210		$ (2,210)		$ 39,000

the basic data for sales, purchases, cost of goods sold, inventories, returns, and discounts are found in Illustration 12.4. The rest are assumed amounts.

The interest revenue is considered to be revenue of the clothing department since it arises from interest charged on extended payment credit sales. As previously noted, these are virtually all in the clothing department.

Federal income taxes are allocated between the two departments at the effective rate on the entire taxable earnings of the company. In this instance this rate is 35 percent ($21,000/$60,000).

CONTRIBUTION TO INDIRECT EXPENSES

Interpreting Departmental Loss

When an earnings statement is prepared that presents net earnings by departments, one or more departments may show a loss. Such a situation exists for the Furnishings Department in Illustration 12.7. Almost automatically the question will arise: Should the department showing the loss be closed? This question cannot be answered without further analysis.

Effect of Eliminating a Department

Before a proper decision can be made about the closing of a department, a detailed analysis of all of the operating expenses and other revenues must be made to determine which will be eliminated if the department is eliminated. A statement showing the assumed amounts of expenses and revenues that would be eliminated if the Furnishings Department was eliminated is shown in Illustration 12.8.

Effect on Sales and Cost of Goods Sold if Department Is Closed. Obviously, if the Furnishings Department was eliminated, all of its sales

ILLUSTRATION 12.8

BAXTER COMPANY
Estimated Effect on Earnings from Discontinuing the Furnishings Department

	Current Amounts	If Dept. Is Discontinued	
		Eliminated	Not Eliminated
Revenues:			
Net sales..............................	$120,000	$120,000	
Total..........................	$120,000	$120,000	
Expenses:			
Cost of goods sold......................	$ 74,800	$ 74,800	
Building occupancy.....................	16,000		$16,000
Promotion.............................	6,000	3,000	3,000
Salesmen..............................	11,000	11,000	
Buying................................	8,600		8,600
Administrative.........................	7,000		7,000
Total..........................	$123,400	$ 88,800	$34,600

revenue would disappear. Also, it should be quite obvious that the cost of goods sold would be eliminated if the department was closed.

Direct Expenses Eliminated. Operating expenses are then analyzed and classified into those which would be eliminated and those which would not be eliminated if the department was closed. Illustration 12.6 provides this information. If the classification of expenses according to direct and indirect categories has been properly completed, the analysis will show that all direct departmental expenses are eliminated. The criterion employed in classifying expenses into the direct and indirect categories was whether they would be eliminated if the department was closed. The expenses which would cease if the department is closed are sometimes referred to as "escapable" expenses.

Indirect Expenses Continue. As the statement in Illustration 12.8 shows, none of the building occupancy expense would disappear. Half of the promotion expense would disappear. If the department is closed, it is assumed the salesman will be released. Thus, all of the salesman's compensation expenses would be eliminated. Buying and administrative costs would continue at their previous amounts. For this reason these expenses which would continue are sometimes called "inescapable" expenses.

After the effect of closing the department on every revenue and expense is known, an estimated earnings statement can be prepared. Illustration 12.9 shows what the expected levels of revenues, expenses, and net earnings would be if the Furnishings Department is eliminated. (See Illustrations 12.6, 12.7 and 12.8.)

ILLUSTRATION 12.9

BAXTER COMPANY
Estimated Earnings Statement for Year Ending June 30, 1979
Assuming the Furnishings Department Was Eliminated

Net sales		$480,000
Cost of goods sold		279,200
Gross margin		$200,800
Operating expenses:		
Selling		
Building occupancy	$ 24,000	
Promotion	25,000	
Salesmen	39,000	
Buying	43,000	
Total	$131,000	
Administrative		
General administrative	$ 42,000	
Total	$ 42,000	
Total Operating Expenses		$173,000
Net operating earnings		$ 27,800
Interest revenue		1,000
Net earnings before taxes		$ 28,800

Earnings Statement Showing Departmental Contribution to Indirect Expenses

The above analysis shows that earnings statements showing net earnings by departments can lead to improper decisions if not used with caution and supplemented by additional analyses. As shown above, a decision to close the Furnishings Department would have been wrong. It would have resulted in reducing net earnings before taxes by $31,200. This is the difference between the $60,000 shown in Illustration 12.7 and the $28,800 shown in Illustration 12.9.

The reliability of net earnings as an indicator of departmental profitability can also be questioned since departmental net earnings can be affected by changes in factors entirely beyond or outside the department. To illustrate, assume that in a given company the annual building depreciation expense of $18,000 is allocated to Departments A and B on the basis of net sales (even though this is not an advisable practice). In 1978, both A and B had net sales of $500,000 and each was charged with $9,000 of building depreciation. If, in 1979, A and B have sales of $500,000 and $400,000, A will be charged with $10,000 of depreciation and B with $8,000. Note that the charge to A will increase over 10 percent (from $9,000 to $10,000) *solely because B's sales decreased.*

For reasons such as this and because many arbitrary allocations are involved in determining departmental net earnings, many accountants view this process as a futile, useless exercise to be avoided at all times. On the other hand, basing decisions on gross margin may be equally incorrect because it omits so many important variable expenses from consideration. The alternative suggested is the preparation of earnings statements which show the individual department's contributions to the indirect expenses of the company. Such an earnings statement for the Baxter Company, is presented in Illustration 12.10.

This statement clearly shows that the Furnishings Department is contributing $31,200 toward the indirect expenses of the company. It does not show the misleading loss of $2,210 reported in the earnings statement showing net earnings by departments (Illustration 12.7).

Reliability of Contribution to Overhead. The departmental contributions to overhead amounts can be computed with a fairly high degree of accuracy as they avoid all arbitrary allocations of expenses. They represent the most relevant and objective information obtainable for use by top management in appraising the relative contributions of the various departments to the profitability of the company.

But note that a department's contribution to indirect expenses should not be used by top management in appraising the department manager's performance. A fundamental principle of management is to hold individuals responsible only for that which they are given authority to control.

ILLUSTRATION 12.10

BAXTER COMPANY
Earnings Statement with Departmental Contributions to Indirect Expenses
For Year Ended June 30, 1979

	Clothing Department	Furnishings Department	Total
Net sales...............................	$480,000	$120,000	$600,000
Cost of goods sold........................	279,200	74,800	354,000
Gross Margin............................	$200,800	$ 45,200	$246,000
Interest revenue.........................	1,000		1,000
Total............................	$201,800	$ 45,200	$247,000
Direct expenses:			
Promotion..............................	$ 13,000	$ 3,000	$ 16,000
Salesmen...............................	39,000	11,000	50,000
Administrative..........................	7,000		7,000
Total Direct Expenses................	$ 59,000	$ 14,000	$ 73,000
Contribution to indirect expenses............	$142,800	$ 31,200	$174,000
Indirect expenses:			
Building occupancy........................			$ 24,000
Promotion..............................			12,000
Buying................................			43,000
Administrative..........................			35,000
Total Indirect Expenses..............			$114,000
Net earnings before income taxes............			$ 60,000
Federal income taxes......................			21,000
Net Earnings............................			$ 39,000

A department manager may not have the authority to control the level of some of a department's direct expenses—his or her own salary, for example. Consequently, any report used in evaluating a department manager's performance (as distinct from the department's performance) should contain revenues and expenses carefully classified into those controllable and those not controllable by the department manager. (This topic is the subject of Chapter 17.)

Other Factors for Consideration

Factors other than financial data must often be considered when analyzing a department's contribution to the overall operations of a company. Many of these factors are quite intangible and cannot be measured with any degree of accuracy, but they nevertheless do exist. Also some care must be exercised even when evaluating the meaning of financial data.

Nonmonetary Factors in Deciding Whether to Eliminate a Department. Sales may often be made in many departments simply because a customer was attracted by the advertising of another department. And sales of several departments may be affected if a company fails to maintain a given department.

The cost of goods and services to the department store may vary somewhat according to the volume purchased (quantity discounts). Closing a certain department may reduce volume to such an extent that higher costs are incurred in other departments. Consequently, it would be a mistake to assume that decisions such as the closing of a department can be based solely on information contained in accounting records. Also, the alternative uses of resources enter into the decision-making process. For example, a decision not to close a department may be changed if the alternative is to accept a relatively attractive offer to lease the space occupied. This simply highlights the fact that different data are needed on which to base different decisions.

Nonmonetary Factors in Evaluating Managerial Performance.   In the short run, earnings (as measured through accounting) seldom reflect satisfactorily the degree of managerial success. For instance, a manager may have canceled all training and development programs for the human resources. Essential research and development efforts may have been reduced or eliminated. Or, customers may have been antagonized through some action such as sending nasty letters to good but slow-paying customers. The consequences of these actions may not become apparent in the earnings figures for several years. In fact, in the short run some of these actions would tend to increase earnings. Thus, it is important also to use nonmonetary measures to evaluate managerial performance. Information on product development (leading to product leadership), employee attitudes, personnel development, and social or public responsibility are all helpful in appraising departmental and companywide performance.

SUMMARY

Because of the variety of products and services sold in many retail businesses, information by departments, divisions, or product lines is needed. Usually such information is used for internal decision making (product pricing, expansion, closing a department, or evaluating manager effectiveness) rather than being released to the public. The desired information relative to a department will usually include some measure of profitability, such as gross margin, net earnings, or the department's contribution to indirect expenses.

Many accountants advocate the use of the department's contribution to indirect expenses as a measure of performance. The amount by which a department's revenues exceed its direct expenses is its contribution to indirect expenses.

Normally, departmental gross margins can be readily computed since information relative to sales, sales returns, sales allowances, purchases, purchase returns, purchase allowances, purchase discounts, transportation-in, and inventories is rather easily accumulated by departments.

Departmental inventories often are determined through use of the retail method. This method makes use of the fact that merchandise is tagged with its retail price and that records are maintained as to original markup, additional markup, and markdown. The reliability of the ending inventory determined under the retail method is tested periodically by the taking of a physical inventory.

Ideally, expenses should be allocated according to benefits received. But it is usually easier to charge the expense to the department causing it to be incurred. Expenses may also be allocated according to budgeted amounts. In every instance of allocation, the goal is to allocate according to some fair and reasonable basis.

Extreme care must be exercised when using departmental net earnings in decision making because of the arbitrary allocations employed. Also, when departmental net earnings are computed, a given department may consistently show a loss which must be interpreted with care. A department may be producing enough revenue to cover all of its direct expenses and to make a contribution to the indirect expenses of the business. Eliminating the department will reduce revenues more than expenses and reduce overall net earnings.

A decision to close a department should not be made solely on the basis of the department's contribution to indirect expenses. Other factors may be influential.

Department managers should be held responsible only for those revenues and expenses which they are given the power to control.

QUESTIONS AND EXERCISES

1. Why might the top management of a retailing company be interested in having accounting information by departments?

2. The managers of the shoe departments of Bryon's and Harold's Department Stores met at a Chamber of Commerce luncheon. Bryon's Department Store computes net earnings by departments, while Harold's computes only gross margins by departments. The two managers soon found themselves disagreeing as to which is the better approach to measuring department performance. Somewhat amazingly they both found themselves arguing that the other's method of measuring "doesn't mean very much." Which manager, if either, is right? Why?

3. Distinguish between variable and fixed expenses and between direct and indirect departmental expenses.

4. What is meant by the term contribution to indirect expenses? Of what significance is it?

5. What would be your reaction to a proposal that the receiving department's expenses be allocated on the basis of the cost of the net purchases to the jewelry and the clothing departments of a store having only these two departments?

6. What would you suggest as a reasonable basis for allocating the following expenses to departments: (a) real property taxes, (b) salesmen's salaries when salesmen work in more than one department, (c) advertising in newspapers and through radio and television stations, and (d) the chief accountant's salary?

7. The X-J Department Store accumulates all of its transportation-in expense and allocates it monthly to the various departments on the basis of the ratio of each department's net purchases relative to total net purchases. What is your reaction to this procedure?

8. Why is it generally inadvisable to compute a department store's inventory on a storewide rather than individual department basis?

9. Bond Company purchased 100 pairs of gloves at $4 per pair which it priced at $6 per pair. After selling 20 pairs at $6, it repriced the gloves at $6.25 and sold 40 pairs at this price. A special sale was then held during which the gloves were priced at $5.50. After the sale was over, the remaining 10 pairs were priced at $6. Compute the total amount of (a) initial markup, (b) net additional markup, and (c) net markdown.

10. Determine the ending inventory at cost, using the retail inventory method, from the following:

	Cost	Selling Price
Beginning inventory	$105,000	$ 195,000
Purchases	954,000	1,566,000
Purchase returns	12,000	22,500
Sales		1,200,000
Sales returns		6,000
Markdowns		24,000
Markups		18,000
Transportation-in	6,900	

11. From the following data, compute the department's (a) gross margin, (b) contribution to indirect expenses, and (c) net earnings. Also compute (d) the department manager's controllable margin (excess of revenues over controllable costs):

Sales	$200,000
Direct operating expenses	40,000
Indirect operating expenses	30,000
Cost of goods sold	120,000

Of the department's expenses, $12,000 of the direct expenses and all of the indirect expenses are not controllable by the department manager.

12. M Company's Departments A and B occupy 6,000 and 4,000 square feet of floor space on the first floor, while Department C and M's administrative offices occupy 7,500 and 2,500 square feet of floor space on the second floor of a building owned by M. Space on the first floor has an estimated rental value of $2 per square foot; second floor space, $1.60 per square foot. Compute the amount of M's $27,000 of building occupancy cost that should be allocated to each department and to the administrative offices.

13. If the earnings before income taxes of a given company are $80,000 and the income taxes are $32,000, how much should be allocated to each of Departments A, B, and C if their before-tax net earnings (loss) are $50,-000, $60,000, and $(30,000)?

14. Department C of the Black Department Store shows a loss after tax credit of $40,000. If the income taxes are approximately 50 percent of before-tax net earnings and the allocated indirect expenses of the department are $94,000, does it appear desirable to eliminate the department? Why?

PROBLEMS

12–1. Garner, Inc., allocates expenses and revenues to the two departments that it operates. It extends credit to customers under a revolving charge plan whereby all account balances not paid within 30 days are charged at the rate of 1½ percent per month.

Given below are selected expense and revenue accounts and some additional data needed to complete the allocation of the expenses and the one revenue amount.

Expenses and Revenue Allocation Bases

Revolving charge service revenue (net sales)...............	$16,000
Building occupancy expenses (space occupied weighted by value of space occupied).............................	68,000
Buying expenses (net purchases).........................	21,000
General administrative expenses (number of employees in department).......................................	30,000
Insurance expense (relative average inventory plus cost of equipment in each department)........................	3,000
Depreciation (depreciation rate times cost of equipment in each department).....................................	2,500

	Dept. R	Dept. S	Total
Sales (net)............................	$100,000	$150,000	$250,000
Square feet of floor space occupied........	40,000	20,000	60,000
Value per square foot of floor space.......	$1.50	$1.25	
Purchases (net)........................	$ 75,000	$100,000	$175,000
Number of employees..................	4	6	10
Average inventory......................	$ 15,000	$ 20,000	$ 35,000
Cost of equipment and fixtures...........	$ 10,000	$ 15,000	$ 25,000

Required:

a. Prepare a schedule showing the allocation of the above items to Departments R and S.

b. Which of the allocation bases is (are) susceptible to criticism for failing to consider pertinent factors?

12–2. The Gehrke Company records purchases on the net price basis. The following financial facts pertain to the January, 1979, operations for one department:

	Cost	Retail
Markdowns................................		$ 8,000
Markups..................................		27,000
Sales.....................................		550,000
Transportation-out.......................	$ 23,000	
Sales returns.............................		9,000
Discounts lost............................	4,600	
Purchase returns.........................	14,000	18,000
Transportation-in.........................	12,000	
Inventory, January 1......................	10,000	15,000
Purchases................................	404,100	610,000

Required:

a. Compute the cost of the January 31, 1979, inventory using the retail method.

b. Indicate how this method can be used as a control device.

12–3. The June 30, 1979, trial balance of Phillips, Inc., is as shown on the following page.

Additional Data:

(1) Physical inventories at June 30, 1979, at retail prices are: Department D, $36,000; Department E, $35,000; the ratio of cost to retail in Department D is 66⅔ percent and in Department E is 60 percent as determined from application of the retail inventory method.

(2) Bad debts (considered an administrative expense) are estimated at 1 percent of sales less returns and allowances.

(3) Depreciation on building at 2½ percent per annum and on furniture and fixtures at 10 percent per annum is to be recognized and treated as selling expense and administrative expense in the ratio of 70 percent and 30 percent.

(4) Selling supplies are expensed when purchased. Unused supplies at June 30, $1,000.

(5)   Purchase discounts are to be allocated on the basis of purchases less returns and allowances.

(6)   Federal income taxes are to be estimated at 40 percent of before-tax net earnings.

PHILLIPS, INC.
Trial Balance
June 30, 1979

	Debits	Credits
Cash..	$ 42,000	
Accounts receivable...........................	78,000	
Allowance for doubtful accounts................	1,400	
Inventory—Department D.......................	26,000	
Inventory—Department E.......................	19,000	
Prepaid expenses..............................	5,000	
Land...	30,000	
Building......................................	200,000	
Allowance for depreciation—building.............		$ 80,000
Furniture and fixtures..........................	75,000	
Allowance for depreciation—furniture and fixtures...		37,500
Accounts payable..............................		32,500
Other accrued payables.........................		12,500
Capital stock.................................		125,000
Retained earnings.............................		101,900
Sales—Department D...........................		248,000
Sales—Department E...........................		377,000
Sales returns and allowances—Department D.......	8,000	
Sales returns and allowances—Department E........	17,000	
Purchases—Department D.......................	139,000	
Purchases—Department E.......................	231,000	
Purchase returns and allowances—Department D....		4,000
Purchase returns and allowances—Department E....		6,000
Purchase discounts............................		7,000
Transportation-in—Department D................	10,000	
Transportation-in—Department E................	16,000	
Selling expenses—control.......................	85,000	
Administrative expenses—control................	64,000	
Service charge revenue.........................		15,000
	$1,046,400	$1,046,400

Required:

a.   Prepare an earnings statement showing departmental gross margins but with net earnings computed only for the company as a whole for the year ended June 30, 1979.

b.   Prepare a short schedule showing gross margins and gross margin rates by departments. Which is the "better" department?

12–4.   Use the data in Problem 3 and the following data. The selling and administrative expenses for the year consist of—

| | | Direct Departmental | | |
	Total	Dept. D	Dept. E	Indirect
Selling expenses				
Selling salaries and related items..	$30,000	$15,000	$10,000	$ 5,000
Advertising..................	15,000	4,000	6,000	5,000
Buying......................	25,000	2,000	3,000	20,000
Depreciation.................	8,750	2,500	2,750	3,500
Other.......................	14,000	2,000	2,000	10,000
Total..................	$92,750	$25,500	$23,750	$43,500
Administrative expenses				
Officers' salaries..............	$30,000			$30,000
Office salaries.................	25,000	$ 2,000	$ 4,000	19,000
Bad debts....................	6,000			6,000
Depreciation.................	3,750			3,750
Other.......................	9,000	500	500	8,000
Total..................	$73,750	$ 2,500	$ 4,500	$66,750

The indirect selling salaries are to be allocated on the basis of direct selling salaries, while indirect advertising is to be allocated on the basis of direct advertising. Indirect buying expenses are to be allocated on the basis of net purchases, and indirect other selling expenses are to be allocated on the basis of net sales. The indirect depreciation charged to selling expenses is to be allocated on a 4:3 ratio to D and E.

The depreciation charged to administrative expenses is to be allocated one third to D and two thirds to E. The remaining indirect administrative expenses are to be allocated on the basis of net sales as is the revenue from service charges on accounts receivable.

Required:

a. Prepare a schedule showing the allocated indirect selling expenses by departments. At the bottom of this schedule add in the direct departmental selling expenses to get the total selling expenses by departments.
b. Repeat part (*a*) above for administrative expenses. ▮
c. Prepare an earnings statement showing net earnings by departments. Use the totals derived by departments in parts (*a*) and (*b*) for the operating expenses.

12–5. Use the data in Problems 3 and 4. Assume that a careful analysis of the bad debts and of the service charge revenues shows that Department E is responsible for 75 percent of each of these.

Required:

a. Prepare an earnings statement showing departmental contributions to indirect expenses.

b. Comment briefly on any differences noted in using contribution to indirect expenses rather than gross margin as a measure of departmental performance.

12–6. The new president of the Baker Company is giving serious consideration to discontinuing Department B. He notes that the earnings statements of the past few years show the department operating at a loss. He also notes that the other two departments seem quite badly crowded and in need of additional space. He doubts, however, that the closing of Department B will increase the sales of these two departments. In condensed form, the earnings statement for the year ending June 30, 1979, is:

	Dept. A	Dept. B	Dept. C	Total
Net sales...................	$300,000	$240,000	$100,000	$640,000
Cost of goods sold.............	$190,000	$150,000	$ 60,000	$400,000
Selling expenses...............	40,000	60,000	20,000	120,000
Delivery expenses..............	8,000	6,000	2,500	16,500
Buying expenses...............	15,000	8,000	5,500	28,500
Occupancy expenses............	14,000	12,000	6,000	32,000
Administrative expenses.........	12,000	12,000	5,000	29,000
Total Expenses...........	$279,000	$248,000	$ 99,000	$626,000
Net earnings from operations.....	$ 21,000	$ (8,000)	$ 1,000	$ 14,000
Financial charges earned.........	4,000	3,000	1,250	8,250
Net earnings before taxes........	$ 25,000	$ (5,000)	$ 2,250	$ 22,250
Federal income taxes............	5,500	(1,100)	495	4,895
Net Earnings (Loss).............	$ 19,500	$ (3,900)	$ 1,755	$ 17,355

The president of the company has asked you to express your opinion on the desirability of the contemplated closing of Department B. He tells you that he believes that all of the selling expenses and half of the buying, delivery, and administrative expenses charged to Department B will be eliminated upon the closing of the department. Also, all of the financial charges earned and allocated to Department B will be eliminated if the department is closed.

Required: State your opinion on the desirability of closing Department B. Support your opinion with a schedule showing what the net earnings after taxes for the company as a whole would have been if Department B had been closed at the start of the accounting year ending June 30, 1979.

12–7. Assume that the earnings statement in Problem 6 is for the Hughes Department Store, Inc., and is representative of the past several years. The department manager in Department B wishes to go into business for himself and has made an offer to the company to lease the space and the fixtures now being used by Department B. He offers an annual rental of 9 percent of net sales. The company would be expected to provide the space and the fixtures; to keep them in a reasonable state of repair; to provide the heat, light, and air-conditioning services; and to provide the necessary delivery services. The lessee will be responsible for all other services and expenses necessary to operate the department.

You have been asked to review this proposal, to analyze the expenses, and to report on whether it should be accepted. Your analysis of the various expenses incurred reveals the following:

The direct delivery expenses for Departments A, B and C are $2,400, $1,200, and $1,400; all of the rest are indirect. The direct occupancy costs are $4,400, $1,400, and $2,000; all of the rest are indirect. The direct selling expenses are $30,000, $52,000, and $15,000.

The buying expenses are direct to the extent of $11,000, $4,000, and $3,000. All of the administrative expenses are allocated, although bad debts have consistently been 2 percent of net sales of each department.

Required:

a.   State your conclusion regarding whether the offer to lease should be accepted and support your conclusion with comparative financial data.

b.   Cite several other factors that should be considered in reaching a decision.

12–8.   The president of the Spearman Company is very concerned over the fact that he is unable to generate any net earnings from department 3. He has devoted considerable time and a disproportionate part of the expenditures of the business to this department and it still shows a loss. He has reached the point where he is considering closing the department and expanding his other two departments equally into the space now occupied by department 3. He believes, however, that this move will neither increase the sales nor lower the costs of the other two departments but will simply relieve some overcrowding. In condensed form the earnings statement for the year ended September 30, 1979, is:

	Dept. 1	*Dept. 2*	*Dept. 3*	*Total*
Net sales.....................	$240,000	$160,000	$80,000	$480,000
Cost of goods sold.............	$160,000	$100,000	$50,000	$310,000
Advertising expense............	8,000	6,000	8,000	22,000
Salesmen's salaries.............	20,000	14,000	6,000	40,000
Delivery expense...............	6,000	4,000	2,000	12,000
Buying expense.................	12,000	8,000	4,000	24,000
Occupancy expense.............	10,000	5,000	5,000	20,000
Administrative expense..........	15,000	10,000	7,000	32,000
Total Expenses.............	$231,000	$147,000	$82,000	$460,000
Net earnings before income taxes..	$ 9,000	$ 13,000	$(2,000)	$ 20,000
Income taxes (credit)...........	1,980	2,860	(440)	4,400
Net Earnings (Loss).............	$ 7,020	$ 10,140	$(1,560)	$ 15,600

Advertising expense is direct to the extent of $6,000 to each of the three departments, while the balance is allocable equally to 1 and 3. All of the salesmen's salaries and related expenses are direct. Delivery expense is all indirect and is allocated on the basis of sales; no reduction is expected if department 3 is closed. Buying expenses are allocated on the basis of purchases ($180,000, $120,000, and $60,000). If department 3 is discontinued, these expenses will be reduced by $4,000. Occupancy expenses are all indirect and fixed and are allocated on the basis of square feet of space occupied (10,000, 5,000, and 5,000). 1 and 2 will each take equal amounts of the space formerly occupied by 3 if 3 is closed. Administrative expenses are direct to the extent of $8,000, $2,000, and $4,000 to 1, 2, and 3. The indirect expense is allocated on the basis of estimated direct administrative officer time spent on each department which is in the ratio of 7:8:3.

An offer has been received from the Tie Company, a nationwide retailer of men's ties, to lease the space now occupied by department 3. The Tie Company offers to sign a long-term lease calling for a flat annual rental of $3,000 plus 5 percent of net sales, with the Spearman Company to provide the space and to pay all costs of heating, lighting, and air conditioning. The Tie Company states that it normally generates sales of $120,000 annually from a location such as this.

The change in expenses resulting from leasing the space now occupied by department 3 will be the same as if department 3 was eliminated except that the advertising in departments 1 and 2 can be reduced by $1,000 in each department due to the heavier advertising of the Tie Company. Deliveries will be made by the Spearman Company for Tie Company without charge, and no change in the level of these expenses is anticipated. The equipment and fixtures now used in department 3 have only a nominal value and will be sold. The proceeds will be used to redecorate the space for the lessee, so that no change in the level of expenses not already mentioned above is expected from this move.

Required:

a. Present an earnings statement for the year ended September 30, 1979, showing the departmental earnings that would have resulted if 3 had been closed during the year and departments 1 and 2 had occupied the vacated space.

b. State your conclusion as to whether the offer to lease should be accepted after preparing schedules comparing the alternatives.

c. What other factors should be taken into consideration before a final decision is reached?

chapter 13

Earnings Measurement in Manufacturing Companies

To this point, discussion of the accounting for inventories and earnings determination has been limited to retailers and wholesalers. Such firms have only one type of inventory—merchandise available for sale. Now attention is turned toward a company that makes rather than buys the goods that it sells.

A manufacturing company's operations can be classified broadly as (1) manufacturing or production, (2) selling or marketing, and (3) administrative or general. The determination of selling and administrative expenses under the accrual basis of accounting has been discussed, especially in Chapter 12. Now, in this chapter and the next two, its application to manufacturing operations is described and explained.

MANUFACTURING OPERATIONS

Generally, in manufacturing operations, the objective is to use resources and incur costs to produce goods that can be sold at a profit. Raw materials are acquired, processed by men and machines to convert them into finished goods, and then delivered to customers. For example, a furniture manufacturer converts lumber, cloth, foam rubber, and other raw materials into chairs, tables, sofas, and so on. The conversion process requires not only the services of employees who work on the goods, but other services such as those received from machines.

A major goal of the accounting system of a manufacturer is to provide information on the cost of producing the finished products. This information is needed to determine the expense, cost of goods sold, in earnings determination; and the current asset, inventories, in reporting on financial position. But the system must also provide management with information needed for other uses such as the pricing of products, the control of assets, and the appraisal of the performance of individuals and segments of a company. Thus, the system provides information for financial reporting (financial accounting) and for management decision making (managerial accounting).

Elements of Manufacturing Cost

The costs of manufacturing a product include the cost of (1) direct materials, (2) direct labor, and (3) manufacturing overhead (also called indirect factory costs, factory overhead, or factory burden).

Direct Materials.   The basic materials that are physically included in the finished product, that are clearly traceable to the product, and whose manufacture caused their usage are called direct materials. Thus, iron ore is a direct material to a steel company, while steel is a direct material to the automobile manufacturer. But some minor materials are not accounted for as direct materials. For example, glue and thread used in manufacturing furniture may not be accounted for as direct materials simply because it is not practical to trace these items to the finished product. They would be described as *supplies* or *indirect materials* and accounted for as manufacturing overhead.

Direct material costs include the cost of the actual quantity of materials used, priced at net invoice price, plus delivery costs. Some firms also include storage and handling costs. Discounts taken should be deducted from gross invoice price to arrive at net cost. The method of pricing inventories, such as Fifo, Lifo, and average (discussed in Chapter 3) also affects the measurement of direct materials cost.

Direct Labor.   The services of employees who actually work on the materials to turn them into finished products are called direct labor. The direct labor costs of a product includes those labor costs that are clearly traceable or readily identifiable with the product or caused by the manufacture of the product. Evidence that a labor cost is directly related to a product can be established by showing that the amount of labor cost incurred varies closely with the number of units produced. Thus, the services of the machinist, the assembler, the cutter, and the painter are classified as direct labor. But some labor services may not be accounted for as direct labor, even though they vary directly with the number of units of product manufactured because they are difficult to trace or it is too costly to trace them. These services are broadly described as *indirect labor* and are accounted for as manufacturing overhead. Materials handling costs may be an example.

Direct labor cost is usually measured by multiplying the number of hours of services received by the wage rate per hour. The actual cost of direct labor is usually considerably higher than this amount because of other costs such as employer's payroll taxes, pension costs, paid vacations, paid sick leaves, and other so-called "fringe" benefits. These fringe benefits may amount to as much as 25 to 50 percent of the hourly wage paid. Although sometimes accounted for as a part of the direct labor cost, these costs are more commonly included in manufacturing overhead.

Manufacturing Overhead. This cost category includes all costs incurred in the manufacture of a product, other than those costs accounted for as direct materials and direct labor. They are costs that must be incurred, but which cannot be clearly traced to the product. As already noted, manufacturing overhead may include the costs of certain direct materials and direct labor because of the difficulty or impracticability of tracing them to specific units of product. They are direct costs that are accounted for as indirect costs.

Manufacturing overhead does not include selling and administrative expenses. Selling expenses are incurred to *sell* or dispose of the product, not to produce it. Administrative expenses generally relate to the overall management of a company. But to the extent that they relate to the management of factory operations, they are included in manufacturing overhead. Thus, a firm's manufacturing overhead may include the following:

Indirect labor, such as materials handling, supervision, engineering and maintenance.

Repair labor and parts for factory buildings and machinery.

Cleaning and maintenance supplies used in the factory.

Indirect materials of various types—glue, thread, nails, and so forth.

Insurance, taxes, and rent of factory buildings and machinery.

Heat, light, and power.

Depreciation on factory buildings and machinery; small tools.

Pensions, employer payroll taxes, and other fringe benefits of factory employees.

The above classification of manufacturing costs is basic to all cost accounting systems. A clear understanding of it will aid in the study of manufacturing accounting and of cost systems.

Some Cost Terminology

The sum of the direct materials and direct labor costs incurred to manufacture a product is often referred to as the product's *prime* cost. The sum of a product's three elements of cost is called *product* cost or *inventory* cost. These relationships are shown graphically in Illustration 13.1.

As its name implies, product cost is the sum of the factory costs incurred to produce it. It is the amount at which completed goods are carried

ILLUSTRATION 13.1

Elements of Product Cost

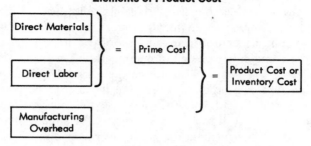

in inventory and the amount used to measure the expense, cost of goods sold, when the products are sold.

THE FLOW OF PRODUCTION COSTS

The Cost Flowchart

The cost accounting systems employed by manufacturing firms tend to have a similar general framework simply because the products manufactured flow through the firm in a similar order. Raw or basic materials are acquired; direct labor services and other factory services are employed to convert the direct materials into finished products ready for sale. The accounting records are set up in such a way as to show a flow of costs through the records that matches the physical flow of product through the company. These relationships are shown graphically in Illustration 13.2.

Physically, the goods move from the raw materials storeroom to the production department where they are processed or converted into

ILLUSTRATION 13.2

Cost and Product Flows

Flow of Products

| Raw Materials Storeroom | → | Production Department | → | Finished Goods Warehouse | → | Delivered to Customers |

Flow of Costs

| Direct Materials Inventory | → | Work-in-Process Inventory | → | Finished Goods Inventory | → | Cost of Goods Sold |

Direct Labor   Manufacturing Overhead

finished goods. They are next moved to the finished goods warehouse and then delivered to customers. The accounting records show the flow of costs from the Materials Inventory into Work in Process Inventory where the costs of direct labor and other factory services are added. When the goods are completed, their costs are moved to the Finished Goods Inventory account and, finally, upon sale they are transferred to the Cost of Goods Sold account.

Because it acquires raw materials, processes them, and carries finished products on hand, the accounting records and the financial statements of a manufacturing company typically will show three types of inventories: Materials, Work in Process, and Finished Goods. At any given time the amount in each of these accounts will depend on many factors including the availability of materials and the level of customer demand.

ACCOUNTING FOR COST AND REVENUE FLOWS

Since knowledge of the general flow of costs through a manufacturing company is of considerable value in understanding a cost system (discussed in Chapter 14), an example using dollar amounts is presented in Illustration 13.3. To begin the illustration, it is assumed that the inventories of the Brice Company as of July 1, 1979 were:

Materials inventory............................	$10,000
Work in process inventory......................	20,000
Finished goods inventory.......................	40,000

Further data with respect to the company's activities for July are given below.

The Flow of Direct Materials Costs

In the month of July, $40,000 of materials were purchased and $30,000 were issued to production from storeroom. The entries required (numbered to key to the entries in the T-accounts in Illustration 13.3) are:

(1)	Materials Inventory................................	40,000	
	*Accounts Payable..............................		40,000
	To record purchases of raw materials on account.		

   *Not shown in Illustration 13.3.

(2)	Work in Process Iventory...........................	30,000	
	Materials Inventory............................		30,000
	To record direct materials issued to production.		

Note how, in Illustration 13.3, the costs of the materials flow into the Materials Inventory account, and then flow out when the materials are issued to production. The balance in the Materials Inventory account of

ILLUSTRATION 13.3

Cost and Revenue Flowchart

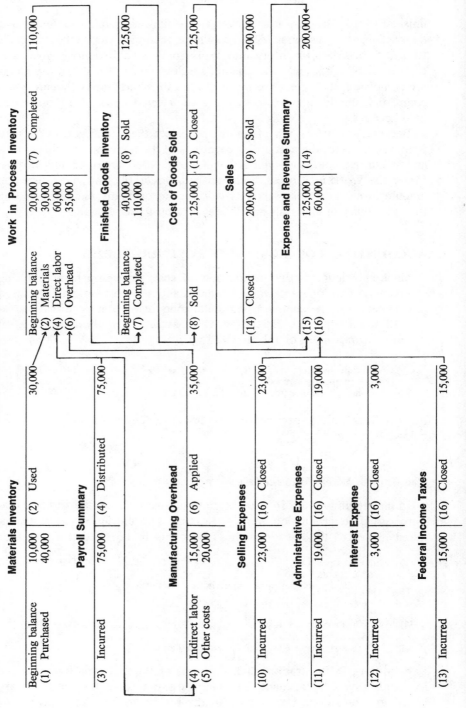

$20,000 would be reported as a current asset on the statement of financial position prepared at the end of the accounting period.

The Flow of Labor Costs

For efficient division of the work involved in accounting for employee services, two groups of clerical employees are likely to be involved. One group is concerned with determining the gross wages of each employee, the various deductions from gross pay, and the determination and payment of the net pay due—an area often referred to as *payroll accounting*. A second group is concerned with *labor cost accounting*, that is, determining what amounts of labor cost are to be charged to which accounts.

Under such an arrangement, an account common to both groups is needed to tie together the separate accounting activities. In Illustration 13.3, this account is called Payroll Summary, although it is given a wide variety of titles in actual practice. The account is debited when payrolls are prepared by the payroll department, and credited when the labor costs are distributed by the factory accounting department.

The factory payroll for the period amounted to $75,000, of which $60,000 is direct labor cost, the remainder of $15,000 is indirect factory labor cost. As required by law and union contract, $3,500 of FICA taxes (commonly called social security taxes), $8,000 of federal income taxes, and $500 of union dues were withheld from the employees' wages earned. The formal entries required (and keyed 3 and 4 in Illustration 13.3) are as follows:

```
(3)  Payroll Summary....................................  75,000
          *FICA Taxes Withheld............................          3,500
          *Federal Income Taxes Withheld..................          8,000
          *Union Dues Withheld............................            500
          *Accrued Payroll................................         63,000
     To record factory payroll and the various withholdings.

     *Not shown in Illustration 13.3.

(4)  Work in Process Inventory...........................  60,000
     Manufacturing Overhead..............................  15,000
          Payroll Summary................................         75,000
     To distribute labor costs for the period.
```

The amounts withheld will be paid, on the employees' behalf, to the federal government and to the union at some later date. The Payroll Summary account has a zero balance (as it normally will) because the labor directly traceable to products has been charged to Work in Process ($60,000), and the remainder ($15,000) treated as indirect factory labor and charged to Manufacturing Overhead. Because they are not relevant to a discussion of the flow of costs, the various liability accounts credited when the payroll was recorded are not shown in Illustration 13.3.

The Flow of Overhead Costs

The indirect factory costs for the period consisted of:

Repairs....................	$1,000	Utilities....................	$4,000
Property taxes..............	1,500	Insurance..................	2,000
Equipment rent.............	2,500	Building depreciation.:::......	5,500
Payroll taxes...............	3,500		

Entry (5) shows the formal recording of these costs:

```
(5)  Manufacturing Overhead............................... 20,000
         *Cash.............................................    1,000
         *Accounts Payable.................................    4,000
         *Accrued Property Taxes Payable...................    1,500
         *Unexpired Insurance..............................    2,000
         *Prepaid Rent.....................................    2,500
         *Allowance for Depreciation.......................    5,500
         *Accrued Payroll Taxes Payable....................    3,500
      To record the incurrence of indirect factory costs.
      *Not shown in Illustration 13.3.
```

Appropriate entries would also be made in subsidiary accounts or records for each type of manufacturing overhead cost incurred. Once again, the various accounts credited are not shown since they add little to the showing of cost flows.

Entry (6) shows the assignment of manufacturing overhead to production:

```
(6)  Work in Process Inventory............................. 35,000
         Manufacturing Overhead.........................          35,000
      To assign overhead to work in process inventory.
```

The assignment of overhead to work in process is a problem which will be dealt with later in this chapter in some depth. For purposes of Illustration 13.3, it is assumed that all overhead incurred in a period is assigned to the production of the period.

The Flow of Finished Goods

As shown in Illustration 13.3, for product costing purposes, Work in Process Inventory is charged with the material, labor, and overhead costs of producing goods. When the goods are completed and transferred out, an entry is made to transfer their cost from Work in Process Inventory to Finished Goods Inventory. If goods costing $110,000 were completed and transferred, the required entry is:

```
(7)  Finished Goods Inventory............................. 110,000
         Work in Process Inventory.......................          110,000
      To record transfer of completed goods.
```

The various ways in which this $110,000 could be determined are discussed in the next chapter.

Let us assume that finished goods costing $125,000 were sold on account for $200,000. Entries are now required to record the sale of the goods and to transfer the cost of the goods sold out of the Finished Goods Inventory account. The required entries are:

(8) Cost of Goods Sold................................ 125,000
         Finished Goods Inventory........................   125,000
      To record the cost of the goods sold.

(9) *Accounts Receivable.............................. 200,000
         Sales.......................................   200,000
      To record sales on account.
      *Not shown in Illustration 13.3.

Since we are concerned only with costs, expenses, and revenues, only the credit to the Sales account in entry 9 is shown in Illustration 13.3.

To complete the explanation of the entries in the accounts in Illustration 13.3, assume that selling expenses (sales salaries, advertising, travel, etc.) of $23,000, administrative expenses (salaries, legal fees, etc.) of $19,000, interest expense of $3,000, and federal income taxes of $15,000 were incurred in July. The required entries are:

(10) Selling Expenses..................................... 23,000
          *Various asset and liability accounts................   23,000
       To record selling expenses incurred in July.

(11) Administrative Expenses.............................. 19,000
          *Various asset and liability accounts................   19,000
       To record administrative expenses incurred in July.

(12) Interest Expense..................................... 3,000
          *Accrued Interest Payable..........................   3,000
       To record interest expense incurred in July.

(13) Federal Income Tax Expense.......................... 15,000
          *Federal Income Taxes Payable......................   15,000
       To record estimated income taxes for July.
       *Not shown in Illustration 13.3.

Subsidiary records would be maintained detailing the various types of selling and administrative expenses incurred. They are omitted here to keep the illustration brief. The credits in entries 10 and 11 would, of course, be to accounts such as Cash, Accounts Payable, Salaries Payable, the various salary withholding accounts, Allowance for Depreciation, and so on. They are omitted here, as are the credits in entries 12 and 13, to keep attention directed toward costs, expenses, and revenues.

Although the accounts are usually closed formally only at the end of the accounting year, entry 14 records the closing of the Sales revenue account for the month of July.

(14) Sales... 200,000
             Expense and Revenue Summary..................   200,000
       To close sales revenue.

Entries 15 and 16 complete the closing process:

(15) Expense and Revenue Summary..................... 125,000
         Cost of Goods Sold............................   125,000
     To close Cost of Goods Sold.

(16) Expense and Revenue Summary..................... 60,000
         Selling Expenses...............................   23,000
         Administrative Expenses.........................   19,000
         Interest Expense...............................   3,000
         Federal Income Tax Expense.....................   15,000
     To close other expense accounts.

As a technical point, the accounting for the costs of manufacturing operations ends with entry 7. The other entries are included to provide a complete set of entries showing the accounting for the earnings-seeking activities of a manufacturing company.

FINANCIAL REPORTING BY MANUFACTURING COMPANIES

In General

The statement of financial position of a manufacturer differs from that of a merchandiser because the manufacturer's statement may show separately the inventories of materials, work in process, and finished goods as well as factory supplies, whereas the merchandiser shows only merchandise inventory. It may also show, as intangible assets, patents and trademarks relating to the products manufactured and sold, and may contain greater detail in the property, plant, and equipment section because of the ownership of assets used in manufacturing. But no problem unique to the manufacturer is encountered in the preparation of the statement of financial position. The same holds for the statement of retained earnings and the statement of changes in financial position.

The Earnings Statement

The preparation of the earnings statement for a manufacturer may be considerably more complex than for a merchandising firm simply because the manufacturer incurs so many additional costs in producing goods rather than buying them ready for sale. Because of this greater detail, a question may arise as to how detailed the earnings statement should be. To a large extent, the answer depends upon to whom the statement is to be shown.

If the earnings statement is to be published, it may be in very condensed form, like the one shown in Illustration 13.4 which reports on the activities just discussed (Illustration 13.3). The period covered is assumed to be the month of July 1979. Although it is generally required that com-

ILLUSTRATION 13.4

Earnings Statement of a Manufacturer

BRICE COMPANY
Earnings Statement for the Month Ended July 31, 1979

Sales...		$200,000
Cost of goods sold...........................	$125,000	
Selling expenses.............................	23,000	
Administrative expenses......................	19,000	
Interest expense.............................	3,000	
Federal income taxes.........................	15,000	185,000
Net Earnings.................................		$ 15,000

parative data (the earnings statement for July 1978) be included when financial statements are released to the general public, such data are omitted here.

The same type of earnings statement could be used in reporting to top management and to the board of directors. When so used, it is likely to be in comparative form, containing comparable period data for last year, and to contain budgeted data. It is also likely to be supplemented with a statement of cost of goods manufactured and sold and with schedules showing the details of the selling and administrative expenses, complete with comparative and budgeted data.

The Statement of Cost of Goods Manufactured and Sold

Illustration 13.5 contains the statement of cost of goods manufactured and sold for the Brice Company for the month of July 1979. Note how it shows the costs incurred during the month for materials, labor, and overhead and describes this total as "Cost to manufacture." By adding the July 1 work in process inventory and subtracting the July 31 inventory of work in process, the cost of the goods manufactured (completed) during the period is shown. When the July 1 finished goods inventory is added to this amount, the cost of the goods available for sale is obtained. Subtracting the ending finished goods inventory from the cost of the goods available for sale yields the cost of goods sold. At this stage in the statement, note that there is some similarity to the cost of goods sold section of a merchandiser's earnings statement:

Merchandiser: Beginning inventory + cost of purchases − ending inventory = cost of goods sold.

Manufacturer: Beginning finished goods inventory + cost of goods manufactured − ending finished goods inventory = cost of goods sold.

ILLUSTRATION 13.5

BRICE COMPANY
Statement of Cost of Goods Manufactured and Sold
For the Month Ended July 31, 1979

Direct materials.............................		$ 30,000
Direct labor..................................		60,000
Manufacturing overhead:		
Indirect labor...........................	$15,000	
Building depreciation.......................	5,500	
Utilities.................................	4,000	
Payroll taxes.............................	3,500	
Equipment rent...........................	2,500	
Insurance................................	2,000	
Property taxes............................	1,500	
Repairs..................................	1,000	35,000
Cost to manufacture........................		$125,000
Work in process, July 1, 1979.................		20,000
		$145,000
Work in process, July 31, 1979...............		35,000
Cost of goods manufactured...................		$110,000
Finished goods, July 1, 1979..................		40,000
Cost of goods available for sale................		$150,000
Finished goods, July 31, 1979.................		25,000
Cost of Goods Sold..........................		$125,000

The statement in Illustration 13.5 could be expanded to show the computation of the cost of the direct materials used by including the following:

Materials inventory, July 1, 1979...........................	$10,000
Materials purchased...................................	40,000
Materials available....................................	$50,000
Materials inventory, July 31, 1979........................	20,000
Direct materials used (all materials used were direct)........	$30,000

The statement would then continue with the $60,000 of direct labor.

Careful attention should be paid to the terminology used in the statement of cost of goods manufactured and sold. Note the similarity between the terms "Cost to manufacture" and "Cost of goods manufactured." The former consists of the costs of all resources put into the manufacturing operation in the period. The latter consists of the cost of the goods completed and includes "Cost to manufacture" and the change in the Work in Process inventory from the beginning to the end of the month.

A GRAPHIC SUMMARY

The discussion of a manufacturer's manufacturing, marketing, and administrative activities that lead to the recognition of net earnings is summarized graphically in Illustration 13.6. Several important implications of the accounting for these activities should be noted.

ILLUSTRATION 13.6

A Manufacturing Company's Total Operations

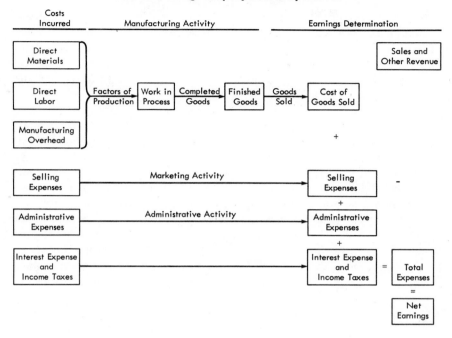

First, the accounting for the costs of the manufacturing operations is an integral part of the overall accounting system of the company. No separate system is used to accumulate manufacturing cost information.

Secondly, the period in which a given cost is recognized as an expense may differ sharply according to whether the cost is considered a manufacturing cost or a marketing or administrative cost. For example, the salary a salesman earned in July is considered an expense of the month of July and affects net earnings for July. Selling and administrative costs are recognized as expenses in the period incurred and for this reason are called *period* costs. But all, a part, or none of a factory inspector's July salary may be included in July's expenses. Because it is treated as a product cost and charged to Work in Process Inventory it then becomes a part of the cost of the goods completed and transferred to Finished Goods Inventory. It has an impact upon net earnings only in the period in which the goods that were inspected are sold. Until they are sold, the salary is included as part of the cost of the Work in Process Inventory or Finished Goods Inventory, both of which are current assets. If inventories are large relative to sales, many months may go by before this salary has an effect on net earnings.

MANUFACTURING OVERHEAD RATES

To focus on the general pattern of cost flows shown in Illustration 13.3, certain problems in accounting for manufacturing overhead were not discussed. These problems arise primarily because the costs of a wide variety of factory services having no common physical basis of measurement must be allocated to many different products. By their nature and for practical reasons, such costs are not traceable to or identifiable with any given unit of product.

Before directing attention to these problems, the terms *cost center, production center,* and *service center* need to be introduced and defined. A cost center is an accounting unit of activity for accumulating costs having a common objective. That is, the items of cost recorded as having been incurred by a given cost center all seek to accomplish the same objective or purpose. Thus, the costs incurred in the assembly department of a furniture manufacturer seek to bring about the assembly of furniture and can, therefore, be allocated to the products assembled. A cost center in which work is performed on units of product is called a production center. A service center is a cost center in which work indirectly related to the goods produced is performed. A tool room, maintenance department, power plant, and even the company cafeteria are examples of service centers.

General Procedures

Illustration 13.7 depicts graphically the general procedures followed in loading indirect factory costs on the units of product manufactured by a

ILLUSTRATION 13.7

Manufacturing Overhead Allocated to Products

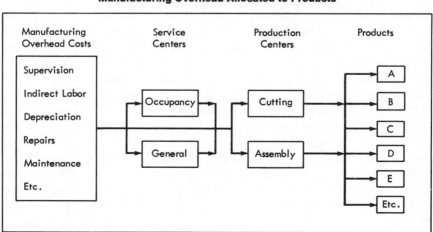

company producing a line of unfinished redwood patio furniture. Manufacturing operations are conducted in two production centers, cutting and assembly, and two service centers, building occupancy and general.

The general procedures followed in allocating overhead to products consist of three steps:

1. All manufacturing overhead costs incurred in a period are charged initially to one and only one service center or production center. In this way, the sum of the overhead charged to the four centers equals the total overhead incurred in a period. Thus, the cost of supplies used is charged to the center where they are consumed, indirect labor cost is charged to the center where the employee works, and so on. All overhead costs incurred to house factory operations, such as building depreciation, taxes, and insurance, are charged to the occupancy center. All overhead costs not traceable to or identifiable with one of the other three centers are charged to the general service center. Section I of Illustration 13.8 shows this initial assignment of overhead costs to the four cost centers of our patio furniture manufacturer.

2. The total overhead costs accumulated in the service centers are now reassigned to the production centers. The objective is to ultimately accumulate all overhead costs in production centers only. Some service center costs, such as those incurred to generate electricity or steam, may be charged to other cost centers on the basis of the metered amounts actually consumed. Repair costs may be charged on a "time and materials" basis. Still other costs will have to be allocated on some reasonable basis such as square feet of floor space occupied, number of employees, dollars of payroll cost, or some other measure of activity. The guiding principle

ILLUSTRATION 13.8

Allocating Overhead to Products

	Production Centers		Service Centers		
	Cutting	Assembly	Occupancy	General	Total
I. Initial Assignment					
Cost Element					
Indirect labor.................	$ 3,000	$ 2,500	–0–	$ 5,000	$10,500
Depreciation..................	2,000	1,000	$ 4,000	500	7,500
Other.......................	10,000	8,500	6,000	9,500	34,000
	$15,000	$12,000	$10,000	$15,000	$52,000
II. Service Center Costs					
Reassigned					
Occupancy...................	5,000	4,000	(10,000)	1,000	
General.....................	10,000	6,000		(16,000)	
Total Overhead Costs..........	$30,000	$22,000	–0–	–0–	$52,000
III. Allocations to Products					
Direct labor hours.............	7,500	5,000			
Manufacturing overhead					
rate per direct labor hour......	$ 4.00	$ 4.40			

is to allocate service center costs to the production centers that benefitted from or caused the incurrence of these costs. The allocation of indirect costs was dealt with in Chapter 12 and, for this reason, is discussed only briefly here.

The Step Method. A special problem was faced in reassigning service center costs in Illustration 13.8, Section II. The two service centers rendered services not only to the production centers, but to each other. This implies that some of the costs of each service center should be allocated to the other service center. The question then is: How does one avoid an almost endless process of allocating costs back and forth between the two service centers? One practical solution is to allocate such costs in a prescribed order. Start with one service center, allocate its costs to the production and other service centers; now choose a second service center and allocate its cost. Make no allocation of its costs to the first service center. Proceed in this manner until all service center costs have been allocated. This is known as the *step* method. But accountants disagree on how to determine the order in which the sevice centers' costs are to be allocated. Some argue the most costly service center should be allocated first simply because it provides the most services. Yet others suggest allocating the least significant center first. Significance is judged by the number of cost centers serviced by a given service center. If this test cannot be used, significance can be determined by the dollar amounts of costs incurred. This procedure is used in Illustration 13.8 and results in the occupancy center's costs being allocated first. The allocation was based on relative square feet of floor space occupied: 50 percent to cutting, 40 percent to assembly, and 10 percent to general. The general service center's costs ($16,000) are then allocated on the basis of prime costs (direct materials + direct labor) charged to the two production centers ($50,000 cutting and $30,000 assembly). Thus, the allocations are: cutting, $5/8$ of $16,000, or $10,000; assembly $3/8$ of $16,000, or $6,000.

3. The total overhead, now accumulated in production centers only, is allocated to the units of product worked on in each center. It is seldom possible to divide the number of units of product into the total overhead costs of a production center to allocate overhead to products for two reasons: (1) different products may be involved—our furniture factory makes benches and tables of different sizes, as well as settees, chairs, chaise lounges, and so forth, and (2) some products may be only partially completed. But all of the products do have things in common: They all have direct materials costs, direct labor costs, have been worked on for a number of direct labor hours, and may have required a certain amount of machine time. This leads to the computation of an *overhead rate,* wherein the overhead incurred is expressed as an amount per some unit of activity, such as the direct labor hours used in Section III of Illustration 13.8. In

computing overhead rates, the objective is to use a measure of activity that is closely related to the amount of overhead incurred.

After the overhead rates have been computed, overhead cost can readily be allocated to products. For example, if the production of 100 tables required 10 direct labor hours in the cutting department and 20 hours in the assembly department, the total overhead charged to these tables would be:

$$
\begin{array}{llr}
\text{Cutting:} & 10 \times \$4.00 = & \$\ 40.00 \\
\text{Assembly:} & 20 \times \$4.40 = & \underline{88.00} \\
\text{Total Overhead} & & \underline{\underline{\$128.00}}
\end{array}
$$

Predetermined Overhead Rates

In the above discussion, overhead rates were determined at the end of a period (say, a month). But, although some companies follow such a procedure, it is far more common to use a *predetermined* overhead rate to allocate overhead to production. The rate is usually set at the beginning of the year. The reasons for this more common practice include:

1. Overhead costs are seldom incurred uniformly throughout the year as, for example, heating costs will be large in winter. No useful purpose is served in allocating less cost to a unit produced in the summer than one produced in the winter.
2. The volume of goods produced may vary from month to month with accompanying sharp fluctuations in average unit cost if some overhead costs are fixed.
3. Unit costs of production are known sooner. Using a predetermined rate, overhead costs can be assigned to production when direct materials and direct labor costs are assigned. Without a predetermined rate, unit costs would not be known until the end of the month or even much later if bills for overhead costs are late.
4. It requires less time and effort to compute one annual rate rather than 12 monthly rates.

Computing Predetermined Overhead Rates. The mechanics of computing predetermined overhead rates are the same as those used for actual rates except for the use of budgeted rather than actual levels of costs and levels of activity. Budgeted overhead costs are first estimated and charged to the various cost centers. Budgeted service center costs are then reassigned to production centers. Budgeted production center costs are then divided by the estimate of the level of activity to compute the predetermined rates. These budget estimates will normally be available as part of the company's budgeting process, which is discussed in Chapter 18.

Choosing the level of activity to be used in setting predetermined overhead rates is a special problem that is dealt with in an appendix to this chapter. But it should be clearly recognized that the estimate of volume can have a significant effect on overhead rates, especially if there are substantial fixed overhead costs. To illustrate, assume that overhead is completely fixed at $100,000. The overhead rate would be $10 per direct labor hour if volume was estimated at 10,000 direct labor hours. It would be only $5 using an estimate of volume of 20,000 direct labor hours.

Underapplied or Overapplied Overhead. When overhead is applied to production using predetermined rates, the manufacturing overhead account is credited with estimated amounts applied to work in process inventory. This follows because the rate is based on estimates when it is established. Under these circumstances, it is highly unlikely that the actual costs debited to the account will exactly equal the overhead applied and credited to the account. A debit balance will remain if actual overhead exceeds applied overhead and overhead will be underapplied or underabsorbed. A credit balance will remain if applied overhead exceeds actual overhead, and overhead will be overapplied or overabsorbed.

Refer to Illustration 13.3, page 322. If overhead is allocated to production using a predetermined rate of 50 percent of direct labor cost, entry 6 on page 324 would read:

Work in Process Inventory	30,000	
Manufacturing Overhead		30,000

Since $35,000 of actual overhead costs were charged to Manufacturing Overhead, the account now has a $5,000 debit balance representing underapplied overhead for the period.

Reasons for Underapplied or Overapplied Overhead. Underapplied or overapplied overhead may be a result of unexpected events such as price changes, a severe winter, or excessive repairs. Or overhead items may be used inefficiently. But underapplied overhead is more likely to be caused by incurring costs at a higher level than that set in the typical "tight" budget. On the other hand, overapplied overhead is likely to be the result of operating at a higher actual level than that used in setting the overhead rate and to the existence of fixed overhead costs.

Disposition of Underapplied or Overapplied Overhead. Any under- or overapplied overhead balance can be carried forward in interim statements of financial position if the probability exists that it will be reduced or offset by future operations. At year end, any remaining balance could be allocated to Work in Process Inventory, Finished Goods Inventory, and Cost of Goods Sold by recomputing the cost of production for the year using actual overhead rates.

As an alternative, charging underapplied overhead off as a loss of the period has particular merit if it results from idle capacity or from unusual circumstances. But, as a practical matter, underapplied or overapplied overhead is frequently transferred to Cost of Goods Sold. Little distortion of net earnings or of assets results from this treatment if the amount transferred is small or if most of the goods produced during the year were sold. Thus, the entry to dispose of the $5,000 of underapplied overhead in the example would read:

Cost of Goods Sold	5,000	
Manufacturing Overhead		5,000

SUMMARY

The three main elements of product cost are the costs of direct materials, direct labor, and manufacturing overhead. The cost of direct materials and direct labor can usually be traced to or physically identified with a product. The manufacture of the product causes the firm to incur these costs and production of the product is expected to be benefitted by their incurrence. All other manufacturing costs are called manufacturing overhead. Many of these costs are indirect costs because they cannot be traced to an individual product. Manufacturing overhead may also include, for reasons of expediency and materiality, costs of items that could be traced to or physically identified with a product. Manufacturing overhead is also referred to as indirect factory costs, even when it contains costs that can be traced to production.

A manufacturer's accounting system shows the flow of costs in a manner that matches the flow of goods through the plant from storeroom to production to finished goods to customers. It typically contains three inventory accounts: Materials, Work in Process, and Finished Goods.

The financial reporting of a manufacturer differs from that of a retailer in that it includes a statement of cost of goods manufactured and sold. The cost system providing information for this statement is a part of the company's accounting system. Such a system distinguishes between product costs and period costs.

Manufacturing overhead is allocated to products by use of predetermined overhead rates. These rates are set initially by assigning all overhead to production or service centers. Service center costs are then reassigned to production centers. Production center costs (including assigned service center costs) are then allocated to products using overhead rates obtained by dividing such costs by estimates of the level of activity, such as direct labor hours.

The use of rates determined in advance to assign overhead to production usually results in underapplied or overapplied overhead. As a practical matter, such balances are closed to Cost of Goods Sold at the end of the year.

APPENDIX: OVERHEAD RATES AND THE LEVELS OF ACTIVITY

Setting overhead rates, especially when large amounts of fixed overhead costs are incurred, involves the difficult problem of choosing the level of activity to be used. As already demonstrated, it would be possible to wait until the end of the period and use actual rates to apply overhead to production. Thus, if $100,000 of fixed overhead costs were incurred and 10 units were produced, the overhead cost per unit would be $10,000. If 1,000 units were produced, it would be $100. And the wide fluctuation in unit cost would be due solely to the differing number of units produced.

But suppose the plant was designed to produce 100,000 units per period. Now might it not be logical to argue that the overhead to be absorbed by each unit is $1 ($100,000 ÷ 100,000) and that any underabsorbed overhead from producing less than 100,000 units is a loss from idle capacity? Many accountants would so argue. Thus, the issue is: What level of activity should be used in setting overhead rates?

Possible Levels of Activity

Among the different levels of activity that might be used, the three most commonly found in practice today are:

(1) Practical capacity—the maximum attainable output of a plant. It is theoretical capacity less allowance for the fact that individuals can seldom achieve perfection. Its use results in only the costs of the facilities actually used being charged to production. If a plant operated at 60 percent of capacity, 60 percent of its fixed costs would be charged to production, and the remaining 40 percent would be treated as a period cost (expense).

(2) Normal capacity or activity—the level of activity expected to prevail over the long run, say, three to five years. Its use is based on the belief that over the long run all manufacturing costs are to be absorbed in production and recovered through sale of the goods.

(3) Expected activity—the estimated level of activity for the coming period. This level of activity has the objective of absorbing all fixed overhead for a period in the production of that period.

The Level of Activity Problem Illustrated

To illustrate, consider the data in the following schedule. Assume that fixed overhead costs are $480,000 per period and that variable overhead costs amount to $1.50 per direct labor hour over a range of 40,000 to 100,000 hours.

	Direct Labor Hours for the Year	Budgeted Overhead for the Year		
		Variable	Fixed	Total
Practical capacity.............	100,000	$150,000	$480,000	$630,000
Normal capacity..............	80,000	120,000	480,000	600,000
Expected activity.............	60,000	90,000	480,000	570,000

From these data, three predetermined overhead rates could be computed as follows:

1. Practical capacity rate: $630,000 ÷ 100,000 = $6.30 per direct labor hour.
2. Normal capacity rate: $600,000 ÷ 80,000 = $7.50 per direct labor hour.
3. Expected activity rate: $570,000 ÷ 60,000 = $9.50 per direct labor hour.

Note that in each of these rates variable overhead accounts for $1.50 of the total rate. If the overhead costs incurred during the year amounted to $480,000 fixed and $75,000 variable and actual direct labor hours of services received amounted to 50,000 hours, the actual overhead rate would be $11.10 ($555,000 ÷ 50,000).

Note further the differing amounts of overhead that would be absorbed depending upon the level of activity used in setting the rate when 50,000 hours of direct labor services were received:

Practical capacity-based rate: 50,000 × $6.30 = $315,000
Normal capacity-based rate: 50,000 × $7.50 = 375,000
Expected activity-based rate: 50,000 × $9.50 = 475,000

If the overhead allocated to production varies, it follows that underapplied overhead will vary. This, in turn, means that unless all goods produced are sold in the period of manufacture, inventories and net earnings will differ because a different level of activity was used in setting overhead rates.

QUESTIONS AND EXERCISES

1. A manufacturing company's activities may be broadly classified into three major functions. Identify these classifications and indicate why it is important that costs associated with one function not be included with those of another.
2. Identify the three elements of manufacturing cost and indicate the distinguishing characteristics of each.
3. Why might a company claim that the total cost of employing an individual is $10.30 per hour even though the employee's wage rate is only

$6.50? How should the items making up this difference be classified? Why?

4. In general, what is the relationship between cost flows in the accounts and the flow of product through the plant?

5. In general terms, outline the basic design of every cost system.

6. Explain the nature and manner in which the Payroll Summary account is used.

7. Explain why the application of overhead to production through use of a predetermined rate is almost a necessity.

8. What are the major reasons why overhead costs incurred will differ from the overhead applied to production? What is probably the primary reason for overapplied overhead?

9. Under what theory is overhead considered properly applied to production?

10. What are two possible dispositions of a year-end balance of underapplied overhead? Explain why a third possibility exists for a balance existing at the end of any period less than a year.

11. What is the general content of a statement of cost of goods manufactured and sold? What is its relationship to the earnings statement?

12. What is a cost center? A production center? A service center?

13. How is the problem of re-assigning service center costs resolved when a company has two service centers that render services to each other?

14. Outline the general procedures used in accounting for factory overhead costs that result in such costs being applied to production.

15. During a given week $50,000 of direct materials and $5,000 of indirect materials were issued to various production departments. Give the necessary journal entry.

16. What levels of capacity or activity are used in setting overhead rates? Of what significance is the choice of any given level?

17. A company budgeted its overhead for the year 1979 at $400,000 ($100,-000 fixed and $300,000 variable) based on normal activity of 200,000 direct labor hours. At the end of 1979, manufacturing overhead was over-absorbed $3,000 while actual direct labor hours amounted to 202,000. Explain why manufacturing overhead was overabsorbed.

18. May a cost be a direct cost of a center and yet be indirect to what was accomplished in the center? Give an example.

PROBLEMS

13–1. Given below are selected data for the Burns Company for the month of May:

Direct labor costs incurred............................	$170,000
Direct materials issued...............................	150,000
Work in process inventory, May 1.....................	130,000
Work in process inventory, May 31....................	190,000
Total manufacturing costs charged to production in May............................	760,000

Required:

a. Compute the amount of manufacturing overhead charged to production in May.

b. Give the journal entry to record the cost of the goods completed and transferred to Finished Goods Inventory in May.

13–2. The following data relate to the Hanson Company for the month of June 1979:

(1) Materials purchased on account, $24,000.

(2) Direct materials issued, $28,000.

(3) Repairs and maintenance on factory buildings and equipment, $3,000.

(4) Factory depreciation, taxes, and utilities, $20,800.

(5) Factory payroll for June, $18,000, including $1,600 of indirect labor.

(6) Overhead rate is 110 percent of direct labor cost.

(7) Cost of goods completed and transferred, $78,000.

(8) Cost of goods sold, $80,000.

The June 1, 1979 inventory account balances were:

Materials...................	$ 8,000
Work in process..............	20,000
Finished goods...............	6,000

Required:

a. Prepare a cost flowchart similar to the one illustrated in the text.

b. Compute the amount of under- or overapplied overhead for the month of June.

13–3. Selected data for the Burns Company for June 1979, are:

Materials inventory, June 1....................	$ 21,000
Materials purchased..........................	52,000
Materials inventory, June 30..................	5,000
Direct labor cost............................	30,000
Work in process inventory, June 1.............	7,000
Work in process inventory, June 30............	51,000
Cost of goods sold...........................	102,000
Finished goods inventory, June 1..............	41,000
Finished goods inventory, June 30.............	22,000
Sales.......................................	165,000
Selling and administrative expenses...........	35,000

Required:

a. Give journal entries to record the cost of the materials used and the cost of the goods completed.

b. Compute the amount of manufacturing overhead charged to production in June.

    c. Prepare a condensed earnings statement supported by a schedule showing the cost of the goods manufactured and sold.

13–4. The following are selected data of the Steinman Company for the year ended December 31, 1979:

	January 1	December 31
Inventories		
Work in process......................	$101,600	$ 79,200
Finished goods........................	130,800	116,400
Direct labor cost incurred.................		482,400
Selling expenses incurred..................		200,800
Direct materials used......................		310,400
General and administrative expenses		
incurred.............................		234,000
Manufacturing overhead overabsorbed		
for year..............................		600

Manufacturing overhead is applied to production at a rate equal to two-thirds of direct labor cost assigned.

Required: Prepare a statement of cost of goods manufactured and sold.

13–5. The following data summarize the operations of the Gross Corporation for the year 1979:

Materials inventory		Work in process inventory	
Balance, 1/1............	$ 2,000	Balance, 1/1............	$ 8,100
Received..............	12,000	Costs added:	
Issued (all direct)........	10,000	Materials..............	10,000
Finished goods		Direct labor...........	30,000
Balance, 1/1............	7,900	Overhead applied.......	60,000
Cost of goods sold.......	97,000	Completed goods........	99,100
Sales....................	192,000		
Selling and admin.			
expenses..............	55,000		

Manufacturing overhead incurred consisted of the following:

Indirect labor.................................	$ 2,500
Supplies used.................................	1,500
Depreciation..................................	10,000
Heat, light and power..........................	4,000
Repairs.......................................	4,500
Property taxes.................................	4,000
Maintenance...................................	6,500
Supervision...................................	12,000
Insurance.....................................	2,000
Rent...	8,000
Miscellaneous.................................	1,000

The Manufacturing Overhead account was closed at year end to Cost of Goods Sold but this amount is not included in the $97,000 cost of goods sold amount given above.

Required: Prepare a condensed earnings statement supported by a detailed statement of cost of goods manufactured and sold.

13–6. Following are selected transactions of the Hanes Company for May, 1979:

(1) Materials purchased on account, $36,000.

(2) Direct materials issued to Department A, $16,000; to Department B, $18,000.

(3) Manufacturing overhead incurred: Department A, $30,000; Department B, $26,000.

(4) Manufacturing payroll for the month, $33,000.

(5) Payroll distributed: direct labor to Department A, $14,000; to Department B, $16,000; indirect labor in Department A, $1,000; in Department B, $2,000.

(6) Overhead rates: Department A, 200 percent of direct labor cost; Department B, 150 percent of direct labor cost.

(7) Goods costing $66,000 were completed in Department A and transferred to Department B.

(8) Goods costing $134,000 were completed in Department B and transferred to Finished Goods.

(9) Goods costing $146,000 were sold for $210,000.

May 1 inventory balances were.

Materials..	$12,000
Work in process—Department A..................	18,000
Work in process—Department B..................	22,000
Finished goods..................................	30,000

Required: Set up T-accounts for Materials Inventory, Payroll Summary, Manufacturing Overhead, Work in Process Inventory—Department A, Work in Process Inventory—Department B, Finished Goods Inventory, Cost of Goods Sold, and Sales. Enter in these accounts that portion of the above data that affects these accounts. Key your entries to the numbered items above.

13–7. The budget prepared for 1979 for the Banke Company shows the following expected overhead costs for each of three production and two service centers:

Production Center	
A...	$40,000
B...	30,000
C...	50,000
Service Center	
I...	20,000
II..	14,000

Overhead rates are to be established for each of the three production centers. The costs charged to Service Center II are to be reassigned to the other four cost centers on the basis of the amounts of overhead costs charged initially to these four centers. The costs charged to Service Center I are then to be reassigned to the three production centers on the basis of square feet of floor space occupied: A—10,000; B—5,000; C—5,000. Overhead rates are then to be established based on direct labor costs, which are budgeted: A—$18,333; B—$38,500; C—$30,250.

Required:

a.   Compute the overhead rates for 1979 for each of Banke's three production centers.
b.   Actual overhead and direct labor costs for January were:

	Production Centers			*Service Centers*	
	A	*B*	*C*	*I*	*II*
Actual overhead..............	$3,000	$2,000	$5,000	$2,000	$1,200
Actual direct labor cost........	1,400	2,900	3,000		

Compute the overapplied or underapplied overhead for each production center for January.

13–8.   (Based on Appendix)
   Budgeted data for the Mason Company's fiscal year beginning July 1, 1979, are as follows:

Level of Activity	*Direct Labor Hours*	*Budgeted Overhead*
Practical Capacity................	300,000	$1,080,000
Normal activity..................	240,000	960,000
Expected activity................	160,000	800,000

Required:

a.   Compute the predetermined overhead rates that might be used by Mason to apply overhead to production.
b.   Assume that in July, 1979, 20,000 hours of direct labor services were received and that $92,000 of overhead costs were incurred. Compute the amount of overhead that would be applied to production if overhead rates were based on each of the above levels of activity, as well as the amount applied based on actual activity.
c.   Explain the significance of the differing amounts in your answer to (b).

chapter 14

Cost Systems—Job Order and Process

Presented and discussed in the previous chapter were (1) the general framework of a cost system, (2) the three main types of manufacturing cost and their general flow pattern, (3) the problems faced in applying overhead to production, and (4) the reporting upon operations of a manufacturing company. Little attention was paid to the procedures and accounting records used in accumulating costs or to the problem of determining unit costs for completed and partially completed units of product. How these costs are determined depends upon the type of cost system employed.

Thus, attention in this chapter is directed to the two major types of cost accumulation systems found in practice—the *job order* or *job cost* system and the *process cost* system. In each system the goal is to determine the unit costs of the products manufactured. As already noted, unit costs are needed to determine the cost of the goods sold and the cost of the ending inventories of work in process and finished goods. They may also be used to determine payments to be received under contracts based on "full" cost and in setting selling prices.

JOB ORDER COST SYSTEMS

Timely and Useful Information

When a job order cost system is used, costs are accumulated by individual jobs, or batches of output. A job may consist of 1,000 chairs, 10 sofas, 5 miles of highway, a single machine, a dam, or a building. A job cost system is generally used when goods are produced to meet a customer's particular needs, such as constructing a house. Job costing is also used in other types of construction, in motion pictures, and in job printing.

Under job order costing a running record of the costs incurred on a job is kept in order to provide management with cost data on a timely basis. For example, it may want to know the cost of producing 100 desks when the desks are completed. It can also receive reports as often as it desires, even daily, on such matters as materials used, labor costs incurred, goods completed, total and detailed production costs, and whether production costs are in line with expectations.

Basic Records in Job Costing

Illustration 14.1 shows the basic records or source documents used in a job order cost system. These include:

1. The *job order sheet* on which is summarized all of the costs—direct materials, direct labor, and applied overhead—of producing a given job or batch of products. It is the key document in the system and is used to control production costs by comparing actual costs with budgeted costs. One sheet is maintained for each job and the file of job order sheets for unfinished jobs is the subsidiary ledger for the Work in Process Inventory account. When the goods are completed and transferred, the job order sheets are transferred to a completed jobs file and the number of units and their unit costs recorded on inventory cards supporting the Finished Goods Inventory account.
2. The *stores* (or *materials*) card, one of which is kept for each type of direct and indirect materials maintained in inventory. It shows the quantities (and costs) of each type of materials received, issued, and on hand for which the storekeeper is responsible. When a job is put into production, direct materials are ordered from the storeroom on a form known as a *materials requisition,* which shows the types, costs, and quantities of the materials ordered.
3. The *work* (or *time*) ticket which shows who worked on what job for how many hours and at what wage rate. All of each employee's daily hours must be accounted for on one or more work tickets.
4. The *manufacturing overhead cost sheet* which summarizes the various types of factory indirect costs incurred. One sheet is maintained for each production center and each service center, as described in Chapter 13.
5. The *finished goods card* or *record,* one of which is maintained for each type of product manufactured and sold. Each card contains a running record of units and costs of products received, sold, and on hand.

The general flow of costs through the general ledger accounts of a firm using a job order cost system is shown in Illustration 14.2. This illustration should be studied carefully and related to documents used to record costs that are shown in Illustration 14.1 to gain a full understanding of a job order cost system.

Job Order Costing—An Example

To illustrate the operation of a job order cost system, especially the tie between the general ledger accounts and the subsidiary records, an extended numerical example is presented below. The example covers the month of July for which the beginning inventories were:

Materials inventory (Material A, $10,000; Material B,
  $6,000; various indirect materials, $4,000)................ $20,000
Work in process inventory (Job No. 106: Direct materials,
  $4,200; Direct labor, $5,000; Overhead, $4,000)........... 13,200
Finished goods inventory (500 units of product AB at
  a cost of $11 per unit)................................ 5,500

The example further assumes that Job No. 106 was completed in July, and that, of the two jobs started in July (Nos. 107 and 108), only Job No. 108 is incomplete at the end of July. The transactions, and the journal entries to record them, are given below.
(1) Purchased $10,000 of material A and $15,000 of material B on account.

Materials Inventory...................................... 25,000
  Accounts Payable.....................................   25,000
  To record purchase of direct materials.

(2) Issued direct materials: Material A to Job No. 106, $1,000; to Job No. 107, $8,000, to Job No. 108, $2,000; Material B to Job No. 106, $2,000, to Job No. 107, $6,000, to Job No. 108, $4,000. Indirect materials issued to all jobs, $1,000.

Work in Process Inventory............................... 23,000
Manufacturing Overhead.................................. 1,000
  Materials Inventory..................................   24,000
  To record direct and indirect materials issued.

(3) Factory payroll for the month, $25,000; social security and income taxes withheld, $4,000.

Payroll Summary... 25,000
  Various liability accounts for taxes withheld..............   4,000
  Accrued Wages Payable...............................   21,000
  To record factory payroll for July.

ILLUSTRATION 14.1

Basic Records in a Job Orders Cost System

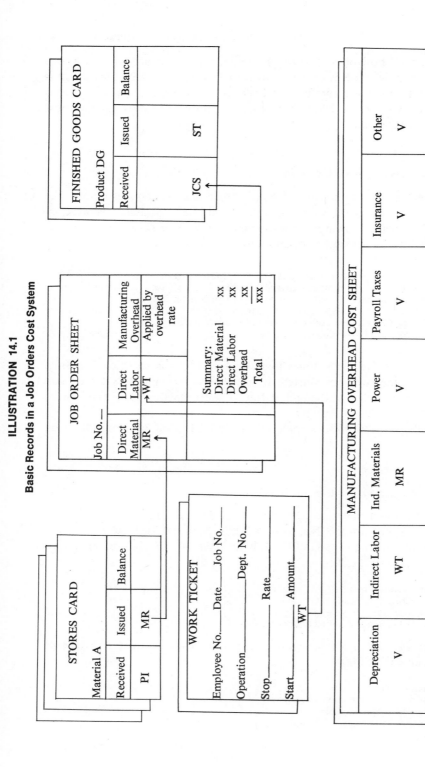

FINISHED GOODS CARD

Product DG

Received	Issued	Balance
JCS	ST	

JOB ORDER SHEET

Job No. ___

Direct Material	Direct Labor	Manufacturing Overhead
MR	WT	Applied by overhead rate

Summary:
Direct Material	xx
Direct Labor	xx
Overhead	xx
Total	xxx

STORES CARD

Material A

Received	Issued	Balance
PI	MR	

WORK TICKET

Employee No.___ Date___ Job No.___

Operation___ Dept. No.___

Stop___ Rate___

Start___ Amount___

WT

MANUFACTURING OVERHEAD COST SHEET

Depreciation	Indirect Labor	Ind. Materials	Power	Payroll Taxes	Insurance	Other
V	WT	MR	V	V	V	V

Code to Source Documents:
PI Purchase invoice or voucher.
MR Materials requisition.
WT Work ticket.
JCS Job cost sheet.
ST Sales ticket or invoice.
V   Various forms, invoices, journal entries for accruals and prepayments.

ILLUSTRATION 14.2
Job Order System Cost Flows

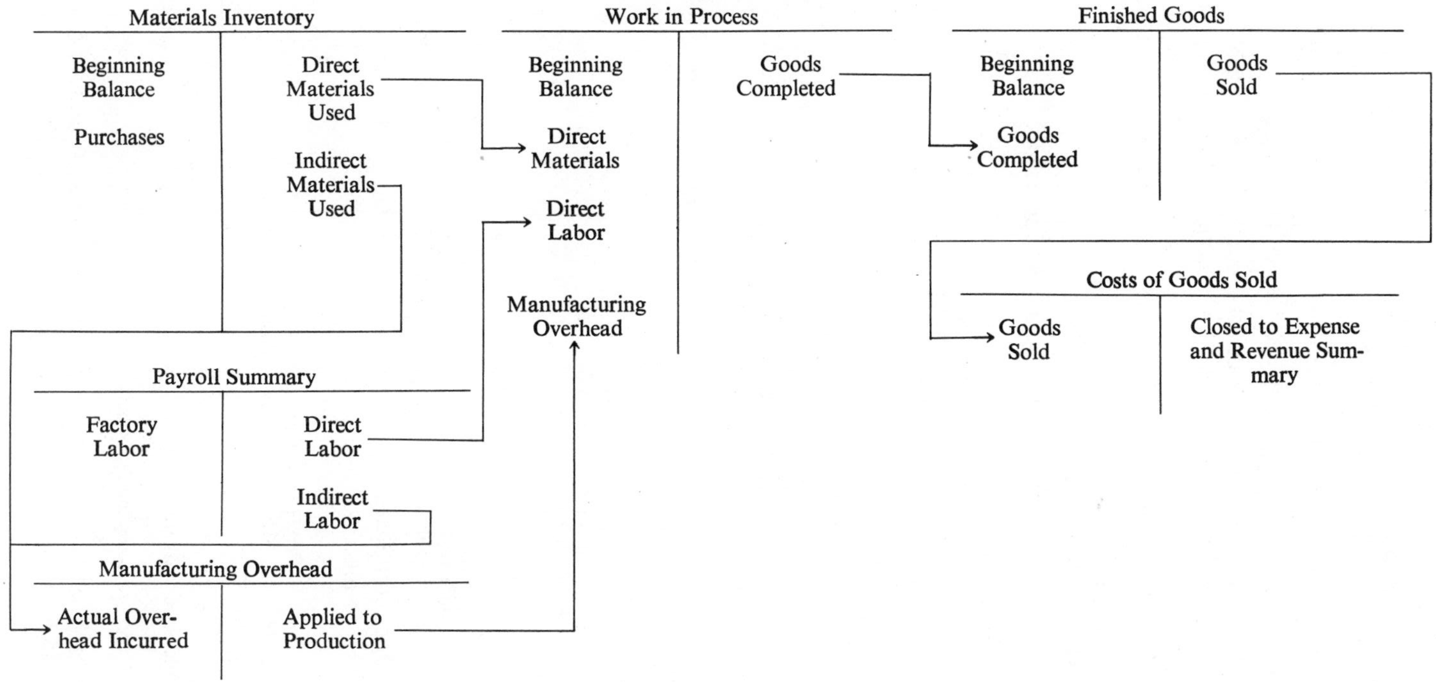

Materials Inventory

Beginning Balance
Purchases

Direct Materials Used
Indirect Materials Used

Payroll Summary

Factory Labor

Direct Labor
Indirect Labor

Manufacturing Overhead

Actual Overhead Incurred

Applied to Production

Work in Process

Beginning Balance
Direct Materials
Direct Labor
Manufacturing Overhead

Goods Completed

Finished Goods

Beginning Balance
Goods Completed

Goods Sold

Costs of Goods Sold

Goods Sold

Closed to Expense and Revenue Summary

(4) Factory payroll paid, $19,000.

```
Accrued Wages Payable....................................  19,000
   Cash................................................           19,000
      To record cash paid to factory employees in July.
```

(5) Payroll costs distributed: direct labor, $20,000 (Job No. 106, $5,000; Job No. 107, $12,000; Job No. 108, $3,000); indirect labor, $5,000.

```
Work in Process Inventory................................  20,000
Manufacturing Overhead..................................   5,000
   Payroll Summary......................................           25,000
      To distribute factory labor costs incurred.
```

(6) Other manufacturing overhead costs incurred:

```
      Repairs (on account)...................................  $ 1,000
      Property taxes accrued.................................    4,000
      Heat, light, and power (on account).....................    2,000
      Depreciation..........................................    5,000
                                                              $12,000
```

```
Manufacturing Overhead..................................  12,000
   Accounts Payable......................................            3,000
   Accrued Property Taxes Payable.........................            4,000
   Allowance for Depreciation.............................            5,000
      To record manufacturing overhead costs incurred.
```

(7) Manufacturing overhead applied to production (at rate of 80 percent of direct labor cost):

```
      Job No. 106 (.80 × $5,000)..............................  $ 4,000
      Job No. 107 (.80 × $12,000).............................    9,600
      Job No. 108 (.80 × $3,000)..............................    2,400
                                                              $16,000
```

```
Work in Process Inventory................................  16,000
   Manufacturing Overhead................................           16,000
      To record application of overhead to production.
```

(8) Jobs completed and transferred to finished goods storeroom (see page 350 for details):

```
      Job No. 106 (4,000 units of product DG @ $6.30)..........  $25,200
      Job No. 107 (10,000 units of product XY @ $3.56)..........   35,600
                                                              $60,800
```

```
Finished Goods Inventory.................................  60,800
   Work in Process Inventory.............................           60,800
      To record completed production for July.
```

(9) Sales on account for the month: 500 units of product AB for $8,000, cost, $5,500; 10,000 units of product XY for $62,000, cost, $35,600 (Job No. 107).

```
Accounts Receivable....................................... 70,000
    Sales.................................................        70,000
    To record sales on account for July.

Cost of Goods Sold....................................... 41,100
    Finished Goods Inventory...............................        41,100
    To record cost of goods sold in July.
```

After the above entries have been posted to the accounts of the company, the Work in Process Inventory and Finished Goods Inventory accounts would appear (in T-account form) as follows:

Work in Process Inventory

July 1 balance	13,200	Job No. 106 completed	25,200
Direct materials used	23,000	Job No. 107 completed	35,600
Direct labor cost incurred	20,000		
Overhead applied	16,000		

Finished Goods Inventory

July 1 balance	5,500	500 units of AB sold	5,500
Job No. 106 completed	25,200	10,000 units of XY sold,	
Job No. 107 completed	35,600	(Job No. 107)	35,600

The Work in Process Inventory account has a balance at July 31 of $11,400, which agrees with the total costs charged thus far to Job No. 108, as is shown in Illustration 14.3. These costs consist of direct materials $6,000, direct labor $3,000, and manufacturing overhead of $2,400. The Finished Goods Inventory account has a balance at July 31 of $25,-200. The finished goods card for product DC supports this amount (see Illustration 14.3) showing that there are indeed units of product DG on hand having a total cost of $25,200.

Note that the entries in the ledger accounts given above are often made from summaries of costs and thus entered only at the end of the month. On the other hand, to keep management informed as to costs incurred, the details of the various costs incurred are recorded more frequently, often daily.

The above example should be studied until the real advantages of using overhead rates (including predetermined rates) are clear (see Chapter 13). Three jobs were worked on during the month. One (No. 106) was started last month and completed in July. One (No. 107) was started and completed in July. And one (No. 108) was started, but not finished in July. Each required different amounts of direct materials and direct labor (and, perhaps, different types of direct labor). Under these conditions, there is simply no way to apply overhead to products without the use of a rate based on some level of activity. Note also that the use of a predetermined overhead rate permits the computation of unit costs of jobs 106 and

ILLUSTRATION 14.3

Supporting Inventory Cards and Job Order Sheets

STORES CARD Material A		
Received	Issued	Balance
		$10,000
$10,000		20,000
	$1,000	19,000
	8,000	11,000
	2,000	9,000

STORES CARD Material B		
Received	Issued	Balance
		$ 6,000
$15,000		21,000
	$2,000	19,000
	6,000	13,000
	4,000	9,000

JOB ORDER SHEET (Product DG)   Job No. 106

Date	Direct Materials	Direct Labor	Manufacturing Overhead
July 1 July	$4,200 A: 1,000 B: 2,000 $7,200	$ 5,000 5,000 $10,000	$4,000 4,000 $8,000

Job completed (4,000 units of product DG @ $6.30) Total Cost $25,200.

JOB ORDER SHEET (Product XY)   Job No. 107

Date	Direct Materials	Direct Labor	Manufacturing Overhead
July	A: $ 8,000 B: 6,000 $14,000	$12,000	$9,600

Job completed (10,000 units of product XY @ $3.56) Total Cost $35,600.

JOB ORDER SHEET (Product OR)   Job No. 108

Date	Direct Materials	Direct Labor	Manufacturing Overhead
July	A: $2,000 B: 4,000	$3,000	$2,400

Job incomplete (1,000 unit of product OR) Cost to date $11,400

FINISHED GOODS CARD Product AB		
Received	Issued	Balance
		$5,500
	$5,500	–0–

FINISHED GOODS CARD Product DG		
Received	Issued	Balance
$25,200		$25,200

FINISHED GOODS CARD Product XY		
Received	Issued	Balance
$35,600		$35,600
	$35,600	–0–

107 at the time of their completion rather than waiting until the end of the month. But this advantage is secured only at the cost of keeping more detailed records of the costs incurred. As we shall see below, the other major cost system—process costing—requires far less record keeping with the result that the computation of unit costs is more complex.

PROCESS COST SYSTEMS

Many businesses manufacture quantities of rather similar products (paint, paper, chemicals, glass, rubber, and plastic) on a continuous basis rather than by specific batches or jobs. There is no specific order for a stated number of units; production is continuous over the year or several years. Since there is no job, costs cannot be accumulated for the job. Rather, costs must be accumulated for each process a product undergoes on its way to completion. This calls for another type of cost system, one that yields unit costs by *processes* or *departments* for stated periods of *time* rather than by jobs without regard to time periods. Here the processes or departments serve as cost centers for which costs are accumulated. Such a system is known as a *process cost system*.

Basic System Design

Process cost systems have the same general design as that shown in Illustration 14.2. Separate accounts are kept for the materials, labor, and overhead costs incurred, as in a job order system. These costs are then transferred to work in process. But a process cost system usually has more than one Work in Process Inventory account. Such an account is kept for each process a product undergoes to determine the cost of each process. For example, the manufacture of a product may take place in seven departments as follows:

If so, the process cost system will probably have seven Work in Process Inventory accounts and the flow of costs through these accounts will match the flow of the actual units of product through the plant.

A model of the flow of costs in the accounting system for a simpler manufacturing process, that will serve as a basis for explaining process cost systems, is shown in Illustration 14.4.

Accounting for Overhead. In process costing, manufacturing overhead will be initially recorded in supporting records or accounts established for

ILLUSTRATION 14.4

Cost Flows in a Process Cost System

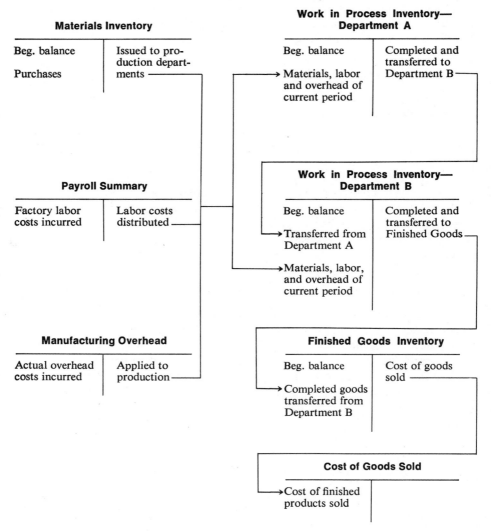

the various producing and service centers. Service center costs will then be allocated to the producing centers. Then, either the actual overhead incurred for the period (usually a month) will be applied to the work in process inventory accounts, or overhead will be applied through use of a predetermined rate. If the quantity of units produced and the amounts of overhead costs incurred are roughly equal through time, applying actual overhead to production will yield reasonable product costs. But, if production and the amounts of overhead costs incurred are not fairly stable, the use of a predetermined rate will prevent the reporting of sharp differences in monthly unit costs. For example, if all production employees took their two-week paid vacations in July, units costs in July might be considerably higher than in June.

Process Costing Illustrated

Assume that a company sells a chemical product which it processes in two departments. In Department A the basic materials are crushed, powdered, and blended; in Department B the product is tested, packaged and labeled and transferred to finished goods. The production and cost data for the month of June are:

	Department A	Department B
Units started, completed, and transferred..........	11,000	9,000
Units on hand at June 30, partially completed......	–0–	2,000
Beginning inventory.........................	$ –0–	$ –0–
Direct materials.............................	16,500	1,100
Direct labor................................	5,500	5,900
Actual manufacturing overhead.................	4,500	5,600
Applied manufacturing overhead................	4,400	5,900

From the above data, the Work in Process Inventory—Department A account can be constructed and will appear as follows. Since all of the units started were completed and transferred, it follows that all of the costs assigned to Department A should be transferred to Department B. And the unit cost in the department is computed simply by dividing total costs of

Work in Process Inventory—Department A

Direct materials	16,500	Transferred to Department B—	
Direct labor	5,500	11,000 units @ $2.40	26,400
Overhead (80% of direct labor cost)	4,400		

$26,400 by the 11,000 units completed and transferred to get an average unit cost for the month of $2.40.

But the computations are seldom this simple. One complication is faced whenever partially completed beginning and ending inventories are present. Assume that Department B's Work in Process Inventory account for June, before recording the cost of the units transferred out, is as follows:

Work in Process Inventory—Department B

Transferred from Department A	26,400
Direct materials	1,100
Direct labor	5,900
Overhead (100% of direct labor)	5,900

The task now faced is to divide the total costs charged to the department in June, $39,300, between the units transferred out and those remaining on hand in the department. The $39,300 cannot be divided by 11,000 to get an average unit cost because the 11,000 units are not alike; 9,000 are finished, but 2,000 are only partially finished. The problem is solved through use of the concept of equivalent units of production.

Equivalent Units.   Essentially, the concept of equivalent units involves expressing a given number of partially completed units as a smaller number of fully completed units. For example, it holds that 1,000 units brought to a 50 percent state of completion are the equivalent of 500 units that are 100 percent complete. It is assumed that the same amount of costs must be incurred to bring 1,000 units to a 50 percent level of completion as would be required to complete 500 units.

The first step in applying the equivalent units concept to Department B is to determine the stage of completion of the unfinished products. And, because it may differ for each element of cost, it must be ascertained separately for materials, labor, overhead and transferred in costs. All direct materials are added at the beginning of the processing in Department B. Thus, the ending inventory is 100 percent complete as to materials. Since the units transferred out must be complete, equivalent production for materials is 11,000 units—9,000 transferred out and 2,000 on hand 100 percent complete. Next assume that the 2,000 units are, on the average, 50 percent complete as to conversion costs (labor and overhead). Equivalent production, then, is 10,000 units—9,000 units transferred and 2,000 units brought to a 50 percent completion state, which is the equivalent of 1,000 fully complete units.

The unit costs of the processing in Department B can now be computed:

Cost Element	Total Cost	Equivalent Units	Current Unit Cost
Materials.....................................	$1,100	11,000	$0.10
Labor..	5,900	10,000	0.59
Overhead....................................	5,900	10,000	0.59
Total unit cost of Department's processing.................			$1.28

With unit costs computed, the $39,300 of costs charged to Department B's Work in Process account can now be divided between costs transferred out and costs remaining as the cost of the department's ending inventory:

Cost of units completed and transferred (9,000):			
From Department A—9,000 × $2.40.....................		$21,600	
Added by Department B—9,000 × $1.28................		11,520	$33,120
Cost of ending work in process inventory (2,000):			
From Department A—2,000 × $2.40.....................		$ 4,800	
Added by Department B:			
Materials (2,000 × 100% × $0.10).....................	$200		
Labor (2,000 × 50% × $0.59).........................	590		
Overhead (2,000 × 50% × $0.59).....................	590	1,380	6,180
Total costs accounted for..			$39,300

The above schedule shows that a transfer of $33,120 of costs from Department B's Work in Process Inventory account must be made. Note how the schedule shows, and takes into account, the stage of completion of the ending inventory. This inventory is complete as to materials and costs transferred in from Department A, and 50 percent complete as to processing (labor and overhead). The completed units will be carried in the finished goods inventory at a cost of $3.68 each ($2.40 + $1.28, or $33,120 ÷ 9,000 units) until sold. At this time they will be charged to the Cost of Goods Sold expense account. The unit costs of production ($2.40 in Department A and $1.28 in Department B) are watched closely by management with explanations sought for unexpected month-to-month variations.

The journal entries to record the costs incurred by manufacturing operations for the month of June are as follow:

(1) Work in Process Inventory—Department A............... 16,500
     Work in Process Inventory—Department B............... 1,100
        Materials Inventory.............................   17,600
     To record materials placed in production in June.

(2) Payroll Summary...................................... 11,400
        (Various withholding accounts and accrued wages
        payable)..   11,400
     To record factory payroll for June.

(3) Work in Process Inventory—Department A............... 5,500
     Work in Process Inventory—Department B............... 5,900
        Payroll Summary.................................   11,400
     To distribute factory labor costs (assumed that all such
     costs are chargeable directly to production departments).

(4) Manufacturing Overhead.............................. 10,100
        (Various accounts—cash, accounts payable, accruals,
        and allowances for depreciation)...................   10,100
     To record actual overhead costs incurred in June.

(5) Work in Process Inventory—Department A............... 4,400
     Work in Process Inventory—Department B............... 5,900
        Manufacturing Overhead..........................   10,300
     To apply overhead to production using predetermined
     rates based on direct labor cost: Department A, 80%;
     Department B, 100%.

(6) Work in Process Inventory—Department B............... 26,400
        Work in Process Inventory—Department A..........   26,400
     To record transfer of goods from Department A to
     Department B.

(7) Finished Goods Inventory............................. 33,120
        Work in Process Inventory—Department B...........   33,120
     To record transfer of completed goods from Department B
     to finished goods.

Assuming that 6,000 units were sold in June at a price of $10 per unit, the following entries would be required:

```
(8)  Accounts Receivable...............................  60,000
       Sales.........................................              60,000
     To record sales on account.

(9)  Cost of Goods Sold.................................  22,080
       Finished Good Inventory.........................              22,080
     To record cost of goods sold in June, 6,000 units @ $3.68.
```

The Cost of Production Report

The computation of unit costs is even more complex when there are both beginning and ending inventories in a department. This problem, and the key report in process cost accounting, is developed and discussed in this section.

The following data are for Department 3 of A Company for the month of June, 1979:

Units

Units in beginning inventory, complete as to materials, 60% complete as to conversion..	6,000
Units transferred in from Department 2...............................	18,000
Units completed and transferred out................................	16,000
Units in ending inventory, complete as to materials, 50% complete as to conversion..	8,000

Costs

Cost of beginning inventory:		
Cost transferred in from preceding department in May.....	$12,000	
Materials added in May in Department 3................	6,000	
Conversion costs (equal amounts of labor and overhead)...	3,000	$21,000
Costs transferred in from preceding department in June......		37,200
Costs added in Department 3 in June:		
Materials...	$18,480	
Conversion (equal amounts of labor and overhead)........	18,000	36,480
Total costs in beginning inventory and placed in production in Department 3 in June..............................		$94,680

How the total of $94,680 of costs charged to Department 3 in June is divided between the cost of the units transferred out and the cost of the units remaining on hand in inventory is shown in Illustration 14.5. This report is discussed by explaining the four steps usually undertaken to prepare it.

1. Trace the physical flow of the actual units into and out of the department. The section headed "Units" in Illustration 14.5 shows that 6,000 units were on hand at the beginning of June and that 18,000 units were transferred in, making a total of 24,000 units that must be accounted for. Of these 24,000 units, 16,000 were completed and

ILLUSTRATION 14.5

Cost of Production Report

A COMPANY
Cost of Production Report
For the Month of June, 1979

Units	Actual Units	Equivalent Units		
		Transferred-in	Materials	Conversion
Units in beginning inventory........	6,000			
Units transferred in...............	18,000			
Units to be accounted for........	24,000			
Units completed and transferred.....	16,000	16,000	16,000	16,000
Units in ending inventory*..........	8,000	8,000	8,000	4,000
Units accounted for.............	24,000	24,000	24,000	20,000

Costs	Transferred-in	Materials	Conversion	Total
Costs in beginning inventory...........	$12,000	$ 6,000	$ 3,000	$21,000
Costs transferred in...................	37,200			37,200
Costs added in department 3..........		18,480	18,000	36,480
Costs to be accounted for...........	$49,200	$24,480	$21,000	$94,680
Equivalent units (as above)............	24,000	24,000	20,000	
Unit costs.........................	$2.05	$1.02	$1.05	$4.12
Costs in ending inventory.............	$16,400	$ 8,160	$ 4,200	$28,760
Costs transferred out.................	32,800	16,320	16,800	65,920
Costs accounted for...............	$49,200	$24,480	$21,000	$94,680

* Inventory is complete as to materials, 50 percent complete as to conversion.

transferred out, 8,000 were retained, partially completed, in the department.

2. The actual units are converted to equivalent units. Illustration 14.5 shows the procedures followed to compute *average* unit costs. Other procedures would be used if unit costs on a Fifo or Lifo basis were desired. Equivalent units, under the average method, consist of units completed and transferred plus the equivalent units in the ending inventory, or 24,000 for the costs of units transferred in and materials, and 20,000 for conversion costs. Note that these amounts include units fully or partially completed last month and on hand in Department 3's beginning inventory. The reason for this is explained in step 3.

3. Compute unit costs for each element of cost, using the equivalent units computed above and the total costs charged to the department. Under the average method, this involves dividing the equivalent units of production for the period, including those in the beginning inventory, into the costs charged to the department, including the costs of the begin-

ning inventory. Thus, the costs of the beginning inventory are treated as if incurred in the current period. And the equivalent units of production in the beginning inventory are treated as if produced in the current period. In this way, the average cost procedure avoids many fine details that emerge under Fifo or Lifo that are of little practical value. As shown in Illustration 14.5, average unit costs for June are: costs transferred in, $2.05; materials costs, $1.02; conversion costs, $1.05. As already noted, management watches these costs closely.

4. The equivalent units transferred out and in inventory can now be multiplied by the unit costs computed to divide the total costs charged to the department into costs to be transferred out and costs that remain in the department's work in process inventory account. Thus, the cost of the ending inventory would be computed as follows:

8,000 equivalent units transferred in @ $2.05	$16,400
8,000 equivalent units of materials costs @ $1.02	8,160
4,000 equivalent units of conversion costs @ $1.05	4,200
Total Cost of Ending Inventory	$28,760

The total cost of the units completed and transferred out can be computed in the same way and, as shown, amounts to $65,920. The sum of the cost of the ending inventory and the cost of the units transferred out must equal the total of the costs charged to the department, which was used in step 3 to compute unit costs. Thus, a built-in check upon the accuracy of the procedures followed is provided.

SUMMARY

The job order cost system and the process cost system are the two major types of cost accumulation systems used by manufacturing companies.

In a job order system, costs are accumulated by jobs without regard for the time period in which the job was worked on and completed. The costs of completing a job—direct materials, direct labor, and manufacturing overhead—are recorded in some detail on a subsidiary work in process record known as a job order sheet. The costs of direct materials and direct labor can be traced to specific jobs through use of materials requisitions and work tickets. Manufacturing overhead is applied using a predetermined rate. In this way, unit costs can be computed for a job as soon as it is completed, even though a number of different jobs may have been worked on at the same time in the same period.

Process cost systems are used to gather the costs of manufacturing large quantities of similar products on a continuous basis. Costs are accumulated for each of the processes a product undergoes on its way to completion. As a result, a process cost system is likely to have a number of Work in Process accounts with one account kept for each processing center. Manufacturing overhead may be applied to production through use of a predetermined rate or on an actual basis.

Unit costs are computed for each department for materials, labor, and overhead. Unit costs are computed using the equivalent units of production in a department for a period. Under the average (rather than the Fifo or Lifo) method, equivalent production consists of the number of units completed and transferred plus the equivalent units of work done on the ending inventory. Average unit costs are then computed by dividing the total costs charged to a department for a period, including the cost of the beginning inventory, by the department's equivalent production, including that in beginning inventory, for the period. The unit costs and the equivalent units produced are then used to divide the total costs charged to a department between the costs to be transferred out and the costs remaining in the department as the cost of the ending inventory.

The cost of production report summarizes both the units and costs charged to a department. It shows how these units and costs were accounted for either by transfer to the next department or remaining in the department. It also shows the department's current unit costs for materials, labor, and overhead and the total unit cost. Variations in period-to-period unit costs are closely watched by management. Explanations may be required for unexpected differences.

QUESTIONS AND EXERCISES

1. Briefly contrast the job order and process cost systems. Indicate the types of manufacturing firms that might use each.

2. Assume that the Byron Company employs a job order cost system and that it incurred the following labor costs in the month of July. Indicate how these costs should be recorded:

Wages earned by painters, cutters, and assemblers.............. $15,000
Supervisors' salaries.. 4,000
Repairmen's wages... 1,200
Wages paid for standby employees............................   400

3. How might the predetermined overhead rate used in a job order cost system be of value to management in bidding on the manufacture and sale of certain products?

4. An objective of a cost system is the compilation of unit costs. Of what use are unit costs to management?

5. What are the basic underlying records or documents in a job order cost system? What function does each serve?

6. The Work in Process account of the Carter Company for a given period is as follows:

Work in Process

Direct materials	200,000	Goods completed	700,000
Direct labor	200,000		
Manufacturing overhead	500,000		

The cost of the direct materials in the ending inventory is $130,000. If manufacturing overhead is applied through use of a rate based on direct labor cost, what is the overhead cost of the ending inventory?

7. The Gold Company, which uses a job order cost system, has just completed a job for State Bank—a special order for 200 gold-plated mechanical pencils. Direct material cost was $500; direct labor cost—200 hours at $5 per hour. Budgeted direct labor for this year was $400,000, while overhead was budgeted at $1,000,000. If the overhead rate is expressed as a percentage of direct labor cost, what is the total cost and the unit cost of the bank's order?

8. Should the overtime premium paid for direct labor on a specific job be charged to the job worked on? Give examples supporting both a "yes" and a "no" answer.

9. What is a process cost center? What is the reason for recognizing these cost centers in the accumulation of costs?

10. What is meant by the term "equivalent units"? Why must equivalent units be computed?

11. Under what circumstances would the equivalent units for materials differ from the equivalent units for conversion? When would they be the same?

12. What basic information is provided by a cost of production report?

13. In Department A, materials are added uniformly throughout processing. The beginning inventory was considered 50 percent complete as was the ending inventory. Assume there were 1,000 units in the beginning inventory, 3,000 in the ending inventory, and that 16,000 units were completed and transferred. If average unit costs are to be computed, what is the equivalent production for the period?

14. If, in Question 13, the total costs charged to the department amounted to $70,000, including the $2,010 cost of the beginning inventory, what is the cost of units completed and transferred?

PROBLEMS

14–1. Job No. 210 has, at the end of the second week in May, an accumulated total cost of $4,200. In the third week, $1,000 of direct materials were used on the job together with $10 of indirect materials; 200 hours of direct labor @ $8 per hour were worked on the job, while indirect factory labor amounted to $2,500 for the week; manufacturing overhead is applied at a rate of $4.50 per direct labor hour. Job No. 210 was the only job worked on in the week and was completed just prior to the end of the weekly work shift.

Required:

a. Compute the total cost of Job No. 210.
b. Give the journal entry required upon its completion.

14–2. The Able Company began business on June 1, engaged in the following activities, and incurred the following costs in June:

Raw materials purchased..............................	$12,000
Factory payroll costs incurred (all employees are paid	
$5 per hour)..	10,500
Factory indirect costs (other than indirect labor)...........	3,800

The costs charged to the three jobs worked on in June were:

	Job No. 101	Job No. 102	Job No. 103
Direct materials..................	$2,000	$3,500	$2,500
Direct labor.....................	2,000	4,500	3,500
Overhead applied at $2 per			
direct labor hour...............	?	?	?

Job No. 101 was completed and sold for $8,000; Job No. 102 was completed, but not sold; Job No. 103 is incomplete. No other costs were incurred.

Required:

a. Compute the June 30 balance for each of the three inventory accounts.
b. Prepare an earnings statement for the month of June.

14–3. Hardy Company uses a job order cost system, applying overhead through use of a predetermined rate based on direct labor hours in Department A and machine hours in Department B. A job may be worked on in either Department A or B. Budget estimates for 1979 are:

	Department A	Department B
Direct labor cost.....................	$48,000	$56,000
Manufacturing overhead..............	72,000	96,000
Direct labor hours...................	12,000	16,000
Machine hours......................	8,000	24,000

Detailed cost records show the following for Job No. 105 which was completed in 1979:

	Department A	Department B
Materials used.......................	$110.00	$34.00
Direct labor cost....................	42.00	72.00
Direct labor hours...................	10	20
Machine hours......................	6	16

Required:

a. Compute the overhead rates for 1979 for Departments A and B.
b. Compute the amount of overhead applied to Job No. 105 in each department.

    c. Compute the total and unit cost of the 20 units in Job No. 105.

    d. Assume the bases upon which the rates were predetermined were switched between the two departments. What would be the difference in the total cost of the Job No. 105?

    e. The actual operating results for 1979 were:

	Department A	Department B
Actual manufacturing overhead.............	$74,000	$98,000
Actual direct labor hours..................	12,100	16,100
Actual machine hours.....................	8,200	24,600

Ignore the assumption in part (*d*). Compute the under- or overapplied overhead for each department for the year.

14–4. Wyatt Company employs a job order cost system. As of January 1, 1979, its records showed the following inventory balances:

Raw materials and supplies.....................	$ 45,000
Work in process..............................	86,000
Finished goods (25,000 units @ $4)..............	100,000

The work in process inventory consisted of two jobs:

Job No.	Materials	Direct Labor	Manufacturing Overhead	Total
212..................	$15,000	$20,000	$10,000	$45,000
213..................	17,000	16,000	8,000	41,000
	$32,000	$36,000	$18,000	$86,000

Summarized below are production and sales data for the company for 1979.

(1) Raw materials and supplies purchased, $160,000.

(2) Factory payroll costs incurred, $340,000.

(3) Factory indirect costs incurred (other than indirect labor and indirect materials): depreciation, $10,000; heat, light, and power, $4,000; miscellaneous, $6,000.

(4) Raw materials and supplies requisitioned: direct materials for Job No. 212, $26,000, for Job No. 213, $48,000, and for Job No. 214, $80,000; supplies (indirect materials) requisitioned, $4,000.

(5) Factory payroll distributed: direct labor to Job No. 212, $40,000, to Job No. 213, $80,000, and to Job No. 214, $120,000; indirect labor, $100,000.

(6) Overhead is assigned to work in process at the same rate per dollar of direct labor cost as in 1978.

(7) Job Nos. 212 and 213 were completed.

(8) Sales for the year amounted to $600,000; cost of goods sold, $344,000.

Required:

    a. Prepare journal entries to record the above transactions.

    b. Prepare all closing entries for which you have information.

c. Set up T-accounts for Materials Inventory, Payroll Summary, Manufacturing Overhead, Work in Process Inventory, Finished Goods Inventory, and Cost of Goods Sold. Post those parts of the entries made in (a) and (b) that affect these accounts.

d. Show that the total of the costs charged to incomplete jobs agrees with the balance in the Work in Process Inventory account.

14–5. Following are cost and production data of the Reed Company's Department Y, in which all material is added at the beginning of the production process and in which the weight of the finished product is equal to the weight of the raw materials used:

Work in process, June 1, 400 pounds (¼ complete as
   to conversion):
   Raw materials...................................... $1,600
   Direct labor..   200
   Manufacturing overhead..............................   300
                                    $2,100

Raw materials placed in production in June, 2,000 lbs......... 8,000
Direct labor, 600 hours @ $4.80......................... 2,880
Overhead applied, 150% of direct labor cost................. 4,320
Work in process inventory, June 30, 600 pounds,
   (⅔ complete as to conversion)........................   ?

Required: Using the above data, compute:

a. The number of pounds of product transferred out of Department Y in June.

b. The unit cost for the month per equivalent unit for materials, labor, and overhead using the average cost method.

c. The cost of the product transferred out of Department Y in June.

d. The cost of the ending work in process inventory in Department Y.

14–6. Floyd Company produces small tools in large quantities. It determines unit costs through use of a process cost system. Given below are production and cost data for the handle department for the month of June:

	Units	Materials Cost	Conversion Costs
Inventory, June 1........................	20,000	$1,790	$2,200
Placed in production in June.............	60,000	5,410	9,560
Inventory, June 30......................	30,000	?	?

The June 1 inventory was complete as to materials and 50 percent complete as to conversion. The June 30 inventory was complete as to materials and 20 percent complete as to conversion.

Required:

a. Compute the number of units transferred.

b. Compute equivalent production for June for materials and conversion.

c. Compute average unit costs for June for materials and conversion.
d. Compute the cost of the units transferred.
e. Compute the cost of the ending inventory.
(Hint: All of the above can be included in a cost of production report for the department for June, if you prefer to prepare one.)

14–7. White, Inc. uses a process cost system to accumulate the costs it incurs to produce aluminum awning stabilizers. The costs incurred in the finishing department are shown for the month of May. The May 1 inventory consisted of 30,000 units, fully complete as to materials, 80 percent complete as to conversion. Its total cost of $240,000 consisted of $180,000 of costs transferred in from the molding department, $25,000 of finishing department material costs, and $35,000 of conversion costs.

Costs from molding department (excluding costs in beginning inventory).............................		$600,000
Costs added in finishing department in May (excluding costs in beginning inventory):		
Materials..	$ 53,000	
Conversion.......................................	109,480	162,480
		$762,480

The finishing department received 100,000 units from the molding department; 106,000 units were completed and transferred; 24,000 units, complete as to materials and 60 percent complete as to conversion, were left in the May 31 inventory.

Required: Prepare a cost of production report for the finishing department for the month of May.

14–8. The Stein Company uses a process cost system to account for the costs incurred in making its single product, a health food called Build-up. This product is processed first in Department K and then in Department L, with materials added in both departments. Production for May was as follows:

	Department K	Department L
Units started or transferred in..................	200,000	150,000
Units completed and transferred out............	150,000	120,000
Stage of completion of May 31 inventory:		
Materials....................................	100%	80%
Conversion..................................	50%	40%
Direct materials costs........................	$120,000	$ 21,600
Conversion costs............................	350,000	237,600

There was no May 1 inventory in either department.

Required:
a. Prepare a cost of production report for Department K for May.
b. Prepare a cost of production report for Department L for May.

chapter **15**

Standard Costs and
Variable Costing

STANDARD COSTS

In the previous chapter, job order and process cost systems were shown to have a primary goal of gathering actual historical cost data that are used mainly in inventory measurement and earnings determination. But because these data say little about how efficiently operations were conducted, many firms find it helpful to introduce standard costs into their job order or process cost systems.

Nature of Standard Costs

A standard cost is a carefully predetermined measure of what a cost *should be* under stated conditions. It is not merely an estimate of what a cost will be; it is more in the nature of a goal to be sought. If properly set, the attainment of a standard represents the securing of a reasonable level of performance.

Standards are set in many ways, but to be of any real value they must be more than mere estimates derived from extending historical trends into the future. Usually engineering and time and motion studies are undertaken to determine the amount and quality of the material needed, the amount and degrees of skill in the labor required, as well as the other services required to produce a unit of product. Knowledge of the actual working conditions in a plant is required. Also, general economic conditions must be studied because they will affect the costs of materials and the other services that must be purchased. The goal is to set a standard cost for each unit of product to be manufactured by determining the standard costs of the direct materials, direct labor, and factory overhead needed to produce it. The standard direct materials cost is made up of a standard number of units of each material required multiplied by a standard price for each. Similarly, the standard direct labor cost consists of the standard number of hours of direct labor needed multiplied by the standard labor or wage rate. The standard overhead cost of a unit is usually based upon a predetermined rate which is computed from standard (budgeted) overhead costs and standard production, although it may be expressed as a rate per unit of some measure of activity such as direct labor hours. Thus, in both a standard cost system and an actual cost system, overhead is assigned to production through use of a predetermined rate. The two systems differ in that an actual cost system collects actual costs for materials and labor while a standard cost system gathers standard costs and transfers these costs through the system into finished goods.

Advantages of Using Standard Costs

A number of benefits are attached to the use of a standard cost system. These include (1) cost control, (2) provision of information useful in managerial planning and decision making, (3) more reasonable inventory measurements, (4) cost savings in record keeping, and (5) possibly some reductions in the costs incurred.

Cost control is secured largely by setting standards for each type of cost incurred—materials, labor, and overhead. The amounts by which actual costs differ from standard are recorded in *variance* accounts. These variances provide a starting point in appraising the effectiveness of managers in controlling the costs they incur and for which they are held responsible. For example, for such purposes, it is far more useful to know that actual direct materials costs of $52,015 in a certain center exceeded standard by $6,015 than merely to know that actual materials costs amounted to $52,015. Thus, a standard cost system highlights *exceptions,* that is, instances where things are not proceeding as planned. Further investigation will reveal whether the exception is caused by factors under management control or not. For example, the exception, the variance, may be caused by inefficient use of materials or, it may be the result of inflation. In either case, the standard cost system has served as an early warning system by highlighting a potential problem for management. On the other hand, little attention is usually paid to actual costs when such costs differ only slightly from standard.

If management develops appropriate standards and succeeds in controlling costs, future actual costs should be fairly close to standard. When this is true, standard costs can be used in preparing budgets and in estimating costs for bidding on jobs.

In a standard cost system, all units of a given product are carried in inventory at the same unit cost. It seems logical that physically identical units should have the same cost. But under an actual cost system, unit costs for batches of identical products may differ because more labor and overhead were assigned to one batch simply because a machine was out of adjustment when the batch was produced. Under a standard cost system, such costs would not be included in inventory. Rather, they would be charged to variance accounts. These accounts are discussed below.

Although standard cost systems may appear to require more detailed record keeping than an actual cost system, actually the reverse is true. For example, in a job order system, detailed accounts or records must be kept of the various types of materials used on each job as well as the various types and quantities of labor services received. In a standard cost system, standard cost sheets may be printed in advance showing quantities, unit costs, and total costs for the materials, labor, and overhead needed to produce a given amount of a certain product. Thus, when a job is started, the job order sheet shows the complete array of costs that apply to it. There is no need to post individual materials requisitions to individual job order sheets. One entry can be made at the end of the month for the total materials used. Also, since inventories are carried at standard cost, the problems of assumed cost flows—Lifo, Fifo, and so forth—disappear.

The use of standard costs may result in employees becoming quite cost conscious and seeking improved methods of completing their tasks. This may result in additional cost savings.

Computing Variances

As noted above, a variance exists when standard costs differ from actual costs. It is logical to look upon a variance as favorable when actual costs are less than standard costs, and to view the variance as unfavorable when actual costs exceed standard. But it does not follow automatically that these terms should be equated with good and bad. Such an appraisal should be made only after the causes of the variance are known.

Since variances cannot serve as essential elements in cost control until they have been isolated, attention is directed first to the computation of the dollar amount of a variance. The discussion and illustrations that follow are based upon the activities of the Case Company which manufactures and sells a single product which has the following standard costs:

Materials—5 sheets @ $6.00	$30.00
Direct labor—2 hours @ $10.00	20.00
Manufacturing overhead—2 direct labor hours @ $5.00	10.00
Total standard cost per unit	$60.00

Additional data regarding the productive activities of the company will be presented as needed.

Materials Variances

The standard materials cost of any product is simply the standard *quantity* of materials that should be used multiplied by the *price* that should be paid for those materials. From this it follows that actual costs may differ from standard costs for materials because of the quantity of materials used or the price paid for the materials. This suggests the need to isolate two variances for materials—a price variance and a usage variance. But there are other reasons for so doing. First, different individuals may be responsible for each—a purchasing agent for the price variance, and a production foreman for the usage variance. Second, the materials may not be purchased and used in the same period. The variance associated with the purchase should be isolated in the period of purchase, that associated with usage should be isolated in the period of use. As a general rule, the sooner a variance can be isolated, the greater its value in cost control. And, finally, it is unlikely that a single materials variance—the difference between the standard cost and the actual cost of the materials used—would be of any real value to management.

Materials Price Variance.   The standard price for material meeting certain engineering specifications is usually set after consultation between the purchasing and accounting departments. Consideration will, of course, be given to current market conditions, vendors' quoted prices, the optimum size of a purchase order, and to other factors. The purchase of materials at a price other than standard gives rise to a materials price variance. The dollar amount of the materials price variance (MPV) is the difference between actual price (AP) and standard price (SP) multiplied by the actual quantity (AQ) of materials purchased. In equation form, the materials price variance is:

$$MPV = (AP - SP) \times AQ$$

To illustrate, assume that the Case Company was able, because of the entry into the market of a new foreign supplier, to purchase 60,000 sheets of material at a price of $5.90 each, for a total cost of $354,000. Since the standard price is $6 per sheet, the materials price variance using the above formula is:

$$MPV = (AP - SP) \times AQ$$
$$MPV = (\$5.90 - \$6.00) \times 60,000$$
$$MPV = -\$0.10 \times 60,000$$
$$MPV = -\$6,000.$$

The materials price variance of $6,000 is considered favorable since the materials were acquired for a price less than standard. (Why it is expressed as a negative amount will be explained later.) If the actual price had exceeded standard price, the variance would be considered unfavorable because more costs were incurred than allowed by the standard. The entry to record the purchase of the materials is:

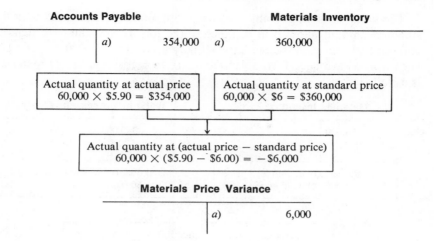

Note that the Accounts Payable account shows the actual debt owed to suppliers, the Materials Inventory account shows the *standard price* of the actual quantity of materials purchased, while the Materials Price Variance account shows the difference between actual price and standard price multiplied by the actual quantity purchased.

Materials Usage Variance.   Since it is largely a matter of physical aspects or product specifications, the standard quantity of materials to be used in making a product is usually set by the engineering department. But if the quality of materials used varies with price, the accounting and purchasing departments may take part in special studies to find the "right" quality.

The materials usage variance shows whether the amount of materials used was more or less than the standard amount allowed. It shows only differences from standard caused by the quantity of materials used; it does not include price variances. Thus, it equals actual quantity at standard price less standard quantity at standard price. Or, in shorter form, the materials usage variance (MUV) is equal to actual quantity used (AQ) minus standard quantity allowed (SQ) multiplied by standard price (SP):

$$MUV = (AQ - SQ) \times SP$$

To illustrate, assume that the Case Company used 55,500 sheets of materials to manufacture 11,000 units of product for which the standard quantity allowed is 55,000 sheets ($5 \times 11,000$). Since the standard price of the material is $6 per sheet, the materials usage variance of $3,000 would be computed as follows:

$$MUV = (AQ - SQ) \times SP$$
$$MUV = (55,500 - 55,000) \times \$6$$
$$MUV = 500 \times \$6$$
$$MUV = \$3,000$$

The variance is unfavorable because more materials were used than the standard amount allowed in completing the job. If the standard quantity allowed had exceeded the quantity actually used, the materials usage variance would have been favorable. The entry to record the use of materials is as follows:

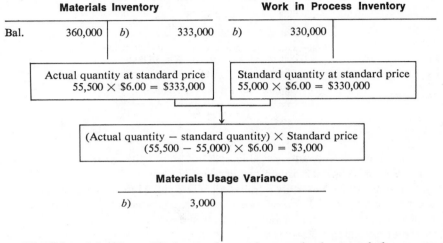

The Materials Usage Variance shows the standard cost of the excess materials used. Note, also, that the Work-in-Process inventory account contains standard quantities and standard prices.

The equations for both of the above materials variances were expressed in a manner so that positive amounts were unfavorable variances and negative amounts were favorable variances. Unfavorable variances are debits in variance accounts because they add to the costs incurred, which, of course, are recorded as debits. Similarly, favorable variances are shown as negative amounts because they are reductions in costs. It follows that they are recorded in variance accounts as credits. And this format will be used in this text. But a word of caution is in order. Far greater understanding is achieved if a variance is determined to be favorable or unfavorable by reliance upon reason or logic. If more materials were used than standard, or if a price greater than standard was paid, the variance is unfavorable. If the reverse is true, the variance is favorable.

Labor Variances

The standard labor cost of any product is equal to the standard quantity of labor time allowed multiplied by the wage rate that should be paid for this time. Here again it follows that the actual labor cost may differ from standard labor cost because of the quantity of labor used, the wages paid for labor, or both. Both of the labor variances relate to the same period because labor services cannot be purchased in one period, stored, and then used in the next period.

Labor Rate Variance. The labor rate variance shows how much the actual labor cost of a product differed from its standard cost because actual pay rates differed from standard rates. In this respect, it is similar to the materials price variance. Typically, actual wage rates are set in bargaining between a firm and the employees' union.

The dollar amount of the labor rate variance (LRV) is computed by multiplying the difference between the actual rate (AR) paid and the standard rate (SR) allowed by the actual hours (AH) of labor services received:

$$LRV = (AR - SR) \times AH$$

To continue our Case Company example, assume that the direct labor payroll of the company consisted of 22,200 hours and a total cost of \$233,100 (an average actual hourly rate of \$10.50). With a standard labor rate of \$10 per hour, the labor rate variance is:

$$LRV = (AR - SR) \times AH$$
$$LRV = (\$10.50 - \$10.00) \times 22,200$$
$$LRV = \$0.50 \times 22,200$$
$$LRV = \$11,100$$

The variance is positive and unfavorable since the actual rate paid exceeded the standard rate allowed. If the reverse were true, the variance would be favorable. The recording of the variance will be presented after the labor time variance has been illustrated and discussed.

Labor Time Variance. The labor time (or efficiency) variance is, in effect, a quantity variance. It shows whether the actual labor time required to complete a period's output or a given job was more or less than the standard amount allowed. The standard amount of labor time needed to complete a product is usually set by the firm's engineering department. It may be based on time and motion studies and may be the subject of bargaining with the employees' union.

The labor time variance (LTV) is computed by multiplying the difference between the actual hours (AH) required and the standard hours (SH) allowed by the standard rate (SR) per hour, or

$$LTV = (AH - SH) \times SR$$

To illustrate, assume that the 22,200 hours of labor time received from its employees by the Case Company resulted in production with a standard labor time of 22,000 hours. Since the standard labor rate is \$10 per hour, the labor time variance is \$2,000 (unfavorable), computed as follows:

$$LTV = (AH - SH) \times SR$$
$$LTV = (22,200 - 22,000) \times \$10$$
$$LTV = 200 \times \$10$$
$$LTV = \$2,000$$

The variance is unfavorable since more hours than standard were required to complete the period's production. If the reverse had been true, the variance would be favorable.

A graphic illustration may aid in understanding the relationship between standard and actual labor cost and the computation of the labor variances. Illustration 15.1 is deliberately not drawn to scale and is based upon the following data relating to the Case Company's factory operations:

Standard labor time per unit................................ 2 hours
Equivalent units produced in period........................ 11,000 units
Standard labor rate per direct labor hour.................... $10
Total direct labor wages paid (at average rate of $10.50
  per hour)... $233,100
Actual direct labor hours received........................ 22,200 hours

The standard labor time allowed for the period's output was 22,000 hours (11,000 units at 2 hours per unit). The standard labor cost of the output then is $220,000 (22,000 hours at $10 per hour, the standard labor rate). The labor time variance is the standard cost of the extra hours of labor required [(22,200 − 22,000) × $10], or $2,000. The actual labor rate is $10.50 per hour. The labor rate variance then is the 50¢ per hour ($10.50 − $10.00) of above standard wages paid multiplied by the standard hours allowed (22,000) and, by convention, the above standard wages paid per hour on the extra hours required (200)—the shaded area in the upper right-hand corner of the rectangle. The variation from standard shown by this shaded area is actually caused by both extra hours and above standard wages per hour. But, as shown, it is included in the labor rate variance as this variance is based on actual hours worked.

The entry to charge Work in Process Inventory with direct labor cost

ILLUSTRATION 15.1

Standard Labor Cost and Labor Variances

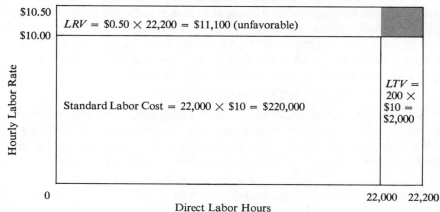

and to set up the two labor variances for the Case Company would be as follows:

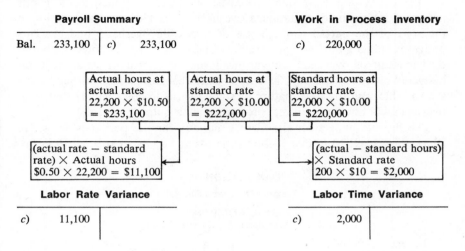

Payroll Summary				Work in Process Inventory	
Bal.	233,100	*c)*	233,100	*c)*	220,000

Actual hours at actual rates
22,200 × $10.50
= $233,100

Actual hours at standard rate
22,200 × $10.00
= $222,000

Standard hours at standard rate
22,000 × $10.00
= $220,000

(actual rate − standard rate) × Actual hours
$0.50 × 22,200 = $11,100

(actual − standard hours) × Standard rate
200 × $10 = $2,000

Labor Rate Variance		Labor Time Variance	
c)	11,100	*c)*	2,000

With the above entry, the gross wages earned by direct production employees ($233,100) is distributed: $220,000 (the standard labor cost of the production) to Work in Process Inventory and the balance to the two labor variance accounts. Note that the labor rate variance is not caused by paying employees more wages than they are entitled to receive. The more likely reason is that employees with different pay rates can complete the same task and that too much of the higher hourly rated employee time was used on a given job. Also, if some overtime premium pay is expected in setting standards, then variation from expected amounts can cause a labor rate variance. But, typically, the hours of labor employed are more likely to be under the control of management, and for this reason the labor time variance is more closely watched.

Summary of Labor Variances. The accuracy of the computation of the two labor variances can be readily checked by comparing their sum with the difference between actual and standard labor cost for a period. In the Case Company illustration this difference was:

Actual labor cost incurred..............................	$233,100
Standard labor cost allowed............................	220,000
Total labor variance (unfavorable)....................	$ 13,100

This $13,000 is made up of two labor variances, both unfavorable:

Labor time variance (200 × $10)........................	$ 2,000
Labor rate variance (22,200 × $0.50)...................	11,100
Total labor variance (unfavorable)....................	$13,100

Overhead Variances

In a cost system using standard costs, overhead is applied to the goods produced by means of a standard overhead rate. This rate is set prior to the start of the period through use of a flexible overhead budget. This budget is called a flexible (or variable) budget because it shows the budgeted amount of overhead for various levels of output or volume. Total budgeted overhead will vary as output varies because some overhead costs are variable. But the fixed nature of some overhead costs means that total overhead will not vary in direct proportion with output.

The flexible budget for the Case Company for the period is shown in Illustration 15.2. Note that it shows the overhead costs expected to be in-

ILLUSTRATION 15.2

Flexible Overhead Budget

CASE COMPANY
Flexible Manufacturing Overhead Budget

	90%	100%	110%
Percent of capacity.......................	90%	100%	110%
Direct labor hours......................	18,000	20,000	22,000
Variable overhead:			
Indirect materials.......................	$ 7,200	$ 8,000	$ 8,800
Power...............................	9,000	10,000	11,000
Royalties.............................	1,800	2,000	2,200
Other................................	18,000	20,000	22,000
Total variable overhead..............	$36,000	$ 40,000	$ 44,000
Fixed overhead:			
Insurance............................	$ 4,000	$ 4,000	$ 4,000
Property taxes........................	6,000	6,000	6,000
Depreciation..........................	20,000	20,000	20,000
Other................................	30,000	30,000	30,000
Total fixed overhead.................	$60,000	$ 60,000	$ 60,000
Total manufacturing overhead.............	$96,000	$100,000	$104,000

curred at three levels of activity: 90 percent, 100 percent, and 110 percent of capacity. For product costing purposes, one level of activity must be chosen and a rate set based on that level. The level chosen is called the standard volume of output and in our example is assumed to be at 100 percent of capacity, at which level 20,000 direct labor hours of services are expected to be used. The standard overhead rate then is $5 per direct labor hour and consists of $2 per hour of variable and $3 per hour of fixed overhead. Note that the variable rate is $2 per hour at all three levels while the fixed overhead rate decreases from $3.33 ($60,000 divided by 18,000 hours) to $3 to $2.73 ($60,000 divided by 22,000 hours) as volume expands.

Standard overhead rates per direct labor hour at 100 percent of capacity:

Variable ($40,000 ÷ 20,000 hours) = $2
Fixed ($60,000 ÷ 20,000 hours) =   3
Total standard manufacturing overhead rate $5

To continue our illustration, assume that the Case Company incurred $108,000 of actual manufacturing overhead costs in the period in which 11,000 units of product were produced and for which the standard labor allowed is 22,000 hours. These actual costs would be debited to Manufacturing Overhead and credited to a variety of accounts such as Accounts Payable, Allowance for Depreciation, Unexpired Insurance, Accrued Property Taxes Payable, and so on. The entry to record the application of $110,000 of overhead to production (22,000 hours @ $5 per hour) would be:

Manufacturing Overhead   **Work in Process Inventory**

Bal.   108,000 | *d*)   110,000   *d*)   110,000

Actual costs   Overhead applied: stan-
  incurred   dard labor hours at
                      standard overhead rate:
                      22,000 × $5 = $110,000

The above accounts show that manufacturing overhead has been over-applied to production by the $2,000 credit balance in the Manufacturing Overhead account. This balance can also be called the *net overhead variance*. It can be analyzed and broken down into a number of variances, of which we will illustrate only two: the overhead volume variance and the overhead budget variance.

The Overhead Volume Variance.   The overhead volume variance (OVV) results from a combination of two factors: (1) the existence of fixed overhead costs, and (2) operating at a level of activity different from that used in setting the standard overhead rate. It shows whether plant assets were used more or less than expected. It is computed as the difference between (*a*) the budgeted fixed overhead (*BFO*) for the standard direct labor allowed for the actual volume achieved and (*b*) the standard fixed overhead (*SFO*) applied to production. Hence,

$$OVV = BFO - SFO$$

In the Case Company illustration, the 11,000 units produced in the period have a standard labor allowance of 22,000 hours. The flexible budget in Illustration 15.2 shows that the budgeted fixed overhead for 22,000 direct labor hours is $60,000. The standard fixed overhead applied to production is 22,000 hours at $3 per hour, or $66,000. The overhead volume variance then is:

$$OVV = BFO - SFO$$
$$OVV = \$60,000 - \$66,000$$
$$OVV = -\$6,000.$$

This variance is considered favorable because standard fixed overhead absorbed in the period's output exceeded the budgeted fixed overhead for the period. That the variance is favorable can also be seen from the fact that the period's output (11,000 units) exceeded the standard volume (10,000) that was used in setting the standard overhead rate.

The Overhead Budget Variance.   The overhead budget variance (also called the spending or controllable variance) shows in one amount how efficiently operations were conducted in the sense of the prices paid for and the amounts of the overhead services used. It shows for overhead a variance that is similar to a combined price and usage variance for materials or labor. The overhead budget variance (OBV) is equal to the difference between total actual overhead costs (AO) and total budgeted overhead costs (BO) for the *actual* output attained. Since the total actual overhead was $108,000 and the total budgeted overhead was $104,000 (from Illustration 15.2) for 11,000 units (22,000 standard direct labor hours), the overhead budget variance is computed as follows:

$$OBV = AO - BO$$
$$OBV = \$108,000 - \$104,000$$
$$OBV = \$4,000$$

The variance is unfavorable because actual overhead costs were $108,000 while, according to the flexible budget, they should have amounted to only $104,000. If the reverse had been true, the variance would be considered favorable.

The relationship between actual, absorbed, and budgeted overhead and the two overhead variances is presented graphically in Illustration 15.3. It shows that budgeted overhead, y, for any volume level is equal to a fixed amount of overhead, a, plus an amount of variable overhead that is equal to the variable overhead rate, b, times the number of units of volume, x, that is, $y = a + bx$. The line "absorbed overhead" shows the amount of overhead that would be applied to production at different volumes using the standard overhead rate. At standard volume (the volume used in setting the standard overhead rate), absorbed and budgeted overhead are equal (the two lines intersect). With output of less than standard volume,

ILLUSTRATION 15.3

Actual, Absorbed, and Budgeted Overhead Costs

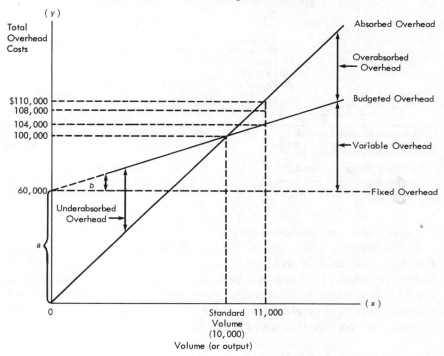

the graph shows that underabsorbed overhead is expected, while over-absorbed overhead is expected if actual volume exceeds standard volume.

The numerical data in Illustration 15.3 pertain to the Case Company. They show that at standard volume of 10,000 units (20,000 standard direct labor hours) budgeted and absorbed overhead are equal at $100,-000. With actual output at 11,000 units, absorbed overhead is $110,000, while budgeted overhead is $104,000 giving rise to a favorable volume variance of $6,000. Actual overhead amounts to $108,000 while it should have been only $104,000 and this yields an unfavorable budget variance of $4,000. The net overhead variance is $2,000, favorable, and is the sum of the $6,000 favorable volume variance and the $4,000 unfavorable budget variance.

Recording Overhead Variances. If desired, a formal entry can be made in the accounts showing the two parts of the net overhead variance, the $2,000 overabsorbed overhead balance. The entry for the Case Company would be (the debits and credits keyed with the letter (*e*):

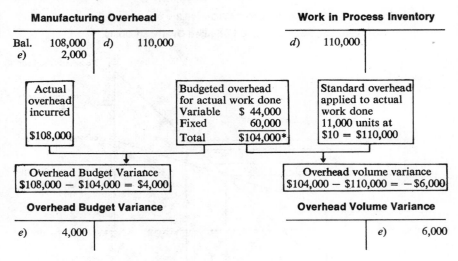

* From flexible budget. See Illustration 15.2

In the entry recorded in the T-accounts, the debit to Manufacturing Overhead of $2,000 reduces that account to a zero balance. The overhead budget variance is recorded as a debit in an account of that title because the $4,000 variance is unfavorable. And the $6,000 favorable overhead volume variance is recorded as a credit in an account of that title. The accounts now contain an analysis of the net overhead variance.

Goods Completed and Sold

To complete our Case Company example, assume that 11,000 units were completed and transferred to finished goods, that 10,000 units were sold on account at a price equal to 160 percent of standard cost, that there was no beginning or ending work in process inventory, and that there was no finished goods beginning inventory. In the T-accounts below, entry f shows the transfer of the standard cost of the units completed, $660,000 (11,000 at $60), from Work in Process Inventory to Finished Goods Inventory. Entry g records the sales for the period, while entry h records the cost of the goods sold.

Work in Process Inventory

b)	Materials	330,000	f)	Completed	660,000
c)	Labor	220,000			
d)	Overhead	110,000			

Finished Goods Inventory

f)	Completed	660,000	h)	Sold	600,000

Accounts Receivable		Cost of Goods Sold	
g) 960,000		*h)* Sold 600,000	

Sales	
	g) 960,000

Since it has been charged with the standard cost of the materials, labor, and overhead put into production, the entry to record the transfer of the standard cost of the completed units, $660,000 (11,000 at $60), reduces the Work in Process Inventory account to a zero balance. Note that the Finished Goods Inventory account is charged with the standard cost of the goods completed and credited with the standard cost of the goods sold. Thus, the ending inventory consists of the units actually on hand (1,000) at their standard cost of $60 each, or $60,000. Sales for the period amount to 10,000 units at $96.00 each (160% of $60).

Investigating Variances from Standard

Once variances are isolated, management must decide which ones should be investigated further. Since so many variances occur they cannot all be investigated, management needs some selection guides. Possible guides include (1) the absolute size of the variance, (2) the size of the variance relative to the cost incurred, and (3) the type of cost incurred, that is, whether it is considered controllable or noncontrollable. The opinions of knowledgeable operating personnel should be sought.

Any analysis of variances is likely to disclose some variances that are controllable within the company and others that are not. Prices paid for materials purchased may be largely beyond the control of the buyer. But amounts used may be controllable internally. Also, although separate variances are isolated, they are not always as independent as they may appear. An unfavorable labor rate variance may result from using higher paid employees in a certain task; but this may result in a favorable labor time variance from greater productivity and possibly a favorable materials usage variance because the more skilled employees caused less spoilage. It follows that variances should be investigated carefully before being used to appraise the performance of a given individual or department.

Disposing of Variances from Standard

At the end of the year, variances from standard may be (1) viewed as losses due to inefficiency and closed to the Expense and Revenue Summary account or (2) allocated as adjustments of the recorded cost of work in process inventory, finished goods inventory, and cost of goods sold. Theoretically, the alternative chosen should depend upon whether the standards set were reasonably attainable standards and whether the variance was controllable by company employees. An unfavorable materials price variance caused by an unexpected price change may be considered an added cost since it is likely to be uncontrollable. On the other hand, there is little merit in treating the fixed costs of idle plant capacity as anything but a loss. As a practical matter, and especially if they are small, the variances are usually closed to the Cost of Goods Sold account rather than allocated. Since they typically are unfavorable (due to the common practice of setting "tight" standards), this tends to reduce reported net earnings below the amounts that would be reported if the variances were treated as cost elements and allocated to the inventory accounts and cost of goods sold.

Entry i in the T-accounts below reflects this practical disposition of the variances in our continuing example of the Case Company:

Materials Price Variance				Materials Usage Variance				Labor Rate Variance			
i)	6,000	a)	6,000	b)	3,000	i)	3,000	c)	11,100	i)	11,100

Labor Time Variance				Overhead Budget Variance				Overhead Volume Variance			
c)	2,000	i)	2,000	e)	4,000	i)	4,000	i)	6,000	e)	6,000

Cost of Goods Sold	
h)	600,000
i)	8,100

In journal entry form, entry i would read as follows:

Materials Price Variance	6,000	
Overhead Volume Variance	6,000	
Cost of Goods Sold	8,100	
Materials Usage Variance		3,000
Labor Time Variance		2,000
Overhead Budget Variance		4,000
Labor Rate Variance		11,100
To close variance accounts.		

Variances are not reported separately in statements released to the public; they are simply included in the reported cost of goods sold amount.

In statements prepared for internal use, the variances may be listed separately after the cost of goods sold at standard cost amount.

VARIABLE COSTING

Absorption versus Variable Costing

Currently, the most commonly accepted theory of product costing holds that the cost of producing a product includes direct materials, direct labor, and an apportioned share of the many manufacturing overhead costs. The latter include costs such as factory depreciation and taxes which tend to remain fixed over varying ranges of output. Other costs, such as supplies and power, may vary with production volume. Despite differences in their variability, all of these costs are attached to the units of product manufactured and then traced from work in process inventory to finished goods inventory and finally to cost of goods sold. This method of assigning costs to products is called *absorption* or *full costing* and is the method generally required for tax purposes.

Because all costs, including fixed overhead costs, are applied to production under full costing, variations in unit product cost may result solely from variations in production volume. If fixed costs are $100,000 and 10,000 units are produced, unit fixed cost is $10; if volume is 20,000, unit fixed cost is $5. Because these variations are not controllable at the production level and may obscure other significant variations in cost, they can be excluded from product cost through use of a costing technique referred to as variable, direct or marginal costing.

Under variable costing, all manufacturing costs must first be classified as fixed or variable—that is, those that do and those that do not vary with production volume. Examples are given above of variable and fixed overhead costs. Direct materials and direct labor costs also are usually completely variable. All variable costs are assigned to production and become part of the unit costs of the products produced. All fixed costs are assumed to be costs of the production period and are not charged to production but are considered an expense for the year. They are called *period costs* as contrasted to variable costs which are called *product costs.*

Variable and Absorption Costing Compared

The differences between variable and full costing can be seen by means of an example comparing the earnings statement that would result from the application of each technique to the same data. Assume the following data:

Beginning inventory........	0	Variable costs (per unit)	
Production (units).........	10,000	Direct materials............	$2.00
Sales (units)...............	9,000	Direct labor...............	1.00
Fixed costs		Manufacturing overhead....	0.30
Manufacturing overhead..	$ 6,000	Total................	$3.30
Selling expenses.........	15,000		
Administrative expenses..	12,000	Variable selling expenses	
		(per unit)...............	$0.20
		Selling price (per unit)........	$8.00

Earnings Statement under Variable Costing.   Under variable costing the earnings statement for the year would be as is shown in Illustration 15.4. Note that all of the fixed manufacturing costs are considered costs of the period and are not included in inventories.

Earnings Statement under Conventional Costing.   Illustration 15.5 contains the earnings statement that would be prepared under full costing. Note that the fixed manufacturing costs are included as part of product cost and some of these costs are included in the ending inventory.

The ending inventory is priced at so-called "full cost." That is, its cost includes fixed manufacturing overhead. Since the total cost of producing 10,000 units is $39,000, then the unit cost is $3.90 and the 1,000 units in inventory are carried at $3,900. Also, under the conventional earnings statement approach, no line of distinction is drawn between fixed and variable selling expenses, and no attempt is made to compute the amount by which sales revenue exceeds the variable costs of the period. Thus, the total selling expenses for the period consisting of $15,000 of fixed expenses and variable expenses of $1,800 (9,000 units at $0.20) are shown as one lump-sum amount.

Different Valuations for Inventory.   Net earnings under full costing amount to $8,100 and are $600 less, at $7,500, under variable costing. Similarly, the inventory under variable costing is $600 less, at $3,300. In any situation in which the beginning inventories are the same, increasing

ILLUSTRATION 15.4
Earnings Statement under Variable Costing

Sales (9,000 units at $8)...............................		$72,000
Cost of goods sold		
Variable production costs incurred		
(10,000 units at $3.30)............................	$33,000	
Less: Inventory (1,000 units at $3.30)..................	3,300	29,700
Manufacturing margin..................................		$42,300
Variable selling expenses (9,000 units at $0.20).............		1,800
Marginal earnings.....................................		$40,500
Period costs		
Manufacturing overhead.............................	$ 6,000	
Selling expenses....................................	15,000	
Administrative expenses.............................	12,000	33,000
Net Earnings...		$ 7,500

ILLUSTRATION 15.5

Earnings Statement under Conventional Costing

Sales (9,000 units at $8)............................		$72,000
Cost of goods sold		
Variable costs of production (10,000 units at $3.30)......	$33,000	
Fixed overhead costs............................	6,000	
Total costs of producing 10,000 units..............	$39,000	
Less: Inventory (1,000 units at $3.90)...............	3,900	35,100
Gross margin on sales...............................		$36,900
Operating expenses		
Selling ($15,000 fixed plus 9,000 at $0.20 each)..........	$16,800	
Administrative..................................	12,000	28,800
Net Earnings.....................................		$ 8,100

the value attached to the ending inventory will increase the amount of net earnings (before taxes) reported.

The $600 difference in net earnings can be explained in yet another way. The fixed manufacturing overhead for the period was $6,000. Of the 10,000 units produced, 9,000 were sold and 1,000 are in inventory. Under full costing, 90 percent of the fixed costs is in cost of goods sold and 10 percent is in inventory ($0.10 \times \$6,000 = \$600$). Under variable costing, none is in inventory, all are in expense.

Analysis is more complicated when both beginning and ending inventories are involved. But the difference in net earnings can be determined by ascertaining whether the amount of fixed overhead in inventory under full costing increased or decreased from the beginning to the end of the year. If it increased, net earnings under variable costing will be less. If it decreased, more. As a general guide, the difference in earnings can be related to the *change* in inventories. Assuming a relatively constant level of production, if inventories are increased, production exceeded sales and the net earnings reported under variable costing will be less than under full costing. Conversely, if inventories are decreased, sales exceeded production, and net earnings under variable costing will be larger than under full costing.

Variable Costing—Pro and Con

Variable costing is not at present considered an acceptable method of costing for earnings measurement and for inventory valuation, nor is it allowed for tax purposes. It is considered unacceptable because it does not include in inventory all costs of producing the goods and because it misstates the period's charges against revenues. Currently accepted practice requires that all costs of producing a given product be, to the extent possible, attached to that product and treated as expenses only when the product is sold.

Advocates of variable costing prefer to treat the fixed manufacturing costs as part of the costs of being ready to produce. Such costs, they contend, should be charged to the period and not to the production of the period; that is, the relationship between such costs and production is so remote that they should be expensed in the period incurred. In this way, variable costing avoids the reporting of fluctuations in net earnings found under full costing when *production* varies from period to period. Net earnings should be a function of sales, not of production, or so the advocates of variable costing maintain.

The type of information accumulated under variable costing, especially the classification of costs as fixed and variable, is undoubtedly of considerable utility to management in gaining a thorough understanding of the relationships between cost, volume, and earnings. And certainly the responsibility for and the control of costs are more readily determined and secured through a proper classification of costs. Variable costing is undoubtedly a useful management tool; and for this reason its usage is likely to increase.

SUMMARY

Standard costs may be introduced on either a full cost or variable cost basis into either job cost or process cost systems as one means of attempting to appraise the efficiency with which operations are conducted. Standard costs are carefully predetermined measures of what costs should be, not merely estimates. The setting of standards often will involve engineering and time and motion studies and knowledge of working conditions within a plant as well as knowledge of general economic conditions.

The advantages secured from using standard costs include cost control, information useful in managerial planning, more rational inventory values, cost savings in recordkeeping, and, possibly, a general reduction in the amounts of costs incurred.

Typically, at least the following variances from standard cost will be computed:

1. Materials price variance = (actual price − standard price) × actual quantity.
2. Materials usage variance = (actual quantity − standard quantity) × standard price.
3. Labor rate variance = (actual rate − standard rate) × actual hours.
4. Labor time variance = (actual hours − standard hours) × standard rate.
5. Overhead volume variance = (budgeted fixed overhead − standard fixed overhead applied to production).

6. Overhead budget variance = (actual overhead − budgeted overhead for actual volume).

Variances may be isolated at different steps in the accounting process. As a general rule, the sooner a variance can be isolated, the better it serves as a means of cost control. Although they may be allocated to work in process inventory, finished goods inventory, and cost of goods sold at the end of a period, variances, as a practical matter, are usually closed to the Cost of Goods Sold account.

Under full costing, some part of all of the costs incurred to produce a product, including fixed manufacturing overhead, is attached to each unit produced. Under an alternative, called variable costing, fixed overhead costs are not applied to production but are treated as period costs, that is, as expenses when incurred. The two cost concepts, when applied to the same data, generally will yield different net earnings amounts which will be a result of the use of different amounts for beginning and ending work in process and finished goods inventories.

Variable costing, by stressing the distinction between fixed and variable costs, provides information useful in discerning the relationships between costs, volume, and earnings. But the measurements it generates for inventories and net earnings are not considered generally acceptable at this time.

QUESTIONS AND EXERCISES

1. What is a standard cost? What is the primary objective of employing standard costs in a cost system? What are some of the other advantages of using standard costs?

2. How can it be maintained that the use of standard costs permits the application of the principle of management by exception?

3. What are some of the problems surrounding the interpretation of variances in a standard cost system?

4. What might be a plausible explanation for a given company having a substantial favorable materials price variance and a substantial unfavorable materials usage variance?

5. What is the usual cause of an unfavorable labor rate variance? What other labor variance is isolated in a standard cost system? Of the two variances, which is more likely to be under management control? Explain.

6. Identify the type of variance indicated by each situation below and whether it is a favorable or unfavorable variance.
    a. The cutting department of a company during the week ending July 15 cut 12 size S cogged wheels out of three sheets of 12-inch high-tempered steel. Usually three wheels of such size are cut out of each sheet.

b. A company purchased and installed a new expensive cutting machine to handle expanding orders. This purchase and the related depreciation had not been anticipated when the overhead rate was set.

c. Edwards, the band saw operator, was on vacation last week. Lands took his place for the normal 40-hour week. Edwards' wage rate is $5.40 per hour, while Lands' is $5.20 per hour. Production was at capacity last week and the week before.

7. Is the overhead budget variance essentially a "price" or a "usage" variance? Explain.

8. Theoretically, how should variances from standard be disposed of? What is typically their practical disposition?

9. Distinguish between full costing and variable costing. Distinguish between period costs and product costs under variable costing.

10. On what generally accepted accounting theory is full costing based? How does this help to explain variations through time in unit costs under full costing?

11. Is variable costing acceptable for external reporting purposes? Explain.

12. Why might internal management find variable costing quite useful even though it might not be acceptable for general financial reporting purposes or for tax purposes?

PROBLEMS

15–1. Payroll and production records of the First Company for a given month show:

Actual direct labor payroll (19,800 hours) $81,180
Standard labor allowed per unit, 2 hours @ $4 per hour 8
Equivalent production for the month (in units) 10,000

Required: Compute the labor rate and time variances for the month.

15–2. During the month of May a department completed 2,000 units of a product which had a standard material cost of 4,000 square feet at $0.40 per square foot. The actual material used consisted of 4,050 square feet at an actual cost of $1,660.50, while the actual purchases of this material amounted to 6,000 square feet at a total cost of $2,460.

Required: Using T-accounts, prepare entries for the (*a*) purchase of the materials and (*b*) for the issuance of materials to production.

15–3. The following data relate to the manufacturing activities of the Glen Company for the month of May:

Standard volume (in units) 50,000
Actual production (in units) 40,000
Budgeted fixed overhead (for the month) $30,000
Variable overhead rate (per unit) . . . . $ 2.00
Actual fixed overhead $30,400
Actual variable overhead $78,300

Required: Compute the overhead budget variance and the overhead volume variance for the month.

15–4. The standard cost variance accounts of the Martin Company at the end of its fiscal year had the following balances:

Materials Usage Variance (unfavorable)	$ 4,000
Materials Price Variance (unfavorable)	5,000
Labor Rate Variance (favorable)	3,000
Labor Time Variance (unfavorable)	11,000
Overhead Volume Variance (unfavorable)	6,000
Overhead Budget Variance (favorable)	1,000

Required: Set up T-accounts for the above variances; enter the above balances in these accounts; then prepare one entry to record the closing of these variance accounts in the manner in which they are usually disposed of in practice.

15–5. The monthly budgeted fixed overhead of the Detroit Plant of the Collier Company is absorbed into production using a rate based upon standard volume of 200,000 units of output per month. The flexible budget for the month for overhead allows $150,000 for fixed overhead and $1 per unit of output for variable overhead. Actual fixed overhead for the month consisted of $151,200.

Required: Compute the overhead budget variance and the overhead volume variance assuming actual production in units and actual variable overhead in dollars were:
a. 150,000 and $152,000.
b. 220,000 and $225,400.

15–6. The George Company experienced the following results of operations in the month of May:

Units produced	20,000
Units sold	18,000
Direct materials consumed	$50,000
Direct labor costs	40,000
Fixed overhead cost	24,000
Variable overhead cost	32,000

Required: Assuming no beginning or ending work in process inventories and no beginning finished goods inventory, compute cost of goods sold under (*a*) variable costing and (*b*) full costing.

15–7. The following data are for the Stein Company for the year 1979:

Sales (10,000 units)	$100,000
Direct materials used (12,000 units at $3)	36,000
Direct labor cost incurred	12,000
Variable manufacturing overhead incurred	3,600
Fixed manufacturing overhead incurred	4,800
Variable selling and administrative expenses	6,000
Fixed selling and administrative expenses	20,000

One unit of direct materials goes into each unit of finished goods. The only beginning or ending inventory is the 2,000 units of finished goods on hand at the end of 1979. Variable and fixed overhead rates (based on 100 percent of capacity of 12,000 units) were $.30 and $.40 respectively.

Required: Prepare an earnings statement under—
   a.   Variable costing.
   b.   Full costing.

15–8.   The Guy Art Company manufactures a number of ceramic figurines which, although produced in six colors, are still sufficiently similar to be considered one product for standard costing purposes. The standard cost of each figurine is:

> Direct materials:
> 2 lbs. of clay at $0.40............................ $0.80
> 4 oz. of coloring pigment at $1.25................ 5.00
> Direct labor (.10 hours at $5.00).................. 0.50
> Overhead:
> Fixed... 0.30
> Variable...................................... 0.40
> $7.00

In May, 50,000 units were manufactured and 48,000 units sold. Detailed data relative to production are summarized as follow:

> Materials purchased:
> 102,000 lbs. of clay at $0.38
> 210,000 oz. of coloring pigment at $1.26
> Materials used:
> 101,050 lbs. of clay; 200,500 oz. of coloring pigment
> Direct labor: 5,030 hours at $5.10
> Fixed overhead: $18,200
> Variable overhead: $20,350

The fixed overhead assigned to production is based upon standard volume of 60,000 units per month. There were no beginning or ending inventories of work in process.

Required: From the above data, compute the following:

a.   The standard costs for materials, labor, and overhead for the production in May.
b.   The standard cost of the goods completed.
c.   The standard cost of the goods sold.
d.   Six variances from standard for the month.

chapter 16

The Behavior and Analysis
of Costs; Capital Budgeting

AN INTRODUCTION TO INCREMENTAL ANALYSIS

The Behavior of Costs

Knowledge of the behavior and nature of costs is crucial to management for decision-making purposes. Two basic categories of costs are generally used—variable and fixed. *Variable costs* (see Illustration 16.1, part A) are those which vary directly with changes in volume. Certain production costs, such as raw materials and the labor used to convert the raw materials into finished products, vary directly with production volume, while sales commissions vary directly with sales volume.

Fixed costs (see Illustration 16.1, part B) are those which do not vary over wide variations in the level of output. They are often described as time-related costs. That is, they will be incurred simply because of the passage of time if the company expects to continue to operate. Depreciation (when computed on a time basis), property insurance, property taxes, and (usually) administrative salaries are examples of time-related costs and, therefore, are fixed costs.

Besides these two basic categories of variable and fixed costs there are two other types of costs which are in part fixed and in part variable. These include semivariable (or semifixed) costs (see Illustration 16.1, part C) and step variable (or step fixed) costs (see Illustration 16.1, part D).

An example of a semivariable cost occurs when a given amount of maintenance cost has to be incurred while a plant is completely idle. Once production is underway, additional maintenance costs vary with produc-

ILLUSTRATION 16.1

Four Types of Cost Patterns

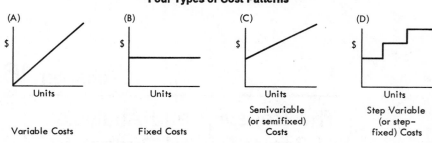

(A)	(B)	(C)	(D)
Variable Costs	Fixed Costs	Semivariable (or semifixed) Costs	Step Variable (or step– fixed) Costs

tion volume. These costs may be (and usually are) separated into their fixed and variable components as shown:

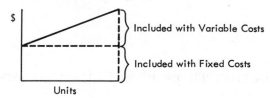

When divided in this way the top part fits the variable cost pattern as shown in Illustration 16.1, part A). The bottom part fits the fixed cost pattern as shown in Illustration 16.1, part B).

The other type, step variable costs, are handled in one of two ways. The first is to assume that the relationship is a straight-line relationship as depicted below by the slanted dotted line:

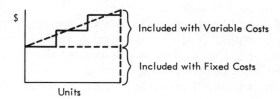

When this method is used, the costs may be separated into their fixed and variable components as was shown for semivariable costs.

When step variable costs are present and there are very few steps (one or two usually) it is sometimes useful to treat the costs as "step fixed." To illustrate, assume that between 0–40 percent of capacity a cost is $20,000 and over 40 percent of capacity it becomes $50,000 as shown:

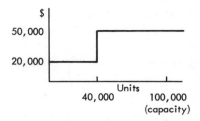

In this situation it is useful to merely change total fixed costs for the two different ranges—0–40 percent of capacity and 40 to 100 percent of capacity. (Problem 2 of this chapter deals with this situation.)

Thus even though there are four different types of cost patterns, it has been shown that two basic categories—variable and fixed—may be used to include all of them. Before proceeding, one other comment is in order. Some costs do not fit a straight-line pattern: that is, they have a curvilinear pattern. For purposes of the analysis of costs these costs are *assumed* to have straight-line relationships. The necessity for making this assumption will become evident as you proceed through this chapter.

Cost-Volume-Earnings Analysis

In planning future operations, a type of analysis sometimes referred to as cost-volume-earnings analysis is undertaken. In such an analysis, the company's break-even point is calculated. A company is said to break even for a given period if the sales revenue and the costs charged to that period are exactly equal. As a result, no element of earnings or loss remains. Thus, the break-even point is defined as that level of operations at which revenues and costs are equal.

To undertake a careful and accurate cost-volume-earnings analysis requires knowledge of costs and their behavior as volume changes. Management must be able to distinguish among the different types of costs involved in its operations. Of course, the types and quantities of cost data accumulated will depend on the costs of obtaining the data compared to the benefits resulting from more refined information. Within this constraint, it is desirable to compute break-even points for each area of decision making within the company. Some important classifications of cost data for breakeven analysis are by product, territory, salesman, class of customer, and method of selling.

Several procedures are available for calculating a break-even point. It may be expressed in (1) dollars of sales revenue, (2) number of units sold, or (3) as a percentage of capacity.

Assume that a company manufactures a single product which it sells for $20. Fixed costs per period total $40,000, while variable costs are $12

392   A Survey of Basic Accounting

per unit, or 60 percent of sales price. A linear relationship between variable costs and sales revenue is assumed to exist. Thus, variable costs are, within a given range of sales activity or sales volume, a constant percentage of sales. In this example, variable costs are 60 percent of sales. The sales revenue needed then to break even is:

$$\text{Sales } (S) = \text{Fixed Costs } (FC) + \text{Variable Costs } (VC)$$

Fixed costs are known to be $40,000, while variable costs as a percentage of sales are equal to 0.60S. Substituting, then, the equation becomes:

$$S = \$40,000 + 0.60S$$
$$0.40S = \$40,000$$
$$S = \$40,000 \div 0.40$$
$$S = \$100,000$$

Sales at the break-even point are $100,000 and this can easily be proven. At that level fixed costs will be $40,000 and variable costs will be $60,000 (0.60 × $100,000). The break-even point in units can be computed by dividing total sales revenue at the break-even point by the selling price per unit ($100,000 ÷ $20 = 5,000 units).

If desired, the break-even point can be expressed in terms of capacity. Newspaper reports often refer to the break-even point of the steel industry, or of a company in that industry, as being a stated percentage of capacity, for example, 65 percent. If, in the example presented above, the output capacity of the plant was 25,000 units, the break-even point in terms of plant capacity is 20 percent (5,000 ÷ 25,000).

The Break-Even Chart

The chart in Illustration 16.2 presents graphically the break-even point for the above company. Each break-even chart (or analysis) is assumed valid only for a specified *relevant range* of volumes. For volumes outside of these ranges, incurrences of different costs will alter the assumed relationship. For example, if only a few units were produced the variable costs per unit would probably be quite high (in spite of the assumption of a strictly linear relationship within the relevant range). Also, to produce more than 10,000 units it may be necessary to add to plant capacity, thus incurring additional fixed costs, or to work extra shifts incurring overtime charges and other inefficiencies. In either case, the cost relationships first assumed are no longer valid. The illustration is based on the data presented previously which are *relevant* for output from 500 to 10,000 units; below 500 and beyond 10,000 units these data may not be relevant.

The chart in Illustration16.2 shows that the break-even volume of sales is $100,000 (5,000 units at $20). At this level of sales, fixed costs of $40,000 and variable costs of $60,000 are exactly equal to sales revenue.

ILLUSTRATION 16.2

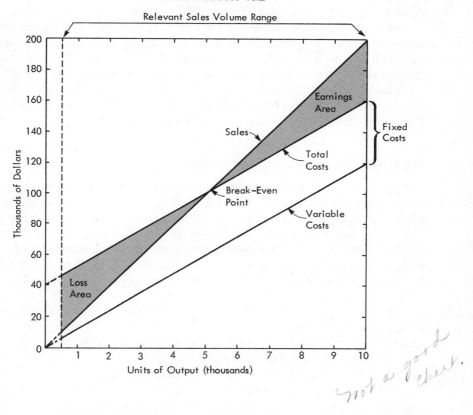

If plant capacity is 25,000 units, the break-even point expressed as a percentage of capacity is 20 percent.

The cost-volume-earnings chart shows that a period of complete idleness would produce a loss of $40,000, the amount of fixed costs, while output of 10,000 units would produce net earnings of $40,000. Other points which can be read show that with sales of 7,500 units total revenue would be $150,000. At that point, total costs would amount to $130,000, leaving net earnings of $20,000. The increase in average earnings per unit as sales volume increases beyond the break-even point can also be noted. At a volume of 7,500 units, average earnings per unit are $2.67 ($20,000 ÷ 7,500). At a volume of 10,000 units, average earnings would be $4 per unit ($40,000 ÷ 10,000 units). The reason for this, of course, is that each unit sold adds $20 to revenues but only $12 to costs (only the variable costs are incurred as additional units are sold). Average per-unit earnings increase rather quickly because the fixed costs associated with the revenues are spread over an increasing number of units. Average earnings per unit will continue to rise as long as the margin of difference for each additional unit sold is higher than average earnings per unit. Below the break-even point, the average loss per unit increases as volume declines.

The break-even point can be lowered by increasing the selling price per unit, decreasing the total fixed costs, or decreasing the variable cost per unit. This can be seen by studying Illustration 16.2 and visually imagining that the slope of the sales line increases, the distance between the variable costs and total costs lines diminishes, or the slope of the variable costs line decreases. The effect of each of these is to lower the break-even point. Taking opposite actions will increase the break-even point.

The Contribution to Fixed Costs Concept

The contribution to fixed costs is defined as the amount by which revenue exceeds the variable costs incurred in securing that revenue. Because it is used in analyzing changes in either direction from an existing volume of output, it is often referred to as the marginal contribution to fixed costs or simply the *marginal contribution* or *contribution margin*. It may be computed for a given number of units (or dollars of sales) or per unit or per dollar of sales. The marginal contribution is also called marginal income.

Using the preceding data (selling price per unit of $20 and variable costs per unit of $12 with total fixed costs of $40,000), the marginal contribution per unit is $8. The sale of one additional unit will add $20 to total revenues, $12 to total costs, and $8 to net earnings (ignoring income taxes). From this information the break-even point in units can be computed. Each unit contributes $8 to the coverage of fixed costs, and fixed costs total $40,000. Thus the sale of 5,000 units will be necessary to cover the fixed costs. The formula is:

Break-Even Point in Units = Fixed Costs ÷ Marginal Contribution per Unit

At the break-even point the total marginal contribution will equal the total fixed costs as shown in Illustration 16.3.

The break-even point in terms of dollars of sales can also be computed by dividing the fixed costs per period by the marginal contribution rate or the marginal earnings rate. This rate is computed by dividing the marginal contribution by sales price per unit. In the above data it is 40 percent ($8 ÷ $20); and the break-even point is $100,000 of sales revenue ($40,000 ÷ 0.40). This 40 percent rate is also sometimes referred to as the earnings/volume ratio.

In addition, the net earnings at any level of output can be computed as the contribution per unit multiplied by the number of units sold, less the total fixed costs. Using the above data, the net earnings at the 80 percent level of capacity can be determined. First multiply 8,000 units (0.80 × 10,000) by $8, obtaining $64,000. Then subtract the fixed costs

ILLUSTRATION 16.3

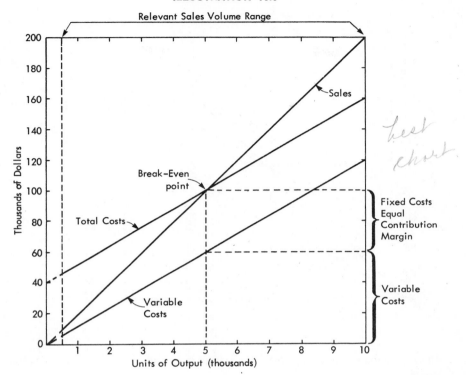

Relevant Sales Volume Range

(chart with Y-axis "Thousands of Dollars" ranging 0 to 200, X-axis "Units of Output (thousands)" ranging 1 to 10; lines labeled Sales, Total Costs, Variable Costs; Break-Even point; right-side brackets labeled "Fixed Costs Equal Contribution Margin" and "Variable Costs")

of $40,000, leaving net earnings of $24,000. In this case the contribution margin more than covers total fixed costs. The remainder is net earnings (ignoring income taxes) as shown in Illustration 16.4.

Rather than applying break-even analysis to the entire operations of a company for a given time period, it can be used to analyze the cost-volume-earnings relationship for a venture or project. Suppose that one of the major airlines wanted to know the number of seats which would have to be sold on a certain flight for the flight to break even. To solve this problem the costs would have to be identified and separated into fixed and variable categories.

The fixed costs are those that would not vary with different levels of seats filled. These would include such costs as: fuel required to fly the plane with crew (no passengers) to destination; depreciation on the plane and facilities utilized on this flight; salaries of crew members, gate attendants, and maintenance and refueling personnel; and other miscellaneous fixed costs.

The variable costs would include those costs which vary directly with the number of passengers. These might include costs such as: extra fuel consumed per passenger; food and beverage included in the price of the

ILLUSTRATION 16.4

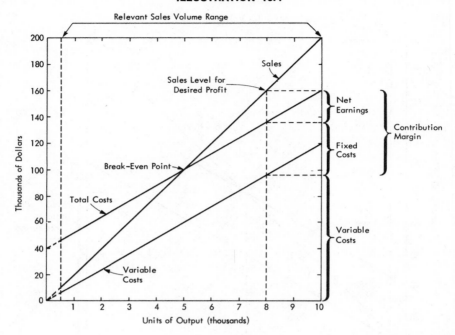

ticket; baggage handling costs per passenger; and miscellaneous variable costs.

Assume that after analyzing the various costs and classifying them as fixed or variable, the fixed costs for a given flight are $12,000. The variable costs are $25 per passenger. Assume also that there are 300 seats on the aircraft and that tickets are sold at $125.

The break-even point can be expressed in dollars, number of passengers, or in percent of capacity.

The sales revenue needed to break even is:

$$Sales\ (S) = Fixed\ Costs\ (FC) + Variable\ Costs\ (VC)$$
$$S = \$12,000 + .2S$$
$$.8S = \$12,000$$
$$S = \$15,000$$

The break-even point in terms of number of passengers is:

$$BEP\ (units) = \frac{FC}{Contribution\ Margin}$$
$$BEP = \frac{\$12,000}{\$125 - \$25}$$
$$BEP = 120\ Passengers$$

The break-even point in percent of capacity is:

$$\frac{BEP\ (units)}{Total\ Capacity\ (units)} = \frac{120\ passengers}{300\ passengers} = 40\ percent$$

Using Cost-Volume-Earnings Analysis. Although cost-volume-earnings analysis alone is insufficient to support managerial decision making, basic cost-volume-earnings relationships should be understood by management. Knowledge of such relationshps may help to determine (1) the level of sales volume that is needed to generate some desired level of net earnings, (2) whether to increase sales promotion costs in an effort to increase sales volume, (3) whether an order at a lower-than-usual price should be accepted, and (4) whether plant facilities should be expanded. Planning, in general, is facilitated by careful study of break-even charts. Indeed, it has been said that management, to be successful, must become "break-even minded." To illustrate using the data cited earlier, if management wished to generate $24,000 net earnings, the chart in Illustration 16.4 shows that sales volume must be 8,000 units, $160,000, or 80 percent of capacity. But assume that management has the opportunity to operate at 100 percent of capacity if it will increase its fixed costs by investing $10,000 in a sales promotion contract. Will it be profitable for management to make such an investment? The chart in Illustration 16.5 shows that it will, provided the cost and revenue estimates are correct and the objective of management is to maximize net earnings.

Limitations of Cost-Volume-Earnings Analysis. Cost-volume-earnings analysis, whether undertaken graphically or through the use of a formula, has certain shortcomings. It presents an overly simplified picture of op-

ILLUSTRATION 16.5

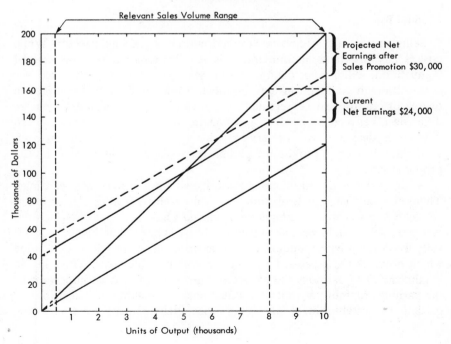

erations and is obviously more reliable for a business which produces and sells only *one* product. The picture presented by a break-even chart will change, for example, with changes in selling price, with changes in the mixture of the products sold, and with changes in the efficiency of labor and in the efficiency of the use of materials. In other words, the break-even chart or formula presents the volume-cost-earnings relationship for a particular set of data. It is also based upon some qualifying assumptions. The most questionable of these are that additional units can continue to be sold at the stated selling price and that variable costs remain a constant amount per unit as volume changes. The assumption also is made that output and sales volume are about the same; that is, that most production flows directly through to sales.

SPECIAL COST STUDIES FOR DECISION MAKING

Accounting records usually are designed to provide full cost data. Such cost data are suitable for such general purposes as determination of net earnings, control of costs, and managerial planning in general. There are occasions, however, when management faces problems which require consideration of only selected cost data. In such instances total costs are somewhat irrelevant and special cost studies are necessary to help provide the data required for decisions. Several types of such managerial problems will now be considered.

Product Pricing

Selling prices are seldom determined entirely by a single factor. While cost is an important determinant, it is readily apparent that because of competition, selling price cannot in all cases be set high enough to recover cost. Although competition may establish a maximum level for prices, a degree of control can be retained by the seller through establishment of differences between its product and competing products. Sometimes such differences take the form of services which accompany its product, such as certain warranty provisions, rather than physical differences in the product itself.

A high price is not in all cases the price which will maximize earnings. There may be some good substitutes for the product. If a high price is set, customers may switch to competing products. Thus, the quantity which the company sells would decline substantially. Assuming that fixed costs are truly fixed, the greatest amount of net earnings will be provided by a price which provides the greatest total margin over variable costs. Thus, in the maximization of earnings the expected volume of sales is as important as the earnings margin per unit of product sold. In making any decision regarding the establishment of selling price, management must seek the combination of price and volume which will produce the largest net earnings. This is often difficult to do in an actual situation since management may not know how many units can be sold at each price.

Product Pricing in Different Markets.   Not infrequently management is faced with the opportunity to sell its product in two or more different markets at two or more different prices. Price discrimination is unlawful under the Robinson-Patman Act unless it is justified by differences in costs of production, delivery, or selling. But since such cost differences often exist, a single product may be marketed at more than one selling price.

The desirability of keeping physical facilities and personnel working at capacity is obvious. Good business management requires keeping the cost of idleness of personnel and facilities at a minimum. When operations are at a level less than full capacity, additional business should be sought. Such additional business may be accepted at prices lower than average unit costs because only the additional, or marginal, costs need be matched against the additional revenue provided. Such costs will be for the most part variable costs such as materials and labor. But the possibility exists that certain near-fixed costs—that is, semivariable costs—will also be increased. Regardless of the classification of the costs affected by the increased volume, one point is clear. It is the comparison of marginal or incremental revenue with marginal costs—*not* the average costs—that is the important consideration.

Obviously the effect on regular sales of accepting a special order at a lower-than-usual price must be considered. If regular sales are to be unharmed by the acceptance of such a special order, it is essential that separate markets exist, such as in the case of a foreign and a domestic market.

To illustrate, assume that a given company produces and sells a single product at a variable cost of $8 per unit. Annual capacity is 10,000 units, and annual fixed costs total $48,000. The selling price is $20 per unit, and production and sales are budgeted at 5,000 units.

Thus, budgeted net earnings are $12,000, computed as follows:

Sales (5,000 @ $20)		$100,000
Costs		
Fixed	$48,000	
Variable (5,000 @ $8)	40,000	88,000
Net Earnings		$ 12,000

An order for 3,000 units is received from a European distributor at a price of $10 per unit. This is only half the regular selling price per unit, and also less than the average cost per unit of $17.60 ($88,000 ÷ 5,000 units). The $10 price offered, however, exceeds variable cost per unit by $2. If the order is accepted, net earnings will be $18,000, computed as follows:

Sales (5,000 units at $20; 3,000 units at $10).............		$130,000
Costs		
Fixed..	$48,000	
Variable (8,000 units at $8).........................	64,000	112,000
Net Earnings...		$ 18,000

To continue to operate at 50 percent of capacity would produce net earnings of only $12,000 (sales of $100,000, less fixed costs of $48,000 and variable costs of $40,000). Thus, a contribution of $2 per unit will result from acceptance of the order, and net earnings will be increased by $6,000. Because the regular market is unlikely to be affected by the export of the product at a sharply reduced price, the order should be accepted.

In summary, variable costs set a floor for selling price in marginal or incremental analyses such as those described above. Even if price exceeds variable costs only slightly, the additional business will make a contribution to earnings.

If the number of product units demanded increases substantially as its price is decreased—that is, if the demand is elastic—reduction of selling price will bring about an increase in total revenue and a decrease in unit costs through increased volume in the industry. It should be recognized, however, that price cutting is not without its dangers. If the demand for the product is inelastic, reduction of price would reduce total revenues. "Contribution pricing" of marginal business often brings short-term increases in earnings. Such pricing should be appraised in the light of long-range effects on the entire price structure of the company and the industry.

Elimination of Products

It is not uncommon for business management to face occasionally the question of elimination or retention of given products. To assist in the solution of such a problem, a special study of costs may be called for. Since the earnings statement does not automatically associate costs with given products, costs must be reclassified into those which would be changed by the elimination and those which would remain unaffected. In effect, one must simply assume elimination and compare the reduction in revenue with the eliminated costs. Costs which would be eliminated are *direct costs* to that product. Costs which would not be eliminated are *indirect costs* to that product.[1] Usually such costs as materials and labor will be eliminated and are therefore direct costs. Many other expenses of the selling and administrative group will remain unaffected and are therefore indirect costs

---

[1] In Chapter 13 the terms *direct* materials and *direct* labor were used. These are traditional titles used in cost accounting literature. The direct costs of a product would include these but might also include some of the manufacturing overhead costs, such as the foreman's salary if this position would cease to exist if the product were discontinued.

to that product. Some other costs are partly direct and partly indirect to that product. It must be remembered that if revenue exceeds direct costs, a product is making a contribution to earnings through its contribution to covering indirect costs. For a product it is most likely that all variable costs are direct in that they would be eliminated and all fixed costs are indirect since they would not be eliminated. Costs can only be direct or indirect *in relation* to a *certain cost objective*. The salary of a production foreman for instance may be an indirect cost to a particular product but a direct cost to the production department. If, for example, Product I is eliminated, the indirect costs now covered by sales of Product I will become additional costs of all other products.

To illustrate, assume that elimination of Product R is being considered by management. Product R provides revenue of only $100,000 annually, while the costs with which it is charged by acceptable accounting methods amount to $110,000, producing a loss of $10,000. Assume that a careful analysis of the costs reveals that if Product R was dropped, the reduction in costs would be $80,000, and $30,000 of the cost would continue to be incurred. The latter costs would increase the burden on the remaining products of the company by $30,000 if Product R was dropped. It is easily seen that Product R, even though producing no net earnings, has been contributing $20,000 ($100,000 − $80,000) annually to the net earnings of the business and that its elimination could be a costly mistake if there were no more profitable use of the resources that would be released from not producing Product R.

Discontinuing Sales to a Customer

Retention of a given segment of business is usually advisable if its revenue exceeds its direct costs. But elimination may be in order if there is a more profitable alternative use of resources. Assume, for example, that revenues from customers whose orders total less than $20,000 annually exceed the direct costs involved but by substantially less than on sales to larger customers. Since the larger customers furnish business which provides a higher margin of revenue over direct costs, it may be advisable to apply greater sales effort to the more productive customers and to discontinue salesmen's visits to the customers whose purchases are small.

Make-or-Buy Decisions

Another application of incremental cost analysis lies in whether to make or buy a part or material used in the manufacture of a product. In such a case a comparison is made between the price which would be paid for the part if it was purchased and the additional costs which would be incurred if the part was to be manufactured. If almost all of the costs of manufacture are fixed and would exist in any case, it is likely that manufacture rather than purchase of the part or material would be more economical.

To illustrate, assume that a company is manufacturing a part used in its final product at a cost of $6. Cost components are materials, $3; labor, $1.50; fixed factory costs, $1.05; and other variable factory costs $0.45. The part could be purchased for $5.25. Since the fixed overhead would presumably continue even if the part was purchased, manufacture of the part should be continued. The added costs of manufacturing amount to only $4.95 ($3.00 + $1.50 + $0.45). This is 30 cents per unit less than the purchase price of the part.

Nonquantifiable Factors

In some cases the relative cost of manufacture as opposed to purchase may be only a minor consideration. Some other factors for consideration are the competency of existing personnel to undertake manufacture of the part or material, the availability of working capital, and the cost of any borrowing that may be necessary.

There also may be nonquantifiable reasons for retaining a loss-producing product or customer. Management must consider the effect of elimination or retention on the sales of other products. An unprofitable product may be retained to provide a full line for customers. For example, even if flashbulbs were known to be sold at a loss in a retail drugstore, their sales would probably be continued in order to be able to offer a complete line of photographic products. Likewise, certain services may be retained because of the effect of their elimination on sales of other products. An example is unprofitable warranty work done by a retail automobile dealer. Buyers of new automobiles like to be assured that warranty service facilities are available at their dealer's place of business for the cars they purchase. Even if the service is provided at a loss, it may be wise to retain it.

CAPITAL EXPENDITURE DECISIONS

A capital expenditure is an expenditure benefiting more than the current period. A revenue expenditure is one benefiting only the current period. Usually a capital expenditure involves the commitment of funds for a relatively long period of time through acquisition of land or buildings, or other depreciable or amortizable assets. Decisions regarding capital expenditures are among the most important that can be made by the management of a company. The effects of a given decision may be felt for many years. The type of data needed for informed decision making in this area usually must be developed through special studies.

To illustrate, assume that a company has two machines in operation which were purchased four years ago at a cost of $15,000 each. The machines have an estimated total service life of 10 years, and each will produce 20,000 units of product annually. The annual total cost of production derived from both of these machines is:

Depreciation (both machines) ($30,000 ÷ 10)...............	$ 3,000
Labor...	8,000
Repairs...	800
Other..	1,200
	$13,000

A new machine is now available on the market at a price of $13,200, less a trade-in allowance of $1,200 ($600 each). This machine, which has an estimated life of six years, will produce 40,000 units annually at reduced labor and repair costs as follows:

Depreciation..	$ 2,000
Labor..	5,000
Repairs..	400
Other..	2,900
	$10,300

For sake of simplicity of illustration and because of their possible complexity, the effects of federal income tax regulations (despite their relevance) are ignored in the above data and will be ignored in subsequent illustrations. Thus, the comparison of the costs of the two alternatives shows a considerable savings in costs from the use of the new machine. But are these costs the relevant costs to be compared in deciding between the two alternatives? Actually, they are not since no distinction is made between out-of-pocket costs and sunk costs.

Out-of-Pocket and Sunk Costs

An out-of-pocket cost is a cost which requires the future utilization of resources. That is, it requires future payment and for this reason can be looked upon as an impending outflow of cash. Labor and repairs are examples of out-of-pocket costs. Sunk costs are past commitments of funds about which nothing can be done at the present time. The price paid for a machine the minute the machine is acquired represents a sunk cost. Its amount cannot be changed regardless of whether the machine is scrapped or used. Thus, depreciation is a sunk cost, as are depletion and the amortization of other assets such as leaseholds and patents. A sunk cost is a *past cost,* while an out-of-pocket cost is a *future cost.* Only the out-of-pocket costs (the future cash outlays) are relevant to the decision in this example. The out-of-pocket costs of the old machines are:

Labor...	$ 8,000
Repairs..	800
Other...	1,200
	$10,000

The annual out-of-pocket costs of the new machine are:

Capital outlay ($13,200—$1,200) ÷ 6......................	$ 2,000
Labor...	5,000
Repairs..	400
Other...	2,900
	$10,300

The outlay for the new machine is an out-of-pocket cost before it is made. In other words, it is an expenditure which must be made before production can be secured from the new machine. The amount is only $12,000 because a total trade-in allowance of $1,200 is granted for the old machines if the new is purchased. The above schedules make it clear that it will be more costly to acquire the new machine than to continue the old in operation. For the six-year period, the required production can be secured for $60,000 (6 × $10,000) from the old machines. A total expenditure of $61,800 (6 × $10,300) must be made if the new machine is acquired. Based upon the above data alone, investment of funds in the new machine does not appear to be a wise decision.

The Payback Period

To assist in deciding whether funds should be expended for a given asset or project, the *payback period* of the outlay is often computed. The payback period is that period of time during which net cash savings or benefits must continue in order to equal the initial net cash outlay. The computation of the payback period ignores the initial capital outlay in determining annual net cash savings or benefits. It, in effect, answers the question: How long will it take the new machine, if purchased, to pay for itself?

The payback period for the new machine in the preceding illustration may be computed from the following data:

	Old Machines	New Machine
Labor..	$ 8,000	$5,000
Repairs......................................	800	400
Other costs..................................	1,200	2,900
Annual out-of-pocket costs..................	$10,000	$8,300

The savings in annual out-of-pocket costs amount to $1,700. Dividing the net capital outlay for the new machine, $12,000, by the annual saving of $1,700 reveals that approximately seven years would be required for the new machine to pay for itself. According to the data in the illustration, the new machine will last only six years. Therefore, it will not pay for itself through savings in production costs and should not be purchased.

When the annual benefits are not level in amount it is necessary to calculate the payback period by accumulating the benefits. For instance, assume a proposal yields net cash benefits of $5,000, $4,000, and $3,000, respectively, for the first three years and has an initial outlay of $10,000. The payback period would be 2⅓ years since by the end of the second year $9,000 would have been recovered and it would take one-third of the next year to accumulate another $1,000. It is assumed that net cash inflows are received evenly throughout each year. Thus after four months of the third year, one-third of the total inflow from that year would have been received.

There are several important defects in the payback period analysis which limit its usefulness. First, it ignores the period of time beyond the payback period. For example, consider two alternative capital outlay proposals, each requiring an initial outlay of $20,000. Proposal A will return $5,000 per year for four years, a total return of $20,000. Its payback period is thus four years. Proposal B will return $4,000 for eight years, a total return of $32,000. But its payback period is five years. Accepting Proposal A simply because of its shorter payback period would be a mistake.

The payback period type of analysis also ignores the time value of money. For example, consider the following net cash receipts expected at the end of each year of life of two capital outlay proposals:

	Proposal X	Proposal Y
First year	$10,000	$ 6,000
Second year	8,000	8,000
Third year	6,000	10,000
Total	$24,000	$24,000

If the cost of each proposal is $24,000, then each has a payback period of three years. But common sense says that the two are not equal. Money has a time value because it usually can be reinvested to increase earnings. Since the larger amounts are received earlier under Proposal X, it is preferable to Y.

The deficiencies in the payback approach have led to the development of more sophisticated techniques. They embrace the use of compound interest and the determination of present values, concepts which were discussed in the appendix to Chapter 6.

The Present Value or Discounted Cash Flow Approach

Rarely is the preferred alternative obvious when competing capital outlay proposals are expected to yield different amounts of net cash inflows in different future periods. What we need is a procedure for formalizing our choice in all situations. One procedure is to find the present value of each proposal by discounting its expected future net cash inflows at some rate of interest. This procedure is based upon the simple notion that any rational person would, other things being equal, prefer to have one dollar today than one dollar at some future date. Further, if we know the appropriate interest rate, we can find the value today (the present value) of any cash receipt at any date in the future.

The rate of interest to be used in discounting expected cash flows from any investment proposal is the subject of a rather technical and complex estimation procedure which will not be discussed here. Instead, it will simply be assumed that there is a minimum desirable rate of interest or return sought by management in all capital expenditures.

To return to our previous example of Proposals X and Y, if it is assumed that the desired rate of return is 20 percent, the present value of each of the two proposals, X and Y, can be computed. The present value of one dollar due in one, two, and three years at 20 percent is $0.833, $0.694, and $0.579 (see Table II in the Appendix). Multiplying each of the above amounts by the appropriate present value multiplier produces the following total present values for X and Y:

	Proposal X	Proposal Y
First year	$ 8,330	$ 4,998
Second year	5,552	5,552
Third year	3,474	5,790
Total	$17,356	$16,340

As should have been expected, Proposal X has the greater present value and, other things being equal, will be more desirable.

The Profitability Index. But suppose that other things are not equal. Assume Proposal X has an initial outlay requirement of $15,000, while that for Proposal Y is only $13,500. Which proposal is now preferable? The answer to this question can be found by computing a *profitability index*. The profitability index is computed by dividing the present value of the expected net cash benefits from the proposal by the present value of its initial outlay (which is the amount that must be paid out immediately).

The profitability index of X is 1.16 ($17,356 ÷ $15,000) and for Y it is 1.21 ($16,340 ÷ $13,500). Now Proposal Y is the preferred proposal.

In this manner all possible proposals can be evaluated and ranked according to their desirability. Presumably only those proposals having a profitability index greater than or equal to 1.00 will be eligible for adoption. Those with a lower index will not yield the desired minimum rate of return. That is, the present value of the expected cash benefits is less than the required initial cash outlay.

The Time-Adjusted Rate of Return Approach

The "time-adjusted rate of return method" is also called the "discounted rate-of-return method." The method involves finding a rate of return that will equate the future expected net cash inflows or benefits from an investment with the cost of the investment. If the rate of return equals or exceeds the minimum rate of return that management requires on investments (ideally, the cost of capital), then the investment would be acceptable for further consideration. Alternatively, if the rate of return is less than the minimum rate of return, the proposal is unacceptable.

Assume next that management is considering several competing proposals (only one of which can be accepted). The project with the highest rate of return should be accepted, assuming its rate of return is above that required by management and that there are no other reasons why it should not be selected.

The rate of return that equates future expected net cash inflows (after taxes) from an investment with the cost of the investment can be approximated with the aid of present value tables. To illustrate such an approximation, assume that a company is considering a $50,000 investment that is expected to last 25 years (with no salvage value). It is expected that the investment will yield $10,000 a year (after-tax effects) for the next 25 years.

The first step in determining the rate of return involves computing the payback period. In this instance, the payback period is five years ($50,000 investment ÷ $10,000 annual cash flow). Next, examine Table III on page 518 which presents the present value of $1 received annually for n years. Since the investment is expected to yield returns for 25 years, look at the 25 periods row in the table. Notice that the factor of 4.948 in that row is nearest to the payback period of 5 that was just computed.[2] The 4.948 figure involves an interest rate of 20 percent.

If the annual return of $10,000 is multiplied by the 4.948 factor the result is $49,480 which is just under the $50,000 cost of the asset. Con-

---

[2] Each figure (or factor) in Appendix Table III shows the ratio of the present value of a stream of net cash benefits to an investment of $1 made at the present time for various combinations of numbers of periods and discount rates.

sequently, it is possible to say that the actual rate of return is slightly less than 20 percent.

So far we only have examined a situation in which expected cash flows are level (the same amount each year). What happens when returns are not level? In such instances, a trial and error procedure is employed. The following example illustrates such a procedure:

Assume that a company is considering a $150,000 project that is expected to last four years and yield the following returns (ignoring scrap value):

At the End of	Net Cash Inflow
Year 1......................	$ 10,000
Year 2......................	20,000
Year 3......................	40,000
Year 4......................	130,000
Total....................	$200,000

The average annual net cash inflow is $50,000 ($200,000 ÷ 4). The payback period (based on average net cash inflow) can then be computed, which in this instance is 3 ($150,000 ÷ $50,000). Examining the table of present value of $1 received for 4 years (Table III on page 518) notice that 3.037 is the closest figure to the payback period in the 4 year row. But in this instance yields are not level. The returns are actually the greatest during the later years of the asset's life. Since the early returns have the largest present value, it is likely that the rate of return will be less than the 12 percent rate that corresponds to the annuity factor of 3.037. Consequently, we can try various interest rates that are less than 12 percent. It may take several attempts to arrive at the percentage which yields a present value which is the closest to the initial outlay of $150,000. By trial and error we find that the rate of return that we are attempting to find is actually slightly higher than 8 percent. The following computation reveals why this is true:

	Return	Present Value at 8%	Present Value of Net Cash Benefits
Year 1...............	$ 10,000	.926	$ 9,260
Year 2...............	20,000	.857	17,140
Year 3...............	40,000	.794	31,760
Year 4...............	130,000	.735	95,550
			$153,710

Since $153,710 is greater than $150,000, a discount rate of slightly more than 8 percent is needed to yield a present value for the net cash benefits of $150,000. If the returns had been greater during the earlier years of the asset's life, we would have looked for the correct rate of return among rates that were higher than 12 percent.

The last two methods described for project evaluation are theoretically superior to the payback method of project selection. (But they are also more difficult to apply.) If one could calculate precisely the cost of capital and use this as management's required rate of return, there would be no need to choose between these two methods. But in the real world it is difficult to calculate precisely the cost of capital.

Since there is some question as to the accuracy of the cost of capital percentage, some argue that the time-adjusted rate of return method is preferable to the net present value method. This is because under the time-adjusted rate of return method the cost of capital figure (management's required return, ideally) is only used as a *cutoff point* in determining which projects are acceptable for further consideration, while under the net present value method the cost of capital is used *in the calculation* of the present value of the benefit and, if wrong, can affect the *ranking* of the various projects (thus causing management to select projects which are really less profitable than other projects). For our purposes, we will treat both methods as being equally correct.

The Postaudit

A postaudit of all implemented capital projects should be conducted. Ideally, a disinterested party should perform this follow-up audit. Specifically, management is interested in finding out how the implemented project compared to its expectations.

The postaudit ideally should be performed early in the life of an implemented project. But enough time should have elapsed for all of the operational "bugs" to be ironed out. Actual operating costs should be determined. Management wants to know if estimated costs are accurate and if all costs were considered. In addition, actual net cash benefits should be compared to the estimated amounts. Any discrepancies in either costs or revenue estimates should be analyzed. This experience will help in analyzing future capital expenditure proposals.

The above discussion of the analyses and data needed in deciding among alternative courses of action regarding capital expenditures is obviously simplified and shortened. The topic is treated at length in more advanced finance and accounting texts. No mention has been made of a number of other factors which must be considered in making any capital expenditure decision. Some of these factors are the relative safety of various types of equipment and employee satisfaction and morale. These factors are obviously extremely difficult to quantify.

SUMMARY

Accurate and appropriate incremental analysis depends heavily upon knowledge of the behavior of costs relative to changes in volume. As a minimum, costs should be classified as variable or fixed for such analytical purposes.

The management of a company will often engage in a type of short-run analysis of its operations known as cost-volume-earnings analysis which will include the computation of the break-even point. The break-even point can be computed in a variety of ways and expressed in terms of dollars of sales revenue, units of product sold, or percentage of capacity and may be presented graphically in a break-even chart.

The elementary type of break-even analysis discussed and illustrated in this text presents a simplified picture of a business organization's operations that is most reliable when only one product is produced and sold. It is based upon the assumptions that (1) selling price remains constant as volume changes, (2) variable costs remain constant per unit as volume changes, (3) there is no change in the technical efficiency in operations, and (4) the company maintains a rather stable inventory level, that is, most production flows directly through to sales. These assumptions are assumed to be reasonable over a relevant range of production. Knowledge of the relationships between costs, volume, and earnings is valuable to management in making decisions regarding plant expansion, product pricing, promotional expenditure levels, and so forth.

The break-even point can be lowered by increasing the selling price, decreasing the total fixed costs, or decreasing the variable costs per unit. Taking opposite actions will increase the break-even point.

Of particular interest to management is the marginal contribution derived from the sale of a unit of product. This marginal contribution can be used to determine the break-even point and to determine the expected net earnings at any level of output. It can also be used in decisions regarding such matters as pricing, possible addition or deletion of product lines, and whether the serving of certain customers should be discontinued.

Incremental analysis is also used in make-or-buy decisions in which attention is centered only on those costs and revenues that will be different as a result of the alternative courses of action.

Informed capital expenditure decision making requires knowledge of the sunk and out-of-pocket costs in the alternatives faced. The decision to be made involves a comparison of the immediate out-of-pocket outlay which must be made in order to realize certain expected savings in out-of-pocket costs in the future. The decision on whether to replace an existing asset can be facilitated through computation of the proposed replacement's payback period. The payback period approach, however, suffers from a failure to consider the time period beyond the payback period and it also ignores the time value of money.

Alternative capital expenditure proposals having different cash flows for different periods of time can be readily compared through the determination of the present value of their cash flows and the computation of a profitability index. The proposal having the higher profitability index value is to be preferred.

The time-adjusted rate of return method involves finding a rate of return that will equate the future expected net cash benefits from an investment with the cost of the investment. If the time-adjusted rate equals or exceeds the minimum rate of return that management requires on investments then the investment is acceptable for further consideration. The time-adjusted rate can be approximated with the aid of present value tables.

QUESTIONS AND EXERCISES

1. What is meant by break-even point? What factors must be taken into consideration in determining it?
2. Why might a business wish to lower its break-even point? How would it go about lowering the break-even point? What effect would you expect the mechanization and automation of production processes to have upon the break-even point?
3. Compute the break-even point for a company in which fixed costs amount to $175,000 and variable costs are 65 percent of sales. Also prepare the cost-volume-earnings chart for the company.
4. Lane Company is currently producing and selling 20,000 units of a given product at $20 per unit. Its average cost of production and sale is $14. It is contemplating raising volume to 50,000 units at which level selling price would be reduced to $16. At this level average cost per unit will be $13. At which level should it seek to operate?
5. If a given company has fixed costs of $50,000 and variable costs of production of $6.75 per unit, how many units will have to be sold at a price of $9.25 each for the company to earn $25,000? Solve algebraically and graphically.
6. In the process of manufacturing gasoline, certain tars are produced which have only a nominal value. Further processing costs for the tars are incurred, and then the tars are sold. The average cost per pound is 6 cents, while sales are made at 5 cents. How would you determine whether this processing of the tars should be discontinued?
7. What relationship has relevant range to break-even analysis?
8. Why is break-even analysis considered appropriate only for short-run decisions?
9. A company is seeking an additional product to manufacture in presently idle space in a building which it owns. The company currently heats and maintains the entire building. One new product under consideration would require the addition of a number of new employees and some equipment. Indicate how you would proceed to reach a decision with regard to adding the product.

10. Suppose that the average fixed cost per unit of a given product is $2 and that the product is being sold at a price which covers only $0.80 of the fixed cost. Should the manufacture and sale of the product be discontinued? Why?

11. Why might an American manufacturer sell its product in South America for a price considerably under that which it receives in the United States?

12. You are the president of a small corporation and are currently purchasing a part needed in the product you manufacture and sell. You are considering manufacturing this part yourself. What factors should be taken into consideration in reaching your decision?

13. Give an example of an out-of-pocket cost and a sunk cost by describing a situation in which both are encountered.

14. A machine is currently being considered for purchase. The salesman attempting to sell the machine says that it will pay for itself in five years. What does he mean by this statement?

15. Project A has a payback period of four years, while Project B's payback period is only three years. Why can it be maintained that Project B is preferable? How might it be argued that insufficient information is available on which to base a decision regarding which is preferable?

16. Given the following information compute the payback period for the new machine if its cost is $40,000. (Ignore income taxes.)

	Old Machine	New Machine
Depreciation	$ 4,000	$ 2,000
Labor	10,000	9,000
Repairs	1,500	500
Other costs	1,100	600
	$16,600	$12,100

17. What is the profitability index and of what value is it?

18. Compute the profitability index for the following two proposals assuming a desired minimum return of 16 percent. (The present value of $1 at 16 percent due in one year is $0.862; in two years, $0.743; in three years, $0.641; and in four years, $0.552.)

	Proposal M	Proposal O
Initial outlay	$8,000	$12,600
Cash flow		
First year	5,000	6,000
Second Year	4,000	6,000
Third year	3,000	4,000
Fourth year	0	3,000

Which is the preferred proposal? Why?

19. The Welby Company is considering investing $100,000 in a new machine that is expected to last four years and yield $25,000, $50,000, $25,000, and $60,000 in years 1, 2, 3, and 4, respectively. Ignore income taxes and scrap value, calculate the time adjusted rate of return.

PROBLEMS

16–1. Two companies, West, Inc., and East Company, are competitors. West, Inc., has just installed the latest automated equipment so that its fixed costs are $600,000. East Company operates a run-down plant with only $300,000 of fixed costs.

Both companies have $1,000,000 in sales with earnings of 20 percent.

Required:

a. Compute earnings for the two companies assuming a 10 percent drop in sales. Show calculations in condensed earnings statement form.

b. In the situation described, which company can bid lower to re-gain lost sales? Why?

16–2. The productive capacity of the plant of the Jackson Corporation is 200,000 units, at which level of operations its variable costs amount to $320,000. When the plant is completely idle, fixed costs amount to $80,000. At 60 percent of capacity and below, its fixed costs are $136,000; and at levels above 60 percent of capacity, its fixed costs are $200,000.

Required:

a. Determine the company's break-even point, assuming that its product sells at $5 per unit. (Assume that in order to sell 200,000 units the price would have to be $5.)

b. Using only the data given, at what level of operations would it be more economical to close the factory than to operate? In other words, at what level will operating losses approximate the losses if the factory is completely closed down? Solve both algebraically and graphically.

c. Assume that when the Jackson Corporation is operating at 60 percent of capacity, a decision is made to reduce the selling price from $5 per unit to $4 per unit in order to increase its sales. At what percentage of capacity must the company operate in order to be profitable at the reduced sales price?

d. Assume that when the Jackson Corporation is operating at 60 percent of capacity, an order is received from the Overseas Sales Corporation for 80,000 units at $3 each. If its present market for 120,000 units would not be affected, should the order be accepted? Show computations in support of your answer.

16–3. *a.* The Foster Company sells its product at $10 per unit; the variable costs of producing and selling it amount to $6 per unit; fixed costs are $210,000 per year. Determine the company's break-even point in dollars of sales revenue.

  b. In 1979 the Morgan Company's sales were $750,000 and its variable costs amounted to $187,500. The company's break-even point is at a sales volume of $800,000. Determine the amount of its fixed costs. What were the net earnings for 1979?

  c. What would have been the net earnings of the Morgan Company, part (*b*) above, if the 1979 sales volume had been 10 percent higher but selling prices had remained unchanged?

  d. What would have been the net earnings of the Morgan Company, part (*b*) above, if 1979 variable costs had been 10 percent lower on a per-unit basis?

  e. What would have been the net earnings of the Morgan Company, part (*b*) above, if fixed costs in 1979 had been 10 percent lower?

  f. Determine the break-even point for the Morgan Company on the basis of the data given in (*d*) above; in (*e*) above.

16–4. Following are sales and other operating data for the three products made and sold by the Bentley Company:

	Total	Product A	Product B	Product C
Sales.................	$400,000	$200,000	$125,000	$75,000
Manufacturing costs				
Fixed...............	$ 60,000	$ 25,000	$ 12,500	$22,500
Variable............	250,000	120,000	100,000	30,000
Total.............	$310,000	$145,000	$112,500	$52,500
Gross margin..........	$ 90,000	$ 55,000	$ 12,500	$22,500
Selling expenses				
Fixed...............	$ 7,500	$ 2,500	$ 2,500	$ 2,500
Variable............	25,000	7,500	5,000	12,500
Administrative expenses				
Fixed...............	10,000	2,500	1,500	6,000
Variable............	10,000	5,000	1,500	3,500
Total.............	$ 52,500	$ 17,500	$ 10,500	$24,500
Operating Earnings..	$ 37,500	$ 37,500	$ 2,000	$(2,000)

In view of the operating loss shown above for Product C, the company's management is considering dropping that product. Assuming that the volume of sales now obtained from sale of Product C would be lost to the company if Product C were dropped and that all of the variable costs and $3,000 of the fixed costs are direct costs, would you recommend elimination of Product C? None of the fixed costs for Products A and B are direct costs. Give supporting computations.

16–5. Based upon the information given in problem 4, determine if it would be profitable to alter the product mix if (assume that total amount of fixed expenses will not change):

a. Dropping product C allows the company to produce and sell $75,000 more of product B at the existing selling price and variable cost per unit of product B.

b. Dropping product C allows the company to produce and sell $75,000 more of product A at existing prices.

c. What does this tell you about the company's current product mix? Show supporting contribution margins.

16–6. The Bhada Company owns five identical machines which it uses in its manufacturing operations, each of which cost $10,000 two years ago and has an estimated life of five years and no salvage value. A new type of machine has become available, each of which has the same productive capacity as the five machines the company now owns; and the company is considering purchase of one of the new machines to replace its five old machines. The new machine, if purchased, will cost $54,000, is estimated to last three years, and will have a salvage value at the end of that time of $6,000. A trade-in allowance of $2,000 is available for each of the old machines. The new machine is capable of producing 100,000 units annually.

Following is a comparison of operating costs per unit:

	Five Old Machines	New Machine
Repairs.....................................	$0.151	$0.019
Depreciation.............................	0.100	0.160
Power.......................................	0.042	0.023
Other operating costs......................	0.036	0.011
Operating cost per unit....................	$0.329	$0.213

Required: Use the payback method for parts (a) and (b).

a. Do you recommend replacement of the old machines? Support your answer with computations, disregarding all other factors except those reflected in the data given above.

b. If the old machines were already fully depreciated, would your answer be different? Why?

c. Assume (for the sake of simplicity) that cash flows for operating costs fall at the end of each year and that 16 percent is an appropriate rate for discounting purposes. Using the discounted cash flow approach, present a schedule showing whether the new machine should be acquired.

16–7. Dressel Company is evaluating three alternative investments, each of which has a cost of $5,000 and from which the following cash flows are expected:

	Periods		
Investment	*1*	*2*	*3*
A.........................	$7,500		
B.........................	3,810	$3,810	
C.........................	2,700	2,700	$2,700

Required:

a. Compute the present value of each of the above investments using a 6 percent rate and rank them from highest to lowest.

b. Repeat part (*a*) using a 16 percent rate.

c. If the order of ranking changes between (*a*) and (*b*), explain why.

16–8. a. Slocum Corporation is now operating at capacity and reports sales of $300,000, variable costs of $180,000, fixed costs of $50,000, and net earnings of $70,000. If the company invests $300,000 in additional machinery and equipment with a useful life of 10 years, it is estimated that sales can be increased by $100,000. Should the company make the additional investment in plant facilities? Show computations to support your answer.

b. Operating data of the Guy Corporation are as follows: sales, $900,000; fixed costs, $160,000; variable costs, $450,000; and net earnings $290,000. A proposed addition to the company's plant is estimated by the sales manager to increase sales by a maximum of $600,000. The company's cost accountant states that the proposed addition will increase the company's fixed costs by $320,000 per year. Do you recommend that the proposed expansion be undertaken? Support your answer with computations.

16–9. The Buchanan Delivery Company is considering replacement of 10 of its delivery vans which originally cost $7,500 each and on each of which $4,500 of depreciation has been accumulated. They were originally estimated to have service lives of 10 years and no salvage value, and each travels an average of 50,000 miles per year. The 10 new vans, if purchased, will cost $8,000 each, will be driven 50,000 miles each per year, and will have no salvage value at the end of their four-year estimated useful life. A trade-in allowance of $500 is available for each of the old trucks.

Following is a comparison of costs of operations:

	Old Vans	*New Vans*
Fuel, lubricants, etc.......................	$0.081	$0.059
Tires..................................	0.015	0.015
Repairs................................	0.063	0.048
Depreciation............................	0.015	0.040
Other operating costs (variable)............	0.032	0.029
Operating cost per mile...................	$0.206	$0.191

Required:

a. Do you recommend replacement of the old vans? Support your answer with computations, and disregard all factors not related to the cost data given above.
b. If the old vans were already fully depreciated, would your answer be different? Why?
c. Assume (for simplicity) that all cash flows for operating costs fall at the end of each year and that 18 percent is an appropriate rate for discounting purposes. Using the discounted cash flow approach, present a schedule showing whether new vans should be acquired.

16–10. The Natho Company is considering three different investments. Listed below are some data related to these investments.

Investment	Initial Outlay	Expected Net Cash Inflow Per Year	Expected Life of Proposal
1	$50,000	$20,000	3 years
2	60,000	10,000	15 years
3	80,000	8,000	40 years

Management requires a minimum return on investments of 10 percent.

Required: Rank these three proposals using the following selection techniques. (Ignore income taxes and scrap value.)

a. Payback method.
b. Discounted cash flow and profitability index.
c. Time-adjusted rate of return.

chapter 17

Responsibility Accounting —For Evaluation of Managers

INTRODUCTION TO RESPONSIBILITY ACCOUNTING

A responsibility accounting system seeks to provide information to evaluate each manager on the revenue and expense items over which he or she has primary *control* (the authority to influence). Each accounting report contains only (or at least clearly segregates) those items which are controllable by the responsible manager. This is the fundamental principle of responsibility accounting. It should be clear from this description that the business entity must be well-organized so that responsibility is assignable to individual managers. Clear lines of authority and responsibility must exist throughout the organization. The various managers of the company, their responsibility level, and the lines of authority existing within an entity should be as clearly defined as shown in the organization chart in Illustration 17.1. If clear areas of authority cannot be determined, it is very doubtful that responsibility accounting can be implemented. Lines of authority should follow a specified path. For example, a plant supervisor may report to a plant manager, who reports to a vice president of manufacturing, who is responsible to the president. The president is ultimately responsible to the stockholders or their elected representatives, the board of directors. In a sense, the president is responsible for all revenue and expense items of the firm since at the presidential level all items are fully controllable. But the president must usually delegate authority to various managers since it is impossible to keep fully informed about the day-to-day operating details of each of the segments.

ILLUSTRATION 17.1

**Illustration of a Corporate Functional Organization Chart
Including Four Levels of Management**

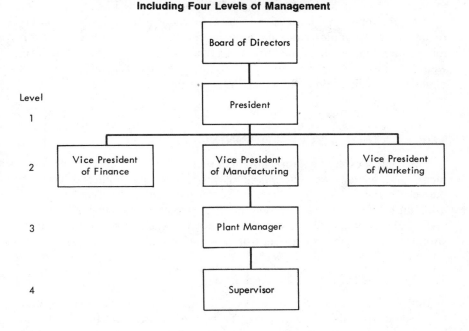

Reference is often made to levels of management. The president is usually considered the first-level manager. All the managers who report directly to the president are second-level managers. Notice on the organizational chart (in Illustration 17.1) the individuals within a given level are on a horizontal line across the chart. But it is not to be assumed that all managers within a certain level have equal authority and responsibilty. The relative authority of managers in a given position will vary from firm to firm.

While the president may delegate much decision-making power, there are some revenue and expense items that may be exclusively under the president's control. For example, large capital (plant and equipment) expenditures may be approved only by the president. Hence, depreciation, property taxes, and other related expenses should not be designated as the plant manager's responsibility since these costs are not primarily under the plant manager's control. The controllability criterion is crucial to the content of the reports for each manager. For example, at the supervisor level, perhaps only direct materials and direct labor are appropriate for the task of measuring performance. But at the plant manager level many other costs, not controllable at a lower level, are controllable and therefore included in the performance evaluation of the plant manager. As reports are addressed to higher management levels, more and more items will be considered controllable. (At this point it would be useful to you to turn to pages 429, 430, and 431 and study Illustrations 17.4, 17.5, and 17.6 to see how the reports prepared for different levels of responsibility are inter-related.) For example, if raw material purchasing is a centralized function for all the plants, then the vice president in charge of manufacturing would be held responsible for this activity. The managers of the various plants will not be evaluated for purchasing results since they have no voice in purchasing decisions.

THE CONTROL CYCLE—PLANNING

The control cycle is comprehensive in that it includes planning, measurement, and evaluation. The *planning process* is accomplished through budgeting; the *measurement process* is the mechanism for feedback; and *evaluation* is the means for determining (from measurements reported versus plans) what action to take. These three elements together constitute the control cycle—for control or accomplishment of results.

The Budget—Planning for Future Earnings

Budgeting is essentially the act of charting a course which will satisfy the goals of the business enterprise. To be most effective, a budget should be assembled from the various segments (or identifiable units) of the entity. These segments may be departments, divisions, service centers, or product lines. A budget dictated from top management and then divided into segmental budgets is rarely as successful because it usually is not accepted willingly by those upon whom it is imposed.

All levels of management from the president to the production supervisor usually should participate in the formulation of a budget in order to increase the chances that it will be accepted by them. Typically, but not always, a master budget for the entire entity is formulated by assembling the component budgets submitted from the segmental level. These segmental budgets are reviewed by higher level managers before they are submitted to a central planning committee. This committee combines the various segmental budgets into a master budget which reflects the plan of the company as a whole. The goals and objectives of the firm must be clear and explicit to all levels of management. In addition, goals and objectives of the *segments* within the firm must be balanced and integrated so that the goals and objectives of the *firm* can be met. Earnings maximization from the viewpoint of each segment may not lead to total company earnings maximization. For instance, segment A may decide to buy units from outside the company at a cost of $10 per unit instead of acquiring them from segment B at an internal "transfer" price of $12 per unit. If segment

B's variable cost of producing a unit is less than $10 per unit, the company as a whole is worse off from segment A's buying from the outside. (Transfer prices are explained in more detail later in the chapter.)

A master budget (earnings plan) by itself cannot be implemented directly in most companies. In order to make the master budget operational, planned future earnings must be broken down into the various segmental revenues and expenses. Segment A, for instance, may have a goal of $2,000,000 gross margin for 1979, with controllable operating costs not to exceed $500,000. The segmental budgets enable the individual managers to see the plan for their segment. The segmental budget must be sufficiently detailed so that the personnel of the various segments of the firm will know exactly what are the segmental goals. In final form, the master budget will plot the company's future course as a plan to achieve desired earnings. These earnings will, of course, be for the total entity. (Budgeting is discussed in much more detail in Chapter 18.)

THE CONTROL CYCLE—MEASUREMENT AND EVALUATION

After a plan has been developed, it is necessary to compare actual results with the plan periodically. As pointed out earlier, the manager must be able to exercise primary control over an item before being held responsible for it. Unfortunately, controllability is rarely absolute. Quite frequently, some factors which change the amount of a budgeted item are beyond the control of a manager. For example, the imposition of a 10 percent excise tax by a governmental authority may decrease the sales of certain items in a particular segment. Even though the manager is given authority to control the sales revenue, in this case external factors beyond the manager's control have altered the actual results. Internal factors may also be present. For example, raw material usage may be excessive because, in an effort to save money, the purchasing department bought low-quality materials. Most revenue or expense items have some elements of noncontrollability in them. In an ideal sense, managerial control means that the manager can make decisions which will change the *quantity* or the *price* of a revenue or an expense item. The theoretical requirement that a manager have absolute control over items for which he or she is held responsible often must be compromised. The manager is usually responsible for items where *relative* control is present. Relative control means that the manager has the *predominant* control over most of the factors which influence a given budget item. The use of relative control may lead to some motivational problems, since the manager is evaluated on results that may not reflect that manager's efforts. Nevertheless, most budget plans assign control on a relative control basis in order to develop and use segmental budgets.

As a practical matter, the psychological appeal of measuring results in terms of earnings has led many companies to plan on the basis of *segmental earnings* and not *controllability*. This approach increases the burden on top management in evaluating results. Care must be taken not to censure a manager when results deviate from the planned earnings program because of noncontrollable factors. The division of revenue and expense items into controllable and noncontrollable components at a particular management level is not clear-cut in many cases. Under some circumstances, a specific item may be controllable by a manager while in others it may not be. The problem of indirect expense allocation in computing segmental earnings is particularly troublesome since allocated expenses are almost never subject to control by the segment manager. Although ideally they should be based on benefit or cause, this often is not possible and such allocations tend to be quite arbitrary.

RESPONSIBILITY CENTERS—EXPENSE (OR COST) CENTERS

Various references have been made to the *segments* of a business enterprise. Examples of segments are divisions, departments, product lines, and service centers. The organization of appropriate business segments is crucial to successful budgeting. The segments of a business enterprise must be defined according to function or product line. For example, companies have traditionally been organized along functional lines. The segments or departments performed a specified function (e.g., marketing, finance, purchasing, production, shipping). Recently, large firms have tended to organize segments according to product line (e.g., the electrical products division, the shoe department, the food division). These segments are to a degree autonomous, self-contained units, each with the various functional units contained within itself. The accounting system must be structured to gather information for each segment. There are three possible reporting bases for evaluating business segments: the expense (or cost) center, the earnings (or profit) center, and the investment center. The characteristics of a specific segment will limit the selection of an appropriate reporting basis.

Managers of expense centers are held responsible only for specified expense items. The distinguishing feature of expense centers is that they produce no direct revenue from the sale of goods or services. Examples of expense centers are service centers (e.g., the maintenance department, computer section, and the accounting department) or intermediate production facilities which produce parts for assembly into a finished product. Although the concept of an expense center appears simple, implementation is difficult.

Because accounting records are often maintained for earnings determination purposes rather than for responsibility purposes, costs of these centers are often categorized as *direct* and *indirect* rather than as *controllable* and *noncontrollable*. In understanding the meaning of the terms, direct costs and indirect costs, one must always keep in mind the frame of reference.

As stated previously, if a cost can be directly traced to a unit under consideration (division, department, product line, or service center), it is a direct cost *with respect to* that unit and would be eliminated if the unit ceased to exist. An indirect cost is one that cannot clearly be identified with the unit under consideration. Therefore it only becomes a part of its total costs *through allocation*. Such allocations can sometimes be made on a very logical and supportable basis (such as benefit received). But at other times they can only be made on a very arbitrary basis such as floor space, volume of sales, and so on.

Thus, whether a particular cost is direct or indirect depends on the unit under consideration. The cost of supplies may be a direct cost of a particular department, but may not be a direct cost of any of the products produced. Similarly, the depreciation of the factory building would be a direct cost of the manufacturing division, but would be an indirect cost of any department or service center within the building or of any product line manufactured in the building.

Now, how do these terms relate to the concept of controllability that is necessary to responsibility accounting? Since *direct* costs are clearly identified with the unit under consideration, there is a *tendency* for these items also to be controllable by the manager of that unit. And, since indirect costs become costs of a unit only through allocation, there is a *tendency* for these items to be noncontrollable by the manager of the unit under consideration. They are controllable at some higher level, as is true for all costs. But care must be taken not to equate direct, variable, and controllable costs. A cost such as the salary of the supervisor of a unit may be direct, fixed, and noncontrollable at the supervisor's level. The salary of the janitor in that unit may be direct, fixed, and controllable at the supervisor's level. But many costs are direct, variable, and controllable in a given unit within an organization.

The appropriate goal of an expense center is not necessarily the short-run minimization of expense for any given level of output, but rather the long-run minimization of expense. The time period examined must also be specified. For example, a product foreman could eliminate maintenance costs during a short period of time. This would cause total short-term costs to be lower. But in the long run, costs might be higher due to more frequent machine breakdowns.

Since earnings are not measured for an expense center, there is no reason to include *noncontrollable* costs which are not relevant in measuring the expense control performance of its manager. For example, depreciation (if computed on a time basis) need not be included in the expense report for the department manager since this particular item is not controllable at that level and the manager consequently should not be held accountable for it.

RESPONSIBILITY CENTERS—EARNINGS CENTERS

Because managers are motivated by basing rewards upon earnings, the calculation of segmental earnings has considerable appeal. Accordingly, in an increasing number of firms, the segments are organized as earnings centers (having both revenues and expenses). Since the master budget for the firm culminates in a projection of expected earnings, it is convenient to identify portions of these earnings with their sources in various segments or divisions. Since segmental earnings are usually defined as segmental revenue minus related expenses, the manager must be able to *control* both of these categories. That is, the manager must have the authority to attempt to control selling price, sales volume, and all of the reported expense items. The manager's authority over all of these measured items is essential to proper performance evaluation. All of the potential problems noted in regard to expense centers, of course, apply as well to earnings centers.

Earnings center organization may be appropriate when the firm is quite large with several autonomous divisions. Being autonomous, each division would have its own manufacturing, marketing, purchasing, personnel, and other functional segments usually found in a self-sufficient business. See Illustration 17.2 for an example of an organizational chart of a company organized along product lines. Notice that even in these larger firms some functional areas such as finance or research and development

ILLUSTRATION 17.2
Organization Chart of Corporation Organized along Product Lines

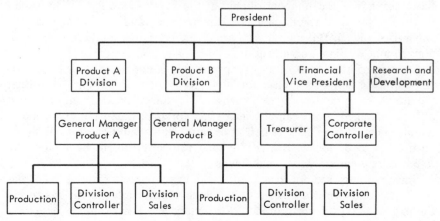

ILLUSTRATION 17.3

Organization Chart of Corporation Functionally Organized

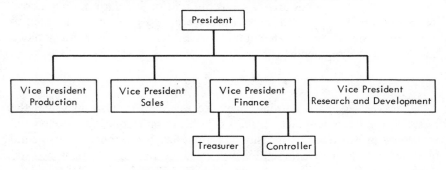

remain centralized at the company level. The allocation of these central corporate expenses to individual earnings centers is often illogically justified as necessary for calculating segmental earnings. Evaluating a segment manager's performance is complicated by these allocations since they are beyond the manager's control. Because of the inherent duplication of functional areas most small- and medium-sized firms cannot be efficiently organized according to product lines. The earnings center concept, accordingly, is inappropriate for these smaller companies. See Illustration 17.3 for an example of the organization chart of a company functionally organized.

Transfer Prices

When a division or segment does not sell its output to outside parties but only to other segments, it is necessary to establish a *transfer price* which must be "paid" by the other segment so that the producing segment can have a measured "revenue." This enables the producing segment to become an earnings center rather than an expense center.

In effect, the transfer price is recorded as revenue of one segment and cost of the other segment. No cash charges hands and the accounting entry on the corporate books resembles an internal adjustment. For example, a segment that manufactures a specialized part used in the assembly of a finished product may have no outside market for that part. A transfer price such as $20 per unit must be charged to the assembly segment in order to measure segmental revenue for the segment manufacturing the part. It is essential that the segment manager have some degree of control over the transfer price. If the manager does not have any control over transfer price and output volume the use of a profit measure may be undesirable for motivational purposes. Ideally, a transfer price would represent the cost of the part or service if purchased from an outside party. But this market "price" is often not available. In this case, the transfer price is sometimes determined on some cost basis. Examples of cost-based transfer prices are standard full cost or standard marginal cost. These costs may or may not have a predetermined profit margin added to compute the transfer price. In still other cases transfer prices are negotiated between the two segments.

Suboptimization

Whenever segmental earnings are used as a performance measure, the effect on total company net earnings of attempting to maximize individual segmental profits must be measured. Emphasizing divisional or segmental earnings may lead to competition among units to the detriment of total company earnings. This is called suboptimization. For instance, the manager of a segment may attempt to reduce costs of the division in a way that results in a reduction in the quality of output or services provided to other units in the organization. This may cause inefficiencies and increasing costs in these other units and reduce company profits.

This situation can be resolved in most instances by making segmental goals congruent with (or in agreement with) company goals. Efforts should be made to avoid "rewarding" segments for actions which can be detrimental to overall company performance.

RESPONSIBILITY CENTERS—INVESTMENT CENTERS

Closely related to the earnings center concept is the concept of an investment center. Each segment is considered an investment center which is evaluated on the basis of the rate of return that it can earn on a specified investment base. Rate of return is computed by dividing segmental earnings by the appropriate investment base. For example, a segment that earns $100,000 on an investment base of $1,000,000 is said to have a rate of return on investment of 10 percent. Of course, all of the problems inherent in the expense center and the earnings center concepts are present in the investment center concept. In addition to these problems, there is a question as to the appropriate investment base that should be utilized in calculating return on investment.

The logic for using investment centers as bases for performance evaluation is that segments with larger resources should produce more earnings than segments with smaller amounts of resources. By calculating rates of return for performance evaluation, the relative effectiveness of a segment is measured. Thus, the segment with the highest percentage return is presumably the most effective in utilizing its resources. When the absolute amount of earnings is used to measure performance, larger segments will have a distinct advantage over smaller segments.

Normally the list of assets available to the segment make up the base;

there are differences of opinion among accountants as to whether (1) depreciated assets should be shown at cost or after deducting accumulated depreciation, (2) leased facilities should be included in the investment base, and (3) how the list of assets should be valued.

After the appropriate investment base is selected and valued to the satisfaction of the manager, problems can remain since most segment managers have limited control over certain items. For instance, capital expenditure decisions are often made by the top-level management of the company. Another problem area may exist if the firm has a centralized credit and collection segment. The manager may have little control over the amount of accounts receivable shown as segment assets. It is usually argued that all segments are treated the same and that the inclusion of noncontrollable items in the investment base is therefore appropriate. But it is important that the segment managers agree to this proposition in order to avoid adverse reactions.

RESPONSIBILITY REPORTS

A unique feature of a responsibility accounting system is the amount of detail in the various reports issued to the different levels of management. For example, a performance report to a particular supervisor would include the dollar amounts, actual and budgeted, of all the revenue and expense items under that supervisor's control. But the report issued to the plant manager would show only the totals from all the supervisors' reports and any additional items subject to the plant manager's control, such as the plant administrative expense. The report to the vice president of manufacturing would contain only the totals of all the plants. Because a responsibility accounting system selectively condenses data, the report to the president does not consist of stapling together all the plant supervisor reports. Only the summary totals of the subordinate levels are reported (see Illustration 17.6 on page 431). This lack of detail which seems a hindrance to performance analysis actually results in the practice of "management by exception." Since modern business enterprises are becoming increasingly complex, it has become necessary to filter and condense accounting data so that they may be analyzed quickly. Most executives do not have the time to study detailed accounting reports searching for problem areas. Reporting only summary totals highlights those areas that need attention, so that the executive can make more efficient use of available time.

The reports issued under the responsibility accounting system are interrelated since the totals from one level are carried forward in the report to the next higher management level. The control reports submitted to the president include all revenue and expense items (in summary form) since the president is responsible for controlling the profitability of the entire firm.

The condensation which occurs at successive levels of management is justified on the basis that the appropriate manager will take the necessary corrective action. Hence, performance details need not be reported except to the particular manager. The manager should be able to describe to the immediate supervisor action that was taken to correct an undesirable situation. For example, if direct labor cost has been excessively high in a particular department, the supervisor should seek to correct the cause of this variance. The plant manager, upon noticing the unfavorable total budget variance of the department, will investigate. The supervisor should be able to respond that the appropriate corrective action was taken. Hence, it is not necessary to report to the vice president of manufacturing that a particular department within one of the plants is not operating satisfactorily, since the plant manager has already attended to the matter. If the plant as a whole under a plant manager has been performing poorly, then the summary totals which have been reported to the vice president of manufacturing will disclose this situation and an investigation of the plant manager's problems might be indicated.

Noncontrollable Items

In preparing responsibility accounting reports, there are two basic ways of handling revenue or expense items which are noncontrollable at the manager's level. First, they may be omitted entirely from the reports. At the management level at which these items become controllable they are then included in that report. As a result each level of reports contains only those items which are controllable at that level. But there is some appeal in including all revenue and expense items which can be traced directly or allocated indirectly to a particular manager. This method represents a full-costing approach. Care must be taken to separate controllable from noncontrollable items in such reports.

Timeliness of Reports

In order for accounting reports to be of maximum benefit they must be timely. That is, reports should be prepared as soon as possible after the end of the performance measurement period. Timely reports allow prompt corrective action to be taken. Reports that are excessively delayed lose their effectiveness as control devices. For example, a report on the previous month's operations that is not received until the end of the current month is virtually useless for analyzing poor performance areas and taking corrective action. Reports should be issued regularly. Regular reports are desirable since trends can be spotted. The appropriate management action can be initiated before major problems occur. Regularity is also important so that the managers will rely on the reports and become familiar with their contents.

Simplicity of Reports

Reports should be relatively simple. Care should be taken to avoid using confusing terminology. Particularly at lower levels of management, aggregate dollar amounts may not be sufficient. Results should also be expressed in physical units when appropriate. The budgeted standard should be reported as well as actual results. Often a year-to-date analysis is included in addition to the current period so that the manager can see performance to date. The inclusion of budget variances is desirable so that relative performance can be ascertained. By carefully analyzing budget variances the significant deviations from the budgeted plan are highlighted. Variance analysis allows management to spot problem areas quickly. The use of variances is helpful in applying the management-by-exception principle.

RESPONSIBILITY REPORTS—ILLUSTRATION

The following illustrations are designed to show how responsibility accounting reports in an organization are interrelated.

Assume an organization with four management levels of which the president, vice president (manufacturing), plant manager, and supervisor are representative (see Illustration 17.4). The fourth level is considered

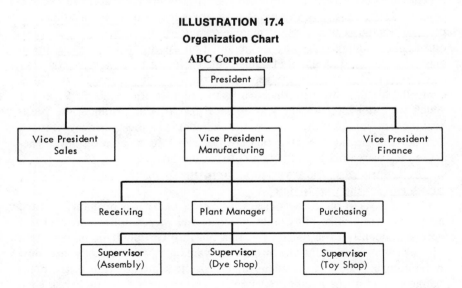

ILLUSTRATION 17.4

Organization Chart

ABC Corporation

ILLUSTRATION 17.5

Responsibility Reports

ABC Corporation

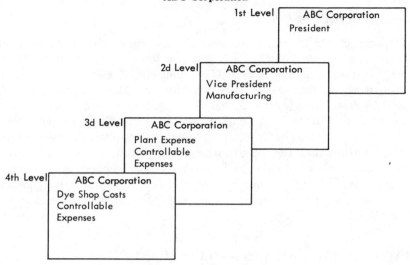

to be the supervisor and so on up to the first level, the president (as shown in Illustration 17.5).

The reports shown in Illustration 17.6 contain only controllable expenses. Notice that only the totals from the supervisor's responsibility report are included in the plant manager's report. In turn, only the totals on the plant manager's report are included on the report for the vice president, and so on. The detailed data from the lower level reports are summarized and carried onto the report for the next higher level. Also, new controllable costs are introduced into the reports for levels 3, 2, and 1 which were not included on a lower level report. For instance, the president's office expense, included as the first item on the president's report, and the vice-president's salaries were not reported at a lower level (because they were not controllable at a lower level).

The reports also show variation from the budgeted amounts for the month and for the year to date.

On the basis of the reports (see Illustration 17.6) it is probable that the supervisor would take immediate action to see why supplies and overtime were significantly over the budget this month. The plant manager might ask the supervisor what the problems were and whether they are now under control. The vice president might ask the same question of the plant manager (and of the head of receiving). And the president might ask each of the vice presidents why the budget was exceeded this month.

ILLUSTRATION 17.6
Responsibility Report

4th level ABC Corporation
Supervisor
Dye Shop

	Amount		Over or (Under) Budget	
Controllable Expenses	This Month	Year to Date	This Month	Year to Date
Repairs and maintenance.........	$ 200	$ 1,000	$ 10	$ 40
Supplies.......................	180	850	80	95
Tools.........................	100	300	(10)	81
Overtime......................	200	450	80	14
Total (Include in report for next higher level).......	$ 680	$ 2,600	$ 160	$ 230

3rd level ABC Corporation
Plant Manager

	Amount		Over or (Under) Budget	
Controllable Expenses	This Month	Year to Date	This Month	Year to Date
Plant manager's office expense.....	$ 800	$ 9,100	$ (50)	$ (100)
Dye shop costs.................	680	2,600	160	230
Toy shop costs.................	1,000	5,000	80	130
Assembly......................	400	1,300	60	240
Salaries of supervisors...........	5,000	25,000	–0–	–0–
Total (Include in report for next higher level).......	$ 7,880	$ 43,000	$ 250	$ 500

2nd level ABC Corporation
Vice President: Manufacturing

	Amount		Over or (Under) Budget	
Controllable Expenses	This Month	Year to Date	This Month	Year to Date
Vice President's office expense.....	$ 2,840	$ 9,500	$ (50)	$ (800)
Plant departmental costs..........	7,880	43,000	250	500
Purchasing.....................	380	2,500	100	200
Receiving......................	700	3,000	300	900
Salaries of plant manager and heads of purchasing and receiving......................	7,000	35,000	–0–	–0–
Total (Include in report for next higher level).......	$18,800	$ 93,000	$ 600	$ 800

1st level ABC Corporation
President

	Amount		Over or (Under) Budget	
Controllable Expenses	This Month	Year to Date	This Month	Year to Date
President's office expense.........	$ 1,000	$ 5,000	$ 100	$ 200
Vice President: Manufacturing....	18,800	93,000	600	800
Vice President: Sales.............	8,700	19,000	400	800
Vice President: Finance..........	4,000	15,000	800	900
Vice Presidents' salaries..........	9,000	45,000	–0–	–0–
Total....................	$41,500	$177,000	$1,900	$2,700

SUMMARY

The attributes of reports issued under a responsibility accounting system can be summarized as follows. The detail of each report is appropriate to the level of management to which it is addressed. The detail will decrease at higher levels of management since corrective action should have been taken at the immediate supervisor level. Reports are interrelated since summary totals, both actual and standard, are carried forward to the next higher level report. The report to the president will compare actual results to the master budget. All items of expense and revenue will be summarized in the president's budget report since the president is responsible for the profitability of the firm.

It is essential to separate controllable and noncontrollable items under a full-cost approach. Reports must be timely to enhance usefulness. That is, they must be prompt and issued on a regular basis. Since all levels of management use the accounting reports, they must be easy to understand. Reports using confusing accounting terminology are not understandable by lower level managers. In order to aid understandability, reports should also use both dollar amounts and physical units when possible.

Both standard and actual results for the evaluation period must be included. It is a desirable practice to include both the results of the current period and the year-to-date results so that the manager can monitor performance to date and make decisions to improve future results. Responsibility accounting reports should allow the *causes* of variances to be analyzed. But every level of report need not contain complete details. The immediate supervisor should take the necessary corrective action. Only those areas which show poor performance should be investigated.

QUESTIONS AND EXERCISES

1. What is the fundamental principle of responsibility accounting?
2. Why can expense allocation be a problem in computing segmental earnings?
3. Describe a segment of a business enterprise that is best treated as an expense center. List four indirect expenses that may be allocated to such an expense center.
4. What type of organization is most appropriate to an earnings center organization?
5. What is a transfer price? List three possible transfer prices that can be used.
6. What is the logic of using an investment center as a basis for performance evaluation?
7. List five important factors that should be considered in designing reports for a responsibility accounting system.

8. Baxter Co. manufactures refrigerators. Below are listed several costs that occur in a shop. Indicate whether or not the shop foreman can control each of the listed items.
   a. Depreciation
   b. Repairs
   c. Small tools
   d. Supplies
   e. Bond interest

9. Compare and contrast an expense and an investment center.

10. Define control. Indicate some of the practical problems of implementing the concept of control.

PROBLEMS

17–1. a. The Dexter Company manufactures swim suits. The company's business is seasonal so that between August and December usually 10 skilled manufacturing employees are "laid off." In order to improve morale the financial vice president suggests that these 10 employees not be laid off in the future. Instead it is suggested that they work in general labor from August to December but still be paid their manufacturing wages of $6 per hour. General labor personnel earn $3 per hour.

Required: What are the implications of this plan to the assignment of costs to the various segments of the business?

   b. The Lange Company builds new homes. Mr. Jones is in charge of the construction department. Among other things he hires and supervises the carpenters and other workmen who build the homes. The Lange Company does not do its own foundation work. The construction of the foundations is done by subcontractors hired by Mr. Smith of the procurement department.

   The Lange Company is about to start the development of a 300 home community. Mr. Smith hires the Weak Company to build the foundations on the homes. On the day construction is to begin, the Weak Company goes out of business. Consequently, construction is delayed six weeks while Mr. Smith hires a new subcontractor.

Required: Which department should be charged with the cost of the delay in construction? Why?

17–2. The Nance Corporation has three product plants (X, Y, and Z). These plants are treated as responsibility centers. The following summarizes the results for the month of March 1979:

Plant	Revenue	Expenses	Investment Base (gross assets)
X	$1,000,000	$ 500,000	$10,000,000
Y	2,000,000	800,000	15,000,000
Z	3,000,000	1,100,000	32,000,000

Required:

a. If the plants are treated as earnings centers, which plant manager appears to have done the best job?

b. If the plants are treated as investment centers, which plant manager appears to have done the best job? (Assume that plant managers are evaluated in terms of rate of return on gross assets.)

c. Do the results of earnings center analysis and investment center analysis give different findings? If so, why?

17–3. You are given the following information relevant to the Monroe Company for the year ended December 31, 1979.

Controllable Expenses	Plant Manager Budget	Plant Manager Actual	Vice President of Manufacturing Budget	Vice President of Manufacturing Actual	President Budget	President Actual
Office Expense............	$3,000	$4,000	$ 5,000	$ 7,000	$10,000	$ 7,000
Printing Shop............	2,000	2,000				
Iron Shop................	1,000	900				
Toaster Shop.............	8,000	7,000				
Purchasing...............			10,000	11,000		
Receiving................			5,000	6,000		
Inspection...............			8,000	7,000		
Sales Manager...........					80,000	70,000
Controller...............					60,000	50,000
Treasurer................					40,000	30,000
Personnel Manager.......					20,000	30,000

Note: The company is functionally organized.

Required: Prepare the responsibility accounting reports for three levels of management—plant manager, vice president of manufacturing, and president.

17–4. John Calachi is supervisor of department 29 of the Farrow Company. The annual budget for the department is as follows:

	Annual Budget for Department 29
Small tools...............................	$ 9,000
Set up....................................	10,000
Direct labor..............................	11,000
Direct materials..........................	20,000
Supplies..................................	5,000
Supervision...............................	30,000
Property taxes............................	5,000
Property insurance........................	1,000
Depreciation: machinery...................	2,000
Depreciation: building....................	2,000
Total..................................	$95,000

Required: Identify the budget items that are controllable by Mr. Calachi. Mr. Calachi's salary of $20,000 is included in supervision. The remaining $10,000 in supervision is the salary of the assistant supervisor who is directly responsible to Mr. Calachi.

17–5.   The Trace Corporation is organized by product divisions. The following data are for the Hand Tool Division which manufactures and sells hand tools.

	Data for year ended *Dec. 31, 1979*
Sales...	$10,000,000
Variable costs of the division.......................	4,000,000
Fixed costs which are traceable directly to the Hand Tool Division	
Controllable...............................	1,000,000
Noncontrollable.............................	2,000,000
The following costs have been allocated to the division by corporate headquarters:	
Interest expense.............................	400,000
Executive office overhead.....................	600,000

Required:

a.   Compute the net earnings for the year.
b.   Compute controllable net earnings for the year.

17–6.   You are given the following information relating to Mitchell Company for the year ended December 31, 1979. The company is organized according to functions.

Controllable *Expenses*	Shop "A" Supervisor		Plant Manager		Vice President of Manufacturing		President	
	Budget	*Actual*	*Budget*	*Actual*	*Budget*	*Actual*	*Budget*	*Actual*
Office Expense......	$2,000	$1,000	$ 4,000	$ 4,000	$ 7,000	$ 6,000	9,000	8,500
Supervision.........	3,000	4,000						
Supplies (manufacturing)...	4,000	4,000						
Tools..............	5,000	7,000						
Shop "B"...........			10,000	10,000				
Shop "C"..........			9,000	12,000				
Purchasing.........					14,000	17,000		
Receiving..........					15,000	15,000		
Inspection.........					16,000	8,000		
Sales Manager......							60,000	64,000
Controller.........							50,000	47,000
Treasurer..........							30,000	32,000
Personnel Manager...							70,000	65,000

Required: Prepare the responsibility accounting reports for the four levels of management—supervisor, plant manager, vice-president of manufacturing, and president. Discuss the results, indicating where you think these individuals might focus their attention as a result of the responsibility reports.

chapter 18

Budgeting—For Planning and Control

THE BUDGET

Time and money are scarce resources to all individuals and organizations. Effective utilization of either requires planning. But planning alone is insufficient. Control must also be exercised to see that the plan, if feasible, is actually carried out. A tool widely used to motivate members of the organization to plan and control the use of scarce resources is a budget. A budget is simply a plan of action for a given period of time. It may be a formal written document; it may exist in the mind of one person. For example, an individual may decide to spend $3.50 and two hours of time to see a given movie on a given night.

Uses for Budgets

In business, a budget is simply a plan showing how management intends to acquire and use resources and how it intends to control the acquisition and use of resources in a coming time period. It shows how an organization intends to achieve a given objective. Yet it is actually more than that. It is a device which enables an organization to evaluate the expected results of a given period's activities before they take place. For example, the planned activities of a period will yield an expected amount of earnings or loss. The amount may be completely unsatisfactory causing the organization to make wholesale revisions in plans. Thus the organizational unit exercises control over its own future.

Budgets should also be used to motivate individuals, encouraging them to strive vigorously to achieve stated goals. The consensus of opinion is that the best way to achieve this is to have those who are expected to live by the budget also have a role in preparing it.

Many other benefits result from the preparation and use of budgets. The activities of the business are better coordinated; individual members of the management become aware of the problems of other members of the management; employees may become cost conscious and seek to conserve resources; the waste of resources is quickly revealed; the business enterprise is forced to maintain an adequate accounting system; greater knowledge of the behavior of costs is secured; the organization plan of the enterprise may be reviewed more often and changed where needed; and a breadth of vision, which might not otherwise be developed, is fostered.

Uncertainty with regard to future developments is a poor excuse for failure to budget; in fact, the less stable the conditions the more necessary and desirable is budgeting. Obviously, stable operating conditions permit greater reliance upon past experience and perhaps reduce the need for future planning.

Types of Budgets

It is actually incorrect to speak of *the* budget. Typically, many individual budgets will be prepared and used. But basically budgets are classified into two types. One type is known as the *forecast* or *master budget,* which is sometimes called the *master profit* or *earnings plan.* The master budget consists of a series of projected earnings statements and statements of financial position indicating the overall goals of the enterprise. The projections in these statements are supported by schedules containing the necessary details.

The second type of budget is the *control* or *responsibility budget* which was discussed in the preceding chapter. These budgets are measures against which to monitor and judge the performance of a manager or other individual. The modern trend in budgeting is to look upon control or responsibility budgets as underlying parts of the master budget. The same data are needed for both; they need only be aggregated in different ways. For instance, the cost of materials used to produce a product will be charged both to the product as a part of its cost and to the supervisor who had control over the cost.

A third type of budget is the capital budget, which was discussed in Chapter 16.

Budgetary Procedures

Budget periods vary in length, but usually they coincide with the accounting period. Normally, the budget period is broken into months or quarters; and the greater the uncertainty expected, the more likely is this to be the case. On the other hand, plans for expenditures for plant and equipment may cover many years.

Budgets are plans for the future, but they are based in large part on the past. Therefore, in the preparation of a budget, accounting data related to the past play an important part. Allowances, of course, are made for probable future developments. The necessary close relationship between the budget and the accounting system can be readily seen. The accounts must be designed to facilitate the preparation of the budget and the usual financial statements as well as the numerous reports—cost and financial—that are prepared quarterly, monthly, weekly, or even daily to facilitate the exercise of operational control.

The principle of charging with responsibility only those to whom authority is delegated is important in classifying accounts and budgetary items. For example, every cost should be the responsibility of some individual, and efficient budget and accounting systems will assist greatly in fixing that responsibility. During the budget period, repeated comparisons of accumulated accounting data and budgeted projections should be made and the differences investigated. But it should be noted that budgeting is not a substitute for management and that a budget is not self-operating. Instead, the budget is designed as merely a tool—but an important one—for exercising control.

THE MASTER BUDGET

The projected statement of financial position in the master budget depends upon many items in the projected earnings statements. Thus, the projected earnings statement must be prepared before the projected statement of financial position. The projected earnings statement is often referred to as the *operating budget*. The projected statement of financial position is called the *financial budget*. A number of supporting budgets are usually prepared. The sales budget is the key budget supporting the operating budget. Illustration 18.1 presents a flowchart of the financial planning process. It can serve as a frame of reference for the following discussion.

The Sales Budget

Because of its primary importance, careful study and analysis must precede the preparation of the sales budget. The expected general level of economic activity in the economy as a whole for the budget period must be taken into consideration. The prospects of the industry of which the company is a member must also be considered. These prospects may be influenced in varying degrees by population growth, income per capita, new construction, population migration, prices of inputs, and so forth. For

ILLUSTRATION 18.1

**A Flowchart of the Financial Planning Process
(an overview)**

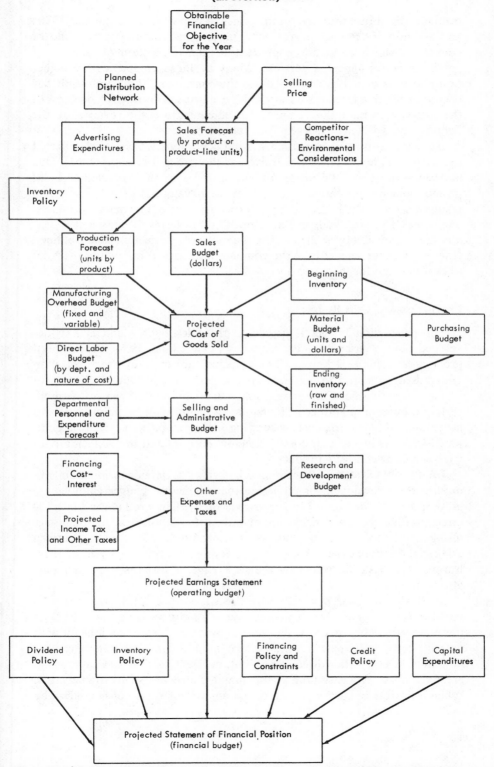

instance, the abrupt increases in the prices of imported oil in the mid 1970s had a significant impact on the sales projections of oil refineries and of companies which consume oil products in the production or delivery of goods or performance of services. Many of these companies set higher prices to pass their higher costs on to the consumer. The usual result has been that fewer units are sold at the higher price. The relative position of the company in the industry must next be considered and reviewed in the light of any expected or actively sought changes.

Allowances must be made for varying conditions which affect different products or different territories as well as the strength of competitors. Due allowance must also be made for any changes in the expected level of promotional expenditures. Quotas may be developed for salesmen as a result of sales analyses according to territories, size of customers, products, and so on. The sales budget is developed first in terms of units and is usually the responsibility of the sales manager. Sales projection data obtained from the various segments of the company are critical in making the total sales projection for the company.

Production and Cost Budgets

The production budget is geared to the sales budget and is also developed first in terms of units. Unit costs can seldom be developed until production volume is known. The principal objective of the production budget is to synchronize, in terms of time and quantity, the production of goods and their sale. Careful scheduling must be undertaken to maintain certain minimum quantities of inventory on hand while avoiding excessive accumulation. Also, the cost of carrying inventory on hand must be compared with the higher unit costs frequently encountered in producing relatively small batches of a product.

The Flexible Budget.   A technique known as *flexible* or *formula* budgeting has been developed for preparing the production budget (although it may be used for certain other purposes as well). The production budget is often subdivided into budgets for materials, for labor, and for manufacturing overhead. A flexible budget, for example, may contain (among others) the estimates of costs at varying levels of output as shown in Illustration 18.2. (As illustrated on the next page, a formula approach may also be used.)

In Illustration 18.2 materials and direct labor are considered a strictly variable cost. Supplies are also considered a strictly variable cost, although there are probably few costs that vary in an exact linear relationship with output. Power is largely a variable cost as it is assumed that beyond a minimum level it varies directly with output. Depreciation and supervision are fixed costs, while insurance and maintenance are semivariable costs. When a flexible budget is prepared, the amount of costs considered to be

ILLUSTRATION 18.2

	Volume (percent of capacity)			
Element of Cost	70%	80%	90%	100%
Materials.....................	$70,000	$80,000	$90,000	$100,000
Direct Labor..................	35,000	40,000	45,000	50,000
Manufacturing Overhead:				
Supplies...................	4,200	4,800	5,400	6,000
Power.....................	11,500	13,000	14,500	16,000
Insurance..................	4,500	4,500	5,000	5,000
Maintenance................	12,000	13,000	14,000	14,800
Depreciation................	20,000	20,000	20,000	20,000
Supervision.................	28,000	28,000	28,000	28,000

the budget amount in monitoring and appraising performance is read from the flexible budget for the actual level of output experienced.

Using the Flexible Budget. As an illustration of a way in which a flexible budget may be used, assume that a departmental budget is prepared based on the expectation of producing 100,000 units of product—the 100 percent of capacity level. Under such expectations, the budgeted amount for supplies would be $6,000, or $0.06 per unit. If, at the end of the period, the actual amount of supplies consumed amounted to $5,600, the first impression is that of a favorable variance of $400. But if the production of the period was only 90,000 units, there was actually an unfavorable variance of $200. The flexible budget shows that at 90 percent of capacity (90,000/100,000) the supplies that should have been consumed amount to only $5,400. Consequently, there appears to have been some inefficiency involved in the use of supplies, and a *budget* variance of $200 ($5,600 − $5,400) is said to exist. A budget variance is defined as the difference between an actual amount experienced at a certain level of operations and the budgeted amount *for that same level of operations.* Budget variances may thus be viewed as indicators or indices of efficiency since they emerge from a comparison of "what was" with "what should have been."

The use of flexible or formula budgets makes it unnecessary to revise budget estimates when production volume differs from that expected. In the case of directly variable costs, the proper budget amount can be read from the flexible budget or obtained through interpolation. In the case of certain semivariable costs which are partially fixed and partially variable, the budget amount for any level of operations can be computed using the following formula:

Budget Amount = Fixed Costs + (x Cents per Unit of Volume × Volume)

More complicated formulas are needed if the relationship between costs and volume above a minimum level of costs is not linear, that is, if the costs do not vary linearly with production.

Other costs may change only when a sufficiently large increase in production occurs as, for example, when one additional inspector must be added for each 20 percent of capacity utilized. Such step-variable costs can usually be read directly from the flexible budget.

The preparation of budgets for selling expenses and for general administrative expenses is similar to that of preparing the manufacturing budget. Several supporting budgets may be involved, such as budgets for advertising, office expenses, and payroll department expenses. In each case the supporting budget may show the fixed expenses and the variable expenses at various levels of sales volume.

THE MASTER BUDGET ILLUSTRATED

To illustrate the processes involved in developing the overall master profit plan for a company, an example based on the Dart Company is presented in the following pages. The Dart Company manufactures and sells a single product. Sales vary widely throughout the year, but production is scheduled uniformly throughout the year. Highly skilled labor is required to produce the product. The company has determined that it is less costly to carry and control heavy inventories during a part of the year than to lose skilled employees who may seek other employment while laid off.

The statement of financial position of the Dart Company as of December 31, 1978, is as shown in Illustration 18.3. A master budget is to be developed for the calendar year 1979. To be included in the master budget are an operating budget by quarters and a financial budget as of the end of each quarter. For illustrative purposes, only the budgets for the first two quarters will be developed.

To prevent the illustration from becoming unduly complicated, certain simplifying assumptions will be made as the illustration progresses. These assumptions in no way detract from the validity of the illustration in showing the basic features of developing the master budget.

The Operating Budget in Units

The operating budget is first developed in terms of units rather than dollars. Since revenues and the bulk of the costs to be incurred will vary with volume, forecasts of revenues and costs can be more easily derived after quantities are established. Sales for the year are forecast at 100,000 units. Quarterly sales are expected to be 20,000, 35,000, 20,000, and 25,000 units. In line with company policy of stabilizing production, the 100,000 units will be produced uniformly throughout the year at the rate of 25,000 units per quarter. A simplifying assumption made at this time is that there are no beginning or ending work in process inventories. A more realistic assumption would be that work in process inventories remain stable throughout the year. But this would still involve the computation of

ILLUSTRATION 18.3

DART COMPANY
Statement of Financial Position
December 31, 1978

Assets

Current Assets:

Cash..		$ 130,000	
Accounts receivable...........................		200,000	
Inventories			
Raw materials.............................	$ 40,000		
Finished goods............................	130,000	170,000	
Prepaid expenses.............................		20,000	$ 520,000
Property, Plant, and Equipment:			
Land..		$ 60,000	
Buildings....................................	$1,000,000		
Less: Allowance for depreciation...............	400,000	600,000	
Machinery and equipment.....................	$ 600,000		
Less: Allowance for depreciation...............	180,000	420,000	1,080,000
Total Assets..........................			$1,600,000

Liabilities and Stockholders' Equity

Current Liabilities:

Accounts payable............................		$ 80,000	
Accrued liabilities............................		160,000	
Federal income taxes payable..................		100,000	$ 340,000
Stockholders' Equity:			
Capital stock (100,000 shares of $10 par			
value).....................................		$1,000,000	
Retained earnings............................		260,000	1,260,000
Total Liabilities and Stockholders'			
Equity............................			$1,600,000

equivalent units of production and possibly different unit costs for the beginning inventory of the year when completed.

From the above data, a schedule of budgeted sales and production in terms of units is prepared, as shown in Illustration 18.4.

Note the fluctuation in the ending inventory which must be accepted if

ILLUSTRATION 18.4

DART COMPANY   Schedule I-a
Planned Sales and Production
(in units of product)

	Quarter Ending	
	March 31, 1979	June 30, 1979
Production planned................................	25,000	25,000
Sales forecast.......................................	20,000	35,000
Increase (decrease) in finished goods inventory...........	5,000	(10,000)
Planned beginning finished goods inventory.............	10,000*	15,000
Planned ending finished goods inventory................	15,000	5,000

   * Actual on January 1.

sales vary and the management policy of stable production is to be implemented. Thus, the finished goods inventory serves the function of absorbing the difference between production and sales. A management decision has been made that it is less costly to deal with fluctuating inventories than fluctuating production.

The Operating Budget in Dollars

The operating budget is now converted from units into dollars. A forecast of expected selling prices must be made. In addition, an analysis of costs must be made along the lines previously outlined. The forecasted selling prices and costs are as shown in Illustration 18.5.

Note that the above costs are classified according to whether they are variable or fixed in nature and are budgeted accordingly. That is, variable costs are budgeted as a constant dollar amount per unit, while fixed costs are budgeted only in total.

In an actual situation the budget estimates presented in Illustration 18.5 would be presented in a number of separate budgets. Manufacturing overhead would be budgeted by responsibility centers or departments with the strong probability that flexible budgets would be prepared for each center. In this way budget information would be developed for use in the master budget which could and would be used as a standard by which the performance of each department or center is appraised.

A schedule showing the development of the forecasted cost of goods manufactured and sold is now prepared. This is shown in Illustration 18.6.

Separate schedules would now be prepared for all of the selling and administrative expenses. Here again the individual budgets could be prepared for responsibility centers so that budget estimates useful in developing the master budget and for appraising the performance of the center are developed simultaneously. Flexible budgets could be prepared here as well as for manufacturing overhead. These budgets will not be illustrated here; the data which would be found in them will simply be entered in total in

ILLUSTRATION 18.5

DART COMPANY   Schedule I-b
Budget Estimates of Selling Price and Costs
for the Quarters Ending March 31, and June 30, 1979

Forecasted selling price... $	20
Manufacturing costs	
Variable (per unit manufactured)	
Raw material...	2
Direct labor..	6
Overhead..	1
Fixed overhead (total each quarter)...........................	75,000
Selling and administrative expenses	
Variable (per unit sold)....................................	2
Fixed (total each quarter)..................................	100,000

ILLUSTRATION 18.6

DART COMPANY   Schedule I-c
Planned Cost of Goods Manufactured and Sold

	Quarter Ending	
	March 31, 1979	June 30, 1979
Planned beginning finished goods inventory	$130,000*	$180,000
Planned cost of goods manufactured		
Raw materials (25,000 × $2)	$ 50,000	$ 50,000
Direct labor (25,000 × $6)	150,000	150,000
Variable overhead (25,000 × $1)	25,000	25,000
Fixed overhead (Schedule I-b)	75,000	75,000
Cost of goods manufactured (25,000 units at $12)	$300,000	$300,000
Planned goods available for sale	$430,000	$480,000
Planned ending finished goods inventory:		
(15,000 at $12)†	180,000	
(5,000 at $12)		60,000
Planned cost of goods sold	$250,000	$420,000

* Actual on January 1.
† First-in, first-out procedure assumed. The $12 cost is made up of raw materials of $2, direct labor of $6, variable overhead of $1, and fixed overhead of $3 $\left(\frac{\$75,000}{25,000 \text{ units}}\right)$

the operating budget for each of the first two quarters as is shown in Illustration 18.7.

All of the items appearing in the operating budget have been previously explained and discussed except the income tax accrual. This is budgeted at an assumed level of 50 percent of net earnings before taxes.

As noted previously, if the operating budget does not reveal the desired net earnings, new plans will have to be formulated and new budgets developed. But the purpose of preparing such a plan is to gain some knowl-

ILLUSTRATION 18.7

DART COMPANY   Schedule I
Projected Earnings Statement
for Quarters Ending March 31, and June 30, 1979

	Quarter Ending	
	March 31, 1979	June 30, 1979
Forecasted sales (20,000 and 35,000 at $20)	$400,000	$700,000
Cost of goods sold (Schedule I-c)	250,000	420,000
Gross margin	$150,000	$280,000
Selling and administrative expenses		
Variable (20,000 and 35,000 at $2)	$ 40,000	$ 70,000
Fixed (Schedule I-b)	100,000	100,000
Total Expenses	$140,000	$170,000
Net earnings before income taxes	$ 10,000	$110,000
Estimated federal income taxes (50%)	5,000	55,000
Net Earnings	$ 5,000	$ 55,000

edge of what the outcome of a period's activities will be prior to their actual occurrence.

Preparing the Financial Budget

The preparation of a projected statement of financial position would ordinarily involve an analysis of each account appearing in that statement. The beginning balance would be taken from the statement of financial position at the start of the budget period. The effect of any planned activities on the account would then be taken into consideration. Many of the accounts will be affected by items appearing in the operating budget and by either cash inflows or outflows. The complexities encountered in many cases will require the preparation of work sheets. Such a technique will not be employed here; rather the individual accounts will be analyzed in a series of schedules.

Inventories. The first of these schedules shows the planned purchases and inventory of raw materials.

The raw materials inventory had been built up above the normal level of one half of next quarter's planned usage because of a strike threat in the supplier company. This threat has now passed, and the inventory will be reduced in the first quarter to the normal planned level. Illustration 18.8 shows the planned material purchases and inventories for the Dart Company for the first two quarters of 1979.

The planned usage of materials and the cost per unit were secured from Schedule I-c, Illustration 18.6. Since quarterly production is planned at 25,000 units, enough materials for 12,500 units are to be maintained on hand at the end of each quarter. Since the cost is $2 per unit of finished product, the planned ending inventory of raw materials is $25,000. The inventory at the end of the first quarter is, of course, the beginning inventory of the second quarter.

The finished goods inventories have already been projected in Schedule

ILLUSTRATION 18.8

DART COMPANY
Schedule II-a
Planned Material Purchases and Inventories

	Quarter Ending	
	March 31, 1979	June 30, 1979
Planned usage (25,000 × $2)	$50,000	$50,000
Planned ending inventory (one half of next quarter's planned production)	25,000	25,000
Planned raw materials available for use	$75,000	$75,000
Inventory at beginning of quarter	40,000*	25,000
Planned purchases for the quarter	$35,000	$50,000

* Actual on January 1.

ILLUSTRATION 18.9

DART COMPANY

Analyses of Accounts Credited as a Result of
Incurrence of Material Purchases and Operating Costs

	Total	Accounts Payable	Accrued Liabilities	Prepaid Expense	Allowance for Depreciation	
					Building	Equipment
Purchases or operating costs, quarter ending March 31						
Raw materials	$ 35,000	$ 35,000				
Direct labor	150,000		$150,000			
Overhead	100,000	16,000	60,000	$ 6,000	$ 5,000	$ 13,000
Selling and administrative expense	140,000	5,000	130,000	2,000	1,000	2,000
Total	$425,000	$ 56,000	$340,000	$ 8,000	$ 6,000	$ 15,000
Beginning balances		80,000	160,000	20,000Dr.	400,000	180,000
		$136,000	$500,000	$12,000Dr.	$406,000	$195,000
Deduct						
Planned cash payments		(80,000)	(330,000)			
Planned balances, March 31		$ 56,000	$170,000	$12,000Dr.	$406,000	$195,000
Purchases or operating costs, quarter ending June 30						
Raw materials	$ 50,000	$ 50,000				
Direct labor	150,000		$150,000			
Overhead	100,000	13,000	64,000	$ 5,000	$ 5,000	$ 13,000
Selling and administrative expense	170,000	10,000	154,000	3,000	1,000	2,000
Total	$470,000	$ 73,000	$368,000	$ 8,000	$ 6,000	$ 15,000
Total including March 31 balances		$129,000	538,000	$ 4,000Dr.	$412,000	$210,000
Add/Deduct						
Planned cash payments		(56,000)	(354,000)	10,000		
Planned balances, June 30		$ 73,000	$184,000	$14,000Dr.	$412,000	$210,000

I-c, Illustration 18.6, and can be taken from this schedule when the financial budget is actually prepared.

Accounts Affected by Operating Costs. Individual schedules could be prepared for each of the accounts affected by operating costs. But for illustrative purposes, a schedule combining the analyses of all the accounts affected by material purchases or operating costs is shown in Illustration 18.9.

Schedule II-b, Illustration 18.9, provides a considerable amount of information needed in constructing financial budgets for the quarters ended March 31, 1979, and June 30, 1979. The balances for both dates for Accounts Payable, Accrued Liabilities, Prepaid Expenses, the Allowance for Depreciation—Building, and the Allowance for Depreciation—Equipment are developed in the schedule. In addition, data needed in order to project the cash balances at both dates are also included in the form of cash payments on Accounts Payable, Accrued Liabilities, and for Prepaid Expenses.

Accounts Receivable. The next schedule to be prepared is shown in Illustration 18.10. This schedule is prepared under the assumption that 60 percent of the current quarter's sales are collected in that quarter plus all of the uncollected sales of the prior quarter. Several other simplifying assumptions are made, namely, that there are no sales returns or allowances, discounts, or uncollectible accounts. Obviously, in an actual planning situation, allowance may have to be made for these items. It is also assumed that all sales are made on a credit basis.

The beginning balance for the second quarter is, of course, the ending balance for the first quarter. Planned sales were secured from Schedule I, Illustration 18.7.

The projected cash collections by quarters in Schedule II-c will be used in preparing the cash budget or cash flow statement.

Federal Income Taxes Payable. A separate schedule could be prepared showing the changes in the Federal Income Taxes Payable account. It will

ILLUSTRATION 18.10

DART COMPANY   Schedule II-c
Planned Accounts Receivable Collections and Balances

	Quarter Ending	
	March 31, 1979	June 30, 1979
Planned balance at beginning of quarter..............	$200,000*	$160,000
Planned sales for period...........................	400,000	700,000
Total...	$600,000	$860,000
Projected collections during quarter..................	440,000	580,000
Planned balance at end of quarter...................	$160,000	$280,000

* Actual on January 1.

be omitted here. The balances reported in the financial budgets presented are derived under the assumption that one half of the liability shown in the December 31, 1978, statement of financial position ($100,000) is paid in each of the first two quarters of 1979. The accrual for the current quarter is added (see Illustration 18.7). Thus, the balance at March 31, 1979, is $100,000 − $50,000 + $5,000 = $55,000. The balance at June 30, 1979, is $55,000 − $50,000 + $55,000 = $60,000. At June 30 the balance is equal to simply the accrual for the current year of $5,000 for the first quarter and $55,000 for the second quarter.

Cash Budget

Sufficient information has now been accumulated so that the cash flow projection statement or cash budget for the two quarters may now be prepared. The statement merely consists of adding planned cash inflows to and deducting planned cash outflows from the actual or planned cash balance at the beginning of the quarter. The result is the planned balance at the end of the quarter, as shown in Illustration 18.11.

ILLUSTRATION 18.11

DART COMPANY   Schedule II-d
Planned Cash Flows and Cash Balances

	Quarter Ended	
	March 31, 1979	June 30, 1979
Planned balance at beginning of quarter..............	$130,000*	$ 90,000
Planned cash receipts		
Collections of accounts receivable (Schedule II-c).......	440,000	580,000
	$570,000	$670,000
Planned cash disbursements		
Payment of accounts payable (Schedule II-b).........	$ 80,000	$ 56,000
Payment of accrued liabilities (Schedule II-b).........	330,000	354,000
Payment of federal income tax liability (see above)....	50,000	50,000
Payment of dividends..............................	20,000	40,000
Expenses prepaid (Schedule II-b)...................	0	10,000
Total disbursements.........................	$480,000	$510,000
Planned balance at end of quarter....................	$ 90,000	$160,000

* Actual on January 1.

Statement of Retained Earnings

In order to tie the operating budget and the financial budget together, a schedule showing the changes in retained earnings and the projected retained earnings balance at the end of each of the first two quarters of 1979 can be prepared. Such a schedule is shown in Illustration 18.12.

ILLUSTRATION 18.12

DART COMPANY   Schedule II-e
Planned Changes in and Balance of Retained Earnings

	Quarter Ended	
	March 31, 1979	June 30, 1979
Planned balance at beginning of quarter..............	$260,000*	$245,000
Add: Planned net earnings.........................	5,000	55,000
	$265,000	$300,000
Less: Planned dividends...........................	20,000	40,000
Planned balance at end of quarter..................	$245,000	$260,000

* Actual on January 1.

The Financial Budgets

The financial budgets for the quarters ended March 31, 1979, and June 30, 1979, are now prepared and are as shown in Schedule II, Illustration 18.13.

The completion of the financial budgets for the two quarters completes the preparation of the master budget. *Management now has on hand information which will assist it in appraising the policies it has instituted prior to these policies being actually implemented.* If the results of these policies, as shown by the master budget, are unsatisfacory, the policies can be changed before serious difficulty is encountered. For example, in the Dart Company illustration, management desired to stabilize production. The master budget shows that production can be stabilized even though sales fluctuate widely. The planned ending inventory at June 30 may be considered somewhat low in view of the fluctuations in sales, but management does have advance information of this fact.

Plant and Equipment Budgets

No purchases of plant and equipment items were budgeted in the above illustration, except that repairs and maintenance are assumed to be included in the overhead budget. Plant and equipment budgets frequently are prepared for a single year and for several years in advance. Careful budgeting of major plant expenditures is needed in order to avoid the substantial amounts of overcapacity which have plagued several major industries in the past.

A Word of Caution

There is a tendency to regard the mere preparation of a budget as sufficient to achieve organizational goals. But if the budgetary process does not result both in the setting of proper goals and the commitment of the

ILLUSTRATION 18.13

| DART COMPANY | | Schedule II |
Projected Statements of Financial Position

	March 31, 1979	June 30, 1979
Assets		
Current Assets:		
Cash...	$ 90,000	$ 160,000
Accounts receivable............................	160,000	280,000
Inventories		
Raw materials................................	25,000	25,000
Finished goods...............................	180,000	60,000
Prepaid expenses..............................	12,000	14,000
Total Current Assets......................	$ 467,000	$ 539,000
Property, Plant, and Equipment:		
Land...	$ 60,000	$ 60,000
Buildings ($1,000,000 less allowance for depreciation of $406,000 and $412,000)...................	594,000	588,000
Equipment ($600,000 less allowance for depreciation of $195,000 and $210,000)...................	405,000	390,000
Total Property, Plant, and Equipment........	$1,059,000	$1,038,000
Total Assets.........................	$1,526,000	$1,577,000
Liabilities and Stockholders' Equity		
Current Liabilities:		
Accounts payable.............................	$ 56,000	$ 73,000
Accrued liabilities............................	170,000	184,000
Federal income taxes payable...................	55,000	60,000
Total Current Liabilities......................	$ 281,000	$ 317,000
Stockholders' Equity:		
Capital stock (100,000 shares of $10 par value)......	$1,000,000	$1,000,000
Retained earnings.............................	245,000	260,000
Total Stockholders' Equity.................	$1,245,000	$1,260,000
Total Liabilities and Stockholders' Equity.	$1,526,000	$1,577,000

individuals involved to the achievement of those goals, it is likely to be a failure. A budget can be imposed from the top or it can be developed with the participation of all those whose behavior is supposed to be affected by it. The latter method seems to have a far greater chance for success in most situations. An individual's actions and decisions are more likely to be subject to the "control" of the budget if he helped develop it and, at least implicitly, agreed that the plan was reasonable and could be achieved.

SUMMARY

Budgets are primarily tools used to plan and control the use of scarce resources to achieve certain objectives. They allow an organization to evaluate the results of a given period's activities before they take place. Budgets are used to motivate individuals, departments, cost centers, or divisions. Other benefits likely to flow from the preparation and adoption of budgets include better coordination of activities, increased cost consciousness on the part of employees, and better knowledge of cost behavior patterns.

In building budgets, every cost should be the responsibility of the individual who has authority to control it. These individuals should have a role in budget preparation. Frequent comparisons between budgeted and actual costs should be made during the budget period and, where appropriate, reasons for differences investigated.

The preparation of a master budget involves the preparation of the operating budget and the financial budget. The operating budget is based on the key sales budget and the cost and production budgets. Flexible budgets may be prepared for a number of different costs so that budgeted amounts for different levels of output will be readily available for comparison with actual results. In this way, the flexible budget becomes a valuable tool in appraising performance.

The operating budget is first expressed in terms of units of planned sales and production and then converted into dollars through the use of planned selling prices and costs. With planned costs and sales computed, the planned cost of goods manufactured and sold can be computed and the projected earnings statement (the operating budget) prepared.

The preparation of the financial budget requires the preparation of schedules showing (1) planned material purchases and inventories, (2) planned accounts receivable collections and balances, (3) planned cash flows and balances, (4) planned plant and equipment changes and balances, (5) planned changes and balances in retained earnings, and (6) planned changes and balances in other statement of financial position accounts, and the planning of federal income tax accruals and payments. The preparation of the projected statement of financial position, the operating budget already having been prepared, completes the preparation of the master budget.

The participation of all those whose behavior is expected to be influenced by the budget should be sought in its preparation. This should motivate the individuals to achieve the goals and allow their decisions and actions to be controlled by the budget.

QUESTIONS AND EXERCISES

1. Indicate three ways in which budget information will be useful to management.
2. What are the two major budgets in the master budget? Which should be prepared first? Why?
3. Distinguish between forecast and responsibility budgeting.

4. What is a flexible budget? What is meant by formula budgeting?

5. The budget established at the beginning of a given period carried an item for supplies used in the amount of $40,000. At the end of the period, the supplies used amounted to $44,000. Can it be concluded from these data that either there was inefficient use of supplies or care was not exercised in purchasing the supplies?

6. The Stanton Shoe Company has decided to produce 60,000 pairs of shoes at a uniform rate throughout 1979. The sales department of Stanton Shoe Company has estimated sales for 1979 according to the following schedule:

	Sales in Units
First quarter	16,000
Second quarter	13,000
Third quarter	15,000
Fourth quarter	21,000
Total for 1979	65,000

If the December 31, 1978, inventory is estimated to be 10,000 pairs of shoes, prepare a schedule of planned sales and production for the first two quarters of 1979.

7. Assume that the original expectation held by a company for the year was to operate at the 100 percent level of capacity, for which the budgeted power cost (a strictly variable cost) for a given department was $16,000. At the end of the year, actual production amounted to 80 percent of capacity and the actual power cost was $13,200. Relative to the efficient use of power, what was the amount of the budget variance and was it favorable or unfavorable?

8. The budgeted amount of maintenance cost for a given department was $22,000 based upon an expectation of operating at the 180,000 units of output level. The $22,000 includes $4,000 of fixed maintenance costs. At the end of the year, actual maintenance costs amounted to $17,700 and 140,000 units were actually produced. Compute the amount of the budget variance and indicate whether it was favorable or unfavorable.

9. How do the terms planning, controlling, and motivating relate to the budgetary process?

10. Mr. Smith is considering constructing a budget and imposing it on his small machine shop organization. Do you have any advice for him?

PROBLEMS

18–1. The Dillon Corporation prepares monthly operating and financial budgets. The operating budgets for June and July 1979, are based on the following data:

	Units Produced	Units Sold
June	100,000	90,000
July	90,000	100,000

All sales are at $10 per unit. Raw materials, direct labor, and variable overhead are estimated at $1, $2, and $1 per unit, while fixed overhead is budgeted at $180,000 per month. Operating expenses are budgeted at $200,000 plus 10 percent of sales, while federal income taxes are budgeted at 50 percent of net operating earnings. The inventory at June 1 consists of 50,000 units with a cost of $5.70 each.

Required:

a. Prepare monthly budget estimates of cost of goods sold assuming Fifo.
b. Prepare operating budgets for June and July. (Use a single amount for cost of goods sold—as derived in your answer to part *a*.)

18–2. The Minmier Company prepares monthly operating and financial budgets. Estimates of sales (in units) are made for each month. Production is scheduled at a level high enough to take care of current needs and to carry into each month one half of that month's unit sales. Raw materials, direct labor, and variable overhead are estimated at $2, $4, and $1 per unit; and fixed overhead is budgeted at $154,000 per month. Sales for April, May, June, and July are estimated at 50,000, 60,000, 80,000, and 60,000 units. The inventory at April 1 consists of 25,000 units with a cost of $8.20 per unit.

Required:

a. Prepare a schedule showing the budgeted production in units for April, May, and June, 1979.
b. Prepare a schedule showing the budgeted cost of goods sold for the same three months assuming the Fifo method is used for inventories.

18–3. Net operating earnings for the Harwood Company for 1978 were determined as follows:

Sales.....................................		$1,000,000
Cost of goods sold		
Raw materials.........................	$200,000	
Direct labor..........................	150,000	
Fixed overhead........................	100,000	
Variable overhead.....................	60,000	510,000
Gross margin.............................		$ 490,000
Selling expenses		
Variable..............................	$ 60,000	
Fixed.................................	90,000	150,000
		$ 340,000
General and administrative expenses		
Variable..............................	$ 80,000	
Fixed.................................	120,000	200,000
Net operating Earnings...................		$ 140,000

An operating budget is prepared for 1979 with sales forecasted at a 20 percent increase solely from volume. Raw materials, direct labor, and all costs labeled variable above are completely variable. Fixed costs are expected to continue as above except for a $20,000 increase in fixed general and administrative costs.

Actual operating data for 1979 are:

Sales	$1,150,000
Raw materials	235,000
Direct labor	175,000
Fixed overhead	102,500
Variable overhead	67,500
Variable selling expense	69,000
Fixed selling expense	91,000
Variable general and administrative expense	95,000
Fixed general and administrative expense	145,000

There were no beginning or ending work in process or finished goods inventories.

Required:

a.   Compute the break-even point using 1978 data.
b.   Prepare a budget report comparing the 1979 operating budget with actual 1979 data.
c.   Prepare a budget report which would be useful in appraising the performance of the various persons charged with responsibility to provide satisfactory earnings. (Hint: Prepare budget data on a flexible basis.)
d.   Comment on the difference revealed by the two reports.

18–4.   Following is a summary of operating data of the Gentry Company for the year 1979:

Sales		$2,500,000
Cost of goods sold		
Direct materials	$500,000	
Direct labor	450,000	
Variable manufacturing overhead	100,000	
Fixed manufacturing overhead	300,000	1,350,000
		$1,150,000
Selling expenses		
Variable	$125,000	
Fixed	100,000	225,000
		$ 925,000
General and administrative expenses		
Variable	$ 50,000	
Fixed	450,000	500,000
Net Operating Earnings		$ 425,000

Sales volume for 1980 is budgeted at 90 percent of 1979 volume with no expectation of price change. The 1980 budget amounts for the various other costs and expenses differ from those reported in 1979 only for the expected volume change in the variable items.

The actual operating data for 1980 are:

Sales.	$1,950,000
Direct materials	455,000
Direct labor	412,500
Variable manufacturing overhead	87,500
Fixed manufacturing overhead	302,500
Variable selling expenses	165,000
Fixed selling expenses	97,500
Variable general and administrative expenses	46,000
Fixed general and administrative expenses	447,500

Required:

a. Prepare a report comparing the operating budget for 1980 with the actual results for that year.

b. Prepare a budget report which would be useful in pinpointing the responsibility for the poor showing in 1980. (Hint: Prepare budget data on a flexible budget basis.)

c. Comment on the differences revealed by the two budget comparisons.

18–5. Nash Corporation prepares annual budgets by quarters for its fiscal year ending June 30. Given below, in summary form, are the data from its December 31, 1978, statement of financial position:

Assets

Cash	$ 23,000
Accounts receivable	60,000
Allowance for doubtful accounts	(2,000)
Inventories	26,000
Prepaid expenses	2,000
Furniture and equipment	30,000
Allowance for depreciation	(2,000)
	$137,000

Liabilities and Stockholders' Equity

Accounts payable	$ 20,000
Accrued liabilities	6,000
Notes payable, 8% (due 1982)	80,000
Capital stock	50,000
Retained earnings (deficit)	(19,000)
	$137,000

All of the stock of Nash Corporation was recently acquired by Frank Haney after the corporation had suffered losses for a number of years. After the purchase, Mr. Haney loaned substantial sums of money to the corporation, which still owes him $80,000 on an 8 percent note. Because of these past losses there are no accrued federal income taxes payable, but future earnings will be subject to taxation.

Mr. Haney is quite anxious to withdraw $20,000 from the corporation (as a payment on the note payable to him) but will not do so if it reduces the corporation's cash balance below $20,000. Thus, he is quite interested in the budgets for the quarter ending March 31, 1979.

Additional data:

(1) Sales for the coming quarter are forecasted at $200,000, for the following quarter at $250,000. All sales are priced to yield a gross margin of 40 percent. Inventory is to be maintained on hand at the end of any quarter in an amount equal to 20 percent of the goods to be sold in the next quarter. All sales are on account, and 95 percent of the December 31, 1978, receivables plus 70 percent of the current quarter's sales will be collected during the quarter ending March 31, 1979.

(2) Selling expenses are budgeted at $8,000 fixed plus 6 percent of sales; $4,000 will be incurred on account, $11,000 accrued, $4,500 from expiration of prepaid rent and unexpired insurance, and $500 from allocated depreciation.

(3) Purchasing expenses are budgeted at $5,800 fixed plus 5 percent of purchases for the quarter; $1,500 will be incurred on account, $8,000 accrued, $2,300 from expired prepaid expenses, and $200 from allocated depreciation.

(4) Administrative expenses are budgeted at $7,000 plus 2 percent of sales; $500 will be incurred on account, $6,000 accrued, $2,200 from expired prepayments, $300 from allocated depreciation, while bad debts are estimated at 1 percent of sales.

(5) Interest accrues at 8 percent on the notes payable and is credited to Accrued Liabilities.

(6) All of the beginning balances in Accounts Payable and Accrued Liabilities will be paid during the quarter plus 80 percent of the current increases in Accounts Payable and all but $5,600 of the current accrued liabilities. A $3,000 insurance premium is to be paid prior to March 31, and a full year's rent of $24,000 is due on January 2.

(7) Federal income taxes are budgeted at 50 percent of net earnings before taxes. The taxes should be accrued separately and no payments are due in the first quarter.

Required:

a. Prepare an operating budget for the quarter ending March 31, 1979, including supporting schedules for planned purchases and operating expenses.

b. Prepare a financial budget for March 31, 1979. A supporting schedule analyzing accounts affected by purchases and operating expenses, a schedule showing planned accounts receivable collections and balances, and a schedule showing planned cash flows and cash balances should be included. (Note: All purchases are made on account.)

c. Will Mr. Haney be able to collect $20,000 on his note?

18–6. The following statement of financial position account balances are for the Talbert Corporation as of December 31, 1980:

Assets

Cash...	$ 20,000
Accounts receivable............................	40,000
Allowance for doubtful accounts................	(3,000)
Inventories....................................	50,000
Prepaid expenses..............................	6,000
Land..	50,000
Buildings and equipment......................	150,000
Allowance for depreciation....................	(20,000)
	$293,000

Liabilities and Stockholders' Equity

Accounts payable..............................	$ 30,000
Accrued liabilities (including income taxes)........	20,000
Capital stock.................................	200,000
Retained earnings............................	43,000
	$293,000

The Talbert Corporation has been expanding very rapidly in recent years. Sales in the last quarter of 1980 amounted to $200,000 and are projected at $250,000 and $400,000 for the first two quarters of 1981. This expansion has created a very tight cash position. Management is especially concerned about the probable cash balance at March 31, 1981, since payment in the amount of $30,000 for some new equipment must be made upon delivery on April 2. The current cash balance of $20,000 is considered to be the minimum workable balance.

Additional Data:

(1) Purchases, all on account, are to be scheduled so that the inventory at the end of any quarter is equal to one third of the goods expected to be sold in the coming quarter. Cost of goods sold averages 60 percent of sales.

(2) Selling expenses are budgeted at $10,000 fixed plus 8 percent of sales: $2,000 is expected to be incurred on account, $24,000 accrued, $2,800 from expired prepayments, and $1,200 from allocated depreciation.

(3) Purchasing expenses are budgeted at $7,000 fixed plus 5 percent of purchases; $1,000 will be incurred on account, $13,000 accrued, $1,100 from expired prepayments, and $900 from allocated depreciation.

(4) Administrative expenses are budgeted at $12,500 fixed plus 3 percent of sales; $2,000 will be incurred on account, $11,000 accrued, $1,100 from expired prepayments, and bad debts equal to 2 percent of current sales, and $900 from allocated depreciation.

(5) Federal income taxes are budgeted at 50 percent of net operating earnings before taxes and are accrued in Accrued Liabilities. Payments on these taxes are included in the payments on Accrued Liabilities discussed below.

(6) All December 31, 1980, Accounts Payable will be paid in the current quarter plus 80 percent of current credits to this account. All of the December 31, 1980, accrued liabilities will be paid in the current quarter except for $6,000. Of the current quarter's accrued liabilities, all but $24,000 will be paid during the quarter.

(7) Cash outlays for various expenses normally prepaid will amount to $8,000 during the quarter.

(8) All sales are made on account; 80 percent of the sales are collected in the quarter in which made, and all of the remaining sales are collected in the following quarter except for 2 percent which are never collected. The allowance for doubtful accounts shows the estimated amount of accounts receivable at December 31, 1980, arising from 1980 sales which will not be collected.

Required:

a. Prepare an operating budget for the quarter ending March 31, 1981. Supporting schedules for planned purchases and operating expenses should be included.

b. Prepare a financial budget for March 31, 1981. Include supporting schedules analyzing accounts credited for purchases and expenses, showing planned cash flows and cash balance, and showing planned collections on and balance of accounts receivable.

c. Will sufficient cash be on hand April 2 to pay for the new equipment? Explain.

chapter 19

Taxes and Tax Considerations in Decision Making

INTRODUCTION

A business is subject to various taxes. For some of them the business is principally concerned with the provisions of the law applying to them so that proper entries can be made to record any expense and the liability for payment. Payroll taxes, property taxes, and sales taxes generally fall into this category. There is little opportunity for minimizing or delaying any expense associated with these taxes. And for certain of these taxes the business merely performs a collection function since the taxes are levied on employees and customers.

Income taxes are in a different category and are the subject of this chapter. Federal income taxes came into being in 1913 and have been used to stimulate or dampen the economy and to encourage or discourage certain activities as well as to raise governmental revenues.

INCOME TAXES

The rates of taxation on earnings by the federal government alone are 70 percent for certain portions of personal income and 48 percent for certain portions of corporate earnings. Because of these relatively high rates (and also the increased possibility of legally avoiding or delaying the incurrence of these taxes), the businessman is concerned not only with correctly accounting for these taxes but also with making decisions which will tend to minimize their effect on earnings.

The Tax Reform Act of 1976 has been called the most extensive tax-reform measure in many years. Except where otherwise described, the provisions and rates applicable to the 1976 tax year are used in this text.

460

Federal Income Tax Withheld

Under the federal "pay-as-you-go" income tax collection system, most individuals must pay (partially or in full) their federal income taxes on wages as the wages are received throughout the year. They cannot wait until they file an income tax return and at that time pay the entire annual amount of the tax. The tax is withheld by the employer from the wages of employees at the time wage payments are made. Withheld taxes are periodically remitted by the employer to a depository bank or to the Internal Revenue Service.

The Internal Revenue Code requires that employers withhold federal income taxes, in whole or in part, from wages of employees. However, certain portions of a person's remuneration are exempt from withholding of taxes.

The amount of the income tax to be withheld from the pay of each employee depends on (1) the amount of the employee's earnings, (2) the frequency of the payroll period, and (3) the income exempt from taxation as determined by the number of exemptions of the employee. Briefly, the exemptions of an employee are as follows:

One for himself and one for his spouse (if married and assuming the filing of a joint return which will be explained later) plus:

1. One more for each of them who is 65 or over.
2. One more for each of them who is blind.
3. One more for each closely related person (son or daughter, or descendant of either; father or mother, or ancestor of either; stepson or stepdaughter; brother, sister, stepbrother, or stepsister; stepfather or stepmother; son or daughter of a sister or brother; brother or sister of father or mother; brother- or sister-in-law, father- or mother-in-law, son- or daughter-in-law) or person (excluding certain unrelated persons) living in taxpayer's home as a member of the household and who is dependent on the taxpayer. The person claimed as a dependent must have less than $750 gross income during the year unless he is under nineteen or is a full-time student. The person must also, in most cases, receive more than one half of his support from the taxpayer to qualify as a dependent.

Normally, $750 of income is exempted from taxation for each personal exemption claimed. Withholding tax rates and tables are constructed accordingly. For the tax years 1976 and 1977 a credit equal to the greater of $35 for each taxpayer and each dependent or 2 percent of the first $9,000 of taxable income was granted.

Every company is required to maintain payroll records for its employees, setting forth (among other items) the names and addresses of persons employed during the year, their social security numbers, exemptions, gross wages earned, taxes withheld, other deductions, and dates and amounts of net take-home pay.

After the end of each calendar year the company must furnish employees a summary of the above information so that they can use it to prepare their personal federal income tax returns. This information also serves the purpose of providing the Internal Revenue Service with data for determining whether taxpayers have filed proper income tax returns.

Accounting for Federal Income Tax Withheld

To illustrate the accounting entries for the federal income tax withheld, assume that there is one employee whose gross wages during the last month of 1976 are $1,000 and that the tax to be withheld is $110.40.

The required entry for the payment of salary is:

Salaries Expense		Federal Income Tax Withheld		Cash	
1,000			110.40	Bal. xxx	889.60

Remittance of Amounts Due

If the total income taxes withheld plus social security taxes exceed $100 per month, the employer must pay the total not later than the 15th day of the following month. Otherwise the remittance for three months may be made after the end of each quarter.

PERSONAL FEDERAL INCOME TAXES

The requirements as to who must file a federal income tax return are somewhat complicated. Basically, persons with a gross annual income of $750 or more should check the law to see if they are required to file.

The taxpayer's income from sources such as wages, dividends, interest, proprietorship earnings, partnership earnings, and net rents is totaled and is called *gross income.* Gross income less certain deductions is equal to *adjusted gross* income. These deductions are usually business expenses relating to the production of gross income.

Allowable personal deductions for contributions, interest, taxes levied directly against the taxpayer, casualty and theft losses exceeding $100 for each incurrence, *limited* medical expenses, *limited* political contributions and "nonbusiness" expenses are subtracted from the adjusted gross income. Instead of deducting these items, the taxpayer may take the *standard deduction,* which is the larger of the percentage standard deduction or the low income allowance. The percentage standard deduction is 16 percent of adjusted gross income up to a maximum of $2,400 for single persons and $2,800 for married persons filing a joint return. A married taxpayer

ILLUSTRATION 19.1

Determination of Taxable Income for an Individual Taxpayer

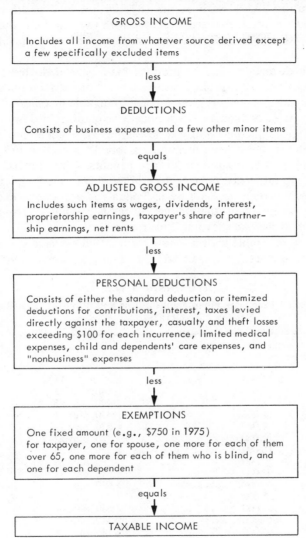

filing a separate return will receive a maximum standard deduction of $1,400. The law also provides for a flat amount low income allowance which is designed to remove poverty level taxpayers from the tax rolls. Under the Tax Reform Act of 1976, the allowance is $1,700 for a single person and $2,100 for married persons filing a joint return ($1,050 for a married person filing a separate return). This means that a single taxpayer could earn up to $2,450 and pay no tax ($1,700 low income allowance plus $750 personal exemption). A married couple with no dependents could earn up to $3,600 with no tax ($2,100 low income allowance plus two $750 exemptions). A married couple with two children could earn up to $5,100 with no tax ($2,100 low income allowance plus four $750 exemptions).

When the deductions and exemptions have been deducted from gross income, the balance is taxable income. Illustration 19.1 outlines the computations required to convert gross income to taxable income.

Unless an item of income is specifically exempted by law, it must be included in gross income. Only a few types of income are exempted, including interest on state and municipal bonds, social security benefits, and workmen's compensation insurance benefits. Gifts, inheritances, and proceeds of life insurance policies are not taxable to the recipient.

The federal income tax paid by individuals is a personal expense, not a business expense. The actual amount of tax is computed through the use of tables such as the one shown in Illustration 19.2.

Besides the rate table shown below for married taxpayers, the law also provides special rates for unmarried individuals, married individuals filing

ILLUSTRATION 19.2
Married Taxpayers Filing Joint Returns and Surviving Spouses
(1976)

Taxable Income		Pay	Of Excess Over
Over	But Not Over		
	$ 1,000	14%	
$ 1,000 —	2,000	$ 140, plus 15%	— $ 1,000
2,000 —	3,000	290, plus 16	— 2,000
3,000 —	4,000	450, plus 17	— 3,000
4,000 —	8,000	620, plus 19	— 4,000
8,000 —	12,000	1,380, plus 22	— 8,000
12,000 —	16,000	2,260, plus 25	— 12,000
16,000 —	20,000	3,260, plus 28	— 16,000
20,000 —	24,000	4,380, plus 32	— 20,000
24,000 —	28,000	5,660, plus 36	— 24,000
28,000 —	32,000	7,100, plus 39	— 28,000
32,000 —	36,000	8,660, plus 42	— 32,000
36,000 —	40,000	10,340, plus 45	— 36,000
40,000 —	44,000	12,140, plus 48	— 40,000
44,000 —	52,000	14,060, plus 50	— 44,000
52,000 —	64,000	18,060, plus 53	— 52,000
64,000 —	76,000	24,420, plus 55	— 64,000
76,000 —	88,000	31,020, plus 58	— 76,000
88,000 —	100,000	37,980, plus 60	— 88,000
100,000 —	120,000	45,180, plus 62	— 100,000
120,000 —	140,000	57,580, plus 64	— 120,000
140,000 —	160,000	70,380, plus 66	— 140,000
160,000 —	180,000	83,580, plus 68	— 160,000
180,000 —	200,000	97,180, plus 69	— 180,000
200,000 —		110,980, plus 70	— 200,000

separate returns (and trusts and estates), and taxpayers qualifying as "heads of households." Generally, persons in this latter category are certain unmarried or legally separated persons (and those married to nonresident aliens) who maintain a residence for a relative or a dependent.

There is a maximum marginal tax rate of 50 percent on all personal services income. Personal services income includes wages, salaries, professional fees, pensions, annuities, deferred compensation and other compensation for personal services actually rendered.

The following illustration for arriving at taxable income for the year 1976 is for an individual filing a joint return who is in business and who also has other income. He is married, and he and his wife, both under age 65, have two children under 19 years of age. The parents provide more than one half of the children's support.

Sales...		$200,000
Deduct: Cost of goods sold...........................	$130,000	
Expenses..................................	40,000	170,000
Net earnings from business operations..................		$ 30,000
Net earnings from a partnership.......................		8,000
Interest on bank deposits.............................		500
Adjusted gross income...............................		$ 38,500
Personal deductions:		
Contributions to church............................	$ 1,600	
Interest on personal loans..........................	150	
Property taxes on residence........................	525	
State sales tax.....................................	265	
Political contribution...............................	100	
Uninsured fire loss (excess over $100)...............	400	
	$ 3,040	
Exemptions: Taxpayer, wife, two children at $750 each...	3,000	6,040
Taxable Income.....................................		$ 32,460

The amount of tax would be computed as follows:

$$
\begin{aligned}
\text{Tax} &= \$8,660 + 42 \text{ percent of amount over } \$32,000 \\
&= \$8,660 + 0.42 \, (\$460) \\
&= \$8,660 + \$193.20 - 2\% \text{ of the first } \$9,000 \text{ of taxable income} \\
&= \$8,853.20 - \$180 \\
&= \$8,673.20
\end{aligned}
$$

Capital Gains and Losses

Since long-term gains on the sale of capital assets receive favored tax treatment, taxpayers are continually searching for ways to report income as long-term capital gains. To qualify gains as long-term, the capital assets giving rise to these gains must have been held for more than six months. (This is increased to nine months for taxable years beginning in 1977, and twelve months for taxable years beginning in 1978 and therefore.) The rate applicable to many of these gains is equal to one half of the rate on ordinary income or 25 percent, whichever is *less*. Long-term gains which aggregate to more than $50,000 ($25,000 in the case of a married person filing a separate return) may be taxed at a rate as high as 35 percent. Gains that do not qualify as long-term are classified as short-term gains and are taxed as ordinary income.

Capital assets commonly held by taxpayers include stocks, bonds, homes, and land. The tax code defines capital assets as all items of property *other than* inventories in a trade or business, trade accounts and notes receivable, copyrights, government obligations due within one year and issued at a discount, and real or depreciable property used in a trade or business.

Even though real or depreciable items of property used in a trade or business and certain other properties are *not* capital assets, the gains may be considered net long-term capital gains for tax purposes. The recognized gains on the sale or exchange of these assets would have to exceed the recognized losses from such sales for them to be recognized as net long-term capital gains. These assets are often described as section "1231" assets, referring to the number of the section of the Internal Revenue Code which grants this treatment.

The gain or loss is equal to the difference between the selling price of the capital asset and its "basis." Generally, the basis is equal to cost less depreciation taken, but the rules governing the proper determination of the basis are extremely complex and are beyond the scope of this book.

Long-term capital gains are taxed as follows: Assume that a taxpayer has net long-term capital gains of $4,000 and that his marginal tax bracket is 41 percent. He would only be taxed on *one half* of the gain, or $2,000. The tax paid on the gain would be:

$$\$2,000 \times 41 \text{ Percent} = \$820$$

The rate of tax compared to the entire amount of the gain is:

$$\frac{\$820}{\$4,000} = 20.5 \text{ Percent}$$

This is exactly one half of the rate of tax if the gain had been classified as ordinary income.

Sometimes the rate is even less than one half of the normal rate. For instance, assume the same situation as above except that the taxpayer has a marginal tax rate of 66 percent. The tax would be $1,000, computed as the lesser of $2,000 × 66 percent ($1,320) or $4,000 × 25 percent ($1,000), since the gain is subject to a maximum tax of 25 percent.

FEDERAL INCOME TAX STATUS OF PARTNERSHIPS

The federal income tax as such is imposed on that party which is entitled to the income. The party may be an individual, corporation, estate, or trust but not a partnership. *The partnership as such does not pay a federal income tax.* Each partner is liable for federal income tax on his or her share of the net earnings of the partnership. Partners report their share of the partnership net earnings on their individual return.

Even though a partnership is not a taxpayer, it is required to file an information return. This return is necessary to provide information to the Intenal Revenue Service so that it can ascertain whether or not the partners have reported their proper share of the partnership earnings on their individual returns.

Corporate Federal Income Taxes

Most corporations organized for profit must file a federal income tax return and pay a corporation income tax on their net earnings. Nonprofit organizations, specifically exempted by law, do not file an income tax return but must file an annual return of information.

Net Earnings before Taxes versus Taxable Income

Net earnings before taxes (as shown on the earnings statement) and taxable income (as shown in the corporation's tax return) need not necessarily agree. There are various reasons why they might differ. Some of these are:

1. Certain items of revenue and expense included in the computation of business earnings are excluded from the computation of taxable income. For instance, interest earned on state, county, or municipal bonds is not subject to tax. Only "ordinary" and "necessary" business expenses and "reasonable" amounts of salaries can be deducted for tax purposes. Life insurance premiums are not deductible if the corporation is the beneficiary, and proceeds received from life insurance policies are not taxed. Costs of attempting to influence legislation are not deductible.

2. The timing of recognition of items of revenue and expense often varies for tax purposes from the timing used in determining business earnings. Interpretations of the tax code have generally held that revenue received in advance is taxable when received and that current expenses based on estimates of future costs (such as costs of performance under service contracts) are not deductible until actually incurred. An exception is bad debts expense. Also, different elective methods may be used for tax purposes than are used for financial statements. For instance, the corporation may be using straight-line depreciation for book purposes and a different method for tax purposes. This is a very common practice.

For a given corporation, the reconciliation between earnings before taxes and taxable income may appear as shown below. The treatment of long-term capital gains is different for corporations than for individuals. For corporations, the maximum rate of tax on all net long-term capital gains is 30 percent. They cannot take the lesser of one half the ordinary tax rate and the capital gains rate as is permitted for individuals.

Net earnings before taxes per earnings statement..........		$74,000
Add:		
Life insurance premiums paid.........................	$ 700	
Service revenue received in advance....................	5,000	
Estimated expenses under service contracts..............	1,000	6,700
		$80,700
Deduct:		
Interest on *New York State Bonds*......................	$3,000	
Difference in depreciation for tax-purposes ($8,000) and		
for book purposes ($6,000)..........................	2,000	5,000
Taxable Income................................		$75,700

The Revenue Act of 1971 included two provisions that are of particular importance to businessmen. The investment credit of the 1960s was reinstated. This permitted taxpayers to deduct 7 percent of the cost of acquisition of machinery and equipment (under certain conditions) from their tax liability in the year of purchase. Also included was a provision allowing a 20 percent speedup in allowable depreciation deductions. These two provisions were included in an attempt to stimulate the economy. For the 1975 tax year the investment credit was increased to 10 percent. The Tax Reform Act of 1976 extended the 10 percent rate through December 31, 1980.

In 1974, an ordinary business corporation was subject to two federal income taxes—the normal tax and the surtax. The normal tax (of 22 percent) applied to the first $25,000 of taxable income. Both taxes (the normal tax of 22 percent and a surtax of 26 percent) applied to all taxable income over $25,000. Thus, if a corporation had $40,000 of taxable income, the first $25,000 was taxed at 22 percent and the other $15,000 was taxed at 48 percent. A "temporary" reduction in these rates was in effect for the 1975 tax year. For 1975, the first $25,000 of taxable income was taxed at 20 percent, the next $25,000 at 22 percent, and the remainder at 48 percent. The Tax Reform Act of 1976 extended these rates through December 31, 1977.

City and State Income Taxes

Many governmental units, such as cities and states, impose an income tax which may or may not be similar to the federal income tax. It is normally based on the net earnings of the single proprietor, partnership, or corporation. It should be noted that normally the partnership will be subject to a city or state income tax, whereas it is not subject to the federal income tax.

THE EFFECT OF INCOME TAXATION ON MANAGEMENT DECISION MAKING

Management strives to maximize earnings available for common stockholders per share of common stock outstanding. In recent years corporations have been taxed at rates ranging from 48 percent to 52 percent on certain portions of their taxable income. Management can affect the timing of the recognition of revenues and the incurrence of some expenses and thus affect the timing of taxable income. Since money has "time value," there is an incentive for management to defer the incurrence and payment of income taxes.

Form of Business Organization

The earnings of a proprietorship or partnership are considered income to the individual owners whether they are distributed or not. There is no tax on the business entity itself. Salaries to owners and distributions of earnings are treated the same under the tax law. In fact, salaries are merely considered a means of distributing earnings.

The corporate form of organization creates another taxpayer. The corporation itself is taxed on its earnings. Only when dividends are paid are the stockholders taxed for corporate earnings and then only to the extent of the dividends received. This situation is often described as the double taxation of corporate earnings. Shareholders in high tax brackets often prefer that the corporation retain the earnings rather than paying dividends (although there are limits, and penalties are imposed for unreasonable accumulations of earnings) so that they may later sell their shares with the gain being taxed at capital gains rates (generally a maximum of 25 percent) rather than at the ordinary income rates (up to 70 percent).

Under the tax law, certain corporations with a limited number of stockholders may elect to be taxed as partnerships. Under this option there is no tax levied on the corporation itself. Instead, all taxable income "flows through" to the individual owners and each pays individual income taxes on his or her share. This tends to negate to some extent the tax implications of the form of organization, although most corporations do not qualify to elect this option.

Size of Organization

The owners may also use the corporate form to establish more than one entity, each of which is taxed at 20 percent on the first $25,000, 22 percent of the next $25,000, and 48 percent on amounts over $50,000 of earnings (using 1975–77 rates) rather than organizing as one entity. For instance, one corporation with $125,000 of taxable earnings could be taxed as follows:

$$20\% \text{ on the first } \$25,000 \quad\quad = \$\ 5,000$$
$$22\% \text{ on the next } \$25,000 \quad\quad = \quad\ 5,500$$
$$48\% \text{ on the remainder of } \$75,000 = \quad 36,000$$
$$\overline{\$46,500}$$

Organized as five separate corporations, each with $25,000 of taxable income, the tax may only be 20 percent of $125,000, or $25,000. But unless there are good business reasons for multiple corporations (other than tax reasons), the tax benefit may be reduced or completely disallowed. Certain groups of corporations, controlled by the same five or fewer persons, lost this benefit as of 1975.

Financing Arrangements

There are a number of ways of financing business growth. Three external means are by issuing common stock, preferred stock, or bonds.

Different tax effects result from the use of bonds rather than stock to finance business growth as was illustrated in Chapter 6. You should recall that dividends on common and preferred stocks are not deductible in arriving at taxable income (although as of this writing there was some discussion of making these deductible). But interest paid on obligations is a deductible business expense in computing taxable income. This tax advantage tends to create a bias toward financing growth through the issuance of bonds rather than by issuing preferred or common stock. Illustration 19.3 supports this contention.

Assume that the Burgess Company is planning to issue $200,000 (at face value) of securities to finance construction of a new building. It is considering issuing either preferred stock with an 8 percent dividend rate on par value or bonds with an 8 percent interest rate. Assume that either obligation can be issued in the market at its face value.

The higher earnings available for common stockholders if the bonds are issued result from the "tax shield" of $7,680 ($16,000 × 48 percent) due to the deductibility of interest payments.

ILLUSTRATION 19.3
Tax Effects of Comparative Forms of Financing

		Preferred Stock		*Bonds*
Earnings before interest and taxes.........		$140,000		$140,000
Less: Interest at 8% of $200,000...........		0		16,000
Taxable income.......................		$140,000		$124,000
Taxes 20% on first $25,000.............	$ 5,000		$ 5,000	
Taxes 22% on next $25,000.............	5,500		5,500	
Taxes 48% on remainder...............	43,200	53,700	35,520	46,020
Earnings after taxes......................		$ 86,300		$ 77,980
Less: Preferred dividends (8% of				
$200,000)............................		16,000		0
Earnings available for common share-				
holders............................		$ 70,300		$ 77,980

Of course there are other considerations in deciding on the method of financing to use. Some of them are the supply and demand conditions in the capital market for bonds and for preferred stock (perhaps one could be issued above its face value and the other below its face value), the amounts of debt already employed, and the stability of earnings. Interest on debt must usually be paid when due if the common stockholders are to retain control of the company, while dividends on preferred stock do not have to be declared and paid. Therefore, the increased risk associated with the issuance of bonds may more than negate the tax advantage.

Capital Expenditure Decisions

When computing the relative benefits of alternative investments in resources which will benefit future periods, one should use after-tax cash inflows and outflows. (The present-value concept involved in making capital expenditure decisions was covered in Chapter 16.) Differences in timing of the tax deductions can affect these decisions. For instance, assume two alternatives have identical *before*-tax net cash inflows, but one expenditure can be deducted immediately for tax purposes, while the other must be spread over a long period of time. The first alternative will have a higher present value since the tax savings in the year of expenditure can be reinvested and can earn a rate of return during the ensuing years. A specific example is an expenditure on research and development versus one to acquire machinery. Expenditures on such items as research and development and advertising are deductible immediately, while the cost of machinery must be depreciated over time.

The use of different methods of depreciation for tax purposes can affect whether a capital expenditure project is a viable one. For instance, assume that a company is evaluating a capital project with an initial cost (after the investment credit has been deducted) of $20,000, an estimated useful life of four years, and no scrap value. The company has set a minimum required return of 20 percent. Net revenues (defined as revenue less all other expenses except depreciation and taxes) of $10,000 per year will result from the project. If straight-line depreciation were used in determining taxable income, the project would, as shown in Illustration 19.4, yield

ILLUSTRATION 19.4

Year	1 Net Revenues	2 Depreciation	3 Col. 1 − Col. 2 Taxable Income	4 Tax at 48%	5 Col. 1 − Col. 4 Net Cash Inflow
1.........	$10,000	$ 5,000	$ 5,000	$2,400	$ 7,600
2.........	10,000	5,000	5,000	2,400	7,600
3.........	10,000	5,000	5,000	2,400	7,600
4.........	10,000	5,000	5,000	2,400	7,600
Total.....	$40,000	$20,000	$20,000	$9,600	$30,400

an annual net cash inflow of $7,600. The present value of the net cash inflow of $7,600 per year for four years is found as follows:

Annuity × Present Value Factor* = Present Value of Benefits
$7,600   2.589 $19,676.40

* Found in Table III in the Appendix. Use four periods and 20 percent column.

Since the cost ($20,000) exceeds the present value of the benefits ($19,676.40), the project should be rejected.

Now assume that the company elects to use the sum-of-the-years'-digits method of depreciation for tax purposes. The project now becomes desirable as shown in the calculations in Illustrations 19.5 and 19.6. The present value of the stream of net cash inflows is calculated as shown in Illustration 19.6.

ILLUSTRATION 19.5

Year	1 Net Revenues	2 Depreciation*	3 Col. 1 − Col. 2 Taxable Income	4 Tax at 48%	5 Col. 1 − Col. 4 Net Cash Inflow
1.........	$10,000	$ 8,000	$ 2,000	$ 960	$ 9,040
2.........	10,000	6,000	4,000	1,920	8,080
3.........	10,000	4,000	6,000	2,880	7,120
4.........	10,000	2,000	8,000	3,840	6,160
Total.....	$40,000	$20,000	$20,000	$9,600	$30,400

* Depreciation is calculated by apportioning 4/10 of the $20,000 depreciable cost to year 1, 3/10 to year 2, 2/10 to year 3, and 1/10 to year 4.

ILLUSTRATION 19.6

Year	Net Cash Inflow	× Present Value Factor*	= Present Value of Benefits
1................	$9,040	0.833	$ 7,530
2................	8,080	0.694	5,608
3................	7,120	0.579	4,122
4................	6,160	0.482	2,969
			$20,229

* From Table II of the Appendix. Use 20 percent column for periods 1, 2, 3, and 4.

Now the present value of the benefits ($20,229) exceeds the initial cost ($20,000) and the decision could be just the opposite from before. The only variable that caused this reversal in the decision is the depreciation method used in computing tax payments.

Tax Considerations in Mergers

A provision of the tax law permits corporations to carry losses back three years and forward seven years. This means that if a company has a loss in a given year it can apply it against taxable earnings of other years and recover some or all of the taxes it paid during those years. In doing this it must apply the loss to the oldest year first, then the next oldest, and so on until the loss has been completely "used up" by offsetting it against ordinary taxable income of these years. The corporation recomputes its taxes for those previous years using the rates then in effect.

An illustration may be helpful. For purposes of this illustration it will be assumed that the first $25,000 of taxable income is taxed at 20 percent, the next $25,000 is taxed at 22 percent, and all amounts in excess of $50,000 are taxed at 48 percent. Assume the amounts of taxable income (or loss) shown below:

Year	Taxable Income (or loss)	Taxes Paid	Taxes Recovered
1975	$ 15,000	$ 3,000	$3,000
1976	20,000	4,000	4,000
1977	5,000	1,000	1,000
1978	(100,000)	–0–	–0–
1979	40,000	–0–	–0–
1980	10,000	–0–	–0–
1981	30,000	4,000	–0–
1982	50,000	10,500	–0–
1983	60,000	15,300	–0–

The loss of $100,000 in 1978 would first be offset against the $15,000 of income in 1975, then the $20,000 in 1976, and next the $5,000 in 1977. The company would recover the taxes previously paid of $8,000 (which is equal to $40,000 times 20 percent). At this point it would have a carry-forward of $60,000. It would apply $40,000 of this toward taxable income in 1979 and therefore pay no taxes in that year. This leaves $20,000 of the carry-forward remaining. $10,000 of this would be used to offset income in the next year (1980), and the other $10,000 would be applied against 1981 taxable income.

If the carry-forward had not been used up by the end of the seventh year of carry-forward, the remaining portion would have been lost. The provision has encouraged profitable firms to merge with firms having losses. The acquiring firm could then apply those losses against its *own* profits and thereby have some tax-free earnings. There are certain requirements which must be satisfied which have made this practice applicable in fewer situations in recent years.

Lessening the Tax Burden on Stockholders and Executives

In determining dividend policy, management may be influenced at least in the part by the fact that cash dividends are taxable income to the recipient while most stock dividends on common stock are nontaxable.

The tax burden on executives can be minimized in several ways. Executives can be granted certain types of stock option plans which will enable a portion of their "income" to be taxed at capital gains rates. There are also deferred compensation plans which allow executives to receive (and be taxed on) a certain portion of their earnings after retirement when they are likely to be in a lower tax bracket.

Accounting Methods

Cash versus Accrual Basis. The tax law allows a business to use a modified cash basis of accounting in determining taxable income *unless* inventories are a significant factor in producing earnings. (The basis is described as "modified" because long-term assets cannot be charged to expense when purchased nor can all prepaid expenses be deducted when paid.) The accrual basis is mandatory for firms having substantial inventories. Since the timing of revenues and expenses is altered by the use of these two different methods, an executive may determine that either the cash or the accrual basis offers a tax advantage to the company.

Accounting for Inventories. There are several different ways of accounting for inventories. (See Chapter 3.) Each of them assumes a different flow of costs and thus results in different taxable income if used for tax purposes. In recent years many firms have adopted Lifo (last-in, first-out). The last goods purchased are assumed to be the first ones sold. Under this method, during periods of rising prices, the most recent *higher* costs are charged against revenues and the asset, inventory, is shown at lower earlier costs. The result is lower net earnings and lower taxes. The tax law requires that a company use the Lifo method for financial statement purposes if it intends to use it for tax purposes.

Depreciation Methods. The tax law permits the use of various methods of depreciation. Two of the best known of these are the sum-of-the-years'-digits method and the uniform-rate-on-declining-balance method. Both of these methods result in depreciation charges higher than those under the straight-line method during the early life of an asset and lower charges during the later years. The use of these methods for tax purposes results initially in lower taxes because taxable income is lower during the early life of the asset. The tax savings in early years can be reinvested and thus increase the earnings per share available for common stockholders for the entire period.

Numerous other examples could be given for showing that business decisions are influenced greatly by their tax effects, but this discussion was intended to be illustrative rather than comprehensive. With the advent of relatively high tax rates, tax planning became an essential function of management.

The tax laws are extremely complicated and are constantly changing.

Those who desire to stay current with the status of the law, and with the interpretations of the law made by courts, must specialize in this area.

Avoidance versus Evasion

There is a distinct important difference between tax avoidance and tax evasion. Tax avoidance is the reduction in tax payments as a result of understanding and correctly applying the provisions of the tax law. It is completely legal and should be encouraged. Ignorance of rightful deductions only serves to place an unfair and unintended burden on certain taxpayers.

Tax evasion is a different matter. Evasion is the illegal concealment of taxable revenues or the exaggeration or falsification of expenses, exemptions, or credits, or all of these for the purpose of escaping taxes.

INCOME TAX ALLOCATION

As already discussed, taxable income and net earnings before income taxes (for simplicity, pretax earnings) may differ sharply for a number of reasons. In fact, the tax return may show a loss, while the earnings statement shows positive net earnings. This raises questions as to what amount of income taxes should be shown in the earnings statement. The answer lies in the nature of the items causing the difference between taxable income and pretax earnings. Some of the differences are *permanent*—interest earned on municipal bonds is never taxable but is always included in net earnings. Such differences cause no problem—the estimated actual amount of income taxes payable for the year is shown on the earnings statement even though this results in reporting only $1,000 of income taxes on $100,000 of pretax earnings.

The reasons for other differences between taxable income and pretax earnings are called *timing differences*—that is, items which will be included in both taxable income and in pretax earnings but in *different periods*. The items involved thus will have a tax effect. When this is true, generally accepted accounting principles require that *tax allocation* procedures be applied to prevent the presentation of possibly misleading information.

To illustrate, assume (1) that a firm acquires for $200,000 a machine whose estimated life is four years with no salvage value expected; (2) that it uses the straight-line depreciation method for financial reporting purposes and the sum-of-the-years'-digits methods for tax purposes; (3) that net earnings before depreciation and income taxes for each year of the machine's life will be $150,000; (4) that there are no other items which cause differences between pretax earnings and taxable income; and (5) that the tax rate is 50 percent (to simplify the illustration).

Under these circumstances, the actual tax liability for each year will be as shown in Illustration 19.7.

If the amounts of income taxes computed above were shown in the earnings statements for the years 1977–80, net earnings would be as shown in Illustration 19.8. To report net earnings as declining this sharply in the circumstances described would, under generally accepted accounting principles, be considered quite misleading. Especially objectionable is the reporting of sharply increased net earnings for 1977 brought about by deducting only $35,000 of income taxes on $100,000 of pretax earnings when the current tax rate is 50 percent and all of the items making up the

ILLUSTRATION 19.7

	1977	1978	1979	1980	Total
Earnings before depreciation and income taxes..........	$150,000	$150,000	$150,000	$150,000	$600,000
Depreciation (sum-of-the years'-digits basis)..........	80,000	60,000	40,000	20,000	200,000
Taxable income.............	$ 70,000	$ 90,000	$110,000	$130,000	$400,000
Income Taxes..............	$ 35,000	$ 45,000	$ 55,000	$ 65,000	$200,000

ILLUSTRATION 19.8

	1977	1978	1979	1980	Total
Earnings before depreciation and income taxes..........	$150,000	$150,000	$150,000	$150,000	$600,000
Depreciation (straight-line method)................	50,000	50,000	50,000	50,000	200,000
Earnings before income taxes..	$100,000	$100,000	$100,000	$100,000	$400,000
Income taxes...............	35,000	45,000	55,000	65,000	200,000
Net Earnings...............	$ 65,000	$ 55,000	$ 45,000	$ 35,000	$200,000

$100,000 will appear on the tax return. Under such circumstances, it is contended that the income taxes should be $50,000. This is supported by drawing attention to the fact that there is no actual reduction in taxes. Total income taxes for the four years will be $200,000. Therefore, any taxes not paid in the early years of the machine's life will be paid later— note the $65,000 of taxes in 1980—when, as the accountant puts it, the timing differences reverse. That occurs, in this case, when depreciation is less per tax return than for financial reporting purposes.

Consequently, tax allocation procedures should be applied in the above circumstances. Under such procedures, the earnings statement for each of the four years would show:

	Each Year	Total for Four Years
Earnings before depreciation and income taxes...............	$150,000	$600,000
Depreciation..	50,000	200,000
Earnings before income taxes...........................	$100,000	$400,000
Income taxes...	50,000	200,000
Net Earnings...	$ 50,000	$200,000

Under tax allocation, reported net earnings are $50,000 per year. Note especially that reported income taxes are $50,000 in each year which seems logical when pretax earnings are $100,000 and the tax rate is 50 percent.

The entries to record the income tax expense, the income taxes payable, the income taxes paid, and the changes in the deferred income taxes payable are summarized in the T-accounts below. The (1) refers to 1977, the (2) to 1978, and so forth.

Federal Income Tax Expense	Federal Income Taxes Payable	Deferred Federal Income Taxes Payable
(1) 50,000	(1a) 35,000 | (1) 35,000	(3) 5,000 | (1) 15,000
(2) 50,000	(2a) 45,000 | (2) 45,000	(4) 15,000 | (2) 5,000
(3) 50,000	(3a) 55,000 | (3) 55,000	
(4) 50,000	(4a) 65,000 | (4) 65,000	

The entries keyed with the letter *a* indicate the debits made to record the actual cash paid in settlement of the federal income tax liability. Note that the amount of expense recognized remained constant at $50,000 even though the tax liability increased from $35,000 for 1977 to $65,000 for 1980 by $10,000 increments. The normalizing of the tax expense for each year was accomplished by entries in the Deferred Federal Income Taxes Payable account. As can be seen, the tax expense for the four years is $200,000, and the tax payments for the four years also sum to $200,000. The only difference is that the tax expense is not charged to the year in the same amount as the actual liability for the year. Note, also, that in our simplified example the Deferred Federal Income Taxes Payable account has a zero balance at the end of four years.

Actual business experience has shown that once a Deferred Federal Income Taxes Payable account is established; it is seldom decreased or reduced to zero. The reason is that most businesses acquire new depreciable assets, at perhaps higher prices. The result is that depreciation for tax purposes continues to be greater than depreciation for financial reporting purposes, and the balance in the Deferred Federal Income Taxes Payable account also continues to grow. For this reason, many accountants seriously question the validity of tax allocation in circumstances such as those described above. But discussion of this controversial issue must be left to a more advanced text.

In some instances, taxable income will be greater than pretax earnings because of timing differences such as when rent collections received in advance are taxed before they are considered earned revenue for accounting purposes. Application of tax allocation procedures in such circumstances will give rise to a balance in an asset account titled Deferred Federal Income Taxes or possibly Prepaid Federal Income Taxes.

SUMMARY

Since business firms are subject to various kinds of taxes, their managements are concerned with accounting correctly for these taxes. They also want to know how they can make decisions which will minimize their adverse effects on earnings.

Persons with a gross annual income of $750 or more should check the law to see if they are required to file a federal income tax return. From the reported gross income, certain deductions are allowed in arriving at taxable income. Also, certain exemptions are allowed. The federal income tax paid by individuals is a personal expense rather than a business expense.

For individual taxpayers, gains on the sale of capital assets and certain other business assets are given favored tax treatment (if they were held more than nine months in 1977 and twelve months in 1978). The rate applicable to many long-term gains is equal to one half of the rate on ordinary income or 25 percent, whichever is less, although gains of over $50,000 may be taxed at a rate as high as 35 percent.

Most corporations organized for profit must file a federal income tax return and pay a corporation income tax on their net earnings. (Partnerships, as such, do not pay a federal income tax.)

Net earnings before taxes as shown on the earnings statement and taxable income as shown in the corporation's tax return need not agree. Certain items of revenue and expense included in the computation of business earnings are excluded from the computation of taxable income, and vice versa. Also, the timing of the recognition of items of revenue and expense often varies for tax purposes from the timing used in determining business earnings.

The maximum rate of taxation on all net long-term capital gains for corporations is 30 percent. They cannot take the lesser of one half of the ordinary tax rate or the capital gains rate as is permitted individuals.

For 1976 the corporation income tax rates were as follows: 20 percent on the first $25,000, 22 percent on the next $25,000, and 48 percent on all amounts over $50,000. As of this writing it could not be determined how long these new "temporary" rates would be in effect.

Management decisions regarding the form of organization, size of the organization, financing arrangements, capital expenditure decisions, mergers, and methods of accounting for the transactions all have an impact on the amount and timing of income tax payments. Since money has "time" value, there is an incentive to defer the incurrence and payment of income taxes.

The estimated amount of income taxes payable for a period as taken from a company's tax return may not be the proper amount of income taxes to report in the earnings statement. Taxable income and net income before income taxes (pretax earnings) may differ sharply because of *permanent* and *timing* differences.

Generally accepted accounting principles require that the tax effect of an item be included in income taxes in the year in which the item is included in the earnings statement—a process called *tax allocation*. Under tax allocation, the amount of income taxes reported in the earnings statement will not differ sharply from an amount computed by applying the current period's tax rate to pretax earnings unless permanent differences are involved. The amount of net earnings reported may be misleading if income taxes do not bear this functional relationship to pretax earnings.

QUESTIONS AND EXERCISES

1. How are the net earnings of a partnership taxed by the federal government?

2. You overhear three men arguing. Their discussion proceeds as follows:
   No. 1—"Management should strive to maximize earnings after taxes."
   No. 2—"Management should strive to maximize the total dollar amount of earnings available for common stockholders."
   No. 3—"Management should strive to maximize earnings per share available for common stockholders."
   Are they all saying essentially the same thing? If not, with which one do you most nearly agree and why?

3. While the corporate form of organization may have other advantages, it certainly does not offer a tax advantage for the stockholders of a corporation. Comment.

4. A friend states, "Why all the fuss about deferring revenues and recognizing expenses sooner for tax purposes? All net taxable earnings are eventually taxed anyway. It is only a matter of putting off the payment. I don't think these manipulations are worth the effort." Comment.

5. What are capital assets? Of what significance is it that an asset is considered a capital asset for tax purposes?

6. What factors might cause net earnings before taxes on a corporation's earnings statement to differ from its taxable income?

7. Name some specific types of management decisions in which tax considerations play an important part.

8. Classified among the long-term liabilities of the A Corporation is an account titled Deferred Federal Income Taxes Payable. Explain the nature of this account.

9. Paul Daly is 68 years old, and his wife is 65 years old and blind. They have three sons, ages 22, 24, and 29. The son who is 22 is a full-time student in college and earns $1,800 per year. His parents contribute $2,000 per year toward his living expenses. The other two sons are self-supporting. How many exemptions are Paul and his wife entitled to on their joint return?

10. Refer to the tax rate table in Illustration 19.2. Assume you are married and that you earn $440,000 in one year and have no taxable income for the next three years. (Your deductions and exemptions are nominal and therefore may be ignored.) What would be the difference in total taxes paid if you could spread the income over a four-year period rather than recognizing the entire amount in one year (assuming the rates for the four-year period were constant)? How much would the total tax be if you could spread it over eight years and had no other taxable income?

11. Describe how an individual taxpayer arrives at the amount of taxable income. Once taxable income has been determined how is the amount of tax payable determined?

12. Review the situation portrayed in Illustrations 19.4, 19.5, and 19.6 on pages 471–72. Explain why using an accelerated depreciation method for tax purposes could "turn around" the decision on this capital expenditure project.

13. Differentiate between timing differences and permanent differences regarding taxable income and pretax earnings. Why are income tax allocation procedures necessary?

14. What is one of the problems encountered in the use of tax allocation procedures involving the Deferred Federal Income Taxes Payable account?

PROBLEMS

19–1. The Loeb Company had the following amounts of taxable earnings (loss) in the years indicated:

1975	$40,000
1976	20,000
1977	60,000
1978 See parts (a), (b), and (c) below	
1979	50,000
1980	10,000
1981	50,000
1982	70,000
1983	80,000
1984	65,000

Assume that the tax rate was 20 percent on the first $25,000 of taxable income, 22 percent on the next $25,000, and 48 percent on all amounts over $50,000 in each of the above years.

Required:

a. If the loss in 1978 was $120,000, how much would the company recover in back taxes?

b. If the loss in 1978 was $200,000, how much would the company have to pay in taxes for the period 1979–84?

c. If the loss in 1978 was $420,000, how much would the company have to pay in taxes for the period 1979–84?

19–2. The Strawser Corporation had the taxable income shown below.

Required:

a. Compute the amount of federal income tax in each year at the rate in effect each year. (The assumed rates are ones which have been in effect at some time in the past—before 1976.)

b. How much would the total tax for the four years have been reduced had the company been able to shift $100,000 of taxable income from year 1 to years 2 and 3 ($50,000 each year)?

		Tax Rate	
Year		On First $25,000 of Taxable Income	Additional Tax on Portion of Taxable Income over $25,000
1	$140,000	30%	22%
2	125,000	22	28
3	75,000	22	26
4	100,000	22	26

c. The company used the straight-line method of depreciation resulting in depreciation expense of $40,000 each year. If it had used one of the accelerated methods of depreciation, the depreciation charges would have been $64,000, $48,000, $32,000, and $16,000 for years 1, 2, 3, and 4, respectively. What would have been the amount of tax savings?

d. There would have been no tax savings in part (c) if the rates had not changed in years 2 and 3. Would you be indifferent to the method of depreciation if the rates had not changed? Explain.

e. What would have been the tax savings if $60,000 of the taxable income of year 4 could have qualified as a long-term capital gain (use a 30 percent capital gains rate)?

19–3. The Susan Company needed almost $300,000 in cash to construct a new building. The financial officer for the company discovered that the amount could be raised by issuing $300,000 (face value) of bonds with an interest rate of 8 percent, or preferred stock of the same total par value but with a dividend rate of only 6 percent. The preferred stock is convertible into common stock but conversion is not expected for a number of years. Which alternative results in greater earnings available for common shareholders in the immediate future assuming:

a. Earnings before interest and taxes (which equal taxable income before interest) of $100,000 and 1975–77 corporation tax rates.

b. Earnings before interest and taxes (all taxable income before interest) of $30,000 and the same tax rates as in part (a)?

c. How do you explain the difference?

19–4. Individuals A and Z are going to operate a business under the corporate form. A is married, and Z is not. They are trying to decide if they should request that they be taxed as a partnership. Each has itemized deductions greater than the maximum allowable standard deduction. A files a joint return and each expects taxable income from sources as follows:

*Taxable Income from Other Sources
after Deducting Personal Deductions
and Exemptions*

A......................... $ 4,000
Z.........................   410,000

(Z's income is virtually all from investments.) A is to receive a salary of $10,000 from the business. All earnings are to be reinvested in the business. Assume the following expectations: total revenues, $1,000,000 (all taxable); business expenses (other than salaries and all tax deductible), $950,000; taxes are at the 1975–77 rates. The computation of earnings after business taxes is as follows:

Business Earnings after Taxes	*Partnership*		*Corporation*	
Total revenues...............		$1,000,000		$1,000,000
Less: Owners' salaries........ $ –0–*			$ 10,000	
Other business expenses... 950,000	950,000		950,000	960,000
Earnings before taxes.........		$ 50,000		$ 40,000
Less: Taxes on business entity:				
20% on first $25,000........			$ .5,000	
22% on remainder..........			3,300	8,300
Earnings after Taxes..........		$ 50,000		$ 31,700

* Partners' salaries are not deductible as business expenses for tax purposes but are viewed as distributions of earnings. If taxed as a partnership each party is to be credited with one half of the partnership earnings.

Required:

a. Using the tax table in Illustration 19.2 of this chapter, determine the proportionate share of the taxes levied directly or indirectly on the actual or implied share of earnings of individual A if the business were taxed as a partnership and, alternatively, as a corporation. Do the same for individual Z assuming his personal tax is equal to $53,090 plus 70 percent of taxable income *above* $100,000. If the business is to be taxed as a corporation you should allocate one half of the corporation taxes to each party.

b. How do you think the individuals would vote in deciding whether or not to be taxed as a partnership?

19–5. Saada Corporation had taxable income of $135,000 in each year from year 1 through year 4. The $135,000 for year 2 includes the gain on sale of land referred to in (*b*) below.

Required:

a. Compute the amount of federal corporate income tax. The tax rates in effect were as shown below. (The assumed rates are ones which have been in effect at some time in the past—before 1975–77.)

Year	On First $25,000 of Taxable Income	Additional Tax on Portion of Taxable Income over $25,000
1	30%	22%
2	30	22
3	22	28
4	22	26

b. In year 2, a plot of land was sold at a short-term capital gain of $40,000. If the gain had qualified as a long-term capital gain in year 2, what would the tax saving have been? (Use a 30% capital gains rate.)

c. The company could have taken $80,000 of certain tax-deductible expenses in year 1 rather than $40,000 in each of years 2 and 3. Compute the difference in taxes that this would have made. Explain the results.

19–6. The records of the B. E. Law Corporation show the following for the calendar year just ended:

Sales	$475,000
Interest earned on—	
State of New Jersey Bonds	3,000
City of Miami Bonds	1,500
Essex County, Ohio, School District No. 2 Bonds	375
Cost of goods sold and other expenses	315,000
Loss on sale of capital asset	3,000
Gain on sale of capital asset acquired two years ago	7,500
Allowable extra depreciation deduction for tax purposes	4,500
Dividends declared	15,000
Revenue received in advance, considered taxable income of this year	3,000
Contribution made to influence legislation (included in the $315,000 listed above)	300

Required:

a. Present a schedule showing the computation of taxable income.

b. Compute the amount of the corporation's tax that was payable for the current year. (Assume 1975–77 tax rates. Also assume the company acquired $100,000 of new equipment during the year and qualified for the full amount of investment credit as a reduction in taxes.)

19–7.   The Jackson Company will have earnings before depreciation and income taxes of $200,000 each year for the period 1977–1980. The company acquires a machine for $320,000, which is expected to last four years and have no salvage value at the end of that period. For financial accounting purposes the company uses the straight-line depreciation method, and for tax purposes it uses the sum-of-the-years'-digits method. Assume that the tax rate is 40 percent (for the sake of simplicity) and that there are no other items which cause differences between pretax earnings and taxable income.

Required:

a.   Prepare a schedule showing the actual tax liability for each year.
b.   Calculate the income tax expense that should be shown each year assuming income tax allocation procedures are to be used.
c.   Prepare journal entries to record the tax expense and tax liability for each year.
d.   Show how the entries prepared in part (c) would be summarized in T-accounts. How would the amounts appearing in these accounts eventually be disposed of?

chapter 20

The Accounting System—
Electronic Equipment
Applications

INTRODUCTION

The search for both greater accuracy and speed in the operation of accounting systems has presented a persistent challenge to the accounting profession. This challenge has been met over the years through the use of more sophisticated devices to aid in the recording, processing, and reporting of accounting data. Two historical stages can be isolated in this process: (1) the development of electromechanical accounting machines which permitted simultaneous journalizing, posting to ledger cards, and accumulation of totals for control but which still required manual handling of records at each step; and (2) the transition to computerized accounting systems which permit virtually simultaneous internal processing of transaction data and preparation of summary reports and statements without the need for manually handling records at each step.

The first of these stages resulted in removing the need for laborious hand posting to ledger accounts, but highly repetitive individual decisions were still required regarding the choice of the proper accounts to be used (i.e., the correct entry) for each transaction. The developments of the second stage have permitted human participation to be limited to the preparation of input (transaction) data and the set of instructions telling the computer how these data should be processed. The input data are automatically transmitted to the appropriate accounts, which have been stored by the computer. If properly programmed, the computer is capable of journalizing and posting a great number of transactions, in any order, and with great speed and a high degree of accuracy.

Because it processes data so rapidly, it is not unusual for a computer to be characterized as nothing more than a very large and very rapid adding machine or calculator. But such a description is incomplete. Computers are capable of storing much more than the single total which is stored by an adding machine. Some computers are able to perform the operation of adding two numbers together 500,000 or more times in one second. What distinguishes a computer from an adding machine or a calculator, however, is its ability to accept instructions for the processing of any transaction data, to store those instructions, and to execute them any number of times precisely in the prescribed sequence. The computer uses elementary numerical logic to alter the sequence of instructions by observing the outcome of a numerical or alphabetic comparison. An example of the use of such a comparison is an instruction to test whether the cash balance is zero before each transaction and to continue processing cash disbursements only if the balance is greater than zero. Thus, an electronic computer is a powerful tool for carrying out data prcessing operations. It has the capability to remain accurate even at very high calculating speeds. And since sets of operating instructions are given to the computer at the outset, human effort is conserved. The performance of repetitive tasks, routine numerical decision making, and certain types of logical decision making is taken over by the computer.

The remainder of this chapter provides a closer view of electronic computers, the ways in which they can be used to process data efficiently, some of the equipment available, and the preparations required before data can be submitted for processing. First, we take a closer look at the computer and the external equipment utilized for input and output. Next, some useful concepts are presented regarding problem programming and the operation of the computer. Finally, three examples have been included which illustrate the way in which computers can be used to solve accounting and data processing problems. These examples describe both the internal processing of the data and the external steps necessary in carrying out the data processing applications.

EQUIPMENT

The *punched card* (Illustration 20.1) is the basic input medium for some electronic data processing (EDP) systems. This card measures 3¼ inches by 7⅜ inches and contains 80 vertical columns and 12 horizontal rows into which information may be punched. Data is sensed according to the punches contained in the card. Note that each letter, number, and symbol has a unique combination of punches. Each of the numbers has a single punch in the row corresponding to its value (for example, the number "6" is represented by a punch in the row numbered "6" of column 32). Each letter is represented by two punches, and more special characters require three punches. The particular code used to punch the card

ILLUSTRATION 20.1
Punched Card

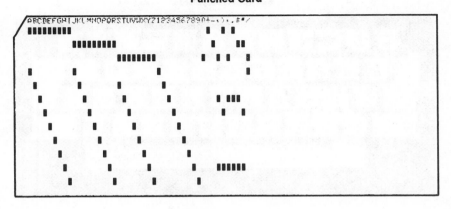

in Illustration 20.1 is called the Hollerith code because it was first used by Herman Hollerith in the 1880s while he was employed by the U.S. Census Bureau. There are other combinations of punches which can be used to denote these same symbols, but we will not be concerned with them here.

Punching is normally done with a *keypunch* (Illustration 20.2) which has a keyboard (Illustration 20.3) similar to that of a typewriter. A keypunch operator reads data from source documents such as sales tickets, invoices, and inventory records, and with this machine, punches the data into specified positions on the card.

The card and source documents then go to a verifier which is similar to

ILLUSTRATION 20.2
Keypunch

ILLUSTRATION 20.3
Keypunch Keyboard

a keypunch in appearance. The operator of this machine keys the same data into the card, but the machine, rather than punching, checks for accuracy. If the "punches" of the verifier agree with the punches in the card, a notch is placed on the right side of the card. If the two punches do not match in a given column, a notch is placed above that column. An incorrect card is then corrected or a new one punched, and in either case it is verified again before being processed further.

INPUT AND STORAGE DEVICES

Since today's high-speed computers can process data much more rapidly than they can read data, it is desirable to speed up the input process whenever possible. While the punched card is currently the most convenient medium for original input, it is also one of the slowest media. The maximum speed with which the data contained on punched cards can be read into the computer is about 100,000 characters per minute, while many computers can execute up to a million operations per *second*. If punched cards are used as the direct input medium, then the computer will waste much time waiting for the data to be read in. For this reason, most installations with large computers use a small computer which is equipped with a card reader/punch unit to transfer information from the cards to a more efficient input medium, usually *magnetic tape* or a *magnetic disk*. The tape or disk then serves as input to the main computer system. The processors of these media are capable of transmitting bits of data at over one hundred times the speed of the card reader.

Magnetic tape is similar to the tape used for an ordinary tape recorder, but is wider, of a much higher quality, and more expensive. A reel of tape, when in use, is mounted onto a tape drive which is under the control of a computer (Illustration 20.4). The tape drive can be used to read from or

ILLUSTRATION 20.4

Tape Drive

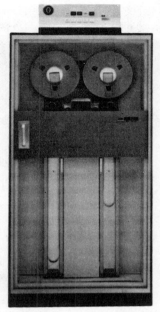

write on the tape. Magnetic tape is a very convenient and compact storage medium as well as being very useful for input and output purposes. The major disadvantage of magnetic tape as an input/output medium for computers is its *serial access* feature. This means that if the tape drive is reading from the beginning of a tape and data near the end of the tape are needed, the tape drive must physically move all of the intervening tape past the reading head before the desired data are located. This process can take as long as 4 or 5 minutes.

The *access time* (the time required to retrieve an item of information from storage) can be reduced greatly by utilizing *random access* storage devices. The random access feature eliminates the need for the sequential processing of data before the desired information is found. Each item of information has a specific predetermined address which can be located directly; no other data need be read or processed. The address consists of a number which designates the location of the data. Desired information can be retrieved after a time interval which is, in the general case, much shorter than that experienced with serial access equipment. Access (retrieval) time is usually reduced to fractions of a second. The word "random" indicates that the data can be retrieved in a random order: no consideration need be given to the sequential ordering of the data or data requests.

One type of random access storage device is the magnetic disk (Illustration 20.5, three units in center). This type of device has been in use for

ILLUSTRATION 20.5
System 360/Model 40 Computer

several years but recently its speed and efficiency have been greatly improved.

A fast and expensive type of storage device is magnetic core storage. This type of storage is a part of the computer and will be discussed when the computer itself is discussed.

The decision about which types and amounts of storage are required in any computer installation is one which involves trade-offs between speed and cost. In some circumstances, a serial access device (the least expensive but generally slowest) may be as efficient as the more expensive random access input and storage device. A firm which uses the computer in such a way as to require the use of most of the sequential data on a tape would gain little by reading the same sequence with more expensive equipment. But an inventory system which must be able to provide information on the status of any of 10,000 parts at any time may well justify the extra cost of a random access memory device. In this case the use of tapes is almost certain to involve a great deal of time-consuming tape movement.

Finally, *tape-to-card* and *tape-to-printer* converters exist which permit computer output in the form of magnetic tapes to be converted into punched cards or printed pages.

THE COMPUTER

The computer consists of three basic components: a storage unit, an arithmetic unit, and a processing unit. Attached to these units may be some of the peripheral equipment already discussed. The peripheral equipment or input/output unit is used mainly to feed unprocessed information into and receive processed information from the computer. The way in which these components are connected and controlled varies from computer to computer.

Illustration 20.6 shows a schematic design of a simple computer system. The numbered arrows indicate the basic flow of data and instructions. The raw data are entered into the system by means of some type of peripheral equipment, for example, tape drives (1) are stored in memory until needed (2), and are called for when needed (3) and transmitted to the arithmetic unit (4) where the required arithmetic operations are performed for output preparation (7 and 8). Most problems will require that the data processed in the arithmetic unit be stored in memory to become the raw data of another processing stage.

The storage unit (sometimes called core storage) of a computer is its internal memory system. It is the most expensive component of the computer both in terms of original acquisition and maintenance costs. To determine the optimum size of internal core storage, the speed and cost factors must be considered in the same way they were when internal input and storage devices were selected. Problems that require a lot of storage space during the running of the computer can use disks and tape units for temporary external storage. A computer word is that set of characters which occupies a single storage location in the memory unit and which is treated as a unit by the computer.

The arithmetic unit of a computer contains devices which perform arithmetic operations and generally process the data. This unit does the computing.

The processing unit of a computer is the governing unit which interprets

ILLUSTRATION 20.6

The Main Components of a Computer System

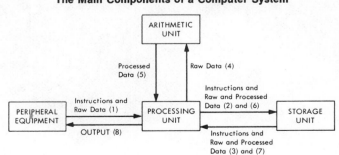

the program (the set of instructions submitted to the computer which specifies the operations to be performed and their correct sequence), makes decisions, and alters the program if so instructed by the program itself. This unit can do only what it has been told to do by the program. If it reaches a situation for which it has been given no explicit instructions, it will instruct the computer to halt operations. (In actual circumstances, most systems have built-in master programs which will cause the program to stop when this situation occurs.) After finding and correcting the problem situation, if possible, the computer operator can restart the processing by means of a console which allows him to exercise control over the computer when necessary.

The computer must be given very explicit instructions for every possible event. It cannot find a solution to problems which arise during the execution process. It can execute only the steps which a programmer has devised to reach a solution. The important step of programming will be considered after a brief discussion of small computers.

Small Computers

The IBM System/3 computer (see Illustration 20.7) is a smaller third-generation computer than IBM's System/360 (see Illustration 20.5) and

ILLUSTRATION 20.7

IBM System/3 Computer

Keyboard   Ledger Card Printer   Computer

System/370. The smaller computer is best suited for smaller businesses. The major advantages of the smaller computer are its low cost, compactness, and flexibility; it also provides direct access storage.

There are basically two types of systems for the smaller computer—a card system and a disk system. One of the unique items appearing with the System/3 is a 96-column card. The 96-column card holds 20 percent more characters than the 80-column card, but it is only one-third the size of an 80-column card.

A multifunction card unit is also available with the System/3. This piece of equipment combines the functions of a card reader, punch, sorter, collator, and interpreter in one compact device.

One model of the System/3 uses an operator keyboard console as the primary input device. This model is also useful for commercial data processing—especially accounts receivable, billing, inventory control and sales analysis.

In contrast to IBM's System/360, the System/3 is much smaller—it occupies only slightly more space than an office desk. Thus, it seems natural that the System/3 can be rented or purchased for a much lower price than the System/360. Although the System/3 was designed primarily to meet the needs of small businesses, it can be used as a processing terminal by medium-size and large organizations. For instance, the System/3 can be used as a processing terminal at branch offices so that data can be communicated from the System/3 (at branch offices) to an IBM System/360 located at the main office.

The primary types of input media for the System/3 are magnetic disk, the 96-column card, and direct data entry through a keyboard that looks like a typewriter. On the other hand, the System/360 uses 80-column cards, magnetic tape, magnetic disk, magnetic drum, data cell, and direct data entry as the primary input devices.

The System/3 is easier for the small business to use than the System /360. It was designed to be used by people who have not had any prior experience with computers. RPG II, which stands for Report Program Generator II, is a problem-oriented programming language that was developed especially for the IBM System/3. It is a very easy-to-learn and easy-to-use programming language. COBOL, FORTRAN, BASIC and Assembler languages can also be used with certain models of the System/3. With the System/3, RPG II is typically used for accounting applications and BASIC for mathematical applications. COBOL, FORTRAN, RPG, Assembler, and PL/1 (Programming Language 1) are programming languages that can be used with the System/360. PL/1 is a relatively new language designed for both commercial and scientific applications.

One important characteristic of the System/360 is its capacity for growth which seems virtually unlimited, particularly in comparison with the System/3, whose growth possibilities are definitely limited. In addition, the System/3 can execute only 28 basic instructions whereas the System /360 can execute over 100 or 200 instructions. Thus, as a small business expands, the owner or manager will probably decide to rent or purchase a larger computer such as a System/360.

PROGRAMMING A PROBLEM FOR COMPUTER PROCESSING

So far we have discussed the computer only in terms of its ability to process data according to a set of instructions which has somehow been accepted and stored in memory. The detailed manner in which these instructions are given to the computer, in the form of a program, is beyond the scope of our interest here. But a brief introduction to the nature of programming will be useful so that the steps which precede data processing activities can be understood.

Nearly all modern digital computers perform operations internally by testing the position of electronic switches which have two alternatives (much like a light switch which can only be on or off). All of the many complex operations which a computer can perform are accomplished by nothing more than combinations of these two positions, or binary switches, in various patterns or circuits. The combination of all instructions in a program constitutes a master circuit, which the computer then executes one step at a time.

Since it is very difficult to communicate with the computer in terms of these binary switches, it is customary for a computer system to be able to interpret computer languages and transform instructions written in them into internal circuitry. For example, each computer has its own machine language, which is a series of special codes by which elementary processing operations are specified. These languages have the advantage of being very rapidly converted by the computer into internal instructions, but machine language programs are difficult to prepare and use and ordinarily cannot be transferred from one computer to another (even to other computer models produced by the same manufacturer).

Another group of languages has been written with the goal of making the transition from one machine to another less difficult. Languages such as FORTRAN and COBOL, known as compiler languages, can be interpreted by many computers with only minor modifications required between systems. FORTRAN (for FORmula TRANslator) was developed especially to be compatible with scientific work; FORTRAN instructions are similar to algebraic formulas (see Illustration 20.8). COBOL (for COmmon Business Oriented Language) was developed with instructions consisting of English phrases, (see Illustration 20.9) so that combinations of instructions form readable sentences and paragraphs. When programs which have been written in a compiler language are submitted to a computer, a specialized program known as a compiler translates the program into the appropriate machine language which the computer can interpret more efficiently. The computer languages, then, are intermediary languages which serve to bridge the gap between everyday speech and mathematics on the one hand and machine languages on the other. It should be noted, however, that it is possible to write programs in terms of machine languages, and occasionally this is done.

Illustration 20.8 gives a program, written in FORTRAN, which could be used to solve a compound interest problem. The amount of principal in this case is $1,000, the annual interest is 5 percent, interest is computed once a year, the period of time is 20 years. The answers desired are the amounts to which the $1,000 would accumulate at the end of each of the

ILLUSTRATION 20.8

FORTRAN Program for Solving Compound
Interest Problems

```
P = 1000.00
R = 0.05
PRINT 3
3FORMAT(1HO,2X,4HYEAR,2X,10HBALANCE($))
DO 7N = 1,20
S = P*(1.0 + R)**N
PRINT 5,N,S
5FORMAT(1H,2X,13,4X,F8.2)
7CONTINUE
STOP
```

20 years if the principal remains untouched and the interest is not withdrawn but left to earn additional interest—that is, is compounded.

The first two lines inform the computer that the principal is $1,000 and the interest rate is 5 percent. The next two cause the following heading to be printed at the top of the print-out page: YEAR BALANCE($). The following five lines cause the computations to be carried out, one year at a time for 20 years, and the answers desired to be printed under the printed heading. The statement $S = p*(1.0 + R)**N$ is a translation of the compound interest formula $S = P(1.0 + R)^n$. S is the sum at the end of period n. The PRINT statement indicates that the year involved and the accumulated sum at the end of that year shall be printed in the format (i.e., physical arrangement) specified by the FORMAT statement. Finally, the STOP statement causes the computer operations to cease after all of the desired computations have been performed and the results printed.

The printout will be similar to the following:

YEAR	BALANCE ($)
1	1050.00
2	1102.50
3	1157.63
.	.
.	.
.	.
20	2653.30

Illustration 20.9 shows a COBOL program written to do the same things done by the FORTRAN program in Illustration 20.8.

Executing a Program

Once a particular problem has been translated into one of the available computer languages and the data have been punched into cards and transmitted to and stored within the computer, it is possible to instruct the computer to execute the program. During the execution of any program, the computer may be occupied with any one of the three major activities: input, processing, and output.

The input phase encompasses all of those operations which result when the program requires data which must be provided by some external source such as a tape unit, magnetic disk, or card reader. Input involves the transmission of data from these external sources to the internal storage of the computer. Once there, the data are available for immediate use in processing.

The *processing* phase is totally internal. During this phase the computer executes the computational and analytical instructions contained in the program in the order which has been specified. If any logical tests are included in the program, it is possible for the data to cause the order or the content of these instructions to be altered.

The *output* phase results in the writing of processed information on some external medium, usually a magnetic tape. Any output created in this manner may then be processed through the auxiliary computer in order to convert the tape impulses into printed pages or punched cards. (Printers and card punches customarily are not attached directly to the main system for the same reason that card readers are not—their operating speed is much slower than that of magnetic tape drives. If they were used the computer would waste valuable processing time in reading out the processed data.)

If you will refer to Illustration 20.7, you will note that step (1) is the input stage, steps (2) through (7) are the processing stage, and step (8) is the output stage.

With any real problem, it is unlikely that these three phases can be accomplished in their entirety in any simple sequence. In fact, there may be several input phases during the execution of a program, just as there

ILLUSTRATION 20.9

**COBOL Program for Solving Compound
Interest Problems**

```
IDENTIFICATION DIVISION.
PROGRAM-I.D. 'COMPOUND-INTEREST'
ENVIRONMENT DIVISION
CONFIGURATION SECTION
SOURCE-COMPUTER. IBM-360
OBJECT-COMPUTER. IBM-360
INPUT-OUTPUT SECTION
FILE-CONTROL
   SELECT PRINT-FILE ASSIGN TO UT-S-WRITEM
DATA DIVISION
FILE SECTION
FD  PRINT-FILE
      LABEL RECORDS ARE OMITTED
01  PRINT-REC.
      05   CC PIC XXX
      05   YEAR PIC Z9
      05   FILLER PIC XXXX
      05   BALANCE PIC 999999.99
01  PRINT-LINE PIC X(130)
WORKING-STORAGE-SECTION
77  W-YEAR PIC 99 VALUE ZERO
77  INT-RATE PIC V99 VALUE .05
77  W-BALANCE PIC 999999V99 VALUE 1000
77  W-SUM PIC 999999V99 VALUE ZERO
77  O-O-C PIC XXX VALUE 'NO'
      88  OUT-OF-CARDS VALUE 'YES'

PROCEDURE DIVISION
      OPEN OUTPUT PRINT-FILE
      MOVE SPACES TO PRINT-LINE
      MOVE' YEAR  BALANCE($)' TO   PRINT-LINE
      WRITE PRINT-LINE
      PERFORM PROCESS-PARA UNTIL W-YEAR > 20
      CLOSE PRINT-FILE
      STOP RUN

PROCESS-PARA.
      ADD 1 TO W-YEAR
      COMPUTE W-SUM = W-BALANCE*(1 + INT-RATE)
         ** W-YEAR
      MOVE SPACES TO PRINT-REC
      MOVE W-SUM TO BALANCE W-BALANCE
      MOVE W-YEAR TO YEAR
      WRITE PRINT-REC
```

may be any number of individual processing or output operations. Typically, a whole series of input-processing-output cycles will constitute the total program. The manner in which these are combined is again a question of efficiency and speed.

Flowcharts

A flowchart is a graphic representation of the correct sequential order of the steps involved in the solution of a problem. It is prepared by the systems analyst or programmer before the actual preparation of the program. The symbols shown in Illustration 20.10 are commonly used in flow charting. These symbols are connected by lines with arrows to indicate the correct processing sequence. Examples of flowcharts will be given in the discussion of computer application examples.

ILLUSTRATION 20.10
Flowchart Symbols

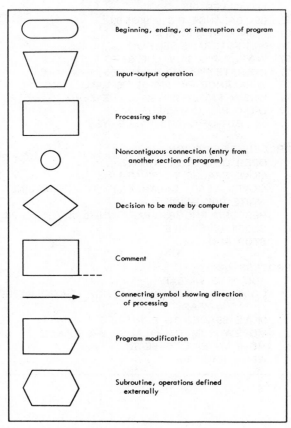

Beginning, ending, or interruption of program

Input–output operation

Processing step

Noncontiguous connection (entry from another section of program)

Decision to be made by computer

Comment

Connecting symbol showing direction of processing

Program modification

Subroutine, operations defined externally

EXAMPLES OF COMMON ELECTRONIC DATA PROCESSING APPLICATIONS TO ACCOUNTING

The discussion so far has covered some of the data processing and computer equipment which is available and the manner in which problems are programmed and executed. But to lend reality to the discussion, three examples of electronic data processing applications to accounting are described in the remainder of this chapter. The examples cover the processing of payroll, accounts receivable, and inventory records, respectively. For each example both a list of the operations needed to prepare data for processing by the computer and to complete the processing after the computer run, and a flow chart of the processing which actually takes place in the computer have been included. The former are the operations which you would see if you were able to stand in a data processing installation and watch the processing of the payroll, accounts receivable, or inventory data.

Nearly all applications of data processing, and particularly those which involve the accounting process, make considerable use of *files*. A file is any grouping of similar items of data arranged in some identifiable order. For example, the ledger account Cash is a file; the data are the individual cash transactions; and the sequence is time. The use of files is particularly relevant in the following examples since the program causes the same basic processing to be performed on each of the many employee records in the payroll file, customer records in the accounts receivable file, and parts records in the inventory file. The processing which occurs is undertaken in order to *update* these files; the end result is a new cumulative file created by the computer.

Payroll

Processing of payroll records was one of the first accounting functions to which computers were applied. The computer is well suited to the routine and easily defined procedures in payroll processing.

External Processing. Processing of payroll records begins when the employee time records or slips are collected and taken to the keypunch room. Here keypunch operators punch into cards the information contained on these records (step 1 in Illustration 20.11). The punched cards are then verified by keying the data from the time records into a verifier. This procedure is extremely important because the greatest proportion of errors in input from EDP systems results from incorrectly prepared input. (It should be noted that systems exist whereby data can be transmitted directly from the keypunch to magnetic tape, thereby eliminating the punched card.)

The punched and verified cards are next sorted by employee number (and possibly by department or factory number as well). One reason for

ILLUSTRATION 20.11

Payroll EDP Procedures

1. Punch cards from employee time records.
2. Verify punched cards.
3. Sort cards by employee number (often done by the computer).
4. Use collator to check sequence of cards (usually done by the computer).
5. Use card reader to transcribe data from cards to magnetic input tape.
6. Load input, payroll year-to-date, payroll master, and output tapes, onto tape drives.
7. Process data.
8. Unload payroll master, new updated year-to-date master, paycheck, and report tapes.
9. Print checks.
10. Print payroll report.
11. Store new payroll master tape and updated year-to-date master tape in library.

using employee numbers rather than names is evident here: two passes on a sorter are required for each column containing an alphabetic character (because there must be two punches to represent an alphabetic character), while only one pass is needed for each column containing a number. Also, a person can be uniquely identified by fewer numbers or digits than there are letters in a name.

The sorted cards are then placed in a collator and checked for sequence. If the sort operation has been performed correctly, the sequence checking operation will go to completion without interruption. But if the operator of the sorter has been careless, the collator will halt when it finds a card out of sequence.

When the cards have been sequence checked, they are fed through a card reader (attached to a small computer), which transfers the information contained on the cards to magnetic tape for input to a larger computer. (The importance of correct sequence will be explained during the discussion of the internal processing flow chart.)

The magnetic tape which contains the input data for the current period (referred to from now on as the payroll input tape) is mounted onto a tape drive connected to the larger computer. The payroll year-to-date (YTD) master tape and the payroll master tape are mounted onto other tape drives. (The content of these tapes is explained more fully in the discussion that follows.) Three or more scratch (blank or nonsaved) tapes are then mounted onto other tape drives. The internal processing is next performed and the output written on the scratch tapes. The new updated YTD master is one output tape. The information to be printed on the paychecks is written on a paycheck tape, and the payroll report data are written on the third output tape.

After the processing has been completed, the paycheck tape and report tape are removed from the main system and mounted onto tape drives connected to the auxiliary computer which controls the printer. The blank paycheck forms are loaded into the printer, and the checks are prepared from the information contained on the output tape. The checks are then unloaded from the printer, burst (separated), signed, and distributed to the distribution points (in the factory).

Payroll report forms (or multipurpose paper) are next loaded into the printer. The report is printed, and the different copies are separated and distributed to the appropriate offices (treasurer, factory superintendent, factory comptroller, and department heads, for example).

The new updated YTD payroll master tape is placed in the magnetic tape library, ready for use when the next payroll is processed. The payroll master tape is also returned to the library.

Internal Processing. The internal processing of payroll records begins with the loading of the payroll master, payroll YTD, and payroll input tapes onto tape drives. The program which controls the processing operations may be stored internally in the memory unit or externally on tape. If it is on tape, this tape is also loaded onto a tape drive, and the proper commands are given for the storage of the program in the internal memory unit where the necessary internal circuits are created. The program can then be executed.

The payroll master tape contains the information which pertains to individual employees and which is needed for payroll processing. These data are recorded in sequence by employee number and include the employee's name, social security number, pay rate, number of dependents claimed, other information concerning withholding taxes, and amounts of deductions for such items as insurance, bonds, and union dues. This tape must be kept up to date, but it is assumed here that the payroll master is updated in a separate operation.

The payroll YTD tape contains the year-to-date totals by employee, department, or any other appropriate classification, for all payroll data: gross pay, withholding taxes, FICA tax, unemployment insurance, net pay, and the various employee-requested deductions.

The payroll input tape, as described above, is created from the employee time records.

Before the processing of the payroll records begins, the registers which will accumulate the total gross pay, FICA tax, unemployment tax, withholding tax, other deductions, and net pay data are all set to zero; see Illustration 20.12(**2**).[1] As each record is processed, each employee's gross pay will be added to the total gross pay accumulator. The other amounts contained on individual paychecks will be added to the proper accumulators.

The processing begins when the computer reads one employee record (the current data for one employee) from the payroll input tape (**2**). The

---

[1] Boldface numbers parallel numbers in illustrations throughout this chapter.

ILLUSTRATION 20.12

Payroll—Internal Processing Flow Chart

The reader who has had much experience drawing flow charts will recognize that certain steps in this flow chart and in the others illustrated in the chapter have been highly summarized and that simplifying assumptions concerning the organization of the input data have been made. Since the purpose is to give only a brief introduction to the process of flow charting, it is felt that greater precision would serve only to confuse the student who has had no prior experience in this area.

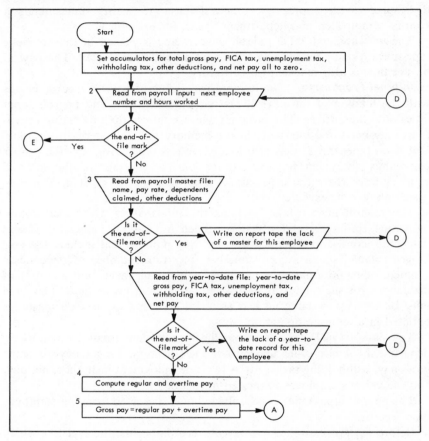

ILLUSTRATION 20.12 (continued)

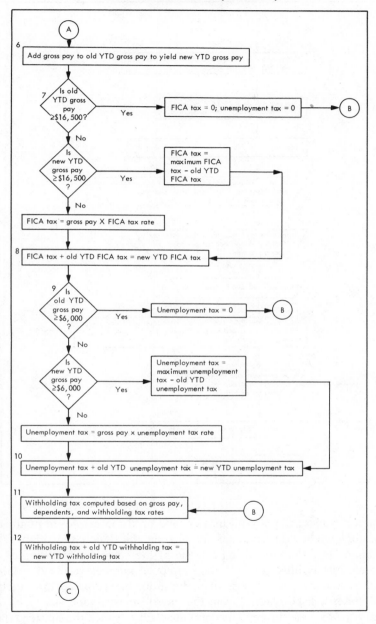

ILLUSTRATION 20.12 (concluded)

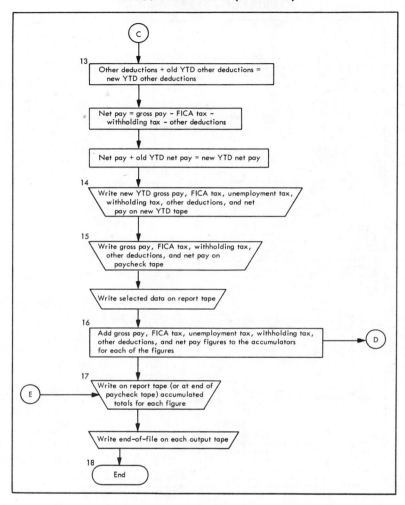

computer advances the payroll master tape until the employee number on the master matches the employee number in the data just read from the input tape. Here the crucial importance of the correct sequencing of employee records is illustrated. If the employee number received from the input tape is out of order (less than the immediately preceding number), the computer will be reading from the payroll master tape at a point past the entry for that employee. The computer will advance the master tape in an attempt to locate the employee number, but since the employee number has already been passed, the computer will read to the end of the tape and stop (probably after indignantly informing the operator that "employee number XXXX is not entered on the payroll master").

If the data are in the correct sequence and the computer finds the entry for the current employee number on the master tape, the computer then reads from it the rate of pay for this employee (3). With this information and the hours worked data from the input tape, the current regular pay and overtime pay are computed and added together to obtain current gross pay (4 and 5).

The YTD tape is now advanced to the entry for this employee. The old YTD gross pay and old YTD FICA balances are read from the YTD tape. The current gross pay is then added to the old YTD gross pay to obtain the new YTD gross pay (6). Note that if the payroll master and YTD records were stored on a magnetic disk, the input cards could be in any order since the records could then be retrieved at random.

The computer now makes its first decision. It compares the old YTD gross pay with the amount $16,500 (7). If it is greater than or equal to $16,500, both the current FICA and the current unemployment taxes are set to 0, and the computer continues the processing with the calculation of withholding taxes. If the old YTD gross pay is less than $16,500, the computer compares the new YTD gross pay with the amount of $16,500. If the new YTD gross pay is greater than or equal to $16,500, the current FICA tax is set to the *maximum* FICA tax minus the old YTD FICA tax. The new YTD FICA tax is then set to maximum FICA tax, and the computer continues the data processing with the computation of unemployment tax. If the new YTD gross pay is less than $16,500, the current FICA tax is computed by multiplying the FICA rate by the current gross pay and is then added to the old YTD FICA tax to obtain the new YTD FICA tax (8).

The next decision is for the purposes of computing the employer's liability for unemployment tax. It is assumed that a combined unemployment tax rate of 3.4 percent (effective January 1, 1977) is in effect for the first $6,000 earned by each employee. (The $6,000 base is effective January 1, 1978.)

If the old YTD gross pay is $6,000 or more, the current unemployment tax is set to 0, and the computer proceeds to the withholding tax computation (9). If the new YTD gross pay is $6,000 or more but the old was not, the current unemployment tax is set to maximum unemployment tax minus old YTD unemployment tax. Otherwise the current unemployment tax is equal to the *rate* times the current gross pay. In either case, the current unemployment tax is added to the old YTD unemployment tax to obtain the new YTD unemployment tax (10).

To compute withholding taxes, the computer first reads the data (dependents claimed or special instructions) from the payroll master, then applies the computation (set by the program) to those data and the current gross pay. The old YTD withholding tax figure is updated (11 and 12).

The computer then reads from the payroll master and enters in its memory the deductions requested by the employee (such as insurance or union dues) (13). The total of all withholdings and deductions is then subtracted from gross pay to arrive at net pay. The current figures for the deductions and net pay are added to the corresponding old YTD amounts to obtain the new updated YTD data. All of the new YTD data are then entered on the new YTD tape (14).

The information for the employee's paycheck is then entered on the output tape which will be used to print the paychecks (15). The individual data are accumulated for the payroll report. Some information may be written on the report tape (which is usually a tape separate from the paycheck tape). The program then instructs the computer to read the next employee record (16).

When the last employee record has been processed, the summary data which pertain to the payroll report are entered on the report tape (17). The computer then puts a mark, called an end-of-the-file mark, on each output tape to indicate the end of the useful portion of the tape (18).

The process which has been described here is a typical procedure for using a computer to process payroll data. Many other procedures are in use, but the purpose here was to give the student an idea of the operations necessary to process payroll records using a computer.

While the system described above requires key punch operators to manually punch the time data into punched cards, it should be noted that equipment does exist which allows these data to be transferred directly from time clocks to the computer. Such systems require that each employee possess a disk which contains data such as name and employee number. Upon arrival at and departure from work each day, the employee will insert the disk in a special time clock. The data contained on the disk and the arrival or departure time data will then be transmitted directly to the computer which will cause them to be stored until processing is begun.

Accounts Receivable

The recording of the numerous accounts receivable transactions is another accounting process to which EDP may be profitably applied. Many companies use a magnetic tape master accounts receivable file, but the following example has been prepared to illustrate the use of a master file kept on punched cards.

External Processing. The punching and verifying steps (Illustration 20.13) encountered in the processing of accounts receivable records are exactly the same as those used for payroll processing. But when accounts receivable data are processed, two types of input cards are produced. One type is punched from invoices on shipments to customers and represents increases in the Accounts Receivable account. The second type is punched from copies of receipts issued to customers and represents decreases in the Accounts Receivable account. The punched and verified cards are sorted either by account number or by name. Here again the use of account numbers will save time in sorting.

ILLUSTRATION 20.13

Accounts Receivable EDP Procedures

1. Punch input cards from invoices and receipts.
2. Verify cards punched in 1.
3. Sort input cards by account number or account name.
4. Obtain accounts receivable masters from file.
5. Merge input cards behind masters.
6. Transfer merged file to magnetic tape.
7. Process on computer.
8. Print accounts receivable report from output tape.
9. Punch new masters from output tape.
10. Store new accounts receivable master file.

The Accounts Receivable master punched card file contains the account number (or name) and the balance which every account receivable of the company had at the last updating. This file is taken from storage to the collator where the current input invoice and receipt cards are merged behind the corresponding masters. In other words, all input cards for a particular account are placed directly behind the master card for that account. This operation results in an automatic sequence check since the collator will halt if it comes to a card out of sequence in either file. Actually the sequence is not as important here as it was in payroll. The important point to remember to insure correct processing when using master *card* files is that the subsidiary cards are behind the correct masters.

An auxiliary computer with card reader is next used to transfer the input data from the merged file to magnetic tape. This tape (or tapes) is then mounted onto a tape drive connected to the main computer for processing. Two scratch tapes for output will also be mounted: one for the accounts receivable report and one for the updated master file.

The internal processing is performed, the two output tapes are removed and mounted onto tape drives connected to the auxiliary computer, and the data on the report tape are then printed and the reports separated and distributed. The new accounts receivable master file is next punched by the card punch attached to the auxiliary computer from the second output tape. Finally, the master file is placed in storage.

Internal Processing. Before the accounts receivable records are processed, the registers used to accumulate the delinquent account and outstanding account totals are set to zero (Illustration 20.14 (1)). As each record is processed, each delinquent account balance will be added to that accumulator and each account balance will be added to the outstanding account accumulators.

The computer reads one record from the input tape. If it represents a master card, the old balance is read into memory (2). If it is a receipt, the amount is subtracted from this old balance, and if it is an invoice, the

ILLUSTRATION 20.14

Accounts Receivable—Internal Processing Flow Chart

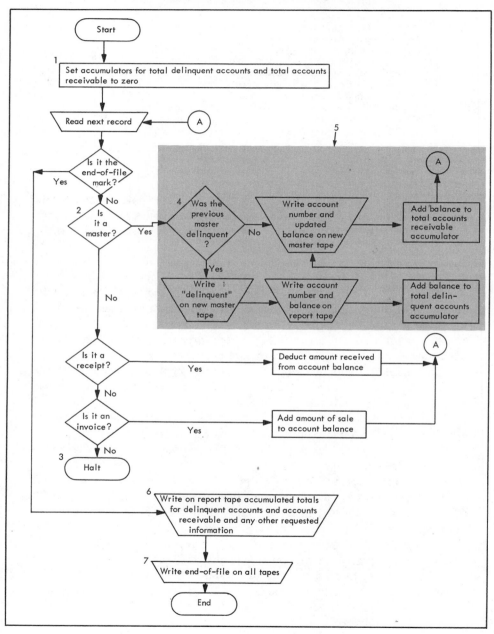

amount is added to the balance. If the record read is none of these and is not an end-of-file mark, an incorrect type of record has been written on the input tape and the processing will halt (**3**). The console operator would then determine the nature of the error, make any needed corrections, and cause the processing to resume.

After all the records which pertain to one account (here called "previous account") have been read and processed and the next master record (here called "next master") is encountered, the previous account is tested for delinquency (**4**). If the old balance of the account (the balance contained in the old master file) was delinquent (past due), the word "delinquent" or some symbol, the updated account balance, and the account number are all written on the new master output and report tapes. The updated balance is also added to the total delinquent accounts and total accounts receivable accumulators. If the old balance was not delinquent, the updated account balance and the account number are written on the new master output tape, and the balance is added to the total accounts receivable accumulator (shaded area **5**).

The transaction records for the next master are then read and processed, and the cycle continues until the end-of-file mark is encountered (**6**). (The last record before the end-of-file mark must be a master record which contains a zero balance. This record is for a nonexistent account but must be present so that all of the data for the preceding master record are processed.) After the last true account processed has been tested for delinquency and the appropriate data have been written on the appropriate output tapes, the summary of transactions and other pertinent information are written on the report tape. "End-of-file" is written on all output tapes and internal processing is complete (**7**).

Again, this is only one common method of processing accounts receivable. Many other types of information (for example, itemized transactions and inactive accounts) can be obtained very easily and without excessive cost through this type of processing. Note that the master file in this example is a card file. One reason for using cards rather than tape might be the desire to refer to the account balances manually between updatings. Or, with some modification, the punched output card may be the bill sent to the customer. If the master were on tape, it would be necessary to have printed listings available for reference.

Inventory

The use of a random access file will now be illustrated for the processing of inventory transaction data. The inventory master is maintained on a magnetic disk and the transaction data are recorded on punched cards.

External Processing. The inventory master will contain for each inventory item the part number, the number on hand as of the last update and their cost, the reorder point, and the quantity to be ordered when necessary.

The first step described in Illustration 20.15 is again the punching of input cards from source documents. These cards are verified and written on magnetic tape. This input is mounted onto a tape drive connected to the main computer, the inventory master magnetic disk is obtained and mounted onto a disk drive, and internal processing is carried out.

A report of inventory activity, such as total purchases and total withdrawals for a particular period, can be obtained by processing the input data for that period using a separate program. An order list can be produced at any time from the inventory master by the use of a separate program which determines those items that have a balance below a predetermined reorder point.

ILLUSTRATION 20.15
Inventory EDP Procedures

1. Punch purchase and issue information from invoices or other source documents.
2. Verify cards punched in step 1.
3. Obtain inventory master magnetic disk.
4. Transfer input cards to magnetic tape.
5. Process on computer.
6. Prepare inventory report and order list.
7. Store updated inventory master file.

Internal Processing. The computer reads one record from the input tape (**1**), see Illustration 20.16. If it represents a purchase, the amount is added to the balance of that particular inventory item as retrieved from the magnetic disk (**2**). If it represents a withdrawal, the amount is subtracted from the balance (**3**). Another record is then read. If the record read is neither a purchase nor a withdrawal record and is not an end-of-file mark, an incorrect record has been written on the input tape. The processing would halt and the console operator would proceed as described in the accounts receivable example (**4**).

After a transaction has been processed, the new balance on hand of the item is written on the magnetic disk, thus replacing the old balance.

It would be quite easy to change the above into a real-time system in which the inventory master file would be updated immediately when a change takes place. Instead of card input, typewriter consoles connected directly to the computer would be used to enter inventory changes as they take place.

ILLUSTRATION 20.16
Inventory—Internal Processing Flowchart

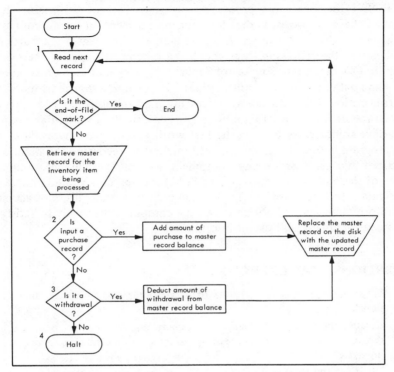

SUMMARY

Recent advances in mechanical and electronic data processing equipment have enabled the accountant to manipulate and summarize data in a much faster manner. A number of different accounting or data processing machines must be carefully integrated to form a system which will solve the organization's need for accurate and timely information with a minimum of cost.

The major advancement in this field has been the advent of the computer. When selecting a system, the manager must consider the three basic phases of computer execution: (1) input, (2) processing, and (3) output. The speed of most input and output devices has been substantially slower than the speed of the central processing unit: thus the phrases "input bound" or "output bound" are heard quite often in data processing centers emphasizing the processing constraints. Higher speed input and output devices are now becoming available; but the trade-off for speed includes large increases in cost.

Various conversational languages have been developed to aid computer programming. FORTRAN is primarily scientific oriented, while COBOL is business data processing oriented. One of the main advantages of these languages is that they can be used on almost all computers with only slight modification. In constructing a program for a particular application, the following steps should be taken: (1) specify the desired output; (2) determine sources of input data; (3) consider other uses of the same data in providing information; (4) prepare a flowchart indicating all transaction steps, decisions, processing, and output; and (5) translate the flowchart into a programming language. Usually a particular program will have some errors in it on the first writing; thus it is important to test the program before discarding the old method of recording the data.

Electronic data processing equipment will relieve the accountant of some of the more routine aspects of bookkeeping. This should enable the accountant to give more thought to the needs of various users of accounting information and the ability to use the computer effectively in satisfying the need for timely and useful information.

QUESTIONS AND EXERCISES

1. What are the three basic units of a computer and what are their functions?

2. Discuss the major arguments a company might consider in deciding to replace its manual data processing system with an electronic data processing system.

3. What are the most commonly used forms of input into a computer? What are the factors which might induce a user to choose one form over another? Evaluate and rank these forms of computer input in terms of the factors you have chosen.

4. Which forms of computer storage are of the serial access type and which are of the random access type? Which forms are generally more expensive per unit of storage? What is the advantage of a random access system?

5. Broadly, how is the binary system utilized in the internal circuitry of a computer?

6. Explain the advantages of programming in compiler languages (FORTRAN, COBOL, etc.) over programming in machine languages.

7. List and explain the three basic phases of computer program execution.

8. What are the most commonly used forms of computer output? Evaluate these forms in terms of the factors a purchaser of a new computer installation might consider.

9. What is a flowchart? What is its function in the data processing cycle?

10. What are the major advantages of a small computer similar to the IBM System/3?

11. What is a multi-function card unit?

PROBLEMS

20-1. The Maka Company is a small enterprise which sells five household appliances—mixers, can openers, disposals, orange squeezers, and percolators—directly to consumers on a door-to-door basis. Five salesmen, Jones, Smith, Stevens, Frank, and Charles sell these appliances in the Alpha Sales District. Salesmen record each sale of one appliance on a sales order which has spaces for the salesman's name, the item sold, the price, and other information. At the end of each day, salesmen deliver their sales orders for the day to the district sales office. There, the information contained in the sales order is punched into cards. At the end of the month, the sales order cards are totaled and sent on to the central sales office. The sales manager of the Alpha Sales District would like to have his total monthly sales broken down by salesman and by appliance, and he requests appropriate reports from the central sales office. The central sales office has a small computer which normally accepts punched card input and delivers printed output. Develop a simple flow chart for a program to break down the Alpha Sales District sales.

20-2. Develop a flowchart for the interest computation on page 495.

20-3. Utilizing the illustration of inventory processing, page 510, list the EDP procedures necessary to produce an order list. Prepare a flowchart of the internal processing necessary to produce the list.

20-4. The City of Hydrolock is preparing its monthly billings for water usage. A card which contains name, ID number, and number of gallons used is punched for each customer. If a customer has used less than 100 gallons, the bill is $25.00. If the customer has used more than 200 gallons, the bill is $100.00. Otherwise, the bill is $70.00. A computer printout is obtained which lists each customer, ID number, and the billing for the month. After all the customers have been listed, the next line of output contains totals accumulated for (1) the number of customers billed and (2) the total amount of billings.

Develop a flowchart for a program to compute each customer's billing, accumulate the total number of billings and the total amount of billings, and print the information described above.

20-5. A bank has a deck of input cards that has been merged with a master file of punched cards so that all the cards for one customer are grouped together. Each card contains (1) an account number, (2) the customer's name, (3) an amount which represents either an account balance, a receipt, or a withdrawal, and (4) a code. The codes are: M for master
R for receipt
W for withdrawal
Develop a flowchart for a program to update the master file.

Appendix

TABLE 1

Amount of 1
(at compound interest)
$(1 + i)^n$

Periods	2%	2½%	3%	4%	5%	6%
1.....	1.02	1.025	1.03	1.04	1.05	1.06
2.....	1.040 4	1.050 625	1.060 9	1.081 6	1.102 5	1.123 6
3.....	1.061 208	1.076 891	1.092 727	1.124 864	1.157 625	1.191 016
4.....	1.082 432	1.103 813	1.125 509	1.169 859	1.215 506	1.262 477
5.....	1.104 081	1.131 408	1.159 274	1.216 653	1.276 282	1.338 226
6.....	1.126 162	1.159 693	1.194 052	1.265 319	1.340 096	1.418 519
7.....	1.148 686	1.188 686	1.229 874	1.315 932	1.407 100	1.503 630
8.....	1.171 659	1.218 403	1.266 770	1.368 569	1.477 455	1.593 848
9.....	1.195 093	1.248 863	1.304 773	1.423 312	1.551 328	1.689 479
10.....	1.218 994	1.280 085	1.343 916	1.480 244	1.628 895	1.790 848
11.....	1.243 374	1.312 087	1.384 234	1.539 454	1.710 339	1.898 299
12.....	1.268 242	1.344 889	1.425 761	1.601 032	1.795 856	2.012 196
13.....	1.293 607	1.378 511	1.468 534	1.665 074	1.885 649	2.132 928
14.....	1.319 479	1.412 974	1.512 590	1.731 676	1.979 932	2.260 904
15.....	1.345 868	1.448 298	1.557 967	1.800 944	2.078 928	2.396 558
16.....	1.372 786	1.484 506	1.604 706	1.872 981	2.182 875	2.540 352
17.....	1.400 241	1.521 618	1.652 848	1.947 901	2.292 018	2.692 773
18.....	1.428 246	1.559 659	1.702 433	2.025 817	2.406 619	2.854 339
19.....	1.456 811	1.598 650	1.753 506	2.106 849	2.526 950	3.025 600
20.....	1.485 947	1.638 616	1.806 111	2.191 123	2.653 298	3.207 135
21.....	1.515 666	1.679 582	1.860 295	2.278 768	2.785 963	3.399 564
22.....	1.545 980	1.721 571	1.916 103	2.369 919	2.925 261	3.603 537
23.....	1.576 899	1.764 611	1.973 587	2.464 716	3.071 524	3.819 750
24.....	1.608 437	1.808 726	2.032 794	2.563 304	3.225 100	4.048 935
25.....	1.640 606	1.853 944	2.093 778	2.665 836	3.386 355	4.291 871
26.....	1.673 418	1.900 293	2.156 591	2.772 470	3.555 673	4.549 383
27.....	1.706 886	1.947 800	2.221 289	2.883 369	3.733 456	4.822 346
28.....	1.741 024	1.996 495	2.287 928	2.998 703	3.920 129	5.111 687
29.....	1.775 845	2.046 407	2.356 566	3.118 651	4.116 136	5.418 388
30.....	1.811 362	2.097 568	2.427 262	3.243 398	4.321 942	5.743 491
31.....	1.847 589	2.150 007	2.500 080	3.373 133	4.538 039	6.088 101
32.....	1.884 541	2.203 757	2.575 083	3.508 059	4.764 941	6.453 387
33.....	1.922 231	2.258 851	2.652 335	3.648 381	5.003 189	6.840 590
34.....	1.960 676	2.315 322	2.731 905	3.794 316	5.253 348	7.251 025
35.....	1.999 890	2.373 205	2.813 862	3.946 089	5.516 015	7.686 087
36.....	2.039 887	2.432 535	2.898 278	4.103 933	5.791 816	8.147 252
37.....	2.080 685	2.493 349	2.985 227	4.268 090	6.081 407	8.636 087
38.....	2.122 299	2.555 682	3.074 783	4.438 813	6.385 477	9.154 252
39.....	2.164 745	2.619 574	3.167 027	4.616 366	6.704 751	9.703 507
40.....	2.208 040	2.685 064	3.262 038	4.801 021	7.039 989	10.285 718

TABLE II

Present Value of 1
(at compound interest)

$$\frac{1}{(1 + i)^n}$$

Periods	2%	2½%	3%	4%	5%	6%
1.....	0.980 392	0.975 610	0.970 874	0.961 538	0.952 381	0.943 396
2.....	0.961 169	0.951 814	0.942 596	0.924 556	0.907 029	0.889 996
3.....	0.942 322	0.928 599	0.915 142	0.888 996	0.863 838	0.839 619
4.....	0.923 845	0.905 951	0.888 487	0.854 804	0.822 702	0.792 094
5.....	0.905 731	0.883 854	0.862 609	0.821 927	0.783 526	0.747 258
6.....	0.887 971	0.862 297	0.837 484	0.790 315	0.746 215	0.704 961
7.....	0.870 560	0.841 265	0.813 092	0.759 918	0.710 681	0.665 057
8.....	0.853 490	0.820 747	0.789 409	0.730 690	0.676 839	0.627 412
9.....	0.836 755	0.800 728	0.766 417	0.702 587	0.644 609	0.591 898
10.....	0.820 348	0.781 198	0.744 094	0.675 564	0.613 913	0.558 395
11.....	0.804 263	0.762 145	0.722 421	0.649 581	0.584 679	0.526 788
12.....	0.788 493	0.743 556	0.701 380	0.624 597	0.556 837	0.496 969
13.....	0.773 033	0.725 420	0.680 951	0.600 574	0.530 321	0.468 839
14.....	0.757 875	0.707 727	0.661 118	0.577 475	0.505 068	0.442 301
15.....	0.743 015	0.690 466	0.641 862	0.555 265	0.481 017	0.417 265
16.....	0.728 446	0.673 625	0.623 167	0.533 908	0.458 112	0.393 646
17.....	0.714 163	0.657 195	0.605 016	0.513 373	0.436 297	0.371 364
18.....	0.700 159	0.641 166	0.587 395	0.493 628	0.415 521	0.350 344
19.....	0.686 431	0.625 528	0.570 286	0.474 642	0.395 734	0.330 513
20.....	0.672 971	0.610 271	0.553 676	0.456 387	0.376 889	0.311 805
21.....	0.659 776	0.595 386	0.537 549	0.438 834	0.358 942	0.294 155
22.....	0.646 839	0.580 865	0.521 893	0.421 955	0.341 850	0.277 505
23.....	0.634 156	0.566 697	0.506 692	0.405 726	0.325 571	0.261 797
24.....	0.621 721	0.552 875	0.491 934	0.390 121	0.310 068	0.246 979
25.....	0.609 531	0.539 391	0.477 606	0.375 117	0.295 303	0.232 999
26.....	0.597 579	0.526 234	0.463 695	0.360 689	0.281 241	0.219 810
27.....	0.585 862	0.513 400	0.450 189	0.346 817	0.267 848	0.207 368
28.....	0.574 375	0.500 878	0.437 077	0.333 477	0.255 094	0.195 630
29.....	0.563 112	0.488 661	0.424 346	0.320 651	0.242 946	0.184 557
30.....	0.552 071	0.476 743	0.411 987	0.308 319	0.231 377	0.174 110
31.....	0.541 246	0.465 115	0.399 987	0.296 460	0.220 359	0.164 255
32.....	0.530 633	0.453 770	0.388 337	0.285 058	0.209 866	0.154 957
33.....	0.520 229	0.442 703	0.377 026	0.274 094	0.199 873	0.146 186
34.....	0.510 028	0.431 905	0.366 045	0.263 552	0.190 355	0.137 912
35.....	0.500 028	0.421 371	0.355 383	0.253 415	0.181 290	0.130 105
36.....	0.490 223	0.411 094	0.345 032	0.243 669	0.172 657	0.122 741
37.....	0.480 611	0.401 067	0.334 983	0.234 297	0.164 436	0.115 793
38.....	0.471 187	0.391 285	0.325 226	0.225 285	0.156 605	0.109 239
39.....	0.461 948	0.381 741	0.315 754	0.216 621	0.149 148	0.103 056
40.....	0.452 890	0.372 431	0.306 557	0.208 289	0.142 046	0.097 222

TABLE II (continued)

8%	10%	12%	14%	16%	18%	20%
0.926	0.909	0.893	0.877	0.862	0.847	0.833
0.857	0.826	0.797	0.769	0.743	0.718	0.694
0.794	0.751	0.712	0.675	0.641	0.609	0.579
0.735	0.683	0.636	0.592	0.552	0.516	0.482
0.681	0.621	0.567	0.519	0.476	0.437	0.402
0.630	0.564	0.507	0.456	0.410	0.370	0.335
0.583	0.513	0.452	0.400	0.354	0.314	0.279
0.540	0.467	0.404	0.351	0.305	0.266	0.233
0.500	0.424	0.361	0.308	0.263	0.225	0.194
0.463	0.386	0.322	0.270	0.227	0.191	0.162
0.429	0.350	0.287	0.237	0.195	0.162	0.135
0.397	0.319	0.257	0.208	0.168	0.137	0.112
0.368	0.290	0.229	0.182	0.145	0.116	0.093
0.340	0.263	0.205	0.160	0.125	0.099	0.078
0.315	0.239	0.183	0.140	0.108	0.084	0.065
0.292	0.218	0.163	0.123	0.093	0.071	0.054
0.270	0.198	0.146	0.108	0.080	0.060	0.045
0.250	0.180	0.130	0.095	0.069	0.051	0.038
0.232	0.164	0.116	0.083	0.060	0.043	0.031
0.215	0.149	0.104	0.073	0.051	0.037	0.026
0.199	0.135	0.093	0.064	0.044	0.031	0.022
0.184	0.123	0.083	0.056	0.038	0.026	0.018
0.170	0.112	0.074	0.049	0.033	0.022	0.015
0.158	0.102	0.066	0.043	0.028	0.019	0.013
0.146	0.092	0.059	0.038	0.024	0.016	0.010
0.135	0.084	0.053	0.033	0.021	0.014	0.009
0.125	0.076	0.047	0.029	0.018	0.011	0.007
0.116	0.069	0.042	0.026	0.016	0.010	0.006
0.107	0.063	0.037	0.022	0.014	0.008	0.005
0.099	0.057	0.033	0.020	0.012	0.007	0.004
0.092	0.052	0.030	0.017	0.010	0.006	0.004
0.085	0.047	0.027	0.015	0.009	0.005	0.003
0.079	0.043	0.024	0.013	0.007	0.004	0.002
0.073	0.039	0.021	0.012	0.006	0.004	0.002
0.068	0.036	0.019	0.010	0.006	0.003	0.002
0.063	0.032	0.017	0.009	0.005	0.003	0.001
0.058	0.029	0.015	0.008	0.004	0.002	0.001
0.054	0.027	0.013	0.007	0.004	0.002	0.001
0.050	0.024	0.012	0.006	0.003	0.002	0.001
0.046	0.022	0.011	0.005	0.003	0.001	0.001

TABLE III
Present Value of an Annuity of 1

$$1 - \frac{\dfrac{1}{(1+i)^n}}{i}$$

Periods	2%	2½%	3%	4%	5%	6%
1.....	0.980 392	0.975 610	0.970 874	0.961 539	0.952 381	0.943 396
2.....	1.941 561	1.927 424	1.913 470	1.886 095	1.859 410	1.833 393
3.....	2.883 883	2.856 024	2.828 611	2.775 091	2.723 248	2.673 012
4.....	3.807 729	3.761 974	3.717 098	3.629 895	3.545 951	3.465 106
5.....	4.713 460	4.645 829	4.579 707	4.451 822	4.329 477	4.212 364
6.....	5.601 431	5.508 125	5.417 191	5.242 137	5.075 692	4.917 324
7.....	6.471 991	6.349 391	6.230 283	6.002 055	5.786 373	5.582 381
8.....	7.325 481	7.170 137	7.019 692	6.732 745	6.463 213	6.209 794
9.....	8.162 237	7.970 866	7.786 109	7.435 332	7.107 822	6.801 692
10.....	8.982 585	8.752 064	8.530 203	8.110 896	7.721 735	7.360 087
11.....	9.786 848	9.514 209	9.252 624	8.760 477	8.306 414	7.886 875
12.....	10.575 341	10.257 765	9.954 004	9.385 074	8.863 252	8.383 844
13.....	11.348 374	10.983 185	10.634 955	9.985 648	9.393 573	8.852 683
14.....	12.106 249	11.690 012	11.296 073	10.563 123	9.898 641	9.294 984
15.....	12.849 264	12.381 378	11.937 935	11.118 387	10.379 658	9.712 249
16.....	13.577 709	13.055 003	12.561 102	11.652 296	10.837 770	10.105 895
17.....	14.291 872	13.712 198	13.166 119	12.165 669	11.274 066	10.477 260
18.....	14.992 031	14.353 364	13.753 513	12.659 297	11.689 587	10.827 604
19.....	15.678 462	14.978 891	14.323 799	13.133 939	12.085 321	11.158 117
20.....	16.351 433	15.589 162	14.877 475	13.590 326	12.462 210	11.469 921
21.....	17.011 209	16.184 549	15.415 024	14.029 160	12.821 153	11.764 077
22.....	17.658 048	16.765 413	15.936 917	14.451 115	13.163 003	12.041 582
23.....	18.292 204	17.332 111	16.443 608	14.856 842	13.488 574	12.303 379
24.....	18.913 926	17.884 986	16.935 542	15.246 963	13.798 642	12.550 358
25.....	19.523 457	18.424 376	17.413 148	15.622 080	14.093 945	12.783 356
26.....	20.121 036	18.950 611	17.876 842	15.982 769	14.375 185	13.003 166
27.....	20.706 898	19.464 011	18.327 032	16.329 586	14.643 034	13.210 534
28.....	21.281 272	19.964 889	18.764 108	16.663 063	14.898 127	13.406 164
29.....	21.844 385	20.453 550	19.188 455	16.983 715	15.141 074	13.590 721
30.....	22.396 456	20.930 293	19.600 441	17.292 033	15.372 451	13.764 831
31.....	22.937 702	21.395 407	20.000 429	17.588 494	15.592 811	13.929 086
32.....	23.468 335	21.849 178	20.388 766	17.873 552	15.802 677	14.084 043
33.....	23.988 564	22.291 881	20.765 792	18.147 646	16.002 549	14.230 230
34.....	24.498 592	22.723 786	21.131 837	18.411 198	16.192 904	14.368 141
35.....	24.998 619	23.145 157	21.487 220	18.664 613	16.374 194	14.498 246
36.....	25.488 843	23.556 251	21.832 253	18.908 282	16.546 852	14.620 987
37.....	25.969 453	23.957 318	22.167 235	19.142 579	16.711 287	14.736 780
38.....	26.440 641	24.348 603	22.492 462	19.367 864	16.867 893	14.846 019
39.....	26.902 589	24.730 344	22.808 215	19.584 485	17.017 041	14.949 075
40.....	27.355 479	25.102 775	23.114 772	19.792 774	17.159 086	15.046 297

TABLE III (*continued*)

8%	10%	12%	14%	16%	18%	20%
0.926	0.909	0.893	0.877	0.862	0.847	0.833
1.783	1.736	1.690	1.647	1.605	1.566	1.528
2.577	2.487	2.402	2.322	2.246	2.174	2.106
3.312	3.170	3.037	2.914	2.798	2.690	2.589
3.993	3.791	3.605	3.433	3.274	3.127	2.991
4.623	4.355	4.111	3.889	3.685	3.498	3.326
5.206	4.868	4.564	4.288	4.039	3.812	3.605
5.747	5.335	4.968	4.639	4.344	4.078	3.837
6.247	5.759	5.328	4.946	4.607	4.303	4.031
6.710	6.145	5.650	5.216	4.833	4.494	4.192
7.139	6.495	5.937	5.453	5.029	4.656	4.327
7.536	6.814	6.194	5.660	5.197	4.793	4.439
7.904	7.103	6.424	5.842	5.342	4.910	4.533
8.244	7.367	6.628	6.002	5.468	5.008	4.611
8.559	7.606	6.811	6.142	5.575	5.092	4.675
8.851	7.824	6.974	6.265	5.669	5.162	4.730
9.122	8.022	7.120	6.373	5.749	5.222	4.775
9.372	8.201	7.250	6.467	5.818	5.273	4.812
9.604	8.365	7.366	6.550	5.877	5.316	4.844
9.818	8.514	7.469	6.623	5.929	5.353	4.870
10.017	8.649	7.562	6.687	5.973	5.384	4.891
10.201	8.772	7.645	6.743	6.011	5.410	4.909
10.371	8.883	7.718	6.792	6.044	5.432	4.925
10.529	8.985	7.784	6.835	6.073	5.451	4.937
10.675	9.077	7.843	6.873	6.097	5.467	4.948
10.810	9.161	7.896	6.906	6.118	5.480	4.956
10.935	9.237	7.943	6.935	6.136	5.492	4.964
11.051	9.307	7.984	6.961	6.152	5.502	4.970
11.158	9.370	8.022	6.983	6.166	5.510	4.975
11.258	9.427	8.055	7.003	6.177	5.517	4.979
11.350	9.479	8.085	7.020	6.187	5.523	4.982
11.435	9.526	8.112	7.035	6.196	5.528	4.985
11.514	9.569	8.135	7.048	6.203	5.532	4.988
11.587	9.609	8.157	7.060	6.210	5.536	4.990
11.655	9.644	8.176	7.070	6.215	5.539	4.992
11.717	9.677	8.192	7.079	6.220	5.541	4.993
11.775	9.706	8.208	7.087	6.224	5.543	4.994
11.829	9.733	8.221	7.094	6.228	5.545	4.995
11.879	9.757	8.233	7.100	6.231	5.547	4.996
11.925	9.779	8.244	7.105	6.234	5.548	4.997

Index

This book has been set in 10 and 9 point Times Roman, leaded 2 points. Chapter numbers are in 16 and 24 point Helvetica and chapter titles are in 18 point Helvetica. The size of the type page is 27 by 45½ picas.